OHIO JUVENILE LAW

Baldwin's OHIO HANDBOOK SERIES

by William A. Kurtz and Paul C. Giannelli

Second Edition

Banks–Baldwin Law Publishing Company

ISBN 0-8322-0263-0

Dedication

To Jeanne, Andrew, Molly, David, and Barbara

W. A. K.

To Helen and Ben

P. C. G.

Foreword

In 1988 Senate Bill 89, the Ohio legislature significantly modified its juvenile laws. The definition of abused child was changed to include mental injury, and the definition of dependent child now includes children whose *siblings* have been abused or neglected. For the first time, the Juvenile Court may issue telephone ex parte orders authorizing the taking of a child into custody. Other changes include the creation of an entirely new dispositional alternative—long term foster care—and more stringent judicial review of case plans and dispositional orders.

This book is the only one of its kind in Ohio. First published in 1985, it quickly became the leading reference for Ohio's juvenile courts and practitioners. The Second Edition carries on this tradition. Direct and easy to understand, it offers complete, up-to-date analysis of reported and unreported caselaw and recent legislation, including 1988 House Bill 643 (provisions effective June 30, 1989) as well as Senate Bill 89 (effective January 1, 1989). New Text sections discuss agreements for temporary and permanent custody, and the newly-required case plans and reasonable efforts determinations.

Each author brings special expertise to the book: as Deputy Court Administrator for Cuyahoga County Juvenile Court, William A. Kurtz is one of Ohio's leading authorities on juvenile law and practice; and, as Albert J. Weatherhead III and Richard W. Weatherhead Professor of Law at Case Western Reserve University School of Law, Paul C. Giannelli is widely respected for his knowledge of evidence, juvenile law, and criminal law. Together, they outline and explain every phase of juvenile proceedings, from intake to disposition, covering juvenile victims of abuse, neglect, and dependency as well as children accused of being delinquent, unruly, and juvenile traffic offenders.

For ready reference in office or courtroom, Revised Code Chapter 2151, the Rules of Juvenile Procedure, and the Ohio Rules of Evidence are reprinted from *Baldwin's Ohio Revised Code Annotated.* A Glossary of technical and legal terms and a Bibliography of selected books, reports, and articles guide readers in further understanding and research. Cross references, a Table of Cases, and a comprehensive Index provide fast access to the material.

We acknowledge with appreciation the contributions of our editorial and production staffs—especially Virginia Luttenton, Kevin S. Lister, Alice Rice, and Louise Wohlgemuth—in preparing the Second Edition for publication.

The Publisher

Cleveland, Ohio
April 1989

Preface

This handbook is designed to provide a succinct treatise on Ohio juvenile law. It is also intended as a single convenient source for legal materials most often used in juvenile court proceedings: Revised Code Chapter 2151, "Juvenile Court"; the Rules of Juvenile Procedure (annotated); and the Ohio Rules of Evidence. The text covers over 1,000 judicial decisions, both reported and unreported, from Ohio and federal courts.

Although the juvenile courts in Ohio have jurisdiction over a variety of civil and criminal cases, this book focuses only on those falling within the court's jurisdiction because of something that a child has done or failed to do (delinquent, unruly, and juvenile traffic offender cases) or something that someone else has done or failed to do (neglected, dependent, and abused child cases). Through an analysis of reported and unreported cases and the pertinent statutes and rules, all steps in the juvenile court process are traced—from the assumption of jurisdiction over a child to the termination of that jurisdiction. Where appropriate, reference is also made to the IJA-ABA Standards and the laws of other jurisdictions.

The handbook includes both a glossary of legal terms and a bibliography of selected books, articles, and reports that will further aid readers in their research and understanding of juvenile law. In addition to a Table of Cases and a Table of Laws and Rules Construed, a detailed Index is provided to facilitate access by subject. Popular names of legal concepts as well as common everyday phrases are included.

William A. Kurtz
Paul C. Giannelli

Cleveland, Ohio
April 1989

Table of Contents

Abbreviations

A	Atlantic Reporter
A(2d)	Atlantic Reporter, Second Series
Abs	Ohio Law Abstract
AD(2d)	Appellate Division Reports, Second Series
Akron L Rev	Akron Law Review
ALR2d	American Law Reports Annotated, Second Series
ALR3d	American Law Reports Annotated, Third Series
ALR4th	American Law Reports Annotated, Fourth Series
ALR Fed	American Law Reports Annotated, Federal
Am	Amended; Amendment
Am Bar Assn Jour	American Bar Association Journal
Am Crim L Rev	American Criminal Law Review
Am Jur 2d	American Jurisprudence, Second Series
Annot	Annotation
App	Appellate Court
App	Ohio Appellate Reports
App(2d)	Ohio Appellate Reports, Second Series
App(3d)	Ohio Appellate Reports, Third Series
App R	Rules of Appellate Procedure (Ohio)
Ariz	Arizona Reports
Ariz App	Arizona Appeals Reports
Art	Article
Bd	Board
BU L Rev	Boston University Law Review
Cal(2d)	California Reports, Second Series
Cal(3d)	California Reports, Third Series
Cal App(2d)	California Appellate Reports, Second Series
Cal App(3d)	California Appellate Reports, Third Series
Calif L Rev	California Law Review
Cal Rptr	California Reporter
Capital L Rev	Capital University Law Review
Case WRU Law Rev	Case Western Reserve University Law Review
CC(NS)	Ohio Circuit Court Reports, New Series
CD	Ohio Circuit Decisions
Cf.	Compare
Ch	Chapter
Cin L Rev	Cincinnati Law Review
Cir	Circuit Court
Civ R	Rules of Civil Procedure (Ohio)
Clev Bar J	Cleveland Bar Journal
Clev Mar L Rev	Cleveland-Marshall Law Review
Clev St L Rev	Cleveland State Law Review
Colo	Colorado Reports

Colum Hum Rts L Rev	Columbia Human Rights Law Review
Cornell L Rev	Cornell Law Review
CP	Common Pleas Court
Crim R	Rules of Criminal Procedure (Ohio)
Ct	Court
D	Decisions (Ohio)
Dayton L Rev	University of Dayton Law Review
DC	District Court
Del Super	Delaware Superior Court
Dist	District
DR	Disciplinary Rules, Code of Professional Responsibility
EC	Ethical Considerations, Code of Professional Responsibility
Ed	Edition; Editor
ED	Eastern District
eff.	Effective
e.g.	for example
Evid R	Ohio Rules of Evidence
F	Federal Reporter
F(2d)	Federal Reporter, Second Series
Fam Ct	Family Court
Fam L Quar	Family Law Quarterly, American Bar Association
Fla	Florida Reports
Fla App	Florida Appellate Court Reports
FSupp	Federal Supplement
Ga	Georgia Reports
Ga App	Georgia Appeals Reports
GC	General Code of Ohio
Gov Jud R	Supreme Court Rules for the Government of the Judiciary
H	House Bill
Harv L Rev	Harvard Law Review
Hawaii	Hawaii Reports
HB	House Bill
Id.	Idem (the same)
Idaho	Idaho Reports
IJA-ABA	Institute of Judicial Administration—American Bar Association
Ill	Illinois Reports
Ill(2d)	Illinois Reports, Second Series
Ill App(3d)	Illinois Appellate Court Reports, Third Series
Ill. Laws	Laws of Illinois
Ind	Indiana Reports
Ind App	Indiana Court of Appeals Reports
Ind L Rev	Indiana Law Review
Iowa L Rev	Iowa Law Review
J Crim L	Journal of Criminal Law and Criminology
J Fam L	Journal of Family Law
Juv	Juvenile Court
Juv R	Rules of Juvenile Procedure (Ohio)
Kan	Kansas Reports
La	Louisiana Reports
LEd	Lawyers' Edition, United States Supreme Court Reports

LEd(2d)	Lawyers' Edition, United States Supreme Court Reports, Second Series
LSC	Legislative Service Commission
Mass	Massachusetts Reports
Md	Maryland Reports
Md App	Maryland Appellate Reports
Me L Rev	Maine Law Review
Mercer L Rev	Mercer Law Review
Mich	Michigan Reports
Mich App	Michigan Appeals Reports
Mich L Rev	Michigan Law Review
Minn	Minnesota Reports
Minn L Rev	Minnesota Law Review
Misc	Ohio Miscellaneous Reports
Misc(2d)	Ohio Miscellaneous Reports, Second Series
Mo	Missouri Reports
Mun	Municipal Court
n.	note
Natl L J	National Law Journal
NC	North Carolina Reports
NC App	North Carolina Court of Appeals Reports
NCCD	National Council on Crime and Delinquency
NCL Rev	North Carolina Law Review
ND	Northern District
NE	Northeastern Reporter
NE(2d)	Northeastern Reporter, Second Series
Neb	Nebraska Reports
Nev	Nevada Reports
NH	New Hampshire Reports
NJ	New Jersey Reports
NJ Super	New Jersey Superior Court Reports
NM	New Mexico Reports
Nor Ky L Rev	Northern Kentucky Law Review
NP(NS)	Ohio Nisi Prius Reports, New Series
NW(2d)	Northwestern Reporter, Second Series
NW L Rev	Northwestern Law Review
NY(2d)	New York Reports, Second Series
NY Misc	New York Miscellaneous Reports
NYS(2d)	New York Supplement, Second Series
NYU L Rev	New York University Law Review
OAC	Ohio Administrative Code
OAG	Opinions of Attorney General
OBar	Ohio Bar Reports
OBR	Ohio Bar Reports
O Const	Ohio Constitution
Ohio North L Rev	Ohio Northern University Law Review
Ohio St L J	Ohio State Law Journal
OJur 2d	Ohio Jurisprudence, Second Series
OJur 3d	Ohio Jurisprudence, Third Series
Okla Crim	Oklahoma Criminal Reports
Okla Crim App	Oklahoma Court of Criminal Appeals
OO(3d)	Ohio Opinions, Third Series
Or	Oregon Reports

Or App	Oregon Reports, Court of Appeals
OS	Ohio State Reports
OS(2d)	Ohio State Reports, Second Series
OS(3d)	Ohio State Reports, Third Series
P	Pacific Reporter
P(2d)	Pacific Reporter, Second Series
Pa	Pennsylvania State Reports
Pa Super	Pennsylvania Superior Court Reports
PINS	Persons in Need of Supervision
PL	Public Laws
PR	Puerto Rico Reports
Prob	Probate Court
RC	Ohio Revised Code
Rev	Revision
RI	Rhode Island Reports
S	Senate Bill
San Diego L Rev	San Diego Law Review
SB	Senate Bill
SCt	United States Supreme Court Reporter
SD	Southern District
SE(2d)	Southeastern Reporter, Second Series
So(2d)	Southern Reporter, Second Series
Stan L Rev	Stanford Law Review
St. Mary's L J	St. Mary's Law Journal
sub nom	under the name
supp	supplement
Supreme Court Rev	Supreme Court Review
SW(2d)	Southwestern Reporter, Second Series
Tenn Code Ann	Tennessee Code Annotated
Tex Civ App	Texas Civil Appeals Reports
Traf R	Traffic Rules (Ohio)
UCD L Rev	U.C. Davis Law Review
US	United States Supreme Court Reports
USC	United States Code
US Const	United States Constitution
USCS	United States Code Service
Utah	Utah Reports
U Tol L Rev	University of Toledo Law Review
v	versus; volume
Va	Virginia Reports
vol	volume
Vt	Vermont Reports
Wash(2d)	Washington Reports, Second Series
Wash App	Washington Appellate Reports
WD	Western District
Wh	Wharton's Reports (Pennsylvania)
Wm & Mary L Rev	William and Mary Law Review
WRU L Rev	Western Reserve University Law Review
W Va	West Virginia Reports
Wyo Stat	Wyoming Statutes

TEXT

Text Outline

Chapter 1
Introduction

1.01   Development of juvenile courts
   (A) Early history
   (B) Philosophy
   (C) 1925-1966

1.02   United States Supreme Court cases
   (A) *Kent v United States*
   (B) *In re Gault*
   (C) *In re Winship*
   (D) *McKeiver v Pennsylvania*
   (E) Double jeopardy and confession cases
   (F) Neglect cases
   (G) Preventive detention
   (H) School searches
   (I) Related cases

1.03   Future directions

1.04   Ohio experience

Chapter 3
Subject Matter Jurisdiction

3.01   General provisions

3.02   Delinquent child

3.03   Juvenile traffic offender

3.04   Unruly child

3.05   Neglect, dependency, and abuse: attachment of jurisdiction

3.06   Neglected child
   (A) Definition
   (B) Abandonment
   (C) Faults or habits
   (D) Proper or necessary care
   (E) Special care

Chapter 5
Police Investigations

Chapter 7
Pre-Adjudication Procedures

Chapter 9
Transfer of Jurisdiction

Chapter 15
Post-Disposition Issues

Chapter 1

Introduction

1.01   Development of juvenile courts

(A) Early history

Illinois established the first juvenile court in 1899.[1] The purpose clause of the enabling Act directed that "the care, custody and discipline of a child shall approximate as nearly as may be that which should be given by its parents, and in all cases where it can properly be done the child [shall] be placed in an improved family home and become a member of the family by legal adoption or otherwise."[2]

The Act contained a number of features that influenced the development of the juvenile court system in this country. First, the Act established a separate court for cases involving children under sixteen alleged to be delinquent, dependent, or neglected. A delinquent child was defined as a child under sixteen "who violates any law of this state or any city or village ordinance." Noncriminal misbehavior was added to the definition of delinquency in 1901.[3] Second, the enabling Act established special procedures for juvenile cases. Third, the Act prohibited the detention of a child under twelve years of age in a jail or police station and required the separation of juveniles and adults when placed in the same institution. Fourth, it provided for probation officers to investigate cases and supervise juveniles placed on probation.

Within six years of the passage of the Illinois Act, thirty states enacted juvenile court legislation.[4] By 1925 every state but two had a juvenile court.[5] Today, every jurisdiction has a juvenile court system. The Juvenile Justice and Delinquency Prevention Act of 1974[6] governs juvenile court practice in federal courts.[7]

(B) Philosophy

The doctrine of parens patriae underlies the philosophy of the juvenile court system.[8] The concept that "the state is the higher or the ultimate parent of all of

---

[1]Illinois Juvenile Court Act of 1899. 1899 Ill. Laws 131.

[2]1899 Ill. Laws 137.

[3]Schultz, *The Cycle of Juvenile Court History*, 19 Crime & Delinquency 457 (1973).

[4]Paulsen, *Kent v. United States: The Constitutional Context of Juvenile Cases*, 1966 Supreme Court Rev 167, 169.

[5]President's Commission on Law Enforcement and Administration of Justice, *Task Force Report: Juvenile Delinquency and Youth Crime* 3 (1967).

[6]18 USC 5031 to 18 USC 5042.

[7]See generally Sessions and Bracey, *A Synopsis of the Federal Juvenile Delinquency Act*, 14 St. Mary's L J 509 (1983); Treatment of juvenile alleged to have violated law of United States under Federal Juvenile Delinquency Act, 58 ALR Fed 232 (1982).

[8]"In the branch of civil law that deals with issues of equity, under the medieval English doctrine of *parens patriae*, court sponsors found the appropriate legal precedent

the dependents within its borders"[9] was used to justify the commitment of children to reform school as early as 1839.[10]

The juvenile court movement was based on a distinct philosophy, the keystone of which was rehabilitation. In the words of two early commentators, "Its purpose is not to punish but to save."[11] Commenting on the practice which existed prior to the adoption of the juvenile court, another early authority wrote, "What was lacking was the conception that a child that broke the law was to be dealt with by the state not as a criminal but as a child needing care, education, and protection."[12]

In order to achieve the goal of rehabilitation, the reformers argued for a separate court for children. According to the reformers, the criminal court system had failed to assist the delinquent child.[13] Oriented primarily toward punishment, the criminal court simply did not focus on the proper issue. It "did not ask how he had come to do the particular act which had brought him before the court. It put but one question, 'Has he committed this crime?' It did not inquire, 'What is the best thing to do for this lad?' "[14]

From its inception, this separate court existed as a civil, not criminal, court. Consequently, children subject to its jurisdiction remained unfettered with the stigma of a criminal conviction. To further protect the child, juvenile records were considered confidential, and the court's proceedings remained closed to the public. Moreover, the juvenile court system discarded the procedures applicable in criminal cases.[15] Section 5 of the original Illinois Act provided that "the court shall proceed to hear and dispose of the case in a summary manner."[16] The juvenile court judge would act "as a wise and merciful father."[17] Despite the lack of procedural safeguards, the courts repeatedly upheld the constitutionality of juvenile court procedures.[18]

The early reformers also placed great reliance on the methodologies of the social sciences to bring about the rehabilitation of juveniles: "[T]he Juvenile

---

to champion their expansive view of juvenile courts as instruments of moral and social uplift." Schlossman, *Juvenile Justice: History and Philosophy*, in 3 Encyclopedia of Crime and Justice 961, 962 (Kadish ed 1983).

[9]Mack, *The Juvenile Court*, 23 Harv L Rev 104 (1909).

[10]Ex parte Crouse, 4 Wh 9 (Pa 1839).

[11]Flexner and Oppenheimer, *The Legal Aspect of the Juvenile Court* 9 (1922) (Children's Bureau Pub No. 99).

[12]Lou, *Juvenile Courts in the United States* 18 (1927).

[13]"[T]he reformers generally rejected deterrence and retribution as adequate notions to justify criminal sanctions. A criminal law based on such principles had failed to suppress crime and was cruel to individuals because of its failure to individualize treatment." Paulsen, *Kent v. United States: The Constitutional Context of Juvenile Cases*, 1966 Supreme Court Rev 167, 169.

[14]Mack, *The Juvenile Court*, 23 Harv L Rev 104, 107 (1909).

[15]"The proceedings were divested of almost all features which are attached to a criminal proceeding. . . . In short, the chancery practice was substituted for that of the criminal procedure." Lou, *Juvenile Courts in the United States* 20 (1927).

[16]1899 Ill. Laws 133.

[17]Mack, *The Juvenile Court*, 23 Harv L Rev 104, 107 (1909).

[18]E.g., Lindsay v Lindsay, 257 Ill 328, 100 NE 892 (1913); Ex parte Sharp, 15 Idaho 120, 96 P 563 (1908); Commonwealth v Fisher, 213 Pa 48, 62 A 198 (1905); Mill v Brown, 31 Utah 473, 88 P 609 (1907).

Court is conceived in the spirit of the clinic; it is a kind of laboratory of human behavior."[19] As another early commentator observed:

> The Juvenile Court is conspicuously a response to the modern spirit of social justice. It is perhaps the first legal tribunal where law and science, especially the science of medicine and those sciences which deal with human behavior, such as biology, sociology, and psychology, work side by side. . . . The methods which it uses are those of social case work.[20]

Several commentators have attacked the view that the juvenile court movement was the product of a reform effort designed to improve the lot of juveniles. For example, A. M. Platt has written:

> Child saving may be understood as a crusade which served symbolic and ceremonial functions for native, middle-class Americans. The movement was not so much a break with the past as an affirmation of faith in traditional institutions. Parental authority, home education, rural life, and the independence of the family as a social unit were emphasized because they seemed threatened at this time by urbanism and industrialism. The child savers elevated the nuclear family, especially women as stalwarts of the family, and defended the family's right to supervise the socialization of youth.[21]

In a later section of his book, he commented:

> It is inaccurate to regard the child savers as liberal reformers and their opponents as staunch conservatives, for the authoritarian impulse was implicit in the child-saving movement. . . . In effect, only lower-class families were evaluated as to their competence, whereas the propriety of middle-class families was exempt from investigation and recrimination.[22]

Platt's view of the early reformers, however, has not gone unchallenged.[23]

(C) 1925-1966

From the creation of the first juvenile court in 1899 until 1966, the United States Supreme Court never decided a juvenile court case. The Court did consider whether a juvenile's confession was admissible in evidence in two cases during this period,[24] but both cases involved criminal trials. As noted above, by

---

[19]Van Waters, *The Socialization of Juvenile Court Procedure*, in Hoag and Williams, Crime, Abnormal Minds and the Law 158 (1923).

[20]Lou, *Juvenile Courts in the United States* 2 (1927).

[21]Platt, *The Child Savers: The Invention of Delinquency* 98 (2d ed 1977).

[22]*Id.* at 135. See also Fox, *Juvenile Justice Reform: An Historical Perspective*, 22 Stan L Rev 1187, 1229 (1970):

> In summary, the 1899 Illinois Act (1) restated the belief in the value of coercive predictions, (2) continued nineteenth-century summary trials for children about whom the predictions were to be made, (3) made no improvements in the long-condemned institutional care furnished these same children, (4) codified the view that institutions should, even without badly needed financial help from the legislature, replicate family life, and that foster homes should be found for predelinquents, and (5) reinforced the private sectarian interests, whose role long had been decried by leading child welfare reformers in the area of juvenile care.

[23]See Schultz, *The Cycle of Juvenile Court History*, 19 Crime & Delinquency 457 (1973). See also Schlossman, *Juvenile Justice: History and Philosophy*, in 3 Encyclopedia of Crime and Justice 961 (Kadish ed 1983).

[24]See Gallegos v Colorado, 370 US 49, 82 SCt 1209, 8 LEd(2d) 325 (1962); Haley v Ohio, 332 US 596, 68 SCt 302, 92 LEd 224 (1948).

1925 the juvenile court system was firmly established. One commentary on these years provides the following picture:

> From 1925 until . . . 1966, juvenile courts operated without legal oversight or monitoring. Many would say that juvenile courts in this period were not really courts at all. There was little or no place for law, lawyers, reporters and the usual paraphernalia of courts; this is not at all surprising because the proponents of the Juvenile Court movement had specifically rejected legal institutions as appropriate to the rehabilitation of children.[25]

It would be a mistake, however, to conclude that nothing of significance occurred during this interval. In 1962, New York enacted the Family Court Act. This Act established a separate classification for noncriminal misbehavior— Persons in Need of Supervision (PINS). This classification aimed to distinguish PINS from delinquents, thereby eliminating the stigma attached to the delinquency label for the PINS child.[26] The Act also established a bifurcated hearing procedure, the first stage focusing on the facts of the case and the second on disposition. In addition, a state-financed system of law guardians was established; limits were placed on pretrial detention; and the right to remain silent was recognized.[27] As one court commented, these provisions "are indicative of legislative recognition of the fact that such proceedings, resulting as they do in a loss of personal freedom, are at the very least quasi-criminal in nature."[28]

Thus, there emerged a middle ground between the lack of procedural safeguards characteristic of the early juvenile courts and the rigorous adherence to procedural rights found in adult trials.

CROSS REFERENCES

Merrick-Rippner, Ohio Probate Law (4th ed), Text Ch 217

1.02 United States Supreme Court cases

(A) Kent v United States

In 1966, the United States Supreme Court in *Kent v United States*[29] examined the juvenile court system for the first time. *Kent* involved proceedings to transfer a child's case from the juvenile court to a criminal court for trial as an adult.[30] The Court's language in *Kent* signaled the end of the era when juvenile courts could be described as "not really courts." Referring to the doctrine of parens patriae, Justice Fortas wrote, "But the admonition to function in a 'parental' relationship is not an invitation to procedural arbitrariness."[31] Then he stated:

---

[25]Wadlington, Whitebread, and Davis, *Cases and Materials on Children in the Legal System* 198 (1983).

[26]*IJA-ABA Juvenile Justice Standards, A Summary and Analysis* 33 (2d ed 1982).

[27]Paulsen, *The Constitutional Domestication of the Juvenile Court*, 1967 Supreme Court Rev 233, 244.

[28]In re Gregory W. and Gerald S., 19 NY(2d) 55, 62, 277 NYS(2d) 675, 224 NE(2d) 102 (1966).

[29]Kent v United States, 383 US 541, 86 SCt 1045, 16 LEd(2d) 84 (1966).

[30]For a further discussion of the transfer process, see Text Ch 9, Transfer of Jurisdiction.

[31]Kent v United States, 383 US 541, 555, 86 SCt 1045, 16 LEd(2d) 84 (1966).

> While there can be no doubt of the original laudable purpose of juvenile courts, studies and critiques in recent years raise serious questions as to whether actual performance measures well enough against theoretical purpose to make tolerable the immunity of the process from the reach of constitutional guaranties applicable to adults. There is much evidence that some juvenile courts ... lack the personnel, facilities and techniques to perform adequately as representatives of the State in a *parens patriae* capacity, at least with respect to children charged with law violation. There is evidence, in fact, that there may be grounds for concern that the child receives the worst of both worlds: that he gets neither the protections accorded to adults nor the solicitous care and regenerative treatment postulated for children.[32]

Although some of the Court's language indicated that *Kent* involved only an issue of statutory interpretation, the opinion also referred to constitutional principles: "[W]e do hold that the [transfer] hearing must measure up to the essentials of due process and fair treatment."[33]

(B) In re Gault

Any doubts about the Court's intention to apply due process safeguards to juvenile court practice were resolved in *In re Gault*,[34] a decision which changed the nature of juvenile court proceedings. According to the Court, "[N]either the Fourteenth Amendment [due process] nor the Bill of Rights is for adults alone."[35] Soon after *Gault* was decided, one court aptly observed, "The Supreme Court has recently revolutionized the procedural aspects of juvenile court proceedings."[36]

The Court in *Gault* questioned the underpinnings of the juvenile court system. The doctrine of parens patriae, according to the Court, was suspect: "[I]ts meaning is murky and its historic credentials are of dubious relevance."[37] The term delinquent "has come to involve only slightly less stigma than the term 'criminal' applied to adults."[38] The "claim of secrecy ... is more rhetoric than reality."[39] Incarceration, "whether it is called 'criminal' or 'civil,' " is nevertheless "a deprivation of liberty."[40] The Court went on to hold that in an adjudicatory hearing to determine delinquency, a child has the right to be notified of the charges, the right to be represented by counsel, the right to confront witnesses who testify against him, and the privilege against compelled self-incrimination.[41]

Two further aspects of the Court's opinion are noteworthy. First, the Court did not believe its decision would ruin the juvenile court system: "[T]he observance of due process standards, intelligently and not ruthlessly administered, will not compel the States to abandon or displace any of the substantive benefits

---

[32]*Id.* at 555-56.

[33]*Id.* at 562. For a further discussion of *Kent*, see Text 9.01, In general.

[34]In re Gault, 387 US 1, 87 SCt 1428, 18 LEd(2d) 527 (1967).

[35]*Id.* at 13.

[36]Kent v United States, 401 F(2d) 408, 409 (DC Cir 1968).

[37]In re Gault, 387 US 1, 16, 87 SCt 1428, 18 LEd(2d) 527 (1967).

[38]*Id.* at 24.

[39]*Id.*

[40]*Id.* at 50.

[41]For a further discussion of *Gault*, see Text Ch 11, Adjudicatory Hearings.

of the juvenile process."[42] Second, the Court limited its holding to delinquency proceedings, and then only to the adjudicatory hearing:

> We do not in this opinion consider the impact of these constitutional provisions upon the totality of the relationship of the juvenile and the state. We do not even consider the entire process relating to juvenile "delinquents." For example, we are not here concerned with the procedures or constitutional rights applicable to the pre-judicial stages of the juvenile process, nor do we direct our attention to the post-adjudicative or dispositional process.[43]

Thus, the *Gault* Court, while using broad language, issued a narrow ruling, limited to specified rights at the adjudicatory stage of delinquency cases.[44] Nevertheless, the ramifications of the decision were not so limited. As one court remarked: "[T]he language of [*Gault*] exhibits a spirit that transcends the specific issues there involved."[45]

(C) In re Winship

In 1970, the Court returned to the examination of juvenile court procedure. In *In re Winship*[46] the Court held that the "beyond a reasonable doubt" standard of proof applicable in adult criminal cases also applied in delinquency cases where a child's liberty was at issue. The Court repeated some of the themes articulated in *Gault*. It rejected the civil-criminal label found in juvenile law jurisprudence: "We made clear [in *Gault*] that civil labels and good intentions do not themselves obviate the need for criminal due process safeguards in juvenile courts."[47] Again, the Court stressed that its decision would not destroy the "beneficial aspects of the juvenile process."[48]

(D) McKeiver v Pennsylvania

The Court's next case, *McKeiver v Pennsylvania,*[49] considered the right to trial by jury. Unlike its prior decisions, however, the Court declined to extend this constitutional guarantee to juvenile cases. In reviewing its prior decisions, the Court pointed out that it had not held that "*all* rights constitutionally assured to an adult accused of crime also are to be enforced or made available to the juvenile in his delinquency proceeding."[50] In particular, the Court noted that it had yet to hold that a delinquency proceeding was a "'criminal prosecution,' within the meaning and reach of the Sixth Amendment."[51] Instead, the Court had relied on the more flexible Due Process Clause in its prior cases.

---

[42]In re Gault, 387 US 1, 21, 87 SCt 1428, 18 LEd(2d) 527 (1967).

[43]*Id.* at 13. On this issue the Court also wrote, "The problems of pre-adjudication treatment of juveniles, and of post-adjudication disposition, are unique to the juvenile process; hence what we hold in this opinion with regard to the procedural requirements at the adjudicatory stage has no necessary applicability to other steps of the juvenile process." *Id.* at 31 n.48.

[44]See McKeiver v Pennsylvania, 403 US 528, 538-39, 91 SCt 1976, 29 LEd(2d) 647 (1971).

[45]In re Urbasek, 38 Ill(2d) 535, 541, 232 NE(2d) 716 (1967). See also Kemplen v Maryland, 428 F(2d) 169, 172 (4th Cir Md 1970).

[46]In re Winship, 397 US 358, 90 SCt 1068, 25 LEd(2d) 368 (1970).

[47]*Id.* at 365-66.

[48]*Id.* at 366. See Text 11.10, Burden of proof.

[49]McKeiver v Pennsylvania, 403 US 528, 91 SCt 1976, 29 LEd(2d) 647 (1971).

[50]*Id.* at 533.

[51]*Id.* at 541. The Sixth Amendment provides:

The Court also remarked that in its prior cases it had insisted that its decisions "not spell the doom of the juvenile court system or even deprive it of its 'informality, flexibility, or speed.' "[52] These concerns led the Court to conclude that the right to jury trial would adversely affect the juvenile court system. The Court, however, repeated its belief that the "civil-criminal" distinction was not a controlling factor[53] and that the "fond and idealistic hopes of the juvenile court proponents and early reformers of three generations ago have not been realized."[54] Still, the Court was "reluctant to say that, despite disappointments of grave dimensions, [the juvenile court system] still does not hold promise . . . [or] that the system cannot accomplish its rehabilitative goals."[55]

(E) Double jeopardy and confession cases

The concern that the Court's refusal to recognize the right to jury trial in *McKeiver* might signal an end to its scrutiny of the juvenile court system did not last long. In *Breed v Jones*,[56] a 1975 decision, the Court held the Double Jeopardy Clause,[57] which protects an individual from being tried twice for the same offense, applicable to juvenile court proceedings: "We believe it is simply too late in the day to conclude . . . that a juvenile is not put in jeopardy at a proceeding whose object is to determine whether he has committed acts that violate a criminal law and whose potential consequences include both the stigma inherent in such a determination and the deprivation of liberty for many years."[58] Again, the Court rejected the civil-criminal distinction.[59] Although the Court did not find double jeopardy violations in two subsequent cases,[60] it also did not back away from its position in *Breed* that the clause applied to juvenile cases.

In another delinquency case, the Court considered the applicability of *Miranda v Arizona*[61] to a juvenile's confession. In *Fare v Michael C.*,[62] the Court held that a child's request for his probation officer was not an automatic invocation of the Fifth Amendment's privilege against self-incrimination.[63]

In all criminal prosecutions, the accused shall enjoy the right to a speedy and public trial, by an impartial jury of the State and district wherein the crime shall have been committed, which district shall have been previously ascertained by law, and to be informed of the nature and cause of the accusation; to be confronted with the witnesses against him; to have compulsory process for obtaining witnesses in his favor, and to have the Assistance of Counsel for his defense.

[52]McKeiver v Pennsylvania, 403 US 528, 534, 91 SCt 1976, 29 LEd(2d) 647 (1971).
[53]*Id.*
[54]*Id.* at 543-44.
[55]*Id.* at 547. See Text 11.07, Jury trials.
[56]Breed v Jones, 421 US 519, 95 SCt 1779, 44 LEd(2d) 346 (1975).
[57]The Fifth Amendment provides that no person shall "be twice put in jeopardy of life or limb" for the same offense.
[58]Breed v Jones, 421 US 519, 529, 95 SCt 1779, 44 LEd(2d) 346 (1975).
[59]*Id.*
[60]Illinois v Vitale, 447 US 410, 100 SCt 2260, 65 LEd(2d) 228 (1980); Swisher v Brady, 438 US 204, 98 SCt 2699, 57 LEd(2d) 705 (1978).
[61]Miranda v Arizona, 384 US 436, 86 SCt 1602, 16 LEd(2d) 694 (1966) (The Fifth Amendment requires that, prior to interrogation, a person in custody be informed of the right to remain silent and the right to the presence of counsel.).
[62]Fare v Michael C., 442 US 707, 99 SCt 2560, 61 LEd(2d) 197 (1979).
[63]For a discussion of the admissibility of confessions, see Text 5.04, Interrogations.

(F) Neglect cases

The Supreme Court's initial juvenile court cases dealt with delinquency proceedings, and when the Court granted due process rights in these cases, it carefully limited its holdings to delinquency cases. In the 1980's, however, the Court addressed due process issues in nondelinquency cases. For example, in *Lassiter v Department of Social Services*[64] the Court examined the applicability of due process rights in neglect cases. *Lassiter,* however, involved only one type of neglect proceeding—that involving the permanent termination of parental rights. Finding a parent's interest in such a proceeding to be "a commanding one,"[65] the Court held that due process may require the appointment of counsel for indigent parents. The *Lassiter* holding requires assessing the right to counsel on a case-by-case basis.

Santosky v Kramer[66] also involved proceedings to terminate parental custodial rights permanently. The issue before the Court was whether the "preponderance of evidence" standard, the burden of proof applied in civil cases, satisfied due process requirements in termination proceedings. The Court held that it did not: "In parental rights termination proceedings, the private interest affected is commanding; the risk of error from using a preponderance standard is substantial; and the countervailing governmental interest favoring that standard is comparatively slight."[67] Accordingly, the Court held that due process required "clear and convincing" proof in termination proceedings.

(G) Preventive detention

In *Schall v Martin*[68] the Court upheld the constitutionality of pretrial preventive detention for accused juvenile delinquents. As in its prior cases, the Court again attempted to "strike a balance—to respect the 'informality' and 'flexibility' that characterize juvenile proceedings . . . and yet to ensure that such proceedings comport with the 'fundamental fairness' demanded by the Due Process Clause."[69] Thus, at the same time the Court wrote that "[t]here is no doubt that the Due Process Clause is applicable in juvenile proceedings,"[70] it also reaffirmed the state's parens patriae interest: "The State has 'a *parens patriae* interest in preserving and promoting the welfare of the child,' . . . which makes a juvenile proceeding fundamentally different from an adult criminal trial."[71] Specifically, the Court held that preventive detention served a legitimate state objective and that the procedural safeguards provided—notice, a hearing, counsel, and a statement of reasons—satisfied due process requirements.

---

[64]Lassiter v Department of Social Services, 452 US 18, 101 SCt 2153, 68 LEd(2d) 640 (1981).

[65]*Id.* at 27. See Text 11.03, Right to counsel, guardian ad litem.

[66]Santosky v Kramer, 455 US 745, 102 SCt 1388, 71 LEd(2d) 599 (1982).

[67]*Id.* at 758. See Text 11.10, Burden of proof. For a discussion of reasonable efforts to place child with his parents, see Text 13.04, Reasonable efforts determination.

[68]Schall v Martin, 467 US 253, 104 SCt 2403, 81 LEd(2d) 207 (1984).

[69]*Id.* at 263.

[70]*Id.*

[71]*Id.* For a discussion of the state's parens patriae interest in unborn children, see Text 3.06(D), Proper or necessary care.

(H) School searches

In *New Jersey v T.L.O.*[72] the Court considered the constitutionality of a school search. In that case a student was taken to the principal's office for smoking in the lavatory. A search of her purse revealed cigarettes as well as marijuana, a discovery that led to the initiation of delinquency proceedings. Initially, the Court declared the Fourth Amendment applicable to school searches, thereby rejecting the view that school officials were private citizens, acting in loco parentis, and thus not subject to the Fourth Amendment.[73]

Next, the Court focused on the requirements of the Fourth Amendment in the school setting. In this context, the student's legitimate expectations of privacy are balanced against the school's legitimate need to maintain an environment in which learning can take place. The Court found that the warrant and probable cause requirements imposed too high a burden on the proper functioning of school officials. The Court went on to rule that "reasonable suspicion" is the controlling standard in determining the constitutionality of these searches.[74]

(I) Related cases

The Court has decided several cases that relate to the juvenile court policy of confidentiality. *Davis v Alaska,*[75] a criminal case, involved the cross-examination of a prosecution witness regarding his juvenile record. Although the Court recognized the legitimacy of the state's protective policy concerning juveniles, it found that the "State's policy interest in protecting the confidentiality of a juvenile offender's record cannot require yielding of so vital a constitutional right as the effective cross-examination for bias of an adverse witness."[76] In sum, the Sixth Amendment right of confrontation outweighed the state's protective policy, at least under the facts of that case.

Smith v Daily Mail Publishing Co[77] involved a conflict between juvenile court confidentiality and the First Amendment's freedom of press guarantee. In *Smith*, two newspapers were indicted for violating a criminal statute that prohibited publication, without court approval, of the name of any person charged as a juvenile offender. The Court held that the state's interest in protecting the child through a policy of confidentiality did not outweigh the significant First Amendment rights involved. The Court, however, also emphasized the limited nature of its decision:

> Our holding in this case is narrow. There is no issue before us of unlawful press access to confidential judicial proceedings . . . ; there is no issue here of privacy or prejudicial pretrial publicity. At issue is simply the power of a state to punish the truthful publication of an alleged juvenile delinquent's name lawfully obtained by a newspaper. The asserted state interest cannot

---

[72]New Jersey v T.L.O., 469 US 325, 105 SCt 733, 83 LEd(2d) 720 (1985).
[73]*Id.* at 336.
[74]*Id.* at 341-42. See Text 5.03, Search and seizure.
[75]Davis v Alaska, 415 US 308, 94 SCt 1105, 39 LEd(2d) 347 (1974).
[76]*Id.* at 320. For a discussion of the right of confrontation, see Text 11.12, Evidence. See also Text 15.04(A), Confidentiality, use in other proceedings.
[77]Smith v Daily Mail Publishing Co, 443 US 97, 99 SCt 2667, 61 LEd(2d) 399 (1979).

justify the statute's imposition of criminal sanctions on this type of publication.[78]

A prior case, *Oklahoma Publishing Co v District Court of Oklahoma*,[79] involved a pretrial order prohibiting the news media from publishing the name or photograph of a child charged as a delinquent for second-degree murder. The child's name was obtained at a detention hearing, which the press was permitted to attend. The Court held that the press could not be prohibited from publishing information lawfully obtained during open court proceedings.

CROSS REFERENCES

Text 3.06(D), Ch 5, 9, 11, 13.04, 13.06(A), 13.07, 15.04(A)

Merrick-Rippner, Ohio Probate Law (4th ed), Text Ch 217

1.03 Future directions

There have been many calls for changes in the juvenile court system. In 1967, the year of the *Gault* decision, the Report of the President's Commission on Law Enforcement and Administration of Justice was published. The Report concluded that the reformers' initial hopes for the juvenile court system remained unrealized: "It has not succeeded significantly in rehabilitating delinquent youth . . . or in bringing justice and compassion to the child offender."[80] The Report disagreed with the reformers' view that delinquency was rooted in the individual. According to the Report, "[D]elinquency is not so much an act of individual deviancy as a pattern of behavior produced by a multitude of pervasive societal influences well beyond the reach of the actions of any judge, probation officer, correctional counselor, or psychiatrist."[81] The Report's proposals for reform have been summarized as "diversion, due process, and deinstitutionalization."[82] In short, the state should minimize harm to the child by "interfering in their lives as infrequently and unobtrusively as community safety . . . will allow."[83]

A recent reform effort is the Juvenile Justice Project, sponsored by the Institute of Judicial Administration and the American Bar Association.[84] The Standards published by the Project recommend a number of significant reforms.

---

[78]*Id.* at 105-06. For a discussion of confidentiality of juvenile court records, see Text 15.04(A), Confidentiality, use in other proceedings.

[79]Oklahoma Publishing Co v District Court of Oklahoma, 430 US 308, 97 SCt 1045, 51 LEd(2d) 355 (1976).

[80]President's Commission on Law Enforcement and Administration of Justice, *The Challenge of Crime in a Free Society* 80 (1967). The Commission published a separate volume on juvenile justice—*Task Force Report: Juvenile Delinquency and Youth Crime* (1967).

[81]*Id.*

[82]Tonry, *Juvenile Justice and the National Crime Commissions*, in Pursuing Justice for the Child 281, 290-91 (Rosenheim ed 1976). In 1976, another national crime commission issued its own report on juvenile justice: National Advisory Committee on Criminal Justice Standards and Goals, *Juvenile Justice and Delinquency Prevention* (1976).

[83]Tonry, *Juvenile Justice and the National Crime Commissions*, in Pursuing Justice for the Child 281, 291 (Rosenheim ed 1976).

[84]See *IJA-ABA Juvenile Justice Standards, A Summary and Analysis* (2d ed 1982). For symposia on the Standards, see 57 BU L Rev 617-776 (1977); 52 NYU L Rev 1014-1135 (1977).

First, the Standards recommend the abolition of juvenile court jurisdiction over noncriminal misbehavior or status offenses: "A juvenile's acts of misbehavior, ungovernability, or unruliness which do not violate the criminal law should not constitute a ground for asserting juvenile court jurisdiction over the juvenile committing them."[85] This recommendation goes beyond earlier reforms, which called for the deinstitutionalization of status offenders. It is one of several recommendations aimed at limiting juvenile court jurisdiction.

Second, the Standards recommend restrictive criteria for state intervention in neglect cases: "In general, coercive intervention is limited [under the Standards] to situations where the child has suffered, or is likely to suffer, serious harm."[86] Again, this recommendation would limit the reach of juvenile court jurisdiction.

Third, the Standards recommend that delinquency dispositions be determinate and proportional to the seriousness of the offense.[87] The Standards "reject the use of indeterminancy as a governing principle of juvenile sentencing."[88] Indeterminate sentences are based on the theory of rehabilitation, the guiding principle of the early reformers who created the first juvenile courts. Thus, this recommendation represents a significant break with the original juvenile court philosophy.

Fourth, the Standards recommend procedural changes which would enhance the "visibility and accountability of decision making."[89] For example, in delinquency cases the Standards propose public trials[90] and jury trials on request.[91] These recommendations would further reduce the differences between delinquency proceedings and criminal trials.

Moreover, some commentators continue to question the underlying justifications for the juvenile court system:

> [T]he juvenile court has been effectively criminalized in that its current administrative assumptions and operations are virtually indistinguishable from those of adult criminal courts. At the same time, however, the procedures of the juvenile court often provide protections for juveniles less adequate than those afforded adult criminal defendants. As a result, juveniles receive the worst of both worlds, and the reasons for the very existence of a separate juvenile court are called into question.[92]

1.04   Ohio experience

As early as 1869, the Ohio Supreme Court recognized the state's authority to commit children to reform schools.[93] According to the court, the "authority of

---

[85]*IJA-ABA Standards Relating to Noncriminal Misbehavior* 23 (1982).

[86]*IJA-ABA Standards Relating to Abuse and Neglect* 4 (1981).

[87]*IJA-ABA Juvenile Justice Standards, A Summary and Analysis* 22-23 (2d ed 1982).

[88]*IJA-ABA Standards Relating to Dispositions* 26 (1980). See also *IJA-ABA Standards Relating to Juvenile Delinquency and Sanctions* 41 (1980).

[89]*IJA-ABA Standards for Juvenile Justice: A Summary and Analysis* 23 (2d ed 1982).

[90]*IJA-ABA Standards Relating to Adjudication* 70 (1980).

[91]*Id.* at 51.

[92]Feld, *Criminalizing Juvenile Justice: Rules of Procedure for the Juvenile Court,* 69 Minn L Rev 141, 142 (1984).

[93]Prescott v State, 19 OS 184 (1869).

the state, as *parens patriae*, to assume the guardianship and education of neglected homeless children, as well as neglected orphans, is unquestioned."[94]

Ohio also became one of the first states to enact juvenile court legislation, establishing the Cuyahoga County Juvenile Court in 1902[95] and extending the system statewide by 1906.[96] This legislation governed juvenile court practice until 1937 when Ohio adopted the Standard Juvenile Court Act.[97] As in other jurisdictions, the constitutionality of this legislation was upheld by the courts.[98] The right to counsel,[99] the privilege against self-incrimination,[100] trial by jury,[101] and the right to bail[102] were all held inapplicable to juvenile proceedings. The traditional arguments were offered to support these decisions: juvenile proceedings "are civil in nature and not criminal" and are "for the purpose of correction and rehabilitation and not for punishment."[103]

The pre-*Gault* view of the juvenile court system is captured in the following commentary by an Ohio juvenile court judge:

> The doctrine of *parens patriae*, which justifies those procedures in the juvenile court which seem superficially to conflict with the constitutional liberties of the person, requires that the court act as a wise and kindly parent would in dealing with his own children, toward those children who are brought before the court.[104]

Similar language is found in judicial opinions: "The Juvenile Court is wholly beneficent in its purpose. Its objective is to redeem and save erring children and youth."[105] "The philosophy ... is not to consider the child ... a criminal but rather to take him in hand for the purpose of protecting him from evil influences. The state thus becomes the *parens patriae* of the child on the theory that he needs protection, care and training."[106]

This picture, of course, changed dramatically after *Gault* was decided in 1967.[107] Major revisions in the Juvenile Code were enacted in 1969.[108] Reform efforts in the 1970's resulted in legislative changes in 1976, 1980, 1981, and

---

[94]Cincinnati House of Refuge v Ryan, 37 OS 197, 204 (1881). See also In re Tailford, 95 OS 411, 116 NE 1086 (1917) (Petition denied on authority of *Ryan*.); Bleier v Crouse, 13 App 69 (Hamilton 1920); State ex rel Fortini v Hoffman, 12 App 341 (Hamilton 1920).

[95]95 Ohio Laws 785 (1902).

[96]97 Ohio Laws 561 (1904); 98 Ohio Laws 314 (1906); 99 Ohio Laws 192 (1908).

[97]See Whitlatch, *The Juvenile Court—A Court of Law*, 18 WRU L Rev 1239 (1967).

[98]E.g., Ex parte Januszewski, 196 F 123 (SD Ohio 1911); Leonard v Licker, 3 App 377 (Richland 1914).

[99]Cope v Campbell, 175 OS 475, 196 NE(2d) 457 (1964), overruled by In re Agler, 19 OS(2d) 70, 249 NE(2d) 808 (1969).

[100]State v Shardell, 107 App 338, 343, 153 NE(2d) 510 (Cuyahoga 1958).

[101]In re Darnell, 173 OS 335, 182 NE(2d) 321 (1962).

[102]State ex rel Peaks v Allaman, 66 Abs 403, 115 NE(2d) 849 (CP, Montgomery 1952).

[103]Cope v Campbell, 175 OS 475, 477-78, 196 NE(2d) 457 (1964), overruled by In re Agler, 19 OS(2d) 70, 249 NE(2d) 808 (1969).

[104]Young, *A Synopsis of Ohio Juvenile Court Law*, 31 Cin L Rev 131, 136 (1962). See also Harpst, *Practice in Cuyahoga County Juvenile Court*, 10 Clev-Mar L Rev 507 (1961).

[105]In re Heist, 27 Abs 1 (Juv, Hamilton 1938).

[106]State v Shardell, 107 App 338, 340, 153 NE(2d) 510 (Cuyahoga 1958).

[107]See In re Agler, 19 OS(2d) 70, 249 NE(2d) 808 (1969) (discussing changes in Ohio law as a result of *Gault*).

[108]See Willey, *Ohio's Post-Gault Juvenile Court Law*, 3 Akron L Rev 152 (1970).

1988. The changes adopted in 1976,[109] 1980,[110] and 1988[111] dealt primarily with proceedings involving neglected, dependent, and abused children. In order to insure that permanent planning would be made for children in the custody of child-care agencies, provisions were added to the Code requiring these agencies to submit periodic reviews to the juvenile court detailing the efforts which had been made to rehabilitate the family, including a recommendation for the permanent custody of the child.[112] Other amendments mandated the drafting of written case plans specifying the actions required of the parents in order to regain custody of their child, as well as the services and treatment that would be offered by the agency to achieve this goal.[113] Standards governing the procedures and findings required in proceedings involving the termination of parental rights were also adopted.[114]

The legislative changes in 1981[115] had a twofold effect: the deinstitutionalization of unruly children and delinquent-misdemeanants, and the increased control over delinquent-felons through institutionalization for prescribed minimum periods.[116] The powers and duties of the juvenile court and the Department of Youth Services with regard to delinquents were redefined.[117] With the assistance of state subsidies, local communities were given responsibility for developing programs for unruly children and delinquent-misdemeanants, primarily through diversion from the juvenile court to appropriate community agencies.[118] The resources of the state were restricted to delinquent-felons, who were thought to require a more secure setting for treatment and rehabilitation, as well as for the protection of the public.[119]

Because of apparent dissatisfaction with the results of prior legislative efforts,[120] and in order to insure Ohio's compliance with federal mandates,[121] in 1988 the General Assembly enacted comprehensive changes in the laws governing neglect, dependency, and abuse proceedings.[122] These changes cover a wide variety of procedural and substantive issues which significantly impact on

---

[109]1976 H 156, eff. 1-1-77.

[110]1980 H 695, eff. 10-24-80. See Blank, *Reunification Planning for Children in Custody of Ohio's Children Services Boards: What Does the Law Require?*, 16 Akron L Rev 681 (1983); Christoff, *Children in Limbo in Ohio: Permanency Planning and the State of the Law,* 16 Capital L Rev 1 (1986).

[111]1988 S 89, eff. 1-1-89.

[112]RC 2151.416 (former RC 5103.151, amended and recodified by 1988 S 89, eff. 1-1-89). See Text 15.01(F), Commitment to child care agency, custody review proceedings.

[113]RC 2151.412. See Text 13.04, Reasonable efforts determination; Text 13.05, Case plans.

[114]RC 2151.413, RC 2151.414. See Text 13.06(A), Dispositional alternatives; Text 13.06(B), Motion for permanent custody.

[115]HB 440 (1981).

[116]RC 2151.355. See Text 13.07, Delinquent child; Text 13.08, Unruly child.

[117]See Text 13.07(A)(4), Commitment to Ohio Department of Youth Services; Text 15.01(E), Commitment to Ohio Department of Youth Services, early release.

[118]RC 5139.34. See Text 7.02, Diversion, youth services grant.

[119]For a discussion of amendments proposed in 1977-78, see Willey, *The Proposed Ohio Juvenile Code of 1977-78*, 39 Ohio St L J 273 (1978).

[120]1976 H 156, eff. 1-1-77; 1980 H 695, eff. 10-24-80.

[121]PL 96-272, Adoption Assistance and Child Welfare Act of 1980.

[122]1988 S 89, eff. 1-1-89.

the operations of juvenile courts and county departments of human services. The overall intent of the legislation is to prevent "foster care drift" by, among other things, establishing maximum time limits under which children may remain in the custody of public and private child care agencies,[123] and increasing the responsibilities of juvenile courts to review and oversee the permanency planning efforts of these agencies.[124]

In addition to substantive law changes, the Ohio Supreme Court, pursuant to its constitutional rulemaking authority, promulgated the Ohio Rules of Juvenile Procedure in 1972. The Ohio Constitution provides, "The Supreme Court shall prescribe rules governing practice and procedure in all courts of the state, which rules shall not abridge, enlarge, or modify any substantive right. . . . All laws in conflict with such rules shall be of no further force or effect after such rules have taken effect."[125] Thus, the court is empowered to promulgate procedural, but not substantive, rules. The line between substance and procedure, however, is a difficult one to draw[126] and may vary depending on the context in which these terms are used.[127] There are several instances in which the Juvenile Code, RC Chapter 2151, and the Juvenile Rules contain provisions that are both substantive and procedural.[128] Moreover, conflicts exist between the Code and the

---

[123]RC 2151.353(F), (G), RC 2151.415. See Text 13.06(A)(1)(b), Time restrictions on protective supervision.

[124]RC 2151.412, RC 2151.416, RC 2151.417, RC 2151.419, RC 5103.15. See Text 13.04, Reasonable efforts determination; Text 13.05, Case plans.

[125]O Const Art IV, § 5(B). See also Krause v State, 31 OS(2d) 132, 285 NE(2d) 736 (1971). For a discussion of the effect of a statute establishing a procedural principle which is enacted after the promulgation of a supreme court rule on the same subject, see Browne, *Civil Rule 1 and the Principle of Primacy: A Guide to the Resolution of Conflicts Between Statutes and the Civil Rules*, 5 Ohio North L Rev 363 (1978). See also In re Vickers Children, 14 App(3d) 201, 14 OBR 228, 470 NE(2d) 438 (Butler 1983) (Juvenile Rules control over subsequently enacted inconsistent statutes purporting to govern procedural matters.).

[126]E.g., State v Douglas, 20 OS(3d) 34, 35, 20 OBR 282, 485 NE(2d) 711 (1985) (Procedure for determining whether to transfer a child to the adult court for criminal prosecution is governed by RC 2151.26 and Juv R 30.); Linger v Weiss, 57 OS(2d) 97, 386 NE(2d) 1354 (1979) (Time limits set forth in Juv R 29(A) and Juv R 34(A) are procedural, not substantive.), cert denied 444 US 862, 100 SCt 128, 62 LEd(2d) 83 (1979); In re Vickers Children, 14 App(3d) 201, 14 OBR 228, 470 NE(2d) 438 (Butler 1983) (Requirements for bifurcated hearings contained in Juv R 29 and 34 control over RC 2151.414 in permanent custody cases.); In re Therklidsen, 54 App(2d) 195, 376 NE(2d) 970 (Franklin 1977) (Ten-day period of limitation in Juv R 29(A) is procedural.); In re Corona, No. 40992 (8th Dist Ct App, Cuyahoga, 8-20-81) (Failure to adhere to the time limits in Juv R 29(F) is a procedural irregularity and thus does not affect the court's jurisdiction.). Contra State v Newton, No. F-82-17 (6th Dist Ct App, Fulton, 6-10-83) (If no detention hearing is held within seventy-two hours and no adjudicatory hearing is held within ten days, the complaint must be dismissed.).

See also Giannelli, *Ohio Evidence Manual*, Author's Comment § 102.05 (1987); Note, *Substance and Procedure: The Scope of Judicial Rule Making Authority in Ohio*, 37 Ohio St L J 364 (1976).

[127]Gregory v Flowers, 32 OS(2d) 48, 290 NE(2d) 181 (1972).

[128]See Kameya and Pringle, *A Comparative Analysis of Chapter 2151 Ohio Revised Code and the Ohio Rules of Juvenile Procedure* (Federation for Community Planning, Cleveland, Ohio, June 19, 1980).

Rules with respect to issues that cannot be easily characterized as either substantive or procedural.[129]

Other conflicts exist within the Rules themselves[130] and between the Juvenile Rules and the Traffic Rules when applied to juvenile traffic offender cases.[131]

The Ohio juvenile court system is not without its critics. One commentator, while acknowledging that the reform efforts to date show "a picture of progress toward a better Juvenile Justice System,"[132] advocated further change:

> The litany of judicial abuse has been long and will continue until adequate monitoring of the juvenile court system is accomplished by both appellate courts and the public. Legislation establishing appropriate appellate standards will be needed, as well as legislation opening juvenile courts to the press and public. While open juvenile courts include possible negative potential, some courts, both in Ohio and out-of-state, have been open for years without any adverse effect on the system or the juvenile therein.[133]

CROSS REFERENCES

Text 7.02, 13.04 to 13.08, 15.01(E), (F)

---

[129]E.g., RC 2151.281 and Juv R 4(B) (requirements for appointment of guardian ad litem); RC 2151.314 and Juv R 7(F) (time limitations for detention and shelter care decisions);RC 2151.312(B) and Juv R 7(H) (authority to detain juveniles in adult facilities).

[130]The most obvious conflict concerns the time limits for conducting an adjudicatory hearing for a child who is in detention or shelter care. Juv R 29(A) requires the hearing within ten days of the filing of the complaint. However, Juv R 16(A) provides that when service of summons is made by certified mail, the hearing date may not be less than twenty-one days after the date of the mailing, and when service is made by publication, the hearing date may not be less than fourteen days after the date of publication. Because a child's parents are parties to a juvenile court proceeding (Juv R 2(16)) and must be served with summons (Juv R 15(A)), a conflict exists where a child is in detention or shelter care and a parent resides in another state (necessitating certified mail service) or the parent's whereabouts is unknown (requiring service by publication).

[131]Pursuant to Juv R 1 and Traf R 1 and Traf R 2, juvenile traffic offender proceedings are governed by both sets of rules. Several conflicts exist, including Juv R 7 and Traf R 4 (governing the granting of bail as opposed to the standards for detaining children); Juv R 15, Juv R 16 and Traf R 6 (form and service of summons and warrants); Juv R 29 and Traf R 8(D) (explanation of rights); Juv R 27 and Traf R 9 (provision for jury trials); Juv R 29(C) and Traf R 10 (permissible pleas); Juv R 40 and Traf R 14 (use of referees and whether they must be attorneys).

[132]Willey, *The History of Juvenile Law Reform in Ohio Since Gault,* 12 Ohio North L Rev 469, 471 (1985).

[133]*Id.* at 590.

Chapter 3

Subject Matter Jurisdiction

3.01   General provisions

Under the jurisdictional statute, RC 2151.23(A)(1), the juvenile court has exclusive original jurisdiction concerning any child[1] who on or about the date specified in the complaint is alleged to be a juvenile traffic offender or a delinquent, unruly, abused, neglected, or dependent child.[2] Because this jurisdiction is both exclusive and original, all complaints regarding these children must be initially filed and processed in the appropriate juvenile court. Only after the juvenile court has assumed jurisdiction may any other type of court obtain jurisdiction (e.g., the court of appeals in appellate cases,[3] or the general division of the court of common pleas in cases involving alleged delinquents transferred for criminal prosecution[4]).

Once a juvenile court assumes jurisdiction over a child, no other court of this state (with the possible exception of another juvenile court[5]) may assume jurisdiction over that child until the juvenile court's jurisdiction is terminated.[6] For instance, if a child is adjudged dependent by a juvenile court and is committed to the temporary custody of a county department of human services, and the parents thereafter are granted a divorce by a domestic relations court, that court is without authority to make any orders concerning the child's custody. In this situation the domestic relations court is authorized to certify its jurisdiction over custody and child support matters to the juvenile court if it finds that custody to either parent is not in the child's best interest,[7] or if the juvenile court consents.[8] Absent the best interest determination or juvenile court consent, the

---

[1]For the definition of "child," see RC 2151.011(B)(1); Juv R 2(2); Text 3.10(A), General provisions.

[2]See In re Lippitt, No. 38421 (8th Dist Ct App, Cuyahoga, 3-9-78), holding that RC 2151.23 is not definitional only, and that the juvenile court has exclusive, original jurisdiction over civil neglect cases.

[3]See Text 15.02, Appeals.

[4]See RC 2151.26. See also Text Ch 9, Transfer of Jurisdiction.

[5]See RC 2151.271; Text 7.04(B), Transfer.

[6]Children's Home of Marion County v Fetter, 90 OS 110, 106 NE 761 (1914); In re Small, 114 App 248, 181 NE(2d) 503 (Darke 1960); Hartshorne v Hartshorne, 89 Abs 243, 185 NE(2d) 329 (App, Columbiana 1959); O'Donnell v Franklin County Children Services, No. 80AP-854 (10th Dist Ct App, Franklin, 1-22-81); State ex rel Thompson v Murray, No. CA84-02-010 (12th Dist Ct App, Madison, 8-31-84).

[7]RC 3109.04(A), RC 2151.23(D).

[8]RC 3109.06, RC 2151.23(D).

domestic relations court has no authority to certify its jurisdiction and would simply abstain from entering any child custody or support order.

When a case is certified to a juvenile court, or when a juvenile court otherwise obtains jurisdiction over and enters orders regarding the custody and support of children, that court retains continuing and exclusive jurisdiction over such matters, and its attempted transfer jurisdiction to a domestic relations court is a nullity.[9]

Although the assumption of jurisdiction over a child by a juvenile court precludes another court from assuming jurisdiction over such child, the reverse is not true. Therefore, if a domestic relations court grants custody of a child to a parent by virtue of a divorce decree, a juvenile court may subsequently assume jurisdiction over the child if he is alleged to be delinquent, unruly, neglected, dependent, abused, or a juvenile traffic offender.[10] The rationale for this rule is obvious: since the juvenile court possesses exclusive jurisdiction over these types of cases, denial of such jurisdiction would, in effect, eliminate any judicial means to protect and treat these children.

If a juvenile court obtains prior jurisdiction over a child, but does not issue orders concerning the child's custody, it does not retain continuing jurisdiction over that subject. Under such circumstances, a domestic relations court which grants a divorce has jurisdiction to issue custody orders with respect to that child.[11] Similarly, if a juvenile court terminates a previous custody order, and a probate court then assumes jurisdiction through the appointment of a guardian for the child, the juvenile court is without jurisdiction to grant custody of the child to another person until the guardianship has been terminated.[12]

CROSS REFERENCES

Text 3.10(A), 7.04(B), Ch 9, 15.01, 15.02

Schroeder-Katz, Ohio Criminal Law, Crim R 1, Author's Text
Merrick-Rippner, Ohio Probate Law (4th ed), Text Ch 219, 225

3.02 Delinquent child

RC 2151.02 defines a delinquent child as any child who violates any law of this state, the United States, or any ordinance or regulation of a political subdivision of this state,[13] which would be a crime if committed by an adult (except for traffic offenses), or violates a lawful order of the juvenile court.[14]

---

[9]Hardesty v Hardesty, 16 App(3d) 56, 16 OBR 59, 474 NE(2d) 368 (Franklin 1984); Handelsman v Handelsman, 108 App 30, 160 NE(2d) 543 (Columbiana 1958).

[10]James v Child Welfare Board, 9 App(2d) 299, 224 NE(2d) 358 (Summit 1967); McFadden v Kendall, 81 App 107, 77 NE(2d) 625 (Auglaize 1946); In re Gail L., 12 Misc 251, 231 NE(2d) 253 (Juv, Cuyahoga 1967); In re Jones, 46 Abs 132, 68 NE(2d) 97 (Juv, Muskingum 1946); In re Likens, No. 85 CA 80 (2d Dist Ct App, Greene, 10-24-86).

[11]Huxley v Huxley, No. 1903 (9th Dist Ct App, Wayne, 5-23-84).

[12]In re Miller, 33 App(3d) 224, 515 NE(2d) 635 (Cuyahoga 1986).

[13]See In re DeGeronimo, No. 40089 (8th Dist Ct App, Cuyahoga, 6-28-79), holding that violation of the rules of the Metropolitan Park Board is a delinquent act, since that board is a "political subdivision."

[14]See In re Burgess, 13 App(3d) 374, 13 OBR 456 (Preble 1984), holding that a delinquent child is a child whose conduct would constitute a violation of any criminal

A child who violates a federal law may be processed in either a federal district court or a state juvenile court. There is a preference for the state juvenile court. In order to prosecute a child in a federal court, the Attorney General or a United States Attorney must certify that the appropriate juvenile court does not have or refuses to assume jurisdiction, or does not have adequate programs and services to meet the child's needs.[15]

Although it is generally true that offenses which may be committed by adults constitute delinquent acts if committed by children,[16] there are certain exceptions. Those crimes which, by their terms, apply only to adults are not considered delinquent acts if committed by children. For instance, the crimes of "Corruption of a minor" (RC 2907.04) and "Importuning" (RC 2907.07(C)), which require the actor to be eighteen years of age or older, are not delinquent acts if committed by a person under the age of eighteen.[17] However, a child who commits a crime which specifies only that the victim must be a child could properly be charged as a delinquent. For example, the crimes of "Disseminating material harmful to juveniles" (RC 2907.31), "Pandering obscenity involving a minor" (RC 2907.321), "Deception to obtain matter harmful to juveniles" (RC 2907.33(A)), "Contributing to delinquency of a child" (RC 2919.24), "Endangering children" (RC 2919.22),[18] and "Interference with custody" (RC 2919.23(A)(1)), which all require that the object of the offense be a person under eighteen years of age, are delinquent acts if committed by a child since the subject of these offenses may be any "person."

A substantial percentage of delinquency complaints involve drug and alcohol offenses. Courts have held that possession of liquor[19] or hallucinogens[20] by a child is an act of delinquency. Since the purchase of liquor is a crime if committed by an adult between the ages of eighteen and twenty-one,[21] and the purchase of beer is a crime if committed by an eighteen year old,[22] either would constitute a delinquent act if committed by a child. However, it could be argued that possession of less than one hundred grams of marihuana, which is a minor misdemeanor if committed by an adult,[23] would not be a delinquent act if committed by a child. The strength of this argument rests on the interpretation given to RC 2925.11(D), which provides that "[a]rrest or conviction [of an

---

statute, even a statute different from the one included in the delinquency complaint. See also In re Crowe, No. CA10055 (2d Dist Ct App, Montgomery, 2-23-87).

[15]18 USC 5032 et seq.

[16]E.g., State v Lee, No. 44902 (8th Dist Ct App, Cuyahoga, 2-10-83) (possession of fireworks and marihuana); In re Pollard, No. 44061 (8th Dist Ct App, Cuyahoga, 12-17-81) (arson); State v Majoros, No. 42062 (8th Dist Ct App, Cuyahoga, 11-13-80) (riot, disorderly conduct); In re White, No. 40971 (8th Dist Ct App, Cuyahoga, 7-31-80) (failure to report a crime, complicity to murder).

[17]However, it is arguable that a child may be unruly for committing these offenses. See RC 2151.022; In re J.P., 32 Misc 5, 287 NE(2d) 926 (CP, Stark 1972).

[18]This often involves the situation where a teen-age babysitter administers unwarranted disciplinary measures to a child.

[19]State v Butler, 38 Abs 211 (Juv, Tuscarawas 1943).

[20]In re Baker, 18 App(2d) 276, 248 NE(2d) 620 (Hocking 1969), modified by 20 OS(2d) 142, 254 NE(2d) 363 (1969).

[21]RC 4301.63.

[22]Id.

[23]RC 2925.11(C)(3).

adult] for a minor misdemeanor violation of this section does not constitute a criminal record." Attorneys representing alleged delinquents charged with possession of marihuana have asserted that since conviction of the offense does not lead to a "criminal record" for an adult, the offense is not a "crime" as used in the definition of a delinquent child.[24] The better position, however, is that possession of marihuana is a crime for an adult since it is included within Title 29 ("Crimes—Procedure") and is listed under the statute which classifies offenses.[25] Although the conviction of an adult for possession of marihuana does not constitute a criminal record, possession is still a crime for an adult and thus a delinquent act for a child.[26]

Because the dispositional alternatives available to the juvenile court depend, in part, on whether the delinquent child has committed a felony or misdemeanor (according to adult standards),[27] there is added significance accorded those crimes which are elevated from misdemeanors to felonies based on an adult's prior conviction for a similar offense. For instance, if an adult is convicted of a misdemeanor theft offense (RC 2913.02) and is subsequently convicted of a second theft offense, the second conviction constitutes a felony regardless of the value of the property stolen.[28] Since RC 2913.02 speaks in terms of a conviction of a crime rather than an adjudication of delinquency, it would appear that this principle would not apply to juvenile court proceedings since such proceedings are not criminal and a juvenile is incapable of committing a crime.[29] However, the Ohio Supreme Court has held that a prior adjudication of delinquency predicated on a theft offense constitutes a previous conviction of theft under RC 2913.02.[30] Thus, a subsequent theft offense adjudication would amount to a delinquent-felony, permitting the juvenile court to commit the child to the legal custody of the Department of Youth Services.[31] The Supreme Court based its decision on a presumption that the legislature intended the juvenile court to have a greater number of choices regarding dispositions for children who have continuing difficulties with the law.[32]

---

[24]RC 2151.02. However, the child may be charged as an unruly child. See RC 2151.022; Text 3.04, Unruly child.

[25]RC 2901.02(A) and (G) include minor misdemeanors.

[26]See State v Lee, No. 44902 (8th Dist Ct App, Cuyahoga, 2-10-83), wherein a delinquency adjudication for possession of marihuana was upheld, although the issue of whether it constituted a delinquent act was not raised.

[27]For instance, under RC 2151.355(A)(4) and (5), only a delinquency adjudication for commission of a felony may lead to a commitment to the Ohio Department of Youth Services. See also RC 2151.26, concerning the transfer of a child to criminal court for trial as an adult if the child is charged with a delinquent-felony offense. See Text 13.07(A)(4), Commitment to Ohio Department of Youth Services.

[28]RC 2913.02(B).

[29]State v Weeks, 37 App(3d) 65, 523 NE(2d) 532 (Franklin 1987); In re Estate of Birt, 18 Misc(2d) 7, 18 OBR 407, 481 NE(2d) 1387 (CP, Preble 1983); In re Agler, 19 OS(2d) 70, 249 NE(2d) 808 (1969).

[30]In re Russell, 12 OS(3d) 304, 12 OBR 377, 466 NE(2d) 553 (1984).

[31]RC 2151.355(A). See Text 13.07(A)(4), Commitment to Ohio Department of Youth Services.

[32]Prior to this decision, the appellate courts were split concerning this issue. The First District (In re Russell, No. C-820533 (1st Dist Ct App, Hamilton, 4-13-83)) and Sixth District (In re Smith, No. L-82-107 (6th Dist Ct App, Lucas, 8-6-82)) held that a subsequent theft offense constituted a delinquent-felony. The Fifth District (State v Lindsay,

Where a child is charged as a delinquent-felon based on a prior adjudication of theft, the prior adjudication becomes an element of the present offense and must be proved by the state beyond a reasonable doubt. This can be accomplished by producing a certified copy of the prior adjudication of delinquency and sufficient evidence to identify the child as the offender named in the prior order.[33]

A child may be found delinquent not only for violating a criminal statute or ordinance, but also for violating a lawful juvenile court order.[34] Thus, if an unruly child (RC 2151.022) is placed on probation and violates the conditions of the probation order, a delinquency complaint may be filed. This provision has stirred considerable controversy since it "transforms" an unruly child into a delinquent one even though the child may not have violated a criminal statute.[35] This was significant when the treatment and dispositional alternatives available for children in Ohio depended in large part on whether such children were delinquent or unruly.[36] However, since 1981, the distinction between a delinquent-felon and a delinquent-misdemeanant has had far more legal and practical significance than the difference between a delinquent child and an unruly child. For instance, only a delinquent-felon may be committed to the legal custody of the Ohio Department of Youth Services,[37] and only a child charged with a delinquent-felony may be transferred to a criminal court for prosecution as an adult.[38] The dispositions permitted for a delinquent-misdemeanant and an unruly child are quite similar.[39] In addition, neither an unruly child nor a child who is delinquent for having violated a court order made in a prior case of unruliness may be held longer than five days in a secure detention setting.[40]

CROSS REFERENCES

Text 3.04, 7.06(D), 9.02(B), 13.06(A), 13.07(A)(4)

Schroeder-Katz, Ohio Criminal Law, Crim R 2, Author's Text
Merrick-Rippner, Ohio Probate Law (4th ed), Text Ch 221

3.03   Juvenile traffic offender

RC 2151.021 defines a juvenile traffic offender as any child who violates any traffic law, ordinance, or regulation (with the exception of parking violations) of

---

No. 1896 (5th Dist Ct App, Richland, 11-6-80)) and Twelfth District (State v Fikes, No. CA82-03-0029 (12th Dist Ct App, Butler, 8-25-82)) held to the contrary.

[33]In re Hayes, 29 App(3d) 162, 29 OBR 191, 504 NE(2d) 491 (Franklin 1986); In re Williams, 31 App(3d) 241, 31 OBR 525, 510 NE(2d) 832 (Franklin 1986); In re Horton, No. 85-AP-183 (10th Dist Ct App, Franklin, 12-17-85).

[34]RC 2151.02(B).

[35]Despite this objection, the statute has been held constitutional against attacks of vagueness and overbreadth. See In re Boyer, No. 34724 (8th Dist Ct App, Cuyahoga, 12-31-75).

[36]See RC 2151.354 and RC 2151.355 prior to amendment by 1981 H 440, eff. 11-23-81.

[37]RC 2151.355. See Text 13.07(A)(4), Commitment to Ohio Department of Youth Services.

[38]RC 2151.26. See Text 9.02(B), Offenses.

[39]RC 2151.355 and RC 2151.354, respectively.

[40]RC 2151.351. See Text 7.06(D), Time restrictions.

this state, the United States, or any political subdivision of this state.[41] This class of children comprises the largest single category of children coming before the juvenile court.

Determining whether a child who commits an offense involving the operation of a motor vehicle should be charged as a delinquent child (RC 2151.02) or a juvenile traffic offender (RC 2151.021) is an issue that has caused some difficulty. It is most important in those cases in which a death has resulted from the child's improper driving, where the child may be responsible for an aggravated vehicular homicide (RC 2903.06) or a vehicular homicide (RC 2903.07). In making this determination, one must consider the nature of the offense involved. If the offense is included in Title 29 ("Crimes—Procedure"), then the child should be charged as a delinquent; if the offense falls under Title 45 ("Motor Vehicles"), the child would fit within the more narrowly defined class of juvenile traffic offender. Thus, the child accused of vehicular homicide, which is a "crime," must be prosecuted as a delinquent, not as a juvenile traffic offender.[42] Since vehicular homicide is a crime which does not depend upon violation of a traffic offense in order to sustain conviction, it would appear that a child who violates a traffic regulation and, in the process, causes the death of another could be charged as both a juvenile traffic offender (for the traffic offense) and a delinquent child (for the criminal offense). However, a court of appeals has held that the traffic offenses of driving while intoxicated and reckless operation are lesser included offenses of aggravated vehicular homicide, so that prosecution for both constitutes double jeopardy.[43]

CROSS REFERENCES

Text 3.02, 7.03(G), 9.06, 11.15, 13.07, 13.09, 15.01(E)

Merrick-Rippner, Ohio Probate Law (4th ed), Text Ch 221

3.04 Unruly child

RC 2151.022[44] defines an unruly child as any child

---

[41]E.g., In re Farinacci, No. 37973 (8th Dist Ct App, Cuyahoga, 11-30-78) (speeding); In re Bernstein, Nos. 33531, 33532 (8th Dist Ct App, Cuyahoga, 1-2-75) (driving while under the influence; reckless operation).

[42]In re Fox, 60 Misc 31, 395 NE(2d) 918 (CP, Highland 1979). Contra State v Gaida, No. 30423 (8th Dist Ct App, Cuyahoga, 3-2-72), holding that it is permissible, but not mandatory, to charge such child as a delinquent. Gaida was decided prior to the 1975 amendments to the Criminal Code, when vehicular homicide was termed "Homicide by Vehicle in the Second Degree" under RC Ch 4511 ("Traffic Laws—Operation of Motor Vehicles"). See also In re Kuchinsky, No. 41944 (8th Dist Ct App, Cuyahoga, 10-23-80), in which a delinquency finding for aggravated vehicular homicide was reversed on other grounds (no proof that act was proximate cause of death).

[43]State v Crowell, No. 42457 (8th Dist Ct App, Cuyahoga, 3-19-81). See, however, State v Konicek, 16 App(3d) 17, 16 OBR 20, 474 NE(2d) 334 (Cuyahoga 1984), which distinguished Crowell in holding that if all the elements of the greater offense have not occurred when the state concludes prosecution for an included offense, prosecution for the greater offense is not thereby barred. See also State v Long, 7 App(3d) 248, 7 OBR 327, 455 NE(2d) 528 (Franklin 1983).

[44]See In re Burgess, No. 3053 (9th Dist Ct App, Lorain, 11-5-80), holding that the unruly statute is not unconstitutionally vague.

(A) Who does not subject himself to the reasonable control of his parents, teachers, guardian, or custodian, by reason of being wayward or habitually disobedient;[45]

(B) Who is an habitual truant from home or school;

(C) Who so deports himself as to injure or endanger the health or morals of himself or others;

(D) Who attempts to enter the marriage relation in any state without the consent of his parents, custodian, legal guardian, or other legal authority;

(E) Who is found in a disreputable place, visits or patronizes a place prohibited by law, or associates with vagrant, vicious, criminal, notorious, or immoral persons;

(F) Who engages in an occupation prohibited by law, or is in a situation dangerous to life or limb or injurious to the health or morals of himself or others;

(G) Who has violated a law applicable only to a child.

Although it would be impossible to list all of the specific types of misbehavior which could be included under this definition, a few examples help to outline the parameters of the statute.

In order to prove a violation of RC 2151.022(A), it must be shown that the child has a pattern of misconduct; one isolated instance of misconduct will not support a charge under this section.[46]

Since RC 2151.022(B) violations must be "habitual," it appears that a child who engages in only occasional school-skipping or class-cutting or who intermittently leaves home without permission is not in violation of this provision.[47]

RC 2151.022(C), which may be the most all-encompassing provision of the statute, is sometimes used when there is insufficient evidence to file a delinquency complaint, but when there is nevertheless some justification for assuming jurisdiction over the child. For example, a child who engages in consensual sexual activity with another child[48] or a child whose parents catch him smoking marihuana may be subject to a "deporting" complaint under this section.

In order to be validly married in Ohio, a male must be at least eighteen years of age and a female must be at least sixteen years of age and have the consent of her parents or guardian.[49] If either attempts to marry without the required

---

[45]See In re Rulison, No. 8-201 (11th Dist Ct App, Lake, 12-7-81), holding that the term "wayward" as used in this section is not unconstitutionally vague.

[46]In re Quillen, No. H-81-11 (6th Dist Ct App, Huron, 12-4-81).

[47]Although the majority of unruly complaints are filed by parents or school authorities, the Cuyahoga County Juvenile Court was once faced with a situation in which the eighteen-year-old husband of a sixteen-year-old girl wished to file an unruly complaint against her for leaving him and returning to her mother. The case, which was resolved informally without official court action, raised many potentially intriguing issues, such as the legal effect of emancipation and the rights of a married female.

[48]Juvenile courts have been criticized for employing a double standard in that more girls than boys are charged with sexual promiscuity. One reason for this disproportionality is that the parents of females are more likely to report such activity than are the parents of males.

[49]RC 3101.01. In an unreported decision from the Summit County Domestic Relations Court, this statute was held to violate Ohio's Equal Rights Amendment because of the differential age requirements. See also Juv R 42(C), which provides that a minor

consent or misrepresents his or her age, that child may be charged pursuant to RC 2151.022(D). Another issue which may arise under this section involves the child who marries after having been adjudged unruly in a prior case and placed on probation subject to the condition that he not attempt to marry without court consent.[50] Although the child may have obtained the requisite parental consent and the marriage is valid,[51] such child could arguably be charged under this section because of the lack of the consent of the "legal authority" (i.e., the court).[52] Alternatively, the child could be charged as a delinquent child for violation of a court order (RC 2151.02(B)).[53]

RC 2151.022(E), which is rarely used, covers the situation where a child frequents bars or associates with gangs.

RC 2151.022(F) covers cases where a child is employed in violation of the child labor laws[54] or is without an age and schooling certificate[55] where one is required. This may include situations in which the child is employed in an occupation which has been found to be hazardous or detrimental to the health and well-being of a child.[56] For example, a child under the age of sixteen years may not be employed in any manufacturing or mining occupation, public messenger service, or any baking occupation in a retail food service.[57] There are also restrictions on the hours of employment, such as a provision prohibiting children from working more than three hours per day on school days.[58]

Examples of RC 2151.022(G) violations include instances in which a child, for the purpose of obtaining material or gaining admission which is harmful to juveniles, either falsely represents or provides false identification concerning his age or marital status.[59] The most typical laws applicable only to children are curfew ordinances, most of which apply to all persons under the age of eighteen. Although the provisions of curfew ordinances vary among municipalities, the following features are common: graduated hours of restriction based on age, greater freedom during summer months and on weekends, applicability to all

---

female who is pregnant or has been delivered of an illegitimate child may, with the consent of the juvenile court and the requisite parental consent, marry the child's father even though either or both are under the statutory minimum age.

[50]See RC 2151.354(A)(2).

[51]RC Ch 3101.

[52]The parent giving consent could possibly be prosecuted for violation of RC 2919.24. In State v Gans, 168 OS 174, 151 NE(2d) 709 (1958), cert denied 359 US 945, 79 SCt 722, 3 LEd(2d) 678 (1959), the Ohio Supreme Court held that where the parents of a female under sixteen years of age actively help her to get married, such help constitutes acts tending to cause the child to become delinquent (RC 2919.24, formerly RC 2151.41).

[53]See Text 3.02, Delinquent child.

[54]RC Ch 4109.

[55]RC Ch 3331.

[56]RC 4109.05(B).

[57]OAC 4101:9-2-02. There are twenty-two separate sections of the Administrative Code restricting the types of jobs a child may legally perform (OAC 4101:9-2-02 to OAC 4101:9-2-23).

[58]RC 4109.07.

[59]RC 2907.33(B). Section (C) of this statute provides that any juvenile who violates section (B) "shall be adjudged an unruly child." This mandatory unruly adjudication is contrary to Juv R 29(F)(2)(d).

public places, and penalties for parents who permit their children to remain out beyond the curfew. Most of these ordinances also incorporate certain exceptions, such as for children accompanied by a parent or responsible adult, children engaged in lawful employment, and children returning home from a school- or church-sponsored event.[60] Although curfew ordinances in other jurisdictions have been attacked on constitutional grounds as being vague[61] and violative of the First Amendment rights of assembly, association, and movement,[62] two Ohio courts of appeals have upheld the constitutionality of curfew ordinances. In *Eastlake v Ruggiero*[63] the court held that a curfew ordinance which restricted children at nighttime was constitutionally valid, since it did not exceed the bounds of reasonableness. In upholding Eastlake's curfew ordinance, the court relied on the general notion that such laws are justified as police regulations necessary to control the activities of minors and to promote the welfare of the community. However, the court reversed the conviction of a parent who "allowed" the child to violate the curfew ordinance, holding that the proof must establish the parent's "actual or constructive knowledge" of the child's violation. In *In re Carpenter*[64] the Franklin County Court of Appeals upheld the validity of a daytime curfew ordinance which prohibited children from being on the public streets when their attendance was required in school. As in *Ruggiero*, the court cautioned that the ordinance must not be unreasonable, arbitrary, or capricious and must bear a real and substantial relationship to the general public welfare.

The IJA-ABA Standards recommend that a child's unruly behavior that does not violate the criminal law should not constitute a ground for asserting juvenile court jurisdiction over the child and that voluntary social services should be substituted for coercive court intervention.[65]

CROSS REFERENCES

Text 3.02, 13.08

Merrick-Rippner, Ohio Probate Law (4th ed), Text Ch 221

---

[60]The Cleveland curfew ordinance (Section 605.14) is typical. Children of the age of twelve or under may not be on the streets, sidewalks, parks, or other public places from darkness to dawn. For children aged thirteen to sixteen, the curfew is 11 p.m. to 5 a.m. The curfew for seventeen year olds is midnight to 5 a.m. It is not a violation of curfew if the child is accompanied by a parent or guardian, or some other responsible person who is twenty-one or older, or a member of his family who is eighteen or older. A parent who permits his child to violate the curfew ordinance is guilty of a minor misdemeanor.

[61]E.g., Hayes v Municipal Court of Oklahoma City, 487 P(2d) 974 (Okla Crim 1971); Seattle v Pullman, 82 Wash(2d) 794, 514 P(2d) 1059 (1973); In re Doe, 54 Hawaii 647, 513 P(2d) 1385 (1973).

[62]Johnson v Opelousas, 488 FSupp 433 (WD La 1980), reversed by 658 F(2d) 1065 (5th Cir La 1981); People v Chambers, 66 Ill(2d) 36, 360 NE(2d) 55 (1976).

[63]Eastlake v Ruggiero, 7 App(2d) 212, 220 NE(2d) 126 (Lake 1966).

[64]In re Carpenter, 31 App(2d) 184, 287 NE(2d) 399 (Franklin 1972).

[65]*IJA-ABA Standards Relating to Noncriminal Misbehavior* 23 (1980).

3.05   Neglect, dependency, and abuse: attachment of jurisdiction

Although parents have a fundamental, constitutionally protected right to raise their children,[66] this right may be forfeited under certain circumstances defined in the neglect,[67] dependency,[68] and abuse[69] statutes.

One issue which seems to be governed by statute,[70] but which has divided the Ohio courts, concerns when the neglect or dependency must exist in order for juvenile court jurisdiction to attach. RC 2151.23(A)(1) provides that the neglect or dependency must exist "on or about the date specified in the complaint." Several cases decided prior to this 1969 statutory amendment held that the dependency or neglect must exist at the time of the hearing.[71] Since 1969, the cases have split on this jurisdictional matter. Several cases have held that the neglect or dependency must be established as of the date specified in the complaint.[72] These cases hold that RC 2151.23(A)(2) implicitly overruled the cases decided prior to the 1969 statutory amendment.[73] According to these cases, if the date of the hearing were to control, it would be possible for the parents to avoid juvenile court jurisdiction by temporarily correcting the neglectful conditions before the hearing date.[74] Other cases, however, have continued to follow the pre-1969 cases by requiring that evidence of neglect or dependency exist at the time of the adjudicatory hearing.[75] These cases hold that the 1969 statutory amendment[76] merely confers jurisdiction on the juvenile court, but that other statutes[77] require the court to find that the child "is" presently (at the time of the hearing) neglected or dependent in order to proceed to adjudication and disposition. According to these cases, it is necessary to establish neglect or

---

[66]E.g., State ex rel Heller v Miller, 61 OS(2d) 6, 399 NE(2d) 66 (1980); In re Cunningham, 59 OS(2d) 100, 396 NE(2d) 1035 (1979); Hughes v Scaffide, 58 OS(2d) 88, 388 NE(2d) 1233 (1979); In re Perales, 52 OS(2d) 89, 369 NE(2d) 1047 (1977).

[67]RC 2151.03.

[68]RC 2151.04.

[69]RC 2151.031.

[70]RC 2151.23(A)(1).

[71]In re Kronjaeger, 166 OS 172, 140 NE(2d) 773 (1957); In re Darst, 117 App 374, 192 NE(2d) 287 (Franklin 1963); In re Minton, 112 App 361, 176 NE(2d) 252 (Darke 1960); In re Burkhart, 15 Misc 170, 239 NE(2d) 772 (Juv, Warren 1968); In re Turner, 12 Misc 171, 231 NE(2d) 502 (CP, Stark 1967); In re Larry and Scott H., 92 Abs 436, 192 NE(2d) 683 (Juv, Cuyahoga 1963).

[72]In re Sims, 13 App(3d) 37, 13 OBR 40, 468 NE(2d) 111 (Preble 1983); In re Siniard, No. C-78-063 (6th Dist Ct App, Lucas, 2-9-79); In re Feldman, No. 34223 (8th Dist Ct App, Cuyahoga, 12-23-75); In re Kidd, No. 34295 (8th Dist Ct App, Cuyahoga, 11-26-75); In re Linger, No. CA-2556 (5th Dist Ct App, Licking, 7-12-79); In re Baby Girl S., 32 Misc 217, 290 NE(2d) 925 (CP, Stark 1972).

[73]See Text 13.06(A)(4), Permanent custody; Text 13.06(B), Motion for permanent custody.

[74]E.g., In re Bennett, No. CA 78-35 (5th Dist Ct App, Muskingum, 4-25-79).

[75]In re Parker, No. 15-79-16 (3d Dist Ct App, Van Wert, 1-26-81); In re Solarz, Nos. 42275, 42359, 42360 (8th Dist Ct App, Cuyahoga, 11-6-80); In re Guthrie, No. CA 6383 (2d Dist Ct App, Montgomery, 2-22-80); In re Justice, 59 App(2d) 78, 392 NE(2d) 897 (Clinton 1978); In re Poth, No. H-81-31 (6th Dist Ct App, Huron, 6-30-82); In re Bishop, 36 App(3d) 123, 521 NE(2d) 838 (Ashland 1987); Young v Young, Nos. CA 86-03-018, 86-03-019 (12th Dist Ct App, Clermont, 1-20-87).

[76]RC 2151.23(A)(1).

[77]RC 2151.03, RC 2151.04, RC 2151.35, RC 2151.353.

dependency both as of the time specified in the complaint and the time of the hearing.[78]

Where permanent custody is at issue, statutory and case law provide definitive standards for making these "timing" decisions.[79]

CROSS REFERENCES

Text 1.02(F), 3.01, 3.06 to 3.08, 13.06(A)(4), (B), 15.01(B)(1)

3.06   Neglected child

(A) Definition

RC 2151.03 defines a neglected child as any child

(A) Who is abandoned by his parents, guardian, or custodian;

(B) Who lacks proper parental care because of the faults or habits of his parents, guardian, or custodian;

(C) Whose parents, guardian, or custodian neglects or refuses to provide him with proper or necessary subsistence, education, medical or surgical care, or other care necessary for his health, morals, or well being;

(D) Whose parents, guardian, or custodian neglects or refuses to provide the special care made necessary by his mental condition;

(E) Whose parents, legal guardian, or custodian have placed or attempted to place such child in violation of sections 5103.16 and 5103.17 of the Revised Code.

A child who, in lieu of medical or surgical care or treatment for a wound, injury, disability, or physical or mental condition, is under spiritual treatment through prayer in accordance with the tenets and practices of a well-recognized religion, is not a neglected child for this reason alone.[80]

(B) Abandonment

The abandonment of a child consists of a willful leaving of the child by his parent, with the intention of causing a permanent separation.[81] The parent relinquishes his right to custody either by express agreement or unfavorable circumstances, making parental custody clearly detrimental to the welfare of the child.[82] Thus, the act of placing a child in a children's home[83] or with a relative[84] will not alone support a finding of neglect. Nor will a mother's placement of her

---

[78]E.g., In re Kidd, No. 34295 (8th Dist Ct App, Cuyahoga, 11-26-75).

[79]See Text 13.06(A)(4), Permanent custody; Text 13.06(B), Motion for permanent custody.

[80]The statute is not unconstitutionally void for vagueness. See In re Artler, No. 34723 (8th Dist Ct App, Cuyahoga, 7-15-76); In re Forille, No. L-81-164 (6th Dist Ct App, Lucas, 2-12-82); In re Pethel, No. 79CA25 (4th Dist Ct App, Washington, 11-9-81).

[81]In re Kronjaeger, 166 OS 172, 140 NE(2d) 773 (1957); In re Masters, 165 OS 503, 137 NE(2d) 752 (1956).

[82]In re Perales, 52 OS(2d) 89, 369 NE(2d) 1047 (1977); Gallagher v Gallagher, 115 App 453, 185 NE(2d) 571 (Henry 1962).

[83]Gallagher v Gallagher, 115 App 453, 185 NE(2d) 571 (Henry 1962); In re Dickerson, No. 1529 (4th Dist Ct App, Lawrence, 6-2-82).

[84]In re Reese, 4 App(3d) 59, 4 OBR 109, 446 NE(2d) 482 (Franklin 1982). But see Hughes v Scaffide, 58 OS(2d) 88, 388 NE(2d) 1233 (1979), a habeas corpus proceeding (RC 2151.23(A)(3)) in which the Ohio Supreme Court held that a parent forfeited his paramount right to custody by leaving the child with grandparents for nine years.

illegitimate child for adoption and her subsequent withdrawal of consent to adoption constitute neglect since it does not demonstrate rejection of the child.[85]

(C) Faults or habits

The majority of neglect complaints are processed under RC 2151.03(B), which requires findings that (1) the child lacks proper parental care, and (2) this lack of care is the fault of the parents.

Lack of "proper parental care" is defined by RC 2151.05[86] and is often equated by the courts with an allegedly immoral lifestyle.[87] For example, where the parents frequently engaged in adulterous behavior, were selfish and childish, and regularly told their children terrible things about each other, the children were found to be neglected.[88]

Faults or bad habits by themselves, however, do not constitute neglect. It must also be shown that as a result the child lacks proper care. In the absence of evidence showing a detrimental impact upon the children, the mere fact that a mother is living with her boyfriend in the family home will not justify a finding that the children are neglected.[89] Nor will a mother's interracial marriage in itself establish a lack of proper parental care; there must be a finding of unfitness.[90] Furthermore, the fact that a parent is an alcoholic does not necessarily mean that his children are neglected. A causal link must be shown between the fault of the parent (i.e., alcoholism) and the neglected condition of the child.[91]

Courts have considered the issue of whether temporary placement of a child with relatives constitutes neglect under RC 2151.03(B).[92] Because such temporary placements do not constitute "abandonment" under RC 2151.03(A)[93] nor "illegal placements" under RC 2151.03(E),[94] it has been argued that they are evidence that the child lacks "proper parental care" because of parental "faults and habits."

It has been held that the fact that a child is temporarily living with relatives, by agreement with the mother during a period in which she is unable to care for the child, does not constitute neglect if the child is receiving proper care from

[85]In re Robert O., 95 Abs 101, 199 NE(2d) 765 (Juv, Cuyahoga 1964).

[86]See RC 2151.011(B)(17) for definition of the term "adequate parental care," which is the standard applicable in permanent custody cases (RC 2151.353(A)(4)). See Text 13.04, Reasonable efforts determination.

[87]See In re Hayes, 62 App 289, 23 NE(2d) 956 (Franklin 1939); In re Burrell, 58 OS(2d) 37, 388 NE(2d) 738 (1979).

[88]In re Douglas, 82 Abs 170, 164 NE(2d) 475 (Juv, Huron 1959).

[89]In re Burrell, 58 OS(2d) 37, 388 NE(2d) 738 (1979).

[90]In re Brenda H., 37 Misc 123, 305 NE(2d) 815 (CP, Cuyahoga 1973). See also Palmore v Sidoti, 466 US 429, 104 SCt 1879, 80 LEd(2d) 421 (1984), holding that a divorce court judgment divesting a natural mother of custody of her infant child because of the mother's remarriage to a man of different race violates the Equal Protection Clause of the Fourteenth Amendment.

[91]In re Sims, 13 App(3d) 37, 13 OBR 40, 468 NE(2d) 111 (Preble 1983).

[92]E.g., In re Reese, 4 App(3d) 59, 4 OBR 109, 446 NE(2d) 482 (Franklin 1982).

[93]See Text 3.06(B), Abandonment.

[94]See Text 3.06(F), Illegal placement.

the custodian.[95] In such situations, the state has no interest in assuming guardianship since the obligations of care, custody, and support are being met.

The neglect issue also arises when a child's parent is confined to a mental hospital or prison.[96] The Ohio Supreme Court has held that a mother's confinement in a mental hospital, during which time she had no funds to support her children and was unaware of their whereabouts, did not constitute neglect. Mental illness, which was the reason for the confinement, is involuntary and not willful or blameworthy.[97] Even where the conduct underlying the confinement is voluntary, such as the commission of a crime, neglect cannot be established without additional evidence showing a willful disregard of parental duty or indifference toward the child.[98] Such evidence must relate to the parent's character, morals, faults, or habits, rather than his inability to care for the child as a result of the confinement.[99]

(D) Proper or necessary care

The provisions of RC 2151.03(C)[100] are similar to those of RC 2151.03(B), except that RC 2151.03(C) is more specific. It applies to distinct categories of neglect: a parent's failure or refusal to provide the child with proper subsistence, education, medical or surgical care, or anything else that may be necessary for his health or well-being.

Evidence which shows only that a child is weak and sick, without any sign of physical neglect, will not establish that the parents have failed or refused to provide proper subsistence.[101]

A child is not "educationally" neglected when he is excluded from public school because he has not been vaccinated, where the evidence shows that his parent has attempted to enroll him into a proper public school and has not prevented the vaccination.[102]

Many cases of "educational" neglect[103] involve situations in which parents refuse to send their child to a certified school,[104] instead choosing to educate the

---

[95]In re Reese, 4 App(3d) 59, 4 OBR 109, 446 NE(2d) 482 (Franklin 1982).

[96]In an adoption proceeding under RC 3107.06(B), the Ohio Supreme Court has held that the mere fact of a parent's incarceration does not constitute a willful failure to support a child. In re Adoption of Schoeppner, 46 OS(2d) 21, 345 NE(2d) 608 (1976).

[97]In re Masters, 165 OS 503, 137 NE(2d) 752 (1956). However, under proper circumstances, the parent's mental illness may be grounds for a dependency action pursuant to RC 2151.04(B). See Text 3.07(C), Parents' mental or physical condition.

[98]In re Thomas, Nos. 39494, 39495 (8th Dist Ct App, Cuyahoga, 7-19-79).

[99]Id.

[100]This section has been held constitutional against vagueness attacks. See In re Lippitt, No. 38421 (8th Dist Ct App, Cuyahoga, 3-9-78); In re Artler, No. 34723 (8th Dist Ct App, Cuyahoga, 7-15-76).

[101]In re MacPherson, No. 34106 (8th Dist Ct App, Cuyahoga, 4-3-75). See also State v Earich, 86 Abs 90, 176 NE(2d) 191 (Juv, Columbiana 1961), holding that a father's failure to ask for relief, thus permitting the child to go without proper subsistence, constituted criminal nonsupport.

[102]State v Dunham, 154 OS 63, 93 NE(2d) 286 (1950).

[103]Where the failure to attend school is the fault of the child rather than the parent, the child may be charged as an unruly child under RC 2151.022(B). See Text 3.04, Unruly child.

[104]RC Ch 3321.

child by themselves, through a correspondence school, or by enrolling the child in a noncertified private school.[105] An educational neglect adjudication was reversed where the evidence showed that the parents had unsuccessfully made several requests to their local school district superintendent for information on the requirements of home instruction, since these actions showed that the parents had not willfully refused to perform their parental duties.[106]

The parents' refusal to send their child to a certified school is often based on religious grounds. The United States Supreme Court, in *Wisconsin v Yoder*,[107] has specifically exempted Amish children from attending public schools beyond the eighth grade, ruling that the Wisconsin state compulsory education law infringed upon their First Amendment rights. However, parents may not merely assert religious grounds as justification for not providing their children with an adequate education and properly qualified teachers.[108] In a case involving children who were taught at home, an Ohio court of appeals in *In re Lippitt*[109] held that in order to successfully assert religious grounds as justification for failing to send their children to school, parents must demonstrate how such an education would undermine their religious values and establish that they belong to an accepted religious group which offers a well-structured alternative.

In a similar "educational" neglect case, *In re Miller*,[110] a juvenile court dismissed a neglect complaint involving children who attended school in the basement of a home. The case was distinguishable both from *Yoder*, because the parents' objections to the public school's social and moral environment were not based on religious grounds, and from *Lippitt*, because the children's teacher was certified to teach elementary school subjects. In holding that violation of compulsory school laws does not necessarily constitute neglect, the court found that the children were receiving an adequate education and were thus not "educationally" neglected.[111] If the legislature had intended to equate nonattendance with neglect, it would have specifically so provided.[112]

---

[105]RC Ch 3332.

[106]In re Nicholson, Nos. 386, 387 (4th Dist Ct App, Hocking, 11-1-83). See also State v Schmidt, 29 OS(3d) 32, 29 OBR 303, 505 NE(2d) 627 (1987) (Requirement of RC 3321.04(A)(2) that application be made to the local superintendent of schools for approval of a home education program is constitutional.).

[107]Wisconsin v Yoder, 406 US 205, 92 SCt 1526, 32 LEd(2d) 15 (1972).

[108]In re Lippitt, No. 38421 (8th Dist Ct App, Cuyahoga, 3-9-78).

[109]*Id.*

[110]In re Miller, Nos. 77-11-171 to 77-11-174 (Juv, Carroll 1978).

[111]For a similar decision from another jurisdiction, see In re Rice, 204 Neb 732, 285 NW(2d) 223 (1979).

[112]Instead of proceeding under the neglect statute, many of these nonattendance cases are processed as criminal prosecutions against the parents for failing to send their children to school (RC 3321.38). In fact, the *Yoder* case involved a criminal prosecution of parents under Wisconsin's compulsory attendance laws. Although many of the same legal principles apply, in one sense these cases are easier to prove since it is not necessary to establish that the children are neglected based on the quality of the alternative education. However, the Ohio Supreme Court has twice reversed the convictions of defendants whose children were attending nonchartered religious schools which did not comply with all of the minimum standards established by the State Board of Education. The court focused on the scope of the minimum standards, holding that they were so comprehensive as to abrogate the defendants' fundamental right of religious freedom. State ex rel

A child may be adjudged "medically" neglected when the evidence demonstrates that the child has suffered bruises on the face and buttocks that appear to have been inflicted by severe slaps.[113] Similarly, a mother's failure to provide medical care for her children who have been abused by their father constitutes neglect.[114] However, in reversing a juvenile court's adjudication that a child was neglected based on the "failure to thrive" syndrome, a court of appeals held that neglect was not established where the record overwhelmingly indicated that the mother had regularly sought proper medical treatment (i.e., eight times in a five-month period) for her child.[115]

As in the "educational" neglect cases, religion may be a factor in "medical" neglect cases. The final paragraph of RC 2151.03 exempts from the purview of the statute religious sects, such as Christian Scientists, which provide spiritual treatment in lieu of medical treatment. The typical case involves a child in need of potentially life-saving blood transfusions, whose parents refuse to permit such treatment on religious grounds. A complaint is filed to secure a temporary court order allowing the treatment over the parents' objections and may include an order granting emergency, temporary custody of the child to a county department of human services.[116]

In *In re Clark*,[117] involving a badly burned child in critical need of blood transfusions, the court held that the child's right to live took precedence over the parents' religious beliefs and granted the emergency order.[118] It has been asserted that the "religious exemption" provision of the neglect statute may be interpreted to permit blood transfusions where the religious objections are

---

Nagle v Olin, 64 OS(2d) 341, 415 NE(2d) 279 (1980); State v Whisner, 47 OS(2d) 181, 351 NE(2d) 750 (1976).

[113]In re Artler, No. 34723 (8th Dist Ct App, Cuyahoga, 7-15-76).

[114]In re Sullivan, Nos. 79 AP-893, 79 AP-894 (10th Dist Ct App, Franklin, 12-16-80).

[115]In re Kuhn, No. 80 CA 32 (4th Dist Ct App, Pickaway, 3-1-82).

[116]RC 2151.33; Juv R 13(A). Where an unemancipated child has been removed from the custody of his parents and placed in the temporary custody of a county department of human services, the department may properly consent to surgical treatment for the child without consulting with the parents. Kilgallion v Children's Hospital Medical Center, Nos. C-850644, C-860342 (1st Dist Ct App, Hamilton, 4-15-87). The attorney general has ruled that where a child has been permanently committed to a child welfare board by order of the juvenile court, the board may properly consent to medical and surgical treatment for the child; but where the commitment is temporary, the juvenile court retains jurisdiction over the child and may consent to the treatment (OAG 51-689). See also Freedman, *Consent to Medical Treatment for Minors Under Care of Children Services Board*, 10 Capital L Rev 309 (1980). Under certain circumstances, the child may have the authority to consent to necessary treatment even without parental permission or court order. See Lacey v Laird, 166 OS 12, 139 NE(2d) 25 (1956). See also Zaremski, *Blood Transfusions and Elective Surgery: A Custodial Function of an Ohio Juvenile Court*, 23 Clev St L Rev 231 (1974). Note: The county welfare department was renamed the "county department of human services" by the amendment of RC 329.01 by 1984 H 401, eff. July 20, 1984.

[117]In re Clark, 90 Abs 21, 185 NE(2d) 128 (CP, Lucas 1962).

[118]The United States Supreme Court has often ruled that a state may legitimately regulate religious practices for the protection of society. E.g., Prince v Massachusetts, 321 US 158, 64 SCt 438, 88 LEd 645 (1944); Cantwell v Connecticut, 310 US 296, 60 SCt 900, 84 LEd 1213 (1940).

based only on scripture, since this would be considered a "religious belief" rather than "spiritual treatment."[119]

Alternatively, a court could avoid the problems associated with the "religious exemption" to the neglect statute by finding the child to be dependent in that its "condition or environment is such as to warrant the state, in the interests of the child, in assuming his guardianship."[120] Because the "purpose" section[121] of the Juvenile Code provides that the statutes should be liberally interpreted "[t]o provide for the care, protection, and mental and physical development of children" under the juvenile court's jurisdiction, it appears that these interpretations are proper since they could result in the saving of a child's life.[122]

A more difficult issue arises when a pregnant woman objects to medical or surgical treatment designed to save the life of her unborn fetus. Although there are instances in which trial courts have authorized emergency treatment,[123] there are no reported Ohio appellate cases on the issue. However, there is authority from other jurisdictions upholding the right of the juvenile court to intercede in some circumstances on behalf of the unborn child.[124] Furthermore, an Ohio court has held that a viable unborn fetus is to be considered a child, thereby providing the state with an interest in the child's care, protection, and development.[125]

---

[119]Merrick-Rippner, *Ohio Probate Law* Ch 221 (4th ed 1989).

[120]RC 2151.04(C); In re Willmann, 24 App(3d) 191, 24 OBR 313, 493 NE(2d) 380 (Hamilton 1986). See Text 3.07(D), Condition or environment.

[121]RC 2151.01(A). See also Juv R 1(B)(3).

[122]The argument might also be raised that the language contained in the final paragraph of RC 2151.03 violates either the Free Exercise of Religion Clause or the Establishment Clause of the First Amendment. See Ferrante, *Federation for Community Planning* (March 2, 1983) (unpublished paper). For cases from other jurisdictions upholding the right of the state to place limits on the parents' right to free exercise of religion in similar situations, see Jehovah's Witnesses of Washington v King County Hospital Unit No. 1, 278 FSupp 488 (WD Wash 1967), affirmed by 390 US 598, 88 SCt 1260, 20 LEd(2d) 158 (1968), rehearing denied 391 US 961, 88 SCt 1844, 20 LEd(2d) 874 (1968); In re Jensen, 54 Or App 1, 633 P(2d) 1302 (1981); State v Perricone, 37 NJ 463, 181 A(2d) 751 (1962); People ex rel Wallace v Labrenz, 411 Ill 618, 104 NE(2d) 769 (1952), cert denied 344 US 824, 73 SCt 24, 97 LEd 642 (1952).

[123]E.g., In re Unborn Child Copeland, No. 7910111 (Juv, Cuyahoga 6-9-79).

[124]People v Estergard, 169 Colo 445, 457 P(2d) 698 (1969) held that pending adjudication regarding the paternity of an unborn child, the juvenile court may issue such temporary orders for protection, support, or medical treatment as the child's best interest requires. See also Raleigh Fitkin-Paul Morgan Memorial Hospital v Anderson, 42 NJ 421, 201 A(2d) 537 (1964), cert denied 377 US 985, 84 SCt 1894, 12 LEd(2d) 1032 (1964); Jehovah's Witnesses of Washington v King County Hospital Unit No. 1, 278 FSupp 488 (WD Wash 1967), affirmed by 390 US 598, 88 SCt 1260, 20 LEd(2d) 158 (1968), rehearing denied 391 US 961, 88 SCt 1844, 20 LEd(2d) 874 (1968).

[125]In re Ruiz, 27 Misc(2d) 31, 27 OBR 350, 500 NE(2d) 935 (Juv, Wood 1986). See also State v Gray, No. L-87-204 (6th Dist Ct App, Lucas, 4-29-88) (Mother charged with child endangerment under RC 2919.22(A) for ingesting cocaine during her pregnancy.). See also Note, *Maternal Rights and Fetal Wrongs: The Case Against The Criminalization of "Fetal Abuse,"* 101 Harv L Rev 994 (1988); Sherman, *Keeping Baby Safe from Mom*, Natl L J (October 3, 1988); Sherman, *Plan Would Jail "Fetal Abusers,"* Natl L J (November 4, 1988).

(E) Special care

Very few cases are brought under RC 2151.03(D). They might include instances in which parents fail or refuse to seek available care for a mentally retarded child. Because more often than not these parents are simply unable to find or afford necessary treatment,[126] but would be willing to accept such care if it were provided, these children more properly fit under the dependency statute.[127]

(F) Illegal placement

The very specific provisions of RC 2151.03(E) apply to cases where, pursuant to an agreement transferring parental rights or duties, a child is placed in the temporary or permanent custody of any person, association, or institution not certified by the department of human services without the consent of the department or the court.[128]

In many respects, complaints filed under RC 2151.03(E) may resemble "abandonment" complaints brought under RC 2151.03(A),[129] although illegal placements may involve some temporary custody arrangements, whereas "abandonment" connotes a permanent forfeiture of parental rights.[130]

The temporary commitment of a child to a day-care center, nursery, or babysitter does not involve transfer of legal custody and thus would not constitute an illegal placement.[131] In addition, since RC 5103.16 exempts from its purview placements into the care of persons related by blood or marriage, this section would not cover cases where a child is being raised by a grandparent or other relative.

A child may be adjudged neglected under RC 2151.03(E) where he is placed for adoption, unless the placement is approved by the probate court or is made by a department or organization duly authorized to place children.[132]

A neglect adjudication may also result when a person, organization, hospital, or association which is not approved and certified knowingly becomes a party to the separation of a child from its parents or guardians.[133] Where blood relatives of an unwed mother take temporary legal possession of her child whom she

---

[126]See In re Siniard, No. C-78-063 (6th Dist Ct App, Lucas, 2-9-79), in which the court held that where there was no evidence of the mother's inability to provide for her child's physical needs and where the child was enrolled in a school appropriate for his handicap, the child was not dependent.

[127]RC 2151.04(C). See Text 3.07(D), Condition or environment.

[128]RC 5103.16 also provides that temporary placement with a person related by blood or marriage or in a legally licensed boarding home is legal. See In re Duncan, 62 Abs 173, 107 NE(2d) 256 (App, Preble 1951), holding that a placement in violation of RC 5103.16 does not necessarily constitute dependency. This case was decided under a statute (GC 1352-13, recodified in 1953 as RC 5103.16 and amended in 1969) in which "illegal placements" were included within the definition of dependency. See also In re Whitmer, No. 28098 (8th Dist Ct App, Cuyahoga, 6-2-67); In re Robert O., 95 Abs 101, 199 NE(2d) 765 (Juv, Cuyahoga 1964).

[129]E.g., In re Swentosky, 25 Abs 601, 68 NE(2d) 844 (Prob, Tuscarawas 1937).

[130]See Text 3.06(B), Abandonment.

[131]1952 OAG 159.

[132]RC 5103.16. See In re Harshey, 40 App(2d) 157, 318 NE(2d) 544 (Cuyahoga 1974).

[133]RC 5103.17.

thereafter abandons, the relatives are not knowing parties to the separation of the child from its parent within the meaning of this section.[134]

RC 2151.031(D), the most recent addition to the abuse statute,[135] is the only provision which specifically requires a finding of fault on the part of the parent, guardian, or custodian in order to establish abuse. Prior to its enactment, cases coming within the purview of this provision were initiated under the neglect statute.[136]

CROSS REFERENCES

Text 1.02(F), 3.04, 3.07(C), (D), 3.08, 7.06, 7.07, 13.04, 13.06, 13.10

Merrick-Rippner, Ohio Probate Law (4th ed), Text Ch 205, 221
Giannelli, Ohio Evidence Manual, Author's Comment 501.08, 803.08

3.07   Dependent child

(A) Definition

A dependent child as defined in RC 2151.04 includes any child

(A) Who is homeless or destitute or without proper care or support, through no fault of his parents, guardian, or custodian;

(B) Who lacks proper care or support by reason of the mental or physical condition of his parents, guardian, or custodian;

(C) Whose condition or environment is such as to warrant the state, in the interests of the child, in assuming his guardianship.[137]

(D) To whom both of the following apply:

(1) He is residing in a household in which a parent, guardian, custodian, or other member of the household has abused or neglected a sibling of the child;

(2) Because of the circumstances surrounding the abuse or neglect of the sibling and the other conditions in the household of the child, the child is in danger of being abused or neglected by that parent, guardian, custodian, or member of the household.

Although it is possible for a child to be both neglected and dependent,[138] there is a clear distinction between the two terms.[139] Whereas a neglected child lacks proper care because of the fault of a parent, guardian, or custodian,[140] the

---

[134]In re Tilton, 161 OS 571, 120 NE(2d) 445 (1954).

[135]1988 S 89, eff. 1-1-89.

[136]RC 2151.03.

[137]RC 2151.04(B) was held constitutional in In re Boyer, No. 34724 (8th Dist Ct App, Cuyahoga, 12-31-75). RC 2151.04(C) has also been found to be constitutional. See In re Johnson, No. C-810516 (1st Dist Ct App, Hamilton, 4-28-82); In re Forille, No. L-81-164 (6th Dist Ct App, Lucas, 2-12-82).

[138]State v Griffin, 93 App 299, 106 NE(2d) 668 (Champaign 1952); In re Douglas, 82 Abs 170, 164 NE(2d) 475 (Juv, Huron 1959).

[139]For dispositional purposes there is no difference (RC 2151.353).

[140]In re Kronjaeger, 166 OS 172, 140 NE(2d) 773 (1957); In re East, 32 Misc 65, 288 NE(2d) 343 (CP, Highland 1972); In re Kuhn, No. 80 CA 32 (4th Dist Ct App, Pickaway, 3-1-82).

dependency case focuses instead on the condition or environment of the child.[141]

Despite this difference in focus, parental fault is sometimes present in dependency cases and many of the issues raised in neglect cases may be important in dependency proceedings since both involve a lack of proper care.[142]

(B) Homeless or destitute or without proper care

As the neglect cases demonstrate, as long as the child is receiving appropriate care, he will generally not be found to be neglected. The same principle holds true in dependency cases. Thus, dependency is not established where the facts show only that the child is illegitimate;[143] the child's parents are divorced;[144] the parents are illegally married;[145] the father has been incarcerated in the state penitentiary;[146] the mother is a minor and a ward of the welfare department;[147] or the unmarried mother is openly living with her boyfriend.[148] Although in any one of these instances it may be in the best interest of the child to live with someone other than his parent(s), a finding of dependency requires more.[149] The dependency statute must be read in pari materia with the purpose statute, RC 2151.01 of the Juvenile Code, and with caselaw, both of which give parents the paramount right to custody unless there is a substantial threat of harm to the child's physical or mental health.[150]

Many cases processed under RC 2151.04(A) resemble neglect cases in that parental fault is established. Courts have found dependency where the evidence showed that the mother's home was filthy and chaotic;[151] that the mother was an alcoholic who ignored her child's needs in favor of her abusive husband;[152] and that the father was irresponsible and a drug user.[153] In *In re Feldman*,[154] in which the record showed that the children had an irregular school attendance pattern, that the eight-year-old girl frequently slept in the same bed with her

[141]In re Bibb, 70 App(2d) 117, 435 NE(2d) 96 (Hamilton 1980); In re Darst, 117 App 374, 192 NE(2d) 287 (Franklin 1963); In re East, 32 Misc 65, 228 NE(2d) 343 (CP, Highland 1972); In re Thomas, Nos. 39494, 39495 (8th Dist Ct App, Cuyahoga, 7-19-79); In re Bishop, 36 App(3d) 123, 521 NE(2d) 838 (Ashland 1987).
[142]Although dependency complaints often refer to more than one section of RC 2151.04, each section will be considered separately for purposes of illustration.
[143]In re Gutman, 22 App(2d) 125, 259 NE(2d) 128 (Hamilton 1969) (complaint filed pursuant to RC 2151.04(C)); Smith v Privette, 13 Abs 291 (App, Franklin 1932). See also In re Hobson, 44 Abs 86, 62 NE(2d) 510 (App, Franklin 1945).
[144]Sonnenberg v State, 40 App 475, 178 NE 855 (Franklin 1931).
[145]In re Solarz, Nos. 42275, 42359, 42360 (8th Dist Ct App, Cuyahoga, 11-6-80).
[146]In re Wiseman, No. CA 2797 (5th Dist Ct App, Licking, 9-23-81); In re Konneker, 30 App 502, 165 NE 850 (Summit 1929).
[147]In re Williams, No. 37370 (8th Dist Ct App, Cuyahoga, 4-27-78).
[148]In re Burrell, 58 OS(2d) 37, 388 NE(2d) 738 (1979).
[149]In re Burkhart, 15 Misc 170, 239 NE(2d) 772 (Juv, Warren 1968); In re Larry and Scott H., 92 Abs 436, 192 NE(2d) 683 (Juv, Cuyahoga 1963); Ludy v Ludy, 84 App 195, 84 NE(2d) 120 (Franklin 1948); In re Hayes, 62 App 289, 23 NE(2d) 956 (Franklin 1939).
[150]In re Zerlick, 74 Abs 525, 129 NE(2d) 661 (Juv, Cuyahoga 1955).
[151]In re Hawkins, No. 9-81-6 (3d Dist Ct App, Marion, 9-22-81) (child also found neglected).
[152]In re Sullivan, Nos. 79 AP-893, 894 (10th Dist Ct App, Franklin, 12-16-80).
[153]In re Hyrb, No. 36910 (8th Dist Ct App, Cuyahoga, 12-1-77).
[154]In re Feldman, No. 34223 (8th Dist Ct App, Cuyahoga, 12-23-75).

father, that the father had encouraged her and her ten-year-old brother to keep late hours, that the children were exposed to sexually suggestive materials and were told the details of the rape-murder of their cousin, and that the children frequently administered nonprescription drugs to their father, the children were found to be dependent.

It appears that many dependency cases would more properly fit within the "neglect" statute. As with neglect cases, many dependency cases focus on the lifestyles of the parents. Thus, marital discord,[155] a mother's sexual promiscuity,[156] and adultery[157] have been cited as factors in establishing dependency.

Dependency cases often rely on youthfulness, immaturity, and lack of child-rearing skills on the part of the parents to establish a lack of proper care.[158] Children have been adjudged dependent in cases in which the human services department attempted to provide training and counseling to the mother, who greeted these attempts with hostility, indifference, or a lack of motivation, and learned little if anything about raising a child.[159] A child may also be adjudged dependent when his mother is a high school student, desirous of completing school, unemployed, and living in a home with domestic problems.[160] A nine-month-old child with a seventeen-year-old mother was found to be dependent where the evidence showed that the child had severe burns on the buttocks, back, and hand, had suffered numerous injuries to her eyes and mouth, was underweight, and where the father was insensitive to the child's critical needs.[161]

Financial instability on the part of the parents in combination with other factors often may be sufficient to establish dependency. Thus, where a child's sixteen-year-old mother wished to surrender temporary custody to a children's services agency, and the child's eighteen-year-old father sought custody for himself, the fact that he was almost destitute and was receiving only minimal wages as a probationary employee was considered relevant by the court finding the child dependent.[162]

Although illegitimacy alone is insufficient to establish dependency, where a mother has four illegitimate children who are supported by public funds, the children may be dependent.[163] However, the dependency statute does not

---

[155]In re Parker, No. 15-79-16 (3d Dist Ct App, Van Wert, 1-26-81).

[156]In re Bowman, No. 79AP-798 (10th Dist Ct App, Franklin, 6-26-80); In re East, 32 Misc 65, 288 NE(2d) 343 (CP, Highland 1972).

[157]In re Turner, 12 Misc 171, 231 NE(2d) 502 (CP, Stark 1967).

[158]Such cases are processed under RC 2151.04(C). See Text 3.07(D), Condition or environment.

[159]E.g., In re Bowman, No. 79AP-798 (10th Dist Ct App, Franklin, 6-26-80); In re Philpott, No. 41186 (8th Dist Ct App, Cuyahoga, 6-5-80); In re Heightland, No. 989 (4th Dist Ct App, Athens, 2-18-80); In re Feiler, No. C-780549 (1st Dist Ct App, Hamilton, 10-17-79).

[160]In re Trizzino, No. 40982 (8th Dist Ct App, Cuyahoga, 1-31-80).

[161]In re Holcomb, No. 39694 (8th Dist Ct App, Cuyahoga, 10-4-79) (Complaint based also on RC 2151.04(A). It appears that the child would also be neglected and abused.).

[162]In re McCarthy, No. 38243 (8th Dist Ct App, Cuyahoga, 4-20-78). See also In re Grubbs, No. 43786 (8th Dist Ct App, Cuyahoga, 4-8-82), in which the trial court's dismissal of a dependency complaint filed under RC 2151.04(C) was reversed in part because of the father's past failure to support the child.

[163]In re Dake, 87 Abs 483, 180 NE(2d) 646 (Juv, Huron 1961). See also In re McCall, No. 42420 (8th Dist Ct App, Cuyahoga, 3-5-81).

require that the source of support for the child in question be the parents' own income. As long as the parents are able to provide proper care, even if that entails obtaining financial assistance from the child's paternal grandfather, the child is not dependent.[164]

As in neglect proceedings, the fact that a child is being cared for by relatives is immaterial to the determination of dependency, as long as the relatives are meeting the obligations of care, support, and custody which are owed to a child by his parents.[165] Under such circumstances the child is not "homeless," as defined by RC 2151.04(A), even if the child's parents are deceased[166] or otherwise unable to provide suitable care. However, where the mother was unable to care for her child and the grandparents were elderly and had not cared for any children in twenty-two years, the child was dependent despite the grandparents' willingness to care for her.[167] The mere allegation that a relative may be willing and able to care for a child, with no evidence of ability, is insufficient in challenging a dependency complaint.[168] Furthermore, where a child is being cared for by a nonparent pursuant to a court order, rather than at the parent's request, the parent's lack of interest in assuming responsibility for the child is a factor in determining dependency.[169]

(C) Parents' mental or physical condition

A substantial number of dependency complaints are filed under RC 2151.04(B) based on the mental condition of the child's parent(s). In such cases it must be proven that as a result of the parent's condition the child lacks proper care. Mental condition by itself, however, is insufficient to establish dependency.[170]

For instance, in *In re McCall*,[171] where a mother had been an in-patient at a mental health center, had no relatives able to care for her child, and was still not stable enough to assume parental responsibility after her release, the child was found to be dependent.[172] In *In re Feke*[173] a court of appeals upheld a dependency adjudication where the father had been hospitalized several times with psychological problems and did not have a realistic view of the world, where the mother and both grandmothers were unable to provide a stable environment for the child, and where the child was vehement in his desire to continue to reside

---

[164]In re Solarz, Nos. 42275, 42359, 42360 (8th Dist Ct App, Cuyahoga, 11-6-80).

[165]In re Darst, 117 App 374, 192 NE(2d) 287 (Franklin 1963); In re Crisp, No. 80AP-678 (10th Dist Ct App, Franklin, 2-5-81); In re Escue, No. 1487 (4th Dist Ct App, Lawrence, 5-11-81).

[166]In re Dillon, No. 1499 (4th Dist Ct App, Lawrence, 12-24-81).

[167]In re Howell, No. 79-CA-16 (5th Dist Ct App, Coshocton, 1-31-80).

[168]In re McCarthy, No. 38243 (8th Dist Ct App, Cuyahoga, 4-20-78); In re Grubbs, No. 43786 (8th Dist Ct App, Cuyahoga, 4-8-82).

[169]In re Lee, No. CA-2856 (5th Dist Ct App, Licking, 11-1-82); In re Poth, No. H-81-31 (6th Dist Ct App, Huron, 6-30-82).

[170]In re Larry and Scott H., 92 Abs 436, 192 NE(2d) 683 (Juv, Cuyahoga 1963).

[171]In re McCall, No. 42420 (8th Dist Ct App, Cuyahoga, 3-5-81).

[172]See also In re Kemp, No. 41320 (8th Dist Ct App, Cuyahoga, 6-26-80); In re Philpott, No. 41186 (8th Dist Ct App, Cuyahoga, 6-5-80).

[173]In re Feke, No. 42242 (8th Dist Ct App, Cuyahoga, 3-12-81).

in a foster home.[174] In a third case, *In re Hadsell*,[175] a mother's past history of mental illness and unwillingness to seek counseling and the father's past criminal record and current drug usage supported a finding that their children were dependent. On the other hand, a finding of dependency was reversed in *In re Bibb*,[176] where the record showed that the mother had been frequently hospitalized for depression but had always made proper arrangements for the care of her children at these times.

Although the "mental condition of parents" provision of RC 2151.04(B) is often used to establish dependency, courts are more reluctant to base a finding of dependency on the "physical condition" of parents. Thus, where a mother who had multiple sclerosis had done an excellent job of raising her child, the court's anticipation of future problems could not justify a dependency adjudication.[177]

(D) Condition or environment

Where it is believed that a newborn infant may be dependent, a complaint is usually filed under RC 2151.04(C).[178] Even though the mother may never have had physical custody of the child, the determination of dependency under this section is based on what the child's "condition or environment" would be if the child were returned to the mother.[179] Often these cases involve the child of an unmarried female[180] who is financially and emotionally unable to care for the child and who may have made plans for the baby's adoption but then changed her mind.[181] In some cases, the objectionable nature of the "condition or environment" may be based in part on the fact that the mother herself is a ward of a county human services department.[182] However, this fact alone will not conclusively establish dependency if the mother is able to provide proper care for the child.[183] Other circumstances which have led to a finding of dependency include an unmarried mother's adjudication for the commission of a delinquent-felony leading to her institutionalization, where the child's father is married and the

[174]See also In re Justice, 59 App(2d) 78, 392 NE(2d) 897 (Clinton 1978), which recognized that the potential harm to a child which might result from his separation from his foster parents is a factor supporting a dependency adjudication.

[175]In re Hadsell, No. 41004 (8th Dist Ct App, Cuyahoga, 6-19-80).

[176]In re Bibb, 70 App(2d) 117, 435 NE(2d) 96 (Hamilton 1980).

[177]In re Livingston, No. 1336 (2d Dist Ct App, Clark, 3-16-81).

[178]This provision has been held to be not unconstitutionally vague. Davis v Trumbull County Children Services Bd, 24 App(3d) 180, 24 OBR 270, 493 NE(2d) 1011 (Trumbull 1985).

[179]In re Campbell, 13 App(3d) 34, 13 OBR 36, 468 NE(2d) 93 (Butler 1983); In re Luke, No. 83-CA-09 (5th Dist Ct App, Coshocton, 1-13-84); In re Price, No. 43443 (8th Dist Ct App, Cuyahoga, 11-25-81); In re East, 32 Misc 65, 288 NE(2d) 343 (CP, Highland 1972); In re Turner, 12 Misc 171, 231 NE(2d) 502 (CP, Stark 1967); In re Bryant, No. CA80-11-0125 (12th Dist Ct App, Butler, 1-13-82); In re Bishop, 36 App(3d) 123, 521 NE(2d) 838 (Ashland 1987); In re Likens, No. 85 CA 80 (2d Dist Ct App, Greene, 10-24-86); In re Ruiz, 27 Misc(2d) 31, 27 OBR 350, 500 NE(2d) 935 (Juv, Wood 1986).

[180]However, illegitimacy of the child, in itself, will not support a dependency adjudication. In re Gutman, 22 App(2d) 125, 259 NE(2d) 128 (Hamilton 1969).

[181]E.g., In re Ware, No. 40983 (8th Dist Ct App, Cuyahoga, 7-17-80); In re Baby Girl S., 32 Misc 217, 290 NE(2d) 925 (CP, Stark 1972).

[182]In re Williams, No. 37370 (8th Dist Ct App, Cuyahoga, 4-27-78) (Adjudication also based on RC 2151.04(A).); In re Turner, 12 Misc 171, 231 NE(2d) 502 (CP, Stark 1967).

[183]In re Williams, No. 37370 (8th Dist Ct App, Cuyahoga, 4-27-78).

mother's family is unstable;[184] an unmarried father's involvement in criminal conduct and past failure to support or visit the child, where the mother is not interested in custody;[185] and the refusal of parents, for religious reasons, to allow further medical treatment of their sick child.[186]

Evidence which shows that returning a child to his natural parent would be detrimental to him establishes dependency under RC 2151.04(C) even though the parent is capable of giving proper care and support to other children.[187] For example, harm that would result from removing a child from a foster home is a factor which would support a finding of dependency.[188]

An appellate court reversed a trial court's adjudication of dependency where the facts showed that the child lived with his father and his father's girlfriend in a residence found to be dirty and in disarray; where the child was exposed to nude photographs of his father's girlfriend, with whom he did not get along; and where the child feared his father, who had dressed in women's clothes.[189] The evidence was insufficient to sustain a finding of dependency since there was no evidence of any ill effects on the child, other than his unhappiness.

(E) Child in danger of abuse or neglect

The most recently enacted category of dependency includes circumstances in which a child resides in a household where a sibling has been abused or neglected by a parent, guardian, or custodian, and in which the circumstances surrounding such abuse or neglect and the other conditions in the household indicate that the child is in danger of being abused or neglected.[190] Prior to the enactment of this statutory provision, these types of cases were initiated under the "condition or environment" provisions of the dependency statute.[191]

It is not clear from the language of RC 2151.04(D) whether an adjudication of abuse or neglect of the sibling is a condition precedent to the filing of a dependency complaint concerning the child. However, if the prior adjudication is not required, the sibling's abuse or neglect would have to be proven at the child's adjudicatory hearing in order for the child to be adjudged dependent.

CROSS REFERENCES

Text 3.04, 3.06 to 3.08, 7.06, 7.07, 13.04, 13.06 to 13.08, 13.10

Merrick-Rippner, Ohio Probate Law (4th ed), Text Ch 221

---

[184]In re Turner, 12 Misc 171, 231 NE(2d) 502 (CP, Stark 1967).

[185]In re McCarthy, No. 38243 (8th Dist Ct App, Cuyahoga, 4-20-78). See also In re Luallen, 27 App(3d) 29, 27 OBR 30, 499 NE(2d) 358 (Hamilton 1985).

[186]In re Willmann, 24 App(3d) 191, 24 OBR 313, 493 NE(2d) 380 (Hamilton 1986).

[187]In re Justice, 59 App(2d) 78, 392 NE(2d) 897 (Clinton 1978).

[188]Id.

[189]In re Sweat, No. CA 86-06-040 (12th Dist Ct App, Warren, 6-22-87).

[190]RC 2151.04(D), enacted by 1988 S 89, eff. 1-1-89.

[191]RC 2151.04(C).

3.08   Abused child

The most recently enacted legislative classification of children within the juvenile court's jurisdiction is the abused child,[192] defined by RC 2151.031 as any child who

> (A) Is the victim of "sexual activity" as defined under Chapter 2907. of the Revised Code, where such activity would constitute an offense under that chapter, except that the court need not find that any person has been convicted of the offense in order to find that the child is an abused child;

> (B) Is endangered as defined in section 2919.22 of the Revised Code, except that the court need not find that any person has been convicted under that section in order to find that the child is an abused child;

> (C) Exhibits evidence of any physical or mental injury or death,[193] inflicted other than by accidental means, or an injury or death which is at variance with the history given of it. Except as provided in division (D) of this section, a child exhibiting evidence of corporal punishment or other physical disciplinary measure by a parent, guardian, custodian, person having custody or control, or person in loco parentis of a child is not an abused child under this division if the measure is not prohibited under section 2919.22 of the Revised Code.

> (D) Because of the acts or omissions of his parents, guardian, or custodian, suffers physical or mental injury that harms or threatens the child's health or welfare.

Prior to the enactment of RC 2151.031, cases concerning children who had been physically or sexually abused were considered under the dependency[194] or neglect[195] statutes.

Divisions (A) to (C) of the abuse statute (RC 2151.031) do not require that the abuser be a parent, guardian, or custodian, nor do they require parental fault. All that is necessary is that the child be a victim, regardless of who is responsible for the abuse.[196] However, some courts have held that if the parent has provided care and supervision, the child will not be considered abused if, despite those efforts, someone else abuses him.[197] Thus, a child was not an abused child where the evidence revealed that the child was abused by the mother's boyfriend, who had previously cared for the child properly and from whom the mother had no reason to expect such conduct.[198] In a sense, the abuse statute is more narrowly drawn than either the neglect or dependency statutes. In order to establish neglect or dependency, it is not necessary that a specific person caused the neglect or dependency. A finding of abuse under RC 2151.031(A) (victim of sexual activity) or RC 2151.031(B) (endangered child)

---

[192]RC 2151.031 was enacted in 1975.

[193]The term "mental injury" was added to the statute by 1988 S 89, eff. 1-1-89. Neither the legislature nor the courts have yet defined the term "mental injury."

[194]RC 2151.04. E.g., In re Holcomb, No. 39694 (8th Dist Ct App, Cuyahoga, 10-4-79).

[195]RC 2151.03.

[196]In re Pitts, 38 App(3d) 1, 525 NE(2d) 814 (Knox 1987). See also In re Marshall, No. 12-85-8 (3d Dist Ct App, Putnam, 10-22-87).

[197]Under some circumstances, the child may be dependent or neglected. For discussion of dependency and neglect, see Text 3.05, Neglect, dependency, and abuse: attachment of jurisdiction; Text 3.06, Neglected child.

[198]In re Collier, No. 8AP-825 (10th Dist Ct App, Franklin, 6-4-81). See also In re Dillon Jr., No. 1747 (9th Dist Ct App, Wayne, 10-28-81).

does not require a criminal conviction, but does require that there be sufficient evidence that a criminal offense has occurred.

A finding that a child is abused may be predicated solely on the prenatal conduct of the mother. Thus, a child who is born addicted to heroin because of the mother's regular use of heroin during pregnancy is an abused child, since it is from the point of viability that the state has an interest in the child's care, protection, and development.[199]

RC 2151.031(C) covers situations where the child's injury[200] is nonaccidental or where it is at variance with the explanation given for it, except that corporal punishment or physical discipline administered by a parent or person in loco parentis does not constitute abuse if it is not prohibited by the "endangering children" statute, RC 2919.22. In interpreting RC 2151.031(C), a court of appeals in *Watts v Cuyahoga County Welfare Dept*[201] held that a four-year-old child was abused where the record demonstrated that the mother punished him by whipping him with an electric appliance cord, causing internal injury and external bruises and lacerations. According to the mother, the reason for the whipping, which was not an isolated incident, was that the child had "badmouthed" his relatives. Such punishment was "excessive under the circumstances" and caused "serious physical harm" to the child.

RC 2151.03(D), the most recent addition to the abuse statute,[202] is the only provision which specifically requires a finding of fault on the part of the parent, guardian, or custodian in order to establish abuse. Prior to its enactment, cases coming within the purview of this provision were initiated under the neglect statute.[203]

CROSS REFERENCES

Text 3.05 to 3.07, 7.06, 7.07, 13.04, 13.06, 13.10

Giannelli, Ohio Evidence Manual, Author's Comment 501.08, 601.06, 803.08

---

[199]In re Ruiz, 27 Misc(2d) 31, 27 OBR 350, 500 NE(2d) 935 (Juv, Wood 1986). See also Roe v Wade, 410 US 113, 93 SCt 705, 35 LEd(2d) 147 (1973) for discussion of the issue of viability of a fetus.

[200]The statute also includes situations where the child has died as a result of the abuse. Because abuse is a civil proceeding concerned with the issue of the child's custody, rather than a criminal proceeding against the abuser, it is not readily apparent why the legislature included this category. The reason may be that an adjudication of abuse based on the death of one child may be evidence of the dependency or neglect of his siblings.

[201]Watts v Cuyahoga County Welfare Dept, No. 40584 (8th Dist Ct App, Cuyahoga, 6-12-80).

[202]1988 S 89, eff. 1-1-89.

[203]RC 2151.03.

3.09   Agreements for temporary and permanent custody

(A) Juvenile court has jurisdiction to approve custody agreements

In addition to the juvenile courts' authority to commit neglected, dependent, abused,[204] delinquent,[205] and unruly[206] children to the custody of a public children services agency or private child-placing agency, such as courts have jurisdiction to hear and determine requests for the extension of temporary custody agreements and requests for court approval of permanent custody agreements.[207]

(B) Temporary custody agreements

The parents, guardian, or custodian of a child may enter into an agreement with such public or private agency for placement of the child in the temporary custody of the agency for up to thirty days without court approval; and up to sixty days without court approval if the agreement is executed solely for the purpose of obtaining the adoption of a child who is less than six months of age.[208]

(C) Extension of temporary custody agreements

The agency may request the juvenile court of the county in which the child has a residence or legal settlement[209] to extend the agreement for up to two thirty-day periods.[210] When it files the request for an extension, the agency must file an original case plan or an updated version of the case plan.[211] The juvenile court may grant the requested extension if it finds that such action would be in the child's best interest. At the expiration of the period of extension, the agency must either return the child to his parents, guardian, or custodian, or file a complaint requesting temporary or permanent custody of the child.[212]

(D) Permanent custody agreements

In addition, the parents, guardian, or custodian of a child may enter into an agreement with such public or private agency surrendering the permanent custody of the child to the agency. All such agreements require juvenile court approval, except that an agreement with a private child-placing agency does not require court approval if the agreement is executed solely for the purpose of obtaining an adoption of a child who is less than six months of age on the date of the execution of the agreement.[213] When a request for approval of a permanent surrender agreement is filed, the juvenile court must determine whether

[204]RC 2151.353(A). See Text 13.06, Abused, neglected, or dependent child.

[205]RC 2151.355(A). See Text 13.07, Delinquent child.

[206]RC 2151.354(A). See Text 13.08, Unruly child.

[207]RC 2151.23(A)(8).

[208]RC 5103.15(A)(1).

[209]Although the term "legal settlement" is not defined in the juvenile law, the term has been used in other areas of the law as the equivalent of "residence." See 1943 OAG 473.

[210]RC 5103.15(A)(2). If the agreement was made to obtain the adoption of a child under the age of six months, only one thirty-day extension is permitted. RC 5103.15(A)(3).

[211]RC 5103.15(A)(2). See RC 2151.412; Text 13.05, Case plans.

[212]RC 5103.15(A)(2), (3). Presumably, pending hearing on the complaint, the child must be returned to his parent, guardian, or custodian unless the agency is granted temporary custody pending hearing. See Text 13.06(A), Dispositional alternatives.

[213]RC 5103.15(B)(1).

the agreement is in the child's best interest and may approve the agreement if it finds that it is.[214]

(E) Parental revocation of permanent surrender

A proceeding to procure the consent of the juvenile court is not an adversary proceeding. It is the function of the juvenile court in consenting to a voluntary surrender to insure that the surrender is made by the parent voluntarily, with full knowledge of the legal import of the relinquishment of parental rights and to insure that the child welfare agency does not enter into improvident contracts.[215]

An agreement by a parent with the county board or human services department for permanent surrender of a child prior to consent of the juvenile court is not only revocable by the parent prior to consent of the juvenile court, but such parental revocation operates to dissolve the offer to surrender, and the public agency's continued retention of the child and refusal to return the child to the parent is illegal and gives rise to an action in habeas corpus.[216]

CROSS REFERENCES

Text 3.02, 3.04, 3.06 to 3.08, 7.07, 13.05 to 13.08, 13.10

3.10   Age jurisdiction

(A) General provisions

In determining the juvenile court's age jurisdiction over delinquent, unruly, neglected, dependent, or abused children or juvenile traffic offenders, it is necessary to define the term "child." RC 2151.011(B)(1)[217] provides, in part, that a child is

> a person who is under the age of eighteen years, except that any person who violates a federal or state law or municipal ordinance prior to attaining eighteen years of age shall be deemed a "child" irrespective of his age at the time the complaint is filed or hearing had on the complaint.[218]

Moreover, any child who allegedly commits a delinquent, unruly, or juvenile traffic offense before age eighteen remains under the juvenile court's jurisdiction even if the complaint is not filed or a hearing held until after he reaches age eighteen.[219] It is implicit in the statutes that abuse, neglect, and dependency proceedings must be conducted before the child reaches age eighteen.

---

[214]RC 5103.15(B)(2).

[215]In re Miller, 61 OS(2d) 184, 399 NE(2d) 1262 (1980); In re Permanent Surrender of Anne K., 31 Misc 218, 282 NE(2d) 370 (Juv, Cuyahoga 1969).

[216]Angle v Holmes County Welfare Dept Children's Services Div, 63 OS(2d) 227, 407 NE(2d) 524 (1980).

[217]See also Juv R 2(2).

[218]This statute also excludes from the definition of "child" any person under age eighteen who has been transferred for criminal prosecution pursuant to RC 2151.26 and convicted in that case and who is subsequently charged with the offense of aggravated murder, murder, or a felony of the first or second degree or aggravated felonies of the first and second degree.

[219]RC 2151.27. See also State ex rel Heth v Moloney, 126 OS 526, 186 NE 362 (1933); In re DeGeronimo, No. 40089 (8th Dist Ct App, Cuyahoga, 6-28-79); In re Davis, 87 Abs 222, 179 NE(2d) 198 (Juv, Marion 1961).

Because the statutory definition of "child" contains no minimum age requirement, there is some question as to whether Ohio follows the common law, which makes seven years the minimum age for criminal capacity.[220] This issue has not been directly confronted in any reported Ohio decisions;[221] however, the Ohio Supreme Court has held that a child under the age of fourteen is presumed incapable of committing the crime of rape, rebuttable only on proof that the child has reached the age of puberty.[222] Courts in some jurisdictions which do not have a statutory minimum age have held that since a delinquency complaint is based on the commission of a criminal offense, the common-law presumptions as to criminal capacity should apply, making infancy a proper defense in a delinquency proceeding.[223] Thus, the common-law presumptions of criminal capacity based on age have been extended beyond criminal cases into juvenile proceedings. Other courts, however, have refused to recognize infancy as a relevant factor in juvenile proceedings.[224] These courts argue that since juvenile proceedings are civil rather than criminal and are designed to protect and rehabilitate children rather than to punish them, the traditional concept of incapacity is irrelevant.[225]

With respect to cases in which the child is the victim rather than the offender, an unborn child may be considered a "child" under RC 2151.011 since it is from the point of viability that the state has an interest in the child's care, protection, and development.[226]

The marital status of a child has no bearing on the jurisdiction of the juvenile court.[227] Thus, the fact that a female under the age of eighteen is married does not exempt her from laws pertaining to juveniles,[228] nor does it prevent the prosecution of someone for contributing to her delinquency.[229]

(B) Mistaken or concealed age

RC 2151.25 provides that proceedings against an arrested child must be initiated in the juvenile court; if the child is taken before an adult court judge, that judge must transfer the case to the appropriate juvenile court. Similarly, RC

---

[220]For a discussion of the juvenile court's jurisdiction over an unborn fetus in neglect proceedings, see Text 3.06(D), Proper or necessary care.

[221]Some Ohio juvenile courts have adopted a policy that children under a certain age (usually seven or ten) will not be charged officially with a delinquent or unruly act. If such children need court intervention, the court may proceed unofficially pursuant to Juv R 9; if the child's misbehavior is due to a lack of parental supervision, the child may be alleged to be neglected under RC 2151.03.

[222]In re M.D., 38 OS(3d) 149, 527 NE(2d) 286 (1988).

[223]E.g., In re Gladys R., 1 Cal(3d) 855, 464 P(2d) 127, 83 Cal Rptr 671 (1970); Commonwealth v Durham, 255 Pa Super 539, 389 A(2d) 108 (1978).

[224]E.g., State v D.H., 340 So(2d) 1163 (Fla 1976); K.M.S. v State, 129 Ga App 683, 200 SE(2d) 916 (1973).

[225]For a discussion of the effect that the child's attaining twenty-one years of age has on the continuing jurisdiction of the court, see Text 15.01, Continuing jurisdiction.

[226]In re Ruiz, 27 Misc(2d) 31, 27 OBR 350, 500 NE(2d) 935 (Juv, Wood 1986).

[227]However, pursuant to Juv R 2(16), the child's spouse would be a party to juvenile court proceedings concerning the child.

[228]State v Wilcox, 26 NP(NS) 343 (Juv, Tuscarawas 1926).

[229]State ex rel Meng v Todaro, 161 OS 348, 119 NE(2d) 281 (1954). However, RC 2907.01(I) specifically excludes a married juvenile from the purview of the criminal sex offense statutes (RC Ch 2907) designed to protect juveniles.

2151.26(E) prohibits the prosecution of any child as an adult where the child has committed the offense prior to attaining age eighteen, unless the child has been transferred to the adult court pursuant to law.[230] RC 2151.26(E) further provides that the criminal prosecution of a child as an adult based on the mistaken belief that the child was an adult at the time of the offense is a nullity to which jeopardy does not attach.

Despite these statutory provisions, several courts have held that where a child intentionally misrepresents himself to be an adult or does not object to the assumption of jurisdiction by the adult criminal court, he is deemed to have waived the right to be processed as a child in juvenile court.[231] The rationale of these decisions is that to hold otherwise would permit the child to lie about his age until the conclusion of the adult proceeding and then choose whether or not to reveal his correct age depending on the outcome of the prosecution.

The court in *State ex rel Leis v Black*[232] held that where the adult court determines that the child was under the age of eighteen at the time of the offense, that court may choose either to retain jurisdiction or to transfer it to the juvenile court. In this case, the statutory provision[233] that such a prosecution is a "nullity" apparently was ignored.

(C) Establishment of age jurisdiction

Because the juvenile courts are statutory courts whose jurisdiction depends on the age of the person before them, it has been held that the prosecution's failure to establish age in delinquency cases before resting its case constitutes a failure to invoke the court's subject matter jurisdiction and must result in a dismissal of the complaint.[234] On the other hand, it has also been held that age relates to personal jurisdiction rather than subject matter jurisdiction, so that any objection to the court's assumption of jurisdiction is waived if not raised before the hearing.[235] In *State v Mendenhall*,[236] which was decided prior to the adoption of the Juvenile Rules, the objection was raised by means of a motion to dismiss following the close of the prosecution's case. The courts in *In re Fudge*[237] and *In re Atwell*[238] relied on Juvenile Rule 22(D), which provides that defects in the institution of the proceedings or in the complaint, other than those relating to the jurisdiction of the court or to the charge, must be raised before the hearing or they are waived.[239]

---

[230]See Text 9.03, Procedure (Transfer of Jurisdiction).

[231]Hemphill v Johnson, 31 App(2d) 241, 278 NE(2d) 828 (Montgomery 1972); State v Peterson, 9 Misc 154, 223 NE(2d) 838 (Mun, Cincinnati 1966); Mellot v Alvis, 81 Abs 532, 162 NE(2d) 623 (App, Franklin 1959); Harris v Alvis, 61 Abs 311, 104 NE(2d) 182 (App, Franklin 1950); Ex parte Pharr, 10 App 395 (Hamilton 1919).

[232]State ex rel Leis v Black, 45 App(2d) 191, 341 NE(2d) 853 (Hamilton 1975).

[233]RC 2151.26(E).

[234]State v Mendenhall, 21 App(2d) 135, 255 NE(2d) 307 (Lake 1969).

[235]In re Fudge, 59 App(2d) 129, 392 NE(2d) 1262 (Clark 1977). See also In re Atwell, Nos. 40667, 40719 (8th Dist Ct App, Cuyahoga, 1-17-80).

[236]State v Mendenhall, 21 App(2d) 135, 255 NE(2d) 307 (Lake 1969).

[237]In re Fudge, 59 App(2d) 129, 392 NE(2d) 1262 (Clark 1977).

[238]In re Atwell, Nos. 40667, 40719 (8th Dist Ct App, Cuyahoga, 1-17-80).

[239]See also In re McCourt, No. 1599 (9th Dist Ct App, Medina, 8-12-87).

However, a later court of appeals decision, *In re Auterson*,[240] relied on *Mendenhall* in holding that the trial court should have granted a motion for a judgment of acquittal filed on behalf of a child under Criminal Rule 29, where the prosecution failed to meet its burden of establishing the child's minority.[241] The court reasoned that when the state fails to establish minority, the matter is not within the court's jurisdiction and any judgment rendered in the case is a nullity.

An allegation in the complaint that a child is under the age of eighteen is not enough to establish age jurisdiction.[242] However, where the child appears with counsel and the court observes the child to be of tender age, this may constitute sufficient evidence that the subject is a juvenile.[243] In a delinquency hearing where a court clerk asked the subject if he was seventeen years old at the time of the alleged offense and the subject answered in the affirmative, age jurisdiction was established.[244] Similarly, where the child's counsel agreed to stipulate that the child was a minor, it was unnecessary to establish his age.[245]

CROSS REFERENCES

Text 3.01, 3.06(D), 7.03(E), 9.02(A), 9.03, 15.01

Merrick-Rippner, Ohio Probate Law (4th ed), Text Ch 219
Giannelli, Ohio Evidence Manual, Author's Comment 301.03

---

[240]In re Auterson, No. 1000 (12th Dist Ct App, Clermont, 1-13-82).

[241]Because Juv R 22 seems to control this issue, the court's reliance on the Criminal Rules is questionable.

[242]State v Mendenhall, 21 App(2d) 135, 255 NE(2d) 307 (Lake 1969); In re Auterson, No. 1000 (12th Dist Ct App, Clermont, 1-13-82).

[243]In re Fudge, 59 App(2d) 129, 392 NE(2d) 1262 (Clark 1977).

[244]State v Cunningham, No. 31563 (8th Dist Ct App, Cuyahoga, 11-9-72).

[245]State v Gaida, No. 30423 (8th Dist Ct App, Cuyahoga, 3-2-72).

Chapter 5

Police Investigations

5.01   In general

A number of police investigative techniques implicate constitutional guarantees. For example, arrests and searches involve the Fourth Amendment's proscription against unreasonable searches and seizures; interrogation practices involve the Fifth Amendment privilege against compulsory self-incrimination, the right to counsel, and due process; and identification procedures, such as lineups, involve the right to counsel and due process. Generally, the courts have applied these constitutional rights to juvenile cases.[1]

Evidence obtained in violation of these constitutional guarantees is subject to exclusion at a criminal trial.[2] The United States Supreme Court, however, has recognized a "good faith" exception to the exclusionary rule where the police search pursuant to a warrant.[3] Other aspects of the exclusionary rule relate to standing and the derivative evidence doctrine. Only a person whose constitutional rights have been violated has standing to invoke the exclusionary rule.[4] Moreover, the exclusionary rule applies not only to primary evidence obtained as a direct result of unconstitutional conduct but also to evidence later discovered and found to be derivative of that conduct ("fruit of the poisonous tree").[5] There are several exceptions to the derivative evidence rule. Such evidence will not be excluded if the prosecution can establish that (1) there was an independent source for obtaining the evidence;[6] (2) the evidence would have been

---

[1]See *IJA-ABA Standards Relating to Police Handling of Juvenile Problems* 54-76 (1980); Davis, *Rights of Juveniles* ch 3 (2d ed 1988).

[2]See generally 1 LaFave, *Search and Seizure* ch 1 (2d ed 1987); Katz, *Ohio Arrest, Search and Seizure* ch 3 (2d ed 1987). See also In re Diane P., 110 AD(2d) 354, 494 NYS(2d) 881 (1985) (exclusionary rule applicable in child protective proceedings).

[3]See United States v Leon, 468 US 897, 104 SCt 3405, 82 LEd(2d) 677 (1984); Massachusetts v Sheppard, 468 US 981, 990, 104 SCt 3424, 82 LEd(2d) 737 (1984) ("[T]he exclusionary rule should not be applied when the officer conducting the search acted in objectively reasonable reliance on a warrant issued by a detached and neutral magistrate that subsequently is determined to be invalid.").

[4]Rakas v Illinois, 439 US 128, 99 SCt 421, 58 LEd(2d) 387 (1978); Rawlings v Kentucky, 448 US 98, 100 SCt 2556, 65 LEd(2d) 633 (1980); Alderman v United States, 394 US 165, 174, 89 SCt 961, 22 LEd(2d) 176 (1969) ("Fourth Amendment rights are personal rights which . . . may not be vicariously asserted."). See generally 4 LaFave, *Search and Seizure* § 11.3 (2d ed 1987).

[5]Nardone v United States, 308 US 338, 341, 60 SCt 266, 84 LEd 307 (1939). See generally Katz, *Ohio Arrest, Search and Seizure* § 3.07 (2d ed 1987).

[6]See Murray v United States, ___ US ___, 108 SCt 2529, 101 LEd(2d) 472 (1988); Segura v United States, 468 US 796, 104 SCt 3380, 82 LEd(2d) 599 (1984). See generally 4 LaFave, *Search and Seizure* § 11.4(a) (2d ed 1987).

"inevitably discovered";[7] or (3) intervening events have sufficiently attenuated the taint of the original illegality.[8]

In Ohio, Juvenile Rule 22(D)(3) governs suppression motions.[9] Juvenile Rule 22(F) provides for an appeal by the state if a motion to suppress evidence is granted in delinquency cases.[10]

CROSS REFERENCES

Text 15.02(E)

Katz, Ohio Arrest, Search and Seizure (2d ed), Text 3.06, 3.07, 29.02

5.02   Custody, arrests, and stops

Juvenile Rule 6 sets forth five conditions under which a child may be taken into custody:[11]

(1) Pursuant to a court order;[12]

(2) Pursuant to the law of arrest;[13]

(3) When there are reasonable grounds to believe that the child is suffering from some illness or injury and is not receiving proper care, or is in immediate danger from his surroundings[14] (only a law enforcement officer or authorized officer of the court may take custody on this ground);

(4) When there are reasonable grounds to believe that the child has run away (only a law enforcement or authorized court officer may take custody on this ground); or

---

[7]See Nix v Williams, 467 US 431, 104 SCt 2501, 81 LEd(2d) 377 (1984).

[8]See Rawlings v Kentucky, 448 US 98, 100 SCt 2556, 65 LEd(2d) 633 (1980); Brown v Illinois, 422 US 590, 95 SCt 2254, 45 LEd(2d) 416 (1975). See generally 4 LaFave, *Search and Seizure* § 11.4(a) (2d ed 1987).

[9]See In re Baker, 18 App(2d) 276, 248 NE(2d) 620 (Hocking 1969) (Failure to file a motion to suppress waives objections to the admissibility of evidence.), modified by 20 OS(2d) 142, 254 NE(2d) 363 (1969).

[10]See In re Hester, 1 App(3d) 24, 1 OBR 85, 437 NE(2d) 1218 (Franklin 1981). For a discussion of prosecution's right to appeal, see Text 15.02(E), By the state.

[11]RC 2151.31 also sets forth the conditions under which a child may be taken into custody. In addition, that statute provides, "The taking of a child into custody is not and shall not be deemed an arrest except for the purpose of determining its validity under the constitution of this state or of the United States." In In re James L., 92 Abs 475, 194 NE(2d) 797 (Juv, Cuyahoga 1963), the court held that the law of arrest does not apply in juvenile proceedings because they are "neither criminal nor penal in . . . nature." *Id.* at 478. This view has been rejected by the post-*Gault* cases (In re Gault, 387 US 1, 87 SCt 1428, 18 LED(2d) 527 (1967)).

See also RC 2151.28(D) (service of summons and taking into custody). See generally *IJA-ABA Standards Relating to Police Handling of Juvenile Problems* 62-65 (1980); Davis, *Rights of Juveniles* § 3.1-3.5 (2d ed 1988).

[12]See Juv R 15(D) ("If it appears that summons will be ineffectual or the welfare of the child requires that he be brought forthwith to the court, a warrant may be issued against the child.").

[13]See In re Howard, 31 App(3d) 1, 31 OBR 14, 508 NE(2d) 190 (Hamilton 1987) (warrantless arrest of juvenile on probable cause).

[14]See State v Hunt, 2 Ariz App 6, 406 P(2d) 208 (1965) (five-year-old child in danger).

(5) Where, during the pendency of court proceedings, it appears to the court that the health, welfare, person, or property of the child or others is endangered[15] or that the child may not appear in court.

RC 2151.31 sets forth comparable grounds for taking a child into custody. The statute, however, recognizes several additional grounds. First, an enforcement official investigating compliance with the child labor laws may, under some circumstances, take a child into custody.[16] Second, when there are reasonable grounds to believe that a parent, guardian, custodian, or other household member has abused or neglected another child in the same household and the child is in immediate danger of physical or emotional harm, a law enforcement or authorized court officer may take the child into custody.[17]

Once in custody, the child must (with reasonable speed) be either (1) released to his parent, guardian, or other custodian, or (2) brought to the juvenile court or a court-designated place of detention or shelter care.[18]

In Ohio, the "law of arrest" is governed by statutory and constitutional provisions. An arrest is a seizure of the person within the meaning of the Fourth Amendment, and thus must be based on probable cause; that is, there must be reasonable grounds to believe that a crime has been committed and that the arrestee committed it.[19] According to the United States Supreme Court, an arrest warrant is not constitutionally required if a suspect is arrested in a public place.[20] Although an invalid arrest does not preclude subsequent prosecution,[21] it may nevertheless result in the exclusion of evidence that was the product of that arrest.[22] RC 2935.04 provides that *any person*, upon reasonable cause, may arrest a felony suspect without a warrant. Misdemeanors are treated differently. Under RC 2935.03, only certain law enforcement officers may arrest without a warrant for (1) misdemeanors committed in their presence, or (2) specified drug, theft, and violence offenses not committed in their presence. Criminal Rule 4 governs the issuance and execution of arrest warrants.[23]

In addition to an arrest, the police may "stop and frisk" a suspect based upon reasonable suspicion that criminal activity is afoot.[24] Although an objective standard, "reasonable suspicion" is a lesser standard of proof than probable cause. However, the detention of a person pursuant to a stop is far less intrusive

---

[15]See In re Jones, 114 App 319, 182 NE(2d) 631 (Allen 1961).

[16]RC 2151.31(A)(4).

[17]RC 2151.31(A)(3)(c).

[18]Juv R 7(B). For a discussion of pretrial detention, see Text 7.06, Detention or shelter care.

[19]E.g., In re Tucker, 20 Ill App(3d) 377, 314 NE(2d) 276 (1974); Minor Boy v State, 91 Nev 456, 537 P(2d) 477 (1975). See generally 1 LaFave, *Search and Seizure* ch 3 (2d ed 1987); Katz, *Ohio Arrest, Search and Seizure* ch 5 (2d ed 1987).

[20]United States v Watson, 423 US 411, 96 SCt 820, 46 LEd(2d) 598 (1976).

[21]Gerstein v Pugh, 420 US 103, 95 SCt 854, 43 LEd(2d) 54 (1975); In re Jackson, 46 Mich App 764, 208 NW(2d) 526 (1973).

[22]E.g., In re S., 36 AD(2d) 642, 319 NYS(2d) 752 (1971).

[23]See 2 Schroeder-Katz, *Ohio Criminal Law and Practice*, 2 vols, 1974-1987.

[24]Terry v Ohio, 392 US 1, 88 SCt 1868, 20 LEd(2d) 889 (1968). See 3 LaFave, *Search and Seizure* ch 9 (2d ed 1987); Katz, *Ohio Arrest, Search and Seizure* ch 25 (2d ed 1987).

than an arrest; a stop is a temporary detention at the scene.[25] The courts have applied the stop and frisk doctrine to juveniles.[26]

CROSS REFERENCES

Text 7.06

Schroeder-Katz, Ohio Criminal Law, Crim R 4, Author's Text
Katz, Ohio Arrest, Search and Seizure (2d ed), Text 7.02, 7.03, 9.02, 25.01 et seq.

5.03 Search and seizure

The Fourth Amendment reads:

> The right of the people to be secure in their persons, houses, papers, and effects, against unreasonable searches and seizures, shall not be violated, and no warrants shall issue, but upon probable cause, supported by oath or affirmation, and particularly describing the place to be searched, and the persons or things to be seized.

The Ohio Constitution contains a comparable provision.[27] The United States Supreme Court has applied the Fourth Amendment to juvenile cases.[28]

The threshold question that must be asked when analyzing search and seizure issues[29] is whether the Fourth Amendment applies. If the amendment is applicable, a search warrant and probable cause are usually required. There are, however, several well-recognized exceptions to the warrant requirement.

(A) Applicability of the Fourth Amendment

The Fourth Amendment applies only to governmental searches. Searches by private citizens are not prohibited by the amendment.[30] However, if the police significantly expand upon a private search, it may evolve into a governmental search.[31]

---

[25]See Dunaway v New York, 442 US 200, 99 SCt 2248, 60 LEd(2d) 824 (1979).

[26]E.g., In re James D., 43 Cal(3d) 903, 741 P(2d) 161, 239 Cal Rptr 663 (1987); In re Tony C., 21 Cal(3d) 888, 582 P(2d) 957, 148 Cal Rptr 366 (1978); In re Thomas, No. 45649 (8th Dist Ct App, Cuyahoga, 9-8-83); In re Harvey, 222 Pa Super 222, 295 A(2d) 93 (1972).
See also In re Ronald B., 61 AD(2d) 204, 401 NYS(2d) 544 (1978) (applying stop and frisk doctrine to school officials).

[27]O Const Art I, § 14.

[28]New Jersey v T.L.O., 469 US 325, 105 SCt 733, 83 LEd(2d) 720 (1985). See generally Davis, *Rights of Juveniles* § 3.6 (2d ed 1988).
See also State v Davis, 56 OS(2d) 51, 56, 381 NE(2d) 641 (1978) ("Fourth Amendment applies to minors in the same manner as adults."); In re Morris, 29 Misc 71, 72, 278 NE(2d) 701 (Juv, Columbiana 1971) (Fourth Amendment applies to juveniles.).

[29]The discussion in this section focuses on law enforcement searches. The Fourth Amendment also applies to inspections by welfare officials. See Wyman v James, 400 US 309, 91 SCt 381, 27 LEd(2d) 408 (1971); 3 LaFave, *Search and Seizure* § 10.3(a) (2d ed 1987); Katz, *Ohio Arrest, Search and Seizure* ch 26 (2d ed 1987).

[30]Burdeau v McDowell, 256 US 465, 41 SCt 574, 65 LEd 1048 (1921); State v Morris, 42 OS(2d) 307, 329 NE(2d) 85 (1975), cert denied sub nom McSpadden v Ohio, 423 US 1049, 96 SCt 774, 46 LEd(2d) 637 (1976). See generally Katz, *Ohio Arrest, Search and Seizure* § 3.07 (2d ed 1987).

[31]See Walter v United States, 447 US 649, 100 SCt 2395, 65 LEd(2d) 410 (1980).

Moreover, the Fourth Amendment applies only to certain governmental activities, that is, those activities that intrude upon a citizen's justifiable expectations of privacy.[32] Searches of homes, offices, cars, and containers are covered by the Fourth Amendment, as is electronic surveillance.[33] Police use of informants,[34] beepers,[35] aerial surveillance,[36] sniffing-dogs,[37] or pen registers[38] is not protected by the amendment. Searches of jail cells,[39] open fields,[40] trash,[41] and bank records[42] also fall outside Fourth Amendment protection.[43]

(B) Warrant and probable cause requirements

Searches must be based on probable cause and conducted pursuant to a search warrant unless a recognized exception to these requirements applies.[44] A search warrant must be issued by a neutral and detached magistrate[45] and describe with particularity the place to be searched and the items to be seized.[46]

Probable cause to search requires substantial evidence that the items sought are connected with a crime and that those items are located at the place to be searched. The United States Supreme Court has written, "In dealing with probable cause, however, as the very name implies, we deal with probabilities. These are not technical; they are the factual and practical considerations of everyday life on which reasonable and prudent men, not legal technicians, act."[47] Proba-

---

[32]Katz v United States, 389 US 347, 88 SCt 507, 19 LEd(2d) 576 (1967). See 1 LaFave, *Search and Seizure* ch 2 (2d ed 1987); Katz, *Ohio Arrest, Search and Seizure* § 1.03 (2d ed 1987).

[33]Katz v United States, 389 US 347, 88 SCt 507, 19 LEd(2d) 576 (1967).

[34]United States v White, 401 US 745, 91 SCt 1122, 28 LEd(2d) 453 (1971).

[35]United States v Knotts, 460 US 276, 103 SCt 1081, 75 LEd(2d) 55 (1983). But see United States v Karo, 468 US 705, 104 SCt 3296, 82 LEd(2d) 530 (1984) (Monitoring beeper in a house is protected by the Fourth Amendment.).

[36]California v Ciraolo, 476 US 207, 106 SCt 1809, 90 LEd(2d) 210 (1986).

[37]United States v Place, 462 US 696, 103 SCt 2637, 77 LEd(2d) 110 (1983) (Use of a trained canine to detect drugs in luggage is not a search.).

[38]Smith v Maryland, 442 US 735, 99 SCt 2577, 61 LEd(2d) 220 (1979).

[39]Hudson v Palmer, 468 US 517, 104 SCt 3194, 82 LEd(2d) 393 (1984).

[40]United States v Dunn, ___ US ___, 107 SCt 1134, 94 LEd(2d) 326 (1987); Oliver v United States, 466 US 170, 104 SCt 1735, 80 LEd(2d) 214 (1984); Hester v United States, 265 US 57, 44 SCt 445, 68 LEd 898 (1924).

[41]California v Greenwood, ___ US ___, 108 SCt 1625, 100 LEd(2d) 30 (1988).

[42]United States v Miller, 425 US 435, 96 SCt 1619, 48 LEd(2d) 71 (1976).

[43]See also United States v Dionisio, 410 US 1, 93 SCt 764, 35 LEd(2d) 67 (1973) (A person does not have reasonable expectation of privacy in the sound of his voice.); United States v Mara, 410 US 19, 93 SCt 774, 35 LEd(2d) 99 (1973) (A person does not have a reasonable expectation of privacy in his handwriting.).

[44]Probable cause is not required if a search is based on a validly obtained consent. Reasonable suspicion, not probable cause, is required for a stop and frisk.

[45]See Shadwick v Tampa, 407 US 345, 92 SCt 2119, 32 LEd(2d) 783 (1972); Coolidge v New Hampshire, 403 US 443, 91 SCt 2022, 29 LEd(2d) 564 (1971). See also 2 LaFave, *Search and Seizure* § 4.2 (2d ed 1987).

[46]Maryland v Garrison, 480 US 79, 107 SCt 1013, 94 LEd(2d) 72 (1987). See Steele v United States, 267 US 498, 45 SCt 414, 69 LEd 757 (1925) (place to be searched); Andresen v Maryland, 427 US 463, 96 SCt 2737, 49 LEd(2d) 627 (1976) (items to be seized). See also 2 LaFave, *Search and Seizure* § 4.5, 4.6 (2d ed 1987).

[47]Brinegar v United States, 338 US 160, 175, 69 SCt 1302, 93 LEd 1876 (1949). See also 1 LaFave, *Search and Seizure* ch 3 (2d ed 1987); Katz, *Ohio Arrest, Search and Seizure* § 1.04 (2d ed 1987).

ble cause may be based on hearsay.[48] In order to determine whether information supplied by an informant satisfies the probable cause requirement, the totality of circumstances must be considered, including the informant's credibility, the basis for his knowledge, and the reliability of his information.[49]

(C) Exceptions to the warrant requirement

There are a number of recognized exceptions to the warrant requirement. First, a warrant is not required for a search incident to arrest.[50] At the time of arrest, the police may search the arrestee[51] and the area within his immediate control.[52] A special rule applies when the police arrest an occupant of an automobile; in such a case the police may also search the passenger compartment of the automobile.[53] In addition, the police may inventory the property of an arrestee at the stationhouse if he is to be incarcerated.[54]

Second, the United States Supreme Court has recognized a broad exception for warrantless automobile searches. Automobiles stopped on the highway may be searched at the time of the stop or at the stationhouse if the police have probable cause to believe criminal evidence is in the automobile.[55] This search generally may extend to containers located in the automobile.[56] Validly seized automobiles may also be inventoried by the police at the place of impoundment.[57]

Third, the police may enter a house without a warrant if they are in hot pursuit of a suspect.[58] In the absence of exigent circumstances, however, an arrest warrant is required before the police may enter the home of a person subject to arrest.[59] A search warrant is required when the police enter the house of a third party to effect an arrest.[60]

---

[48]Draper v United States, 358 US 307, 79 SCt 329, 3 LEd(2d) 327 (1959).

[49]Illinois v Gates, 462 US 213, 103 SCt 2317, 76 LEd(2d) 527 (1983). See also Massachusetts v Upton, 466 US 727, 104 SCt 2085, 80 LEd(2d) 721 (1984).

[50]See 2 LaFave, Search and Seizure § 5.2 (2d ed 1987); Katz, Ohio Arrest, Search and Seizure ch 17 (2d ed 1987).

[51]United States v Robinson, 414 US 218, 94 SCt 467, 38 LEd(2d) 427 (1973); Gustafson v Florida, 414 US 260, 94 SCt 488, 38 LEd(2d) 456 (1973).

[52]Chimel v California, 395 US 752, 89 SCt 2034, 23 LEd(2d) 685 (1969). For a juvenile case applying this rule, see In re Marsh, 40 Ill(2d) 53, 237 NE(2d) 529 (1968).

[53]New York v Belton, 453 US 454, 101 SCt 2860, 69 LEd(2d) 768 (1981).

[54]Illinois v LaFayette, 462 US 640, 103 SCt 2605, 77 LEd(2d) 65 (1983).

[55]Florida v Meyers, 466 US 380, 104 SCt 1852, 80 LEd(2d) 381 (1984); Chambers v Maroney, 399 US 42, 90 SCt 1975, 26 LEd(2d) 419 (1970). See also 3 LaFave, Search and Seizure § 7.2 (2d ed 1987); Katz, Ohio Arrest, Search and Seizure ch 19 (2d ed 1987).
For a juvenile case on this issue, see In re M., 487 SW(2d) 502 (Mo 1972).

[56]United States v Ross, 456 US 798, 102 SCt 2157, 72 LEd(2d) 572 (1982).

[57]Colorado v Bertine, 479 US 367, 107 SCt 738, 93 LEd(2d) 739 (1987); South Dakota v Opperman, 428 US 364, 96 SCt 3092, 49 LEd(2d) 1000 (1976).

[58]United States v Santana, 427 US 38, 96 SCt 2406, 49 LEd(2d) 300 (1976); Warden, Maryland Penitentiary v Hayden, 387 US 294, 87 SCt 1642, 18 LEd(2d) 782 (1967).

[59]Payton v United States, 445 US 573, 100 SCt 1371, 63 LEd(2d) 639 (1980). See also Welsh v Wisconsin, 466 US 740, 104 SCt 2091, 80 LEd(2d) 732 (1984) (Entry of a home to arrest for a nonjailable traffic offense does not constitute exigent circumstances.). See generally 2 LaFave, Search and Seizure § 6.1 (2d ed 1987).
For a juvenile case on this issue, see In re Kwok T., 43 NY(2d) 213, 401 NYS(2d) 52, 371 NE(2d) 814 (1977).

[60]Steagald v United States, 451 US 204, 101 SCt 1642, 68 LEd(2d) 38 (1981).

Fourth, the police may seize an item without a warrant if it is in plain view, that is, when the police inadvertently come across incriminating evidence during a lawful search.[61]

(D) Consent searches

Another exception to the warrant requirement is recognized for consent searches. Unlike other exceptions, a search based upon consent also does not require probable cause. A valid consent depends on two factors: (1) whether the consent was voluntary, and (2) whether it was obtained from a person who may validly give consent. The voluntariness of a consent is determined by considering the "totality of all the circumstances," including factors such as the schooling and intelligence of the person consenting and the conduct of the police in obtaining consent.[62] Failure of the police to advise a person that he has the right to refuse to give consent is not determinative; it is merely one factor to be considered in assessing whether the consent is voluntary.[63] Nevertheless, neither mere submission to a claim by the police that they have authority to search[64] nor consent obtained by trickery is a voluntary consent.[65]

Under certain circumstances, a third party may give consent. According to the United States Supreme Court, a third party who possesses common authority over or other sufficient relationship to the premises or effects searched may give a valid consent.[66] Generally, the courts have held that the consent of a parent to the search of a child's room is valid.[67] As one court has stated:

> In his capacity as the head of the household, a father has the responsibility and authority for the discipline, training and control of his children. In the exercise of his parental authority a father has full access to the room set aside for his son for purposes of fulfilling his right and duty to control his son's social behavior and to obtain obedience. . . . Permitting an officer to search a bedroom in order to determine if his son is using or trafficking in narcotics [is] a reasonable and necessary extension of a father's authority and control over his children's moral training, health and personal hygiene.[68]

---

[61]Arizona v Hicks, 480 US 321, 107 SCt 1149, 94 LEd(2d) 347 (1987); Texas v Brown, 460 US 730, 103 SCt 1535, 75 LEd(2d) 502 (1983); Coolidge v New Hampshire, 403 US 443, 91 SCt 2022, 29 LEd(2d) 564 (1971). See generally 3 LaFave, *Search and Seizure* § 7.5 (2d ed 1987); Katz, *Ohio Arrest, Search and Seizure* ch 23 (2d ed 1987).

[62]Schneckloth v Bustamonte, 412 US 218, 227, 93 SCt 2041, 36 LEd(2d) 854 (1973).

[63]*Id.* See generally 3 LaFave, *Search and Seizure* ch 8 (2d ed 1987); Katz, *Ohio Arrest, Search and Seizure* ch 21 (2d ed 1987).

For juvenile cases in which the issue of consent is raised, see In re Ronny, 40 NY Misc(2d) 194, 242 NYS(2d) 844 (Fam Ct 1963). See also State v Davis, 56 OS(2d) 51, 381 NE(2d) 641 (1978) (A minor may consent and thereby waive his Fourth Amendment rights.).

[64]Bumper v North Carolina, 391 US 543, 88 SCt 1788, 20 LEd(2d) 797 (1968); In re Brent, No. 35400 (8th Dist Ct App, Cuyahoga, 2-17-77).

[65]In re Robert T., 8 Cal App(3d) 990, 88 Cal Rptr 37 (1970).

[66]United States v Matlock, 415 US 164, 94 SCt 988, 39 LEd(2d) 242 (1974). See generally 3 LaFave, *Search and Seizure* § 8.3 (2d ed 1987).

[67]E.g., United States v Wright, 564 F(2d) 785 (8th Cir Mo 1977); State v Carder, 9 OS(2d) 1, 222 NE(2d) 620 (1966); State v Bortree, No. 8-80-31 (3d Dist Ct App, Logan, 3-12-82). See generally 3 LaFave, *Search and Seizure* § 8.4(b) (2d ed 1987); Comment, *"Who's Been Searching in My Room?" Parental Waiver of Children's Fourth Amendment Rights,* 17 UCD L Rev 359 (1983).

[68]Vandenberg v Superior Court of Los Angeles County, 8 Cal App(3d) 1048, 1055, 87 Cal Rptr 876 (1970).

Parental consent, however, is not always valid. For example, one court has held that a father's consent to the search of a seventeen-year-old's toolbox was invalid where the son was present and objected: "The father claimed no interest in the box or its contents. He acknowledged that the son was owner, and the son did not consent to the search. Because those facts were known to the police there was no justification ... for their relying on the father's consent to conduct the search."[69]

(E) School searches

The constitutionality of school searches raises a number of Fourth Amendment issues.[70] The United States Supreme Court resolved some of these issues in *New Jersey v T.L.O.*[71] In that case, a student was taken to the vice-principal's office for smoking in the lavatory. A search of her purse revealed cigarettes as well as marijuana. This discovery led to the initiation of delinquency proceedings, at which the constitutionality of the search was challenged.

On review, the Supreme Court upheld the search. Initially, the Court declared the Fourth Amendment applicable to school searches. A number of courts had held that school officials were private citizens, acting in loco parentis, and thus not subject to the Fourth Amendment.[72] In response, the Court wrote:

> Such reasoning is in tension with contemporary reality and the teachings of this Court. ... Today's public school officials do not merely exercise authority voluntarily conferred on them by individual parents; rather they act in furtherance of publicly mandated educational and disciplinary policies. ... In carrying out searches and other disciplinary functions pursuant to such policies, school officials act as representatives of the State, not merely as surrogates for the parents, and they cannot claim the parents' immunity from the strictures of the Fourth Amendment.[73]

Next, the Court focused on the requirements of the Fourth Amendment in the school setting. In this context, the student's legitimate expectations of privacy are balanced against the school's legitimate need to maintain an environment in which learning can take place. The Court found that the warrant requirement imposed too high a burden on the proper functioning of school

---

[69]In re Scott K., 24 Cal(3d) 395, 405, 595 P(2d) 105, 155 Cal Rptr 671 (1979), cert denied sub nom Fare v Scott K., 444 US 973, 100 SCt 468, 62 LEd(2d) 388 (1979). See also Reeves v Warden, Maryland Penitentiary, 346 F(2d) 915 (4th Cir Md 1965); People v Flowers, 23 Mich App 523, 179 NW(2d) 56 (1970).

[70]See generally *IJA-ABA Standards Relating to Schools and Education* 150-59 (1982); Davis, *Rights of Juveniles* § 3.7 (2d ed 1988); 4 LaFave, *Search and Seizure* § 10.11 (2d ed 1987); Parkey, *Fourth Amendment Protections in the Elementary and Secondary School Settings*, 38 Mercer L Rev 1417 (1987); Note, *School Searches Under the Fourth Amendment: New Jersey v. T.L.O.*, 72 Cornell L Rev 368 (1987); Admissibility, in criminal case, of evidence obtained by search conducted by school official or teacher, 49 ALR3d 978 (1973).

[71]New Jersey v T.L.O., 469 US 325, 105 SCt 733, 83 LEd(2d) 720 (1985).

[72]E.g., In re Donaldson, 269 Cal App(2d) 509, 75 Cal Rptr 220 (1969); People v Stewart, 63 NY Misc(2d) 601, 313 NYS(2d) 253 (NY Crim Ct 1970); Commonwealth v Dingfelt, 227 Pa Super 380, 323 A(2d) 145 (1974); Mercer v State, 450 SW(2d) 715 (Tex Civ App 1970).

See also State v Wingerd, 40 App(2d) 236, 318 NE(2d) 866 (Athens 1974) (College officials who searched a dormitory room are private citizens.).

[73]New Jersey v T.L.O., 469 US 325, 336, 105 SCt 733, 83 LEd(2d) 720 (1985).

officials. Similarly, the Court believed that probable cause was too demanding an evidentiary standard in this setting. Instead, the Court held:

> [T]he legality of a search of a student should depend simply on the reasonableness, under all the circumstances, of the search. Determining reasonableness of any search involves a twofold inquiry: first, one must consider "whether the . . . action was justified at its inception" . . .; second, one must determine whether the search as actually conducted "was reasonably related in scope to the circumstances which justified the interference in the first place" . . . . Under ordinary circumstances, a search of a student by a teacher or other school official will be "justified at its inception" when there are reasonable grounds for suspecting that the search will turn up evidence that the student has violated or is violating either the law or the rules of the school. Such a search will be permissible in its scope when the measures adopted are reasonably related to the objectives of the search and not excessively intrusive in light of the age and sex of the student and the nature of the infraction.[74]

The Court's decision in *T.L.O.* clarified two issues: (1) Fourth Amendment protections extend to the schoolhouse; and (2) reasonable suspicion is the controlling standard in determining the constitutionality of these searches. A number of other issues, however, were left unresolved. First, the Court pointed out that its decision was limited to searches by school officials; the decision did not control searches conducted by school officials in conjunction with or at the behest of the police.[75] Second, the case involved the search of a purse, and the Court refused to say whether its rationale extended to searches of lockers, desks, or other school property used for storage by students.[76] For example, some lower courts have held that school officials may validly consent to a search of student lockers.[77] Finally, the Court refused to decide whether the exclusionary rule applied to school searches.[78]

CROSS REFERENCES

Text 1.02(H)

Schroeder-Katz, Ohio Criminal Law, Crim R 41, Author's Text
Katz, Ohio Arrest, Search and Seizure (2d ed), Text 1.03, 1.04, 3.07, 7.04, 13.03, Ch 17 to 23, Ch 26, 27.04

---

[74]*Id.* at 341-42.

[75]*Id.* at 341 n.7. See also Cason v Cook, 810 F(2d) 188 (8th Cir 1987) (Limited role of police liaison officer did not change nature of school search.).

[76]New Jersey v T.L.O., 469 US 325, 337 n.5, 105 SCt 733, 83 LEd(2d) 720 (1985). See also State v Joseph T., 336 SE(2d) 728 (W Va 1985) (Reasonable suspicion standard applied to locker search.).

[77]E.g., State v Stein, 203 Kan 638, 456 P(2d) 1 (1969), cert denied 397 US 947, 90 SCt 966, 25 LEd(2d) 128 (1970); People v Overton, 20 NY(2d) 360, 283 NYS(2d) 22, 229 NE(2d) 596 (1967) (Vice-principal could validly consent to search of student lockers.), remanded 393 US 85 (1968), on remand 24 NY(2d) 522, 301 NYS(2d) 479, 249 NE(2d) 366 (1969). See generally 3 LaFave, *Search and Seizure* § 8.6(e) (2d ed 1987).

[78]New Jersey v T.L.O., 469 US 325, 333 n.3, 105 SCt 733, 83 LEd(2d) 720 (1985). See also State v Young, 234 Ga 488, 216 SE(2d) 586 (1975), cert denied 423 US 1039, 96 SCt 576, 46 LEd(2d) 413 (1975) (The exclusionary rule does not apply to searches conducted by public school officials.); 1 LaFave, *Search and Seizure* § 1.7(b) (2d ed 1987).

5.04 Interrogations

The admissibility of a confession may be challenged on several distinct constitutional grounds.[79] First, a confession may be involuntary and thus violate due process. Confessions obtained by means of physical or psychological coercion are examples of involuntary confessions. Second, a confession may be obtained in violation of the Fifth Amendment's privilege against compelled self-incrimination as defined in *Miranda v Arizona*.[80] Third, a confession may be obtained in violation of the Sixth Amendment right to counsel. Finally, a confession that is the product of an illegal search or seizure under the Fourth Amendment may be excludable as "fruit of the poisonous tree."[81]

(A) Due process

Prior to *Miranda* the United States Supreme Court examined the admissibility of confessions under the Due Process Clause. In deciding these cases, the Court employed a "voluntariness test." Although the *Miranda* decision has overshadowed the voluntariness test, that test remains valid and important in a number of contexts. A statement may be involuntary and therefore inadmissible, even if the *Miranda* requirements are satisfied.[82] Moreover, an involuntary statement cannot be used to impeach a defendant, whereas a statement obtained in violation of *Miranda* may be used for impeachment.[83]

The Court summarized the voluntariness test as follows:

> The ultimate test . . . [is] voluntariness. Is the confession the product of an essentially free and unconstrained choice by its maker? If it is, if he has willed to confess, it may be used against him. If it is not, if his will has been overborne and his capacity for self-determination critically impaired, the use of his confession offends due process.[84]

The voluntariness test is based on the totality of circumstances and includes such factors as the defendant's age, education, intelligence, and mental condition. Other factors focus on police conduct. For example, failure to warn of rights, incommunicado detention, lengthy periods of questioning, use of relays in the interrogation, physical abuse, lack of food or sleep, deceptions, improper advice and promises are all relevant to a voluntariness determination.[85]

---

[79]See In re Hawkins, No. 3430 (9th Dist Ct App, Lorain, 5-11-83) (Juv R 7(A), which requires a person taking a child into custody to bring the child to court, to deliver the child to a place of detention, or to release the child to his parents, does not prohibit the police from questioning a child taken into custody.).

[80]Miranda v Arizona, 384 US 436, 86 SCt 1602, 16 LEd(2d) 694 (1966).

[81]See Taylor v Alabama, 457 US 687, 102 SCt 2664, 73 LEd(2d) 314 (1982); Dunaway v New York, 442 US 200, 99 SCt 2248, 60 LEd(2d) 824 (1979); Brown v Illinois, 422 US 590, 95 SCt 2254, 45 LEd(2d) 416 (1975). See also In re Appeal No. 245, 29 Md App 131, 349 A(2d) 434 (1975) (applying fruit of poisonous tree doctrine to a juvenile case).

[82]See State v Kassow, 28 OS(2d) 141, 277 NE(2d) 435 (1971), vacated on other grounds by 408 US 939, 92 SCt 2876, 33 LEd(2d) 762 (1972).

[83]Compare Mincey v Arizona, 437 US 385, 98 SCt 2408, 57 LEd(2d) 290 (1978) with Harris v New York, 401 US 222, 91 SCt 643, 28 LEd(2d) 1 (1971).

[84]Culombe v Connecticut, 367 US 568, 602, 81 SCt 1860, 6 LEd(2d) 1037 (1961).

[85]See generally 3 Wigmore, *Evidence* 352 n.11 (Chadbourn rev 1970); Note, *Developments in the Law—Confessions*, 79 Harv L Rev 935 (1966); Katz, *Ohio Arrest, Search and Seizure* ch 31 (2d ed 1987).

Two of the Court's voluntariness cases involved juveniles. These juveniles, however, were prosecuted in criminal, not juvenile, court. In *Haley v Ohio*[86] a fifteen year old confessed to murder after several hours of questioning. The Court commented:

> What transpired would make us pause for careful inquiry if a mature man were involved. And when, as here, a mere child—an easy victim of the law—is before us, special care in scrutinizing the record must be used. Age 15 is a tender and difficult age for a boy of any race. He cannot be judged by the more exacting standards of maturity. That which would leave a man cold and unimpressed can overawe and overwhelm a lad in his early teens. This is the period of great instability which the crisis of adolescence produces. A 15-year-old lad, questioned through the dead of night by relays of police, is a ready victim of the inquisition.[87]

In *Gallegos v Colorado*[88] the Court, in holding a confession involuntary, again stressed the differences between juveniles and adults:

> He cannot be compared with an adult in full possession of his senses and knowledgeable of the consequences of his admissions. He would have no way of knowing what the consequences of his confession were without advice as to his rights—from someone concerned with securing him those rights—and without the aid of more mature judgment as to the steps he should take in the predicament in which he found himself. A lawyer or an adult relative or friend could have given the petitioner the protection which his own immaturity could not.[89]

Courts have applied the voluntariness test to juvenile cases: "Use of an involuntary confession in a juvenile court proceeding offends fundamental fairness because of the likelihood of its untrustworthiness."[90]

(B) Miranda

In *Miranda v Arizona*[91] the United States Supreme Court held that custodial interrogation constituted compulsion within the meaning of the Fifth Amendment privilege against compelled self-incrimination. In order to protect the privilege in this context, the Court required the reading of the now familiar *Miranda* warnings. Prior to any questioning the suspect must be warned that (1) he has the right to remain silent; (2) anything he says can be used against him in a court of law; (3) he has the right to the presence of an attorney; and (4) if he cannot afford an attorney, one will be appointed for him prior to any questioning if he so desires.[92] The verbatim recital of the words of the *Miranda* opinion

---

[86]Haley v Ohio, 332 US 596, 68 SCt 302, 92 LEd 224 (1948).

[87]*Id.* at 599.

[88]Gallegos v Colorado, 370 US 49, 82 SCt 1209, 8 LEd(2d) 325 (1962).

[89]*Id.* at 54. See also State v Bell, 48 OS(2d) 270, 277, 358 NE(2d) 556 (1976), modified by 438 US 637, 98 SCt 2977, 57 LEd(2d) 1010 (1978); State v Stewart, 176 OS 156, 198 NE(2d) 439 (1964), cert denied 379 US 947, 85 SCt 443, 13 LEd(2d) 544 (1964).

[90]In re State in re Carlo, 48 NJ 224, 236, 225 A(2d) 110 (1966). See also United States v Ramsey, 367 FSupp 1307 (WD Mo 1973); In re Garth D., 55 Cal App(3d) 986, 127 Cal Rptr 881 (1976); In re Dunlop, Nos. 46822, 46823 (8th Dist Ct App, Cuyahoga, 1-5-84); In re White, No. 40971 (8th Dist Ct App, Cuyahoga, 7-31-80). See generally Voluntariness and admissibility of minor's confession, 87 ALR2d 624 (1963).

[91]Miranda v Arizona, 384 US 436, 86 SCt 1602, 16 LEd(2d) 694 (1966).

[92]*Id.* See generally 1 LaFave and Israel, *Criminal Procedure* ch 6 (1984); Whitebread and Slobogin, *Criminal Procedure* ch 16 (2d ed 1986); Katz, *Ohio Arrest, Search and Seizure* ch 31 (2d ed 1987).

is not required, so long as the warnings fully convey the rights required by *Miranda*.[93] Although the warnings are required in misdemeanor as well as felony cases,[94] the Supreme Court has recognized a "public safety" exception where the warnings are not required.[95]

(1) Custodial interrogation

The *Miranda* rights are triggered by "custodial interrogation." If either custody or interrogation is absent, there is no need to give the warnings. In *Miranda* the Court defined custodial interrogation as follows: "By custodial interrogation, we mean questioning initiated by law enforcement officers after a person has been taken into custody or otherwise deprived of his freedom of action in any significant way."[96] In a later case, the Court equated "custody" with "arrest." According to the Court, "[T]he ultimate inquiry is simply whether there is a 'formal arrest or restraint on freedom of movement' of the degree associated with a formal arrest."[97] Thus, even if the defendant is the focus of the police investigation, the warnings are not required unless he is in custody.[98] Moreover, questioning a suspect at the stationhouse does not necessarily mean that he is in custody.[99]

Even if the defendant is in custody, *Miranda* applies only when he is subjected to "interrogation." Volunteered statements are not subject to *Miranda*.[100] According to the United States Supreme Court, "the Miranda safeguards come into play whenever a person in custody is subjected to either express questioning or its functional equivalent."[101] The latter phrase includes "any words or actions on the part of the police (other than those normally attendant to arrest and custody) that the police should know are reasonably likely to elicit an incriminating response from the suspect."[102]

(2) Waiver

After receiving *Miranda* warnings, a suspect may waive his Fifth Amendment rights and make a statement. The Court in *Miranda* indicated that the prosecution had a heavy burden in establishing a waiver; the failure to request counsel does not constitute a waiver, and a waiver will not be presumed simply from the suspect's silence.[103] If no evidence is introduced at a suppression hearing to

[93]California v Prystock, 453 US 355, 101 SCt 2806, 69 LEd(2d) 696 (1981). See also State v Harris, 48 OS(2d) 351, 359 NE(2d) 67 (1976), vacated on other grounds by 438 US 911, 98 SCt 3148, 57 LEd(2d) 1155 (1978).

[94]Berkemer v McCarty, 468 US 420, 104 SCt 3138, 82 LEd(2d) 317 (1984). See also State v Buchholtz, 11 OS(3d) 24, 11 OBR 56, 462 NE(2d) 1222 (1984).

[95]New York v Quarles, 467 US 649, 104 SCt 2626, 81 LEd(2d) 550 (1984).

[96]Miranda v Arizona, 384 US 436, 444, 86 SCt 1602, 16 LEd(2d) 694 (1966).

[97]California v Beheler, 463 US 1121, 1125, 103 SCt 3517, 77 LEd(2d) 1275 (1983). See also Berkemer v McCarty, 468 US 420, 104 SCt 3138, 82 LEd(2d) 317 (1984); Minnesota v Murphy, 465 US 420, 430-31, 104 SCt 1136, 79 LEd(2d) 409 (1984).

[98]Beckwith v United States, 425 US 341, 96 SCt 1612, 48 LEd(2d) 1 (1976). See also State v Lipker, 16 App(2d) 21, 241 NE(2d) 171 (Lawrence 1968).

[99]Oregon v Mathiason, 429 US 492, 97 SCt 711, 50 LEd(2d) 714 (1977).

[100]State v Perry, 14 OS(2d) 256, 237 NE(2d) 891 (1968).

[101]Rhode Island v Innis, 446 US 291, 300-01, 100 SCt 1682, 64 LEd(2d) 297 (1980).

[102]*Id.* at 301. See also Arizona v Mauro, 481 US 521, 107 SCt 1931, 95 LEd(2d) 458 (1987).

[103]Miranda v Arizona, 384 US 436, 86 SCt 1602, 16 LEd(2d) 694 (1966).

establish a knowing and intelligent waiver, the defendant's statements are inadmissible.[104]

In *North Carolina v Butler*[105] the Court considered the validity of a waiver where the defendant agreed to talk but refused to sign a waiver of rights form. The Court upheld the waiver and commented:

> An express written or oral statement of waiver of the right to remain silent or of the right to counsel is usually strong proof of the validity of that waiver, but it is not inevitably either necessary or sufficient to establish waiver. The question is not one of form, but rather whether the defendant in fact knowingly and voluntarily waived the rights delineated in the *Miranda* case. . . . [M]ere silence is not enough. That does not mean that the defendant's silence, coupled with an understanding of his rights and a course of conduct indicating waiver, may never support a conclusion that the defendant has waived his rights. The courts must presume that a defendant did not waive his rights; the prosecution's burden is great; but in at least some cases waiver can be clearly inferred from the actions and words of the person interrogated.[106]

The Court has found a valid waiver where the defendant was not informed of all the crimes he was suspected of committing,[107] where the defendant was not informed that a lawyer had been retained for him,[108] and where a defendant refused to make a written statement but agreed to discuss a crime.[109]

Once a defendant invokes his right to remain silent or requests an attorney after receiving *Miranda* warnings, questioning must cease. The conditions under which interrogation may resume depend on which right the defendant has invoked. If the suspect indicates a desire to remain silent, but does not request counsel, questioning may resume if the police "scrupulously honor" the initial decision to remain silent. In *Michigan v Mosley*[110] the Court upheld the admission of a statement made during a second interrogation. Both interrogations were preceded by *Miranda* warnings; the defendant invoked the right to remain silent after the first interrogation. The Court emphasized several factors that demonstrated that the defendant's right to remain silent had been scrupulously honored: the second interrogation involved a different crime, was conducted by a different police officer, and occurred after a significant lapse of time. A different rule applies if the defendant requests counsel after receiving warnings. In such a case the prosecution must establish that the defendant (1) initiated the further communication, exchange, or conversation with the police, and (2) validly waived the right to counsel.[111]

---

[104]Tague v Louisiana, 444 US 469, 100 SCt 652, 62 LEd(2d) 622 (1980).

[105]North Carolina v Butler, 441 US 369, 99 SCt 1755, 60 LEd(2d) 286 (1979).

[106]*Id.* at 373. See also State v Scott, 61 OS(2d) 155, 161, 400 NE(2d) 375 (1980).

[107]Colorado v Spring, 479 US 564, 107 SCt 851, 93 LEd(2d) 954 (1987).

[108]Moran v Barbine, 475 US 412, 106 SCt 1135, 89 LEd(2d) 410 (1986).

[109]Connecticut v Barrett, 479 US 523, 107 SCt 828, 93 LEd(2d) 920 (1987).

[110]Michigan v Mosley, 423 US 96, 96 SCt 321, 46 LEd(2d) 313 (1975).

[111]Oregon v Bradshaw, 462 US 1039, 103 SCt 2830, 77 LEd(2d) 405 (1983). See also Arizona v Roberson, ___ US ___, 108 SCt 2093, 100 LEd(2d) 704 (1988); Edwards v Arizona, 451 US 477, 101 SCt 1880, 68 LEd(2d) 378 (1981); Wyrick v Fields, 459 US 42, 103 SCt 394, 74 LEd(2d) 214 (1982).

(3) Impeachment

Impeachment is an attempt to diminish a witness's credibility or worthiness of belief. Statements obtained in violation of *Miranda* may nevertheless be used to impeach a defendant if he testifies at trial.[112] If, however, the statement is involuntary (coerced), it is not admissible, even for impeachment.[113]

Under some circumstances, a defendant's silence also may be used to impeach his trial testimony. In *Doyle v Ohio*[114] the United States Supreme Court held that due process is violated when a defendant is impeached by his silence following *Miranda* warnings:

> [W]hile it is true that the *Miranda* warnings contain no express assurance that silence will carry no penalty, such assurance is implicit to any person who receives the warnings. In such circumstances, it would be fundamentally unfair and a deprivation of due process to allow the arrested person's silence to be used to impeach an explanation subsequently offered at trial.[115]

Doyle applies only when a suspect remains silent after receiving *Miranda* warnings. If he makes a statement, he is subject to impeachment.[116] Moreover, silence prior to arrest[117] or prior to the reading of *Miranda* warnings[118] is admissible for impeachment.

(4) Juvenile cases

The lower courts have applied the *Miranda* requirements to juvenile court proceedings.[119] Interestingly, in *Fare v Michael C.*,[120] its only case involving the application of *Miranda* to juvenile proceedings, the United States Supreme Court suggested that this issue remains undecided:

> [T]his Court has not yet held that *Miranda* applies with full force to exclude evidence obtained in violation of its proscriptions from consideration in juvenile proceedings, which for certain purposes have been distinguished

---

[112]Oregon v Hass, 420 US 714, 95 SCt 1215, 43 LEd(2d) 570 (1975); Harris v New York, 401 US 222, 91 SCt 643, 28 LEd(2d) 1 (1971).

[113]Mincey v Arizona, 437 US 385, 98 SCt 2408, 57 LEd(2d) 290 (1978).

[114]Doyle v Ohio, 426 US 610, 96 SCt 2240, 49 LEd(2d) 91 (1976).

[115]*Id.* at 618. See also State v Williams, 64 App(2d) 271, 276, 413 NE(2d) 1212 (Cuyahoga 1979) ("An indirect comment on the accused's silence can be as devastating as a direct comment on his failure to speak."); State v Eiding, 57 App(2d) 111, 385 NE(2d) 1332 (Cuyahoga 1978).

[116]Anderson v Charles, 447 US 404, 100 SCt 2180, 65 LEd(2d) 222 (1980). See also State v Osborne, 50 OS(2d) 211, 216, 364 NE(2d) 216 (1977) ("If a defendant voluntarily offers information to police, his toying with the authorities by allegedly telling only part of his story is certainly not protected by *Miranda* or *Doyle*."), vacated on other grounds by 438 US 911, 98 SCt 3137, 57 LEd(2d) 1157 (1978); State v Jones, 53 App(2d) 308, 373 NE(2d) 1272 (Summit 1977).

[117]Jenkins v Anderson, 447 US 231, 100 SCt 2124, 65 LEd(2d) 86 (1980). See also State v Sims, 3 App(3d) 321, 3 OBR 441, 445 NE(2d) 235 (Cuyahoga 1981).

[118]Fletcher v Weir, 455 US 603, 102 SCt 1309, 71 LEd(2d) 490 (1982).

[119]E.g., In re R.A.H., 314 A(2d) 133 (DC 1974); In re Creek, 243 A(2d) 49 (App, DC 1968); In re Dennis M., 70 Cal(2d) 444, 450 P(2d) 296, 75 Cal Rptr 1 (1969); State v Whatley, 320 So(2d) 123 (La 1975); State v Loyd, 297 Minn 442, 212 NW(2d) 671 (1973); In re William L., 29 AD(2d) 182, 287 NYS(2d) 218 (1968); In re Robert O., 109 NY Misc(2d) 238, 439 NYS(2d) 994 (Fam Ct 1981); Leach v State, 428 SW(2d) 817 (Tex Civ App 1968). See generally Holtz, Miranda *in a Juvenile Setting: A Child's Right to Silence*, 78 J Crim L 534 (1987).

[120]Fare v Michael C., 442 US 707, 99 SCt 2560, 61 LEd(2d) 197 (1979).

from formal criminal prosecutions. . . . We do not decide that issue today. In view of our disposition of this case, we assume without deciding that the *Miranda* principles were fully applicable to the present proceedings.[121]

The Court went on to hold that a juvenile's request to speak with his probation officer, after receiving *Miranda* warnings, is not a per se invocation of the right to remain silent.

Courts have held that statements made by juveniles are not subject to *Miranda* in the absence of custodial interrogation.[122] Statements made to persons other than police officers are also not covered by *Miranda*.[123] Moreover, statements obtained in violation of *Miranda* are admissible for impeachment.[124]

The test for determining whether a juvenile has waived his *Miranda* rights has divided the courts. Generally, courts have followed one of two approaches. One approach requires the presence of an interested adult—an attorney or a parent—before a child may validly waive his *Miranda* rights.[125] This approach is supported by several studies. One study concludes, "[Y]ounger juveniles as a class do not understand the nature and significance of their *Miranda* rights to remain silent and to counsel. Consequently, their waivers of these rights cannot be considered intelligently, knowingly, and voluntarily made."[126]

The second approach requires a consideration of the "totality of the circumstances" in determining the validity of a waiver, the same standard that applies in adult cases. The United States Supreme Court adopted this approach in *Fare v Michael C.*[127] According to the Court, the totality of the circumstances requires an inquiry that would include "the juvenile's age, experience, education, background, and intelligence, and . . . whether he has the capacity to understand the warnings given him, the nature of his Fifth Amendment rights, and the consequences of waiving those rights."[128]

The Ohio Supreme Court also has adopted the "totality of the circumstances" test. It has held that *Miranda* does not require that "the parents of a minor shall

---

[121]*Id.* at 717 n.4.

[122]E.g., In re Paul T., 15 Cal App(3d) 886, 93 Cal Rptr 510 (1971) (volunteered statement); In re Appeal No 245, 29 Md App 131, 349 A(2d) 434 (1975) (custody); In re Gage, 49 Or App 599, 624 P(2d) 1076 (1980) (no custody). See also In re Killitz, 59 Or App 720, 651 P(2d) 1382 (1982) (Juvenile questioned by police in principal's office was in custody.).

[123]State v Bolan, 27 OS(2d) 15, 271 NE(2d) 839 (1971) (store security officer). See also In re Deborah C., 30 Cal(3d) 125, 635 P(2d) 446, 177 Cal Rptr 852 (1981); R.W. v State, 135 Ga App 668, 218 SE(2d) 674 (1975); In re Simmons, 24 NC App 28, 210 SE(2d) 84 (1974).

[124]In re Welfare of Larson, 254 NW(2d) 388 (Minn 1977); In re Michael P., 50 AD(2d) 598, 375 NYS(2d) 153 (1975); In re Welfare of Noble, 15 Wash App 51, 547 P(2d) 880 (1976).

[125]See Davis, *Rights of Juveniles* § 3.13 (2d ed 1988); *IJA-ABA Standards Relating to Police Handling of Juvenile Problems* 69-73 (1980).

[126]Grisso, *Juveniles' Capacities to Waive Miranda Rights: An Empirical Analysis*, 68 Calif L Rev 1134, 1166 (1980). See also Grisso, *Juveniles' Waiver of Rights* (1981); Ferguson and Douglas, *A Study of Juvenile Waiver*, 7 San Diego L Rev 39 (1970).

[127]Fare v Michael C., 442 US 707, 99 SCt 2560, 61 LEd(2d) 197 (1979).

[128]*Id.* at 725.

be read his constitutional rights along with their child."[129] In applying the totality of the circumstances test, however, the court has recognized the special problems associated with juvenile waivers: "When a minor is sought to be interrogated, the question of whether he intelligently and voluntarily waives his rights cannot always be decided by the same criteria applied to mature adults."[130] The court went on to hold that the relevant factors in determining the validity of a waiver are the child's "age, emotional stability, physical condition, and mental capacity."[131]

Juvenile Rule 3 provides, in part, that no right of a child may be waived without permission of the juvenile court. The courts, however, have held that this provision does not apply to a child's waiver of *Miranda* rights.[132]

(C) Right to counsel

A statement obtained in violation of a criminal defendant's right to counsel is inadmissible. In *Brewer v Williams*[133] the United States Supreme Court wrote, "[O]nce adversary proceedings have commenced against an individual, he has a right to legal representation when the government interrogates him."[134] The right to counsel is a distinct ground for challenging the admissibility of a confession. Thus, even if the *Miranda* requirements are satisfied or are inapplicable, a violation of the Sixth Amendment requires suppression.

The right to counsel differs from the *Miranda* requirements in several respects. First, *Miranda* is triggered by "custodial interrogation." In contrast, the right to counsel is triggered by the initiation of adversary judicial proceedings, such as a formal charge, preliminary hearing, indictment, information, or arraignment.[135] A suspect who is not in custody but who is involved in adver-

---

[129]State v Bell, 48 OS(2d) 270, 276-77, 358 NE(2d) 556 (1976), reversed on other grounds by 438 US 637, 98 SCt 2977, 57 LEd(2d) 1010 (1978).

[130]*Id.* at 277.

[131]*Id.* See also In re Toler, No. 314 (12th Dist Ct App, Preble, 5-4-83); In re Hawkins, No. 3430 (9th Dist Ct App, Lorain, 5-11-83).

In West v United States, 399 F(2d) 467, 469 (5th Cir Fla 1968), cert denied 393 US 1102, 89 SCt 903, 21 LEd(2d) 795 (1969), the court set forth the following factors for consideration in the waiver issue:

> (1) the age of the accused; (2) education of the accused; (3) knowledge of the accused as to both the substance of the charge, if any has been filed, and the nature of his rights to consult with an attorney and remain silent; (4) whether the accused is held incommunicado or allowed to consult with relatives, friends or an attorney; (5) whether the accused was interrogated before or after formal charges had been filed; (6) methods used in interrogation; (7) length of interrogations; (8) whether vel non the accused refused to voluntarily give statements on prior occasions; and (9) whether the accused has repudiated an extra judicial statement at a later date.

[132]In re Hawkins, No. 3430 (9th Dist Ct App, Lorain, 5-11-83); State v Hull, No. 1059 (4th Dist Ct App, Athens, 8-7-81).

[133]Brewer v Williams, 430 US 387, 97 SCt 1232, 51 LEd(2d) 424 (1977).

[134]*Id.* at 401. See also Estelle v Smith, 451 US 454, 101 SCt 1866, 68 LEd(2d) 359 (1981); United States v Henry, 447 US 264, 100 SCt 2183, 65 LEd(2d) 115 (1980); Massiah v United States, 377 US 201, 84 SCt 1199, 12 LEd(2d) 246 (1964).

[135]Brewer v Williams, 430 US 387, 97 SCt 1232, 51 LEd(2d) 424 (1977). See also People v Fleming, 134 Ill App(3d) 562, 480 NE(2d) 1221 (1985) (Right to counsel attached when delinquency petition was filed and arrest warrant issued.); Edwards v Arizona, 451 US 477, 480 n.7, 101 SCt 1880, 68 LEd(2d) 378 (1981).

sary judicial proceedings is entitled to counsel but not *Miranda* warnings.[136] However, when a suspect is in custody and subjected to interrogation before adversary judicial proceedings have begun, the *Miranda* rule applies rather than the right to counsel.

Second, *Miranda* applies only when there is police interrogation—"words or actions . . . that the police should know are reasonably likely to elicit an incriminating response from the suspect."[137] The right to counsel is violated when the police "deliberately elicit" information from the defendant after the initiation of formal proceedings. Although interrogation would satisfy the "deliberately elicit" test, that test is not restricted to interrogation.[138] "By intentionally creating a situation likely to induce . . . incriminating statements,"[139] the government violates the right to counsel. Thus, even when a suspect is unaware that the person to whom he is speaking is a police officer, or an informant, the right to counsel may be violated.[140] However, passive listening by itself does not constitute deliberate elicitation.[141]

The right to counsel may be waived, but the test for a valid waiver is stringent. The prosecution must establish an intentional relinquishment of a known right.[142] The United States Supreme Court has held that the waiver of *Miranda* rights also waives the right to counsel.[143]

CROSS REFERENCES

Text 1.02(E)

Merrick-Rippner, Ohio Probate Law (4th ed), Text Ch 223
Katz, Ohio Arrest, Search and Seizure (2d ed), Text Ch 31

5.05   Identification procedures

Along with confessions and searches, identification procedures play an important role in the police investigation of crime. The use of these procedures raises a number of legal issues.

---

[136]Massiah v United States, 377 US 201, 84 SCt 1199, 12 LEd(2d) 246 (1964).

[137]Rhode Island v Innis, 446 US 291, 301, 100 SCt 1682, 64 LEd(2d) 297 (1980).

[138]*Id.* at 300 n.4 ("The definitions of 'interrogation' under the Fifth and Sixth Amendments, if indeed the term 'interrogation' is even apt in the Sixth Amendment context, are not necessarily interchangeable, since the policies underlying the two constitutional protections are quite distinct."). See also United States v Henry, 447 US 264, 100 SCt 2183, 65 LEd(2d) 115 (1980).

[139]United States v Henry, 447 US 264, 274, 100 SCt 2183, 65 LEd(2d) 115 (1980).

[140]Maine v Moulton, 474 US 159, 106 SCt 477, 88 LEd(2d) 481 (1985); United States v Henry, 447 US 264, 100 SCt 2183, 65 LEd(2d) 115 (1980); Massiah v United States, 377 US 201, 84 SCt 1199, 12 LEd(2d) 246 (1964).

[141]Kuhlmann v Wilson, 477 US 436, 106 SCt 2616, 91 LEd(2d) 364 (1986).

[142]Brewer v Williams, 430 US 387, 404, 97 SCt 1232, 51 LEd(2d) 424 (1977); State v Cowans, 10 OS(2d) 96, 227 NE(2d) 201 (1967). See also Michigan v Jackson, 475 US 625, 106 SCt 1404, 89 LEd(2d) 631 (1986).

[143]Patterson v Illinois, ___ US ___, 108 SCt 2389, 101 LEd(2d) 261 (1988).

(A) Self-incrimination

The United States Supreme Court has limited the Fifth Amendment privilege against compelled self-incrimination[144] to "testimonial or communicative" evidence; the privilege does not prohibit the compelled production of "real or physical" evidence.[145] Accordingly, requiring a suspect to be photographed,[146] appear in a lineup,[147] speak for identification,[148] or provide blood specimens,[149] handwriting exemplars,[150] or fingerprints[151] does not violate the privilege.

(B) Right to counsel

Because of the innumerable ways in which identification procedures can erroneously affect eyewitness identifications[152] and the difficulty of reconstructing these procedures at trial, the United States Supreme Court in *United States v Wade*[153] held that a lineup is a "critical stage" of the criminal process, thereby entitling the defendant to the assistance of counsel under the Sixth Amendment.[154] The presence of counsel, according to the Court, assures that a criminal defendant can effectively challenge a subsequent in-court identification based on a suggestive pretrial identification.[155] In *Kirby v Illinois*,[156] however, the Court restricted the right to counsel, holding that it attaches only "at or after the initiation of adversary judicial criminal proceedings—whether by way of formal charge, preliminary hearing, indictment, information, or arraignment."[157] The

---

[144]US Const Am 5 ("No person . . . shall be compelled in any criminal case to be a witness against himself."). The privilege against compelled self-incrimination applies to state trials. Malloy v Hogan, 378 US 1, 84 SCt 1489, 12 LEd(2d) 653 (1964). The Ohio Constitution also guarantees the privilege against self-incrimination (O Const Art I, § 10).

[145]Schmerber v California, 384 US 757, 764, 86 SCt 1826, 16 LEd(2d) 908 (1966).

[146]*Id.*

[147]United States v Wade, 388 US 218, 87 SCt 1926, 18 LEd(2d) 1149 (1967).

[148]United States v Dionisio, 410 US 1, 93 SCt 764, 35 LEd(2d) 67 (1973).

[149]Schmerber v California, 384 US 757, 86 SCt 1826, 16 LEd(2d) 908 (1966).

[150]United States v Euge, 444 US 707, 100 SCt 874, 63 LEd(2d) 141 (1980); United States v Mara, 410 US 19, 93 SCt 774, 35 LEd(2d) 99 (1973); Gilbert v California, 388 US 263, 87 SCt 1951, 18 LEd(2d) 1178 (1967); State v Ostrowski, 30 OS(2d) 34, 282 NE(2d) 359 (1972), cert denied 409 US 890, 93 SCt 130, 34 LEd(2d) 147 (1972).

[151]See Schmerber v California, 384 US 757, 86 SCt 1826, 16 LEd(2d) 908 (1966).

[152]See generally 1 LaFave and Israel, *Criminal Procedure* ch 7 (1984); Loftus, *Eyewitness Testimony* (1979); Whitebread and Slobogin, *Criminal Procedure* ch 18 (2d ed 1986); Sobel, *Eye-Witness Identification: Legal and Practical Problems* (2d ed 1987); Katz, *Ohio Arrest, Search and Seizure* ch 33 (2d ed 1987).

[153]United States v Wade, 388 US 218, 87 SCt 1926, 18 LEd(2d) 1149 (1967).

[154]US Const Am 6 ("In all criminal prosecutions, the accused shall enjoy the right . . . to have the assistance of counsel for his defence."). The right to counsel applies in state trials. Gideon v Wainwright, 372 US 335, 83 SCt 792, 9 LEd(2d) 799 (1963). The Ohio Constitution also guarantees the right to counsel (O Const Art I, § 10).

[155]United States v Wade, 388 US 218, 87 SCt 1926, 18 LEd(2d) 1149 (1967). See also Gilbert v California, 388 US 263, 87 SCt 1951, 18 LEd(2d) 1178 (1967).

[156]Kirby v Illinois, 406 US 682, 92 SCt 1877, 32 LEd(2d) 411 (1972).

[157]*Id.* at 689. See also Moore v Illinois, 434 US 220, 98 SCt 458, 54 LEd(2d) 424 (1977) (Right to counsel attaches at preliminary hearing.); Edwards v Arizona, 451 US 477, 480 n.7, 101 SCt 1880, 68 LEd(2d) 378 (1981) (indicating this issue is controlled by state law); State v Stricklen, 63 OS(2d) 47, 406 NE(2d) 1110 (1980); State v Sheardon, 31 OS(2d) 20, 285 NE(2d) 335 (1972); State v Kiraly, 56 App(2d) 37, 381 NE(2d) 649

Court also has held that the right to counsel does not apply to photographic displays, even after the commencement of adversary proceedings.[158]

The right to counsel at an identification procedure may be waived. A stringent test determines whether there has been a valid waiver of the right to counsel. The prosecution must establish "an intentional relinquishment or abandonment of a known right or privilege"[159] and the "courts indulge in every reasonable presumption against waiver."[160]

Testimony concerning a lineup identification at which the defendant has been denied the right to counsel is inadmissible.[161] Even if the lineup is constitutionally defective because of the denial of the right to counsel, a subsequent in-court identification may be admissible if the prosecution can establish by clear and convincing evidence that the in-court identification was based upon an independent source.[162] A number of factors are considered when determining whether the in-court identification is derived from an independent source: the witness's prior opportunity to observe the alleged criminal act, the existence of any discrepancy between any prelineup description and the defendant's actual description, any identification prior to the lineup of another person, the identification by picture of the defendant prior to the lineup, the failure to identify the defendant on a prior occasion, and the lapse of time between the alleged act and the lineup identification.[163]

Courts have applied the right-to-counsel requirement to juvenile cases.[164] The precise point at which the right attaches, however, is uncertain. One court has questioned whether juvenile court proceedings could be considered adversarial judicial criminal proceedings under *Kirby*.[165]

(C) Due process

Pretrial identification procedures are also subject to scrutiny under the Due Process Clause.[166] Due process rights are more comprehensive than the right to

---

(Cuyahoga 1977) (Setting bond triggers the right to counsel.); State v Strodes, 42 App(2d) 8, 325 NE(2d) 899 (Clark 1974).

[158]United States v Ash, 413 US 300, 93 SCt 2568, 37 LEd(2d) 619 (1973).

[159]Johnson v Zerbst, 304 US 458, 464, 58 SCt 1019, 82 LEd(2d) 1461 (1938).

[160]Brewer v Williams, 430 US 387, 404, 97 SCt 1232, 51 LEd(2d) 424 (1977). See also State v Hurt, 30 OS(2d) 86, 282 NE(2d) 578 (1972) (waiver of counsel not found), cert denied 409 US 991, 93 SCt 337, 34 LEd(2d) 258 (1972).

[161]Gilbert v California, 388 US 263, 87 SCt 1951, 18 LEd(2d) 1178 (1967).

[162]United States v Wade, 388 US 218, 87 SCt 1926, 18 LEd(2d) 1149 (1967).

[163]*Id.* See also State v Lathan, 30 OS(2d) 92, 282 NE(2d) 574 (1972) (no clear and convincing evidence of independent source); State v Hurt, 30 OS(2d) 86, 282 NE(2d) 578 (1972), cert denied 409 US 991, 93 SCt 337, 34 LEd(2d) 258 (1972); State v Kiraly, 56 App(2d) 37, 381 NE(2d) 649 (Cuyahoga 1977).

[164]In re Carl T., 1 Cal App(3d) 344, 81 Cal Rptr 655 (1969); In re Stoutzenberger, 235 Pa Super 500, 344 A(2d) 668 (1975); In re Daniel T., 446 A(2d) 1042 (RI 1982); In re Holley, 107 RI 615, 268 A(2d) 723 (1970).

See also In re McKelvin, 258 A(2d) 452 (App, DC 1969); In re Spencer, 288 Minn 119, 121 n.1, 179 NW(2d) 95 (1970); In re Carlos B., 86 NY Misc(2d) 160, 382 NYS(2d) 655 (Fam Ct 1976); *IJA-ABA Standards Relating to Police Handling of Juvenile Problems* 73-76 (1980).

[165]See Jackson v State, 17 Md App 167, 300 A(2d) 430 (1973).

[166]See generally 1 LaFave and Israel, *Criminal Procedure* ch 7 (1984); Whitebread and Slobogin, *Criminal Procedure* ch 18 (2d ed 1986); Sobel, *Eye-Witness Identification:*

counsel. For example, due process applies to photographic displays[167] and to lineups conducted prior to the time the right to counsel attaches.[168] In *Stovall v Denno*[169] the United States Supreme Court held that due process requires the exclusion of a pretrial identification where the procedure used is "unnecessarily suggestive and conducive to irreparable mistaken identification."[170] The focus of this test is the reliability of the *procedure* used in the identification. If the procedure is both suggestive and unnecessary, the identification is inadmissible.

In a subsequent case, *Neil v Biggers*,[171] the Court altered the due process test. The new test—whether a substantial likelihood of misidentification has occurred during the identification process—focuses on the reliability of the actual identification rather than on the reliability of the identification procedure itself. In applying this test, courts must consider the "totality of the circumstances," including the opportunity of the witness to view the criminal at the time of the crime, the witness's degree of attention, the accuracy of the witness's prior description of the criminal, the level of certainty demonstrated by the witness at the confrontation, and the length of time between the crime and the confrontation.[172]

The *Biggers* test was further refined in *Manson v Brathwaite*.[173] After citing the factors listed in *Biggers,* the Court commented that these factors must be weighed against the "corrupting effect of the suggestive identification itself."[174] Thus, it appears that the present due process test combines both the *Biggers* and *Stovall* tests.[175]

Courts have applied the due process tests to identifications in juvenile cases.[176]

(D) Fingerprints and photographs

The fingerprinting and photographing of children is governed by RC 2151.313. This statute prohibits the fingerprinting or photographing of children without the consent of the juvenile court except where the child is arrested or taken into custody for committing a felony, in which case the court must be

---

Legal and Practical Problems (2d ed 1987); Katz, *Ohio Arrest, Search and Seizure* ch 33 (2d ed 1987).

[167]See Simmons v United States, 390 US 377, 88 SCt 967, 19 LEd(2d) 1247 (1968). See also State v Kaiser, 56 OS(2d) 27, 381 NE(2d) 632 (1978); State v Moody, 55 OS(2d) 64, 377 NE(2d) 1008 (1978).

[168]Kirby v Illinois, 406 US 682, 92 SCt 1877, 32 LEd(2d) 411 (1972).

[169]Stovall v Denno, 388 US 293, 87 SCt 1967, 18 LEd(2d) 1199 (1967).

[170]*Id.* at 302.

[171]Neil v Biggers, 409 US 188, 93 SCt 375, 34 LEd(2d) 401 (1972).

[172]*Id.*

[173]Manson v Brathwaite, 432 US 98, 97 SCt 2243, 53 LEd(2d) 140 (1977).

[174]*Id.* at 114.

[175]See dissenting opinion of Justice Marshall in *Manson.* See also State v Madison, 64 OS(2d) 322, 415 NE(2d) 272 (1980); State v Moody, 55 OS(2d) 64, 377 NE(2d) 1008 (1978).

[176]In re Carl T., 1 Cal App(3d) 344, 81 Cal Rptr 655 (1969); In re Mark J., 96 NY Misc(2d) 733, 412 NYS(2d) 549 (1979); In re Howard, 31 App(3d) 1, 31 OBR 14, 508 NE(2d) 190 (Hamilton 1987); In re Finley, No. 48356 (8th Dist Ct App, Cuyahoga, 12-20-84); In re Daniel T., 446 A(2d) 1042 (RI 1982). See also *IJA-ABA Standards Relating to Police Handling of Juvenile Problems* 73-76 (1980).

immediately notified.[177] The statute also specifies the conditions under which fingerprints and photographs may be retained,[178] used, or released.[179]

Although a violation of the statute constitutes a misdemeanor,[180] exclusion of evidence is not a remedy.[181] According to the Ohio Supreme Court, the purpose of the statute is not to determine the admissibility of the evidence "but rather to conform to the theory that juvenile proceedings are not criminal in nature."[182]

CROSS REFERENCES

Merrick-Rippner, Ohio Probate Law (4th ed), Text Ch 223
Katz, Ohio Arrest, Search and Seizure (2d ed), Text Ch 33

---

[177]See In re Order Requiring Fingerprinting of a Juvenile, No. 12-027 (11th Dist Ct App, Lake, 11-6-87) (Juvenile may be fingerprinted with court's consent even in the absence of probable cause.).
[178]RC 2151.313(A).
[179]RC 2151.313(B).
[180]RC 2151.99(B).
[181]State v Davis, 56 OS(2d) 51, 381 NE(2d) 641 (1978).
[182]State v Carder, 9 OS(2d) 1, 11, 222 NE(2d) 620 (1966).

Chapter 7

Pre-Adjudication Procedures

7.01   Intake

The intake process commences juvenile court proceedings. At intake, the intake officer decides whether the matter should be handled through official court action or diverted to a community services program. Juvenile Rule 9(A) provides that "[i]n all appropriate cases formal court action should be avoided and other community resources utilized to ameliorate situations brought to the attention of the court."[1] In making this decision, the intake officer first determines whether the facts of the case justify the filing of a complaint and, if so, how to process the case. The facts are presented to the intake worker either directly from the complainant or through written reports supplied by the police, the welfare department, or some other agency.[2] If the facts are legally insufficient to establish grounds for a complaint, the complainant may be referred to an appropriate alternative.[3] However, even if the facts justify the filing of a complaint, the intake worker has several options in handling the matter. These include (1) filing an official complaint;[4] (2) holding an informal mediation conference with the child, his parents, and the victim; or (3) diverting the matter to available community resources. This decision is based on such factors as the seriousness of the offense or behavior (in delinquency, unruly, and juvenile traffic offender cases), the living conditions of the child (in neglect, dependency, and abuse cases), the parties' prior involvement with the court or another agency, the child's age and attitude, and the family dynamics affecting the child.

These evidentiary and social history matters may be "informally screened prior to the filing of a complaint to determine whether the filing of a complaint is in the best interest of the child and the public."[5] In informal court proceed-

---

[1]See In re M.D., 38 OS(3d) 149, 527 NE(2d) 286 (1988), holding that the filing of delinquency charges based on allegations of complicity to rape against a child under the age of thirteen is contrary to RC Ch 2151 and Juv R 9(A) and constitutes a denial of due process of law.

[2]Discovery of these reports is governed by Juv R 24. See Text 7.08(A), From other parties.

[3]For instance, if the facts are insufficient to file a delinquency complaint (RC 2151.02), the alleged victim might be referred to an attorney to explore the possibility of filing a civil action. A parent wishing to file a complaint against his child might be referred to a social service agency if the child's behavior does not fit within the definition of an unruly child (RC 2151.022).

[4]See Juv R 10; Text 7.03(A), Who may file.

[5]Juv R 9(B).

ings, no written pleadings are filed, nor is the case docketed or recorded; but memoranda are maintained in the court's files.[6]

An issue which has not been ruled on by the Ohio appellate courts is whether the parties[7] have a right to counsel at the intake stage. Courts in other jurisdictions have generally denied such a right on the ground that the United States Supreme Court cases, including the constitutional rights of juveniles, have been limited to the adjudicatory stage of the proceedings.[8] In Ohio, the right to counsel may attach at some point in the intake process. Juvenile Rule 4(A) provides that the right to counsel "shall arise when a person becomes a party to a juvenile court proceeding." Juvenile Rule 2(4) defines a "court proceeding" as "all action taken by a court from the earlier of (a) the time a complaint is filed and (b) the time a person first appears before an officer of a juvenile court until the court relinquishes jurisdiction over such child." Thus, if a child attends an informal intake mediation conference conducted by the juvenile court, he is entitled to legal representation.

If the decision is made at the intake stage to handle the matter informally, the issue arises as to whether the complainant has an absolute right to demand that a complaint be accepted. RC 2151.27 and Juvenile Rule 10 provide that "any person having knowledge" that a child is delinquent, unruly, neglected, dependent, or abused or a juvenile traffic offender, "may file a sworn complaint with respect to that child." However, these provisions must be read in conjunction with Juvenile Rule 9(A), which provides that the court has discretion to avoid formal court action "in all appropriate cases." Although the complainant may not compel the filing of a complaint, he may appeal the intake decision to the juvenile judge. As the official who is responsible for maintaining court records[9] and managing the court staff,[10] the judge has the final authority regarding intake decisions.

CROSS REFERENCES

Text 7.03, 7.08(A), 15.02, 15.04

Merrick-Rippner, Ohio Probate Law (4th ed), Text Ch 223

---

[6]In re Douglas, 82 Abs 170, 164 NE(2d) 475 (Juv, Huron 1959). See also RC 2151.18, RC 2151.35.

[7]Juv R 2(16) defines a party as "a child who is the subject of a juvenile court proceeding, his spouse, if any, his parent, or if the parent of a child be himself a child, the parent of such parent and, in appropriate cases, his custodian, guardian or guardian ad litem, the state and any other person specifically designated by the court."

[8]E.g., In re Anthony S., 341 NYS(2d) 11 (Fam Ct 1973); In re H., 71 Misc(2d) 1042, 337 NYS(2d) 118 (Fam Ct 1972).

[9]RC 2151.18. In all counties except those in which the domestic relations division of the common pleas court exercises juvenile jurisdiction, the juvenile judge serves also as the clerk of the juvenile court (RC 2151.12). In Cuyahoga County, the administrative juvenile judge is the clerk of court (RC 2153.08).

[10]RC 2151.13, RC 2153.08, RC 2153.09 (relating to Cuyahoga County Juvenile Court).

7.02   Diversion, youth services grant

In furtherance of the general purpose clauses of the juvenile court statutes and rules[11] and the specific provision of Juvenile Rule 9(A), an increasingly popular alternative at intake is to divert the matter to appropriate "community resources."[12] These include diversion programs operated by the court or an outside agency whose primary purpose is to provide counseling or other treatment to children and their families. Because formal diversion programs are a relatively recent development, there is virtually no caselaw in Ohio concerning the due process rights of those referred to such programs.

A typical diversion program,[13] however, will establish the following guidelines:

(1) A child who is referred to a diversion program may choose instead to have the matter handled officially by the court;

(2) The child is not required to admit the alleged behavior in order to be eligible for diversion;[14]

(3) The child has a right to consult an attorney, retained or appointed, before agreeing to participate in diversion;[15]

(4) Any statements made by the child during participation in a diversion program or during negotiations leading to such participation are inadmissible as evidence in any subsequent judicial proceeding relative to the original charge.

In addition to these due process guidelines, diversion programs may also include the following provisions:

(1) Diversion should only be used as an alternative to court action. Therefore, diversion is inappropriate if there is insufficient evidence to file a complaint or if the matter is not serious enough to justify court action;

(2) Although the wishes of the complainant should be considered, the decision to divert should be based primarily on the child's best interest;[16]

(3) Because a primary purpose of diversion is to prevent official court involvement with the child,[17] diversion is inappropriate if the child already has an official record with the court; and

---

[11]RC 2151.01; Juv R 1(B).

[12]According to the 1982 statistics of the Cuyahoga County Juvenile Court, more than 1,100 cases were referred to some type of diversion program or service agency.

[13]E.g., the diversion guidelines of the Cuyahoga County Juvenile Court, which were based in part on a similar program in Louisville, Kentucky.

[14]This is based on the premise that a confession made to obtain the benefits of diversion is a "compelled" confession which may violate the child's Fifth Amendment privilege against self-incrimination. On the other hand, it has been argued that admission should be a condition to eligibility for diversion because admitting one's misbehavior is essential to rehabilitation.

[15]For a discussion of the right to counsel at the intake stage, see Text 7.01, Intake.

[16]This is authorized by Juv R 9(A) and (B).

[17]There is some research indicating that children who become wards of the court and are labeled delinquent have a high probability of recidivism. E.g., Faust, *Delinquency Labeling, Its Consequences and Implications*, 19 Crime and Delinquency 41 (1973).

(4) If the child voluntarily enters a diversion program and thereafter violates the conditions of his participation, the court may choose to take formal action relative to the original charge.[18]

To further advance the general goal of avoiding official court action whenever possible, juvenile courts may participate with public or private county agencies in delinquency prevention and control programs.[19] The juvenile judge may assign employees to work with such programs and may accept and administer gifts, grants, bequests, and devises made to the court for delinquency prevention.[20]

In addition to diversion and prevention programs, there are a variety of other community resources which the juvenile court may use as alternatives to official court action. RC 5139.34 permits appropriation of funds to the Department of Youth Services. The funds are then channeled to counties as subsidies to establish diagnostic, prevention, diversion, counseling, treatment and rehabilitation programs and nonsecure foster care facilities for alleged or adjudicated unruly or delinquent children or those at risk of becoming unruly or delinquent.[21] Because the purpose of these subsidies is to provide community-based programs for children in need, certain conditions have been placed on the receipt of subsidy money: (1) all programs, with one exception,[22] must be provided in a nonsecure setting;[23] (2) the subsidy may not be used for foster care facilities which have not been certified, licensed, or properly approved;[24] (3) only certain percentages of the subsidy grant may be used for residential facilities having more than twenty beds or for capital improvements;[25] and (4) subsidy funds may not be used to supplant existing county expenditures for the juvenile court or related programs.[26] In determining how the subsidy grant will be spent,[27] a youth services advisory board, jointly established and maintained by each juvenile court and board of county commissioners, provides assistance in formulating an annual comprehensive plan.[28] This plan must be approved by the court and the commissioners,[29] as well as by the Department of Youth Services.[30]

---

[18]Since the speedy trial provisions of RC 2945.71 do not apply to children's cases, the court is permitted to wait a reasonable time before commencing official proceedings. See Text 11.02, Speedy trial.

[19]RC 2151.11.

[20]*Id.*

[21]RC 5139.34(A).

[22]The exception is for diagnostic programs provided in a secure setting, in which no child may be detained for more than two weeks (RC 5139.34(A)).

[23]The term "nonsecure setting" refers to a facility not characterized by the use of physically restricting construction, hardware, and procedures and which provides its residents access to the surrounding community with minimal supervision (OAC 5139-19-02).

[24]RC 5139.34(A).

[25]*Id.*

[26]RC 5139.34(D).

[27]Each county receives a minimum of $50,000 per fiscal year (RC 5139.34(B)(1)); any remaining portion of the department's grant appropriation is distributed to larger counties on a per capita basis (RC 5139.34(B)(2)).

[28]RC 5139.34(C).

[29]*Id.*

[30]RC 5139.34(D).

Although the IJA-ABA Standards encourage intake screening and other non-judicial methods of handling children, they warn against potential misuse of such methods. Because of the virtually unlimited discretion given intake workers, there is the possibility that cases that should be handled officially may be diverted or that cases that do not necessitate any court intervention will be processed through informal intake channels.[31]

CROSS REFERENCES

Text 1.03, 5.04(C), 7.01, 7.07(A), 11.02

Merrick-Rippner, Ohio Probate Law (4th ed), Text Ch 217

7.03   Complaint

(A) Who may file

The instrument that sets forth the allegations which form the basis for juvenile court jurisdiction is the complaint.[32] Unless a complaint is filed, the juvenile court has no jurisdiction to proceed with an adjudicatory or dispositional hearing.[33] The requirements of a complaint are covered both by rule[34] and by statute.[35]

A complaint may be filed by "any person having knowledge"[36] that a child is within the court's jurisdiction. The term "person" is defined as "an individual, association, corporation, or partnership and the state or any of its political subdivisions, departments, or agencies."[37] Although this definition seems to permit any individual to file any type of complaint, there are some restrictions. For instance, a uniform traffic ticket must be used as the complaint in juvenile traffic offense proceedings.[38] Since such tickets may only be issued by law enforcement officers,[39] other persons would not be permitted to file complaints relative to juvenile traffic offenders.

Any person having reason to believe that a child is abused or neglected may report such information to a children services board, county human services department, or municipal or county peace officer.[40] In addition, certain "professionals,"[41] who due to their line of work are likely to come into contact with

---

[31]*IJA-ABA Standards Relating to the Juvenile Probation Function* 2-3 (1980).

[32]Juv R 2(3).

[33]Howser v Ashtabula County Children Services Board, No. 1134 (11th Dist Ct App, Ashtabula, 9-19-83).

[34]Juv R 10.

[35]RC 2151.27.

[36]*Id.*; Juv R 10(A).

[37]Juv R 2(17).

[38]Juv R 10(C); Traf R 3(A).

[39]Traf R 3(C), (E).

[40]RC 2151.421. The statute also includes "any crippled or otherwise physically or mentally handicapped *child* under twenty-one years of age." However, a person between the ages of eighteen and twenty-one is not, according to statute, a "child" (RC 2151.011(B)(1), (2)).

[41]The mandatory provision applies to the following occupations: attorney, physician, intern, resident, dentist, podiatrist, limited practitioner as defined in RC 4731.15, registered nurse, licensed practical nurse, visiting nurse, other health care professional, licensed psychologist, licensed school psychologist, speech pathologist or audiologist,

children, are required to report information regarding abuse or neglect.[42] Upon receipt of such a report, the children services board or county human services department must investigate the allegations within twenty-four hours and determine whether a complaint should be filed or other action taken to protect the child.[43]

The complaint may be based upon "information and belief."[44] In interpreting this term in criminal proceedings, Ohio courts have held that it is not necessary that a complainant or affiant have personal knowledge of the facts constituting the elements of the offense or have observed the commission of the offense.[45] It is sufficient if such person has reasonable grounds to believe that the accused has committed the offense.[46] The complainant or affiant may rely upon the testimony and investigation of others to establish matters not within his personal knowledge.[47]

(B) When to file

If an alleged abused, neglected, or dependent child is taken into custody pursuant to RC 2151.31(D) or is taken into custody pursuant to RC 2151.31(A) without the filing of a complaint, the complaint must be filed with respect to the child before the end of the next business day after the day on which the child was taken into custody.[48] With respect to any other child held in a place of detention or shelter care, the complaint must be filed not later than seventy-two hours after he is placed in detention or shelter care.[49]

(C) Necessary language

The complaint must allege that the child is delinquent, unruly, abused, neglected, dependent, or a juvenile traffic offender[50] and must state in ordinary

---

coroner, administrator or employee of a child day-care center or certified child care agency or children services agency, school employee, school teacher, school authority, social worker, or clergyman, acting in an official or professional capacity (RC 2151.421).

[42]RC 2151.421. If the report is made to a peace officer, the officer must refer it to the county human services department or children services board.

[43]RC 2151.421 also provides certain criminal penalties (i.e., fourth degree misdemeanor for any person required to make the report who fails to do so (RC 2151.99), or for any person who permits the unauthorized dissemination of these confidential reports), establishes evidentiary rules (i.e., waiver of physician-patient privilege), and provides immunity from civil or criminal liability to anyone making the reports. See also Bishop v Ezzone, No. WD-80-63 (6th Dist Ct App, Wood, 6-26-81).

[44]RC 2151.27(A); Juv R 10(B).

[45]Sopko v Maxwell, 3 OS(2d) 123, 209 NE(2d) 201 (1965); State v Villagomez, 44 App(2d) 209, 337 NE(2d) 167 (Defiance 1974); State v Biedenharn, 19 App(2d) 204, 250 NE(2d) 778 (Hamilton 1969).

[46]Sopko v Maxwell, 3 OS(2d) 123, 209 NE(2d) 201 (1965).

[47]State v Villagomez, 44 App(2d) 209, 337 NE(2d) 167 (Defiance 1974). In some counties, the police departments of large municipalities assign to one officer the duty of signing all juvenile court complaints filed by the department.

[48]RC 2151.27.

[49]RC 2151.314.

[50]RC 2151.27(A). For the requirements of permanent custody complaints, see Text 7.03(I), Neglect, dependency, and abuse proceedings.

and concise language the essential facts which bring the case within the court's jurisdiction.[51]

The rule requiring that the complaint specify the type of case involved has generally been followed by the Ohio courts. Thus, a neglect finding based on a dependency complaint[52] and a dependency finding based on a neglect[53] or unruly[54] complaint have been held invalid. Since dependency, neglect, and unruliness involve different conditions, the parent must be provided sufficient notice of the category relied upon.[55] On the other hand, an Ohio court of appeals substituted a finding of dependency for a finding of neglect in a permanent custody case, although dependency had not been alleged in the complaint.[56]

Whether a complaint is sufficiently definite and clear is an issue which has arisen in several cases. A dependency complaint which recited only that the children "appear to be dependent in that their condition or environment is such as to warrant the state, in the interests of the children, in assuming their guardianship" was held to be defective.[57] Such a complaint merely reiterates the wording of the dependency statute (RC 2151.04(C)), without stating the particular facts supporting the complaint.[58]

Dependency complaints which allege some details have generally been upheld against challenges of lack of specificity and definiteness. For example, a complaint which recited the wording of the dependency statute was upheld because it included the following supporting allegations: the parents' unstable living situation, their inability to provide for the child's support or medical care, the putative father's denial of paternity, the mother's lack of education and employment, and the mother's residence in a home fraught with domestic difficulties.[59] Complaints alleging even fewer details have met the requirement of definiteness. A mere allegation of "excessive punishment" has been held sufficient.[60]

---

[51]In re Gault, 387 US 1, 87 SCt 1428, 18 LEd(2d) 527 (1967); Juv R 10(B)(1). RC 2151.27(A) provides that the complaint must "allege the particular facts upon which the allegation . . . is based." These provisions overruled early court decisions which held that a complaint was valid if it merely used the words delinquent, dependent, or neglected, without alleging specific facts. See In re Duncan, 62 Abs 173, 107 NE(2d) 256 (App, Preble 1951); In re Anteau, 67 App 117, 36 NE(2d) 47 (Lucas 1941); In re Hayes, 62 App 289, 23 NE(2d) 956 (Franklin 1939); Smith v Privette, 13 Abs 291 (App, Franklin 1932); In re Decker, 28 NP(NS) 433 (Juv, Tuscarawas 1930).

[52]In re Thomas, Nos. 39494, 39495 (8th Dist Ct App, Cuyahoga, 7-19-79).

[53]In re Flynn, No. 82 AP-750 (10th Dist Ct App, Franklin, 4-12-83); In re Reed, No. CA 1325 (5th Dist Ct App, Tuscarawas, 7-24-79).

[54]In re Osborn, No. CA 1744 (5th Dist Ct App, Richland, 1-16-79).

[55]In re Thomas, Nos. 39494, 39495 (8th Dist Ct App, Cuyahoga, 7-19-79).

[56]In re Sullivan, Nos. 79 AP-893, 894 (10th Dist Ct App, Franklin, 12-16-80).

[57]In re Hunt, 46 OS(2d) 378, 379, 348 NE(2d) 727 (1976). See also In re Baker, No. 6-81-12 (3d Dist Ct App, Hardin, 7-14-82).

[58]In re Hunt, 46 OS(2d) 378, 348 NE(2d) 727 (1976). For similar decisions holding that "boilerplate" complaints which merely recite the wording of the statute are defective, see In re Baker, No. 6-81-12 (3d Dist Ct App, Hardin, 7-14-82); In re Willis, Nos. 7-80-10 to 7-80-12 (3d Dist Ct App, Henry, 12-24-81); In re Parker, No. 15-79-16 (3d Dist Ct App, Van Wert, 1-26-81); In re Reed, No. CA 1325 (5th Dist Ct App, Tuscarawas, 7-24-79); In re Neff, No. 1-78-9 (3d Dist Ct App, Allen, 6-14-78); In re Spears, No. 1200 (4th Dist Ct App, Athens, 12-10-84).

[59]In re Trizzino, No. 40982 (8th Dist Ct App, Cuyahoga, 1-31-80).

[60]In re Brown, No. 3-CA-79 (5th Dist Ct App, Fairfield, 7-20-79).

Moreover, an abuse complaint which did not specifically set forth the dates on which the abusive acts occurred also has been held to satisfy the requirement of definiteness.[61]

The issue of whether a complaint contains "essential facts" arises more often in dependency and neglect proceedings than in delinquency proceedings. In dependency and neglect cases the "facts" are more generalized and the necessary elements are more nebulous than in delinquency cases, which involve a violation of a specific statute or ordinance. However, the requirement of definiteness applies equally to delinquency cases. A delinquency complaint for disorderly conduct which alleges that the child is delinquent, which recites the statutory language of the criminal statute violated, and which describes the alleged conduct with particular facts relative to the time, place, and circumstances of the conduct is valid.[62] While all the facts relied upon to sustain the complaint need not be recited, the material elements of the offense must be stated.[63]

Some courts have liberally interpreted the "necessary language" requirements of Juvenile Rule 10(B)(1). It has been held that the rule is not intended to force a complainant to state in the complaint every fact surrounding each incident described.[64] Thus, in proving its case in a neglect and dependency proceeding, the state is not limited to those facts which are specifically listed in the complaint.[65] Moreover, even though a delinquency complaint designates a particular statute or statutes as being violated by a child, a juvenile court may find, on the basis of the facts alleged and proved, that the child is a delinquent child for the violation of an additional statute.[66] Similarly, a delinquency complaint is sufficient under Juvenile Rule 10(B) to state a charge of complicity when it alleges that the juvenile "knowingly" aided another to commit robbery[67] in violation of RC 2923.03.[68] In *In re Howard*,[69] the court held that a delinquency complaint is sufficient even if it fails to specify exactly what theft offense was committed or attempted, and fails to specify the degree or degrees of culpability applicable to that theft offense.

---

[61]In re Gall, No. 11-85-1 (3d Dist Ct App, Paulding, 6-16-86).

[62]In re Davis, No. CA-1573 (5th Dist Ct App, Tuscarawas, 4-13-82) (Complaint valid even though the only specific facts mentioned related to the date and county, with no facts given relative to the exact time, location, or victim.); In re Corona, No. 40992 (8th Dist Ct App, Cuyahoga, 8-20-81) (Complaint included particular facts relative to exact time and location and included the victims' names.).

[63]State v Burgun, 49 App(2d) 112, 359 NE(2d) 1018 (Cuyahoga 1976).

[64]In re Sims, 13 App(3d) 37, 13 OBR 40, 468 NE(2d) 111 (Preble 1983).

[65]*Id.*

[66]In re Burgess, 13 App(3d) 374, 13 OBR 456 (Preble 1984). The court cautioned that its holding might differ if the complaint were intentionally abbreviated and the testimony at the adjudicatory hearing bore no relationship to the facts alleged in the complaint.

[67]RC 2911.01.

[68]In re Howard, 31 App(3d) 1, 31 OBR 14, 508 NE(2d) 190 (Hamilton 1987). See also In re Swackhammer, No. 1284 (4th Dist Ct App, Ross, 11-26-86).

[69]In re Howard, 31 App(3d) 1, 31 OBR 14, 508 NE(2d) 190 (Hamilton 1987).

(D) Numerical designation of statute

In delinquency and juvenile traffic offense cases, the complaint must contain the numerical designation of the statute or ordinance alleged to have been violated.[70] This requirement refers to the statute or ordinance which defines the particular offense and not to the general statutes which define a delinquent child[71] or a juvenile traffic offender.[72] In *State v Burgun*,[73] a case interpreting a similar provision in Criminal Rule 3, the court held that inclusion of the numerical designation of the applicable criminal statute in a complaint does not cure failure to charge all of the essential elements of the crime.

(E) Identifying information

The complaint must also contain the name and address of the child's parent, guardian, or custodian or, if such name and address is unknown, it must so state.[74] Where a permanent custody order has been entered against the child's parents,[75] it is unnecessary to include their names or addresses in any subsequent complaint because they would no longer be parties to the action.[76] In such cases the name and address of the child's guardian[77] or custodian[78] should be included. Where temporary custody of the child has been granted to one parent or to someone other than the parents,[79] Juvenile Rule 10(B) requires that the names and addresses of both parents as well as that of the custodian be listed in the complaint.

The rationale for requiring the inclusion of the parents' names and addresses is that the parents are parties to any juvenile court proceeding regarding their child,[80] unless their rights have been permanently divested. As parties they are entitled to certain due process safeguards, such as the rights to counsel[81] and notice.[82]

If the name or whereabouts of the child's parent, guardian, or custodian is unknown, the court is required to serve summons on that person by publication.[83]

---

[70]Juv R 10(B)(1).

[71]RC 2151.02.

[72]RC 2151.021.

[73]State v Burgun, 49 App(2d) 112, 359 NE(2d) 1018 (Cuyahoga 1976).

[74]Juv R 10(B)(2).

[75]RC 2151.353(A)(4). See Text 13.06(A)(4), Permanent custody; Text 13.06(B), Motion for permanent custody.

[76]RC 2151.35(D), RC 2151.414(F).

[77]Juv R 2(9) defines a "guardian" as "a court appointed guardian of the person of a child."

[78]Juv R 2(5) defines a "custodian" as "a person who has been granted custody of a child by a court."

[79]RC 2151.353(A). See Text 13.04, Reasonable efforts determination; Text 13.05, Case plans.

[80]Juv R 2(16) also provides that "in appropriate cases" the child's guardian or custodian may also be a party.

[81]See Text 11.03, Right to counsel, guardian ad litem.

[82]See Text 7.05, Summons.

[83]See Text 7.05(C), Methods of service.

(F) Necessity of oath

The complaint must be made under oath.[84] By entry in its journal, the juvenile court may authorize any deputy clerk to administer oaths when necessary in the discharge of his duties.[85] Despite the general rule requiring a sworn complaint, the complaint in juvenile traffic offenses need not be made under oath. Juvenile Rule 10(C) requires that a uniform traffic ticket be used as the complaint in juvenile traffic offense proceedings.[86] Traffic Rule 3(E) requires only that such tickets be "signed" by the law enforcement officer, not sworn to.[87]

Although it is apparent from Juvenile Rule 10(B)(3) and RC 2151.27 that all complaints in non-traffic cases must be made under oath, this requirement has been relaxed in two unreported decisions. In one case, the complainant signed the complaint, but failed to do so under oath. The court held that the complainant had substantially complied with the rule and statute since at all times she realized the effect of signing the complaint and she corroborated at the adjudicatory hearing, under oath, the facts outlined in the complaint.[88] In the other case, the complaint was not even signed. However, the court determined that since the complainant appeared in court at the time the complaint was filed and testified under oath about the allegations in the complaint, the purpose and spirit of the rule had been served.[89]

(G) Juvenile traffic offense

In juvenile traffic offense proceedings, a uniform traffic ticket is used as the complaint.[90] Since juvenile court traffic proceedings are subject to the Ohio Traffic Rules, it is necessary to look at those rules to determine the requirements of a ticket.[91] Unlike other complaints filed in the juvenile court, a traffic ticket need not be sworn to;[92] it may be issued only by a law enforcement officer.[93] A properly issued uniform traffic ticket provides information relative to the time, place, and nature of the alleged violation, a narrative description of the offense, a synopsis of the road, weather, and traffic conditions,[94] and the numerical designation of the statute or ordinance alleged to have been violated.[95] In this respect, the traffic ticket is like other complaints; it informs the parties of the essential facts.

---

[84]RC 2151.27(A); Juv R 10(B)(3). RC 3.20 provides that whenever an oath is required, an affirmation in lieu thereof may be taken by a person having conscientious scruples against taking an oath. An affirmation has the same effect as an oath.

[85]RC 2151.13.

[86]See Text 7.03(G), Juvenile traffic offense.

[87]Prior to the 1975 amendment to Juv R 10, traffic tickets had to be made under oath. See In re Bernstein, Nos. 33531, 33532 (8th Dist Ct App, Cuyahoga, 1-2-75).

[88]In re Lewandowski, No. 85-C-55 (7th Dist Ct App, Columbiana, 8-25-86).

[89]In re Bridges, No. L-85-275 (6th Dist Ct App, Lucas, 6-20-86).

[90]Juv R 10(C).

[91]Traf R 1(A), Traf R 2. See also Text 7.03(D), Numerical designation of statute.

[92]Traf R 3(E).

[93]Traf R 3(C), (E).

[94]See Traffic Rules, Appendix of Forms.

[95]Juv R 10(B)(1).

A uniform traffic ticket for speeding which fails to charge that the speed stated thereon is unreasonable fails to state an offense.[96] However, where a traffic ordinance prohibits driving faster or slower than is reasonable or proper and provides that exceeding any speed limit is prima facie unlawful, a traffic ticket alleging that the offender has exceeded the posted speed limit in effect also alleges that the offender's speed was prima facie unreasonable.[97]

(H) Custody proceedings

RC 3109.27(A) requires every party in a custody proceeding to give information in his first pleading as to the child's present and past addresses and custodians and as to any custody proceedings concerning the child pending in other jurisdictions. This section is made applicable to juvenile court custody proceedings, including neglect and dependency cases, by RC 2151.23(F) and RC 3109.21(C). The Ohio Supreme Court has held that this mandatory jurisdictional requirement applies to a parent bringing an action, but does not apply to a public agency that initiates such an action.[98]

(I) Neglect, dependency, and abuse proceedings

In a case in which a child is alleged to be abused, neglected, or dependent, if the complainant desires permanent custody of the child, temporary custody of the child (whether as the preferred or an alternative disposition), or the placement of the child in long-term foster care, the complaint must contain a prayer specifically requesting permanent custody, temporary custody, or the placement of the child in long-term foster care.[99] If such a prayer is not included in the complaint, such a dispositional order may not be made.[100] As with other complaints, abuse, neglect, and dependency complaints must allege the particular facts on which the allegations of the complaint are based.[101] The standard of definiteness which applies to complaints also applies to motions and applications for permanent custody.[102]

---

[96]Medina v Coles, No. 1571 (9th Dist Ct App, Medina, 7-15-87).

[97]In re Farinacci, No. 37973 (8th Dist Ct App, Cuyahoga, 11-30-78).

[98]In re Palmer, 12 OS(3d) 194, 12 OBR 259, 465 NE(2d) 1312 (1984), cert denied sub nom Pihlblad v Stark County Welfare Dept, 469 US 1162, 105 SCt 918, 83 LEd(2d) 930 (1985). See also Pasqualone v Pasqualone, 63 OS(2d) 96, 406 NE(2d) 1121 (1980); Cook v Court of Common Pleas, 28 App(3d) 82, 28 OBR 124, 502 NE(2d) 245 (Marion 1986).

[99]RC 2151.27(C). See also Juv R 10(D). Although the statutory provision requires this statement only in complaints which allege abuse, dependency, or neglect, the rule applies to any complaint which seeks permanent custody. This includes delinquency and unruly cases since it is legally possible for permanent custody to be ordered in such cases (RC 2151.354(A), RC 2151.355(A)(1)).

[100]RC 2151.353(B).

[101]RC 2151.27(A); Juv R 10(B)(1).

[102]In re Fassinger, 43 App(2d) 89, 334 NE(2d) 5 (Cuyahoga 1974), affirmed by 42 OS(2d) 505, 330 NE(2d) 431 (1975); In re Strowbridge, No. 1574 (4th Dist Ct App, Lawrence, 10-25-82); In re Escue, No. 1487 (4th Dist Ct App, Lawrence, 5-11-81); In re Coulter, No. C-800444 (1st Dist Ct App, Hamilton, 4-29-81); In re Holcomb, No. 39694 (8th Dist Ct App, Cuyahoga, 10-4-79); In re Neff, No. 1-78-9 (3d Dist Ct App, Allen, 6-14-78). But see In re Crose, No. 1055 (2d Dist Ct App, Darke, 10-18-82), holding that RC 2151.27 and Juv R 10(B) concern the sufficiency of complaints, whereas RC 2151.413 governs motions. See also In re Covin, 8 App(3d) 139, 8 OBR 196, 456 NE(2d) 520 (Hamilton 1982); In re Hadsell, No. 41004 (8th Dist Ct App, Cuyahoga, 6-19-80); In re Massie, No. 447 (4th Dist Ct App, Jackson, 3-30-84).

An adjudication of neglect or dependency for the purpose of obtaining permanent custody of a child will not be valid unless there has been a complaint filed containing a prayer requesting permanent custody which sufficiently apprises the parents of the grounds upon which the permanent custody order is to be based.[103] A motion for permanent custody based on a previous dependency adjudication which contains merely an allegation that "it would appear to be in the best interests of said minors that they be placed for adoption" is not sufficiently specific.[104] A "best interest" statement alone does not present the essential facts. A court does not have discretion to grant custody of a child to a third party solely on the ground that the best interest of the child will be promoted thereby.[105]

On the other hand, courts have upheld motions and complaints for permanent custody containing varying degrees of detail. A motion for permanent custody was held to be sufficiently definite when it alleged that the mother had failed to formulate any child-care plans in order to reunite her family, that she was living with but had not married the child's alleged father, and that she had visited her child only twice during the nine-month period that the child was in the temporary custody of the movant.[106] A permanent custody motion which was accompanied by an affidavit detailing the parents' marital troubles, the child's physical abuse, and the father's failure to protect the child was also held to be sufficiently specific.[107] A complaint seeking permanent custody was upheld where it alleged that the children lacked adequate supervision, that the mother was unable to maintain a proper home for the children and had often expressed her inability to care for them, and that she had recently attempted suicide and been admitted to a hospital psychiatric unit for alcohol and drug dependence.[108]

A neglect complaint for permanent custody was held sufficient even though it alleged facts pertaining to a previous temporary custody order that had since been terminated. Although a permanent custody hearing must be based on events occurring since the most recent grant of temporary custody, in this case the mother's continuing uncooperativeness and lack of effort to meet the child's financial and medical needs met this test.[109]

---

[103]In re Fassinger, 43 App(2d) 89, 334 NE(2d) 5 (Cuyahoga 1974), affirmed by 42 OS(2d) 505, 330 NE(2d) 431 (1975); In re Strowbridge, No. 1574 (4th Dist Ct App, Lawrence, 10-25-82); In re Lewis, No. 1573 (4th Dist Ct App, Lawrence, 9-2-82); In re Hutchison, No. 1537 (4th Dist Ct App, Lawrence, 6-9-82); In re Banks, No. L-80-212 (6th Dist Ct App, Lucas, 5-22-81); In re Escue, No. 1487 (4th Dist Ct App, Lawrence, 5-11-81); In re Evener, No. 1065 (4th Dist Ct App, Athens, 9-30-81); In re Osborn, No. CA 1744 (5th Dist Ct App, Richland, 1-16-79); In re Cox, No. 614 (4th Dist Ct App, Highland, 7-18-86).

[104]In re Fassinger, 42 OS(2d) 505, 506, 330 NE(2d) 431 (1975).

[105]Id.; Ludy v Ludy, 84 App 195, 84 NE(2d) 120 (Franklin 1948).

[106]In re Kemp, No. 41320 (8th Dist Ct App, Cuyahoga, 6-26-80).

[107]In re Holcomb, No. 39694 (8th Dist Ct App, Cuyahoga, 10-4-79).

[108]In re Pethel, No. 79CA25 (4th Dist Ct App, Washington, 11-9-81).

[109]In re Bell, No. 17-81-5 (3d Dist Ct App, Shelby, 9-24-81).

Finally, a dependency complaint seeking permanent custody was held to state sufficiently particular facts where it cited only the parents' inability to provide a nurturing physical and emotional environment for the child.[110]

(J) Certification or transfer from another court

When a case concerning a child is transferred or certified from another court, the certification from the transferring court is deemed to be the complaint.[111] "Transferred" cases are those in which a juvenile court of one county turns its jurisdiction of a matter over to a juvenile court of another county pursuant to Juvenile Rule 11.[112] "Certified" cases are typically those in which a juvenile court obtains jurisdiction from a domestic relations court pursuant to RC 2151.23(D)[113] or a probate court pursuant to RC 2151.23(E).[114]

Although a certification from domestic relations court constitutes a complaint, there is a split of authority as to whether a certification to a juvenile court that is not supplemented[115] by another type of complaint gives the juvenile court the jurisdiction to treat the child as a dependent or neglected child. In Birch v Birch[116] the juvenile court had adopted the findings of fact and conclusions of law of the domestic relations court following certification. The juvenile court found the children to be dependent although apparently no dependency complaint had been filed. In affirming the juvenile court's order granting temporary custody to the human services department, the Ohio Supreme Court, in dictum, rejected the argument that the juvenile court could not adopt the domestic relations court's findings of fact and conclusions of law without holding a new hearing. Similarly, in Hartshorne v Hartshorne[117] a court of appeals held that the certification of a divorce action that shows that the children are being neglected amounts to the filing of a neglect complaint under RC 2151.27. The court reasoned that since "any person having knowledge" may file a complaint and the purpose of filing a complaint with the juvenile court is to bring the matter to the court's attention, the certification itself constituted a neglect complaint.

On the other hand, the statutes[118] specify that any disposition made by a juvenile court after a case is certified to it must be made in accordance with RC 3109.04, the general custody statute, and several appellate court decisions have recognized this principle. Courts have held that the juvenile court is not permitted to use the more diverse dispositional alternatives available in other types of

---

[110]In re Blankenship, No. 9901 (9th Dist Ct App, Summit, 4-1-81).

[111]Juv R 10(A).

[112]See Text 7.04(B), Transfer.

[113]See RC 3109.04, RC 3109.06. A domestic relations court may not certify proceedings to a juvenile court under RC 3109.04 unless it finds after a full hearing that custody to either parent is not in the child's best interest. See Haslam v Haslam, No. 544 (7th Dist Ct App, Monroe, 11-6-81).

[114]See RC 2111.46, RC 3107.14.

[115]Juv R 10(A) provides that the juvenile court may order the certification supplemented upon its own motion or that of a party.

[116]Birch v Birch, 11 OS(3d) 85, 11 OBR 327, 463 NE(2d) 1254 (1984).

[117]Hartshorne v Hartshorne, 89 Abs 243, 185 NE(2d) 329 (App, Columbiana 1959).

[118]RC 3109.06. See also RC 2151.23(F)(1).

children's cases[119] unless the certification is supplemented by a complaint alleging dependency, neglect, abuse, delinquency, or unruliness.[120] Moreover, a certification from a domestic relations court which is supplemented by a motion alleging parental unsuitability is not sufficient to constitute a complaint of dependency or neglect.[121] In order for there to be a valid complaint, there must be an allegation that the child is dependent or neglected,[122] as well as a definite statement of the particular, essential facts which the parents will have to defend against.[123]

The authority of a juvenile court to dispose of a case certified from a probate court following the dismissal of an adoption petition (RC 3107.14(D)) is not as clearly defined as it is with a domestic relations court certification. Since probate court certifications result from the dismissal of an action, there would appear to be nothing to certify to the juvenile court. The Ohio Supreme Court has held in State ex rel Clark v Allaman[124] that such a certification, in itself, does not constitute a dependency or neglect complaint, nor even a complaint concerning the child's custody.[125] The court reasoned that there was no language in the statute[126] to indicate that the certification was to be considered a complaint. The only purpose of the certification statute was to provide a method for the juvenile court to conduct an investigation of the custody arrangements and, if warranted, to invoke the juvenile court's jurisdiction by having the appropriate

---

[119]RC 3109.04(A) permits the court to grant custody to either parent, or to both parents jointly, or to a relative, but does not authorize the more wide-ranging dispositions of RC 2151.353, which permits a temporary or permanent commitment to a public child services agency or private child placing agency. Additionally, RC 2151.23(F) provides that the juvenile court shall follow the Uniform Child Custody Jurisdiction Law (RC 3109.21 to RC 3109.36) in exercising its jurisdiction in child custody matters. See also RC 2151.353 (disposition of abused, neglected, or dependent child); RC 2151.354 (disposition of unruly child); RC 2151.355 (disposition of delinquent child). For further discussion of these dispositional alternatives, see Text Ch 13, Disposition of Children's Cases.

[120]In re Snider, 14 App(3d) 353, 14 OBR 420, 471 NE(2d) 516 (Defiance 1984); In re Height, 47 App(2d) 203, 353 NE(2d) 887 (Van Wert 1975). See also In re Carter, No. 78-16 (6th Dist Ct App, Wood, 1-26-79); Union County Child Welfare Bd v Parker, 7 App(2d) 79, 218 NE(2d) 757 (Union 1964); Thrasher v Thrasher, 3 App(3d) 210, 3 OBR 240, 444 NE(2d) 431 (Summit 1981).

[121]Union County Child Welfare Bd v Parker, 7 App(2d) 79, 218 NE(2d) 757 (Union 1964).

[122]RC 2151.27(A).

[123]Id.; Juv R 10(B)(1). Union County Child Welfare Bd v Parker, 7 App(2d) 79, 218 NE(2d) 757 (Union 1964).

[124]State ex rel Clark v Allaman, 154 OS 296, 95 NE(2d) 753 (1950).

[125]This interpretation finds support in a later case, In re Robert O., 95 Abs 101, 199 NE(2d) 765 (Juv, Cuyahoga 1964), which held that the certification in itself does not give the juvenile court jurisdiction to determine the custody of an illegitimate child. However, neither Allaman nor Robert O. mentioned an earlier court of appeals decision, State ex rel Sparto v Williams, 86 App 377, 86 NE(2d) 501 (Darke 1949), affirmed sub nom State ex rel Sparto v Juvenile Court of Drake County, 153 OS 64, 90 NE(2d) 598 (1950), in which it was held that such a certification did confer jurisdiction upon the juvenile court to determine the custody of the child. It should be noted that in Sparto the certification was supplemented by a neglect complaint, although the court indicated that this was not the basis for its decision.

[126]GC 10512-21, now RC 3107.14(D).

complaint filed.[127] However, both *Allaman* and *In re Robert O.*[128] were decided prior to the promulgation of Juvenile Rule 10(A), which provides, in part, that "the certification from the transferring court shall be deemed to be the complaint." In view of the rule and the principles established by cases concerning domestic relations court certifications,[129] it appears that a certification from a probate court following the dismissal of an adoption petition constitutes a complaint for custody, with RC 3109.04 controlling the disposition. RC 3109.04 applies not only to divorce actions, but also to any custody determination in a juvenile court, other than one involving a neglected, dependent, delinquent, or unruly child.[130] If the custody alternatives available to a juvenile court in a case certified from probate court are limited to those in RC 3109.04, any child care agency seeking custody should supplement the certification with a dependency or neglect complaint.[131]

(K) Amendment of pleadings

Juvenile Rule 22(B) provides:

> Any pleading[132] may be amended at any time prior to the adjudicatory hearing. After the commencement of the adjudicatory hearing, a pleading may be amended upon agreement of the parties, or if the interests of justice require, upon order of court. Such order shall where requested grant a party reasonable time in which to respond to an amendment.

---

[127]State ex rel Clark v Allaman, 154 OS 296, 95 NE(2d) 753 (1950).

[128]In re Robert O., 95 Abs 101, 199 NE(2d) 765 (Juv, Cuyahoga 1964).

[129]Thrasher v Thrasher, 3 App(3d) 210, 3 OBR 240, 444 NE(2d) 431 (Summit 1981); In re Height, 47 App(2d) 203, 353 NE(2d) 887 (Van Wert 1975).

[130]In re Height, 47 App(2d) 203, 353 NE(2d) 887 (Van Wert 1975). RC 2151.23(F) was amended in 1984 (1983 H 93, eff. 3-19-84) to provide that the juvenile court shall exercise its jurisdiction in child custody matters in accordance with RC 3109.04. RC 3109.04(A) includes two significant legal principles. First, it limits the juvenile court's choices in granting custody to either a parent, both parents jointly, or another relative. Second, it adopts a "best interest" test for determining who shall receive custody. According to In re Perales, 52 OS(2d) 89, 369 NE(2d) 1047 (1977), an Ohio Supreme Court case decided prior to the statutory amendment, neither of these principles necessarily applies to all juvenile court custody cases brought under RC 2151.23(A)(2). *Perales* involved a custody dispute between a parent and the child's caretaker, who was neither a parent nor a relative. The court held that the nonparent could be awarded custody pursuant to an RC 2151.23(A)(2) action but only if the trial court made a finding of "parental unsuitability," a higher standard than the "best interest" test of RC 3109.04. In juvenile court custody disputes between parents, the "best interest" standard would apply. In re Byrd, 66 OS(2d) 334, 421 NE(2d) 1284 (1981). See also Thrasher v Thrasher, 3 App(3d) 210, 3 OBR 240, 444 NE(2d) 431 (Summit 1981), a juvenile court custody case originating from a domestic relations court certification. The court criticized *Perales* for apparently modifying the construction of RC 3109.04 from a "best interest" test to an "unsuitability" test and felt compelled to hold that the "unsuitability" test adopted by *Perales* must also apply to RC 3109.04 custody actions between a parent and a relative.

[131]Based on In re Perales, 52 OS(2d) 89, 369 NE(2d) 1047 (1977), it appears that the certification could also be supplemented by an application to determine custody under RC 2151.23(A)(2). If a nonparent (including a child human services department or children services board) filed such an application, *Perales* would require a finding of parental unsuitability before custody could be awarded to the nonparent. This is a higher standard than is required in dependency cases and would not permit an award of permanent custody. See Text 13.06(A)(4), Permanent custody; Text 13.06(B), Motion for permanent custody.

[132]A complaint is included under the definition of pleadings (Juv R 22(A)).

Unlike Criminal Rule 7(D), Juvenile Rule 22(B) does not specifically prohibit an amendment from changing the name or identity of the crime charged. In an appellate case, *In re Pollard*,[133] it was argued that amending a delinquency complaint from aggravated arson to arson was improper because it changed the identity of the complaint.[134] The court in that case did not rule on whether a delinquency complaint could be amended to change the crime's name or identity but instead relied on Criminal Rule 31(C) to hold that it was not error to adjudge the child delinquent for arson, since arson is a lesser included offense of aggravated arson. In *State v Gaida*,[135] a pre-Rules case, it was held that amending a complaint to charge a child with being a delinquent instead of a juvenile traffic offender, without objection by counsel, was not prejudicial error. A court may amend a complaint, after all the evidence has been submitted, from one of dependency to one of custody.[136] However, a juvenile court has no authority to amend a neglect complaint by adding a child who was not included in the original complaint.[137]

In adult criminal proceedings, it has been held that a court is without authority to amend an affidavit without a new verification by the affiant.[138] However, the Ohio Supreme Court has held that where counsel has agreed to the amendment and has not objected to the lack of reverification, any objection thereto is waived.[139]

(L) Objections based on defects

The general rule in Ohio is that nonjurisdictional issues which have been neither brought to the attention of nor passed on by a lower court will not be ruled upon by appellate courts.[140] Whether the failure to include the particular facts in a complaint constitutes a jurisdictional defect, which may be raised at any time, is an issue which Ohio courts have not agreed upon.

Juvenile Rule 22(D) provides:

> Any defense, objection or request which is capable of determination without hearing on the allegations of the complaint may be raised before the adjudicatory hearing by motion. The following must be heard before the adjudicatory hearing, though not necessarily on a separate date: . . .

> (2) Defenses or objections based on defects in the complaint (other than failure to show jurisdiction in the court or to charge an offense which objec-

---

[133]In re Pollard, No. 44061 (8th Dist Ct App, Cuyahoga, 12-17-81).

[134]See also In re Burgess, 13 App(3d) 374, 13 OBR 456 (Preble 1984).

[135]State v Gaida, No. 30423 (8th Dist Ct App, Cuyahoga, 3-2-72).

[136]In re Likens, No. 85 CA 80 (2d Dist Ct App, Greene, 10-24-86). See also In re Dolibor, No. 799 (4th Dist Ct App, Ross, 6-15-81).

[137]In re James, No. 30608 (8th Dist Ct App, Cuyahoga, 2-3-72).

[138]State v Jackson, 90 Abs 577, 190 NE(2d) 38 (App, Franklin 1960); Ironton v Bundy, 98 App 416, 129 NE(2d) 831 (Lawrence 1954); Diebler v State, 43 App 350, 183 NE 84 (Richland 1932).

[139]State v Chrisman, 9 OS(2d) 27, 222 NE(2d) 649 (1966).

[140]In re Adoption of McDermitt, 63 OS(2d) 301, 408 NE(2d) 680 (1980); State v Williams, 51 OS(2d) 112, 364 NE(2d) 1364 (1977), vacated in part by 438 US 911, 98 SCt 3137, 57 LEd(2d) 1156 (1978); In re Lee, No. CA-2856 (5th Dist Ct App, Licking, 11-1-82).

tions shall be noticed by the court at any time during the pendency of the proceeding).[141]

Furthermore, Juvenile Rule 22(E) provides that "[a]ll prehearing motions shall be filed by the earlier of (1) seven days prior to hearing, or (2) ten days after the appearance of counsel. The court in the interest of justice may extend the time for making prehearing motions."

In interpreting Juvenile Rule 22(D), the Ohio Supreme Court has held that objections to defects in a complaint must be raised in the juvenile court by an answer, a motion to dismiss, or a request for other relief.[142] The Eighth District Court of Appeals reached the same result with respect to an alleged failure of a delinquency complaint to set forth an offense.[143] It has also been held that the failure to include the particular facts in a permanent custody complaint is not a jurisdictional defect and may be waived if not timely objected to before the adjudicatory hearing pursuant to Juvenile Rule 22(D).[144]

On the other hand, several cases have held that the absence of specific facts in a complaint requesting permanent custody is a jurisdictional matter and may be raised for the first time in the appellate court. These courts reason that RC 2151.23(A)(1), which confers jurisdiction regarding neglected or dependent children, RC 2151.27, which sets forth complaint requirements, and RC 2151.03 and RC 2151.04, which define a neglected and dependent child, respectively, must be read in pari materia, and thus, the jurisdiction of the juvenile court is invoked only when a proper complaint is filed in accordance with these statutes.[145]

CROSS REFERENCES

Text Ch 3, 7.04(B), 7.05, 11.03, Ch 13, 15.04, 15.05

Schroeder-Katz, Ohio Criminal Law, Crim R 3, Author's Text, Crim R 12, Author's Text
Merrick-Rippner, Ohio Probate Law (4th ed), Text Ch 219, 223, 225
Giannelli, Ohio Evidence Manual, Author's Comment 501.08

---

[141]It is a well-settled rule in criminal law that jurisdictional challenges may be raised at any time or by collateral attack (In re Lockhart, 157 OS 192, 105 NE(2d) 35 (1952)). It is questionable whether the phrase "during the pendency of the proceeding" changes this rule for juvenile court proceedings.

[142]In re Hunt, 46 OS(2d) 378, 348 NE(2d) 727 (1976). See also Bridges v Lucas County Children Services Bd, No. L-85-275 (6th Dist Ct App, Lucas, 6-20-86).

[143]In re Corona, No. 40992 (8th Dist Ct App, Cuyahoga, 8-20-81).

[144]In re Crose, No. 1055 (2d Dist Ct App, Darke, 10-18-82); In re Daniels, Nos. 9794, 9795, 9796, 9802 (9th Dist Ct App, Summit, 3-18-81).

[145]In re Hutchison, No. 1537 (4th Dist Ct App, Lawrence, 6-9-82); In re Bryant, No. CA80-11-0125 (12th Dist Ct App, Butler, 1-13-82); In re Moore, No. CA291 (12th Dist Ct App, Preble, 5-20-81). See also In re Baker, No. 6-81-12 (3d Dist Ct App, Hardin, 7-14-82); In re Bundy, No. 1507 (4th Dist Ct App, Lawrence, 7-8-81); In re Nance, No. 1452 (4th Dist Ct App, Lawrence, 10-16-80); Union County Child Welfare Bd v Parker, 7 App(2d) 79, 218 NE(2d) 757 (Union 1964); State ex rel Clark v Allaman, 154 OS 296, 95 NE(2d) 753 (1950).

7.04   Venue

(A) General rules

Complaints in children's cases may be filed either in the county where the child has a residence or legal settlement[146] or in the county where the traffic offense, delinquency, unruliness, neglect, dependency, or abuse occurred.[147] Thus, venue does not depend on having personal jurisdiction over the parents when the alleged conduct takes place outside of their county of residence.[148]

When a complaint is filed in the county of the parent's residence, the court retains jurisdiction even if the summons is not served until after the parent has moved to another county.[149] However, when a child is moved from his resident county to another county and a complaint is immediately filed in the nonresident county, that county does not have venue if neither the child nor his parents reside there and none of the facts underlying the complaint occurred there.[150]

(B) Transfer

A juvenile court acquiring jurisdiction over a child may, on its own motion or the motion of a party,[151] transfer the proceedings to the county of the child's residence either after the filing of the complaint or after the adjudicatory or dispositional hearing.[152] However, a juvenile court may not impose a fine and then transfer the matter to another jurisdiction for further dispositional proceedings. Once a final dispositional order is made, nothing remains to transfer to the other court.[153]

Where other proceedings involving the child are pending in the juvenile court of the county of his residence, transfer to that court is mandatory.[154] When a case against a child is pending in a foreign county, that case must be transferred to the child's home county if at any time prior to the disposition of that case, other proceedings against the child are pending in the home county.[155] In all other cases the decision to transfer is discretionary with the court in which the

---

[146]Pursuant to RC 2151.06, "[A] child has the same residence or legal settlement as his parents, legal guardian of his person, or his custodian who stands in the relation of loco parentis." A child who is a ward of a human services department or children services board is a resident of the county in which the department or board is located.

[147]RC 2151.27(A); Juv R 10(A). State ex rel Burchett v Juvenile Court for Scioto County, 92 Abs 357, 194 NE(2d) 912 (App, Scioto 1962); In re Bowen, No. WD-86-74 (6th Dist Ct App, Wood, 6-30-87).

[148]In re Poth, No. H-81-31 (6th Dist Ct App, Huron, 6-30-82); In re MacPherson, No. 34106 (8th Dist Ct App, Cuyahoga, 4-3-75).

[149]In re Goshorn, 82 Abs 599, 167 NE(2d) 148 (Juv, Columbiana 1959).

[150]State ex rel Burchett v Juvenile Court for Scioto County, 92 Abs 357, 194 NE(2d) 912 (App, Scioto 1962).

[151]"Party" is defined in Juv R 2(16).

[152]RC 2151.271; Juv R 11(A).

[153]In re Sekulich, 65 OS(2d) 13, 417 NE(2d) 1014 (1981). However, it is common practice in Ohio to transfer probation supervision where the residence of the child changes after he is placed on probation. Since this does not involve a second dispositional order, it is proper. See also RC 2151.56 for provisions regarding the cooperative supervision of delinquent juveniles on probation or parole under the Interstate Compact.

[154]RC 2151.271; Juv R 11(B).

[155]State v Payne, No. 81-CA-22 (4th Dist Ct App, Pickaway, 7-28-82).

complaint is originally filed.[156] If either the transferring court or the receiving court[157] finds that the interests of justice and the convenience of the parties so require, the adjudicatory hearing will be held in the county where the complaint was filed.[158] After the adjudicatory hearing, the proceedings may be transferred to the county of the child's residence for disposition and must be transferred if there are proceedings involving the child pending in the resident county.[159] Transfer may also be made if the residence of the child changes.[160]

Certified copies of all legal and social records pertaining to the proceeding must accompany any transfer.[161]

When a complaint concerning an alleged delinquent child is filed in the county of his residence, and that court transfers the proceedings to the common pleas court for criminal prosecution, the child is entitled to be tried in the county where the offense occurred.[162]

CROSS REFERENCES

Text 15.05

Merrick-Rippner, Ohio Probate Law (4th ed), Text Ch 219, 223

7.05 Summons

(A) Issuance to parties

The United States Supreme Court held in *In re Gault*[163] that timely notice must be given to the child and parents sufficiently in advance of scheduled court proceedings to afford a reasonable opportunity to prepare. Ohio law provides that after a complaint has been filed, the court must promptly issue summons to the parties and to any person with whom the child may be residing, requiring them to appear before the court at the time fixed for hearing.[164] The term "party" applies to the child, his spouse, if any, his parent, or if the parent is a

---

[156]RC 2151.271; Juv R 11(A). Squires v Squires, 12 App(3d) 138, 12 OBR 460, 468 NE(2d) 73 (Preble 1983). When a child is on probation in his county of residence, it is reasonable for proceedings initiated in another county to be transferred to his resident county, at least for dispositional purposes. Whether or not transfer is mandatory depends on whether probation is considered a "pending proceeding." One interpretation is that probation is a final dispositional order and, therefore, not a "pending proceeding." On the other hand, because the court of the resident county maintains continuing jurisdiction over a child who is on probation, transfer to that court may be mandatory.

[157]Juv R 11(C) grants to either court the authority to make this determination, whereas RC 2151.271 grants it only to the court of the resident county, as the receiving court.

[158]The practice in Ohio is to conduct the adjudicatory hearing in the county in which the witnesses reside, even though a witness is generally not a "party" (Juv R 2(16)), and someone who is a "party" (i.e., the child) may be inconvenienced thereby.

[159]Juv R 11(B), (C). Such transfer is permitted only if the allegations of the complaint were admitted or proved at the adjudicatory hearing. See Juv R 29(F).

[160]Juv R 11(A).

[161]RC 2151.271; Juv R 11(D).

[162]In re Davis, 87 Abs 222, 179 NE(2d) 198 (Juv, Marion 1961).

[163]In re Gault, 387 US 1, 87 SCt 1428, 18 LEd(2d) 527 (1967).

[164]RC 2151.28(C), RC 2151.35(C); Juv R 15(A). The statutes and rule also provide that a copy of the complaint must accompany the summons. For discussion of complaints, see Text 7.03, Complaint.

child, the parent of such parent, and, where appropriate, his custodian, guardian, or guardian ad litem, the state, and any other person specifically designated by the court.[165] If the person who has physical custody of the child or with whom the child resides is other than the parent or guardian, then the parents or guardian shall also be summoned.[166] Unless the parents of a child are given actual or constructive notice of the proceedings, the jurisdiction of the court does not attach, and any order or judgment rendered in such proceedings is void[167] and open to collateral attack.[168] If the court issues an order committing a child to the permanent custody of an appropriate agency, the parents of that child cease to be parties to that action.[169]

A noncustodial father is a party in juvenile court cases[170] even if he is divorced from the mother or his whereabouts are unknown.[171] Under some circumstances, the father of an illegitimate child may be entitled to notice. In an Illinois dependency case, *Stanley v Illinois*,[172] in which it was undisputed that the putative father was in fact the biological father, that he had lived with his two children all their lives, and that he had supported and reared them, the United States Supreme Court held that the father was a "parent" within the meaning of the Illinois dependency statute and, thus, was entitled to the same due process accorded to other parents.[173] In *In re Ware*[174] an Ohio appellate court has gone even further, holding that even an apparently unconcerned or unknown putative father is entitled to the minimal protection of service by publication in a dependency proceeding. Because such service is central to the court's subject matter jurisdiction, the child's mother may assert the failure of service upon the father.[175]

However, where the complainant is also the child's guardian (e.g., children services board), the mother's assertion that lack of service on the guardian

---

[165]Juv R 2(16). RC 2151.28(B)(1) and RC 2151.314(B)(2) provide that the court's consideration of a relative for appointment as a temporary custodian does not make that relative a party to the proceedings.

[166]RC 2151.28(C). It is not necessary to serve the parents if they have been permanently divested of the child's custody. See Text 7.03(E), Identifying information; Text 13.06(A)(4), Permanent custody; Text 13.06(B), Motion for permanent custody.

[167]In re Corey, 145 OS 413, 61 NE(2d) 892 (1945); Rarey v Schmidt, 115 OS 518, 154 NE 914 (1926), which implicitly overruled Bleier v Crouse, 13 App 69 (Hamilton 1920), which had held that notice to the parent was not a condition precedent to the juvenile court's acquiring jurisdiction over a dependent child.

[168]Lewis v Reed, 117 OS 152, 157 NE 897 (1927); In re Tovar, No. 1701 (4th Dist Ct App, Lawrence, 12-7-84).

[169]RC 2151.35(D), RC 2151.414(F).

[170]In re Koogle, Nos. CA 82-68, CA 82-93 (2d Dist Ct App, Greene, 6-16-83); In re Rule, 1 App(2d) 57, 203 NE(2d) 501 (Crawford 1963).

[171]For requirements for service by publication, see Text 7.05(C), Methods of service.

[172]Stanley v Illinois, 405 US 645, 92 SCt 1208, 31 LEd(2d) 551 (1972).

[173]See also Quillion v Wolcott, 434 US 246, 98 SCt 549, 54 LEd(2d) 511 (1978), holding that where a putative father had provided virtually no care or support to an illegitimate child, a Georgia statute requiring only the mother's consent to adoption of the child did not deny the father due process or equal protection.

[174]In re Ware, No. 40983 (8th Dist Ct App, Cuyahoga, 7-17-80).

[175]Where the identity of the father is unknown, the court would be required to try to serve the father through a "John Doe" publication, usually a futile attempt.

deprived the court of personal and subject matter jurisdiction is unfounded.[176] Moreover, the jurisdiction of the juvenile court was proper in a proceeding to terminate parental rights despite the failure to serve the child's mother. The mother had voluntarily executed a permanent surrender of the child to a private agency and had actual notice of the proceeding via service on her husband, the legal father.[177]

In *In re Palmer*,[178] a dependency case in which foster parents had cared for a child for over two years, it was held that the foster parents were not parties in interest because they had no property or liberty rights which would require a juvenile court to permit their intervention.[179] However, a trial court does not abuse its discretion in allowing foster parents to participate in hearings where their participation assists in fully developing the facts so that a more informal judgment can be made.[180]

A child's grandparents are necessary parties only if (1) they are the child's guardian or custodian;[181] (2) they have obtained through statute, court order, or other means a legal right to custody or visitation with the child;[182] or (3) the parent (their child) is under age eighteen.[183]

Although the child who is the subject of the complaint is a necessary party,[184] a child alleged to be abused, neglected, or dependent shall not be summoned unless the court so directs,[185] and such child may be excused from attending the hearings.[186]

When requested by the judge, or when a child denies the allegations of a complaint, the prosecuting attorney must assist the court by presenting the evidence in support of the allegations of the complaint.[187] In such a case, the prosecuting attorney, as a representative of the state, is also a party.[188]

---

[176]In re Bell, No. 17-81-5 (3d Dist Ct App, Shelby, 9-24-81).

[177]In re Luallen, 27 App(3d) 29, 27 OBR 30, 499 NE(2d) 358 (Hamilton 1985).

[178]In re Palmer, No. CA-6026 (5th Dist Ct App, Stark, 4-12-83).

[179]The appeal of this case was consolidated with the appeal filed by the child's natural mother. The Ohio Supreme Court affirmed the lower court's decision to award custody of the child to the welfare department (now, human services department), thus rendering the appeal by the foster parents moot. See In re Palmer, 12 OS(3d) 194, 12 OBR 259, 465 NE(2d) 1312 (1984), cert denied sub nom Pihlblad v Stark County Welfare Dept, 469 US 1162, 105 SCt 918, 83 LEd(2d) 930 (1985). See also In re Fullmer, No. CA-5153 (5th Dist Ct App, Stark, 10-24-79), holding that foster parents have no standing to challenge a permanent custody request by habeas corpus.

[180]In re Spears, No. 1200 (4th Dist Ct App, Athens, 12-10-84).

[181]Juv R 2(16).

[182]In re Schmidt, 25 OS(3d) 331, 25 OBR 386, 496 NE(2d) 952 (1986). See also In re Miller, No. C-830919 (1st Dist Ct App, Hamilton, 10-24-84); In re Johnson, No. CA-3262 (5th Dist Ct App, Licking, 8-21-87).

[183]Juv R 2(16). In custody proceedings governed by RC 3109.04, a grandparent may become a party if custody to neither parent is in the child's best interest.

[184]Juv R 2(16).

[185]RC 2151.28(C).

[186]RC 2151.35(A); Juv R 27.

[187]RC 2151.40; Juv R 29(E)(1). The rule permits the court to appoint another attorney in lieu of the prosecuting attorney.

[188]Juv R 2(16).

(B) Contents and form

Pursuant to Juvenile Rule 15(B), the summons must contain (1) the name of the person with whom the child is residing, or, if the name is unknown, any name or description by which the person can be identified with reasonable certainty; (2) a summary statement of the complaint and, in juvenile traffic offense and delinquency proceedings, the numerical designation of the applicable statute or ordinance; (3) a statement that any party is entitled to be represented by an attorney and that upon request the court will appoint an attorney for an indigent party entitled to appointed counsel under Juvenile Rule 4(A);[189] and (4) an order to the person to appear at a stated time and place with a warning that the person may lose valuable rights or be subject to court sanction if he fails to appear.[190] The summons must also contain the name and telephone number of the court employee designated by the court to arrange for the prompt appointment of counsel for indigent persons.[191]

If the complaint contains a prayer for permanent custody, temporary custody, or long-term foster care in a case involving an alleged abused, neglected, or dependent child, the summons served on the parents must contain (1) an explanation that the granting of permanent custody permanently divests the parents of their parental rights and privileges; (2) an explanation that an adjudication of abuse, neglect, or dependency may result in an order of temporary custody that will cause the removal of the child from their legal custody until the court terminates temporary custody or orders permanent custody; or (3) an explanation that an order for long-term foster care will cause the removal of the child from the legal custody of the parents if the appropriate conditions are found to exist.[192] If the requisite explanation is not included in the summons, the corresponding dispositional order may not be made.[193] These requirements apply not only to original complaints, but also to motions for permanent custody.[194]

---

[189]Pursuant to RC 2151.28(F), the court may designate a public defender to represent an indigent party. In In re Trizzino, No. 40982 (8th Dist Ct App, Cuyahoga, 1-31-80), the following language, together with the phone number of the public defender's office, was held to sufficiently apprise the parents of their right to counsel:

> You and/or your child have the right to be represented by a lawyer at all stages of the proceedings or the rights to a lawyer may be waived. If you wish to be represented by a lawyer but are financially unable to employ one, you have a right to have a lawyer provided for you.

[190]A similar provision is contained in RC 2151.28(J). The juvenile court has the same power in contempt as do the courts of common pleas (RC 2151.21). See also RC 2705.01 to RC 2705.10; State ex rel Turner v Albin, 118 OS 527, 161 NE 792 (1928).

[191]RC 2151.28(C), RC 2151.314(D), RC 2151.414(A).

[192]RC 2151.28(D).

[193]RC 2151.353(B); In re Fassinger, 43 App(2d) 89, 334 NE(2d) 5 (Cuyahoga 1974), affirmed by 42 OS(2d) 505, 330 NE(2d) 431 (1975). See also In re Snider, 14 App(3d) 353, 14 OBR 420, 471 NE(2d) 516 (Defiance 1984); Reynolds v Ross County Children's Services Agency, 5 OS(3d) 27, 5 OBR 87, 448 NE(2d) 816 (1983); In re Hutchison, No. 1537 (4th Dist Ct App, Lawrence, 6-9-82); In re Bryant, No. CA80-11-0125 (12th Dist Ct App, Butler, 1-13-82); In re Banks, No. L-80-212 (6th Dist Ct App, Lucas, 5-22-81); In re Trizzino, No. 40982 (8th Dist Ct App, Cuyahoga, 1-31-80); In re Reed, No. CA 1325 (5th Dist Ct App, Tuscarawas, 7-24-79).

[194]RC 2151.414(A).

A court has no jurisdiction to award permanent custody when the summons contains only a cursory, confusing notice in fine print regarding the effects of permanent custody.[195] However, in a temporary custody proceeding, the parents were held to have received adequate notice even though the summons did not contain the required explanation.[196] The court determined that both parents had notice of the possibility that their son could be removed from their legal custody because (1) the language of the complaint itself gave that notice;[197] (2) both parties were individually represented by counsel; and (3) neither party objected to the court's exercise of jurisdiction at any time during or after the hearing until a complaint for permanent custody was filed.

It has been held that the failure of a summons to explain adequately the effects of permanent custody is not a jurisdictional matter, but rather a matter of due process.[198]

The summons may also be endorsed with an order directing the person with whom the child is residing to appear personally with the child.[199] A copy of the complaint must accompany the summons.[200]

(C) Methods of service

Juvenile Rule 16(A) provides that service of summons shall be governed by Civil Rules 4(A), (C), and (D), 4.1, 4.2, 4.3, 4.5, and 4.6.[201] Where service is made by certified mail pursuant to Civil Rule 4.1(1), the hearing may not be held before twenty-one days after the date of mailing.[202]

Personal service[203] or residence service[204] may be made in lieu of service by certified mail. Residence service may be perfected by leaving the process at the usual place of residence of the person to be served with a person of suitable age and discretion residing therein.[205]

---

[195]In re Osborn, No. CA 1744 (5th Dist Ct App, Richland, 1-16-79) held that a summons containing the following language in fine print at the bottom was defective: "NOTICE: If the complaint contains a prayer for permanent custody in a neglect or dependency case, the parents are hereby advised that the granting of such custody permanently divests the parents of their parental rights and privileges."

[196]In re Cox, No. 614 (4th Dist Ct App, Highland, 7-18-86).

[197]See Text 7.03(I), Neglect, dependency, and abuse proceedings.

[198]In re King, No. 10165 (9th Dist Ct App, Summit, 11-4-81).

[199]RC 2151.28(E); Juv R 15(C).

[200]Juv R 15(A).

[201]For provisions governing service of subpoenas, see RC 2151.28(J); Juv R 17.

[202]Juv R 16(A). When the child who is the subject of the complaint is in detention or shelter care, this rule conflicts with Juv R 29(A), which requires a hearing within ten days of the filing of the complaint. See Text 7.06(D), Time restrictions. RC 2151.29 provides that the hearing may be held within one week of the date of publication. Because this is a procedural issue, Juv R 16(A) supersedes the statute. See O Const Art IV, § 5(B).

[203]Civ R 4.1(2) provides that in the event of failure to serve personally the party within twenty-eight days, the clerk shall so notify the attorney or party who requested the service. This, too, would be in conflict with the "ten-day" rule of Juv R 29(A), which applies when the child is in detention or shelter care.

[204]Civ R 4.1(3). The rule includes the same "twenty-eight-day" provision discussed in the preceding footnote.

[205]Id. See OAG 70-130 concerning the duty of the sheriff to serve summons, notices, and subpoenas.

Service of process upon a person under the age of sixteen is made by serving either his guardian or the parent or other individual having his care with whom he resides; the child himself may be served if he has no guardian and does not live or reside with a parent or person having his care.[206]

When a party's residence is unknown and cannot be ascertained with reasonable diligence, service must be made by publication in a newspaper of general circulation in the county in which the complaint is filed; if no such newspaper exists, publication may be made in a newspaper of an adjoining county.[207] Before service by publication may be made, an affidavit must be filed with the court averring that service cannot be made because the residence of the party is unknown and cannot with reasonable diligence be ascertained.[208] Service by publication without the filing of such an affidavit does not constitute proper service.[209] Moreover, once there is a challenge to a party's exercise of reasonable diligence, that party must support his claim that he used reasonable diligence to locate the party served by publication.[210] Along with other information about the case, the publication must contain a summary statement of the object of the complaint[211] and, in permanent custody cases, a full explanation of the effect of permanent custody.[212] The date of the hearing stated in the publication must not be less than fourteen days after the date of publication.[213] Service by publication is a method of last resort and the requirements, as specified in Juvenile Rule 16(A) are mandatory and will be strictly enforced.[214]

When service of summons is made by certified mail, personal service, or residence service, there must be a signed certification attesting to the type of service.[215] If service is by publication, the publisher or his agent must file with the court an affidavit showing the fact of publication together with a copy of the notice of publication.[216]

---

[206]Civ R 4.2(2). This rule supersedes RC 2151.28(C), which requires service on the parent, guardian, or custodian for a child under fourteen years of age.

[207]Juv R 16(A).

[208]*Id.* The rule uses the word "defendant" rather than "party" but would apply to any party whose residence is unknown. The term "defendant" is not defined by or otherwise used in the rules.

[209]In re Osborn, No. CA 1744 (5th Dist Ct App, Richland, 1-16-79). Both Juv R 16(A) and this decision overruled In re Veselich, 22 App 528, 154 NE 55 (Cuyahoga 1926), which had held that service by publication on absent parents under former GC 1647 (now RC 2151.27) and former GC 1648 (now RC 2151.28) was sufficient even though an affidavit had not been filed (*Osborn* was based on an interpretation of Civ R 4.4, which is similar to Juv R 16(A), but which does not apply to children's cases.).

[210]In re Miller, 33 App(3d) 224, 515 NE(2d) 635 (Cuyahoga 1986). See also In re Wilson, No. H-84-6 (6th Dist Ct App, Huron, 8-3-84).

[211]Juv R 16(A).

[212]In re Brown, No. 3-CA-79 (5th Dist Ct App, Fairfield, 7-20-79).

[213]Juv R 16(A). When the child who is the subject of the complaint is in detention or shelter care, this rule conflicts with Juv R 29(A), which requires a hearing within ten days of the filing of a complaint. See Text 7.06(D), Time restrictions.

[214]In re Wilson, No. H-84-6 (6th Dist Ct App, Huron, 8-3-84).

[215]Civ R 4.1. In re Osborn, No. CA 1744 (5th Dist Ct App, Richland, 1-16-79).

[216]Juv R 16(A).

(D) Waiver

A party other than the child may waive service of summons by written stipulation.[217] The Ohio Supreme Court has twice considered the issue of waiver under a prior version of the statute (RC 2151.28), which required service of summons "unless the parties voluntarily appear." In *Ex parte Province*[218] the court initially held that where a parent voluntarily appeared with counsel and participated in a dependency hearing regarding her child, she was deemed to have waived her right to prior notice of the hearing.[219] In *In re Frinzl*,[220] a later decision in which the mother participated in a permanent custody proceeding, but was not served with summons until the time of the hearing and was not represented by counsel, the court held that the service was not made sufficiently in advance of the hearing.[221] Thus, the voluntary appearance of a party does not in itself constitute a waiver of service. However, a voluntary appearance may result in a waiver if the party consents and the court permits.[222]

It has also been held that a mother's purported waiver of summons in a permanent custody case is ineffective unless the waiver contains a full explanation of the effects of a permanent custody order.[223]

CROSS REFERENCES

Text 7.03, 7.06(D), 13.06(A), 13.10

Schroeder-Katz, Ohio Criminal Law, Crim R 4, Author's Text
Merrick-Rippner, Ohio Probate Law (4th ed), Text Ch 223

7.06   Detention or shelter care

(A) Appropriate place

When a child is taken into custody,[224] there are several restrictions regarding his detention. The first priority is to release the child to his parents, guardian, or other custodian.[225] If the child is not released, then the place in which he will be held depends to some extent on the type of case involved. As a general rule, no child may be placed in any prison, jail, lockup, or other place where he can come in contact or communication with any adult convicted of crime, under arrest, or

---

[217]RC 2151.28(H). Civ R 4(D) is applicable to children's cases pursuant to Juv R 16(A).
[218]Ex parte Province, 127 OS 333, 188 NE 550 (1933).
[219]See also Mobley v Allaman, 89 Abs 473, 184 NE(2d) 707 (Prob, Montgomery 1961).
[220]In re Frinzl, 152 OS 164, 87 NE(2d) 583 (1949).
[221]See also Union County Child Welfare Bd v Parker, 7 App(2d) 79, 218 NE(2d) 757 (Union 1964).
[222]Juv R 3.
[223]In re Brown, No. 3-CA-79 (5th Dist Ct App, Fairfield, 7-20-79).
[224]For discussion of when an alleged delinquent or unruly child may be arrested, see Text 5.02, Custody, arrests, and stops. For discussion of when an alleged neglected, dependent, or abused child may be taken into custody, see Text 7.07, Temporary orders pending hearing.
[225]RC 2151.311(A); Juv R 7(B)(1). See also *IJA-ABA Standards Relating to Interim Status: The Release, Control, and Detention of Accused Juvenile Offenders Between Arrest and Disposition* 50 (1980).

charged with crime.[226] For children under the age of sixteen, this prohibition also applies to the time when the child is being booked.[227] There are, however, certain limited circumstances under which a child may be jailed. Both statute and rule[228] provide that a child[229] may be detained in an adult facility if a detention home is not available,[230] and then only if the child is over fifteen years of age, the public safety and protection require that the detention be in such a place, and the detention is in a room separated by both sight and sound from adult detainees.[231] If a case is transferred to an adult court for criminal prosecution, the child may be transferred to the appropriate officer or detention facility according to the law governing the detention of adult criminal defendants.[232]

A child alleged to be neglected, abused, or dependent may not be detained in a jail or other detention facility for adults or for children alleged to be delinquent, except by order of the court.[233]

When detention is warranted but placement in jail is inappropriate, a child alleged to be delinquent, unruly, or a juvenile traffic offender may be brought to the court or to a detention or shelter care facility,[234] or may be held in a foster home, in a facility operated by a certified child welfare agency, or in any other suitable place designated by the court.[235] An alleged dependent, neglected, or abused child whose detention is required may be brought either to the court or to a shelter care facility.[236] The major distinction between detention and shelter

---

[226]RC 2151.34; Juv R 7(H). See also Cox v Turley, 506 F(2d) 1347 (6th Cir 1974), which held that keeping a juvenile in a jail with adult inmates violates due process.

[227]RC 341.11.

[228]RC 2151.312(B) and Juv R 7(H), respectively.

[229]The statute uses the term "child" without specifically restricting the provision to a delinquent child. The rule limits the provision to a child alleged to be delinquent. It would appear that the provision also applies to an adjudicated delinquent awaiting disposition.

[230]It is doubtful that a detention home that is filled to capacity would be considered unavailable. See RC 2151.34 to RC 2151.3416 for statutes regulating the operation of detention homes.

[231]RC 2151.312(B). This provision, added to the law in 1981, precludes a juvenile court from placing a child in an adult facility if a detention home is available. Curiously, the statutory amendment did not repeal that part of RC 2151.312(A) which authorizes placement of a child in an adult facility under some circumstances. In addition, Juv R 7(H) retains an almost identical provision.

[232]RC 2151.312(A).

[233]RC 2151.312(C); Juv R 7(H). Because of the strict restrictions on the placement of alleged delinquents in jails, it is doubtful that a juvenile court could ever order an alleged neglected, abused, or dependent child to be placed in a jail or other adult detention facility, despite the statutory language which seems to permit it. Even the placement of such children in detention facilities designed for delinquents should be severely restricted to those times when no shelter care facility is available and when separation from alleged delinquents is possible.

[234]RC 2151.311(A)(2); Juv R 7(B)(2). It has been held that a child may be questioned at a police station before being taken to the court or a place of detention. See In re Hawkins, No. 3430 (9th Dist Ct App, Lorain, 5-11-83).

[235]RC 2151.312(A).

[236]RC 2151.311(A)(2); Juv R 7(B)(2).

care is that detention involves care in a physically restricted facility,[237] whereas shelter care is nonrestrictive.[238]

(B) Admissions

A person delivering a child to a shelter or detention facility must give the admissions officer a signed report stating the reasons for taking the child into custody and for not releasing him and must assist the admissions officer, if necessary, in notifying the child's parent.[239]

Based on this report and any further investigation as is feasible, the admissions officer must make an initial decision as to whether the child should be released or held.[240] The child must be released prior to final disposition except in the following circumstances: (1) when detention or shelter care is required to protect the person and property of the child or others; (2) when the child may abscond or be removed from the court's jurisdiction; (3) when the child has no parent or other person able to provide supervision and care for him and return him to the court when required;[241] or (4) when an order for the child's detention or shelter care has been made by the court.[242]

If the child is admitted to detention or shelter care, the admissions officer must (1) prepare a report containing the time of and reasons for admission;[243] (2) advise the child of his right to telephone parents and counsel, both immediately and at reasonable times thereafter;[244] (3) advise the child of the time, place, and purpose of the detention (or shelter care) hearing;[245] and (4) use reasonable diligence to contact the child's parent, guardian, or custodian and advise him of the place of and reasons for detention; the time allowed for visitation; the time, place, and purpose of the detention hearing; and the right to counsel and to appointed counsel if indigent.[246]

(C) Hearing

When a child has been admitted to a detention or shelter care facility, a detention hearing must be provided[247] within seventy-two hours or the next court day, whichever is earlier, to determine whether further detention or shel-

---

[237]Juv R 2(6).

[238]Juv R 2(20).

[239]Juv R 7(C).

[240]Juv R 7(D).

[241]RC 2151.31(C); Juv R 7(A). The statute applies these standards "prior to the hearing," while the rule applies them "prior to final disposition." The rule recognizes that detention may be required after adjudication, in order to allow time for planning and preparing for the dispositional hearing.

[242]RC 2151.31(C). This final condition is not included in the rules. An example would be a situation in which the court orders a child arrested and detained for his failure to appear for a hearing.

[243]Juv R 7(E)(1).

[244]Juv R 7(E)(2)(a).

[245]Juv R 7(E)(2)(b).

[246]Juv R 7(E)(3).

[247]Juv R 2(7) defines a "detention hearing" as "a hearing to determine whether a child shall be held in detention or shelter care prior to or pending execution of a final dispositional order."

ter care is required.[248] Oral or written notice of the hearing must be given to the child and, if they can be found, to his parents, guardian, or custodian.[249] Prior to the hearing, the parties must be informed (1) of their right to counsel, (2) their right to appointed counsel or a public defender if they are indigent,[250] and (3) the name and telephone number of a court employee who can be contacted during the normal business hours of the court to arrange for the prompt appointment of counsel for any party who is indigent.[251] They must also be advised of the child's right to remain silent with respect to any allegation of delinquency, unruliness, or juvenile traffic offense.[252] The hearing is informal,[253] and any reports filed by the person delivering the child and by the admissions officer, as well as other evidence, may be considered without regard to formal rules of evidence.[254]

In deciding whether to detain or release the child, the court[255] must apply the same standards used when the child is initially taken into custody[256] or brought to a detention or shelter care facility.[257] Thus, the child must be released unless (1) detention or care is required to protect the person or property of the child or others;[258] (2) the child may abscond or be removed from the court's jurisdiction; or (3) the child has no parent, guardian, or other person able to provide supervision and care for him and return him to the court when required.[259] The United States Supreme Court in *Schall v Martin*[260] upheld the validity of a New York statute permitting the preventive detention of alleged delinquents when there is a "serious risk" that such children may commit a crime before their adjudicatory hearing. In holding that the statute was not invalid under the Due Process Clause of the Fourteenth Amendment, the Court reasoned that preventive detention serves the legitimate state objective of protecting the child and society from the hazards of pretrial crime and the procedural safeguards afforded by the statute provide sufficient protection against erroneous detention.

---

[248]RC 2151.314(A); Juv R 7(F). For discussion of the seventy-two-hour and other time limits concerning detained children, see Text 7.06(D), Time restrictions.

[249]RC 2151.314(A); Juv R 7(F)(1).

[250]RC 2151.314(A); Juv R 7(F)(2)(a).

[251]RC 2151.314(A).

[252]*Id.*; Juv R 7(F)(2)(b). The statute applies this right only to "any allegation of delinquency."

[253]RC 2151.314(A).

[254]Juv R 7(F)(3).

[255]In most counties, detention hearings are conducted by referees or other court personnel, rather than by judges.

[256]RC 2151.28(G), RC 2151.31(A); Juv R 6.

[257]Juv R 7(A), (F)(3).

[258]This provision is contained in Juv R 7(A). A similar provision—to protect the child from immediate or threatened physical or emotional harm—is contained in RC 2151.31(C).

[259]RC 2151.31(C); Juv R 7(A). The standards relative to the detention of children, as well as the elements of a detention hearing, have been considered by several federal courts. For example, although Ohio law does not specifically require a probable cause finding at the detention hearing, federal courts in other states whose detention laws are similar to Ohio's have imposed this additional procedural requirement in hearings for alleged delinquent and unruly children. E.g., R.W.T. v Dalton, 712 F(2d) 1225 (8th Cir Mo 1983), cert denied 464 US 1009, 104 SCt 527, 78 LEd(2d) 710 (1983); Moss v Weaver, 383 FSupp 130 (SD Fla 1974), modified by 525 F(2d) 1258 (5th Cir Fla 1976).

[260]Schall v Martin, 467 US 253, 104 SCt 2403, 81 LEd(2d) 207 (1984).

Also, RC 2151.314(B) provides that when the court conducts a detention or shelter care hearing, all of the following apply:

(1) The court must determine whether an alleged abused, neglected, or dependent child should remain in or be placed in shelter care;

(2) The court must determine whether there are any relatives of the child who are willing to be temporary custodians of the child. If any appropriate relatives are found, the court must appoint one of them as the child's temporary custodian instead of using shelter care placement. If the court determines that the appointment of a relative as custodian would not be appropriate, it must issue a written opinion setting forth its reasons and give a copy to all parties; and

(3) The court must make the determination and issue the written findings of fact required by RC 2151.419.[261]

Any decision relating to detention or shelter care may be reviewed at any time upon motion of any party.[262] If a parent, guardian, or custodian did not receive notice of the initial detention hearing and did not appear or waive appearance at the hearing, the court must rehear the matter promptly.[263] The Ohio Supreme Court has held that a parent alleging lack of notice of a shelter care hearing concerning his child must move the juvenile court for a rehearing pursuant to Juvenile Rule 7(G) before seeking a writ of habeas corpus.[264]

Any party or the child's guardian ad litem may file a motion with the court requesting that the child be released from shelter care.[265] The motion must state the reasons why the child should be released and must recite any changes in the situation of the child or the child's parents, guardian, or custodian since the

---

[261]RC 2151.314(B). See also Text 13.04, Reasonable efforts determination. This provision, which became effective on January 1, 1989, as a result of 1988 S 89, raises many questions. Section (1) of division (B), requiring the court to determine whether the child should remain or be placed in shelter care, seems unnecessary since division (A) of the statute already includes this requirement. Moreover, it is unclear whether sections (2) and (3) of division (B), requiring appropriate relative placement and written finds of fact, apply to delinquent and unruly children as well as abused, neglected, and dependent children. The plain language of division (B) seems to extend its application to all children in detention or shelter care. However, S 89 was concerned almost exclusively with abused, neglected, and dependent children, and it is questionable whether the General Assembly intended to include delinquent and unruly children who are in detention. Finally, it is unclear why the General Assembly now mandates a written opinion whenever the court finds that relative placement is inappropriate. In contrast, following an adjudicatory hearing such written opinions are only required if requested. One possible explanation for this apparent disparity is that the General Assembly is strengthening its preference for placement of children with relatives, but has yet to make such changes uniform throughout the Revised Code.

[262]Juv R 7(G). Although this rule focuses on decisions relating to prehearing detention or shelter care, it has been extended to cover post-dispositional matters as well. See Text 15.01, Continuing jurisdiction.

[263]RC 2151.314(A); Juv R 7(G).

[264]Linger v Weiss, 57 OS(2d) 97, 386 NE(2d) 1354 (1979), cert denied 444 US 862, 100 SCt 128, 62 LEd(2d) 83 (1979).

[265]RC 2151.314(C).

shelter care hearing. On filing of the motion, the court must hold another shelter care hearing.[266]

(D) Time restrictions

Both detention and shelter care facilities are intended to provide only temporary care pending adjudication, disposition, or execution of a court order.[267] The law places specific limits on the length of time that a child may be held before certain steps must be taken. Any child admitted to such a facility must be provided a hearing within seventy-two hours after admission, or on the next court day, whichever is earlier, to determine whether detention or shelter care is required.[268] This time limitation may not be extended by the court.[269] A complaint must also be filed within seventy-two hours of the child's admission.[270]

Regardless of when the detention hearing is held or what its outcome is, "no child who is not alleged to be, or adjudicated, delinquent by reason of violating any law, ordinance, or regulation, a violation of which would be a crime if committed by an adult" may be held for longer than five days in a secure setting.[271] Thus, an unruly child may not be held in a secure setting[272] (i.e., a detention home) longer than five days from the time of initial detention to the time of final disposition of the complaint.

If a decision is made at the detention or shelter care hearing to hold the child, the adjudicatory hearing must be held within ten days after the complaint is

---

[266]*Id.* The requirement that the court conduct a hearing if the motion is filed conflicts with Juv R 19, which permits courts to make provision for the determination of motions without oral hearing upon brief written statements of reasons in support and opposition. It also conflicts with Juv R 7(G), which makes such hearings permissible rather than mandatory.

[267]Juv R 2(6), (20).

[268]RC 2151.314(A); Juv R 7(F)(1). The statute does not include the "next court day" provision. For discussion of the detention hearing, see Text 7.06(C), Hearing.

[269]Juv R 18(B).

[270]RC 2151.314(A). Because the nature of the complaint bears on the question of detention, it should be filed prior to the hearing.

[271]RC 2151.351. The quoted material has been interpreted in two disparate ways. The better interpretation is that only those children who are alleged or adjudicated delinquent, as defined in RC 2151.02(A), may be detained in a secure setting beyond five days. This is based on the similarity of the language used in RC 2151.351 and RC 2151.02(A). Under this interpretation, the five-day limitation applies to the detention of a child who is delinquent by reason of violating a court order made in a previous unruly child case (RC 2151.02(B)). On the other hand, it has been argued that violation of a court order constitutes "a crime if committed by an adult." Therefore, a child who is charged as a delinquent, pursuant to RC 2151.02(B), for violating a court order could be detained beyond five days.

[272]RC 2151.351 provides that the term "secure setting" is to be defined in rules adopted by the Department of Youth Services. In OAC 5139-19-02(C), the department has defined "non-secure setting" as "a facility not characterized by the use of physically restricting construction, hardware and procedures and which provides its residents access to the surrounding community with minimal supervision."

filed.[273] Only upon a showing of good cause may the adjudicatory hearing be continued and detention or shelter care extended.[274]

The Ohio Supreme Court held in *Linger v Weiss*[275] that a juvenile court does not lose jurisdiction by failing to adhere to the ten-day time limit set forth in Juvenile Rule 29(A).[276] The court reasoned that since the jurisdiction of the juvenile courts is a creation of statutory law (RC 2151.23) and the juvenile rules govern procedural matters, the rules could not be construed to affect the juvenile court's jurisdiction. In support of its holding, the court cited Juvenile Rule 44, which specifically provides that "[t]hese rules shall not be construed to extend or limit the jurisdiction of the juvenile court."

Whereas the *Linger* decision concerned a child in shelter care, an earlier court of appeals decision, *In re Therklidsen*,[277] ruled similarly regarding a child in detention.[278] In that case, the court held that a procedural rule (Juvenile Rule 29(A)) could not confer the right to a discharge for an alleged delinquent if the court failed to comply with the ten-day rule. There must be specific statutory authority for such a right. On the other hand, another court of appeals in *State v Newton*[279] has held that both the seventy-two-hour (Juvenile Rule 7(F)(1)) and ten-day (Juvenile Rule 29(A)) time limits are mandatory rather than directory, so that a child in detention, who is not provided a timely detention hearing or adjudicatory hearing, is entitled to have the complaint dismissed.[280]

A child who is voluntarily placed in the custody of a children services bureau pending a hearing is in shelter care, but voluntary shelter care placement is not subject to the time limits for detention contained in Juvenile Rules 7 and 29(A).[281]

RC 2151.34, which limits length of detention,[282] provides that a child may not be confined in a place of juvenile detention beyond ninety days, during which time a social history and other pertinent studies and material may be prepared to assist the court in its disposition of the case.

---

[273]Juv R 29(A). See also RC 2151.28(A)(1). Because RC 2151.314 allows up to seventy-two hours for filing the complaint, the adjudicatory hearing may, in some cases, be held thirteen days after the child's admission to the facility.

[274]Juv R 29(A), Juv R 18(B).

[275]Linger v Weiss, 57 OS(2d) 97, 386 NE(2d) 1354 (1979), cert denied 444 US 862, 100 SCt 128, 62 LEd(2d) 83 (1979).

[276]See also In re Price, No. 43443 (8th Dist Ct App, Cuyahoga, 11-25-81).

[277]In re Therklidsen, 54 App(2d) 195, 376 NE(2d) 970 (Franklin 1977).

[278]See also In re Gossick, No. 48088 (8th Dist Ct App, Cuyahoga, 11-15-84).

[279]State v Newton, No. F-82-17 (6th Dist Ct App, Fulton, 6-10-83) (making no reference to either *Linger* or *Therklidsen*).

[280]The court initially held that the dismissal was without prejudice. However, in denying the child's application to reconsider the remedy and dismiss the complaint with prejudice, the court decided that "the facts of the case . . . render it unnecessary to decide that question at this time."

[281]In re Siniard, No. C-78-063 (6th Dist Ct App, Lucas, 2-9-79). See also RC 5153.16(B), which authorizes a children services board or human services department to enter into voluntary agreements with parents with respect to the custody, care, or placement of their children.

[282]The statute makes no specific reference to shelter care, but it is reasonable to assume that it applies to shelter care as well.

(E) Rights and treatment of children

Since a child who is alleged to be delinquent or unruly is not charged with a crime, he is not entitled to bail under Section 9, Article I of the Ohio Constitution.[283] The restrictions on detention and the protection afforded to detained children by the statutes and rules[284] are considered to be an adequate substitute for bail.[285] Nevertheless, a juvenile court may grant bail in its discretion.[286]

A child admitted to a detention or shelter care facility has a right to telephone his parents and counsel both immediately and at reasonable times thereafter.[287] The child may be visited at reasonable visiting hours by his parents, adult family members, pastor, and teachers and at any time by his attorney.[288]

As far as possible, a detention home must be furnished and administered as a family home, in the charge of a superintendent or matron, in a nonpunitive, neutral atmosphere.[289] During the school year, when possible, school-age children must be provided with an educational program comparable to what they would receive in public schools, with competent, trained staff.[290] A child in detention must also be given wholesome and profitable leisure-time activities with trained recreational personnel, as well as necessary medical and mental health services.[291]

In order to control health problems, the supervisor of a shelter or detention facility may provide for a physical examination of a child placed therein.[292]

CROSS REFERENCES

Text 3.01(A), 5.02, 7.07, 13.04, 15.01, 15.04

Merrick-Rippner, Ohio Probate Law (4th ed), Text Ch 217, 223

---

[283]State ex rel Peaks v Allaman, 66 Abs 403, 115 NE(2d) 849 (CP, Montgomery 1952). For discussion of the right to bail pending appeal, see Text 15.02(D), Stay of proceedings, appeal bond; appeal bond.

[284]RC 2151.31 to RC 2151.314; Juv R 7.

[285]See Fulwood v Stone, 394 F(2d) 939 (DC Cir 1967). Although the United States Supreme Court has not ruled specifically on this issue, there is dicta in both In re Gault, 387 US 1, 87 SCt 1428, 18 LEd(2d) 527 (1967) and Kent v United States, 383 US 541, 86 SCt 1045, 16 LEd(2d) 84 (1966), which states that children have no right to bail.

[286]See also RC 2151.311(A)(1), which provides that a person taking a child into custody may release the child to his parents, guardian, or custodian upon a written promise to return the child to court when requested. This requirement is not contained in the corresponding rule, Juv R 7(B).

[287]Juv R 7(E)(2)(a), (J).

[288]Juv R 7(E)(3)(b), (J).

[289]RC 2151.34.

[290]Id. The child's school district, as determined by the court, must pay the cost of educating the child based on the per capita cost of the educational facility within the detention home. See RC 2151.357.

[291]RC 2151.34. The United States Court of Appeals for the First Circuit has decided that a state (Puerto Rico) does not have a constitutional duty to provide rehabilitative treatment to juveniles confined in a detention home. The court rejected the argument that such treatment was mandated by the state's parens patriae interest in children and by the failure to extend to juveniles all due process protections. Santana v Collazo, 714 F(2d) 1172 (1st Cir PR 1983), cert denied 466 US 974, 104 SCt 2352, 80 LEd(2d) 825 (1984).

[292]Juv R 7(I). However, medical treatment is authorized only upon court order. RC 2151.33(A); Juv R 13.

Giannelli, Ohio Evidence Manual, Author's Comment 101.10

7.07   Temporary orders pending hearing

(A) Types of temporary orders permitted

Before a hearing is held on a complaint, the juvenile court is authorized to make such temporary orders as may be necessary, both with respect to the care and custody of a child who is the subject of the complaint and the conduct of others toward that child.[293] For example, an emergency custody order made by a juvenile court was upheld where the evidence showed that the children were dirty, undernourished, and infected.[294]

The court's authority to make temporary orders extends to the provision of emergency medical and surgical treatment for a child upon the certification of one or more reputable practicing physicians.[295] Although such treatment must appear to be "immediately necessary" for the child,[296] it has been held that the emergency need not be absolute; it is enough that the emergency might arise at any minute.[297]

RC 2151.33 provides that a juvenile court, prior to the final disposition of an abuse, neglect, or dependency case, and on the oral or written motion of a party,[298] may issue any of the following temporary orders to protect the best interests of the child:

(1) An order granting temporary custody of the child to a particular party;

(2) An order for the taking of the child into custody pending the outcome of the adjudicatory and dispositional hearing;

(3) An order granting, limiting, or eliminating visitation rights with respect to the child;

(4) An order for the payment of child support for the child and the continued maintenance of any medical, surgical, or hospital policies of insurance for the child that existed at the time of the filing of the complaint or other document;

---

[293]RC 2151.33(A); Juv R 13(A). Notwithstanding these provisions, a county human services department or child services board is mandated to provide emergency care for any child it considers to be in need of such care, without agreement of the parents or commitment of the child (RC 5153.16(G)).

[294]In re Douglas, 82 Abs 170, 164 NE(2d) 475 (Juv, Huron 1959).

[295]RC 2151.33(A); Juv R 13(C). 1951 OAG 689. For a discussion of the court's right to authorize medical or surgical care for a child, despite religious objections of the parents, see Text 3.06(D), Proper or necessary care.

[296]*Id.*

[297]In re Clark, 90 Abs 21, 185 NE(2d) 128 (CP, Lucas 1962). RC 2151.33(A) further provides that the court may order the parents, guardian, or custodian, if financially able, to reimburse the court for expenses involved in providing such treatment and enforce such order through contempt. If the child is a nonresident of the county and the expense cannot be recovered from the parent, guardian, or custodian, the board of county commissioners of the county in which the child has a legal settlement must reimburse the court for the reasonable cost of such treatment.

[298]See RC 2151.33(C) for the notice requirements of the motion.

(5) An order requiring a party to vacate a residence that will be lawfully occupied by the child;

(6) An order requiring a party to attend an appropriate counseling program that is reasonably available to that party; or

(7) Any other order that restrains or otherwise controls the conduct of any party which conduct would not be in the best interest of the child.[299]

(B) Compulsory hearings

If the order was made in an abuse, neglect, or dependency proceeding, the hearing must be conducted within seventy-two hours after the issuance of the order or before the end of the next business day on which it is issued, whichever occurs first.[300]

If the court does not grant an ex parte order pursuant to the motion filed in an abuse, neglect, or dependency case, the court must hold a shelter care hearing on the motion within ten days after the motion is filed.[301]

If a judge or referee issues an ex parte emergency order for taking an alleged abused, neglected, or dependent child into custody,[302] the court must conduct a hearing to determine whether there is probable cause for the emergency order. The hearing must be held before the end of the next business day after the day on which the emergency order is issued, but not later than seventy-two hours after issuance of the order. If the court determines that probable cause does not exist, the child must be released to the custody of his parents, guardian, or custodian.[303] If the court determines that probable cause does exist, the court must (1) ensure that a complaint is or has been filed, (2) conduct a shelter care hearing, and (3) make the determination and issue the written findings of fact required by RC 2151.419.[304] Furthermore, if the court determines at the hearing that there is probable cause to believe that the child is abused, the court may do any of the following: (1) on motion, issue reasonable protective orders with respect to interviewing or deposing the child; (2) order that the child's testimony be videotaped for preservation of the testimony for possible use in any other proceedings in the case; or (3) set any additional conditions with respect to the child or the case involving the child that are in the child's best interest.[305]

(C) Limitations on temporary orders

Wherever possible, the court must provide notice and an opportunity for a hearing prior to issuing the temporary or emergency order.[306] If the record does not reflect circumstances justifying an ex parte proceeding, the court may not

---

[299]RC 2151.33(B).

[300]RC 2151.33(D). This provision also contains the notice requirements for the hearing.

[301]*Id.*

[302]RC 2151.31(D) authorizes referees to grant by telephone an ex parte emergency order authorizing the taking of a child into custody. This in in conflict with Juv R 40, which provides that referees may make only findings and recommendations, not court orders.

[303]RC 2151.31(E). See Text 13.06, Abused, neglected, or dependent child.

[304]RC 2151.31(E).

[305]RC 2151.31(F).

[306]Juv R 13(E); RC 2151.33(D).

issue a temporary custody order without providing notice and an opportunity for a hearing to the child's parents.[307] If, however, it appears to the court that the interest and welfare of the child require immediate action, the court may proceed summarily without notice.[308] After issuing an ex parte order, the court must then give notice of the action it has taken to the parties and any other affected person and must provide them an opportunity for a hearing concerning the continuing effects of the order.[309]

The Ohio Supreme Court held in *Linger v Weiss*[310] that where almost three years elapses between the time of an emergency shelter care order under Juvenile Rule 13 and the adjudicatory hearing, the juvenile court does not lose jurisdiction over the matter of the alleged neglected child for failing to adhere to the time limits mandated by Juvenile Rule 29(A).[311] However, this case was decided prior to the amendments of RC 2151.28(A)(2) and (B)(3),[312] which establish strict time frames for conducting the adjudicatory and dispositional hearings. The failure of a court to hold a dispositional hearing for an abused, neglected, or dependent child within ninety days after the date on which the complaint was filed requires that the complaint be dismissed without prejudice.[313]

Pending the outcome of the adjudicatory and dispositional hearings, the court may not issue an order granting temporary custody of a child to a public children services agency or private child-placing agency unless the court determines and specifically states in the order that the continued residence of the child in his current home will be contrary to his best interest and welfare and makes the determination and issues the written findings of fact required by RC 2151.419.[314] Moreover, any agency that receives temporary custody of a child pursuant to RC 2151.33 is required to maintain in the child's case record written documentation that it has placed the child, to the extent that it is consistent with the best interest, welfare, and special needs of the child, in the most family-like setting available and in close proximity to the home of the parents, custodian, or guardian of the child.[315]

---

[307]Williams v Williams, 44 OS(2d) 28, 336 NE(2d) 426 (1975).

[308]Juv R 13(D); RC 2151.33(D).

[309]Juv R 13(E); RC 2151.33(D).

[310]Linger v Weiss, 57 OS(2d) 97, 386 NE(2d) 1354 (1979), cert denied 444 US 862, 100 SCt 128, 62 LEd(2d) 83 (1979).

[311]In this case, the juvenile court did not conduct the adjudicatory hearing until after a complaint for a writ of habeas corpus had been filed in the court of appeals. (In a footnote, the Supreme Court mentioned that the juvenile court had found the child to be neglected.) This case was appealed to the Licking County Court of Appeals on the basis that the adjudicatory hearing was not timely held. The court of appeals rejected that argument on the ground that the Supreme Court's footnote impliedly looked with favor upon the adjudication. See In re Linger, No. CA-2556 (5th Dist Ct App, Licking, 7-12-79). See also In re Caldwell, No. 420 (7th Dist Ct App, Carroll, 12-13-79), where the court of appeals held that a three-year delay in conducting an adjudicatory hearing, following an order granting emergency custody to a county human services department, did not constitute prejudicial error and did not deprive the court of jurisdiction over an alleged dependent child.

[312]1988 S 89, eff. 1-1-89.

[313]RC 2151.35(B)(1). See Text 13.06(A), Dispositional alternatives.

[314]RC 2151.33(E). See also 42 USC 672.

[315]RC 2151.33(F). See also 42 USC 675.

A temporary custody order issued by a juvenile court pursuant to Juvenile Rule 13 or Juvenile Rule 29 is not a dispositional order under Juvenile Rule 34. Thus, it neither constitutes a final appealable order nor makes a dispositional hearing conducted thereafter a nullity.[316]

CROSS REFERENCES

Text 3.06(D), 13.06

Merrick-Rippner, Ohio Probate Law (4th ed), Text Ch 223

7.08 Discovery

(A) From other parties

Juvenile Rule 24 provides the means by which a party may discover material which is in the possession of an adverse party and includes the right to inspect, copy, or photograph (1) the names and addresses of each witness;[317] (2) copies of any written statements made by any party or witness;[318] (3) transcriptions, recordings, and summaries of any oral statements of any party or witness, except the work product of counsel;[319] and (4) scientific and other reports, photographs, and physical evidence which a party intends to introduce at a hearing.[320]

Ohio courts have held that Juvenile Rule 24 does not permit discovery of police reports in delinquency proceedings.[321] However, RC 2151.352 provides that any report concerning a child who is taken into custody, which is used in any hearing and is pertinent thereto, must for good cause shown be made available to any attorney representing the child or parents, on written request prior to the hearing.[322]

With regard to the type of information that is subject to discovery in neglect, dependency, and abuse proceedings initiated by a county human services department, several Ohio courts have determined that a parent's attorney has a right to inspect or copy a caseworker's file, despite claims of work product and privilege.[323] On the other hand, it has been held that a social worker may not be

---

[316]In re Wayne, Nos. 81AP-631, 81AP-632 (10th Dist Ct App, Franklin, 12-10-81); Morrison v Morrison, 45 App(2d) 299, 344 NE(2d) 144 (Summit 1973).

[317]Juv R 24(A)(1).

[318]Juv R 24(A)(2). This rule is broader than Crim R 16, which does not permit discovery of witnesses' statements.

[319]Juv R 24(A)(3).

[320]Juv R 24(A)(4), (5).

[321]In re Hunter, No. 46019 (8th Dist Ct App, Cuyahoga, 4-5-84). See also State v Workman, 14 App(3d) 385, 14 OBR 490, 471 NE(2d) 853 (Cuyahoga 1984), holding that under Crim R 16(B) police reports are not discoverable in criminal cases.

[322]Juv R 24, *Editor's Comment,* Request for discovery (Juv R 24(A)(2) and (3) would make items such as police reports available to counsel.).

[323]In re Trumbull County Children Services Bd, 32 Misc(2d) 11, 513 NE(2d) 360 (CP, Trumbull 1986); Davis v Trumbull County Children Services Bd, 24 App(3d) 180, 24 OBR 270, 493 NE(2d) 1011 (Trumbull 1985); In re Evans, No. 87 CA 12 (2d Dist Ct App, Miami, 11-23-87); In re Strickland, No. CA 86-07-043 (12th Dist Ct App, Warren, 6-22-87).

compelled to reveal the name of the person who reported an instance of child abuse since such information is confidential under RC 2151.421.[324]

In order to obtain discovery, a party must serve a written request upon the opposing party.[325] If the opposing party is represented by an attorney, the request must be served upon the attorney, unless service upon the party himself is ordered by the court.[326] Requests for discovery must also be filed with the court simultaneously with or immediately after service.[327]

If the request is refused, application may be made to the court for a discovery order, by means of a motion certifying that a request has been made and refused.[328] The court has several options in ruling on the motion. It may order the party to furnish the requested information and may make such discovery reciprocal for all parties, including the party requesting discovery.[329] The court may also deny or limit discovery upon a showing that discovery would jeopardize the safety of a party, witness, or confidential informant, result in perjured evidence, endanger the existence of physical evidence, violate a privileged communication, or impede the criminal prosecution of a child as an adult in bindover proceedings or of an adult charged with an offense arising from the same transaction or occurrence.[330]

Motions for discovery must be heard before the adjudicatory hearing, though not necessarily on a separate date.[331] They must be filed with the court seven days prior to hearing or ten days after the appearance of counsel, whichever is earlier. The court, however, may extend the time in the interest of justice.[332] The failure to file a motion for discovery estops a party from thereafter raising the issue on appeal.[333]

If a party fails to comply with a court order for discovery, the court may grant a continuance, prohibit the party from introducing the material in evidence, or make other appropriate orders.[334] However, it is necessary that the party seeking discovery request the proper order from the court in order to obtain such

---

[324]In re Hicks, No. H-78-7 (6th Dist Ct App, Huron, 11-17-78). See also Pennsylvania v Ritchie, 480 US 39, 107 SCt 989, 94 LEd(2d) 40 (1987), holding that although a defendant has a due process right to access to child protection agency records in a criminal child abuse case, the court may first review these records in camera and remove information not relevant to the defense, including the identity of the reporter.

[325]Juv R 24(A).

[326]Juv R 20(A), (B). The method of service is governed by Civ R 5(B).

[327]Juv R 20(C).

[328]Juv R 24(B). Presumably, the same procedure applies if the request is simply not acted upon, though not technically refused. Juv R 24(A) requires the requested information to be produced "forthwith."

[329]Juv R 24(B). Presumably, the "work product" exception of Juv R 24(A)(3) applies to reciprocal discovery.

[330]Id.

[331]Juv R 22(D)(4).

[332]Juv R 22(E).

[333]State v Lee, No. 44902 (8th Dist Ct App, Cuyahoga, 2-10-83). Although this was a juvenile delinquency case, the decision was based on Crim R 16(B), the adult criminal court counterpart to Juv R 24(B).

[334]Juv R 24(C).

remedies.[335] Where discovery is not provided until immediately before the adjudicatory hearing and the party who requested it agrees to proceed with the hearing after reviewing the material, that party may not claim on appeal that he was denied discovery.[336]

Unlike Criminal Rule 16, Juvenile Rule 24 contains no requirement that disclosures be updated. Therefore, a party seeking current information must either repeat the request or move for an order compelling discovery pursuant to Juvenile Rule 24(B).[337]

An additional device for obtaining discovery is the deposition. Authority to take the deposition of a party or other person may be granted by the court upon good cause shown and upon such conditions as the court may fix.[338]

(B) From court

In addition to providing for the discovery of material in the possession of another party (Juvenile Rule 24), the law permits parties to inspect social history information in the possession of the court.[339] As a general rule, a social history of the child and his family may not be ordered or utilized by the court until there has been an admission or adjudication that the child is neglected, dependent, abused, delinquent, unruly, or a juvenile traffic offender.[340] However, a social history or physical or mental examination may be ordered or utilized at any time after a complaint is filed, under any of the following limited circumstances: (1) upon the request of the party concerning whom it is to be made; (2) where transfer of the child for criminal prosecution[341] is in issue; (3) where the history is necessary to clarify a material allegation of a neglect, dependency, or abuse complaint; (4) where a party's legal responsibility for his acts or his competence to participate in the proceedings is an issue; (5) where a physical or mental examination is required to determine the need for emergency medical care under Juvenile Rule 13;[342] or (6) where the supervisor of a shelter or detention facility authorizes the physical examination of a child placed therein pursuant to Juvenile Rule 7(I).[343]

The right to inspect a social history or physical or mental examination report arises at a reasonable time before any hearing at which it is to be utilized.[344]

---

[335]In re Hester, 3 App(3d) 458, 3 OBR 539, 446 NE(2d) 202 (Franklin 1982). See also In re Bernstein, Nos. 33531, 33532 (8th Dist Ct App, Cuyahoga, 1-2-75).

[336]In re Wyrock, Nos. 41827, 41828, 41904 (8th Dist Ct App, Cuyahoga, 10-23-80).

[337]In re Gilbert, No. CA 86-10-144 (12th Dist Ct App, Butler, 9-28-87).

[338]Juv R 25.

[339]Juv R 32. See also RC 2151.352.

[340]Juv R 32(B). For a discussion of the use of a social history for dispositional purposes, see Text 13.03, Conduct of hearing. For a discussion of the use of a social history at the adjudicatory hearing, see Text 11.11(B), Hearsay.

[341]RC 2151.26; Juv R 30. See Text 9.03(G), Access to reports.

[342]See Text 7.07, Temporary orders pending hearing.

[343]Juv R 32(A). In a permanent custody case, In re Green, 18 App(3d) 43, 18 OBR 155, 480 NE(2d) 492 (Montgomery 1984), it was held that a juvenile court's consideration of a psychological evaluation of a mother did not violate her right as an indigent parent under the Due Process and Equal Protection Clauses, where the evaluation was requested by the mother pursuant to Juvenile Rule 32(A) and was understood to be for the purpose of assisting the juvenile court and not solely for the mother's defense.

[344]Juv R 32(C).

However, this right is more limited and subject to greater restriction than the discovery rights provided by Juvenile Rule 24. While Juvenile Rule 24 permits discovery by all parties and allows inspection, copying, or photographing, Juvenile Rule 32 limits discovery to inspection, and then only by counsel. Upon a showing of good cause, the court may deny or limit the scope of inspection to specified portions of the history or report and may order that all or part of its contents not be disclosed to specified persons.[345] If the court denies or limits inspection, the reasons constituting "good cause" must be stated to counsel.[346]

The Attorney General has ruled that under RC 1347.08 a juvenile court must permit a juvenile or a duly authorized attorney who represents the juvenile to inspect court records pertaining to the juvenile unless the records are exempt under RC 1347.04(A)(1)(e) (investigatory material compiled for law enforcement purposes), RC 1347.08(C) (certain medical, psychiatric, or psychological information), or RC 1347.08(E)(2) (confidential law enforcement investigatory records or trial preparation records).[347]

CROSS REFERENCES

Text 7.07, 9.03(G), 11.11(B), 13.03, 15.04

Schroeder-Katz, Ohio Criminal Law, Crim R 12, Author's Text, Crim R 15, Author's Text
Merrick-Rippner, Ohio Probate Law (4th ed), Text Ch 223
Giannelli, Ohio Evidence Manual, Author's Comment 501.04, 501.09, 501.12

---

[345]*Id.* The constitutionality of these restrictions was considered in J.P. v DeSanti, No. C78-697 (ND Ohio 12-18-78). Although a United States court of appeals ultimately reversed the decision, partly on the basis that the district court should have abstained from deciding those claims, J.P. v DeSanti, 653 F(2d) 1080 (6th Cir 1981), the following language from the district court's opinion and order is worth noting:

> Insofar as Rule 32(C) ... authorizes the Juvenile Court to limit or deny access by a juvenile, his parents or guardian, or his legal counsel to any social history or family record concerning such juvenile prepared pursuant to Rule 32 prior to the juvenile's adjudicatory hearing, Rule 32(C) is inconsistent with the requirements of the Fifth, Sixth, and Fourteenth Amendments to the United States Constitution and the pronouncements of the Supreme Court in *Kent v. United States* and *In re Gault,* ... and is to that extent hereby declared to be unconstitutional. Accordingly, any (such) social history or family record ... shall be made available by the (court) to the juvenile concerned, his parents or guardian, and his legal counsel for inspection and copying upon written request not less than three days prior to the hearing.

[346]Juv R 32(C).
[347]OAG 84-077.

Chapter 9

Transfer of Jurisdiction

9.01   In general

Transfer of jurisdiction refers to the process by which a juvenile court relinquishes jurisdiction and transfers a juvenile case to the criminal courts for prosecution. This process, variously described as waiver, certification, or bindover, has been a unique[1] part of the juvenile court system since the establishment of the first juvenile court in 1899.[2] Although virtually all jurisdictions permit transfer, the criteria and procedures for transfer vary from state to state.[3] Double jeopardy principles preclude the transfer of jurisdiction after a child has been adjudicated delinquent.[4]

The concept of transfer entails a recognition that the juvenile court system should not be available to all children:

> Some acts are so offensive to the community that the arbitrary line drawn at eighteen cannot acceptably be used to protect the alleged wrongdoer. The serious offender should not be permitted to escape the criminal justice system simply because he or she is a day or a year short of eighteen. As age eighteen approaches, credible argument can be made that the juvenile court's always inadequate resources should not be devoted to those youthful wrongdoers whose offenses are so serious or who appear to be so incorrigible as to be unworthy of or beyond help.[5]

---

[1]See Kemplen v Maryland, 428 F(2d) 169, 173 (4th Cir Md 1970) ("There is no proceeding for adults comparable directly to the juvenile jurisdiction waiver hearing.").

[2]Illinois Juvenile Court Act of 1899. 1899 Ill. Laws 131.

[3]See *IJA-ABA Standards Relating to Transfer Between Courts* (1980); Davis, *Rights of Juveniles* ch 4 (2d ed 1980).

[4]See Text 9.06, Double jeopardy.

[5]*IJA-ABA Standards Relating to Transfer Between Courts* 3 (1980). See also In re Mack, 22 App(2d) 201, 203, 260 NE(2d) 619 (Hamilton 1970):

> The purpose of [transfer] is to protect the public in those cases where rehabilitation appears unlikely and circumstances indicate that if the charge is ultimately established society would be better served by the criminal process by reason of the greater security which may be achieved or the deterring effect which that process is thought to accomplish.

This view of transfer proceedings is not universally accepted. Piersma, Ganousis, Volenik, Swanger, and Connell, in *Law and Tactics in Juvenile Cases* 274 (3d ed 1977), have written:

> Others argue that the existence of this loophole [transfer] in the juvenile system indicates a half-hearted commitment to treatment and a continued allegiance to retribution on the part of society, an allegiance that is particularly distasteful because it applies to the very persons whom the separate juvenile court system was designed to protect.

For articles on transfer, see Feld, *The Juvenile Court Meets the Principle of the Offense: Legislative Changes in Juvenile Waiver Statutes*, 78 J Crim L 471 (1987); Thomas and

In Ohio, transfer proceedings are governed by RC 2151.26 and Juvenile Rule 30.[6] Juvenile courts have exclusive jurisdiction over persons under the age of eighteen who are charged with criminal conduct.[7] Only a properly transferred child may be prosecuted in the criminal courts.[8] As one court has stated, "Failure to comply with the provisions of R.C. 2151.26 ... deprives the Court of Common Pleas of jurisdiction over a juvenile defendant."[9] Generally, a hearing is required before a child can be transferred to the criminal courts. However, there is one situation in which a transfer hearing is not required. RC 2151.26(G) provides that a child who has been transferred and convicted and who is subsequently charged with aggravated murder, murder, an aggravated felony of the first or second degree, or a felony of the first or second degree shall be prosecuted as an adult.[10]

Constitutional considerations also affect transfer procedures. In *Kent v United States*[11] the United States Supreme Court considered a challenge to transfer proceedings conducted pursuant to the D.C. Code.[12] Kent was taken into custody for rape. As a sixteen year old, he was subject to juvenile court jurisdiction. The juvenile court, however, transferred his case for trial as an adult. The transfer was accomplished without a hearing or written reasons. In addition, the court failed to provide Kent's attorney with access to Kent's social service file. On review, the Supreme Court held that the transfer proceedings were invalid. According to the Court, transfer is a "critically important"[13] stage of the juvenile process and "there is no place in our system of law for reaching a result of such tremendous consequences without ceremony—without hearing, without effective assistance of counsel, without a statement of reasons."[14]

Bilchik, *Prosecuting Juveniles in Criminal Courts: A Legal and Empirical Analysis*, 76 J Crim L 439 (1985).

[6]There is no direct conflict between the statute and the rule, although each has provisions not found in the other. The Ohio Supreme Court has indicated that the statute and rule should be construed together. See State v Douglas, 20 OS(3d) 34, 35, 20 OBR 282, 485 NE(2d) 711 (1985) ("R.C. 2151.26 and Juv. R. 30 set forth the procedure to be followed by a juvenile court in a bind-over situation."); State v Adams, 69 OS(2d) 120, 123, 431 NE(2d) 326 (1982) ("R.C. 2151.26 and Juv. R. 30 provide the procedural mechanism by which a juvenile offender may be 'bound over' to the adult court.").

[7]RC 2151.23(A)(1). See also RC 2151.25 (transfer of cases from other courts to the juvenile court).

[8]A prosecution in criminal court on the mistaken belief that the child was over eighteen years of age at the time of the offense is a "nullity." RC 2151.26(E). See Text 3.10, Age jurisdiction.

[9]State v Riggins, 68 App(2d) 1, 4, 426 NE(2d) 504 (Cuyahoga 1980). See also State v Taylor, 26 App(3d) 69, 26 OBR 243, 498 NE(2d) 211 (Auglaize 1985) (Failure to comply with notice requirements deprives criminal court of jurisdiction.).

[10]See also RC 2151.011(B)(1).

[11]Kent v United States, 383 US 541, 86 SCt 1045, 16 LEd(2d) 84 (1966).

[12]See generally Paulsen, *Kent v. United States: The Constitutional Context of Juvenile Cases*, 1966 Supreme Court Rev 167. Compare Brown v Wainwright, 537 F(2d) 154 (5th Cir Fla 1976) (*Kent* not retroactive), cert denied 430 US 970, 97 SCt 1656, 52 LEd(2d) 363 (1977) with Kemplen v Maryland, 428 F(2d) 169 (4th Cir Md 1970) (*Kent* retroactive).

[13]Kent v United States, 383 US 541, 556, 86 SCt 1045, 16 LEd(2d) 84 (1966).

[14]*Id.* at 554.

Whether the Court intended to rest its decision in *Kent* on statutory or constitutional grounds is not entirely clear. At one point in the opinion, Justice Fortas wrote, "The Juvenile Court Act and the decisions of the United States Court of Appeals for the District of Columbia Circuit provide an adequate basis for decision of this case, and we go no further."[15] Moreover, the dissenting justices believed the case involved only a statutory issue.[16] Nevertheless, other parts of the Fortas opinion indicate a constitutional basis. One passage reads, "We believe that this result is required by the statute read in the context of constitutional principles relating to due process and the assistance of counsel."[17] In another passage the Court wrote that a transfer hearing "must measure up to the essentials of due process and fair treatment."[18] Significantly, the Court quoted this passage in *In re Gault*[19] and then wrote, "We reiterate this view . . . as a requirement which is part of the Due Process Clause of the Fourteenth Amendment of our Constitution."[20]

Although there are some exceptions,[21] most courts, including the Ohio courts, view *Kent* as establishing constitutional standards.[22] For example, the Third Circuit has stated, "[I]t is our view that *Kent*, particularly in light of the Supreme Court's subsequent opinion in In re Gault . . . sets forth certain principles of constitutional dimension."[23]

CROSS REFERENCES

Text 1.02(A), (B), 3.10, 9.06, 15.05

Merrick-Rippner, Ohio Probate Law (4th ed), Text Ch 223

9.02   Juveniles subject to transfer

RC 2151.26 and Juvenile Rule 30 specify which children are subject to transfer and what criteria apply. Generally, transfer is permitted only for children of specified ages and for certain types of offenses. In addition, the court

---

[15]*Id.* at 556.

[16]*Id.* at 568 (dissenting opinion) ("This case involves the construction of a statute applicable only to the District of Columbia.").

[17]*Id.* at 557.

[18]*Id.* at 562.

[19]In re Gault, 387 US 1, 87 SCt 1428, 18 LEd(2d) 527 (1967).

[20]*Id.* at 30-31.

[21]E.g., State v Steinhauer, 216 So(2d) 214 (Fla 1968), cert denied 398 US 914, 90 SCt 1698, 26 LEd(2d) 79 (1970); In re Bullard, 22 NC App 245, 206 SE(2d) 305 (1974), appeal dismissed 285 NC 758, 209 SE(2d) 279 (1974); Cradle v Peyton, 208 Va 243, 156 SE(2d) 874 (1967), cert denied 392 US 945, 88 SCt 2296, 20 LEd(2d) 1407 (1968).

[22]See State v Adams, 69 OS(2d) 120, 431 NE(2d) 326 (1982); State v Taylor, 26 App(3d) 69, 26 OBR 243, 498 NE(2d) 211 (Auglaize 1985); State v Oviedo, 5 App(3d) 168, 5 OBR 351, 450 NE(2d) 700 (Wood 1982); State v Riggins, 68 App(2d) 1, 426 NE(2d) 504 (Cuyahoga 1980); In re Mack, 22 App(2d) 201, 260 NE(2d) 619 (Hamilton 1970).

[23]United States ex rel Turner v Rundle, 438 F(2d) 839, 841-42 (3d Cir Pa 1971). Accord Oviedo v Jago, 809 F(2d) 326 (6th Cir Ohio 1987); Geboy v Gray, 471 F(2d) 575 (7th Cir Wis 1973); Powell v Hooker, 453 F(2d) 652 (9th Cir Nev 1971), overruled on other grounds by Harris v Procunier, 498 F(2d) 576 (9th Cir Cal 1974); Kemplen v Maryland, 428 F(2d) 169 (4th Cir Md 1970); Inge v Slayton, 395 FSupp 560 (ED Va 1975), appeal dismissed 541 F(2d) 277 (4th Cir Va 1976).

must find that there is probable cause to believe that the child has committed the offense. Where transfer is discretionary, the court must decide whether the child is amenable to treatment in the juvenile system.

The United States Supreme Court has yet to consider the constitutionality of the standards used in transfer proceedings. In *Breed v Jones*[24] the Court commented that it "has never attempted to prescribe criteria for, or the nature and quantum of evidence that must support, a decision to transfer a juvenile for trial in adult court."[25] Constitutional challenges to transfer statutes typically have been based on vagueness grounds, but these challenges generally have been rejected.[26]

(A) Age

A child fifteen years or older *may* be transferred to the criminal courts for trial.[27] Generally, children under fifteen years of age are not subject to transfer. However, a child previously adjudicated delinquent for aggravated murder or murder and alleged to have committed such an act again *must* be transferred, regardless of his age.[28] The child's age at the time of the offense, rather than at the time of the transfer hearing, controls.[29]

(B) Offenses

Discretionary transfer is permitted only if the complaint alleges that the child has committed an act that would constitute a felony if committed by an adult.[30] There are no common-law crimes in Ohio—only statutory crimes.[31] An offense specifically classified as a felony in the Revised Code is a felony regardless of the penalty that may be imposed.[32] Similarly, an offense classified as a misdemeanor is a misdemeanor regardless of the penalty that may be imposed.[33] Any offense not specifically classified is a felony if imprisonment for more than one year may be imposed as a penalty.[34]

---

[24]Breed v Jones, 421 US 519, 95 SCt 1779, 44 LEd(2d) 346 (1975).

[25]*Id.* at 537.

[26]See State v Brown, No. 52757 (8th Dist Ct App, Cuyahoga, 10-8-87). See also Speck v Auger, 558 F(2d) 394 (8th Cir Iowa 1977) (construing the Iowa statute), cert denied 434 US 999, 98 SCt 641, 54 LEd(2d) 495 (1977); Donald L. v Superior Court of Los Angeles County, 7 Cal(3d) 592, 498 P(2d) 1098, 102 Cal Rptr 850 (1972); Davis v State, 297 So(2d) 289 (Fla 1974); State v Gibbs, 94 Idaho 908, 500 P(2d) 209 (1972); State v Smagula, 117 NH 663, 377 A(2d) 608 (1977); In re Bullard, 22 NC App 245, 206 SE(2d) 305 (1974), appeal dismissed 285 NC 758, 209 SE(2d) 279 (1974).

But see State in re Hunter, 387 So(2d) 1086 (La 1980), superseded by La Const Art 5, § 19 as stated in State v Perique, 439 So(2d) 1060 (La 1983). See also People v Fields, 388 Mich 66, 199 NW(2d) 217 (1972). But see People v Peters, 397 Mich 360, 244 NW(2d) 898 (1976).

[27]RC 2151.26(A)(1)(a); Juv R 30(A).

[28]RC 2151.26(A)(2).

[29]See Text 3.10, Age jurisdiction.

[30]RC 2151.26(A); Juv R 30(A). Transfer of a felony charge does not relinquish juvenile court jurisdiction over misdemeanors committed by the child. State ex rel Duganitz v Court of Common Pleas, 23 OO(3d) 572 (App, Cuyahoga 1981), affirmed by 69 OS(2d) 270, 432 NE(2d) 163 (1982).

[31]RC 2901.03(A).

[32]RC 2901.02(D).

[33]*Id.*

[34]RC 2901.02(E).

(C) Probable cause

Before a child may be transferred, the court must find that there is probable cause to believe that he has committed the alleged act.[35] There must be probable cause (1) that a felony has been committed, and (2) that the child is the person who has committed that felony.[36]

(D) Amenability to treatment

RC 2151.26 recognizes two types of transfers: mandatory and discretionary. A child who has previously been adjudicated delinquent for aggravated murder or murder and is alleged to have again committed either of those crimes is subject to mandatory transfer on a finding of probable cause.[37]

The more common type of transfer involves a discretionary decision. Here, before a child may be transferred, the court must find that there are reasonable grounds to believe (1) that he is not amenable to care or rehabilitation or further care or rehabilitation in any facility for delinquent children, and (2) that the safety of the community may require legal restraint for a period extending beyond his majority.[38]

Juvenile Rule 30(E) requires the court to consider the following factors in determining whether a child is amenable to treatment: (1) age,[39] (2) mental and physical health, (3) prior juvenile record,[40] (4) previous efforts to treat or rehabilitate,[41] (5) family environment,[42] and (6) school record.[43] Although the juvenile court must consider all of these factors, "not all of the relevant factors need be resolved against the juvenile in order to justify the transfer."[44] In evaluating the "safety of the community," the court may consider "the nature of the

---

[35]RC 2151.26(A); Juv R 30(A).

[36]See generally *IJA-ABA Standards Relating to Transfer Between Courts* 37-38 (1980); Davis, *The Efficacy of a Probable Cause Requirement in Juvenile Proceedings*, 59 NC L Rev 723 (1981).

[37]RC 2151.26(A)(2).

[38]RC 2151.26(A)(1); Juv R 30(C).

[39]See State v Tilton, No. 384 (7th Dist Ct App, Harrison, 6-23-83) (Due to the maturity of the child, he would not be amenable to treatment as a juvenile.); State v Holt, No. 81AP-661 (10th Dist Ct App, Franklin, 3-30-82) (eighteen years old at time of trial).

[40]See State v Carter, 27 OS(2d) 135, 138, 272 NE(2d) 119 (1971) ("many court appearances"); State v Whiteside, 6 App(3d) 30, 35, 6 OBR 140, 452 NE(2d) 332 (Allen 1982) ("[A]ppellant had a record as a juvenile delinquent."); State v Oviedo, 5 App(3d) 168, 171, 5 OBR 351, 450 NE(2d) 700 (Wood 1982) ("[H]istory of delinquency ... included such charges as petty theft, breaking and entering, receiving stolen property, theft, criminal mischief and criminal damaging.").

[41]See State v Carter, 27 OS(2d) 135, 272 NE(2d) 119 (1971) (prior commitment to correctional school); State v Whiteside, 6 App(3d) 30, 6 OBR 140, 452 NE(2d) 332 (Allen 1982) (prior treatment at Ohio Youth Commission (now, Department of Youth Services)); State v Oviedo, 5 App(3d) 168, 5 OBR 351, 450 NE(2d) 700 (Wood 1982) (prior probation); State v Ridgley, No. L-80-241 (6th Dist Ct App, Lucas, 3-27-81) (four prior commitments to Ohio Youth Commission (now, Department of Youth Services)).

[42]See State v Hawkins, No. 3462 (9th Dist Ct App, Lorain, 6-8-83) (unstable family situation); State v Arnold, No. L-80-269 (6th Dist Ct App, Lucas, 6-12-81) (Family had a long history of antisocial behavior and criminal activity.).

[43]See State v Hawkins, No. 3462 (9th Dist Ct App, Lorain, 6-8-83) (suspended from school eight times); State v Arnold, No. L-80-269 (6th Dist Ct App, Lucas, 6-12-81) (truancy problem and not currently attending school).

[44]State v Oviedo, 5 App(3d) 168, 171, 5 OBR 351, 450 NE(2d) 700 (Wood 1982).

offense, the existence of aggravating circumstances, and the extent of any apparent pattern of anti-social conduct."[45] RC 2151.26(B) requires the court to consider whether the act involved an offense of violence and whether the victim of the alleged offense was sixty-five years of age or older or was permanently and totally disabled at the time of the offense.[46]

The Ohio Supreme Court has written:

> Neither R.C. 2151.25 nor Juv. R. 30 requires the juvenile court to make written findings as to the five factors listed in Juv. R. 30(E). The rule simply requires the court to *consider* these factors in making its determination on the amenability issue. Although the better practice would be to address each factor, as long as sufficient, credible evidence pertaining to each factor exists in the record before the court, the bind-over order should not be reversed in the absence of an abuse of discretion.[47]

One survey of juvenile court judges revealed that the following factors, in the order of the frequency of their listing, were considered in making transfer decisions:

(1) Seriousness of the alleged offense;

(2) Record and history of the juvenile, including prior contacts with police, court, or other official agencies;

(3) Aggressive, violent, premeditated, or willful manner in which the offense was committed;

(4) Sophistication, maturity, emotional attitude of the juvenile;

(5) Proximity of juvenile's age to maximum age of juvenile court jurisdiction;

(6) Existence of more appropriate procedures, services, and facilities in the adult court that would increase the likelihood of reasonable rehabilitation;

(7) The possible need for a longer period of incarceration;

(8) Existence of evidence sufficient for a grand jury indictment;

(9) The trial of the juvenile's associates in the alleged offense in an adult court;

(10) Other factors;

(11) Effect of transfer on public's respect for law enforcement and law compliance; and

(12) Community attitude toward the specific offense.[48]

---

[45]*Id.* at 171-72. See also State v Carter, 27 OS(2d) 135, 272 NE(2d) 119 (1971) (Juvenile court cited aggravated character of offense—armed robbery—in the transfer order.); State v Harris, No. 81AP-299 (10th Dist Ct App, Franklin, 10-6-81) (Court may consider the nature of the offense—aggravated rape and kidnapping.).

[46]See State v Grooms, No. 374 (4th Dist Ct App, Adams, 9-3-81) (seventy-eight-year-old victim).

[47]State v Douglas, 20 OS(3d) 34, 36, 20 OBR 282, 485 NE(2d) 711 (1985). See also Oviedo v Jago, 809 F(2d) 326 (6th Cir Ohio 1987) (Habeas corpus challenge to transfer decision was rejected.).

[48]President's Commission on Law Enforcement and the Administration of Justice, *Task Force Report: Juvenile Delinquency and Youth Crime* 78 appendix (1967). See also Comment, *Waiver of Jurisdiction in Juvenile Courts*, 30 Ohio St L J 132 (1969) (survey-

The IJA-ABA Standards adopt a restrictive approach to transfer, permitting it only for "extraordinary juveniles in extraordinary factual circumstances."[49] The criteria for transfer are (1) the seriousness of the offense; (2) prior record of *adjudicated* delinquency involving the infliction or threat of significant bodily injury; (3) the likely inefficacy of the dispositions available to the juvenile court *as demonstrated by previous dispositions of the juvenile*; and (4) the appropriateness of the services and dispositional alternatives available in the criminal justice system for dealing with the juvenile's problems, and whether they are, in fact, available.[50] The Standards reject "the public interest as a justification for waiver."[51]

CROSS REFERENCES

Text 1.02(E), 3.10, 9.06, 11.15

9.03 Procedure

(A) Hearing and investigation

In Ohio, RC 2151.26 and Juvenile Rule 30 govern the transfer hearing and investigation. In *Kent v United States*,[52] the United States Supreme Court held that "an opportunity for a hearing which may be informal, must be given the child prior to entry of a waiver order." In explaining the hearing requirement, the Court wrote, "We do not mean by this to indicate that the hearing to be held must conform with all of the requirements of a criminal trial or even of the usual administrative hearing; but we do hold that the hearing must measure up to the essentials of due process and fair treatment."[53]

Juvenile Rule 30 establishes a two-step hearing procedure for discretionary transfers. First, a preliminary hearing is held to determine whether there is probable cause to believe the child has committed a felony. The child, the prosecutor, or the court may move for a preliminary hearing.[54] If the court finds probable cause, the proceedings are continued until a full investigation is completed, at which time a second hearing is held to determine whether jurisdiction should be transferred to the criminal courts.

The focus of the second hearing is the amenability of the child to rehabilitation in the juvenile court system. A social history may be prepared and used for this purpose.[55] The "full investigation" required by the rule and statute also

---

ing factors Ohio juvenile judges used in making transfer determinations under prior statute).

[49]*IJA-ABA Standards Relating to Transfer Between Courts* 39 (1980).

[50]*Id.* at 36 (emphasis added).

[51]*Id.* at 37.

[52]Kent v United States, 383 US 541, 561, 86 SCt 1045, 16 LEd(2d) 84 (1966).

[53]*Id.* at 562.

[54]Although a child may move for a hearing, "[t]here is no provision in the rule or in the Revised Code that a child can cause the juvenile court to surrender its jurisdiction." State v Smith, 29 App(3d) 194, 196-97, 29 OBR 237, 504 NE(2d) 1121 (Cuyahoga 1985). Recognizing a child's right to move for transfer raises an issue of waiver because the child is giving up the right to treatment in the juvenile system. See United States v Williams, 459 F(2d) 903 (2d Cir NY 1972) (Child should be advised of his right to be proceeded against as a child and of all the consequences of waiving that right.).

[55]Juv R 32(A)(2).

includes a mental and physical examination by a public or private agency or other qualified person.[56] This examination may be waived by the child, and refusal to submit to the examination constitutes a waiver.[57] Although the mental and physical examinations may be waived, neither the investigation nor the hearing may be waived.[58]

A different procedure governs *mandatory* transfers. A child who is alleged to have committed aggravated murder or murder must be transferred if the court determines (1) that there is probable cause that the child committed the act, and (2) that the child has been previously adjudicated delinquent for aggravated murder or murder.[59]

(B) Right to counsel

Juvenile Rule 4(A) provides for the right to counsel at all juvenile court hearings.[60] The right to counsel at transfer hearings is also constitutionally required.[61] In *Kent* the United States Supreme Court stated that "counsel must be afforded to the child in waiver proceedings"[62] and that "there is no place in our system of law for reaching a result of such tremendous consequences . . . without effective assistance of counsel."[63]

Juvenile Rule 4(A) also provides that in the case of indigency, the child has the right to appointed counsel.[64] This right is also constitutionally required.[65] In criminal trials the Sixth Amendment right to counsel includes the right to appointed counsel for indigent defendants,[66] and in *In re Gault*,[67] the Court held that the appointment of counsel is required in a delinquency adjudication if the child is "unable to afford to employ counsel."

Usually, the right to counsel may be waived. The standard for waiver is an "intentional relinquishment or abandonment" of a fully known right.[68] In Ohio,

---

[56]Juv R 30(B) provides that the mental and physical examination also may be conducted by the Ohio Youth Commission (now, Department of Youth Services). RC 2151.26(A)(3) does not contain this provision.

[57]RC 2151.26(C) (Waiver must be "competently and intelligently made."); Juv R 30(F).

[58]State v Newton, No. F-82-17 (6th Dist Ct App, Fulton, 6-10-83).

[59]RC 2151.26(A)(2).

[60]RC 2151.352 also guarantees the right to counsel.

[61]See Geboy v Gray, 471 F(2d) 575 (7th Cir Wis 1973); Kemplen v Maryland, 428 F(2d) 169 (4th Cir Md 1970); Inge v Slayton, 395 FSupp 560 (ED Va 1975), appeal dismissed 541 F(2d) 277 (4th Cir Va 1976); James v Cox, 323 FSupp 15 (ED Va 1971); Steinhauer v State, 206 So(2d) 25 (Fla 1968), cert denied 398 US 914, 90 SCt 1698, 26 LEd(2d) 79 (1970).

[62]Kent v United States, 383 US 541, 562, 86 SCt 1045, 16 LEd(2d) 84 (1966). See also In re Gault, 387 US 1, 36, 87 SCt 1428, 18 LEd(2d) 527 (1967).

[63]Kent v United States, 383 US 541, 554, 86 SCt 1045, 16 LEd(2d) 84 (1966).

[64]RC 2151.352 also provides for the appointment of counsel in indigency cases. Juv R 2(12) defines "indigent person."

[65]Kemplen v Maryland, 428 F(2d) 169 (4th Cir Md 1970).

[66]See Gideon v Wainwright, 372 US 335, 83 SCt 792, 9 LEd(2d) 799 (1963); Argersinger v Hamlin, 407 US 25, 92 SCt 2006, 32 LEd(2d) 530 (1972); Scott v Illinois, 440 US 367, 99 SCt 1158, 59 LEd(2d) 383 (1977).

[67]In re Gault, 387 US 1, 42, 87 SCt 1428, 18 LEd(2d) 527 (1967).

[68]*Id.* (quoting Johnson v Zerbst, 304 US 458, 464, 58 SCt 1019, 82 LEd(2d) 1461 (1938)).

however, the right to counsel at a transfer hearing may not be waived. Juvenile Rule 3 provides that a child's "right to be represented by counsel at a hearing to determine whether the juvenile court shall relinquish its jurisdiction for purposes of criminal prosecution may not be waived."

The right to counsel includes the right to effective assistance of counsel. This is the rule regarding the Sixth Amendment right to counsel,[69] and the United States Supreme Court's references to "effective assistance" of counsel in *Kent*[70] indicate that the same rule applies to the due process right of counsel in transfer proceedings.[71]

The function of counsel at a transfer hearing is to challenge the evidence offered by the prosecution[72] and to adduce evidence that the child is amenable to treatment in the juvenile system. As one court has commented, "The child's advocate should search for a plan, or perhaps a range of plans, which may persuade the court that the welfare of the child and the safety of the community can be served without waiver."[73]

(C) Notice

Juvenile Rule 30(B) requires that written notice of the time, place, and nature of the transfer hearing be given to the parties at least three days prior to the hearing.[74] Adequate notice is an essential aspect of due process.[75] Notice must be given sufficiently in advance of the hearing to permit adequate preparation.[76] It also must be sufficiently specific to appraise the parties of the nature of the

---

[69]See Strickland v Washington, 466 US 668, 104 SCt 2052, 80 LEd(2d) 674 (1984) (Sixth Amendment requires reasonably effective assistance of counsel.).

[70]Kent v United States, 383 US 541, 558, 86 SCt 1045, 16 LEd(2d) 84 (1966).

[71]See Geboy v Gray, 471 F(2d) 575 (7th Cir Wis 1973) (noting counsel showed a "notable lack of zeal" in attempting to find alternatives to transfer).

[72]See Kent v United States, 383 US 541, 563, 86 SCt 1045, 16 LEd(2d) 84 (1966) ("[I]f the staff's submissions include materials which are susceptible to challenge or impeachment, it is precisely the role of counsel to 'denigrate' such matter.").

[73]Haziel v United States, 404 F(2d) 1275, 1279 (DC Cir 1968). For a discussion of counsel's role at the transfer hearing, see *IJA-ABA Standards Relating to Counsel for Private Parties* 161-68 (1980); Feld, *Juvenile Court Legislative Reform and the Serious Young Offender: Dismantling the "Rehabilitative Ideal,"* 65 Minn L Rev 167 (1981).

[74]See also RC 2151.26(D) (notice to parents or guardian and counsel three days prior to the hearing). This statute differs from Juv R 30(B) in one respect. The statute does not provide for notice to the child, while the rule requires notice to all parties, which would include the child. See Juv R 2(16).

[75]See Wolff v McDonnell, 418 US 539, 94 SCt 2963, 41 LEd(2d) 935 (1974) (prison disciplinary hearings); Morrissey v Brewer, 408 US 471, 92 SCt 2593, 33 LEd(2d) 484 (1972) (parole revocation hearings); Cole v Arkansas, 333 US 196, 68 SCt 514, 92 LEd 644 (1948) (criminal cases); In re Oliver, 333 US 257, 68 SCt 499, 92 LEd 682 (1948) (criminal cases).

[76]See Geboy v Gray, 471 F(2d) 575 (7th Cir Wis 1973); Kemplen v Maryland, 428 F(2d) 169 (4th Cir Md 1970); Miller v Quatsoe, 332 FSupp 1269 (ED Wis 1971). See also In re Gault, 387 US 1, 33, 87 SCt 1428, 18 LEd(2d) 527 (1967) ("Notice, to comply with due process requirements, must be given sufficiently in advance of scheduled court proceedings so that reasonable opportunity to prepare will be afforded.").

charges[77] and the purpose of the hearing.[78] Finally, the proper parties must receive notice.[79]

The notice requirements are mandatory and nonwaivable; failure to comply with the notice requirements precludes a valid transfer.[80]

(D) Standard of proof

Juvenile Rule 30(C) requires the court to find *reasonable grounds to believe* that the child is not amenable to rehabilitation and that the safety of the community may require legal restraint beyond the child's majority.[81] Commenting on this standard, the Ohio Supreme Court has written, "[T]he 'investigation' is not required to show that the child *cannot* be rehabilitated as a juvenile but only that there are reasonable grounds to believe that he cannot be rehabilitated."[82] The court also held that the juvenile court has "considerable latitude within which to determine whether it should retain jurisdiction."[83]

In other jurisdictions, the standard of proof on the issue of nonamenability varies. Some jurisdictions require "substantial evidence," while others require a "preponderance of evidence." Still others have adopted a "clear and convincing evidence" standard,[84] a standard also found in the IJA-ABA Standards.[85]

(E) Evidence

In many jurisdictions the rules of evidence are relaxed in transfer hearings because these hearings are considered dispositional in nature.[86] At least as a general rule, however, in Ohio the Rules of Evidence apply in transfer hearings.

---

[77]See United States ex rel Turner v Rundle, 438 F(2d) 839 (3d Cir Pa 1971). See also In re Gault, 387 US 1, 33, 87 SCt 1428, 18 LEd(2d) 527 (1967) ("Notice, to comply with due process requirements, ... must 'set forth the alleged misconduct with particularity.' ").

[78]See James v Cox, 323 FSupp 15 (ED Va 1971); State v Gibbs, 94 Idaho 908, 500 P(2d) 209 (1972).

[79]See Miller v Quatsoe, 332 FSupp 1269 (ED Wis 1971); Crandell v State, 539 P(2d) 398 (Okla Crim App 1975).

[80]State v Taylor, 26 App(3d) 69, 26 OBR 243, 498 NE(2d) 211 (Auglaize 1985).

[81]See also RC 2151.26(A)(3).

[82]State v Carmichael, 35 OS(2d) 1, 6, 298 NE(2d) 568 (1973), cert denied 414 US 1161, 94 SCt 922, 39 LEd(2d) 113 (1974) (emphasis by the court).

[83]*Id.* (syllabus 1). See also State v Douglas, 20 OS(3d) 34, 36, 20 OBR 282, 485 NE(2d) 711 (1985); State v Whiteside, 6 App(3d) 30, 6 OBR 140, 452 NE(2d) 332 (Allen 1982); State v Leonard, No. CA-5535 (5th Dist Ct App, Stark, 6-3-81) (Juvenile court's transfer decision should be overturned only if unreasonable and arbitrary.); State v Grooms, No. 374 (4th Dist Ct App, Adams, 9-3-81) (Clear and convincing evidence standard is not required.).

[84]See Davis, *Rights of Juveniles* 4-17 (2d ed 1980); In re Winship, 397 US 358, 90 SCt 1068, 25 LEd(2d) 368 (1970), which held that the proper standard of proof in delinquency cases is proof beyond a reasonable doubt, was expressly limited to the adjudicatory hearing. See also State v Carmichael, 35 OS(2d) 1, 298 NE(2d) 568 (1973), cert denied 414 US 1161, 94 SCt 922, 39 LEd(2d) 113 (1974).

[85]*IJA-ABA Standards Relating to Transfer Between Courts* 39 (1980).

[86]See Davis, *Rights of Juveniles* 4-17 (2d ed 1980). But see In re Anonymous, 14 Ariz App 466, 484 P(2d) 235 (1971) (Only competent evidence is admissible.); In re Harris, 218 Kan 625, 544 P(2d) 1403 (1976) (Transfer may not be based on inadmissible hearsay.); People v Morris, 57 Mich App 573, 226 NW(2d) 565 (1975) (Only legally admissible evidence may be introduced.), cert denied 423 US 849, 96 SCt 90, 46 LEd(2d) 72 (1975).

Evidence Rule 101 provides that the Rules of Evidence "govern proceedings in the courts of this state and before court-appointed referees of this state."[87] Accordingly, the Rules of Evidence apply in transfer hearings. There is, however, an important exception. Evidence Rule 101(C)(6) exempts from the Rules of Evidence proceedings in which other rules prescribed by the Ohio Supreme Court govern evidentiary matters. Thus, where the Rules of Evidence are in conflict with any other rule prescribed by the Ohio Supreme Court, the "other rule" prevails. For example, Juvenile Rule 32(A)(2) expressly permits the use of a social history in transfer proceedings, although much of the material contained in a social history would be inadmissible under the Rules of Evidence. Juvenile Rule 2(21) defines the social history as "the personal and family history of a child or any other party to a juvenile proceeding and may include the prior record of the person with the juvenile court or any other court."

Prior to the adoption of the Rules of Evidence, the Ohio Supreme Court in *State v Carmichael*[88] had upheld the use of a social history at a transfer hearing, despite its hearsay character.[89] In that case, however, the court also indicated that the psychiatrists and psychologists whose opinions appeared in the social history could have been called as witnesses: "[T]hey were never called, nor was any effort made to call them by defense counsel, even though counsel had access to those documents for more than two months prior to the hearing."[90]

The issue of whether the right of confrontation applies at a transfer hearing was raised in *State v Riggins*.[91] In that case, the defendant contended that he was denied due process because he was deprived of the opportunity to confront the witnesses against him, i.e., the confession of a codefendant was read into evidence by a police officer. The court overruled this objection because the defendant failed to provide a transcript to support his allegations.[92] Under Evidence Rule 801, the confession of a codefendant is inadmissible hearsay.

(F) Self-incrimination

The privilege against self-incrimination applies in transfer hearings.[93] In *In re Gault*[94] the United States Supreme Court held the privilege applicable to adjudicatory hearings, and in other cases the Court has stated that the privilege is

[87]See generally Giannelli, *Ohio Evidence Manual* § 101.01-.10 (1987).
[88]State v Carmichael, 35 OS(2d) 1, 298 NE(2d) 568 (1973), cert denied 414 US 1161, 94 SCt 922, 39 LEd(2d) 113 (1974).
[89]See also State v Riggins, 68 App(2d) 1, 7, 426 NE(2d) 504 (Cuyahoga 1980) ("The Ohio Supreme Court has held that hearsay evidence is admissible at a relinquishment proceeding in Juvenile Court in the form of psychiatric reports from the Ohio Youth Commission Juvenile Diagnostic Center."); State v Cole, No. CA82-10-0104 (12th Dist Ct App, Butler, 8-31-83).
[90]State v Carmichael, 35 OS(2d) 1, 3-4, 298 NE(2d) 568 (1973), cert denied 414 US 1161, 94 SCt 922, 39 LEd(2d) 113 (1974).
[91]State v Riggins, 68 App(2d) 1, 426 NE(2d) 504 (Cuyahoga 1980).
[92]*Id.* See also People ex rel Guggenheim v Mucci, 77 NY Misc(2d) 41, 352 NYS(2d) 561 (1974) (Due process requires that probable cause determination be based on nonhearsay evidence.), affirmed by 46 AD(2d) 683, 360 NYS(2d) 71 (1974).
For a discussion of the right of confrontation at the adjudicatory hearing, see Text 11.12, Right of confrontation.
[93]R.E.M. v State, 532 SW(2d) 645 (Tex Civ App 1975). See also *IJA-ABA Standards Relating to Transfer Between Courts* 50 (1980).
[94]In re Gault, 387 US 1, 87 SCt 1428, 18 LEd(2d) 527 (1967).

applicable in any proceeding "civil or criminal, formal or informal, where the answers might incriminate [a person] in future criminal proceedings."[95] The Court has also held that a criminal defendant's exercise of his right to remain silent may not be commented upon or used against him.[96]

By testifying at a transfer hearing, the child waives the privilege against self-incrimination. Whether the child's statement may be later used at a criminal trial or at an adjudicatory hearing is unclear. If his statements may be used against him at a later time, the child is placed in an untenable position. He either must give up the privilege or give up his right to be heard at the transfer hearing. The United States Supreme Court considered an analogous situation in *Simmons v United States*,[97] which involved a similar choice facing criminal defendants in suppression hearings:

> Thus, in this case [the defendant] was obliged either to give up what he believed, with advice of counsel, to be a valid Fourth Amendment claim or, in legal effect, to waive his Fifth Amendment privilege against self-incrimination. In these circumstances, we find it intolerable that one constitutional right should have to be surrendered in order to assert another. We therefore hold that when a defendant testifies in support of a motion to suppress evidence on Fourth Amendment grounds, his testimony may not thereafter be admitted against him at trial on the issue of guilt unless he makes no objection.[98]

Several courts have applied this reasoning to transfer hearings: "[C]andid testimony by the juvenile at the fitness hearing should be encouraged to aid in the determination of where best to try the minor; fairness to the minor requires that this testimony not be given at the expense of the privilege against self-incrimination."[99] Accordingly, statements made at a transfer hearing have been held inadmissible at subsequent criminal trials[100] and adjudicatory hearings.[101]

(G) Access to reports

Juvenile Rule 32(C) provides for the right to inspect a social history or report of a mental or physical examination a reasonable time prior to the transfer hearing. The United States Supreme Court in *Kent* held that counsel had a right of access to social service records. The Court left no doubt that the right of

---

[95]Lefkowitz v Turley, 414 US 70, 77, 94 SCt 316, 38 LEd(2d) 274 (1973).

[96]Griffin v California, 380 US 609, 85 SCt 1229, 14 LEd(2d) 106 (1965). See also United States v Robinson, ___ US ___, 108 SCt 864, ___ LEd(2d) ___ (1988) (not a Fifth Amendment violation to comment on an accused's silence in response to defense counsel's tactics); In re Jackson, 21 OS(2d) 215, 257 NE(2d) 74 (1970) (no *Griffin* violation found).

[97]Simmons v United States, 390 US 377, 88 SCt 967, 19 LEd(2d) 1247 (1968).

[98]*Id.* at 394.

[99]Sheila O. v Superior Court, 125 Cal App(3d) 812, 816, 178 Cal Rptr 418 (1981).

[100]Ramona R. v Superior Court, 37 Cal(3d) 802, 693 P(2d) 789, 210 Cal Rptr 204 (1985); Bryan v Superior Court, 7 Cal(3d) 575, 498 P(2d) 1079, 102 Cal Rptr 831 (1972), cert denied 410 US 944, 93 SCt 1380, 35 LEd(2d) 610 (1973); Commonwealth v Ransom, 446 Pa 457, 288 A(2d) 762 (1972).

[101]Ramona R. v Superior Court, 37 Cal(3d) 802, 693 P(2d) 789, 210 Cal Rptr 204 (1985); Sheila O. v Superior Court, 125 Cal App(3d) 812, 178 Cal Rptr 418 (1981) (except for impeachment). See also *IJA-ABA Standards Relating to Transfer Between Courts* 50-51 (1980).

inspection was intended to permit counsel to challenge the accuracy of these reports:

> [I]f the staff's submissions include materials which are susceptible to challenge or impeachment, it is precisely the role of counsel to "denigrate" such matter. There is no irrebuttable presumption of accuracy attached to staff reports. If a decision on waiver is "critically important" it is equally of "critical importance" that the material submitted to the judge ... be subjected ... to examination, criticism and refutation. While the Juvenile Court judge may, of course, receive *ex parte* analyses and recommendations from his staff, he may not, for the purposes of a decision on waiver, receive and rely upon secret information, whether emanating from his staff or otherwise.[102]

Juvenile Rule 32(C) grants the court authority to deny or limit inspection for good cause. The court may also order that the contents of the report be withheld from specified persons. The court, however, must state reasons for its action.

(H) Right to present evidence

Although the Juvenile Rules do not specifically recognize a child's right to present evidence at a transfer hearing, there seems little question that this right exists.[103] The right to counsel, the right to notice,[104] and the right of access to the social history all imply a right to present evidence. In a different context, the United States Supreme Court has commented, "Ordinarily, the right to present evidence is basic to a fair hearing."[105] The Ohio Supreme Court has implicitly recognized this right. In one case the court commented on a defense counsel's failure to make any effort to call witnesses at a transfer hearing.[106]

(I) Statement of reasons

RC 2151.26(F) and Juvenile Rule 30(G) require the court to state reasons if it decides to transfer the child. The United States Supreme Court in *Kent* also required a statement of the reasons:

> Meaningful review requires that the reviewing court should review. It should not be remitted to assumptions. It must have before it a statement of the reasons motivating the waiver including, of course, a statement of the relevant facts. It may not "assume" that there are adequate reasons, nor may it merely assume that "full investigation" has been made. Accordingly, we hold that it is incumbent upon the Juvenile Court to accompany its waiver order with a statement of the reasons or considerations therefor. We do not read the statute as requiring that this statement must be formal or that it should necessarily include conventional findings of fact. But the statement should be sufficient to demonstrate that the statutory requirement of "full investigation" has been met; and that the question has received the careful

---

[102]Kent v United States, 383 US 541, 563, 86 SCt 1045, 16 LEd(2d) 84 (1966).

[103]See Summers v State, 248 Ind 551, 230 NE(2d) 320 (1967); In re Brown, 183 NW(2d) 731 (Iowa 1971); In re Doe, 86 NM 37, 519 P(2d) 133 (1974).

[104]See Wolff v McDonnell, 418 US 539, 564, 94 SCt 2963, 41 LEd(2d) 935 (1974) (Prison disciplinary hearings: "Part of the function of notice is to give the charged party a chance to marshal the facts in his defense.").

[105]*Id.* at 566.

[106]See State v Carmichael, 35 OS(2d) 1, 298 NE(2d) 568 (1973), cert denied 414 US 1161, 94 SCt 922, 39 LEd(2d) 113 (1974). See also State v Yoss, 10 App(2d) 47, 225 NE(2d) 275 (Carroll 1967) (*Kent* requires the juvenile court to consider additional evidence offered by a child in a transfer hearing.).

consideration of the Juvenile Court; and it must set forth the basis for the order with sufficient specificity to permit meaningful review.[107]

In *State v Oviedo*[108] the court held that Juvenile Rule 30(G) is satisfied if the transfer order demonstrates that the "full investigation" requirement has been met and the issue has received the full attention of the court. In contrast, the court in *State v Newton*[109] required more:

> Mere recitation of the conclusory language set forth in Juv. R. 30(C)(1) and (2) is *not* sufficient. Conclusions are not reasons, as contemplated by Juv. R. 30(G). The "reasonable grounds" for the court's belief that a juvenile is not amenable to rehabilitation and that the community's safety may require his legal restraint must be spelled out with reasonable specificity. Stated differently, Juv. R. 30(G) necessitates findings of fact from which to determine the prerequisites in Juv. R. 30(C)(1) and (2) and upon which to base the transfer order.[110]

The Ohio Supreme Court has written:

> Neither R.C. 2151.25 nor Juv. R. 30 requires the juvenile court to make written findings as to the five factors listed in Juv. R. 30(E). The rule simply requires the court to *consider* these factors in making its determination on the amenability issue. Although the better practice would be to address each factor, as long as sufficient, credible evidence pertaining to each factor exists in the record before the court, the bind-over order should not be reversed in the absence of an abuse of discretion.[111]

The Court also stated that Juvenile Rule 30(G) "does not require written findings on each of the five factors listed in Juv. R. 30(E)."[112]

Courts in other jurisdictions have insisted on specific reasons for transfer.[113]

(J) Right to a transcript

Juvenile Rule 37(A) provides for the right to a complete record of all juvenile court hearings upon request. Moreover, one Ohio court, citing due process and equal protection grounds, has held that an indigent child has a right to a transcript in transfer proceedings.[114] The importance of a transcript is illustrated by *State v Riggins*,[115] in which the appellate court overruled an alleged error at a transfer hearing because the "appellant has failed to provide this court

---

[107]Kent v United States, 383 US 541, 561, 86 SCt 1045, 16 LEd(2d) 84 (1966).

[108]State v Oviedo, 5 App(3d) 168, 5 OBR 351, 450 NE(2d) 700 (Wood 1982).

[109]State v Newton, No. F-82-17 (6th Dist Ct App, Fulton, 6-10-83).

[110]*Id.* at 7 (emphasis by the court). See also State v Reuss, No. WD-81-26 (6th Dist Ct App, Wood, 8-7-81) (Bare recitation of factors in Juv R 30(E) is insufficient.).

[111]State v Douglas, 20 OS(3d) 34, 36, 20 OBR 282, 485 NE(2d) 711 (1985).

[112]*Id.* at 36 n.2.

[113]See Summers v State, 248 Ind 551, 230 NE(2d) 320 (1967); Risner v Commonwealth, 508 SW(2d) 775 (Ky 1974); In re Heising, 29 Or App 903, 565 P(2d) 1105 (1977); Knott v Langlois, 102 RI 517, 231 A(2d) 767 (1967). See also *IJA-ABA Standards Relating to Transfer Between Courts* 33-34 (1980).

[114]State v Ross, 23 App(2d) 215, 262 NE(2d) 427 (Greene 1970). See also State v Harris, No. 81AP-299 (10th Dist Ct App, Franklin, 10-6-81) (No due process violation for failure to provide a transcript where defendant did not attempt to use procedure provided in App R 9(C) for a statement of the evidence or proceedings when no transcript is available.).

[115]State v Riggins, 68 App(2d) 1, 426 NE(2d) 504 (Cuyahoga 1980).

with a transcript of the hearing before the Juvenile Court at which this evidence was presented."[116]

(K) Exclusion of the public

Juvenile Rule 27 and RC 2151.35 provide for the exclusion of the general public from juvenile court hearings; only persons with a direct interest in the case may attend. However, in *State ex rel Fyffe v Pierce*[117] the Supreme Court refused to issue a writ of prohibition to close a transfer hearing. The Court pointed out that both the rule and the statute make closure discretionary: "The word 'may' is clearly not mandatory; therefore, the court was not required to close the hearing, but could exercise its discretion."[118] Moreover, the Court found an adequate remedy at law. According to the Court, "If tried as adults, they can move for change of venue to alleviate any unfairness that pretrial publicity may cause. If change of venue is denied, and relators are subsequently convicted, they can appeal."[119]

CROSS REFERENCES

Text 1.02(A), (B), 11.11, 11.12, 15.02(F), 15.04

9.04   Post-transfer issues

(A) Retention of jurisdiction

If the juvenile court decides to retain jurisdiction, it must schedule a hearing on the merits.[120] One court has stated that a juvenile judge is not disqualified from presiding at an adjudicatory hearing because of his involvement in a prior transfer hearing.[121] In contrast, the IJA-ABA Standards recognize a child's right to disqualify the transfer hearing judge from participating in subsequent proceedings: "No matter how fair the waiver judge may be in subsequent proceedings, an impression of unfairness will exist."[122]

(B) Transfer of jurisdiction

If the juvenile court decides to transfer jurisdiction, it will set the terms and conditions for release of the child in accordance with Criminal Rule 46.[123] If the child is in detention, he may be transferred to the appropriate officer or detention facility in accordance with the law governing the detention of adults.[124] The

---

[116]*Id.* at 8. See also Bailey and Rothblatt, *Handling Juvenile Delinquency Cases* 183 (1982) ("Insist that the proceedings be transcribed.").

[117]State ex rel Fyffe v Pierce, 40 OS(3d) 8, ___ NE(2d) ___ (1988).

[118]*Id.* at 9.

[119]*Id.*

[120]Juv R 30(D).

[121]In re Terry H., 1 OBR 377 (CP, Cuyahoga 1982). See also Text 11.09, Impartial judge.

[122]*IJA-ABA Standards Relating to Transfer Between Courts* 49 (1980). See also Donald L. v Superior Court of Los Angeles County, 7 Cal(3d) 592, 598, 498 P(2d) 1098, 102 Cal Rptr 850 (1972) ("[I]f the referee or judge who hears the issue of fitness decides that the minor should be retained in the juvenile court, he may not thereafter properly preside at a contested hearing on the issue of jurisdiction.").

[123]Juv R 30(H). For a discussion of Crim R 46, see 2 Schroeder-Katz, *Ohio Criminal Law and Practice*, 2 vols (1974-1987).

[124]RC 2151.312(A).

criminal court to which jurisdiction has been transferred may not "review the factual findings of the juvenile court on the issue of amenability."[125]

RC 2151.26(F) provides that "transfer abates the jurisdiction of the juvenile court with respect to the delinquent acts alleged in the complaint." This provision appears to require that the juvenile court transfer jurisdiction over *all* delinquent acts before these acts can be prosecuted in the criminal courts. In *State v Adams*,[126] however, the Ohio Supreme Court ruled otherwise. According to the court, once a child is properly transferred, he is considered bound over for all felonies, even if the other felonies have not been subject to transfer proceedings. Moreover, once transferred, a child may be tried in the criminal courts for any subsequent felonies that he has committed.[127] RC 2151.26(G) now provides that once transferred and convicted, a child is automatically subject to criminal court jurisdiction for subsequent charges of aggravated murder, murder, an aggravated felony of the first or second degree, or felonies of the first or second degree. This provision was not applicable at the time the child in *Adams* was transferred.[128]

Once a child is transferred, a grand jury may indict for any offense appropriate under the facts; the grand jury is not limited to the charges filed in juvenile court.[129] Moreover, a criminal defendant's statutory right to a speedy trial does not commence until the juvenile court relinquishes jurisdiction.[130] In addition, a defendant is entitled to good time credit for the time spent in juvenile custody.[131] By pleading guilty in criminal court, a defendant does not waive the right to contest the validity of the transfer decision.[132]

CROSS REFERENCES

Text 11.09, 15.01

9.05   Appeals

In Ohio a juvenile court order transferring jurisdiction to the criminal courts is not a final appealable order.[133] Thus, a transfer order may be challenged on appeal only after trial and conviction in the criminal courts. Similarly, a writ of

---

[125]State v Whiteside, 6 App(3d) 30, 36, 6 OBR 140, 452 NE(2d) 332 (Allen 1982).

[126]State v Adams, 69 OS(2d) 120, 431 NE(2d) 326 (1982).

[127]*Id.*

[128]*Id.* at 126-27 n.3.

[129]*Id.* (A grand jury does not exceed its authority by returning indictments on charges that were not originally filed in juvenile court.); State v Klingenberger, 113 OS 418, 149 NE 395 (1925).

[130]State v Bickerstaff, 10 OS(3d) 62, 67, 10 OBR 352, 461 NE(2d) 892 (1984); State ex rel Williams v Court of Common Pleas, 42 OS(2d) 433, 329 NE(2d) 680 (1975); State v Steele, 8 App(3d) 137, 8 OBR 194, 456 NE(2d) 513 (Franklin 1982); State v Trapp, 52 App(2d) 189, 368 NE(2d) 1278 (Hamilton 1977); State v Young, 44 App(2d) 387, 339 NE(2d) 668 (Franklin 1975).

[131]State v Young, 44 App(2d) 387, 339 NE(2d) 668 (Franklin 1975).

[132]State v Riggins, 68 App(2d) 1, 426 NE(2d) 504 (Cuyahoga 1980).

[133]In re Becker, 39 OS(2d) 84, 314 NE(2d) 158 (1974). Accord State ex rel Torres v Simmons, 68 OS(2d) 118, 428 NE(2d) 862 (1981); State v Whiteside, 6 App(3d) 30, 6 OBR 140, 452 NE(2d) 332 (Allen 1982). See generally Comment, *Juvenile Court and Direct Appeal from Waiver of Jurisdiction in Ohio*, 8 Akron L Rev 499 (1975). For a further discussion of appeals, see Text 15.02, Appeals.

prohibition may not be used to challenge a transfer order.[134] Although a number of jurisdictions permit appeals of transfer orders, the Ohio rule appears to be the majority rule.[135]

The Ohio Supreme Court has provided the following reasons for its position:

> To permit interlocutory review of such an order would obviously delay the prosecution of any proceeding in either the juvenile or the criminal division, with the result that the prospect of a just disposition would be jeopardized. In either proceeding the primary issue is the ascertainment of the innocence or guilt of the person charged. To permit interlocutory review would subordinate that primary issue and defer its consideration while the question of the punishment appropriate for a suspect whose guilt has not yet been ascertained is being litigated in reviewing courts. We are unwilling to sanction such a procedure.[136]

There is, however, a serious disadvantage to this rule. The time consumed during the prosecution of the case in criminal court and during the appellate process may place the defendant beyond the age jurisdiction of the juvenile court. In this event, an appellate court that finds error in a transfer proceeding must either free the improperly transferred individual, because neither juvenile nor criminal court has jurisdiction, or reconstruct the transfer process to determine whether a hearing free from error would have resulted in transfer.[137] The *Kent* case illustrates this problem. By the time the United States Supreme Court reversed Morris Kent's conviction, he was over twenty-one years of age and thus no longer subject to juvenile court jurisdiction. The Court remanded the case to the district court for a de novo consideration of the transfer issue, i.e., a reconstructed waiver hearing.[138] The difficulty with this procedure is that the reconstructed hearing must "attempt to imagine" the child as he was at the time of the original transfer hearing.[139]

CROSS REFERENCES

Text 15.02

9.06   Double jeopardy

In *Breed v Jones*[140] the United States Supreme Court reviewed a California procedure that permitted transfer *after* a child had been found delinquent in an

---

[134]State ex rel Torres v Simmons, 68 OS(2d) 118, 428 NE(2d) 862 (1981).

[135]See *IJA-ABA Standards Relating to Transfer Between Courts* 53 (1980).

[136]In re Becker, 39 OS(2d) 84, 86, 314 NE(2d) 158 (1974), quoting People v Jiles, 43 Ill(2d) 145, 150, 251 NE(2d) 529 (1969).

[137]*IJA-ABA Standards Relating to Transfer Between Courts* 53 (1980).

[138]Kent v United States, 383 US 541, 86 SCt 1045, 16 LEd(2d) 84 (1966). On appeal after remand, the DC Circuit held that Kent had been improperly transferred. See Kent v United States, 401 F(2d) 408 (DC Cir 1968). For other cases requiring a reconstructed waiver hearing, see United States ex rel Turner v Rundle, 438 F(2d) 839 (3d Cir Pa 1971); Kemplen v Maryland, 428 F(2d) 169 (4th Cir Md 1970).

[139]*IJA-ABA Standards Relating to Transfer Between Courts* 53 (1980).

[140]Breed v Jones, 421 US 519, 95 SCt 1779, 44 LEd(2d) 346 (1975).

adjudicatory hearing.[141] The Court held that this procedure violated the Double Jeopardy Clause:[142]

> We believe it is simply too late in the day to conclude . . . that a juvenile is not put in jeopardy at a proceeding whose object is to determine whether he has committed acts that violate a criminal law and whose potential consequences include both the stigma inherent in such a determination and the deprivation of liberty for many years.[143]

In a footnote, however, the Court distinguished the California procedure from a transfer procedure requiring only a finding of probable cause:

> We note that nothing decided today forecloses States from requiring, as a prerequisite to the transfer of a juvenile, substantial evidence that he committed the offense charged, so long as the showing required is not made in an adjudicatory proceeding. . . . The instant case is not one in which the judicial determination was simply a finding of, e.g., probable cause. Rather, it was an adjudication that respondent had violated a criminal statute.[144]

In *Sims v Engle*[145] the Sixth Circuit held that the Ohio procedure operative in that case suffered from the same deficiencies that marked the California procedure in *Breed.* Under that procedure a juvenile court was required to make a delinquency finding prior to transfer.[146] According to the Sixth Circuit, this procedure violated the double jeopardy guarantee:

> Once the Juvenile Court, possessing the jurisdiction and power to enter final orders levying a wide range of possible sanctions, began a hearing, not limited in scope by statute to a preliminary hearing or probable cause hearing, jeopardy attached and appellant possessed the constitutional right to have the Juvenile Court, as the original trier of fact, determine his fate.[147]

----

[141]Several courts have held *Breed* retroactive. See Rios v Chavez, 620 F(2d) 702 (9th Cir Cal 1980); Holt v Black, 550 F(2d) 1061 (6th Cir Ky 1977), cert denied 432 US 910, 97 SCt 2960, 53 LEd(2d) 1084 (1977); Brenson v Havener, 403 FSupp 221 (ND Ohio 1975); In re Bryan, 16 Cal(3d) 782, 548 P(2d) 693, 129 Cal Rptr 293 (1976); State v Turner, No. 39951 (8th Dist Ct App, Cuyahoga, 5-3-79).

Other courts have disagreed. See Jackson v Justices of Superior Court, 549 F(2d) 215 (1st Cir Mass 1977), cert denied 430 US 975, 97 SCt 1666, 52 LEd(2d) 370 (1977); Moore v State, 409 NE(2d) 1181 (Ind App 1980); State v Knowles, 371 A(2d) 624 (Me 1977); Stokes v Commonwealth, 368 Mass 754, 336 NE(2d) 735 (1975).

[142]US Const Am 5 ("[N]or shall any person be subject for the same offence to be twice put in jeopardy of life or limb."). For a further discussion of double jeopardy, see Text 11.15, Double jeopardy.

[143]Breed v Jones, 421 US 519, 529, 95 SCt 1779, 44 LEd(2d) 346 (1975).

[144]*Id.* at 538 n.18.

[145]Sims v Engle, 619 F(2d) 598 (6th Cir 1980), cert denied 450 US 936, 101 SCt 1403, 67 LEd(2d) 372 (1981). Accord State v Turner, No. 39951 (8th Dist Ct App, Cuyahoga, 5-3-79).

[146]See State v Carter, 27 OS(2d) 135, 272 NE(2d) 119 (1971); In re Jackson, 21 OS(2d) 215, 257 NE(2d) 74 (1970).

[147]Sims v Engle, 619 F(2d) 598, 605 (6th Cir 1980), cert denied 450 US 936, 101 SCt 1403, 67 LEd(2d) 372 (1981). See also Johnson v Perini, 644 F(2d) 573 (6th Cir 1981) (*Sims* does not apply if the record plainly establishes that the transfer hearing was limited to a probable cause determination.).

In Du Bose v Court of Common Pleas, 64 OS(2d) 169, 413 NE(2d) 1205 (1980), the court held that the refusal to grant a motion to dismiss on double jeopardy grounds is appealable and thus not subject to a writ of prohibition. The double jeopardy grounds asserted were based on *Breed.*

The statute that the Sixth Circuit found constitutionally defective in *Sims* has since been amended. Unlike the former procedure, the present transfer procedure requires only a finding of probable cause and not a determination of delinquency. The Sixth Circuit has upheld the constitutionality of this procedure: "We reject the contention that the introduction of evidence of probable cause to believe appellant committed the alleged offense without more, transformed the hearing into an adjudicatory proceeding."[148]

CROSS REFERENCES

Text 9.06, 11.15

---

[148]Keener v Taylor, 640 F(2d) 839, 841-42 (6th Cir 1981). Accord State v Salmon, Nos. 43328, 43329 (8th Dist Ct App, Cuyahoga, 5-21-81).

Chapter 11

Adjudicatory Hearings

11.01 In general

The adjudicatory hearing is the fact-determining stage in juvenile cases.[1] It is analogous to the trial in a criminal or civil case. The party with the burden of persuasion is required at this stage to introduce sufficient evidence to sustain its burden of persuasion on the issues before the court—for example, establishing that the child is delinquent, neglected, or dependent. The opposing party, of course, has the right to challenge this evidence through cross-examination and the introduction of its own evidence. The adjudicatory hearing should be distinguished from the dispositional hearing, which is governed by Juvenile Rule 34.[2] Only after there has been an adjudication may the court consider matters relating to disposition.[3] For example, the Supreme Court has written:

> The law commands that the proceedings be bifurcated into separate adjudicatory and dispositional hearings because the issues raised and the procedures used at each hearing differ. The issue at the adjudicatory stage of a dependency case is whether petitioner has proven, by clear and convincing evidence, that the child is in fact dependent. The issue at the dispositional stage involves a determination of what is in the child's best interests. There must be strict adherence to the Rules of Evidence at the adjudicatory stage.

---

[1]Juv R 2(1) defines adjudicatory hearing as a "hearing to determine whether a child is a juvenile traffic offender, delinquent, unruly, neglected, or dependent or is otherwise within the jurisdiction of the court or whether temporary legal custody should be converted to permanent custody."

[2]For a discussion of the dispositional hearing, see Text Ch 13, Disposition of Children's Cases.

[3]Juv R 34 expressly recognizes the distinction between the adjudicatory and dispositional hearings. Juv R 34(A) reads, "The dispositional hearing may be held immediately following the adjudicatory hearing or at a later time fixed by the court." Similarly, Juv R 29 also recognizes the distinction. Juv R 29(F)(2) grants the court several options if the allegations in the complaint are either admitted or proved: The court may (1) enter an adjudication and proceed to disposition, (2) enter an adjudication and continue the matter for disposition for not more than six months, (3) postpone judgment or adjudication for not more than six months, or (4) dismiss the complaint if such action is in the best interests of the child and the community.

Yet, "any evidence that is material and relevant, including hearsay, opinion and documentary evidence," is admissible at the dispositional stage. Juv. R. 34(B)(2).[4]

In Ohio, RC 2151.35 and Juvenile Rule 29 generally govern procedures in adjudicatory hearings. These procedures must comply with due process requirements. In *In re Gault*[5] the United States Supreme Court for the first time held that due process safeguards applied to juvenile adjudicatory hearings. Specifically, the Court held that the right to notice, right to counsel, right of confrontation, and the privilege against compelled self-incrimination applied in delinquency hearings. In subsequent cases, the Court held that the constitutional standard of proof in criminal cases (proof beyond a reasonable doubt)[6] and the Double Jeopardy Clause[7] also applied to delinquency cases. The Court, however, refused to extend the right to jury trial to juvenile cases.[8]

In addition, the United States Supreme Court has considered the due process rights applicable to neglect cases in which the permanent termination of parental rights is at issue. It has held that an indigent parent has the right to appointed counsel under some circumstances[9] and that the state must introduce "clear and convincing" proof before parental rights may be terminated.[10]

Which due process rights the Court would extend to other types of juvenile cases is uncertain. Some lower courts have found the *Gault* rationale applicable to nondelinquency cases. For example, one court has commented, "While an adjudication of unruliness ... is not based upon a finding that the accused committed a crime, we believe it still carries a significant degree of stigmatization, which, when taken together with the possible loss of liberty, mandates application of constitutional safeguards."[11]

CROSS REFERENCES

Text 1.02(B), 11.03, 11.07, 11.10, 11.15, Ch 13

---

[4]In re Baby Girl Baxter, 17 OS(3d) 229, 233, 17 OBR 469, 479 NE(2d) 257 (1985). See also In re Cunningham, 59 OS(2d) 100, 396 NE(2d) 1035 (1979) (emphasizing the differences between the adjudicatory and dispositional stages); In re Pitts, 38 App(3d) 1, 4, 525 NE(2d) 814 (Knox 1987) ("[T]he trial court erred in considering dispositional matters and issues at the adjudication phase."); Elmer v Lucas County Children Serv Bd, 36 App(3d) 241, 246, 523 NE(2d) 540 (Lucas 1987) ("If a hearing is held which is to cover both the adjudicatory and dispositional phases of the proceeding, the court must bifurcate the proceedings into two distinct phases in order to accommodate the different standards of proof.").
For a discussion of this issue, see Text 13.02, Bifurcated hearings.
[5]In re Gault, 387 US 1, 87 SCt 1428, 18 LEd(2d) 527 (1967). For a further discussion of *Gault*, see Text 1.02(B), In re Gault.
[6]In re Winship, 397 US 358, 90 SCt 1068, 25 LEd(2d) 368 (1970). See Text 11.10, Burden of proof.
[7]Illinois v Vitale, 447 US 410, 100 SCt 2260, 65 LEd(2d) 228 (1980); Swisher v Brady, 438 US 204, 98 SCt 2699, 57 LEd(2d) 705 (1978); Breed v Jones, 421 US 519, 95 SCt 1779, 44 LEd(2d) 346 (1975). See Text 11.15, Double jeopardy.
[8]McKeiver v Pennsylvania, 403 US 528, 91 SCt 1976, 29 LEd(2d) 647 (1971). See Text 11.07, Jury trials.
[9]Lassiter v Department of Social Services, 452 US 18, 101 SCt 2153, 68 LEd(2d) 640 (1981). See Text 11.03, Right to counsel, guardian ad litem.
[10]Santosky v Kramer, 455 US 745, 102 SCt 1388, 71 LEd(2d) 599 (1982). See Text 11.10, Burden of proof.
[11]Smith v Grossmann, 6 OBR 83, 88 (SD Ohio 1982).

Merrick-Rippner, Ohio Probate Law (4th ed), Text Ch 223

11.02   Speedy trial

Juvenile Rule 29(A) provides that the adjudicatory hearing for a child in detention or shelter care must be held within ten days of the filing of the complaint.[12] The hearing, however, may be continued upon a showing of good cause. Juvenile Rule 29(A) does not specify a remedy for a violation of the ten-day rule and the cases are in conflict. In *In re Therklidsen*[13] the court held that dismissal was not an appropriate remedy. "In the absence of a specific statutory provision for a discharge constituting a bar to further prosecution, a provision requiring a trial within a certain period of time does not entitle the defendant to discharge."[14] In contrast, the court in *State v Newton*[15] held that Juvenile Rule 29(A)'s time limits were mandatory and that the proper remedy was dismissal without prejudice.[16]

RC 2945.71(C) provides a statutory right to a speedy trial in criminal prosecutions. That section, however, applies only to a "person against whom a charge of felony is pending." Based on this language, the Ohio Supreme Court has ruled the statute inapplicable to juveniles cases. According to the court, the statute applies "only if and when the Juvenile Court relinquishes jurisdiction over the case and transfers it to the appropriate 'adult' court."[17]

In adult cases the Sixth Amendment guarantees the right to a speedy trial in criminal prosecutions.[18] The United States Supreme Court has held that four factors are relevant in determining whether this right has been violated: (1) the length of the delay, (2) the reason for the delay, (3) whether and when the defendant asserted the right to a speedy trial, and (4) whether the defendant has

---

[12]See also RC 2151.28(A)(1). In Linger v Weiss, 57 OS(2d) 97, 386 NE(2d) 1354 (1979), cert denied 444 US 862, 100 SCt 128, 62 LEd(2d) 83 (1979), the Ohio Supreme Court held that a juvenile court does not lose jurisdiction by failing to adhere to the time limits of Juv R 29(A).

[13]In re Therklidsen, 54 App(2d) 195, 376 NE(2d) 970 (Franklin 1977).

[14]*Id.* at 199.

[15]State v Newton, No. F-82-17 (6th Dist Ct App, Fulton, 6-10-83).

[16]See Text 7.06(D), Time restrictions.

[17]State ex rel Williams v Court of Common Pleas, 42 OS(2d) 433, 435, 329 NE(2d) 680 (1975). Accord State v Bickerstaff, 10 OS(3d) 62, 67, 10 OBR 352, 461 NE(2d) 892 (1984). See also State v Reed, 54 App(2d) 193, 194, 376 NE(2d) 609 (Coshocton 1977) ("[T]he statutory speedy trial provisions for adults in Ohio do not apply to juveniles."); In re T.L.K., 2 OO(3d) 324 (CP, Ross 1976) (Juv R 29 controls over statute.).

Other courts have also held that the statute is triggered only after juvenile court jurisdiction has been transferred to the criminal courts. State v Steele, 8 App(3d) 137, 8 OBR 194, 456 NE(2d) 513 (Franklin 1982); State v Trapp, 52 App(2d) 189, 368 NE(2d) 1278 (Hamilton 1977); State v Young, 44 App(2d) 387, 339 NE(2d) 668 (Franklin 1975).

See also State v Robinson, No. 45854 (8th Dist Ct App, Cuyahoga, 8-4-83) (Right to speedy trial commences on date court makes pronouncement of transfer and not date the entry is journalized.).

[18]US Const Am 6 ("In all criminal prosecutions, the accused shall enjoy the right to a speedy and public trial."). The right to a speedy trial applies to state trials. Klopfer v North Carolina, 386 US 213, 87 SCt 988, 18 LEd(2d) 1 (1967). See generally 2 LaFave and Israel, *Criminal Procedure* ch 18 (1984); Whitebread and Slobogin, *Criminal Procedure* ch 25 (2d ed 1986).

The Ohio Constitution also guarantees the right to a speedy trial (O Const Art I, § 10).

suffered actual prejudice from the delay.[19] The sole remedy for a denial of the constitutional right to a speedy trial is dismissal.[20] Courts in other jurisdictions have held that the constitutional right to a speedy trial applies to delinquency cases.[21] Although the Ohio Supreme Court has not yet addressed this issue,[22] one Ohio court has commented, "With respect to the constitutional right to a speedy trial, the rationale and progeny of *In re Gault* ... suggests there is no distinction between adults and juveniles."[23]

RC 2151.28(A)(2) requires an adjudicatory hearing to be held within thirty days of the filing of a complaint in abuse, neglect, and dependency cases. The hearing may be continued for ten days to allow a party to obtain counsel or for thirty days to allow for service on all parties and any necessary evaluation.

CROSS REFERENCES

Text 7.06(D)

11.03   Right to counsel, guardian ad litem

Juvenile Rule 4(A) and RC 2151.352 guarantee the right to counsel for all parties in juvenile court proceedings. Juvenile Rule 15(B)(3) and RC 2151.28(F) require the summons to include a statement informing the parties of the right to counsel. Similarly, Juvenile Rule 29(B)(3) requires the juvenile court judge to inform unrepresented parties of the right to counsel at the commencement of the adjudicatory hearing. In *Gault* the United States Supreme Court commented on the importance of counsel:

> The juvenile needs the assistance of counsel to cope with problems of law, to make skilled inquiry into the facts, to insist upon regularity of the proceedings, and to ascertain whether he has a defense and to prepare and submit it. The child "requires the guiding hand of counsel at every step in the proceedings against him."[24]

---

[19]Barker v Wingo, 407 US 514, 92 SCt 2182, 33 LEd(2d) 101 (1972).

[20]Strunk v United States, 412 US 434, 93 SCt 2260, 37 LEd(2d) 56 (1973).

[21]See R.D.S.M. v Intake Officer, 565 P(2d) 855 (Alaska 1977); J.B.H. v State, 139 Ga App 199, 228 SE(2d) 189 (1976); In re F., 316 NW(2d) 865 (Iowa 1982); In re T., 159 NJ Super 104, 387 A(2d) 368 (App Div 1978); State v Henry, 78 NM 573, 434 P(2d) 692 (1967); In re Anthony P., 104 NY Misc(2d) 1024, 430 NYS(2d) 479 (Fam Ct 1980); Piland v Clark County Juvenile Court Services, 85 Nev 489, 457 P(2d) 523 (1969).

[22]State ex rel Williams v Court of Common Pleas, 42 OS(2d) 433, 435 n.4, 329 NE(2d) 680 (1975).

[23]State v Reed, 54 App(2d) 193, 194, 376 NE(2d) 609 (Coshocton 1977). See also In re Hester, 3 App(3d) 458, 3 OBR 539, 446 NE(2d) 202 (Franklin 1982).

[24]In re Gault, 387 US 1, 36, 87 SCt 1428, 18 LEd(2d) 527 (1967). As the Ohio Supreme Court recognized in In re Agler, 19 OS(2d) 70, 249 NE(2d) 808 (1969), *Gault* overruled prior Ohio cases that held the right to counsel inapplicable to adjudicatory delinquency proceedings. E.g., Cope v Campbell, 175 OS 475, 196 NE(2d) 457 (1964), overruled by In re Agler, 19 OS(2d) 70, 249 NE(2d) 808 (1969).

Juvenile Rule 4(A) also provides that in the case of indigency[25] a party has the right to appointed counsel.[26] Similarly, Juvenile Rule 29(B)(4) requires the court at the adjudicatory hearing to appoint counsel for an indigent party, unless the right to counsel is waived. RC 2151.352 contains a similar but not identical provision; it requires the appointment of counsel pursuant to RC Chapter 120, which governs representation by public defenders.[27] These provisions go beyond federal constitutional requirements.[28] Although the Supreme Court in *Gault* recognized that a child and his parents had the right to appointed counsel if they could not afford counsel,[29] the *Gault* decision applied only to delinquency cases. In *Lassiter v Department of Social Services*[30] the Court held that in some cases due process requires the appointment of counsel for indigent parents where the permanent termination of parental rights is at issue.[31] According to the Court, whether counsel's appointment is constitutionally required must be decided on a case-by-case basis. The Court has yet to decide whether

---

[25]Juv R 2(12) defines an "indigent person" as "a person who, at the time his need is determined, is unable by reason of lack of property or income to provide for full payment of legal counsel and all other necessary expenses of representation."

[26]See RC 2151.352. See also In re Rushing, No. 1518 (4th Dist Ct App, Lawrence, 11-12-81) (RC 2151.352 imposes a mandatory duty upon the trial court to ascertain whether a party is indigent.).

See generally *IJA-ABA Standards Relating to Counsel for Private Parties* (1980); Right of juvenile court defendant to be represented during court proceedings by parent, 11 ALR4th 719 (1982); Right of indigent parent to appointed counsel in proceeding for involuntary termination of parental rights, 80 ALR3d 1141 (1977); Right to and appointment of counsel in juvenile court proceedings, 60 ALR2d 691 (1958).

The right to appointed counsel does not require the appointment of a particular attorney to represent an indigent party. See State ex rel Butler v Demis, 66 OS(2d) 123, 132-33, 420 NE(2d) 116 (1981) ("Pursuant to ... inherent power, a trial judge may decide not to appoint a particular attorney to represent an indigent party in a proceeding before the court."). See also In re Church, No. 1550 (4th Dist Ct App, Lawrence, 5-26-83) (Refusal to appoint counsel of party's choice without stating reasons was an abuse of discretion.).

[27]Pursuant to RC 2151.352, a child, his parents, custodian, or other person in loco parentis, if indigent, is entitled to be represented in all juvenile proceedings by a public defender in accordance with the comprehensive system set forth in RC Ch 120, regardless of whether the outcome of the proceeding could result in a loss of liberty (OAG 84-023).

[28]See In re Kriak, 30 App(3d) 83, 506 NE(2d) 556 (Medina 1986) (Indigent juvenile traffic offender's statutory, but not constitutional, right to counsel was violated.).

[29]In re Gault, 387 US 1, 87 SCt 1428, 18 LEd(2d) 527 (1967). See also McKeiver v Pennsylvania, 403 US 528, 532, 91 SCt 1976, 29 LEd(2d) 647 (1971) (Due process requires "right to counsel, retained or appointed."); In re Agler, 19 OS(2d) 70, 249 NE(2d) 808 (1969) (Constitutional fairness requires provision for counsel at state expense.).

[30]Lassiter v Department of Social Services, 452 US 18, 101 SCt 2153, 68 LEd(2d) 640 (1981).

[31]In State ex rel Heller v Miller, 61 OS(2d) 6, 399 NE(2d) 66 (1980), the Ohio Supreme Court held that both the United States and Ohio Constitutions guarantee the right to counsel on appeal to indigent parents in proceedings to permanently terminate parental rights. In In re Miller, 12 OS(3d) 40, 12 OBR 35, 465 NE(2d) 397 (1984), the court held that there is no constitutional right to counsel in temporary custody proceedings.

the right to counsel is required in other contexts, such as in status offense (unruly) cases.[32]

The right to counsel may be waived.[33] As indicated in *Gault*, the standard for waiving the right to counsel is stringent; there must be an " 'intentional relinquishment or abandonment' of a fully known right."[34] Juvenile Rule 29(B)(3) requires the court to inform the parties of their right to counsel at the beginning of an adjudicatory hearing and to determine whether they intend to waive this right. In discussing a court's responsibility in determining whether a waiver of the right to counsel is valid, the United States Supreme Court has written:

> To discharge this duty properly in light of the strong presumption against waiver of the constitutional right to counsel, a judge must investigate as long and as thoroughly as the circumstances of the case before him demand. The fact that an accused may tell him that he is informed of his right to counsel and desires to waive this right does not automatically end the judge's responsibility. To be valid such waiver must be made with an apprehension of the nature of the charges, the statutory offenses included within them, the range of allowable punishments thereunder, possible defenses to the charges and circumstances in mitigation thereof, and all other facts essential to a broad understanding of the whole matter. A judge can make certain that an accused's professed waiver of counsel is understandingly and wisely made only from a penetrating and comprehensive examination of all the circumstances under which such a plea is tendered.[35]

Some jurisdictions have taken the position that a child cannot waive the right to counsel without the advice of counsel,[36] and the IJA-ABA Standards do not permit the right to counsel to be waived.[37]

The right to counsel includes the right to the effective assistance of counsel.[38] Whether a criminal defendant has been denied this right is judged by a "reason-

---

[32]Compare In re Walker, 282 NC 28, 191 SE(2d) 702 (1972) (no constitutional right to counsel in status offense proceedings) with State ex rel Wilson v Bambrick, 156 W Va 703, 195 SE(2d) 721 (1973) (*Gault* requires right to counsel for juvenile arrested as a runaway.).

[33]See Faretta v California, 422 US 806, 95 SCt 2525, 45 LEd(2d) 562 (1975) (Defendant has a right to represent himself.).

See also In re Bolden, 37 App(2d) 7, 14, 306 NE(2d) 166 (Allen 1973):

> The law does not require continuances to be granted and trials postponed indefinitely until counsel is obtained. The record reveals that the parties were given a reasonable opportunity to obtain same and we find no error of the trial court in not granting a continuance and in proceeding with the trial under these circumstances.

[34]In re Gault, 387 US 1, 42, 87 SCt 1428, 18 LEd(2d) 527 (1967). See also Juv R 3 (waiver of rights).

[35]Von Moltke v Gillies, 332 US 708, 723-24, 68 SCt 316, 92 LEd 309 (1948). See also In re Wilson, No. 11-80-28 (3d Dist Ct App, Paulding, 11-12-81) (Waiver of counsel will not be presumed from a silent record.).

[36]State ex rel J.M. v Taylor, 276 SE(2d) 199 (W Va 1981).

[37]*IJA-ABA Standards Relating to Adjudication* 14 (1980).

[38]McMann v Richardson, 397 US 759, 771 n.14, 90 SCt 1441, 25 LEd(2d) 763 (1970) ("It has long been recognized that the right to counsel is the right to the effective assistance of counsel."). See generally 2 LaFave and Israel, *Criminal Procedure* ch 11 (1984); Whitebread and Slobogin, *Criminal Procedure* ch 31 (2d ed 1986).

See also Williams County Dept of Soc Services v Gilman, No. WMS-81-26 (6th Dist Ct App, Williams, 6-4-82) (RC 2151.352 and RC 2151.353(B) entitle party to effective assistance of counsel in neglect cases.).

ably effective assistance" standard. According to the United States Supreme Court, "When a convicted defendant complains of the ineffectiveness of counsel's assistance, the defendant must show that counsel's representation fell below an objective standard of reasonableness."[39] One type of ineffective assistance involves conflicts of interest.[40] RC 2151.352 provides that if the interests of two or more parties conflict, separate counsel shall be provided for each party. Similarly, Juvenile Rule 4(A) requires the appointment of counsel to represent the child in abuse cases. Moreover, as discussed later in this section, conflicts may arise because an attorney is functioning in dual roles—as counsel and as guardian ad litem.

Juvenile Rule 4(B) provides for the appointment of a guardian ad litem[41] to protect the interests of a child when (1) the child has no parent, guardian, or legal custodian; (2) the interests of the child and the parents may conflict; (3) the parent is under eighteen years of age or appears to be mentally incompetent; or (4) appointment is necessary to meet the requirements of a fair hearing. RC 2151.281 contains a comparable, but not identical, provision. It requires the appointment of a guardian ad litem in all abuse and neglect cases.[42] According to one court, the guardian ad litem for the child should be a person "who can serve uninhibited by any ties or loyalties with either the mother of [the child] or the proposed adoptive parents."[43]

Juvenile Rule 4(C) provides that a guardian ad litem who is an attorney may also serve as counsel. However, in *In re Baby Girl Baxter*,[44] the Supreme Court recognized that these two roles are not always compatible:

> The duty of a lawyer to his client and the duty of a guardian ad litem to his ward are not always identical and, in fact, may conflict. The role of guardian ad litem is to investigate the ward's situation and then to ask the court to do what the guardian feels is in the child's best interest. The role of the attorney is to zealously represent his client within the bounds of the law. . . .

---

[39]Strickland v Washington, 466 US 668, 687-88, 104 SCt 2052, 80 LEd(2d) 674 (1984).

[40]See Cuyler v Sullivan, 446 US 335, 100 SCt 1708, 65 LEd(2d) 333 (1980) (multiple representation); Holloway v Arkansas, 435 US 475, 98 SCt 1173, 55 LEd(2d) 426 (1978).

See also In re Appeal of a Juvenile, 61 App(2d) 235, 401 NE(2d) 937 (Lake 1978) (Juvenile court cannot deny representation by an attorney on the grounds that the attorney is an assistant law director of an adjoining county.).

[41]Juv R 2(10) defines guardian ad litem as a "person appointed to protect the interests of a party in a juvenile court proceeding."

[42]See In re Barzak, 24 App(3d) 180, 24 OBR 270, 493 NE(2d) 1011 (Trumbull 1985) (Appointment of a guardian ad litem is not required in dependency proceedings.); In re Height, 47 App(2d) 203, 353 NE(2d) 887 (Van Wert 1975) (Appointment of guardian ad litem is procedural, not jurisdictional.); In re Church, No. 1550 (4th Dist Ct App, Lawrence, 5-26-83) (Appointment of guardian ad litem is mandatory.); In re Strowbridge, No. 1574 (4th Dist Ct App, Lawrence, 10-25-82); In re Myer, No. 80-CA-10 (5th Dist Ct App, Delaware, 6-16-81).

See also Juv R 4(A) (requiring the appointment of an attorney to represent the child in abuse cases).

[43]In re Christopher, 54 App(2d) 137, 144, 376 NE(2d) 603 (Morrow 1977).

[44]In re Baby Girl Baxter, 17 OS(3d) 229, 17 OBR 469, 479 NE(2d) 257 (1985).

If the attorney feels there is a conflict between his role as attorney and his role as guardian, he should petition the court for an order allowing him to withdraw as guardian. The court should not hesitate to grant such request.[45]

CROSS REFERENCES

Text 15.02(F)

Schroeder-Katz, Ohio Criminal Law, Crim R 44, Author's Text
Merrick-Rippner, Ohio Probate Law (4th ed), Text Ch 223

11.04   Mental competency

Mental competency refers to a criminal defendant's mental condition at the time of trial and should be distinguished from insanity, which refers to the defendant's mental condition at the time of the crime. The United States Supreme Court has held that "the failure to observe procedures adequate to protect a defendant's right not to be tried or convicted while incompetent to stand trial deprives him of his due process right to a fair trial."[46] In federal trials, the test for competency is whether the defendant "has sufficient present ability to consult with his lawyer with a reasonable degree of rational under-standing—and whether he has a rational as well as factual understanding of the proceedings against him."[47]

In Ohio, RC 2945.37 governs the competency issue. Under this statute, a defendant is presumed competent to stand trial unless it is proved by a prepon-derance of the evidence that he is incapable of understanding the nature and objective of the proceedings which have been brought against him or of pres-ently assisting in his defense. This statute, however, applies only to a "criminal action." There is no comparable provision for juvenile cases. Nevertheless, Juvenile Rule 32(A) does provide that the court may order a mental examina-tion where a party's "competence to participate in the proceedings is an issue."

The few courts in other jurisdictions which have considered the issue have applied the competency requirements to juvenile proceedings. As one court has noted, "Since the right not to be tried while incompetent is a due process-fundamental fairness right . . . it should . . . be applicable to juvenile proceed-ings, unless some essential end of the juvenile justice system will be thwarted by its application."[48]

CROSS REFERENCES

Text 1.02(A), (B)

---

[45]*Id.* at 232. See also RC 2151.281(H).

[46]Drope v Missouri, 420 US 162, 172, 95 SCt 896, 43 LEd(2d) 103 (1975). See also Pate v Robinson, 383 US 375, 86 SCt 836, 15 LEd(2d) 815 (1966); State v Chapin, 67 OS(2d) 437, 424 NE(2d) 317 (1981); LaFave and Scott, *Criminal Law* § 4.4 (2d ed 1986).

[47]Dusky v United States, 362 US 402, 402, 80 SCt 788, 4 LEd(2d) 824 (1960).

[48]State in re Causey, 363 So(2d) 472, 476 (La 1978). See also State ex rel Dandoy v Superior Court of County of Pima, 127 Ariz 184, 619 P(2d) 12 (1980); In re Welfare of S.W.T., 277 NW(2d) 507 (Minn 1979); In re Jeffrey C., 81 NY Misc(2d) 651, 366 NYS(2d) 826 (Fam Ct 1975).

See also In re Atwell, Nos. 40667, 40719 (8th Dist Ct App, Cuyahoga, 1-17-80) (Mental competency of child considered.).

11.05   Pleas

Juvenile Rule 29(C) requires the parties to admit or deny the allegations in the complaint. Failure or refusal to admit the allegations constitutes a denial. Juvenile Rule 29(D) governs the procedures applicable if a party enters an admission.[49] If the party denies the allegations or the court does not accept an admission, the case is tried.

In contrast to Criminal Rule 11, Juvenile Rule 29 does not recognize a plea of "no contest."[50] In a criminal case, a plea of no contest does not waive a defendant's right to challenge a pretrial ruling on a motion to suppress evidence. Criminal Rule 12(H) provides that a "plea of no contest does not preclude a defendant from asserting upon appeal that the trial court prejudicially erred in ruling on a pretrial motion, including a pretrial motion to suppress evidence." There is no comparable provision in juvenile cases. Instead, Juvenile Rule 29(D)(2) provides that an admission waives a party's right to challenge the evidence against him.

CROSS REFERENCES

Text 11.06

Schroeder-Katz, Ohio Criminal Law, Crim R 11, Author's Text, Crim R 12, Author's Text

11.06   Uncontested cases

Before the court may accept an admission,[51] it must address the party and decide whether the admission is voluntarily and intelligently made, i.e., with an understanding of the allegations and the consequences of the admission. The court must also insure that the party understands that an admission waives the right to challenge the witnesses and evidence against him, the right to remain silent, and the right to introduce evidence at the hearing.[52] In addition, the court may hear testimony, review documents, and make further inquiry in connection with the plea.

---

[49]See Text 11.06, Uncontested cases.

[50]See In re Green, 4 App(3d) 196, 4 OBR 300, 447 NE(2d) 129 (Franklin 1982); In re Juniper, No. 82AP-13 (10th Dist Ct App, Franklin, 6-15-82); In re Langrehr, No. 2944 (11th Dist Ct App, Trumbull, 11-9-81).

Since the Traffic Rules apply in juvenile traffic offender cases, a child may plead "no contest" in such a case. Traf R 10(A). See also In re Kahan, No. L-82-170 (6th Dist Ct App, Lucas, 10-22-82) (Failure to inform child that no contest plea could result in revocation of driving privileges invalidated plea.).

[51]An admission must demonstrate that the child is in fact delinquent, neglected, or dependent. See In re Hobson, 44 Abs 86, 62 NE(2d) 510 (App, Franklin 1945) (Mere fact that mother desires to place her baby for adoption is not enough to constitute dependency.). See also In re Sims, 13 App(3d) 37, 13 OBR 40, 468 NE(2d) 111 (Preble 1983) (An admission does not bar a parent from participating in an adjudicatory hearing on neglect.).

[52]Juv R 29(D). See also State v Miller, No. 33127 (8th Dist Ct App, Cuyahoga, 1-23-75) (Juv R 29(D) violated where record failed to show that child understood the consequences of his admission to delinquency charges or his right to introduce evidence in his own behalf.).

The procedure for accepting admissions, at least in delinquency cases,[53] is based on the constitutional requirements applicable in criminal trials. In *McCarthy v United States*[54] the United States Supreme Court wrote:

> A defendant who enters such a plea [of guilty] simultaneously waives several constitutional rights, including his privilege against compulsory self-incrimination, his right to trial by jury, and his right to confront his accusers. For this waiver to be valid under the Due Process Clause, it must be "an intentional relinquishment or abandonment of a known right or privilege." ... Consequently, if a defendant's guilty plea is not equally voluntary and knowing, it has been obtained in violation of due process and is therefore void. Moreover, because a guilty plea is an admission of all the elements of a formal criminal charge, it cannot be truly voluntary unless the defendant possesses an understanding of the law in relation to the facts.[55]

Courts in other jurisdictions have applied the constitutional standards relating to guilty pleas in criminal trials to delinquency cases.[56]

The requirements of Juvenile Rule 29(D), however, are not limited to delinquency cases. For example, in a dependency case a court has written:

> The record before us is devoid of any showing that these provisions were complied with. In a case where parental rights are permanently terminated, it is of utmost importance that the parties fully understand their rights and that any waiver is made with full knowledge of those rights and the consequences which will follow.[57]

CROSS REFERENCES

Schroeder-Katz, Ohio Criminal Law, Crim R 11, Author's Text

11.07   Jury trials

Juvenile Rule 27 and RC 2151.35 require the juvenile court to "hear and determine all cases of children without a jury." In contrast, the Sixth Amendment guarantees the right to trial by jury in adult criminal cases.[58] The United States Supreme Court has held this right to be fundamental and therefore

---

[53]See In re Banks, No. L-80-212 (6th Dist Ct App, Lucas, 5-22-81) (Pleading requirements for criminal cases also apply to admissions regarding dependency.); In re Theodore F., 47 AD(2d) 945, 367 NYS(2d) 103 (1975) (applying pleading rules to status offender cases).

[54]McCarthy v United States, 394 US 459, 89 SCt 1166, 22 LEd(2d) 418 (1969).

[55]*Id.* at 466. See also Henderson v Morgan, 426 US 637, 96 SCt 2253, 49 LEd(2d) 108 (1976); Boykin v Alabama, 395 US 238, 89 SCt 1709, 23 LEd(2d) 274 (1969). See generally 2 LaFave and Israel, *Criminal Procedure* ch 20 (1984); Whitebread and Slobogin, *Criminal Procedure* ch 6 (2d ed 1986).

[56]E.g., In re Mary B., 20 Cal App(3d) 816, 98 Cal Rptr 178 (1971); G.M.K. v State, 312 So(2d) 538 (Fla App 1975); In re Appeal No. 544, 25 Md App 26, 332 A(2d) 680 (1975); In re Chavis, 31 NC App 579, 230 SE(2d) 198 (1976), cert denied 291 NC 711, 232 SE(2d) 203 (1977); State ex rel Juvenile Dept of Coos County v Welch, 12 Or App 400, 501 P(2d) 991 (1972), modified by 12 Or App 410, 507 P(2d) 401 (1973); State ex rel J.M. v Taylor, 276 SE(2d) 199 (W Va 1981).

[57]Elmer v Lucas County Children Serv Bd, 36 App(3d) 241, 245, 523 NE(2d) 540 (Lucas 1987).

[58]US Const Am 6 ("In all criminal prosecutions, the accused shall enjoy the right to a speedy and public trial, by an impartial jury."). The Ohio Constitution also guarantees the right to jury trial (O Const Art I, § 5).

applicable to state criminal trials.[59] In *McKeiver v Pennsylvania*,[60] however, the Court held that trial by jury is not a constitutional requirement in juvenile cases. The Court reasoned that mandating jury trials would "remake the juvenile proceeding into a fully adversary process and . . . put an effective end to what has been the idealistic prospect of an intimate, informal protective proceeding."[61]

In *McKeiver* the Court also commented, "If, in its wisdom, any State feels the jury trial is desirable in all cases, or in certain kinds, there appears to be no impediment to its installing a system embracing that feature."[62] A majority of jurisdictions,[63] including Ohio,[64] do not provide for jury trials in juvenile cases. Nevertheless, a number of jurisdictions recognize such a right by statute,[65] and one jurisdiction recognizes it as a matter of state constitutional law.[66]

The IJA-ABA Standards also provide for the right to jury trial upon request. Under the Standards the jury would consist of six persons. The right to a jury trial on demand is supported by the following reasons:

> The importance of the availability of jury trials in juvenile cases goes beyond neutralizing the biased juvenile court judge. A jury trial gives enhanced visibility to the adjudicative process. A jury trial requires the trial court judge to articulate his or her views of the applicable law in the case through jury instructions, thereby facilitating appellate court review of the legal issues involved. Without the focus on legal issues that such an exercise entails, the danger is great that the applicable law may be misperceived or misapplied and that the error will go uncorrected on appeal. In addition, many significant evidentiary protections in the adjudicative process are based on the assumption that preliminary rulings on admissibility will be made by the trial judge and that a jury will receive the evidence only if it has been ruled admissible. When a jury is not present, the evidentiary questions tend to become blurred and appellate review of evidentiary questions is made extremely difficult by the universal presumption that the trial judge disregarded inadmissible evidence and relied only upon competent evidence in arriving at his or her decision.[67]

CROSS REFERENCES

Text 1.02(D)

---

[59]Duncan v Louisiana, 391 US 145, 88 SCt 1444, 20 LEd(2d) 491 (1968).

[60]McKeiver v Pennsylvania, 403 US 528, 91 SCt 1976, 29 LEd(2d) 647 (1971).

[61]*Id.* at 545.

[62]*Id.* at 547.

[63]E.g., In re T.M., 742 P(2d) 905 (Colo 1987); State v Schaaf, 109 Wash(2d) 1, 743 P(2d) 240 (1987).

[64]See State v Ostrowski, 30 OS(2d) 34, 282 NE(2d) 359 (1972), cert denied 409 US 890, 93 SCt 130, 34 LEd(2d) 147 (1972); In re Agler, 19 OS(2d) 70, 249 NE(2d) 808 (1969); Cope v Campbell, 175 OS 475, 196 NE(2d) 457 (1964), overruled by In re Agler, 19 OS(2d) 70, 249 NE(2d) 808 (1969); In re Darnell, 173 OS 335, 182 NE(2d) 321 (1962); Prescott v State, 19 OS 184 (1869); In re Tsesmilles, 24 App(2d) 153, 265 NE(2d) 308 (Columbiana 1970); In re Benn, 18 App(2d) 97, 247 NE(2d) 335 (Cuyahoga 1969). See also Ex parte Januszewski, 196 F 123 (SD Ohio 1911).

[65]See Davis, *Rights of Juveniles* § 5.3 (2d ed 1988). See also Right to jury trial in juvenile court delinquency proceedings, 100 ALR2d 1241 (1965).

[66]R.L.R. v State, 487 P(2d) 27 (Alaska 1971).

[67]*IJA-ABA Standards Relating to Adjudication* 53 (1980).

11.08   Public trials

Juvenile Rule 27 and RC 2151.35 provide for the exclusion of the general public from juvenile court hearings; only persons with a direct interest in the case may attend. RC 2151.352 expressly recognizes a parent's or guardian's right to attend all hearings.[68]

Exclusion of the public from juvenile proceedings is designed to protect the child. As Justice Rehnquist has written:

> It is a hallmark of our juvenile justice system in the United States that virtually from its inception at the end of the last century its proceedings have been conducted outside of the public's full gaze and the youths brought before our juvenile courts have been shielded from publicity. . . . This insistence on confidentiality is born of a tender concern for the welfare of the child, to hide his youthful errors and "bury them in the graveyard of the forgotten past." [69]

In contrast, the Sixth Amendment guarantees the right to a public trial in adult criminal trials.[70] Justice Brennan focused on a child's right to a public trial in *McKeiver v Pennsylvania*,[71] in which the Supreme Court held that the right to jury trial did not apply to juvenile cases. *McKeiver* involved the consolidation of several cases for the purpose of appeal. Justice Brennan concurred in the Court's decision in the Pennsylvania cases, but dissented in the North Carolina cases. In his view, the difference between the two jurisdictions was that Pennsylvania provided the right to a public trial, a right which provided "similar protection" to the right to jury trial:

> The availability of trial by jury allows an accused to protect himself against possible oppression by what is in essence an appeal to the community conscience, as embodied in the jury that hears his case. To some extent, however, a similar protection may be obtained when an accused may in essence appeal to the community at large, by focusing public attention upon the facts of his trial, exposing improper judicial behavior to public view, and obtaining, if necessary, executive redress through the medium of public indignation.[72]

---

[68]See State v Ostrowski, 30 OS(2d) 34, 282 NE(2d) 359 (1972) (Exclusion of parents until they have testified does not violate RC 2151.352.), cert denied 409 US 890, 93 SCt 130, 34 LEd(2d) 147 (1972). But see Text 11.11(C), Separation of witnesses.

[69]Smith v Daily Mail Publishing Co, 443 US 97, 107, 99 SCt 2667, 61 LEd(2d) 399 (1979) (concurring opinion).

[70]US Const Am 6 ("In all criminal prosecutions, the accused shall enjoy the right to a speedy and public trial."). The right to a public trial applies to state trials. In re Oliver, 333 US 257, 68 SCt 499, 92 LEd 682 (1948). See also Gannett Co v De Pasquale, 443 US 368, 99 SCt 2898, 61 LEd(2d) 608 (1979) (Right to public trial may be waived by the accused.); Waller v Georgia, 467 US 39, 104 SCt 2210, 81 LEd(2d) 31 (1984) (Right to a public trial extends to suppression hearings.).

The Ohio Constitution also guarantees the right to a public trial (O Const Art I, § 10).

[71]McKeiver v Pennsylvania, 403 US 528, 91 SCt 1976, 29 LEd(2d) 647 (1971).

[72]*Id.* at 554-55.

For similar reasons, the Alaska Supreme Court has recognized a child's right to public trial as a matter of state constitutional law.[73] The IJA-ABA Standards also provide for the right to public trial in juvenile cases.[74]

In addition to a criminal defendant's Sixth Amendment right to a public trial, the United States Supreme Court has also recognized a First Amendment right of access on the part of the public and press to attend adult criminal trials. In *Richmond Newspapers, Inc v Virginia*[75] the Court wrote, "We hold that the right to attend criminal trials is implicit in the guarantees of the First Amendment; without the freedom to attend such trials . . . important aspects of freedom of speech and 'of the press could be eviscerated.' "[76] Whether the "right of access" applies to juvenile cases is uncertain.[77] One court has held that it does not apply to juvenile proceedings.[78]

CROSS REFERENCES

Text 1.02(D), 11.11(C)

11.09   Impartial judge

Due process guarantees the right to an impartial judge. According to the United States Supreme Court, "A fair trial in a fair tribunal is a basic requirement of due process. Fairness of course requires an absence of actual bias in the trial of cases. But our system of law has always endeavored to prevent even the probability of unfairness."[79]

An issue of impartiality may arise when the same judge who decides the issue of transfer subsequently presides at an adjudicatory hearing. Evidence admissible at a transfer hearing may not be admissible at the adjudicatory hearing. For example, a social history may be considered at the transfer hearing but not at

---

[73]R.L.R. v State, 487 P(2d) 27 (Alaska 1971). But see In re Jesse McM., 105 Cal App(3d) 187, 164 Cal Rptr 199 (1980) (no constitutional right to a public trial in juvenile cases). See also In re L., 24 Or App 257, 546 P(2d) 153 (1976) (statutory right to public trial on request).

[74]*IJA-ABA Standards Relating to Adjudication* 70 (1980). Open hearings in juvenile cases have been proposed in Ohio. See Willey, *The Proposed Ohio Juvenile Code of 1977-1978*, 39 Ohio St L J 273 (1978).

[75]Richmond Newspapers, Inc v Virginia, 448 US 555, 100 SCt 2814, 65 LEd(2d) 973 (1980).

[76]*Id.* at 580. See also Press-Enterprise Co v Superior Court, 478 US 1, 106 SCt 2735, 92 LEd(2d) 1 (1986) (Right of access applies to preliminary hearing.); Press-Enterprise Co v Superior Court of California, 464 US 501, 104 SCt 819, 78 LEd(2d) 629 (1984) (Right of access applies to voir dire examinations of jurors.); Globe Newspaper Co v Superior Court for County of Norfolk, 457 US 596, 102 SCt 2613, 73 LEd(2d) 248 (1982) (Mandatory closure of trial during testimony of sex offense victim unconstitutional.).

[77]See Note, *The Public Right of Access to Juvenile Delinquency Hearings*, 81 Mich L Rev 1540 (1983); Note, *The Right of Access and Juvenile Delinquency Hearings: The Future of Confidentiality*, 16 Ind L Rev 911 (1983).

[78]In re J.S., 140 Vt 458, 438 A(2d) 1125 (1981). See also State ex rel Oregonian Publishing Co v Deiz, 289 Or 277, 613 P(2d) 23 (1980) (State constitution guarantees public and press right of access to juvenile proceedings.); In re Jones, 46 Ill(2d) 506, 263 NE(2d) 863 (1970) (statutory right of news media to attend juvenile proceedings).

[79]In re Murchison, 349 US 133, 136, 75 SCt 623, 99 LEd 942 (1955).

the adjudicatory hearing.[80] Accordingly, some juvenile court statutes preclude, over the objection of the child, the same judge from presiding at both the transfer and adjudicatory hearing.[81] Moreover, the California Supreme Court has written:

> [I]f the referee or judge who hears the issue of fitness [transfer] decides that the minor should be retained in the juvenile court, he may not thereafter properly preside at a contested hearing on the issue of jurisdiction. Basic principles of fairness underlying the Juvenile Court Law require that the minor be protected against premature resolution of the jurisdictional issue on the basis of incompetent background material adduced on the issue of amenability to juvenile court treatment.[82]

The IJA-ABA Standards also adopt this position.[83]

Nevertheless, one Ohio court has stated that a juvenile judge is not disqualified from presiding at an adjudicatory hearing by reason of his involvement in a prior transfer hearing.[84] Judges are often exposed to inadmissible evidence, such as evidence excluded as a result of a motion to suppress, and they are presumed capable of disregarding such evidence.[85]

11.10   Burden of proof

Juvenile Rule 29(E)(4) and RC 2151.35 require proof "beyond a reasonable doubt" in delinquency, unruly, and juvenile traffic offender cases.[86] These same provisions require a less demanding standard of proof—"clear and convincing" evidence—in abuse, neglect, and dependency cases.[87]

---

[80]See Juv R 32.

[81]E.g., Tenn Code Ann § 37-1-134(f) (1984); Wyo Stat § 14-6-237(f) (1977).

[82]Donald L. v Superior Court of Los Angeles County, 7 Cal(3d) 592, 598, 498 P(2d) 1098, 102 Cal Rptr 850 (1972).

[83]*IJA-ABA Standards Relating to Transfer Between Courts* 49 (1980) ("No matter how fair the waiver judge may be in subsequent proceedings, an impression of unfairness will exist.").

[84]In re Terry H., 1 OBR 377 (CP, Cuyahoga 1982).

[85]See In re Diana A., 65 NY Misc(2d) 1034, 319 NYS(2d) 691 (Fam Ct 1971) (The customary ground for disqualification of a judge is personal bias and not prior judicial exposure to the issues or parties.).

[86]The Ohio definition of proof "beyond a reasonable doubt" is found in RC 2901.05(D):

> "Reasonable doubt" is present when the jurors, after they have carefully considered and compared all the evidence, cannot say they are firmly convinced of the truth of the charge. It is a doubt based on reason and common sense. Reasonable doubt is not mere possible doubt, because everything relating to human affairs or depending on moral evidence is open to some possible or imaginary doubt. "Proof beyond a reasonable doubt" is proof of such character that an ordinary person would be willing to rely and act upon it in the most important of his own affairs.

[87]The Ohio Supreme Court has ruled that the Ohio Constitution does not require the "beyond-a-reasonable-doubt" standard in proceedings involving the termination of parental rights. In re Schmidt, 25 OS(3d) 331, 25 OBR 386, 496 NE(2d) 952 (1986).

See generally In re Bishop, 36 App(3d) 123, 521 NE(2d) 838 (Ashland 1987) (Dependency established by clear and convincing evidence.); In re Green, 18 App(3d) 43, 18 OBR 155, 480 NE(2d) 492 (Montgomery 1984) (Dependency established by clear and convincing evidence.); In re Bibb, 70 App(2d) 117, 435 NE(2d) 96 (Hamilton 1980) (Dependency not proved by clear and convincing evidence.); In re Fassinger, 43 App(2d)

In some instances these provisions codify due process requirements; in other instances they go beyond constitutional standards. In *In re Winship*[88] the United States Supreme Court held that the Due Process Clause protects "against conviction except upon proof beyond a reasonable doubt of every fact necessary to constitute the crime . . . charged."[89] This standard, according to the Court, protects against erroneous convictions and assures community respect and confidence in the criminal process; it applies to delinquency proceedings as well as to criminal trials.

In *Santosky v Kramer*[90] the United States Supreme Court considered the standard of proof in neglect proceedings involving the permanent termination of parental rights. According to the Court, the "preponderance of evidence" standard, the typical standard applied in civil litigation, did not satisfy due process: "In parental rights termination proceedings, the private interest affected is commanding; the risk of error from using a preponderance standard is substantial; and the countervailing governmental interest favoring that standard is comparatively slight."[91] The Court went on to require a more demanding standard of proof—clear and convincing evidence—in these cases.

Winship and *Santosky* are the Supreme Court's only juvenile court standard of proof cases. In *Winship* the Court pointed out that it was not deciding the required standard of proof for status offense (unruly) cases,[92] and courts in other jurisdictions are divided over the proper standard in these cases.[93]

Winship speaks only to the prosecution's burden of persuasion with respect to the elements of the charged offense. It does not expressly deal with the burden of persuasion for affirmative defenses.[94] In criminal trials, RC 2901.05 provides that the "burden of going forward with the evidence of an affirmative defense, and the burden of proof, by a preponderance of the evidence, for an affirmative defense, is upon the accused."

CROSS REFERENCES

Text 1.02(C), (F)

89, 334 NE(2d) 5 (Cuyahoga 1974) (Present neglect or dependency not established by clear and convincing evidence.), affirmed by 42 OS(2d) 505, 330 NE(2d) 431 (1975).

[88]In re Winship, 397 US 358, 90 SCt 1068, 25 LEd(2d) 368 (1970). In Ivan v City of New York, 407 US 203, 92 SCt 1951, 32 LEd(2d) 659 (1972), the Court held *Winship* retroactive.

[89]In re Winship, 397 US 358, 364, 90 SCt 1068, 25 LEd(2d) 368 (1970). *Winship* overruled prior Ohio cases on this issue. E.g., In re Agler, 19 OS(2d) 70, 249 NE(2d) 808 (1969) (clear and convincing evidence standard); State v Shardell, 107 App 338, 153 NE(2d) 510 (Cuyahoga 1958) (preponderance of evidence standard).

[90]Santosky v Kramer, 455 US 745, 102 SCt 1388, 71 LEd(2d) 599 (1982).

[91]*Id.* at 758.

[92]In re Winship, 397 US 358, 359 n.1, 90 SCt 1068, 25 LEd(2d) 368 (1970).

[93]Compare In re William D., 36 AD(2d) 970, 321 NYS(2d) 510 (1971) (proof beyond a reasonable doubt) with In re Potter, 237 NW(2d) 461 (Iowa 1976) (clear and convincing evidence).

[94]See Martin v Ohio, 480 US 228, 107 SCt 1098, 94 LEd(2d) 267 (1987) (Allocating burden of proving self-defense to defendant does not violate due process.); Patterson v New York, 432 US 197, 97 SCt 2319, 53 LEd(2d) 281 (1977) (Allocating burden of proving extreme emotional disturbance to homicide defendant does not violate due process.); Mullaney v Wilbur, 421 US 684, 95 SCt 1881, 44 LEd(2d) 508 (1975) (Allocating burden of proving heat of passion to homicide defendant violates due process.).

11.11 Evidence

The Ohio Rules of Evidence apply in the adjudicatory hearing.[95] Evidence Rule 101 provides that the Rules "govern proceedings in the courts of this state and before court-appointed referees of this state." None of the exceptions specified in Evidence Rule 101(C) apply to the adjudicatory hearing. Even prior to the adoption of the Rules of Evidence, the Ohio Supreme Court indicated that evidentiary rules applied in adjudicatory hearings: "We are in complete agreement that at the adjudicatory stage the use of clearly incompetent evidence to prove a youth's involvement is not justifiable."[96] In particular, inadmissible hearsay evidence was prohibited.[97]

Although the Rules of Evidence do not distinguish between the applicability of the Rules in jury and bench trials, there nevertheless is a difference. Many of the exclusionary Rules of Evidence are designed to insulate juries from evidence that is thought to be too unreliable or too inflammatory. Since trial judges are presumed capable of properly evaluating such evidence, exclusionary rules are treated differently in bench trials, at least to the extent that appellate courts will less readily find error in a bench trial than in a jury trial.[98] For example, one court has written, "It is presumed that the Juvenile Court Judge would reject any incompetent and prejudicial evidence and only consider the competent and relevant evidence. A reviewing court may not presume that the trial court deliberately committed error."[99]

Evidence obtained in violation of a child's constitutional rights may be inadmissible at the adjudicatory hearing. Juvenile Rule 22(D)(3) governs the procedure for motions to suppress evidence.[100]

---

[95]In re Baby Girl Baxter, 17 OS(3d) 229, 233, 17 OBR 469, 479 NE(2d) 257 (1985) ("There must be strict adherence to the Rules of Evidence at the adjudicatory stage."). See generally Giannelli, *Ohio Evidence Manual* (1982-1987). See also Applicability of rules of evidence in juvenile delinquency proceedings, 43 ALR2d 1128 (1955).

[96]State v Carmichael, 35 OS(2d) 1, 7, 298 NE(2d) 568 (1973), cert denied 414 US 1161, 94 SCt 922, 39 LEd(2d) 113 (1974).

[97]See In re Agler, 19 OS(2d) 70, 249 NE(2d) 808 (1969); In re Tsesmilles, 24 App(2d) 153, 265 NE(2d) 308 (Columbiana 1970); State v Shardell, 107 App 338, 153 NE(2d) 510 (Cuyahoga 1958).

[98]See State v Eubank, 60 OS(2d) 183, 187, 398 NE(2d) 567 (1979) ("[A] judge is presumed to consider only the relevant, material and competent evidence in arriving at a judgment, unless the contrary affirmatively appears from the record."); State v White, 15 OS(2d) 146, 239 NE(2d) 65 (1968).

[99]In re Baker, 18 App(2d) 276, 283, 248 NE(2d) 620 (Hocking 1969), modified by 20 OS(2d) 142, 254 NE(2d) 363 (1969).

[100]See Text Ch 5, Police Investigations.

(A) Privileges

The law of privilege,[101] including the constitutional privilege against compelled self-incrimination,[102] applies in adjudicatory hearings.[103] The physician-patient[104] and psychologist-client[105] privileges, however, do not apply to physical and mental examinations that are ordered by the court.[106] Moreover, a special exemption from the coverage of a privilege often applies in abuse or neglect cases.[107] While some courts have recognized a parent-child privilege,[108] the majority have not.[109] Although welfare records are confidential,[110] they are not protected by an absolute privilege.[111]

(B) Hearsay

As noted above, the hearsay rule[112] applies in adjudicatory hearings. The right of confrontation is often implicated when hearsay evidence is intro-

---

[101]See Evid R 501. See also RC 2317.02 (attorney-client, physician-patient, clergyman-penitent, husband-wife, counselor-client, and social worker-client privilege), RC 4732.19 (psychologist-client privilege), RC 2739.04 (broadcasters' confidential source privilege), RC 2739.12 (reporters' confidential source privilege). See Giannelli, *Ohio Evidence Manual* § 501.01-.12 (1982).

[102]See Text 11.13, Self-incrimination.

[103]E.g., In re Decker, 20 App(3d) 203, 20 OBR 248, 485 NE(2d) 751 (Van Wert 1984) (applying psychiatrist-patient privileges in dependency and neglect proceeding).

[104]RC 2317.02(B).

[105]RC 4732.19.

[106]See In re Smith, 7 App(3d) 75, 7 OBR 88, 455 NE(2d) 171 (Greene 1982); In re Winstead, 67 App(2d) 111, 425 NE(2d) 943 (Summit 1980).

[107]RC 2151.421.

[108]See In re Agosto, 553 FSupp 1298 (D Nev 1983); In re Application of A. and M., 61 AD(2d) 426, 403 NYS(2d) 375 (1978); People v Fitzgerald, 101 NY Misc(2d) 712, 422 NYS(2d) 309 (1979). See also Idaho Code § 9-203(7) (1988 supp).

See generally Testimonial privilege for confidential communications between relatives other than husband and wife—state cases, 6 ALR4th 544 (1981); Kandoian, *The Parent-Child Privilege and the Parent-Child Crime: Observations on State v. DeLong and In re Agosto,* 36 Me L Rev 59 (1984); Stanton, *Child-Parent Privilege for Confidential Communications: An Examination and Proposal,* 16 Fam L Quar 1 (1982); Watts, *The Parent-Child Privileges: Hardly a New or Revolutionary Concept,* 28 Wm & Mary L Rev 583 (1987); Note, *Parent-Child Loyalty and Testimonial Privilege,* 100 Harv L Rev 910 (1987).

[109]See In re Hawkins, No. 3430 (9th Dist Ct App, Lorain, 5-11-83) (There is no parent-child privilege in Ohio.); In re Grand Jury Proceedings, 842 F(2d) 244 (10th Cir Utah 1988); Port v Heard, 764 F(2d) 423 (5th Cir Tex 1985); United States v Ismail, 756 F(2d) 1253 (6th Cir Mich 1985); In re Terry W., 59 Cal App(3d) 745, 130 Cal Rptr 913 (1976); State v DeLong, 456 A(2d) 877 (Me 1983); Three Juveniles v Commonwealth, 390 Mass 357, 455 NE(2d) 1203 (1983), cert denied sub nom Keefe v Massachusetts, 465 US 1068, 104 SCt 1421, 79 LEd(2d) 746 (1984).

[110]RC 5153.17.

[111]In re Barzak, 24 App(3d) 180, 24 OBR 270, 493 NE(2d) 1011 (Trumbull 1985).

[112]Evid R 801 to Evid R 806. Hearsay is a written or oral statement made by a declarant out of court and offered for the truth of the assertions contained in the statement. See generally Giannelli, *Ohio Evidence Manual* § 801.01 (1982).

See also In re Barzak, 24 App(3d) 180, 24 OBR 270, 493 NE(2d) 1011 (Trumbull 1985) (hearsay inadmissible in dependency cases); In re Vickers Children, 14 App(3d) 201, 14 OBR 228, 470 NE(2d) 438 (Butler 1983) (hearsay inadmissible in neglect cases); In re Sims, 13 App(3d) 37, 13 OBR 40, 468 NE(2d) 111 (Preble 1983) (hearsay inadmissible in neglect cases); In re Crose, No. 1055 (2d Dist Ct App, Darke, 10-18-82) (Hearsay

duced.[113] Together, Evidence Rules 803 and 804 recognize twenty-nine exceptions to the hearsay rule. Perhaps the most important exception in juvenile cases is Evidence Rule 803(8), which governs the admissibility of public records. Police, welfare,[114] and school records[115] are often admissible under this exception. Typically, these records are also self-authenticating[116] and certified copies may be admitted.[117] Hospital and medical records are admissible as business records under Evidence Rule 803(6).[118]

Physical and sexual abuse cases present special problems. Statements made by children in these cases have sometimes been admitted as excited utterances[119] or as statements made for the purpose of medical treatment or diagnoses.[120] Depositions, including videotape depositions, may be admissible in abuse cases[121] and in delinquency cases when specified sex offenses are alleged for victims under eleven years of age.[122] A special open-ended hearsay exception for the statements of a child applies in abuse, neglect, and dependency cases.[123]

A specific rule governs the use of social histories, which often contain hearsay evidence. Juvenile Rule 32(B) provides that a social history may not be used until after an admission or adjudication.

(C) Separation of witnesses

Juvenile Rule 29(E)(2) provides for the separation or exclusion of witnesses upon request. Evidence Rule 615 contains a comparable provision. Evidence Rule 615, however, recognizes exceptions for (1) a party who is a natural person, (2) an officer or employee of a party which is not a natural person designated as its representative by its attorney, and (3) a person whose presence is shown by a party to be essential to the presentation of his cause. Since parents are "parties" to juvenile cases under Juvenile Rule 2(16), Evidence Rule 615 would appear to supersede a prior Ohio case that upheld the exclusion of parents who were also witnesses.[124]

---

evidence is inadmissible in adjudicatory hearings unless it falls within a recognized exception.).

[113]See Text 11.12, Right of confrontation.

[114]In re Lucas, 29 App(3d) 165, 173, 29 OBR 194, 504 NE(2d) 472 (Putnam 1985) (Caseworker's case notes were admitted as public record.).

[115]See Admissibility of school records under hearsay exceptions, 57 ALR4th 1111 (1987).

[116]Evid R 902. See In re Knipp, No. 1388 (4th Dist Ct App, Scioto, 3-28-83) (Georgia state reports that have not been certified as authentic are inadmissible.).

[117]Evid R 1005 (admissibility of certified copies of public records).

[118]See In re Smart, 21 App(3d) 31, 34, 21 OBR 33, 486 NE(2d) 147 (Franklin 1984).

[119]E.g., State v Wallace, 37 OS(3d) 87, 524 NE(2d) 466 (1988); State v Duncan, 53 OS(2d) 215, 373 NE(2d) 1234 (1978); State v Wagner, 30 App(3d) 261, 30 OBR 458, 508 NE(2d) 164 (Cuyahoga 1986); State v Fowler, 27 App(3d) 149, 27 OBR 182, 500 NE(2d) 390 (Cuyahoga 1985).

[120]E.g., United States v Iron Shell, 633 F(2d) 77 (8th Cir SD 1980), cert denied 450 US 1001 (1981).

[121]RC 2151.35(G).

[122]RC 2151.3511.

[123]RC 2151.35(F).

[124]State v Ostrowski, 30 OS(2d) 34, 282 NE(2d) 359 (1972), cert denied 409 US 890, 93 SCt 130, 34 LEd(2d) 147 (1972).

(D) Competency of witnesses

Evidence Rule 601(A) governs the competency of a child witness. Under this rule, children under the age of ten who do not appear capable of "receiving just impressions of the facts and transactions respecting which they are examined, or of relating them truly" are incompetent.[125] Determining the competency of a child witness is a decision that is entrusted to the discretion of the court.[126] One court has written:

> Proper judicial procedure requires the trial judge to conduct a voir dire examination of a child under age ten to determine the child's competence to testify. . . . The trial judge has a duty to conduct the examination when the child is presented to the court and the fact is revealed that the child has not reached age ten.[127]

The parties are entitled to introduce evidence, including expert testimony, on this issue.[128]

RC 2317.01 provides that in an abuse, neglect, or dependency case an examination of a child to determine competency shall be conducted in an office or room other than a courtroom. In addition, only those persons considered necessary by the court for the conduct of the examination or the well-being of the child may be present. The prosecutor, guardian ad litem, or attorney for any party may submit questions for use by the court in determining competency. This provision would permit the exclusion of parties and perhaps counsel. In *Kentucky v Stincer*,[129] the United States Supreme Court ruled that the exclusion of a criminal defendant from a hearing to determine the competency of a child witness did not violate the right of confrontation. The defendant's attorney, however, was present and participated in the hearing.

(E) Expert witnesses

Expert testimony is admissible if scientific, technical, or other specialized knowledge will assist the court and if the witness is qualified by knowledge, skill, experience, training, or education to express an opinion.[130] An expert may base his opinion on personal observation or on evidence admitted at the hearing.[131] The latter situation typically involves the use of a hypothetical question. If it will assist the court, an expert may express an opinion on the ultimate issues in the case.[132]

---

[125]See Huprich v Paul W. Varga & Sons, Inc, 3 OS(2d) 87, 209 NE(2d) 390 (1965); State v Workman, 14 App(3d) 385, 14 OBR 490, 471 NE(2d) 853 (Cuyahoga 1984); State v Lee, 9 App(3d) 282, 9 OBR 497, 459 NE(2d) 910 (Summit 1983); Philpot v Williams, 8 App(3d) 241, 8 OBR 314, 456 NE(2d) 1315 (Hamilton 1983); State v Lewis, 4 App(3d) 275, 4 OBR 494, 448 NE(2d) 487 (Union 1982); In re Black, No. 40247 (8th Dist Ct App, Cuyahoga, 1-25-80). See generally Giannelli, *Ohio Evidence Manual* § 601.05 (1988).

[126]State v Holt, 17 OS(2d) 81, 246 NE(2d) 365 (1969); Huprich v Paul W. Varga & Sons, Inc, 3 OS(2d) 87, 209 NE(2d) 390 (1965).

[127]State v Morgan, 31 App(3d) 152, 154, 31 OBR 241, 509 NE(2d) 428 (Hamilton 1986).

[128]Huprich v Paul W. Varga & Sons, Inc, 3 OS(2d) 87, 209 NE(2d) 390 (1965).

[129]Kentucky v Stincer, 482 US ___, 107 SCt 2658, 96 LEd(2d) 631 (1987).

[130]Evid R 702. See generally Giannelli, *Ohio Evidence Manual* § 702.01 et seq. (1988).

[131]Evid R 703.

[132]Evid R 704.

Testimony by psychologists, caseworkers, and counselors is often admitted in dependency and neglect cases.[133] Medical testimony concerning the "battered child syndrome" is admissible in physical abuse cases.[134] In addition, some courts have admitted expert testimony concerning the "child sexual abuse accommodation syndrome."[135]

In *Ake v Oklahoma*,[136] the United States Supreme Court recognized that an indigent criminal defendant has a due process right to expert assistance in some cases. One court has extended *Ake* to permanent custody proceedings.[137]

(F) Impeachment by prior conviction

Evidence Rule 609 governs impeachment by prior conviction. Evidence Rule 609(D) provides, "Evidence of juvenile adjudications is not admissible except as provided by statute enacted by the General Assembly." RC 2151.358(H) is the applicable statute:

> The disposition of a child under the judgment rendered or any evidence given in court is not admissible as evidence against the child in any other case or proceeding in any other court, except that the judgment rendered and the disposition of the child may be considered by any court only as to the matter of sentence or to the granting of probation.

One court has held that this statute does not apply to the admissibility of juvenile records in juvenile cases.[138]

The courts have considered the applicability of the statute in adult criminal cases on several occasions. In *State v Cox*[139] the Ohio Supreme Court wrote, "Although the General Assembly may enact legislation to effectuate its policy of protecting the confidentiality of juvenile records, such enactment may not impinge upon the right of a defendant in a criminal case to present all available,

---

[133]E.g., In re Green, 18 App(3d) 43, 18 OBR 155, 480 NE(2d) 492 (Montgomery 1984).

[134]E.g., United States v Bowers, 660 F(2d) 527, 529 (5th Cir Ga 1981); State v Durfee, 322 NW(2d) 778, 783-84 (Minn 1982); State v Holland, 346 NW(2d) 302, 307-08 (SD 1984). See also Admissibility of expert medical testimony on battered child syndrome, 98 ALR3d 306 (1980); John, *Child Abuse—The Battered Child Syndrome,* 2 Am Jur Proof of Facts(2d) 365 (1974).

[135]See In re Spears, No. 1200 (4th Dist Ct App, Athens, 12-10-84); United States v Azure, 801 F(2d) 336, 340-41 (8th Cir ND 1986); McCoid, *Expert Psychological Testimony About Child Complainants in Sexual Abuse Prosecutions: A Foray into the Admissibility of Novel Psychological Evidence,* 77 J Crim L (1986).

[136]Ake v Oklahoma, 470 US 68, 105 SCt 1087, 84 LEd(2d) 53 (1985).

[137]In re Brown, No. C-850878 (1st Dist Ct App, Hamilton, 11-26-86).

[138]In re Wyrock, Nos. 41827, 41828, 41904 (8th Dist Ct App, Cuyahoga, 10-23-80); State v Eppinger, No. 30798 (8th Dist Ct App, Cuyahoga, 12-9-71) (RC 2151.358's use of the phrase "any other court" clearly excludes the juvenile court from the restrictions contained in the statute.). See generally Herbert and Sinclair, *Adversary Juvenile Delinquency Proceedings: Impeachment of Juvenile Defendants by the Use of Previous Adjudications of Delinquency,* 8 Akron L Rev 443 (1975).
  See also In re Hayes, 29 App(3d) 162, 29 OBR 191, 504 NE(2d) 491 (Franklin 1986) (Evidence of prior adjudication is admissible as prior conviction to enhance degree of theft offense.).

[139]State v Cox, 42 OS(2d) 200, 327 NE(2d) 639 (1975).

relevant and probative evidence which is pertinent to a specific and material aspect of his defense."[140]

(G) Corroboration rules

The Ohio courts have applied "corroboration" rules in criminal cases. For example, a confession is inadmissible unless there is some independent evidence of the corpus delicti.[141] This rule applies to juvenile cases.[142] In addition, by statute a criminal defendant may not be convicted of conspiracy based solely on the testimony of a co-conspirator, unsupported by other evidence.[143] At one time a similar rule applied to accomplice testimony and complicity prosecutions, but the statute[144] has since been amended.[145]

CROSS REFERENCES

Text 1.02(H), Ch 5, 11.10, 11.12, 11.13, 15.04(A)

11.12　Right of confrontation

The right of confrontation was one of the due process rights expressly applied to adjudicatory hearings in *Gault*: "We now hold that ... a determination of delinquency and an order of commitment to a state institution cannot be sustained in the absence of sworn testimony subjected to the opportunity for cross-examination in accordance with our law and constitutional requirements."[146] Although the *Gault* decision was limited to delinquency cases, there seems little question that due process requires the right of confrontation in most juvenile cases.[147]

---

[140]*Id.* at 204. See also State v Marinski, 139 OS 559, 41 NE(2d) 387 (1942); State v Hale, 21 App(2d) 207, 256 NE(2d) 239 (Franklin 1969). See Giannelli, *Ohio Evidence Manual* § 609.09 (1988).

For a discussion of this issue, see Text 15.04(A), Confidentiality, use in other proceedings.

[141]See State v Black, 54 OS(2d) 304, 376 NE(2d) 948 (1978); State v Edwards, 49 OS(2d) 31, 358 NE(2d) 1051 (1976), vacated in part on other grounds by 438 US 911, 98 SCt 3147, 57 LEd(2d) 1155 (1978); State v King, 10 App(3d) 161, 10 OBR 214, 460 NE(2d) 1383 (Hamilton 1983); State v Ralston, 67 App(2d) 81, 425 NE(2d) 916 (Clermont 1979), vacated on other grounds by 438 US 911, 98 SCt 3147, 57 LEd(2d) 1155 (1978). See generally McCormick, *Evidence* § 145 (3d ed 1984); LaFave and Scott, *Criminal Law* 18 (2d ed 1986).

[142]See In re Toler, No. 314 (12th Dist Ct App, Preble, 5-4-83); In re Way, 319 So(2d) 651 (Miss 1975); In re State in re W.J., 116 NJ Super 462, 282 A(2d) 770 (1971).

[143]RC 2923.01(H).

[144]RC 2923.03(D).

[145]See State v Mullins, 34 App(3d) 192, 517 NE(2d) 945 (Fairfield 1986) (Amendment applies prospectively.).

[146]In re Gault, 387 US 1, 57, 87 SCt 1428, 18 LEd(2d) 527 (1967).

[147]The right of confrontation as a due process requirement applies in a variety of contexts. See Goldberg v Kelly, 397 US 254, 90 SCt 1011, 25 LEd(2d) 287 (1970) (Right of confrontation applies in welfare termination hearings.); Morrissey v Brewer, 408 US 471, 92 SCt 2593, 33 LEd(2d) 484 (1972) (Conditional right of confrontation applies in parole revocation hearings.).

Most of the Supreme Court's cases in this area have focused on the Sixth Amendment Confrontation Clause.[148] There are several aspects to the right of confrontation. At the very least, it guarantees an accused the right to be present during trial. "One of the most basic of the rights guaranteed by the Confrontation Clause is the accused's right to be present in the courtroom at every stage of his trial."[149] This right is implicitly recognized in Juvenile Rule 27[150] and RC 2151.35.[151] The right to be present at the proceedings, however, can be waived by a defendant's obstructive conduct[152] or his voluntary absence after the hearing has commenced.[153]

The right to be present includes the right to "face-to-face" confrontation. The Court has found a Sixth Amendment violation where a screen was used to separate the accused and his alleged child sexual abuse victims during their testimony.[154] However, an important concurring opinion, citing statutes which permit the use of closed-circuit television, indicated that the right to face-to-face confrontation is not absolute; the state interest in protecting the child could outweigh the defendant's right if case-specific findings of necessity are made by the trial court.[155] The Ohio statute, RC 2151.3511, on testifying via closed-circuit television applies when specified sex offenses are charged and the alleged victim is under eleven years of age when the complaint is filed.

The right of confrontation also includes the right of cross-examination. For example, in *Davis v Alaska*[156] an accused was prohibited from cross-examining a prosecution witness concerning the witness's status as a juvenile probationer. This curtailment of cross-examination was based on a state statute designed to protect the confidentiality of juvenile adjudications. On review, the Supreme Court reversed: "The State's policy interest in protecting the confidentiality of a juvenile offender's record cannot require yielding of so vital a constitutional right as the effective cross-examination for bias of an adverse witness."[157]

---

[148]US Const Am 6 ("In all criminal prosecutions, the accused shall enjoy the right . . . to be confronted with the witnesses against him."). The right of confrontation applies to state trials. Pointer v Texas, 380 US 400, 85 SCt 1065, 13 LEd(2d) 923 (1965).

The Ohio Constitution also guarantees the right of confrontation (O Const Art I, § 10).

[149]Illinois v Allen, 397 US 337, 338, 90 SCt 1057, 25 LEd(2d) 353 (1970). See also In re Oliver, 333 US 257, 68 SCt 499, 92 LEd 682 (1948); Lewis v United States, 146 US 370, 13 SCt 136, 36 LEd 1011 (1892).

The right to be present has been applied to juvenile cases. See R.L.R. v State, 487 P(2d) 27 (Alaska 1971).

[150]Juv R 27 provides, "The court may excuse the attendance of the child at the hearing in neglect, dependency, or abuse cases."

[151]RC 2151.35(A) is identical to Juv R 27 in this respect ("The court may excuse the attendance of the child at the hearing in cases involving abused, neglected, or dependent children.").

[152]Illinois v Allen, 397 US 337, 90 SCt 1057, 25 LEd(2d) 353 (1970).

[153]Taylor v United States, 414 US 17, 94 SCt 194, 38 LEd(2d) 174 (1973).

[154]Coy v Iowa, 487 US ___, 108 SCt 2798, 101 LEd(2d) 857 (1988).

[155]*Id.* at 2803 (Justice O'Connor). See also State v Eastham, 39 OS(3d) 307, 530 NE(2d) 409 (1988) (Use of video violated right of confrontation where no particularized findings of necessity established.).

[156]Davis v Alaska, 415 US 308, 94 SCt 1105, 39 LEd(2d) 347 (1974).

[157]*Id.* at 320. See also Smith v Illinois, 390 US 129, 88 SCt 748, 19 LEd(2d) 956 (1968).

The Confrontation Clause also places some limitations on the use of hearsay evidence. The Supreme Court has addressed this issue on several occasions. Because a hearsay declarant is, in effect, a "witness," a literal application of the Confrontation Clause would preclude the prosecution from introducing any hearsay statement, notwithstanding the applicability of a recognized hearsay exception. The Supreme Court, however, has rejected this interpretation: "[I]f thus applied, the Clause would abrogate virtually every hearsay exception, a result long rejected as unintended and too extreme."[158]

The Confrontation Clause could also be interpreted as requiring only the right to cross-examine in-court witnesses and not out-of-court declarants. Under this interpretation, the admissibility of statements falling within any recognized hearsay exception would not violate the confrontation guarantee. But the Court has also rejected this view: "It seems apparent that the Sixth Amendment's Confrontation Clause and the evidentiary hearsay rule stem from the same roots. But this Court has never equated the two, and we decline to do so now."[159]

Instead, the Court has adopted a middle ground. In *Ohio v Roberts*[160] the Court provided the following standard for determining the constitutionality of hearsay statements:

> In sum, when a hearsay declarant is not present for cross-examination at trial, the Confrontation Clause normally requires a showing that he is unavailable. Even then, his statement is admissible only if it bears adequate "indicia of reliability." Reliability can be inferred without more in a case where the evidence falls within a firmly rooted hearsay exception. In other cases, the evidence must be excluded, at least absent a showing of particularized guarantees of trustworthiness.[161]

In later cases, the Court has held that statements admissible under the co-conspirator exception are reliable[162] and that a showing of unavailability is not required for such statements.[163]

The right of confrontation may be waived. In some cases the United States Supreme Court has applied a stringent waiver standard, requiring "an intentional relinquishment or abandonment of a known right or privilege."[164] In other cases the Court has found a waiver by conduct.[165] In *In re Gantt*[166] a juvenile court considered a witness's transfer hearing testimony during the adjudicatory hearing, even though the witness did not testify at that hearing. On

---

[158]Ohio v Roberts, 448 US 56, 63, 100 SCt 2531, 65 LEd(2d) 597 (1980).

[159]Dutton v Evans, 400 US 74, 86, 91 SCt 210, 27 LEd(2d) 213 (1970). See also California v Green, 399 US 149, 90 SCt 1930, 26 LEd(2d) 489 (1970).

[160]Ohio v Roberts, 448 US 56, 100 SCt 2531, 65 LEd(2d) 597 (1980).

[161]*Id.* at 66. See also State v Spikes, 67 OS(2d) 405, 423 NE(2d) 1122 (1981). See Giannelli, *Ohio Evidence Manual* § 801.16 (1982).

[162]Bourjaily v United States, ___ US ___, 107 SCt 2775, 97 LEd(2d) 144 (1987).

[163]United States v Inadi, 475 US 387, 106 SCt 1121, 89 LEd(2d) 390 (1986).

[164]Brookhart v Janis, 384 US 1, 4, 86 SCt 1245, 16 LEd(2d) 314 (1966).

[165]Taylor v United States, 414 US 17, 94 SCt 194, 38 LEd(2d) 174 (1973); Illinois v Allen, 397 US 337, 90 SCt 1057, 25 LEd(2d) 353 (1970).

[166]In re Gantt, 61 App(2d) 44, 398 NE(2d) 800 (Wood 1978).

review, the appellate court held that the child had waived his right of confrontation by failing to object to the use of the transfer hearing testimony.[167]

11.13 Self-incrimination

In *Gault* the United States Supreme Court held the Fifth Amendment privilege against compelled self-incrimination[168] applicable in adjudicatory delinquency proceedings, despite the state's argument that such proceedings were "civil" in nature. According to the Court, proceedings "which may lead to commitment to a state institution, must be regarded as 'criminal' for purposes of the privilege against self-incrimination. To hold otherwise would be to disregard substance because of the feeble enticement of the 'civil' label-of-convenience which has been attached to juvenile proceedings."[169] The Court also has held that the privilege prohibits a court from considering a criminal defendant's failure to testify as evidence of guilt.[170] This rule applies in juvenile cases.[171]

The privilege against self-incrimination may be waived. A child waives the privilege by taking the stand and testifying in his own defense. In *Gault* the Court commented:

> We appreciate that special problems may arise with respect to waiver of the privilege by or on behalf of children, and that there may well be some differences in technique—but not in principle—depending upon the age of the child and the presence and competence of parents. The participation of counsel will, of course, assist the police, Juvenile Courts and appellate tribunals in administering the privilege. If counsel was not present for some permissible reason when an admission was obtained, the greatest care must be taken to assure that the admission was voluntary, in the sense not only that it was not coerced or suggested, but also that it was not the product of ignorance of rights or of adolescent fantasy, fright or despair.[172]

Juvenile Rule 29(B)(5) requires the court to inform parties who have waived the right to counsel of the right to remain silent. In *In re Collins*[173] the court stated that the explanation of the privilege "must include the facts that there is an unqualified right to remain silent, that a statement made may be used against

[167]*Id.* at 48.

[168]US Const Am 5 ("No person ... shall be compelled in any criminal case to be a witness against himself."). The privilege applies in state trials. Malloy v Hogan, 378 US 1, 84 SCt 1489, 12 LEd(2d) 653 (1964). See generally Whitebread and Slobogin, *Criminal Procedure* ch 15 (2d ed 1986).

The Ohio Constitution also guarantees the right against self-incrimination (O Const Art I, § 10).

[169]In re Gault, 387 US 1, 49-50, 87 SCt 1428, 18 LEd(2d) 527 (1967). As the Ohio Supreme Court acknowledged in In re Agler, 19 OS(2d) 70, 249 NE(2d) 808 (1969), *Gault* overruled prior Ohio cases which had held the privilege inapplicable in juvenile cases. See State v Shardell, 107 App 338, 153 NE(2d) 510 (Cuyahoga 1958).

[170]Griffin v California, 380 US 609, 85 SCt 1229, 14 LEd(2d) 106 (1965). But see United States v Robinson, __ US __, 108 SCt 864, __ LEd(2d) __ (1988) (not a Fifth Amendment violation to comment on an accused's silence in response to defense counsel's tactics).

[171]See In re Collins, 20 App(2d) 319, 253 NE(2d) 824 (Cuyahoga 1969); State in re D.A.M., 132 NJ Super 192, 333 A(2d) 270 (App Div 1975).

[172]In re Gault, 387 US 1, 55, 87 SCt 1428, 18 LEd(2d) 527 (1967).

[173]In re Collins, 20 App(2d) 319, 253 NE(2d) 824 (Cuyahoga 1969).

him, and that his refusal to testify will not be held against him."[174] The court also ruled that only the child could waive the privilege: "No case . . . has held that a parent could waive the constitutional right of a minor in a Juvenile Court or criminal case."[175]

CROSS REFERENCES

Text 1.02(B), (H)

Merrick-Rippner, Ohio Probate Law (4th ed), Text Ch 223

11.14   Right to a transcript

Juvenile Rule 37(A) requires a complete record of all juvenile court hearings upon the motion of the court or the request of a party.[176] RC 2151.35 contains a comparable, but not identical, provision.[177] It requires recordings in permanent custody proceedings (RC 2151.414 and RC 2151.353). Juvenile Rule 29(B)(5) requires the court to inform parties who are not represented by counsel that they have the right, upon request, to a record of all proceedings at public expense if indigent.

Although the right to a transcript was raised in *Gault*, the Supreme Court declined to rule on this issue.[178] In a concurring and dissenting opinion, Justice Harlan expressed the view that a "written record, or its equivalent, adequate to permit effective review on appeal or in collateral proceedings" should be required as a matter of due process.[179]

In criminal cases the United States Supreme Court has held, on equal protection and due process grounds, that an indigent is entitled to a free transcript if the state provides the right to appeal.[180] In *State ex rel Heller v Miller*[181] the Ohio Supreme Court extended the right to a transcript to indigent parents in proceedings to permanently terminate parental rights. Similarly, an Ohio court of appeals, citing due process and equal protection grounds, has held that an

---

[174]*Id.* at 322.

[175]*Id.*

[176]Juv R 37(A) also provides that the recording "shall be taken in shorthand, stenotype or by any other adequate mechanical or electronic recording device." It is within the trial court's discretion to determine which method of recording shall be used. In re Glenn, No. 35352 (8th Dist Ct App, Cuyahoga, 1-20-77). However, if an electronic recording device malfunctions, the party's right to a transcript may be infringed. In re Roberts, No. 34232 (8th Dist Ct App, Cuyahoga, 11-13-75).
See also In re Menich, No. 42727 (8th Dist Ct App, Cuyahoga, 3-26-81) (Local rules conditioning right to a transcript upon prepayment of costs are not inconsistent with Juv R 37 where they permit avoidance of costs by filing a poverty affidavit.).
See also Text 15.02(F), Right to transcript and counsel.

[177]See In re Wyrock, Nos. 41305, 41306 (8th Dist Ct App, Cuyahoga, 6-5-80) (Juv R 37(A) supersedes RC 2151.35.).

[178]In re Gault, 387 US 1, 87 SCt 1428, 18 LEd(2d) 527 (1967).

[179]*Id.* at 72.

[180]Griffin v Illinois, 351 US 12, 76 SCt 585, 100 LEd 891 (1956). See also Mayer v Chicago, 404 US 189, 92 SCt 410, 30 LEd(2d) 372 (1971) (right to transcript in cases where a fine is imposed).

[181]State ex rel Heller v Miller, 61 OS(2d) 6, 399 NE(2d) 66 (1980) (right to transcript based on United States and Ohio Constitutions' Due Process and Equal Protection Clauses).

indigent child has a right to a transcript in transfer proceedings.[182] Courts in other jurisdictions have also ruled that juveniles have a constitutional right to a transcript.[183]

CROSS REFERENCES

Text 15.02(F)

Merrick-Rippner, Ohio Probate Law (4th ed), Text Ch 223

11.15 Double jeopardy

The Fifth Amendment protects a criminal defendant from being put in jeopardy twice for the same offense.[184] The Double Jeopardy Clause consists of three separate guarantees: "It protects against a second prosecution for the same offense after acquittal. It protects against a second prosecution for the same offense after conviction. And it protects against multiple punishments for the same offense."[185]

In *Breed v Jones*[186] the Supreme Court held the Double Jeopardy Clause applicable to delinquency proceedings:[187]

> We believe it is simply too late in the day to conclude ... that a juvenile is not put in jeopardy at a proceeding whose object is to determine whether he has committed acts that violate a criminal law and whose potential consequences include both the stigma inherent in such a determination and the deprivation of liberty for many years.[188]

According to the Court, jeopardy attached "when the Juvenile Court, as the trier of the facts, began to hear evidence."[189] *Breed* involved double jeopardy issues relating to transfer proceedings.[190]

---

[182]State v Ross, 23 App(2d) 215, 262 NE(2d) 427 (Greene 1970).

[183]E.g., In re State in re Aaron, 266 So(2d) 726 (La App 1972). See generally Comment, *Appellate Review for Juveniles: A "Right" to a Transcript*, 4 Colum Hum Rts L Rev 485 (1972); Comment, *The Right of an Indigent Juvenile in Ohio to a Transcript at State Expense*, 5 Akron L Rev 117 (1972).

[184]US Const Am 5 ("[N]or shall any person be subject for the same offence to be twice put in jeopardy of life or limb."). The Supreme Court has held that the Double Jeopardy Clause applies to state trials. Benton v Maryland, 395 US 784, 89 SCt 2056, 23 LEd(2d) 707 (1969). See generally 3 LaFave and Israel, *Criminal Procedure* ch 24 (1984); Whitebread and Slobogin, *Criminal Procedure* ch 30 (2d ed 1986).

The Ohio Constitution also prohibits double jeopardy (O Const Art I, § 10).

[185]North Carolina v Pearce, 395 US 711, 717, 89 SCt 2072, 23 LEd(2d) 656 (1969).

[186]Breed v Jones, 421 US 519, 95 SCt 1779, 44 LEd(2d) 346 (1975).

[187]See generally Applicability of double jeopardy to juvenile court proceedings, 5 ALR4th 234 (1981).

[188]Breed v Jones, 421 US 519, 529, 95 SCt 1779, 44 LEd(2d) 346 (1975). *Breed* overruled several Ohio cases that held the Double Jeopardy Clause inapplicable to juvenile cases on the grounds that these cases were civil and not criminal. See In re Mack, 22 App(2d) 201, 260 NE(2d) 619 (Hamilton 1970); In re Whittington, 17 App(2d) 164, 245 NE(2d) 364 (Fairfield 1969).

[189]Breed v Jones, 421 US 519, 531, 95 SCt 1779, 44 LEd(2d) 346 (1975). See also Serfass v United States, 420 US 377, 95 SCt 1055, 43 LEd(2d) 265 (1975) (In a bench trial jeopardy attaches when the first witness is sworn.).

[190]For a discussion of this issue, see Text 9.06, Double jeopardy.

The Court also addressed double jeopardy issues in *Swisher v Brady*,[191] which involved the use of a master. The issue was whether the state's filing of exceptions to a master's proposals required the child to stand trial a second time, i.e., before the juvenile court judge. The Court held that the Maryland procedure involved in *Swisher* did not violate the Double Jeopardy Clause. The Court, however, emphasized several factors regarding the Maryland procedure that were critical to its decision. First, under that procedure the prosecution is not given a "second crack" at winning its case in the proceeding before the juvenile judge: "The State presents its evidence once before the master. The record is then closed, and additional evidence can be received by the Juvenile Court judge only with the consent of the minor."[192] Second, the master's recommendations are not binding; only the juvenile court judge is authorized to enter a judgment.[193]

An issue raised by the dissent in *Swisher*, but not decided by the Court, focused on whether the Maryland procedure violated due process because the juvenile judge, who was the ultimate factfinder, did not personally conduct the trial. The Arizona Supreme Court has held that such a procedure violates due process.[194]

In *Illinois v Vitale*[195] a child was first prosecuted and convicted in criminal court for failure to reduce speed to avoid an accident. A petition was subsequently filed in juvenile court alleging involuntary manslaughter by reckless operation of a motor vehicle. Both the criminal prosecution and the juvenile petition were based on the same incident. The United States Supreme Court held that the test for determining whether two offenses are the same offense for purposes of the Double Jeopardy Clause is the same in criminal and juvenile cases. "The applicable rule is that where the same act or transaction constitutes a violation of two distinct statutory provisions, the test to be applied to determine whether there are two offenses or only one, is whether each provision requires proof of a fact which the other does not."[196] The Court, however, was uncertain whether a careless failure to slow is always a necessary element of manslaughter by automobile under state law and thus remanded the case to the state supreme court.

In *In re Gilbert*[197] an Ohio appellate court held that the Double Jeopardy Clause precluded the prosecution from appealing a verdict in favor of a child after an adjudicatory hearing.[198] Such a postverdict appeal should be distinguished from a pretrial appeal. For example, Juvenile Rule 22(F) provides for the right of appeal by the prosecution where the juvenile court grants a motion

---

[191]Swisher v Brady, 438 US 204, 98 SCt 2699, 57 LEd(2d) 705 (1978).

[192]*Id.* at 216.

[193]*Id.* See also Text 11.16, Referees.

[194]In re Appeal in Pima County, Juvenile Action, 129 Ariz 371, 631 P(2d) 526 (1981) (en banc) (Juvenile judge reversed referee's finding that evidence did not establish offense beyond a reasonable doubt.).

[195]Illinois v Vitale, 447 US 410, 100 SCt 2260, 65 LEd(2d) 228 (1980).

[196]Brown v Ohio, 432 US 161, 166, 97 SCt 2221, 53 LEd(2d) 187 (1977).

[197]In re Gilbert, 45 App(2d) 308, 345 NE(2d) 79 (Summit 1974).

[198]See also In re Hampton, 24 App(2d) 69, 263 NE(2d) 910 (Cuyahoga 1970) (A juvenile court's overruling of a plea in bar on double jeopardy grounds is not a final appealable order.).

to suppress evidence. This rule does not violate the double jeopardy provision because jeopardy has not yet attached[199] and such a ruling is not an acquittal.[200]

In *In re Williams*,[201] a juvenile was charged with felony theft based on prior adjudications for petit theft. The referee sua sponte declared a mistrial because of her own intervention in the examination of a witness concerning the prior adjudications. The appellate court ruled that the Double Jeopardy Clause precluded a retrial for felony theft but not for petit theft.

Whether the Double Jeopardy Clause applies to nondelinquency cases remains uncertain. One court, however, has held that the double jeopardy guarantee bars delinquency proceedings based on conduct that was earlier the subject of a "status" offender proceeding.[202]

CROSS REFERENCES

Text 1.02(E), 9.06, 11.16, 15.02(E)

11.16   Referees

Juvenile Rule 40(A) and RC 2151.16 empower a juvenile court judge to appoint referees[203] to hear juvenile cases.[204] A person who has contemporaneous responsibility for working with or supervising children subject to juvenile court jurisdiction may not be appointed a referee.[205] Neither the rule nor the statute requires the referee to be an attorney. The Traffic Rules, however, require referees to be attorneys,[206] and this provision applies in juvenile traffic offender cases. Where possible, a female referee must be appointed for the trial of females.[207]

Generally, a hearing before a referee is conducted in the same manner as a hearing before a juvenile court judge; the referee is authorized to swear in witnesses and rule on the admissibility of evidence unless the order of reference provides otherwise.[208] The referee is required to submit a report to the juvenile

---

[199]Breed v Jones, 421 US 519, 531, 95 SCt 1779, 44 LEd(2d) 346 (1975).

[200]See United States v Scott, 437 US 82, 98 SCt 2187, 57 LEd(2d) 65 (1978). For a discussion of the state's right to appeal, see Text 15.02(E), By the state.

[201]In re Williams, 31 App(3d) 241, 31 OBR 525, 510 NE(2d) 832 (Franklin 1986).

[202]In re K., 67 Ill App(3d) 451, 384 NE(2d) 531 (1978). See also Garrison v Jennings, 529 P(2d) 536 (Okla Crim App 1974) (Jeopardy attached in status offender hearing based on criminal conduct.).

[203]Juv R 40 is similar but not identical to Civ R 53, which governs the appointment and powers of referees in civil cases. See generally *Baldwin's Ohio Civil Practice*. See also Traf R 14 (referees in traffic cases).

[204]Juv R 40(A) provides that the appointment of a referee may empower him to act in a single proceeding or in a specified class of proceedings or portions thereof. RC 2151.16 provides that referees shall have the usual powers of masters in chancery cases. In State v Eddington, 52 App(2d) 312, 369 NE(2d) 1054 (Marion 1976), the court held that neither of these provisions authorizes the appointment of a referee to hear a case involving an adult charged with child abuse, even though such a case is subject to juvenile court jurisdiction.

[205]Juv R 40(A).

[206]Traf R 14.

[207]RC 2151.16.

[208]Juv R 40(B).

court, and copies of the report must be provided to the parties.[209] The report must set forth the referee's findings and recommendations.[210] The referee's findings of fact must be sufficient to permit the court to make an independent analysis of the issues.[211] The parties may submit objections to the report within fourteen days of the date of filing.[212] The court may then adopt, reject, or modify the report. It may also hear additional evidence, return the report to the referee with instructions, or hear the matter itself.[213] There is, however, no right to an evidentiary hearing before the juvenile court judge.[214]

The referee's report is not binding until approved and entered as a matter of record by the juvenile court judge.[215] As one court has commented, "Although reports of referees may frequently be adopted by the trial court, the rule does not contemplate that the trial court rubber-stamp all reports by referees."[216] RC 2151.31(D), however, appears to give referees the authority to order (rather than merely recommend) the taking of a child into custody.

CROSS REFERENCES

Merrick-Rippner, Ohio Probate Law (4th ed), Text Ch 223

---

[209]See In re Weimer, 19 App(3d) 130, 19 OBR 219, 483 NE(2d) 173 (Cuyahoga 1984) (Failure to provide juvenile with supplemental report is error.); In re Hobson, 44 Abs 86, 90, 62 NE(2d) 510 (App, Franklin 1945) (The "findings and recommendations by the referee are required by statute to be in writing.").

[210]See Nolte v Nolte, 60 App(2d) 227, 396 NE(2d) 807 (Cuyahoga 1978) (Referee's report must contain a statement of facts forming the basis for the referee's recommendation.).

[211]Juv R 40(D)(5).

[212]Juv R 40(D)(2).

[213]*Id.* See In re Langrehr, No. 2944 (11th Dist Ct App, Trumbull, 11-9-81) (A juvenile court's judgment entered before the filing of a referee's report is invalid.).

[214]In re Stall, 36 OS(2d) 139, 304 NE(2d) 596 (1973).

[215]Juv R 40(D)(5). See In re Fusik, No. 41569 (8th Dist Ct App, Cuyahoga, 6-12-80) (Juvenile court referee has no authority to enter a judgment.).

[216]In re Bradford, 30 App(3d) 87, 88, 30 OBR 185, 506 NE(2d) 925 (Franklin 1986).

Chapter 13

Disposition of Children's Cases

13.01   General principles

The juvenile court has wide latitude in the disposition of children's cases.[1] However, there are specific principles which govern the court in the exercise of its discretion. The primary consideration in the disposition of all children's cases is the best interests and welfare of the child.[2] The court must focus its disposition on providing for the care, protection, rehabilitation, and mental and physical development of the child.[3] Whenever possible, the child should be cared for in a family environment, separated from his parents only when necessary for his welfare or in the interests of public safety.[4] Parents have a natural, paramount right to raise their children, the loss of which must be safeguarded by due process protections.[5]

If the child is placed in the guardianship or custody of someone other than his parent, the court must, when practicable, select a person, institution, or agency of the same religious faith as his parents; in case of a difference in the religious faith of the parents, the selection may be based on the religious faith of the child or, if this is not ascertainable, on that of either parent.[6] Where the parent has stated an indifference to the religious upbringing of the child, the county welfare department (now county human services department) which has obtained custody of the child is not required to place the child with persons of the parent's religion.[7]

If a county or district establishes a school, camp, or other facility for the training, treatment, and rehabilitation of children adjudged to be delinquent, dependent, neglected, abused, unruly, or juvenile traffic offenders, the juvenile

---

[1]See RC 2151.353 to RC 2151.356 for the range of dispositional alternatives for each type of children's case.

[2]For a discussion of this issue in the context of permanent custody cases, see Text 13.04, Reasonable efforts determination; Text 13.06(A)(4), Permanent custody.

[3]RC 2151.01(A), (B).

[4]RC 2151.01(C); In re Escue, No. 1487 (4th Dist Ct App, Lawrence, 5-11-81).

[5]State ex rel Heller v Miller, 61 OS(2d) 6, 399 NE(2d) 66 (1980); In re Cunningham, 59 OS(2d) 100, 396 NE(2d) 1035 (1979); In re Perales, 52 OS(2d) 89, 369 NE(2d) 1047 (1977); In re Gutman, 22 App(2d) 125, 259 NE(2d) 128 (Hamilton 1969).

[6]RC 2151.32.

[7]In re Doe, 167 NE(2d) 396 (Juv, Columbiana 1956).

court is responsible for determining which children shall be admitted to the facility, the period of commitment, and removal and transfer from the facility.[8]

Whenever the court makes an order that removes a child from his home or that vests temporary or permanent custody of the child with a nonparent or governmental agency, the court must determine the school district responsible for bearing the cost of the child's education.[9] If a child is placed in a detention home[10] or a juvenile facility established under RC 2151.65, or if he has been committed to the permanent custody of the Department of Youth Services, his school district as determined by the court must pay the cost of the child's education.[11] However, if the child is placed in a private institution, school, residential treatment center, or other private facility, the state must pay the court a subsidy, not to exceed $500 per year, to help defray the expense of educating the child.[12]

CROSS REFERENCES

Text 13.04, 13.06(A)(4), 13.07(B)(8)

Merrick-Rippner, Ohio Probate Law (4th ed), Text Ch 223

13.02   Bifurcated hearings

If the child is found to be within the jurisdiction of the court at the adjudicatory hearing, a dispositional hearing is subsequently held to determine what action should be taken concerning the child.[13] The judge who presided at the adjudicatory hearing must, if possible, preside at the dispositional hearing.[14]

In abuse, neglect, and dependency proceedings, the date for the dispositional hearing must be scheduled by the court at the conclusion of the adjudicatory hearing.[15] The dispositional hearing must be held at least one day but not more than thirty days after the adjudicatory hearing, except that it may be held immediately after the adjudicatory hearing if all parties were served prior to the adjudicatory hearing with all necessary documents, and all parties consent to the immediate hearing.[16] On the request of any party, the court may continue the dispositional hearing to enable a party to obtain or consult counsel.[17] However, the dispositional hearing in neglect, abuse, and dependency cases must be held within ninety days after the complaint was filed, and if the court fails to meet this time limit, it is required to dismiss the complaint without prejudice.[18]

---

[8]RC 2151.65.

[9]RC 2151.357; Juv R 34(C). RC 3313.64 prescribes the manner in which this determination is to be made. See Kenton Bd of Ed v Day, 30 Misc(2d) 25, 30 OBR 289, 506 NE(2d) 1239 (CP, Hardin 1986).

[10]Placement in a detention home may not be used as a final disposition. See Text 13.07(B)(8), Any further disposition that the court finds proper.

[11]RC 2151.357; Christman v Washington Court House School Dist, 30 App(3d) 228, 30 OBR 386, 507 NE(2d) 257 (Fayette 1986); OAG 88-23.

[12]RC 2151.357.

[13]Juv R 2(8); RC 2151.35(B)(1).

[14]Juv R 34(B)(1); RC 2151.35(B)(2)(a).

[15]RC 2151.28(B)(3).

[16]RC 2151.35(B)(1).

[17]*Id.* See also RC 2151.28(B)(3).

[18]*Id.*

In all other cases (e.g., delinquency, unruly, and traffic cases) this hearing may be conducted either immediately after the adjudicatory hearing or at a later date.[19] If the dispositional hearing is held immediately after the adjudicatory hearing, a party may request that the hearing be continued for a reasonable time to obtain or consult counsel.[20] Where a party does not request a continuance, the court may proceed immediately to disposition.[21]

If the juvenile court decides to schedule the dispositional hearing at a later date, such hearing must be conducted within six months of the adjudicatory hearing.[22] However, the Ohio Supreme Court has held in *Linger v Weiss*[23] that the juvenile court does not lose jurisdiction by failing to adhere to the time limits set forth in Juvenile Rule 34(A). The court in *Linger* reasoned that since the Ohio Rules of Juvenile Procedure may not extend or limit the jurisdiction of the juvenile court,[24] a procedural violation has no effect on jurisdictional issues, which are governed by statutory law. Because almost three years had elapsed since the adjudicatory hearing and no dispositional hearing had ever been scheduled,[25] the court relied on Juvenile Rule 34, rather than Juvenile Rule 29(F)(2)(b), in reaching its decision. The same outcome would have resulted if the dispositional hearing had been held in conformity with Juvenile Rule 34(A) but after the six-month limit of Juvenile Rule 29(F)(2)(b).[26] Where an untimely delay occurs between the adjudicatory and dispositional hearings, a party's only recourse is to file a complaint for a writ of procedendo[27] or mandamus,[28] rather than filing an appeal[29] or a writ of habeas corpus.[30]

Ohio law mandates that adjudication and disposition take place at bifurcated hearings.[31] In reversing a permanent custody order made in a dependency case, the Ohio Supreme Court in *In re Cunningham*[32] held that consideration of the child's "best interests" may not enter into the initial factual determination of dependency. That issue becomes a proper focus only when the emphasis has shifted to a consideration of the statutorily permissible dispositional alternatives. A finding of dependency, neglect, or abuse, which is at some point jour-

---

[19]RC 2151.35(A); Juv R 34(A).

[20]Juv R 34(A).

[21]In re Howell, No. 79-CA-16 (5th Dist Ct App, Coshocton, 1-31-80); In re Bolden, 37 App(2d) 7, 306 NE(2d) 166 (Allen 1973).

[22]Juv R 29(F)(2)(b).

[23]Linger v Weiss, 57 OS(2d) 97, 386 NE(2d) 1354 (1979), cert denied 444 US 862, 100 SCt 128, 62 LEd(2d) 83 (1979).

[24]Juv R 44.

[25]There was some question as to whether an adjudicatory hearing had even been held. For discussion of this issue, see Text 7.06(D), Time restrictions.

[26]In re Fusik, No. 41569 (8th Dist Ct App, Cuyahoga, 6-12-80).

[27]See footnote 5 of the Supreme Court's decision in Linger v Weiss, 57 OS(2d) 97, 386 NE(2d) 1354 (1979), cert denied 444 US 862, 100 SCt 128, 62 LEd(2d) 83 (1979).

[28]In re Fusik, No. 41569 (8th Dist Ct App, Cuyahoga, 6-12-80).

[29]*Id.*

[30]Linger v Weiss, 57 OS(2d) 97, 386 NE(2d) 1354 (1979), cert denied 444 US 862, 100 SCt 128, 62 LEd(2d) 83 (1979).

[31]Juv R 29(E)(4), Juv R 34. For a discussion of the need for bifurcated hearings where a motion for permanent custody is filed following a prior adjudication and temporary custody order, see Text 13.04, Reasonable efforts determination; Text 13.06(A)(4), Permanent custody.

[32]In re Cunningham, 59 OS(2d) 100, 396 NE(2d) 1035 (1979).

nalized, must precede the disposition of the case because there are different substantive inquiries to be undertaken in each phase with concomitant differences in evidence and standards of review.[33]

Although prejudice need not be shown in order to justify reversal where the hearings are not bifurcated,[34] it has been held that such error is waived if there is no objection to the combined hearings.[35] Furthermore, where the juvenile court hears some evidence on disposition during the adjudicatory phase but understands the distinction between the two stages, the court does not commit reversible error.[36] This is particularly so where the issues of dependency (adjudication) and custody (disposition) are so interrelated as to make it impossible to conduct a dependency hearing devoid of all dispositional aspects.[37]

CROSS REFERENCES
Text 7.06(D), 13.04, 13.06(A)(4), 15.01(B)(1)

13.03　Conduct of hearing

The dispositional hearing in children's cases shares certain aspects with the adjudicatory hearing. For example, the court may conduct a dispositional hearing in an informal manner and may adjourn the hearing from time to time.[38] In addition, the general public may be excluded, and in neglect, dependency, or abuse cases the child's attendance may be excused.[39] However, whereas the standard of proof at the adjudicatory hearing is proof beyond a reasonable doubt or clear and convincing evidence.[40] the standard of proof in the dispositional portion of the proceedings is by a preponderance of the evidence.[41]

Although the Ohio Rules of Evidence apply to juvenile court proceedings,[42] their applicability at the dispositional stage is somewhat limited. Evidence Rule 101(C)(6) provides that the evidence rules are inapplicable in "proceedings in

---

[33]In re Johnson, No. C-810516 (1st Dist Ct App, Hamilton, 4-28-82); In re Bryant, No. CA80-11-0125 (12th Dist Ct App, Butler, 1-13-82); In re Black, No. C-800021 (1st Dist Ct App, Hamilton, 1-28-81). See also In re Moore, No. CA291 (12th Dist Ct App, Preble, 5-20-81); In re Bowman, No. 79AP-798 (10th Dist Ct App, Franklin, 6-26-80); In re Brown, No. 3-CA-79 (5th Dist Ct App, Fairfield, 7-20-79); In re Darst, 117 App 374, 192 NE(2d) 287 (Franklin 1963); In re Baxter, 17 OS(3d) 229, 17 OBR 469, 479 NE(2d) 257 (1985); In re Pitts, 38 App(3d) 1, 525 NE(2d) 814 (Knox 1987); In re Smart, 21 App(3d) 31, 21 OBR 33, 486 NE(2d) 147 (Franklin 1984).

[34]In re Parker, No. 15-79-16 (3d Dist Ct App, Van Wert, 1-26-81). But see In re Feldman, No. 34223 (8th Dist Ct App, Cuyahoga, 12-23-75), a pre-*Cunningham* case which indicated that prejudice must be shown.

[35]In re Guthrie, No. CA 6383 (2d Dist Ct App, Montgomery, 2-22-80); In re Feldman, No. 34223 (8th Dist Ct App, Cuyahoga, 12-23-75).

[36]In re Bibb, 70 App(2d) 117, 435 NE(2d) 96 (Hamilton 1980); In re Feiler, No. C-780549 (1st Dist Ct App, Hamilton, 10-17-79). See also In re Skaggs, No. 1278 (4th Dist Ct App, Scioto, 1-22-81).

[37]In re Kemp, No. 41320 (8th Dist Ct App, Cuyahoga, 6-26-80); In re Feldman, No. 34223 (8th Dist Ct App, Cuyahoga, 12-23-75).

[38]Juv R 27.

[39]*Id.*

[40]Juv R 29(E)(4); RC 2151.35(A). See Text 11.10, Burden of proof.

[41]Juv R 29(E)(4); In re Willmann, 24 App(3d) 191, 24 OBR 313, 493 NE(2d) 380 (Hamilton 1986).

[42]Evid R 101(A). See Text 11.11, Evidence.

which other rules prescribed by the supreme court govern matters relating to evidence." Both the rules[43] and the statutes[44] governing the procedure for the dispositional hearing in children's cases permit the court to "admit any evidence that is material and relevant, including hearsay, opinion, and documentary evidence."[45] Thus, these types of evidence are properly admitted at dispositional hearings without the restrictions imposed by Evidence Rule 802 and Articles VII and IX of the Rules of Evidence. In addition, Evidence Rule 611(B), governing cross-examination of witnesses, is superseded by RC 2151.35(B)(2)(c) and Juvenile Rule 34(B)(3), which prohibit the cross-examination of medical examiners and investigators who prepare a social history, except on consent of all the parties or the court.[46]

If a social history is prepared or a mental or physical examination is conducted prior to the dispositional hearing, counsel is entitled to inspect the contents of the history or report a reasonable time before the hearing.[47] For good cause shown, the court may deny inspection or may limit its scope to specified portions of the history or report and may order that its contents not be disclosed to specified persons. The court must state its reasons for denial or limitation of inspection or disclosure to counsel.[48]

Any party may offer evidence supplementing, explaining, or disputing the information contained in the social history or other reports utilized by the court at disposition.[49]

A record of all testimony and other oral proceedings is required in all cases where permanent custody of the child may be granted at the original dispositional hearing (RC 2151.353(A)(4)) or pursuant to a motion for permanent custody (RC 2151.414), and in any other proceedings a record must be made upon request.[50] It has been held that the denial of a request for a court reporter is not prejudicial error, since alternative methods of reporting trial proceedings, including a full narrative statement based on Appellate Rule 9(C), are permissible if they place before the appellate court an equivalent report of the events at trial.[51]

At the conclusion of the hearing, the court must advise the child of his right to record expungement (in delinquency and unruly cases) and, where any part of the proceeding was contested, the court must advise the parties of their right to

---

[43]Juv R 34(B)(2)(b).

[44]RC 2151.35(B)(2).

[45]This may include the contents of a social history or report of a mental or physical examination ordered under Juv R 32. See In re Crose, No. 1055 (2d Dist Ct App, Darke, 10-18-82).

[46]See also In re Guthrie, No. CA 6383 (2d Dist Ct App, Montgomery, 2-22-80), holding that where the adjudicatory and dispositional hearings were combined, a parent had a right to call as a witness a psychologist who had prepared a report.

[47]Juv R 32(C); In re Crose, No. 1055 (2d Dist Ct App, Darke, 10-18-82).

[48]Juv R 32(C).

[49]Juv R 34(B)(3). See also In re Simon, No. CA1011 (2d Dist Ct App, Darke, 10-15-80).

[50]RC 2151.35(A). See also RC 2301.20.

[51]In re Holcomb, No. 39694 (8th Dist Ct App, Cuyahoga, 10-4-79), citing Draper v Washington, 372 US 487, 83 SCt 774, 9 LEd(2d) 899 (1963).

appeal.[52] However, failure of the court to advise the child of his right to expungement does not constitute reversible error where no prejudice is shown.[53]

Juvenile Rule 34(C) provides that within seven days of the conclusion of the dispositional hearing, the court must enter an appropriate judgment, including any applicable conditions, and provide a copy of the judgment to any party requesting it.[54] However, it appears that a copy of the judgment must be served on all parties whether or not a request is made. RC 2151.35(B)(3), which applies to abuse, neglect, and dependency proceedings, requires a copy of the judgment to be served on all parties. Moreover, the Ohio Supreme Court has held that within three days of the entry of any final appealable judgment or order, the clerk of courts must serve a notice of the entry on every party who is not in default for failure to appear.[55] Since a dispositional order is a final appealable order,[56] this case would supersede Juvenile Rule 34(C).

CROSS REFERENCES

Text 1.02, Ch 11, 15.02

Schroeder-Katz, Ohio Criminal Law, Crim R 22, Author's Text, Crim R 32, Author's Text
Merrick-Rippner, Ohio Probate Law (4th ed), Text Ch 223
Giannelli, Ohio Evidence Manual, Author's Comment 101.10, 611.04(b), 701.01, 702.07, 802.06, 901.01

13.04   Reasonable efforts determination

At any hearing in which the court removes a child from his home or continues the removal from his home, the court must determine whether the public children services agency or private child placing agency has made reasonable efforts (1) to prevent the removal, (2) to eliminate the continued removal, or (3) to make it possible for the child to return home.[57] Although this requirement is intended to apply mainly to abuse, neglect, or dependency proceedings where such public and private agencies are involved, by the wording of the statute its applicability is extended to other cases under certain circumstances. Thus, the requirement applies in any proceeding (e.g., abuse, neglect, dependency, delinquency, and unruly cases) where the removal order is made at (1) an adjudicatory hearing,[58] (2) an "emergency custody" hearing,[59] or (3) a detention or shelter care hearing.[60] However, if the removal order is made at a dispositional hearing, the reasonable efforts determination is required only if the dispositional hearing was held following an adjudication of abuse, neglect, or depen-

---

[52]Juv R 34(E).

[53]In re Haas, 45 App(2d) 187, 341 NE(2d) 638 (Stark 1975).

[54]See also RC 2151.35(B)(3).

[55]Atkinson v Grumman Ohio Corp, 37 OS(3d) 80, 523 NE(2d) 851 (1988).

[56]See Text 15.02(B), Final orders.

[57]RC 2151.419(A). See 42 USC 672.

[58]RC 2151.419(A). See RC 2151.28(B); Text Ch 11, Adjudicatory Hearings.

[59]RC 2151.419(A). See RC 2151.31(E), RC 2151.33; Text 7.07, Temporary orders pending hearing.

[60]RC 2151.419(A). See RC 2151.314; Text 7.06(C), Hearing.

dency.[61] The burden of proving that reasonable efforts have been made rests with the agency.[62]

The court must issue written findings of fact setting forth the reasonable efforts determination, including a brief description of the relevant services provided by the agency to the family of the child and why those services did not prevent the child's removal from home or enable the child to return home.[63]

CROSS REFERENCES

Text 7.06(C), 7.07, Ch 11, 13.06(A)

13.05   Case plans

(A) Conditions requiring case plan

An agency must prepare and maintain a case plan for any child to whom the agency is providing services and to whom any of the following applies: (1) the agency filed a complaint alleging that the child is abused, neglected, or dependent; (2) the agency has temporary or permanent custody of the child; (3) the child is living at home subject to an order for protective supervision; (4) the child is in long-term foster care.[64]

(B) Time for filing case plan

The case plan must be filed with the court prior to the child's adjudicatory hearing, but no later than thirty days after the earlier of the date on which the complaint was filed or the date on which the child was first placed into shelter care.[65] If insufficient information is available prior to the hearing to complete the plan, the agency must complete the plan by thirty days after the adjudicatory hearing or the date of the dispositional hearing, whichever is earlier.[66]

(C) Court approval and journalization of case plan

In preparing the case plan, the agency must attempt to obtain an agreement among all parties regarding its content. If this is accomplished, and the court approves it, the court must journalize the case plan as part of its dispositional order.[67] If, on the other hand, agreement cannot be reached, or the court does not approve it, the court must decide its contents at the dispositional hearing based on the child's best interest.[68] The journalized case plan will then bind all parties.[69]

---

[61]RC 2151.419(A). See RC 2151.353(H); Text 13.06(A), Dispositional alternatives.

[62]RC 2151.419(A). Although the statute does not indicate the standard of proof, Juvenile Rule 29(E)(4) provides that the issues are to be determined by clear and convincing evidence in dependency, neglect, and abuse proceedings.

[63]RC 2151.419(B).

[64]RC 2151.412(A); 42 USC 671. The Department of Human Services is required to adopt rules concerning the content and format of case plans and procedures for developing, implementing, and changing case plans. RC 2151.412(A)(1), (2).

[65]RC 2151.412(C).

[66]Id.

[67]RC 2151.412(D). See RC 2151.353(D).

[68]RC 2151.412(D).

[69]RC 2151.412(E)(1).

(D) Changing the case plan

Substantive parts of a case plan may not be changed unless approved in advance by all parties.[70] Although it does not define the term "substantive parts," the statute does include the child's placement and the visitation rights of any party as examples of such parts. Within seven days of approval, the proposed change must be submitted to the court, which may, within fourteen days, either approve it or schedule a hearing to be held no later than thirty days after the expiration of the fourteen-day period. If the court takes neither action within the fourteen days, the agency may implement the proposed change. Otherwise, the proposed change may not be implemented without court approval.[71]

If emergency circumstances exist, and an immediate change in the case plan is needed to prevent harm to the child, the agency may implement the change without prior agreement or court approval.[72] Before the end of the next business day after the change is made, the agency must notify all parties and the court. If the agency can obtain an agreement on the change from all parties within seven days after implementing the change, the change must be immediately filed with the court. Once again, the court may either approve it or schedule a hearing within the same time frames that apply to other proposed changes in the case plan.[73] If the agency is unable to obtain an agreement from all parties, the court must schedule a hearing to be held within fourteen days after the agency requests the hearing.[74]

(E) General goals and priorities for case plan

All case plans for children in temporary custody[75] must have the following general goals: (1) consistent with the best interest and special needs of the child, to achieve an out-of-home placement in the least restrictive, most family-like setting available and in close proximity to the home from which the child was removed or the home in which the child will be permanently placed; (2) either to eliminate the need for the out-of-home placement with all due speed so the child can return home, or to develop and implement an alternative permanent living arrangement.[76] If the child is or has been the victim of abuse or neglect, or if the child witnessed the commission in the child's household of abuse or neglect against a sibling, parent, or any other household member, then the case plan for a child in temporary custody must also include a requirement that the child's parents, guardian, or custodian participate in mandatory counseling and any supportive services included in the case plan.[77]

The agency developing the case plan and the court reviewing it must be guided by the following general priorities. A child who is residing with or can be

---

[70]RC 2151.412(E)(2).
[71]Id.
[72]RC 2151.412(E)(3).
[73]Id.
[74]Id. See RC 2151.417.
[75]For children in protective supervision, long-term foster care, or permanent custody, the Department of Human Services must adopt rules setting forth the general goals of case plans. RC 2151.412(F)(2).
[76]RC 2151.412(F)(1).
[77]RC 2151.412(H).

placed with his parents within a reasonable time should remain in their legal custody, even if an order of protective supervision is required.[78] If return to the parents is not feasible, the child should be placed in the legal custody of a suitable member of the child's extended family or, if none exists, a suitable nonrelative.[79] If the above options cannot be implemented, the child should be placed in the temporary custody of an appropriate agency.[80] As a last resort, the child should be committed to the permanent custody of an agency if the agency has a reasonable expectation of placing the child for adoption.[81]

(F) Due process and case plans

A federal district court held that the Due Process Clause of the United States Constitution does not require states to carry out a reunification plan before making a final adjudication of abuse or dependency.[82] The court further held that although federal law[83] provides that the amount of federal tax money granted to states for child welfare programs will be reduced unless the state has a "replacement preventive service program," the statute is a mere funding provision and creates no federal "right" to such a reunification program.

CROSS REFERENCES

Text 1.02(A), (B), 7.03, 13.06(A)(1), (4), (5)

13.06   Abused, neglected, or dependent child

(A) Dispositional alternatives

If a child is adjudicated abused, neglected, or dependent, the court may issue any order described in RC 2151.33.[84] In addition, RC 2151.353(A)[85] authorizes the court to make any of the following dispositional orders:

(1) Place the child in protective supervision;[86]

(2) Commit the child to the temporary custody of a public children services agency, a private child placing agency,[87] either parent, a relative resid-

---

[78]RC 2151.412(G)(1).

[79]RC 2151.412(G)(2), (3).

[80]RC 2151.412(G)(4).

[81]RC 2151.412(G)(5). The statute does not include long-term foster care among any of the priorities.

[82]Lesher v Lavrich, 632 FSupp 77 (ND Ohio 1984), affirmed by 784 F(2d) 193 (6th Cir Ohio 1986).

[83]42 USC 627(b)(3).

[84]RC 2151.35(B)(4). See Text 3.05, Neglect, dependency, and abuse: attachment of jurisdiction; Text 3.06, Neglected child; Text 3.07, Dependent child; Text 3.08, Abused child.

[85]The statute, in a previous but similar version, was held not unconstitutionally vague or broad. In re Williams, 7 App(3d) 324, 7 OBR 421, 455 NE(2d) 1027 (Hamilton 1982).

[86]RC 2151.353(A)(1).

[87]Hereinafter, the terms "public children services agency" and "private child placing agency" will be referred to as "agency." See RC 2151.011(B)(26) and (B)(9), respectively, for definitions of these terms.

ing within or without the state, or a probation officer for placement in a certified foster home[88] or approved foster care;[89]

(3) Award legal custody of the child to either parent or to any other person;[90]

(4) Commit the child to the permanent custody of an agency;[91]

(5) Place the child in long-term foster care with an agency.[92]

(1) Protective supervision

(a) Definition of protective supervision. Protective supervision is an order of disposition in which the court permits a child to remain in the custody of his parents, guardian, or custodian and stay in his home, subject to any conditions and limitations upon the child, his parents, guardian, or custodian, or any other person that the court prescribes, including supervision as directed by the court for the protection of the child.[93] These conditions and limitations include, but are not limited to, any of the following:

(1) The court may order a party, effective within forty-eight hours after the issuance of the order, to vacate the child's home indefinitely or for a specified period of time;

(2) The court may order a party to prevent any particular person from having contact with the child; or

(3) The court may issue an order restraining or otherwise controlling the conduct of any person whose conduct would not be in the child's best interest.[94]

(b) Time restrictions on protective supervision. Any order for protective supervision must terminate one year after the earlier of the date on which the complaint was filed or the date on which the child was first placed into shelter care, unless the agency that prepared the child's case plan files a motion with the court requesting an extension of the dispositional order for up to six months or an extension of a previous extension for up to six months.[95] After conducting a mandatory hearing,[96] the court may grant either extension if it is in the child's best interest. At any time after the order granting an extension is issued, the

---

[88]A foster home is a family home in which a child is received apart from his parents for care, supervision, or training (RC 2151.011(B)(5)). A certified foster home is a foster home operated by persons holding a permit issued under RC 5103.03 to RC 5103.05 (RC 2151.011(B)(6)). Any foster home is considered to be a residential use of property for purposes of municipal, county, and township zoning and is a permitted use in all zoning districts in which residential uses are permitted (RC 2151.418).

[89]RC 2151.353(A)(2). For discussion of agreements for temporary custody, see Text 3.09, Agreements for temporary and permanent custody.

[90]RC 2151.353(A)(3).

[91]RC 2151.353(A)(4).

[92]RC 2151.353(A)(5).

[93]RC 2151.011(B)(16).

[94]RC 2151.353(C).

[95]RC 2151.353(G).

[96]RC 2151.353(G) mandates a hearing when the motion is filed. This conflicts with Juv R 19, which permits the court to make provision by rule or order for the submission and determination of motions without oral hearing upon brief written statements of reasons in support and opposition.

agency may request the court to terminate the order. On receipt of the motion requesting termination, the court must terminate the dispositional order.[97]

(2) Temporary custody

(a) Definition of temporary custody. Temporary custody is defined as legal custody of a child who is removed from his home, which custody may be terminated at any time by the court in its discretion or, if the legal custody is granted in an agreement for temporary custody, by the person who executed the agreement.[98]

(b) Time restrictions on temporary custody and extensions. Any temporary custody order must terminate one year after the earlier of the date on which the complaint was filed or the date on which the child was first placed into shelter care.[99] However, under certain circumstances this termination date may be extended.[100] Not later than thirty days prior to either the scheduled termination date or the scheduled dispositional review hearing date,[101] the agency is required to file a motion with the court requesting any of the following dispositional orders:

(1) An order that the child be returned to his home and the custody of his parents, guardian, or custodian without any restrictions;

(2) An order for protective supervision;

(3) An order that the child be placed in the legal custody[102] of a relative or other interested individual;

(4) An order permanently terminating the parental rights of the child's parents;

(5) An order that the child be placed in long-term foster care;

(6) An order for the extension of temporary custody.[103]

On the filing of the agency's motion, the court must conduct a dispositional hearing on the date set at the initial dispositional hearing.[104] After the dispositional hearing that follows the agency's motion, or at a date after such dispositional hearing that is not later than one year after the earlier of the date on which the complaint was filed or the date on which the child was first placed into shelter care, the court must issue a dispositional order from among those listed in RC 2151.415(A), in accordance with the child's best interest.[105] How-

---

[97]RC 2151.353(G). It appears that a hearing is not required before terminating the order.

[98]RC 2151.011(B)(13). See RC 2151.011(B)(5) and (6) for definitions of foster home and certified foster home.

[99]RC 2151.353(F). For time periods applicable to agreements for temporary custody, see Text 3.09, Agreements for temporary and permanent custody.

[100]RC 2151.415(D).

[101]See RC 2151.415, RC 2151.35(B)(3); Text 3.09, Agreements for temporary and permanent custody.

[102]See RC 2151.011(B)(10) for definition of legal custody.

[103]RC 2151.415(A).

[104]RC 2151.415(B). See RC 2151.35(B)(3).

[105]RC 2151.415(B).

ever, all orders for permanent custody must be in accordance with the statutes governing permanent custody.[106]

If the agency requests an extension of temporary custody for up to six months, it must include in its motion an explanation of the progress on the child's case plan[107] and its expectations of reunifying the child with its family, or placing the child in a permanent placement, within the extension period.[108] The court may extend the temporary custody order for up to six months if, after hearing, it determines by clear and convincing evidence that (1) the extension is in the child's best interest, (2) there has been significant progress on the child's case plan, and (3) there is reasonable cause to believe that the child will be reunified with one of his parents or otherwise permanently placed within the period of extension.[109]

Prior to the end of an extension granted by the court, the agency must file a motion with the court requesting one of the dispositional orders set forth in RC 2151.415(A)(1) to (5), or requesting an additional six-month extension of the temporary custody order.[110] If the agency requests one of the orders set forth in RC 2151.415(A)(1) to (5), or does not file any motion, the court must conduct a hearing[111] and issue an appropriate order of disposition.[112] If the agency requests an additional six-month extension of temporary custody, the court may, after hearing, grant the additional extension if it makes the same findings required for the original six-month extension.[113]

Prior to the end of the second extension of a temporary custody order, the agency must file the same type of motion that it filed with respect to the first extension. The court, after hearing, must then issue the appropriate dispositional order.[114] No further extension of temporary custody may be ordered by the court.[115]

(3) Legal custody

(a) Definition of legal custody. Legal custody is defined as a legal status which vests in the custodian (1) the right to have physical care and control of the child and to determine where and with whom he shall live, and (2) the right and duty to protect, train, and discipline the child and to provide him with food, shelter, education, and medical care, all subject to any residual parental rights, privileges, and responsibilities.[116]

Any person wishing legal custody of a child must, prior to the dispositional hearing, file a motion requesting legal custody of the child.[117] An individual

[106]Id. See RC 2151.413, RC 2151.414; Text 3.09(D), Permanent custody agreements.
[107]See Text 13.05, Case plans.
[108]RC 2151.415(D)(1).
[109]Id. If the court extends temporary custody, upon request it must issue findings of fact.
[110]RC 2151.415(D)(2).
[111]See RC 2151.415(B).
[112]RC 2151.415(D)(2).
[113]Id.
[114]RC 2151.415(D)(3).
[115]RC 2151.415(D)(4).
[116]RC 2151.011(B)(10).
[117]RC 2151.353(A)(3).

granted legal custody must exercise the rights and responsibilities personally unless otherwise authorized by law or by the court.[118]

(b) Definition of residual parental rights. Residual parental rights, privileges, and responsibilities are those remaining with the natural parent after the transfer of legal custody of the child, including but not necessarily limited to the privilege of reasonable visitation, consent to adoption, the privilege to determine the child's religious affiliation, and the responsibility for support.[119]

(4) Permanent custody

The most drastic dispositional alternative available to the juvenile court is to commit an abused, neglected, or dependent child to the permanent custody of a public children services agency or private child placing agency.[120]

(a) Definition of permanent custody. Permanent custody is a legal status which vests in the agency all parental rights, duties, and obligations, including the right to consent to adoption, and divests the natural parents or adoptive parents of any and all parental rights, privileges, and obligations, including all residual rights and obligations.[121] Because the purpose clause (RC 2151.01(C)) of the Juvenile Code expresses a preference that children be cared for in a family environment with their parents, permanent custody should be used only as a last resort. Judicial reluctance to grant permanent custody recognizes the importance of maintaining the family structure and protecting the rights of parents, as well as protecting the child's right to the companionship of his siblings.[122]

(b) Methods by which permanent custody is obtained. Ohio law provides two means by which an authorized agency may obtain permanent custody.[123] The agency may either request permanent custody as part of the initial abuse, neglect, or dependency proceeding,[124] or it may first obtain temporary custody and thereafter file a motion for permanent custody.[125] The court may grant permanent custody as the initial dispositional order if it determines in accordance with RC 2151.414(E) that the child cannot be placed with one of his parents within a reasonable time or should not be placed with either parent, and deter-

---

[118]RC 2151.011(B)(10).

[119]RC 2151.011(B)(11).

[120]RC 2151.353(A)(4).

[121]RC 2151.011(B)(12). See RC 3107.06. When a permanent custody complaint is filed prior to a mother's attempt to petition the probate court for the children's adoption, the mother may not contest the custody determination by interposing her residual adoptive rights. In re Palmer, 12 OS(3d) 194, 12 OBR 259, 465 NE(2d) 1312 (1984), cert denied sub nom Pihlblad v Stark County Welfare Dept, 469 US 1162, 105 SCt 918, 83 LEd(2d) 930 (1985).

[122]In re M., 65 Misc 7, 416 NE(2d) 669 (Juv, Cuyahoga 1979).

[123]An award of permanent custody should not be confused with a permanent surrender action governed by RC 5103.15. Permanent surrender results from a voluntary agreement between a parent and an appropriate agency and does not require a finding that the child is neglected, dependent, or abused. Furthermore, where such an agreement is with a county department of human services, it is revocable by the parent prior to the consent of the juvenile court. See In re Williams, 7 App(3d) 324, 7 OBR 421, 455 NE(2d) 1027 (Hamilton 1982). For discussion of permanent surrenders, see Text 3.09, Agreements for temporary and permanent custody.

[124]RC 2151.353(A)(4).

[125]For discussion of this procedure, see Text 13.06(B), Motion for permanent custody.

mines in accordance with RC 2151.414(D) that the permanent commitment is in the child's best interest.[126] Permanent custody should be granted as the initial disposition only in extreme situations where reunification is not possible.[127]

(c) Circumstances compelling order of permanent custody. The court must consider all relevant evidence before determining that the child cannot be placed with either of his parents within a reasonable time or that he should not be placed with his parents.[128] Such a finding *must* be made if the court finds, by clear and convincing evidence, that any of the following circumstances exist with respect to each of the child's parents:

(1) Following the placement of the child outside his home and notwithstanding reasonable case planning and diligent efforts by the agency to assist the parents to remedy the problems that initially caused the child to be placed outside the home, the parent has failed continuously and repeatedly for a period of six months or more to substantially remedy the conditions causing the child to be placed outside his home. In making this determination, the court must consider parental utilization of medical, psychiatric, psychological, and other social and rehabilitative services and material resources that were made available to the parents for the purpose of changing parental conduct to allow them to resume and maintain parental duties.[129]

(2) The severe and chronic mental illness, severe and chronic emotional illness, severe mental retardation, severe physical disability, or chemical dependency of the parent makes the parent unable to provide an adequate permanent home for the child at the present time and in the foreseeable future.[130]

(3) The parent committed any abuse as described in RC 2151.031, caused the child to suffer any neglect as described in RC 2151.03, or allowed the child to suffer any neglect as described in RC 2151.03 between the date that the original complaint alleging abuse or neglect was filed and the date of the filing of the motion[131] for permanent custody.[132]

(4) The parent has demonstrated a lack of commitment toward the child by failing to regularly support, visit, or communicate with the child when able to do so, or by other actions showing an unwillingness to provide an adequate permanent home for the child.[133]

(5) The parent is incarcerated for an offense committed against the child or a sibling of the child.[134]

---

[126]RC 2151.353(A)(4).

[127]In re Smart, 21 App(3d) 31, 21 OBR 33, 486 NE(2d) 147 (Franklin 1984).

[128]RC 2151.414(E).

[129]RC 2151.414(E)(1). See Drushal v Drushal, No. 10955 (9th Dist Ct App, Summit, 4-20-83).

[130]RC 2151.414(E)(2).

[131]It is presumed that this applies to original complaints requesting permanent custody, as well as motions for permanent custody. See RC 2151.415(A).

[132]RC 2151.414(E)(3). See In re Wellinger, No. 46465 (8th Dist Ct App, Cuyahoga, 10-13-83); In re Lucas, No. 1539 (4th Dist Ct App, Lawrence, 5-17-82).

[133]RC 2151.414(E)(4).

[134]RC 2151.414(E)(5). See In re Espy, Nos. 44202 to 44204 (8th Dist Ct App, Cuyahoga, 7-22-82).

(6) The parent is incarcerated at the time of the filing of the motion for permanent custody or the dispositional hearing of the child and will not be available to care for the child at least eighteen months after the filing of the motion for permanent custody or the dispositional hearing.[135]

(7) The parent is repeatedly incarcerated and the repeated incarceration prevents the parent from providing care for the child.[136]

(8) The parent for any reason is unwilling to provide food, clothing, shelter, and other basic necessities for the child or to prevent the child from suffering physical, emotional, or sexual abuse or physical, emotional, or mental neglect.[137]

(d) Factors for determining the best interest of the child. In determining the best interest of a child at a permanent custody hearing, the court must consider all relevant factors, including but not limited to the following:

(1) The reasonable probability of the child being adopted, whether an adoptive placement would positively benefit the child, and whether a grant of permanent custody would facilitate an adoption;[138]

(2) The interaction and interrelationship of the child with his parents, siblings, relatives, foster parents, and out-of-home providers, and any other person who may significantly affect the child;[139]

(3) The wishes of the child, as expressed directly by the child or through his guardian ad litem, with due regard for the maturity of the child;[140]

(4) The custodial history of the child;[141]

(5) The child's need for a legally secure permanent placement and whether that type of placement can be achieved without a grant of permanent custody to the agency.[142]

In making these determinations, the court may not consider the effect that the granting of permanent custody would have on any parent of the child.[143]

(e) Relationship between "best interests of the child" and "parental unfitness." Long before its codification, the "best interest" standard was recognized as the

---

[135]RC 2151.414(E)(6). See In re Hederson, 30 App(3d) 187, 30 OBR 329, 507 NE(2d) 418 (Summit 1986); In re Davis, No. 388 (4th Dist Ct App, Hocking, 10-11-84).

[136]RC 2151.414(E)(7).

[137]RC 2151.414(E)(8).

[138]RC 2151.414(D)(1).

[139]RC 2151.414(D)(2). Several cases decided prior to the 1989 amendment to the statute (1988 S 89, eff. 1-1-89) held that where the child has become a stranger to the parent and has become psychologically and emotionally attached to foster parents, termination of parental rights may be justified. In re Luke, No. 83-CA-09 (5th Dist Ct App, Coshocton, 1-13-84); In re Wellinger, No. 46465 (8th Dist Ct App, Cuyahoga, 10-13-83); In re Espy, Nos. 44202 to 44204 (8th Dist Ct App, Cuyahoga, 7-22-82); In re Wayne, Nos. 81 AP-631, 81 AP-632 (10th Dist Ct App, Franklin, 12-10-81); In re Justice, 59 App(2d) 78, 392 NE(2d) 897 (Clinton 1978); In re Christopher, 54 App(2d) 137, 376 NE(2d) 603 (Morrow 1977).

[140]RC 2151.414(D)(3).

[141]RC 2151.414(D)(4).

[142]RC 2151.414(D)(5).

[143]RC 2151.414(C).

primary consideration in permanent custody cases.[144] However, there appears to be considerable overlap between the "best interests" test and a "parental fitness" standard. The Ohio Supreme Court held in *In re Perales*[145] that in a custody dispute between a parent and a nonparent under RC 2151.23(A)(2), the welfare of the child is the first consideration, but suitable parents have a paramount right to custody.[146] In effect, the court defined "suitability" in terms of the best interests of the child[147] when it stated that a parent is unsuitable if "a preponderance of the evidence indicates abandonment, contractual relinquishment of custody, total inability to provide care or support, or that the parent is otherwise unsuitable—that is, that an award of custody would be detrimental to the child."[148] Apparently, a "parental unsuitability" finding is not required in a permanent custody proceeding concerning a child who has been adjudicated neglected, dependent, or abused. On the other hand, a custody decision made under RC 2151.23(A)(2) does not require a preliminary finding that the child is neglected, dependent, or abused[149] and is based on a lesser standard of proof— preponderance of the evidence[150] rather than clear and convincing evidence.[151]

In comparing the concepts of "parental unfitness" and "the best interests of the child" as they apply to the disposition of dependency cases, the Ohio Supreme Court in *In re Cunningham*[152] noted a subtle relationship between the two criteria. While elements of parental unfitness figure strongly in the best interests test, elements of the child's best interests weigh in any consideration of whether a parent is fit to have custody of his child. The court emphasized,

---

[144]E.g., In re Cunningham, 59 OS(2d) 100, 396 NE(2d) 1035 (1979); In re Young, 58 OS(2d) 90, 388 NE(2d) 1235 (1979); In re Tilton, 161 OS 571, 120 NE(2d) 445 (1954); Children's Home of Marion County v Fetter, 90 OS 110, 106 NE 761 (1914); Clark v Bayer, 32 OS 299 (1877); Gishwiler v Dodez, 4 OS 615 (1855); In re Espy, Nos. 44202 to 44204 (8th Dist Ct App, Cuyahoga, 7-22-82); In re Poth, No. H-81-31 (6th Dist Ct App, Huron, 6-30-82); In re Banks, No. L-80-212 (6th Dist Ct App, Lucas, 5-22-81); In re Bowman, No. 79AP-798 (10th Dist Ct App, Franklin, 6-26-80); In re Hadsell, No. 41004 (8th Dist Ct App, Cuyahoga, 6-19-80); In re Collier, No. 39343 (8th Dist Ct App, Cuyahoga, 12-13-79); In re Holcomb, No. 39694 (8th Dist Ct App, Cuyahoga, 10-4-79); In re Christopher, 54 App(2d) 137, 376 NE(2d) 603 (Morrow 1977).

[145]In re Perales, 52 OS(2d) 89, 369 NE(2d) 1047 (1977).

[146]In a more recent case, the court held that the best interests standard applies to a custody case between the parents of an illegitimate child. In re Byrd, 66 OS(2d) 334, 421 NE(2d) 1284 (1981). This case also held that an *alleged* natural father, who has participated in the nurturing process of his illegitimate child, has standing to seek custody pursuant to RC 2151.23(A)(2). This decision was apparently overruled by the 1982 revision of RC 3111.13(C) which now states, *"After entry of the judgment or order* (establishing the existence of the parent-child relationship), the father may petition for custody of the child or for visitation rights in a proceeding separate from any action to establish paternity" (emphasis added).

[147]For this interpretation of *Perales*, see Thrasher v Thrasher, 3 App(3d) 210, 3 OBR 240, 444 NE(2d) 431 (Summit 1981).

[148]In re Perales, 52 OS(2d) 89, 98, 369 NE(2d) 1047 (1977). This standard also applies in habeas corpus proceedings involving child custody. Reynolds v Ross County Children's Services Agency, 5 OS(3d) 27, 5 OBR 87, 448 NE(2d) 816 (1983); In re Hua, 62 OS(2d) 227, 405 NE(2d) 255 (1980).

[149]In re Torok, 161 OS 585, 120 NE(2d) 307 (1954).

[150]Juv R 29(E)(4).

[151]*Id.*; RC 2151.35, RC 2151.414(B).

[152]In re Cunningham, 59 OS(2d) 100, 396 NE(2d) 1035 (1979).

however, that the two concepts have different meanings. The fundamental inquiry at the dispositional hearing is what the child's best interests are and not whether the parents of a dependent child are fit or unfit. Because parental unfitness is not a mandatory prerequisite to an award of permanent custody in this type of case, a fit parent is not automatically entitled to custody if the specific needs of the child require termination of parental rights.[153]

A court is not required to grant custody to a blood relative of the child,[154] nor to a specific family requested by the mother, as long as it acts in the child's best interests.[155]

(f) Report of guardian ad litem. A written report of the child's guardian ad litem must be submitted to the court prior to or at the time of the permanent custody hearing, but it need not be submitted under oath.[156]

(g) Findings of fact and conclusions of law. If the court grants permanent custody, the court, on the request of any party, must file a written opinion setting forth its findings of fact and conclusions of law in relation to the proceeding.[157] However, the trial court's failure to make findings of fact and conclusions of law following a grant of permanent custody of a child to an agency does not constitute prejudicial error where the parties agree generally to the facts of the case.[158] Moreover, the determinations to be made by the court in a permanent custody hearing need not be listed in the court's judgment entry.[159] These determinations would be appropriately included within the court's findings of fact and conclusions of law, if they were requested by any of the parties.[160]

(5) Long-term foster care

(a) Definition of long-term foster care. Long-term foster care is a dispositional order pursuant to which both of the following apply:

(1) Legal custody[161] of a child is given to an agency without the termination of parental rights; and

(2) The agency is permitted to make an appropriate placement of the child and to enter into a written long-term foster care agreement with a foster care provider or with any other person or agency with whom the child is placed.[162]

(b) Prerequisites for long-term foster care. In order for a child to be placed in long-term foster care, the agency must request that the court make such an order, and the court must find, by clear and convincing evidence, that long-term foster care is in the child's best interest and that one of the following exists:

[153]*Id.*

[154]Montgomery County Children Services Board v Kiszka, No. 8096 (2d Dist Ct App, Montgomery, 10-3-83); In re Coulter, No. C-800444 (1st Dist Ct App, Hamilton, 4-29-81); In re Baby Girl S., 32 Misc 217, 290 NE(2d) 925 (CP, Stark 1972).

[155]In re Baumgartner, 50 App(2d) 37, 361 NE(2d) 501 (Franklin 1976).

[156]RC 2151.414(C).

[157]RC 2151.353(A)(4). See *id.*

[158]In re Hollins, No. CA-703 (5th Dist Ct App, Guernsey, 3-29-83).

[159]In re Covin, 8 App(3d) 139, 8 OBR 196, 456 NE(2d) 520 (Hamilton 1982).

[160]*Id;* In re Holcomb, No. 39694 (8th Dist Ct App, Cuyahoga, 10-4-79).

[161]The term "legal custody" is defined in RC 2151.011(B)(10).

[162]RC 2151.011(B)(25).

(1) The child, because of physical, mental, or psychological problems or needs, is unable to function in a family-like setting and must remain in residential or institutional care;

(2) The parents of the child have significant physical, mental, or psychological problems and are unable to care for the child because of those problems, adoption is not in the best interest of the child, and the child retains a significant and positive relationship with a parent or relative;

(3) The child is age sixteen or older, has been counseled on the permanent placement options available to him, is unwilling to accept or unable to adopt to a permanent placement, and is in an agency program preparing him for independent living.[163]

Long-term foster care may also be used as a further dispositional alternative after a prior temporary custody order has expired.[164] In such cases, the agency must present to the court evidence indicating why long-term foster care is appropriate for the child, including, but not limited to, evidence that the agency has tried or considered all other possible dispositions for the child.[165] Before a court may place the child in long-term foster care, it must make the same findings required when long-term foster care is requested as an original order of disposition.[166] If the court then makes the long-term foster care order, it must issue a finding of fact setting forth its reasons.[167] Thereafter, the agency may make any appropriate placement for the child and must develop a case plan that is designed to assist the child in finding a permanent home outside of the home of the parents.[168] Moreover, the agency may not remove the child from the residential placement in which the child is originally placed without court approval except under emergency circumstances.[169]

(B) Motion for permanent custody

(1) Circumstances permitting motion for permanent custody

In addition to ordering permanent custody at the dispositional hearing on the original complaint of abuse, neglect, or dependency,[170] permanent custody may be ordered on a motion in cases where the child has been committed to the temporary custody of an agency at a dispositional hearing on the original complaint.[171] With regard to a child who is abandoned or orphaned, the motion may be filed whenever the agency can show that the parents cannot be located and there is no relative able to take legal custody.[172] If the child is not abandoned or

---

[163]RC 2151.353(A)(5). See RC 2151.415(C)(2).
[164]See RC 2151.415(A)(5); Text 13.06(A)(2), Temporary custody.
[165]RC 2151.415(C)(1).
[166]*Id.* See RC 2151.353(A)(5).
[167]RC 2151.415(C)(2)(a).
[168]RC 2151.415(C)(2)(b).
[169]RC 2151.415(G). Apparently, this requirement applies only if long-term foster care follows a prior temporary custody order, and not if long-term foster care is the original dispositional order.
[170]RC 2151.353(A)(4).
[171]RC 2151.413, RC 2151.414.
[172]RC 2151.413(B). Although RC 2151.414 provides that services of summons must be in accordance with RC 2151.29, it appears that service of summons is governed by Juv R 16.

orphaned, or if the parents of an abandoned child are located, the motion may be filed after a period of at least six months has elapsed since a temporary custody order was made or since the initial case plan was filed.[173]

(2) Documentation required for motion for permanent custody

Any agency that files a motion for permanent custody must include in the case plan of the child a specific plan of the agency's actions to seek an adoptive family for the child and to prepare the child for adoption.[174]

It has been held that when a county human services department brings a complaint for permanent custody in the juvenile court, its failure to provide the affidavit required by RC 3109.27(A) is not a jurisdictional defect.[175]

(3) Prerequisites for granting motion for permanent custody

The court may grant permanent custody of the child to the agency if the court determines at the hearing, by clear and convincing evidence, that it is in the best interest of the child to grant permanent custody, and that any of the following apply: (1) the child is not abandoned or orphaned and cannot be placed with either parent within a reasonable time or should not be placed with his parents;[176] (2) the child is abandoned and the parents cannot be located;[177] (3) the child is orphaned and there are no relatives able to take permanent custody.[178]

In making the above determinations, the court is to consider the same factors that it considers when permanent custody is requested at the original dispositional hearing following an adjudication of abuse, neglect, or dependency.[179]

(4) Effect of foster parents as "psychological parents"

Where permanent custody is requested several years after an initial temporary custody order, the passage of time and the resultant psychological and emotional development of the child become especially important in determin-

---

[173]RC 2151.413(A). But see In re Lee, No. CA-2856 (5th Dist Ct App, Licking, 11-1-82), in which the court upheld a permanent custody order even though the motion for permanent custody was filed less than six months after the order of temporary custody. The court based its decision on the fact that the parent in question had not raised this issue at the permanent custody hearing and that she had not been prejudiced by the alleged error because she had refused to meet with the agency's social workers.

[174]RC 2151.413(C).

[175]In re Palmer, 12 OS(3d) 194, 12 OBR 259, 465 NE(2d) 1312 (1984), cert denied sub nom Pihlblad v Stark County Welfare Dept, 469 US 1162, 105 SCt 918, 83 LEd(2d) 930 (1985).

[176]RC 2151.414(B)(1).

[177]RC 2151.414(B)(2). Where the record reveals that the agency holding temporary custody has been unable to maintain contact with the mother because of her frequent changes in address and that the mother has expressed no interest in regaining custody of her children on the infrequent occasions when she has contacted the agency, the mother's conduct constitutes abandonment. In re Fields, No. WMS-82-13 (6th Dist Ct App, Williams, 11-26-82).

[178]RC 2151.414(B)(3). It has been held that this provision pertains only to a situation where the child is found to be an orphan. If the child is not orphaned, Ohio law does not give blood relatives any superior right to custody, particularly where they would not be able to provide adequate parental care for the child's special needs. Montgomery County Children Services Board v Kiszka, No. 8096 (2d Dist Ct App, Montgomery, 10-3-83).

[179]RC 2151.414(C) to (E). See Text 13.06(A)(4), Permanent custody.

ing the child's best interests. Thus, in *In re Christopher*,[180] where the evidence indicated that between the time of the temporary and permanent custody hearings the mother had married, sought counseling, and now demonstrated normal maternal concern for her child, the court properly granted permanent custody on the basis that the separation of the parent and child had resulted in the child becoming a stranger to the parent.[181] In such situations, where there is no strong relationship between the parent and child, the difficult challenge that the resumption of parenthood would demand is a significant factor.[182] In addition, the fact that a child in the temporary custody of a human services department, has become psychologically and emotionally dependent on his foster parents, and has been fully integrated into their family may justify a best interests decision to terminate parental rights.[183]

On the other hand, where a parent has continuous visitation and an ongoing relationship with his children in foster care, the likelihood that the foster parents will become "psychological parents" is negligible.[184] It is up to the agency holding temporary custody to make a conscientious effort to rehabilitate and reunite the family by attempting to maintain contact and communication between parent and child.[185] Thus, difficulties in transportation, where, for instance, the foster home is sixty miles from the mother's home, do not justify the agency's denial of regular and frequent visits between a parent and child.[186]

(5) Effect of failure to implement case plan

Amendments to the permanent custody statute[187] have resolved two questions raised by the prior version of the statute. It is now specifically provided that the juvenile court may not deny an agency's motion for permanent custody solely because the agency failed to implement any particular aspect of the child's case plan.[188] Prior to the enactment of this provision, the cases seemed at odds with the statute. The statute had required the court to decide whether the agency had made a good faith effort to implement reunification plans. Although proof of such good faith effort was a factor to be considered, the *statute* did not specifically require the submission of the reunification plans as a condition precedent to granting the motion for permanent custody. However, the *court*

---

[180]In re Christopher, 54 App(2d) 137, 376 NE(2d) 603 (Morrow 1977).

[181]See also Goldstein, Freud, and Solnit, *Beyond the Best Interests of the Child* (1973), for a discussion of the importance of psychological factors in making child-placement decisions.

[182]In re Philpott, No. 41186 (8th Dist Ct App, Cuyahoga, 6-5-80); In re Christopher, 54 App(2d) 137, 376 NE(2d) 603 (Morrow 1977). See also In re Ferguson, No. 46775 (8th Dist Ct App, Cuyahoga, 12-22-83).

[183]In re Luke, No. 83-CA-09 (5th Dist Ct App, Coshocton, 1-13-84); In re Wellinger, No. 46465 (8th Dist Ct App, Cuyahoga, 10-13-83); In re Espy, Nos. 44202 to 44204 (8th Dist Ct App, Cuyahoga, 7-22-82); In re Wayne, Nos. 81AP-631, 81AP-632 (10th Dist Ct App, Franklin, 12-10-81); In re Justice, 59 App(2d) 78, 392 NE(2d) 897 (Clinton 1978).

[184]In re M., 65 Misc 7, 416 NE(2d) 669 (Juv, Cuyahoga 1979).

[185]See RC 2151.412. See also In re Skaggs, No. 1278 (4th Dist Ct App, Scioto, 1-22-81).

[186]In re Skaggs, No. 1278 (4th Dist Ct App, Scioto, 1-22-81).

[187]RC 2151.414, amended by 1988 S 89, eff. 1-1-89.

[188]RC 2151.414(C).

decisions were unclear regarding whether a plan had to be submitted before a permanent custody order.[189]

(6) Effect of motion for permanent custody on prior adjudications

The statute also now provides that neither the adjudication of abuse, neglect, or dependency nor the grant of temporary custody to the agency that filed the motion is to be readjudicated at the permanent custody hearing or affected by a denial of the motion for permanent custody.[190] Prior to the enactment of this statutory provision, there were conflicting appellate decisions regarding whether the court was required to redetermine the issue of neglect or dependency at a hearing held pursuant to the filing of a motion for permanent custody.[191]

(7) Effect of permanent custody order on biological parents

Once the court issues an order granting permanent custody pursuant to the filing of a motion for permanent custody, the child's biological parents cease to be parties to the action except for purposes of appeal.[192]

CROSS REFERENCES
Text 3.05 to 3.09, 13.05

13.07 Delinquent child

(A) Mandatory dispositions

If a child is adjudged delinquent for any drug abuse offense,[193] disorderly conduct while intoxicated,[194] or driving while intoxicated,[195] the court is required to suspend or revoke the child's temporary instruction permit or probationary operator's license until the child's eighteenth birthday or until the child attends, at the court's discretion, and satisfactorily completes a drivers' intervention program certified pursuant to RC 3720.06.[196] During the time that the child is attending the program, the court must retain the child's permit or license and return it to the child after he satisfactorily completes the program.[197]

---

[189]See, e.g., In re Stewart, No. CA-3075 (5th Dist Ct App, Licking, 2-27-85); In re Miller, No. C-830919 (1st Dist Ct App, Hamilton, 10-24-84); In re Wurtzel, No. 82 CA 31 (4th Dist Ct App, Pickaway, 3-6-84).

[190]RC 2151.414(A).

[191]See, e.g., In re Vickers Children, 14 App(3d) 201, 14 OBR 228, 470 NE(2d) 438 (Butler 1983); In re Jones, 29 App(3d) 176, 29 OBR 206, 504 NE(2d) 719 (Cuyahoga 1985); In re Kiernan, No. CA2744 (5th Dist Ct App, Licking, 9-29-81).

[192]RC 2151.414(F). Presumably, this would also apply where permanent custody is granted at the original dispositional hearing pursuant to RC 2151.353(A)(4).

[193]"Drug abuse offense" is defined in RC 2925.01.

[194]RC 2917.11.

[195]RC 4511.19. It is not clear why the offense of driving while intoxicated is included in the dispositional statute for delinquent children since such offense constitutes a juvenile traffic offense pursuant to RC 2151.021.

[196]RC 2151.355(B). The effective date of 1988 H 643, amending RC 2151.355(B), was suspended by 1989 H 329 until June 30, 1989. See also RC 4507.162. If the child does not yet own a temporary instruction permit or probationary operator's license, he may not be issued one until he satisfactorily completes the program (RC 4507.08).

[197]RC 2151.355(B).

Within ten days after the adjudication, the court must notify the Bureau of Motor Vehicles of the adjudicatory order.[198] If the child satisfactorily completes a drivers' intervention program, the program operator must promptly notify the court,[199] whereupon the court must immediately notify the Bureau of Motor Vehicles.[200]

(B) Discretionary dispositions

(1) Statutory provisions

RC 2151.355(A) provides that if a child is adjudged delinquent, the court may make any of several dispositional orders.[201] A court may make "[a]ny order that is authorized by section 2151.353 of the Revised Code."[202] Pursuant to this dispositional alternative, the court may utilize any disposition allowable for an abused, neglected, or dependent child. This would include commitment of the child to the temporary custody[203] and permanent custody of an authorized agency as long as all required findings have been made.[204] However, it is unclear whether the stringent procedural and substantive safeguards applicable to the commitment of abused, neglected, and dependent children apply to a delinquent child. For instance, RC 2151.353(B) provides that no permanent or temporary custody order may be made unless both the summons and complaint served on the parents contain an explanation of their rights and of the possible consequences of the order. The language of this provision seems to limit its applicability to abuse, neglect, and dependency proceedings. On the other hand, it is arguable that whenever a court treats a delinquent child as an abused, neglected, or dependent child pursuant to RC 2151.355(A)(1), the statutory requirements imposed in the latter proceedings apply. For instance, it is clear that a case plan must be prepared and maintained for a delinquent child who is in the temporary or permanent custody of an appropriate agency.[205]

(2) Probation

A frequently used disposition for a delinquent child is an order of probation under conditions that the court prescribes.[206] "Probation" is defined as a legal status created by court order following an adjudication that a child is delinquent, unruly, or a juvenile traffic offender, whereby the child is permitted to remain in his parent's, guardian's, or custodian's home subject to supervision or under the supervision of any agency designated by the court. The child may be returned to the court for violation of probation at any time during the proba-

---

[198]RC 4507.021(D)(2)(a). Although this order is mandated by the dispositional statute (RC 2151.355(B)), it is made at the adjudicatory hearing, which may be held well before the dispositional hearing (see Juv R 34(A)).

[199]RC 3720.06.

[200]RC 4507.021(D)(2)(b).

[201]Although the disposition of cases is substantive in nature and is thus governed by statute, Juv R 29(F)(2)(d) permits dismissal of the complaint where it is in the best interests of the child and the community, even if the allegations of the complaint are admitted or proven.

[202]RC 2151.355(A)(1).

[203]See RC 5103.10.

[204]RC 2151.353(A)(4).

[205]RC 2151.412(A)(2).

[206]RC 2151.355(A)(2).

tionary period.[207] In all cases in which a child is placed on probation, such child must be provided a written statement of the conditions of probation and must be instructed regarding them.[208] The length of time for which a child is to remain on probation may be fixed at the dispositional hearing or at a later date and may extend until the time the child reaches age twenty-one.[209]

If a child is adjudged delinquent for the offenses of vandalism (RC 2909.05), criminal damaging or endangering (RC 2909.06), or criminal mischief (RC 2909.07), and if restitution is appropriate under the circumstances of the case, the court must require the child to make restitution for the property damage as a condition of probation.[210] Restitution may also be made a condition of probation for any child adjudged delinquent for violation of any other Revised Code section. In such cases, restitution is limited to the amount of any property damage and the value of any property that was the subject of a theft offense.[211] A restitution order may also be appropriate as an independent disposition apart from probation.[212]

Restitution may take many forms, including a cash reimbursement (paid in a lump sum or in installments), the performance of repair work (to restore any damaged property to its original condition), the performance of a reasonable amount of labor for the victim (approximately equal to the value of the property that was damaged or stolen), the performance of community service or community work, or any combination of these forms.[213]

The court's probation department, under the direction of the juvenile judge and the chief probation officer, must keep informed concerning the conduct and condition of each person under its supervision and must report thereon to the judge as he directs.[214] Each probation officer is required to use all suitable methods to aid persons on probation and to bring about improvement in their conduct and condition. The department must maintain full records of its work, which records are considered confidential and not available to the public.[215]

(3) Commitment to county or private facility

Another alternative is to commit the delinquent child to the temporary custody of any school, camp, institution, or other facility for delinquent children

---

[207]RC 2151.011(B)(15).

[208]RC 2151.14; Juv R 34(C). All children placed on probation by the Cuyahoga County Juvenile Court are subject to certain standard conditions such as attending school, obeying parents, and maintaining appointments with the probation officer.

[209]In re DeGeronimo, No. 40089 (8th Dist Ct App, Cuyahoga, 6-28-79). See also Text 15.01(B), Duration and termination of continuing jurisdiction.

[210]RC 2151.355(A)(2). Victims of delinquent acts may also be entitled to compensation from the Reparations Rotary Fund established pursuant to RC 2743.70. See Text 13.07(B)(6), Restitution.

[211]RC 2151.355(A)(2).

[212]RC 2151.355(A)(8). See Text 13.07(B)(6), Restitution.

[213]RC 2151.355(A)(2), (8). Many juvenile courts have established programs which are funded by a state subsidy (RC 5139.34) and which provide delinquents with temporary, part-time jobs in the community. Typically, the majority of the money earned by the child is given directly to the victim, with the child receiving a minimal wage.

[214]RC 2151.14.

[215]Id. For further discussion of the confidentiality of juvenile court records, see Text 15.04(A), Confidentiality, use in other proceedings.

operated by the county, by a district, or by a private agency within or outside the state.[216]

As a general rule, a final order of disposition for a delinquent child may not include confinement in a juvenile detention home.[217] However, a district detention home approved for such purpose by the Department of Youth Services may receive children committed to its temporary custody under this statute and may provide the care, treatment, and training required.[218]

When a county or district operates a school, camp, or other facility for delinquent children pursuant to RC 2151.65, the juvenile court must determine which children are to be admitted to the facility, the duration of their commitment, and the date of release or transfer.[219]

(4) Commitment to Ohio Department of Youth Services

If a child has been adjudicated delinquent for the commission of a felony, he may be committed to the legal custody of the Department of Youth Services for institutionalization, provided that he is at least twelve years of age at the time of the commitment.[220] If the act constitutes an aggravated felony of the third degree or a felony of the third or fourth degree, the commitment is for an indefinite term, a minimum of six months and a maximum period not to exceed the child's attainment of age twenty-one.[221] If the act constitutes an aggravated felony of the first or second degree or a felony of the first or second degree, commitment may be to a secure facility[222] for an indefinite term, a minimum of one year and a maximum period not to exceed the child's attainment of age twenty-one.[223] If the offense constitutes murder or aggravated murder, the child may be committed to a secure facility until he reaches age twenty-one.[224]

The IJA-ABA Standards support the principle of court determinancy with regard to the nature and duration of coercive dispositions. With specific exceptions, the Standards assert that neither correctional authorities nor administrative agencies should be permitted to alter independently the nature and duration of commitment without a judicial order.[225]

Unlike commitments to county, district, or private agencies authorized by RC 2151.355(A)(1) and (3), a commitment to the state-operated Department of

---

[216]RC 2151.355(A)(3).

[217]See Text 13.07(B)(8), Any further disposition that the court finds proper.

[218]RC 2151.34. See In re Hale, No. WD-85-74 (6th Dist Ct App, Wood, 4-25-86).

[219]RC 2151.65.

[220]RC 2151.355, RC 5139.05(A).

[221]RC 2151.355(A)(4). For discussion of the early release provisions, see Text 15.01(E), Commitment to Ohio Department of Youth Services, early release.

[222]The three secure facilities operated by the Department of Youth Services are Cuyahoga Hills Boys School (Warrensville Heights), Indian River School (Massillon), and Training Institution of Central Ohio (Columbus). The remaining six facilities are Buckeye Youth Center (Columbus), Maumee Youth Center (Liberty Center), Mohican Youth Center (Loudenville), Riverview School for Boys (Powell), Scioto Village School (Powell), and Training Center for Youth (Columbus).

[223]RC 2151.355(A)(5).

[224]RC 2151.355(A)(6).

[225]*IJA-ABA Standards Relating to Dispositions* 23 (1980).

Youth Services may only be ordered for a delinquent-felon.[226] In addition, a commitment to the department is usually accompanied by a minimum period of institutionalization,[227] whereas commitment to other agencies is usually for an open-ended period of time. When the court commits a child to the department, the department determines to which facility the child will be sent. The court may not designate a specific institution but instead must specify that the child is to be institutionalized or that the institutionalization is to be in a secure facility, if this is required by RC 2151.355(A)(5) and (6).[228] Commitments to the Department of Youth Services may not exceed the child's attainment of age twenty-one.[229]

An adjudged delinquent committed to the Department of Youth Services, who has been confined as an adult in an adult jail, may be granted credit for time served while waiting for his dispositional hearing.[230]

It is not clear from RC 2151.355(A) whether a court may impose consecutive commitments to the Department of Youth Services concerning a child who is adjudged delinquent for more than one felony offense.[231] An appellate court which was asked to decide this issue determined it to be moot and dismissed the appeal because the department released the appellants prior to the hearing on the appeal.[232]

When a juvenile court commits a child to the Department of Youth Services, it must provide the department with the child's social history and medical records, the section(s) of the Revised Code violated and the degree of violation, and any other of the child's records that the department reasonably requests. A copy of the journal entry ordering the commitment must be sent to the child's school, which, upon receiving the entry, must provide the department with the child's school transcript. Upon releasing the child, the department must provide the court and the school with an updated copy of the child's school transcript and must provide the court with a summary of the child's institutional record. The department must also furnish the court with a copy of any portion of the child's institutional record that the court specifically requests, within five working days of the request.[233]

---

[226]Because the degree of offense is paramount in determining whether and for how long a child may remain in the custody of the Department of Youth Services, plea-bargaining occurs frequently in the juvenile justice system.

[227]For provisions regarding the department's procedures and requirements prior to releasing a child, see Text 15.01(E), Commitment to Ohio Department of Youth Services, early release.

[228]RC 2151.355(D)(1), RC 5139.05.

[229]RC 2151.355(A)(4) to (6), RC 2151.38, RC 5139.05(A). For a discussion of the termination of juvenile court jurisdiction, see Text 15.01(B), Duration and termination of continuing jurisdiction.

[230]In re Smith, 32 App(3d) 82, 513 NE(2d) 1387 (Butler 1986).

[231]For discussion of concept of plural dispositions, see Text 13.07(B), Plural dispositions.

[232]State v Porter, No. CA-3253 (5th Dist Ct App, Licking, 5-4-87).

[233]RC 2151.355(D)(2), RC 5139.05(C).

The Department of Youth Services is eligible to receive educational tuition pursuant to RC 3313.64(I) and RC 3313.64(C)(2) for a child committed to an institution operated by the department.[234]

Under RC 5139.01(A)(3), the department is responsible for payment of medical bills incurred by a child in the department's custody.[235]

(5) Fine

The juvenile court may also impose a fine not to exceed $50 and costs.[236] The juvenile court may tax and collect the same fees and costs as are allowed the clerk of the court of common pleas for similar services, but no fees or costs may be taxed in children's cases except as required by RC 2743.70 or when specifically ordered by the court.[237]

The imposition of a fine and costs often accompanies other dispositions and may include an order directing the child to perform work assignments to earn money to pay the fine and costs.[238] However, since the assessment of a fine and costs constitutes a final order, once it is ordered the court may not also transfer the case to the juvenile court of the child's resident county for further disposition.[239]

A juvenile court may not commit a child who has been adjudged delinquent to a county jail or juvenile detention home upon the failure, refusal, or inability of the child to pay a fine and/or court costs.[240]

(6) Restitution

The child may be ordered to make restitution for all or part of the property damage caused by his delinquent act and for all or part of the value of the property that was the subject of his delinquent theft offense.[241]

Restitution may be made a condition of a probation order[242] or may be ordered independently of any other order. If the court determines that the victim of the child's delinquent act was sixty-five years of age or older, or permanently and totally disabled at the time of the commission of the act, the court must, regardless of whether or not the child knew the victim's age, consider this fact in favor of imposing restitution, but that fact shall not control the court's decision.[243]

It is error for a juvenile court to order restitution without holding an evidentiary hearing on the existence of damages and the proper amount of restitu-

---

[234]OAG 88-23.
[235]Northern Columbiana County Community Hospital Assn v Ohio Dept of Youth Services, 38 OS(3d) 102, 526 NE(2d) 802 (1988).
[236]RC 2151.355(A)(7).
[237]RC 2151.54.
[238]See RC 2151.355(A)(10). See also Text 13.07(B)(2), Probation; Text 13.07(B)(6), Restitution.
[239]In re Sekulich, 65 OS(2d) 13, 417 NE(2d) 1014 (1981).
[240]In re Rinehart, 10 App(3d) 318, 10 OBR 523, 462 NE(2d) 448 (Ross 1983).
[241]RC 2151.355(A)(8).
[242]See RC 2151.355(A)(2). The variety of forms of restitution is discussed in Text 13.07(B)(2), Probation.
[243]RC 2151.355(A)(8).

tion.[244] However, there is no denial of due process or equal protection when the court equally divides damages among three juveniles, who, by their joint and concerted efforts and actions, seriously damaged another's property.[245]

A juvenile court does not have jurisdiction to order a parent to make restitution for the destructive acts of his children, since recovery from the parent may only be gained through a civil suit under RC 3109.09, RC 3109.10,[246] or RC 2307.70.

(7) Termination of driving privileges

The court may suspend or revoke the operator's license issued to the child or suspend or revoke the registration of all motor vehicles registered in the child's name.[247]

(8) Any further disposition that the court finds proper

The catch-all provision allowing the court to impose any other appropriate disposition (RC 2151.355(A)(10)) has often resulted in innovative dispositions designed to meet the specific rehabilitative needs of the child. However, the provision has also resulted in several controversial dispositions, leading the appellate courts to place limits on the juvenile court's discretion. For example, the disposition of a child may not include confinement in a jail or detention home for punishment, for failure to pay a fine or costs, or any other reason.[248] In addition, neither this provision nor any other statute permits the juvenile court to order a parent to pay for the destructive acts of his child.[249]

The authority of a juvenile court to impose an adult sentence on a delinquent who has reached the age of eighteen or twenty-one, pending final disposition, is an issue which has resulted in inconsistent decisions from the appellate courts. In the first reported appellate case which considered the issue, In re Cox,[250] the court held that when a child who had been adjudged delinquent left the jurisdiction of the juvenile court, rendering the court unable to dispose of his case until he was over twenty-one years of age, such child was an adult within the meaning of RC 2151.011(B)(2). As a result, the juvenile court was authorized under RC 2151.355(I) (now RC 2151.355(A)(10)) to treat the person as an adult and to impose the statutory penalty applicable to adults committing the same offense.[251] However, three years later, another court of appeals was confronted with an almost identical case involving a delinquent child who failed to appear for his dispositional hearing, was subsequently arrested after reaching age eighteen, and was sentenced by the juvenile court to six months in jail and fined

[244]In re Hall, No. C-77022 (1st Dist Ct App, Hamilton, 11-16-77).
[245]Daudt v Daudt, No. CA 87-01-003 (12th Dist Ct App, Butler, 6-29-87).
[246]In re Watkins, No. 42409 (8th Dist Ct App, Cuyahoga, 1-22-81); In re Daudt, No. CA 85-11-147 (12th Dist Ct App, Butler, 9-2-86).
[247]RC 2151.355(A)(9). For discussion of this alternative, see Text 13.09, Juvenile traffic offender.
[248]In re Rinehart, 10 App(3d) 318, 10 OBR 523, 462 NE(2d) 448 (Ross 1983); In re Bolden, 37 App(2d) 7, 306 NE(2d) 166 (Allen 1973); OAG 70-143. See also RC 2151.34, which allows confinement of a child in a detention home only "until final disposition."
[249]In re Watkins, No. 42409 (8th Dist Ct App, Cuyahoga, 1-22-81).
[250]In re Cox, 36 App(2d) 65, 301 NE(2d) 907 (Mahoning 1973).
[251]Id.

$1,000. The court held in *In re Day*[252] that since all that remained to be done by the juvenile court was impose a disposition upon his later apprehension, the delinquent youth was still a "child" as defined by RC 2151.011. The court invalidated the juvenile court's commitment order, holding that the statutory phrase "make such further disposition as the court finds proper" does not include treating a delinquent as an adult criminal for dispositional purposes.[253]

The same issue has twice been considered by the Cuyahoga County Court of Appeals, but in neither case had the child failed to appear for hearings prior to reaching age eighteen. In *In re Corona*,[254] the child was seventeen years of age at the time that the delinquency complaint was filed but had reached age nineteen by the time he was adjudged delinquent. The juvenile court imposed a six-month sentence in an adult penal facility. This was appealed on the ground that since the child was over age eighteen at the time of disposition, the juvenile court exceeded its jurisdiction by subjecting him to a greater sentence than that which would have been imposed on an adult violating the same statute.[255] Based on the statutory definition of a child (RC 2151.011(B)(1)) and the catch-all provision allowing the court to order any further disposition it finds proper (RC 2151.355(I), now RC 2151.355(A)(10)), it was held that the juvenile court had not exceeded its jurisdiction in imposing the six-month prison term.[256] Moreover, the court held that RC 2151.34, which prohibits the commitment of any child under eighteen years of age to any prison or jail, was not applicable, since the appellant was over the age of eighteen.[257]

Less than two months after its decision in *Corona*, the same court of appeals in *State v Grady*[258] was asked to determine a similar issue involving a child who had turned eighteen after a delinquency complaint was filed against him for receiving stolen property. After adjudging the child delinquent, the juvenile court imposed a ten-day confinement to county jail. In reversing this disposition, the court of appeals determined that since the child was still a "child" for purposes of RC Chapter 2151, notwithstanding the fact that by the date of the hearing he was eighteen years of age, his disposition was governed by RC 2151.355. The court further ruled that the juvenile court's discretion under RC 2151.355(A)(9) (now RC 2151.355(A)(10)) is not unlimited and that commitment to a jail for adult offenders is not a proper disposition for a delinquent juvenile absent a finding that housing in an appropriate juvenile facility is temporarily unavailable or that the public safety requires it.[259]

---

[252]In re Day, No. 669 (11th Dist Ct App, Geauga, 8-23-76).
[253]*Id.*
[254]In re Corona, No. 40992 (8th Dist Ct App, Cuyahoga, 8-20-81).
[255]The child was adjudged delinquent for disorderly conduct (RC 2917.11), which would be a minor misdemeanor if committed by an adult and carries a maximum penalty of a $100 fine. This case differs from In re Cox, 36 App(2d) 65, 301 NE(2d) 907 (Mahoning 1973) and In re Day, No. 669 (11th Dist Ct App, Geauga, 8-23-76) in that the juveniles in those cases received sentences similar to those which could be imposed on adults for the same offenses.
[256]In re Corona, No. 40992 (8th Dist Ct App, Cuyahoga, 8-20-81).
[257]*Id.*
[258]State v Grady, 3 App(3d) 174, 3 OBR 199, 444 NE(2d) 51 (Cuyahoga 1981).
[259]*Id.*

In reaching its decision, the court in *Grady* indicated that the choice of places to which a court may send a juvenile offender is a legislative, not a judicial, prerogative and that none of the provisions of RC Chapter 2151 permits post-dispositional use of adult facilities to house children. It further reasoned that incarceration of a juvenile offender in a jail or other adult facility is contrary to the rehabilitative approach traditionally intended for juvenile proceedings. The court distinguished *Cox*[260] by limiting it to the special circumstances involved, i.e., the fact that the juvenile in *Cox* had fled the court's jurisdiction in defiance of court order until after he had reached age twenty-one. In a footnote, the *Grady* opinion also distinguished *Corona,* by asserting that none of the issues raised in *Corona* corresponded to the issue decided in *Grady.*[261]

(C) Plural dispositions

Under certain circumstances the court may choose to impose more than one disposition for a child adjudged delinquent, such as restitution (RC 2151.355(A)(8)) and commitment to the Department of Youth Services (RC 2151.355(A)(4)).[262] However, the court's authority to order more than one disposition is not unlimited. In *In re Bolden*,[263] in which a child was adjudged delinquent on three separate assault complaints, the juvenile court judge committed the child to the custody of the Ohio Youth Commission (now Ohio Department of Youth Services) for diagnostic study[264] on one complaint, placed him in the physical care and custody of his parents on the second complaint, and placed him on probation with the court's probation department on the third complaint. On appeal, it was held that plural delinquency findings constitute a finding of a single legal status and permit either one disposition common to all the complaints and findings of delinquency or separate dispositions for each finding based on a single complaint, which findings must be consistent with and not mutually exclusive of each other. Because it was impossible to simultaneously place the child on probation, return him to his parents, and place him in the custody of the Ohio Youth Commission (now Department of Youth Services), the dispositions imposed by the juvenile court were inconsistent. Whether a juvenile court may order consecutive commitments to the Depart-

---

[260]In re Cox, 36 App(2d) 65, 301 NE(2d) 907 (Mahoning 1973).

[261]The two relevant assignments of error in *Corona* were as follows: (1) the court committed prejudicial error in sentencing the appellant to six months in the workhouse for an offense which, if committed by an adult, would result in a fine of no more than $100; and (2) the court committed prejudicial error in sentencing the appellant to jail, since the court had lost jurisdiction over the case. The sole assignment of error in *Grady* was as follows: the court erred in committing a child who was still under the jurisdiction of the juvenile court to a determinate sentence in county jail. Although the assignments of error are somewhat different, the issue of whether a delinquent child who reaches age eighteen prior to disposition may be committed to an adult facility remains clouded. It is noteworthy that in *Grady* a ten-day incarceration in the county jail for receiving stolen property was invalidated even though an adult defendant could have received up to six months' imprisonment for the same offense; in *Corona* a six-month commitment to an adult facility for disorderly conduct was approved even though an adult convicted of the same offense could only have received a maximum $100 fine.

[262]In re Wood, No. 9-84-44 (3d Dist Ct App, Marion, 4-14-86).

[263]In re Bolden, 37 App(2d) 7, 306 NE(2d) 166 (Allen 1973).

[264]RC 2151.355 no longer permits a temporary commitment for diagnostic study.

ment of Youth Services for a child who is found delinquent on more than one felony complaint is an issue which has not yet reached the appellate courts.[265]

In *State ex rel Duganitz v Court of Common Pleas*,[266] involving a child who was charged with several delinquency complaints, some of which were classified as felonies and some misdemeanors, the juvenile court judge transferred the felony complaints to the adult court for criminal prosecution[267] and retained jurisdiction over the disposition of the misdemeanor complaints. This action was approved by a court of appeals because there is no provision for transferring to adult court the trial of juveniles for misdemeanors.

A juvenile court may not impose a fine and court costs on a delinquent child and also transfer the matter to the juvenile court of the child's resident county for further disposition.[268] Since the imposition of a fine pursuant to RC 2151.355 is a final dispositional order, nothing remains for transfer to the other juvenile court.

CROSS REFERENCES

Text 3.02, 13.09, 15.01(B), (E), 15.04(A)

Schroeder-Katz, Ohio Criminal Law, Crim R 32.3, Author's Text
Merrick-Rippner, Ohio Probate Law (4th ed), Text Ch 223

13.08   Unruly child

(A) Mandatory dispositions

If a child is adjudged unruly for any drug abuse offense,[269] disorderly conduct while intoxicated,[270] or driving while intoxicated,[271] the court is required to suspend or revoke the child's temporary instruction permit or probationary operator's license until the child's eighteenth birthday or until the child attends, at the court's discretion, and satisfactorily completes a drivers' intervention program certified pursuant to RC 3720.06.[272] During the time that the child is attending the program, the court must retain the child's permit or license and return it to the child after he satisfactorily completes the program.[273]

---

[265]See also In re Soboslay, Nos. 51872, 51873 (8th Dist Ct App, Cuyahoga, 11-13-86).

[266]State ex rel Duganitz v Court of Common Pleas, 23 OO(3d) 572 (App, Cuyahoga 1981), affirmed by 69 OS(2d) 270, 432 NE(2d) 163 (1982).

[267]See RC 2151.26. See also Juv R 30. Transfer to the adult court is technically not a disposition, since it is a pre-adjudicatory order.

[268]In re Sekulich, 65 OS(2d) 13, 417 NE(2d) 1014 (1981).

[269]"Drug abuse offense" is defined in RC 2925.01.

[270]RC 2917.11.

[271]RC 4511.19. It is not clear why any of these offenses are included in the dispositional statute for unruly children since drug abuse offenses and disorderly conduct while intoxicated are delinquency offenses (RC 2151.02) and driving while intoxicated is a juvenile traffic offense (RC 2151.021).

[196]RC 2151.354(B). The effective date of 1988 H 643, amending RC 2151.354(B), was suspended by 1989 H 329 until June 30, 1989. See also RC 4507.162. If the child does not yet own a temporary instruction permit or probationary operator's license, he may not be issued one until he satisfactorily completes the program (RC 4507.08).

[273]RC 2151.354(B).

Within ten days after the adjudication, the court must notify the Bureau of Motor Vehicles of the adjudicatory order.[274] If the child satisfactorily completes a drivers' intervention program, the program operator must promptly notify the court,[275] whereupon the court must immediately notify the Bureau of Motor Vehicles.[276]

(B) Discretionary dispositions

If the child is adjudged unruly, the court may (1) make any of the dispositions authorized for neglected, dependent, and abused children under RC 2151.353;[277] (2) place the child on probation under such conditions as the court prescribes;[278] or (3) suspend or revoke the child's operator's or chauffeur's[279] license or the registration of all motor vehicles issued to the child.[280]

The statutory section authorizing probation for an unruly child does not contain the directives concerning restitution which apply to probation for a delinquent child. However, it appears that restitution could be made a condition of probation.

If, after making its disposition, the court finds, upon further hearing, that the child is not amenable to treatment or rehabilitation under such disposition, it may make a disposition authorized for a delinquent child under RC 2151.355.[281] This further finding may result from the filing of a motion to review the original order, notice of which must be served in the same manner provided for service of process.[282] A complaint for violation of probation[283] or a delinquency complaint for violation of a court order[284] may also trigger this reexamination of the original disposition.

The order of disposition for an unruly child who is found not amenable to treatment or rehabilitation may not include commitment to the Department of Youth Services, since this disposition is available only for a delinquent-felon.[285] However, it may include any other disposition that the court finds proper.[286]

---

[274]RC 4507.021(D)(2)(a). Although this order is mandated by the dispositional statute (RC 2151.354(B)), it is not made at the adjudicatory hearing, which may be held well before the dispositional hearing (see Juv R 34(A)).

[275]RC 3720.06.

[276]RC 4507.021(D)(2)(b).

[277]RC 2151.354(A). See Text 13.06(A), Dispositional alternatives. For a discussion of whether the procedural requirements applicable to the disposition of neglected, dependent, and abused children would apply to the disposition of delinquent (and unruly) children, see Text 13.07(B)(1), Statutory provisions.

[278]RC 2151.354(A)(2). The same rules governing probation for delinquent children apply to unruly children. See Text 13.07(B)(2), Probation.

[279]This provision which was removed from RC 2151.356 in 1977 is inapplicable to juveniles, since only adults may obtain a chauffeur's license (RC 4507.08).

[280]RC 2151.354(A)(3). The same rules governing a disposition relative to a juvenile traffic offender apply to unruly children. See Text 13.09, Juvenile traffic offender.

[281]RC 2151.354.

[282]Juv R 35(A).

[283]See Juv R 35(B). See also Text 15.01(C), Revocation of probation.

[284]RC 2151.02(B). See Text 3.02, Delinquent child.

[285]RC 2151.355(A)(4) to (6).

[286]RC 2151.355(A)(10). See Text 13.07(B)(8), Any further disposition that the court finds proper.

Text 3.02, 13.04(A), 13.05(A), 13.07, 15.01(C)

Merrick-Rippner, Ohio Probate Law (4th ed), Text Ch 223

13.09   Juvenile traffic offender

(A) Mandatory dispositions

If a child is adjudged a juvenile traffic offender for any drug abuse offense,[287] disorderly conduct while intoxicated,[288] or driving while intoxicated,[289] the court is required to suspend or revoke the child's temporary instruction permit or probationary operator's license until the child's eighteenth birthday or until the child attends, at the court's discretion, and satisfactorily completes a drivers' intervention program certified pursuant to RC 3720.06.[290] During the time that the child is attending the program, the court must retain the child's permit or license and return it to the child after he satisfactorily completes the program.[291]

Within ten days after the adjudication, the court must notify the Bureau of Motor Vehicles of the adjudicatory order.[292] If the child satisfactorily completes a drivers' intervention program, the program operator must promptly notify the court,[293] whereupon the court must immediately notify the Bureau of Motor Vehicles.[294]

(B) Discretionary dispositions

If the child is found to be a juvenile traffic offender, the court may (1) impose a fine not to exceed fifty dollars and costs;[295] (2) suspend or revoke the child's probationary driver's license or the registration of any motor vehicles registered in the child's name for such period as the court prescribes;[296] (3) place the child

---

[287]"Drug abuse offense" is defined in RC 2925.01.

[288]RC 2917.11. It is not clear why drug abuse offenses and disorderly conduct while intoxicated are included in the dispositional statute for juvenile traffic offenders since such offenses constitute delinquency offenses pursuant to RC 2151.02.

[289]RC 4511.19.

[290]RC 2151.356(B). The effective date of 1988 H 643, amending RC 2151.356(B), was suspended by 1989 H 329 until June 30, 1989. See also RC 4507.162. If the child does not yet own a temporary instruction permit or probationary operator's license, he may not be issued one until he satisfactorily completes the program (RC 4507.08).

[291]RC 2151.356(B).

[292]RC 4507.021(D)(2)(a). Although this order is mandated by the dispositional statute (RC 2151.356(B)), it is made at the adjudicatory hearing, which may be held well before the dispositional hearing (see Juv R 34(A)).

[293]RC 3720.06.

[294]RC 4507.021(D)(2)(b).

[295]RC 2151.356(A)(1). Fines imposed upon juvenile traffic offenders must be paid to the general fund of the county treasury pursuant to RC 2949.11, rather than to the county law library association pursuant to RC 3375.52 or RC 3375.53 (OAG 82-062).

[296]RC 2151.356(A)(2), (3). In some juvenile courts, the child's driver's license is restricted for a period of time, permitting the child to drive for limited, specified purposes. The record of any revocation or suspension must be sent to the registrar of the Bureau of Motor Vehicles pursuant to RC 4507.15.

on probation;[297] or (4) require the child to make restitution for all damages caused by his traffic violation or any part thereof.[298]

(C) Violations of seat belt law

Specific dispositional alternatives are provided for children who violate the seat belt law.[299] If a child is found to be a juvenile traffic offender for operating an automobile without wearing a seat belt,[300] he must be fined $20.[301] If he operates an automobile in which a front seat passenger is not wearing a seat belt,[302] he must be fined $10 for each such passenger, up to a maximum of $30.[303] If a child sixteen years of age or older is found to be a juvenile traffic offender for occupying a front seat without wearing a seat belt,[304] he must be fined $10.[305] However, if he is under sixteen he may not be fined, but may be placed on probation.[306] If a child who receives a traffic ticket for violating the seat belt law proves by a preponderance of the evidence that prior to the originally scheduled court appearance he had viewed one of the films developed for the seat belt education program, the court must dismiss the charge and waive the fine, but may impose court costs not to exceed $15.[307]

(D) Institutionalization

An initial dispositional order for a juvenile traffic offender may not include commitment to an institution or agency. However, if after making a disposition, the court finds upon further hearing that the child has failed to comply with the court orders and that his operation of a motor vehicle constitutes a danger to himself and others, it may make any disposition authorized for a delinquent child under RC 2151.355.[308]

(E) Revocation of probationary operator's license

In addition to the juvenile court's authority to revoke a child's driver's license, the Bureau of Motor Vehicles must revoke for a period of one year the probationary operator's license issued to a child between the ages of sixteen and eighteen years if he has, before reaching his eighteenth birthday, been adjudged guilty in juvenile court of committing three separate moving violations in a two-year period.[309] These violations must come within the purview of RC 2903.06, RC 2903.07, RC 4511.02, RC 4511.12, RC 4511.13, RC 4511.15, RC 4511.19

---

[297]RC 2151.356(A)(4). For a discussion of probation as it applies to the disposition of a delinquent child, see Text 13.07(B)(2), Probation.

[298]RC 2151.356(A)(5). For a discussion of restitution as it applies to the disposition of a delinquent child, see Text 13.07(B)(6), Restitution.

[299]RC 4513.263.

[300]RC 4513.263(B)(1).

[301]RC 2151.356(C), RC 4513.99(F).

[302]RC 4513.263(B)(2).

[303]RC 2151.356(C), RC 4513.99(G).

[304]RC 4513.263(B)(3).

[305]RC 2151.356(C), RC 4513.99(H).

[306]RC 2151.356(C). It is not clear from the statute whether the child's age should be determined as of the date of the issuance of the ticket, or the date of the hearing.

[307]RC 2151.356(C), RC 4513.263(F).

[308]RC 2151.356. This would not, of course, include commitment to the Department of Youth Services, which is available only for a delinquent-felon. See Text 13.07(B)(4), Commitment to Ohio Department of Youth Services.

[309]RC 4507.162.

to RC 4511.23, RC 4511.25 to RC 4511.48, RC 4511.57 to RC 4511.65, RC 4511.75, RC 4549.02, RC 4549.021, or RC 4549.03 or of any municipal ordinance relating to the offenses covered in these statutes.[310] RC 4507.162 differs from the general rule governing the disposition of children's cases in that the adjudication on the third violation must occur prior to the child's eighteenth birthday in order for mandatory revocation to apply.[311] The general rule in other cases is that a child who violates a law shall be deemed a child irrespective of his age at the time the complaint is filed or the hearing is had thereon, and any permissible disposition may be made even if the child reaches age eighteen prior to adjudication.[312]

(F) Occupational driving privileges

If a child is adjudicated on a third violation of RC 4511.12, RC 4511.13, RC 4511.15, RC 4511.20 to RC 4511.24, RC 4511.26 to RC 4511.48, RC 4511.57 to RC 4511.65, or RC 451' 75, or any similar municipal ordinance within a two-year period, the court may grant the child occupational driving privileges if the court finds that the child will reach age eighteen before the end of the mandatory suspension period, and further finds reasonable cause to believe that such suspension, if continued beyond the child's eighteenth birthday, will seriously affect his ability to continue in his employment.[313] If granted, the occupational driving privileges take effect on the child's eighteenth birthday, and during the period following that birthday for which the suspension would otherwise be imposed.[314] If a person who has been granted occupational driving privileges violates any conditions imposed by the court,[315] or commits a subsequent violation of the Revised Code sections contained in RC 4507.162(A), the court must revoke the occupational driving privileges, and the registrar must suspend the person's license for a period of one year.[316]

(G) Effect of penalties for adult traffic offenders

Generally, the penalty provisions applicable to an adult traffic offender may not be imposed on a juvenile traffic offender unless expressly permitted by the dispositional statute, RC 2151.356. Thus, a final dispositional order for a juvenile traffic offender may not include commitment to a county jail upon the failure, refusal, or inability of the child to pay a fine and court costs.[317] Nor may such order include incarceration in a juvenile detention home,[318] even if the child has committed a traffic offense which, if committed by an adult, would

---

[310]*Id.*

[311]The attorney general has ruled that the probationary operator's license of a person who commits a third moving traffic violation before his eighteenth birthday, but who neither is convicted of nor pleads guilty to the violation until after his eighteenth birthday, may not be suspended under RC 4507.162 (OAG 79-092). However, the juvenile court may still suspend his license pursuant to RC 2151.356(A)(2).

[312]Juv R 2(2). See Text 3.10, Age jurisdiction; Text 13.07(B)(8), Any further disposition that the court finds proper.

[313]RC 4507.162(C).

[314]*Id.*

[315]See RC 4507.02.

[316]RC 4507.162(D).

[317]OAG 70-143.

[318]OAG 63-553.

require incarceration.[319] Thus, the minimum three-day imprisonment required by RC 4511.99 for an adult convicted of driving while intoxicated pursuant to RC 4511.19 does not apply to a juvenile traffic offender, since it is not specifically provided for in RC 2151.356.[320]

On the other hand, if permitted by the dispositional statute, the court may impose a stricter dispositional order on a juvenile traffic offender than could be imposed on an adult convicted of the same traffic violation.[321] Because the special Code provisions relating to juveniles supersede the more general provisions governing the operation of motor vehicles,[322] a child's driver's license may be suspended for a speeding violation under RC 2151.356(A)(2), whereas an adult's license could not be suspended for the same offense.

Moreover, a juvenile traffic offender is subject to some of the same penalties which are imposed on an adult traffic offender by the Bureau of Motor Vehicles. For instance, the accumulation of points for moving violations applies equally to juvenile and adult traffic offenders.[323] In addition, a juvenile traffic offender is subject to the provisions of RC 4509.01 to RC 4509.78, the Ohio Financial Responsibility Act.[324]

CROSS REFERENCES

Text 3.03, 3.10, 13.07(B)

Merrick-Rippner, Ohio Probate Law (4th ed), Text Ch 223

13.10   Jurisdiction over parents and others, responsibilities to victim

The juvenile court's jurisdiction over the disposition of children's cases may, in some instances, extend beyond the child himself. Under certain circumstances the court may impose orders on the child's parents.[325] For instance, the court may order the parents, if able to do so, to reimburse the court for the expense involved in providing emergency medical or surgical treatment to a child.[326] The court may also order the parents to pay the costs for the services of appointed counsel and guardians ad litem.[327]

---

[319]In re Martin, No. CA-740 (5th Dist Ct App, Ashland, 10-29-81).
[320]Id.
[321]In re Farinacci, No. 37973 (8th Dist Ct App, Cuyahoga, 11-30-78).
[322]Id.
[323]RC 4507.40. Gebell v Dollison, 57 App(2d) 198, 386 NE(2d) 845 (Clermont 1978) held that RC 2151.358 does not prohibit the use of records pertaining to traffic violations, kept pursuant to RC 4507.40 (now RC 4507.021), in a driver's license revocation hearing conducted after the accused has attained majority.
[324]RC 2151.356(D), RC 4509.011. The 1977 amendment to RC 2151.356 and the enactment of RC 4509.011 overrule Lapp v State of Ohio Bureau of Motor Vehicles, No. 1128 (5th Dist Ct App, Muskingum, 9-25-75), which held that RC 4509.31 did not apply to juvenile traffic offenders since, at that time, they were not specifically included within its purview.
[325]For authority of court to impose restrictions on a parent following an order of protective supervision, see RC 2151.353(C) and Text 13.06(A)(1), Protective supervision.
[326]RC 2151.33(A). See St. Thomas Medical Center v Morgan, No. 11618 (9th Dist Ct App, Summit, 8-15-84).
[327]Juv R 4(F). See In re Vaughn, No. 53462 (8th Dist Ct App, Cuyahoga, 10-15-87).

When a child has been committed pursuant to RC Chapter 2151, the court may make an examination regarding the income of the parents, guardian, or person charged with the child's support, and may order that person or persons to pay for the care, maintenance, and education of the child and for expenses involved in providing orthopedic, medical, or surgical treatment for, or special care of, the child.[328] An order requiring a parent to pay the cost of his child's placement without first examining the parent's income is prejudicial error.[329]

In any case where a delinquent child is placed on probation, if the court finds that the custodial parent has failed to exercise reasonable parental control and that such failure is the proximate cause of the child's delinquent act, the court may require the parent to post a recognizance bond in an amount not over $500, conditioned upon the faithful discharge of the parent's duties under the probation order.[330] Under certain circumstances, this bond may be forfeited if the child commits a second delinquent act or violates the conditions of probation, where the parent's failure to exercise his duties is the proximate cause thereof. The proceeds from the forfeited recognizance are applied towards payment of any damages caused by the child or are paid into the county treasury. The court's authority under this section is in addition to that contained in other provisions relating to failure or neglect to exercise proper parental control.[331]

Additionally, the court may grant a restraining order controlling the conduct of a parent, guardian, custodian, or any other party, if it is necessary to control any conduct or relationship which may be harmful to the child and may tend to defeat the execution of a dispositional order. Due notice, the grounds for the application, and an opportunity to be heard must be given to the person against whom the order is directed.[332]

Where a parent has admitted to past use of marijuana and has indicated his intention to continue using it, and where his child has been adjudged delinquent for a drug offense and placed on probation in the custody of his parents, the court may order the custodial parent to submit to a urine analysis test to check for use of marijuana.[333]

The juvenile court's authority over parents and others is not unlimited. The court does not have jurisdiction to order a parent to pay for the destructive acts of his child.[334] Nor may the court order the Ohio Department of Mental Health to pay the cost of caring for a child placed in a private psychiatric hospital.[335]

---

[328]RC 2151.36; Juv R 34(C); OAG 62-2938. Where permanent custody is awarded, the parents are divested of all legal obligations towards the child, including the duty of support. See RC 2151.011(A)(12).

[329]In re Koogle, Nos. CA 82-68, CA 82-93 (2d Dist Ct App, Greene, 6-16-83).

[330]RC 2151.411.

[331]Id.

[332]RC 2151.359; Juv R 34(D). Included under the definition of party in Juv R 2(16) is "any other person specifically designated by the court." By such action, the court would be authorized to order virtually anyone not to associate with the child and would be able to enforce such an order through its contempt powers (RC 2151.21).

[333]In re Dague, No. 87-CA-12 (5th Dist Ct App, Delaware, 10-22-87).

[334]In re Watkins, No. 42409 (8th Dist Ct App, Cuyahoga, 1-22-81); In re Daudt, No. CA 85-11-147 (12th Dist Ct App, Butler, 9-2-86).

[335]In re Hamil, 69 OS(2d) 97, 431 NE(2d) 317 (1982). This case involved a child, charged as a delinquent, who was found "not guilty by reason of insanity," and was

In recognition of the juvenile court's responsibility to protect the welfare of the community,[336] the court is authorized, and in some cases is required, to consider the interests of the victim at the dispositional hearing in delinquency cases. Such consideration may include an order requiring the child to make restitution to the victim of the delinquent act.[337] The victim's status may also be a relevant factor in determining whether to relinquish jurisdiction of an alleged delinquent for the purpose of criminal prosecution.[338] Furthermore, prior to making an order of disposition for a delinquent child, the court must determine whether the victim was sixty-five years of age or older or permanently and totally disabled at the time of the delinquent act and whether the delinquent act would have been an offense of violence if committed by an adult. If the victim was sixty-five years of age or older or permanently and totally disabled at the time the act was committed, regardless of whether the child knew the victim's age, and if the act would have been an offense of violence if committed by an adult, these facts will be considered in favor of imposing commitment of the child,[339] although these facts will not control the court's decision.[340] At any hearing at which a child is adjudicated delinquent, or as soon as possible thereafter, the court must notify all victims that they may be entitled to a recovery under RC 3109.09 (compensatory damages from child's parents for acts of theft or vandalism), RC 3109.10 (compensatory damages from child's parents for willful and malicious assaults committed by the child), and RC 2743.51 to RC 2743.72 (award of reparations).[341]

CROSS REFERENCES

Text Ch 9, 13.06(A)(1), 13.07(B)(6)

Merrick-Rippner, Ohio Probate Law (4th ed), Text Ch 223

---

thereafter determined to be a mentally ill person in need of hospitalization pursuant to RC 2151.23(A)(4).

[336] Juv R 1(B)(3), Juv R 30(C)(2).

[337] See RC 2151.355(A)(2), (8). See also Text 13.07(B)(6), Restitution.

[338] See RC 2151.26(B). See also Text Ch 9, Transfer of Jurisdiction.

[339] See RC 2151.355(A)(3) to (6).

[340] RC 2151.355(C).

[341] RC 2151.355(E).

Chapter 15

Post-Disposition Issues

15.01   Continuing jurisdiction

(A) In general

The continuing jurisdiction of the juvenile court is invoked by motion filed in the original proceeding, notice of which must be served in the manner provided for the service of process.[1] Despite the language of Juvenile Rule 35(A), the label placed on the initiating document is unimportant. Thus, the court's continuing jurisdiction may be invoked by the filing of a new complaint rather than a motion, as long as the parties are given notice and an opportunity to be heard.[2]

The time period provided for certain acts and proceedings is not affected or limited by the expiration of a term of court which in no way affects the authority of a juvenile court.[3]

The grounds for modification and vacation of judgments contained in Civil Rule 60 appear to apply to juvenile court judgments. These grounds include fraud or misrepresentation, lack of jurisdiction, and any other reason justifying relief from the judgment.[4]

A motion invoking the court's continuing jurisdiction, like any other motion, must state with particularity the grounds upon which it is made and must set forth the relief or order sought. It must also be supported by a brief and may be supported by an affidavit. To expedite its business, the court may provide by rule or order for the submission and determination of motions without oral hearing upon brief written statements of reasons in support and opposition.[5]

During the pendency of proceedings pursuant to a motion invoking the court's continuing jurisdiction, a child may be placed in detention in accordance with the provisions of Juvenile Rule 7.[6]

(B) Duration and termination of continuing jurisdiction

(1) Abuse, neglect, and dependency proceedings

Once the court issues an original dispositional order[7] or a further dispositional order following the expiration of a temporary custody order in abuse,

---

[1]Juv R 35(A).

[2]In re Luke, No. 83-CA-09 (5th Dist Ct App, Coshocton, 1-13-84).

[3]Juv R 18(C). For special provisions relating to the Cuyahoga County Juvenile Court, see RC 2153.15. The term of any juvenile court is one calendar year (RC 2151.22).

[4]Civ R 60(B). E.g., In re Frinzl, 152 OS 164, 87 NE(2d) 583 (1949).

[5]Juv R 19.

[6]Juv R 35(C).

[7]See RC 2151.353(A); Text 13.06(A), Dispositional alternatives.

neglect, and dependency proceedings,[8] the court's jurisdiction over the child continues until age eighteen for a child who is not mentally or physically handicapped, age twenty-one for a child who is mentally or physically handicapped, or until the child is adopted.[9] However, the court may make a journal entry retaining jurisdiction over the child and continuing any order of disposition for a specified period of time to enable the child to graduate from high school or vocational school.[10]

On the motion of any party to modify or terminate a dispositional order, or on the court's own motion, the court is required to conduct a further dispositional hearing and may modify or terminate a dispositional order in accordance with the child's best interest.[11] Cases decided prior to the 1989 amendments to the dispositional statutes[12] held that the parent bears the burden to show by clear and convincing evidence that the modification is in the child's best interest.[13] Moreover, it has been held that where a biological parent moves to terminate temporary custody in another that was based on a previous finding of dependency, the parent's present suitability and fitness for the role of parent must be considered in the context of the best interest of the child.[14]

(2) All other proceedings

RC 2151.38(A) provides that when a child is committed to the legal custody of the Department of Youth Services,[15] the juvenile court's jurisdiction with respect to the child terminates except as it relates to early release[16] and aftercare[17] decisions. Moreover, RC 2151.38(A) indicates that if the Department makes a motion to terminate permanent custody,[18] the court may terminate custody at any time prior to the child's attainment of age eighteen.[19]

---

[8]See RC 2151.415(B).

[9]RC 2151.353(E)(1), RC 2151.415(E).

[10]*Id.*

[11]RC 2151.353(E)(2), RC 2151.415(F), RC 2151.417(B). Since this is a dispositional hearing, it appears that the court is not required to relitigate the issue of abuse, neglect, or dependency. This overrules those cases which interpreted the previous versions of the statutes as requiring a readjudication of the child's status. See, e.g., In re Monfreda, No. 740 (12th Dist Ct App, Madison, 5-26-82).

[12]RC 2151.353, RC 2151.415, amended by 1988 S 89, eff. 1-1-89.

[13]In re Patterson, 16 App(3d) 214, 16 OBR 229, 475 NE(2d) 160 (Madison 1984); In re Sopher, No. 50198 (8th Dist Ct App, Cuyahoga, 2-20-86).

[14]In re Christopher, 54 App(2d) 137, 376 NE(2d) 603 (Morrow 1977).

[15]See Text 13.07(B)(3), Commitment to county or private facility.

[16]See RC 2151.38(B); Text 15.01(E), Commitment to Ohio Department of Youth Services, early release.

[17]See RC 2151.38(C); Text 15.01(E), Commitment to Ohio Department of Youth Services, early release.

[18]It is not clear why the statute initially refers to a commitment to the "legal custody" of the department and then, in the same sentence, uses the term "permanent custody." The two terms have significantly different meanings. See RC 2151.011(B)(10) and (12), respectively, for definitions of these terms; Text 13.06(A)(4), Permanent custody. See also RC 2151.355(A)(4) to (6), which uses the term "legal custody" with respect to commitments to the Department of Youth Services.

[19]A prior version of the statute, amended by 1988 S 89, eff. 1-1-89, provided that the court could terminate custody prior to the child attaining age twenty-one. With the reduction to age eighteen, the juvenile court is apparently not authorized to terminate the department's custody of a child who is eighteen, nineteen, or twenty.

A prior version of RC 2151.38(A) provided that all other commitments made by the court were temporary and continued (1) for a period designated by the court, (2) until terminated or modified by the court, or (3) until the child attained the age of twenty-one. Although the statute used the term "commitment," courts generally regarded this provision as authority for the juvenile courts to retain jurisdiction in all cases until the child reached age twenty-one,[20] regardless of whether the child had been committed.[21] When RC 2151.38(A) was amended,[22] this provision was eliminated in its entirety. Therefore, Ohio law provides for the duration and termination of jurisdiction only in abuse, neglect, and dependency cases[23] and in delinquency cases in which the child is committed to the Department of Youth Services.[24] There are no statutory provisions governing the duration and termination of juvenile court jurisdiction in any other type of case.

Although there are no cases interpreting the amended version of RC 2151.38(A), several earlier cases considered the extent of juvenile court jurisdiction when the statute provided for termination of jurisdiction at the child's attainment of age twenty-one. According to one juvenile court, when a child adjudicated delinquent becomes twenty-one years of age during the pendency of appeals from the adjudication, all jurisdiction of the juvenile court terminates and that court has no authority to vacate its previous order of commitment.[25] This issue was discussed by the United States Supreme Court in *Kent v United States*[26] in relation to a Washington D.C. statute which, like the former Ohio statute,[27] provides that the juvenile court may no longer exercise jurisdiction over a child who reaches twenty-one years of age during the period that his appeal is pending final determination.[28] In *Kent* the Supreme Court overturned a juvenile court order transferring jurisdiction over a child from the juvenile court to the district court for prosecution as an adult. Because the child had passed the age of twenty-one years by the time of the Supreme Court's decision, the Court concluded that the juvenile court had lost jurisdiction over the child. Thus, the case was remanded to the district court for a hearing de novo on the issue of waiver.

In *Kent* the juvenile court's waiver order had been effectuated prior to the child's attaining twenty-one years of age. In addition, it was through no fault of the child that he had passed beyond the court's age jurisdiction by the time of the Supreme Court's remand order. It is uncertain whether that part of the *Kent*

---

[20]See, e.g., In re DeGeronimo, No. 40089 (8th Dist Ct App, Cuyahoga, 6-28-79), which held that a juvenile court may place a child on probation until he reaches the age of twenty-one.

[21]The predecessor of RC 2151.38, GC 1643, provided that when a child came into the "custody" of the juvenile court, the court's jurisdiction over the child continued until the child attained twenty-one years of age. A Supreme Court decision interpreting the former statute held that the arrest of a child pursuant to a warrant brought the child into the custody of the court. State ex rel Heth v Moloney, 126 OS 526, 186 NE 362 (1933).

[22]1988 S 89, eff. 1-1-89.

[23]RC 2151.353(E)(1), RC 2151.415(E).

[24]RC 2151.38(A).

[25]In re J.F., 17 Misc 40, 242 NE(2d) 604 (Juv, Cuyahoga 1968).

[26]Kent v United States, 383 US 541, 86 SCt 1045, 16 LEd(2d) 84 (1966).

[27]RC 2151.38.

[28]*Id.* For further discussion, see Text 9.05, Appeals.

decision concerning the termination of the juvenile court's jurisdiction would apply if, through the fault of the child, the juvenile court is unable to enforce its dispositional order until after the child attains the age of twenty-one years. According to an Ohio appellate court case decided prior to the amendment of RC 2151.38(A),[29] when a child who has been adjudicated delinquent leaves the jurisdiction of the juvenile court so that the court cannot dispose of his case until he is over twenty-one years of age, the juvenile court retains jurisdiction and may impose the adult penalty prescribed for the offense for which he was adjudged delinquent. Instead of focusing on the termination of jurisdiction statute,[30] the court in *In re Cox* relied on the statutory definition of "child"[31] for its conclusion that the juvenile court retained jurisdiction. RC 2151.011(B)(1) provides that "child" includes any person who violates a law prior to attaining eighteen years of age, *irrespective* of his age at the time the complaint is filed or a hearing is held.

Based on the *Cox* rationale, it appears that a juvenile court properly assumes jurisdiction over an alleged delinquent child who is not arrested or charged until after he attains the age of twenty-one years (assuming the statute of limitations for the offense has not expired). No child, either before or after reaching eighteen years of age, may be prosecuted in a criminal court as an adult for an offense committed before reaching age eighteen unless he is transferred from the juvenile court pursuant to RC 2151.26(E).[32] Therefore, if the juvenile court were not given jurisdiction over such child, there would be no judicial recourse for his delinquent act.

(C) Revocation of probation

The juvenile court may not revoke a child's probation except after a hearing at which the child is present and is apprised of the grounds for the proposed revocation. All parties to a probation revocation proceeding have a right to retain counsel, or to have counsel appointed if indigent. Probation may not be revoked unless it is found that the child has violated a condition of probation of which he was notified pursuant to Juvenile Rule 34(C).[33] The standard of proof required to establish the violation is not provided by statute or rule. However, in a proceeding charging an unruly child as a delinquent for violation of the conditions of his probation,[34] proof beyond a reasonable doubt would be required.[35]

Although there is no provision specifying the dispositional alternatives available to the court for a child in violation of probation, it appears that any

---

[29]In re Cox, 36 App(2d) 65, 301 NE(2d) 907 (Mahoning 1973).

[30]RC 2151.38.

[31]RC 2151.011(B)(1).

[32]See Text Ch 9, Transfer of Jurisdiction.

[33]Juv R 35(B).

[34]See RC 2151.02(B).

[35]RC 2151.35; Juv R 29(E)(4). But see In re Boyer, No. 34724 (8th Dist Ct App, Cuyahoga, 12-31-75), in which the court stated, "Violation [of probation] is not a separate crime in Ohio (cf. Ohio Revised Code 2951.09) if committed by an adult. However, even if it were criminal in an adult requiring proof beyond a reasonable doubt, such proof was obviously present in this case."

disposition authorized at the time of the original dispositional hearing would be permitted.[36]

(D) Contempt

The juvenile court has the same contempt power as the court of common pleas,[37] as well as the inherent power to punish for contempt.[38] Anyone who is summoned or subpoenaed to appear for a hearing and who fails to do so may be punished for contempt of court.[39] This sanction also applies to a parent who fails to obey a summons ordering him to bring a child to the hearing.[40] However, parents may not be held in contempt if the evidence indicates that they do not know the child's whereabouts.[41]

Contempt is sometimes used to compel a party or witness to answer questions addressed to him. Where the mother of a child who is the subject of a dependency action fails to answer deposition questions[42] after being granted immunity under RC 2945.44, she may be held in contempt. The juvenile court has authority to grant immunity even though no criminal case is pending against the grantee.[43] However, the result is different where immunity has not been granted. For example, a juvenile witness (who was charged with being a delinquent and was under indictment for manslaughter) is not guilty of contempt for refusing to testify in the criminal trial of a defendant charged with selling liquor to a minor in answer to questions about whether he had purchased liquor from the defendant or had seen him sell liquor to minors.[44]

The traditional due process requirements of notice and hearing, which are applicable to contempt proceedings, must be adhered to in a juvenile court action brought against a child for failure to pay court costs ordered by the court.[45]

(E) Commitment to Ohio Department of Youth Services, early release

As a general rule, two legal consequences result from a juvenile court's commitment of a child to the legal custody of the Department of Youth Services: (1) the court's jurisdiction over the child terminates,[46] and (2) the department assumes legal custody of the child until the child attains twenty-one years of age.[47] However, there are several exceptions to these rules. When the depart-

---

[36]For an adult defendant who has violated probation, the court may impose any sentence which might originally have been imposed (RC 2951.09).

[37]RC 2151.21. See RC 2705.01 to RC 2705.10.

[38]State ex rel Turner v Albin, 118 OS 527, 161 NE 792 (1928).

[39]RC 2151.28(J). See also Juv R 15(B)(4), relative to failure to appear in response to a summons, and Juv R 17(G), which provides that the contempt power may be applied against any person who fails to obey a subpoena "without adequate excuse."

[40]See Juv R 15(C).

[41]State v Hershberger, 83 Abs 62, 168 NE(2d) 13 (App, Wayne 1959).

[42]See Juv R 25.

[43]In re Poth, 2 App(3d) 361, 2 OBR 417, 442 NE(2d) 105 (Huron 1981).

[44]In re Newton, 12 App(2d) 191, 231 NE(2d) 880 (Hamilton 1967).

[45]In re Rinehart, 10 App(3d) 318, 10 OBR 523, 462 NE(2d) 448 (Ross 1983).

[46]RC 2151.38(A), RC 5139.05(B). See State v McCallister, No. CA-7264 (5th Dist Ct App, Stark, 12-7-87).

[47]RC 5139.05(B). See also In re Cox, 36 App(2d) 65, 301 NE(2d) 907 (Mahoning 1973).

ment is given permanent custody of a child,[48] it may apply to the committing court for termination of such custody.[49] After notice and hearing, and for good cause shown, the court may terminate permanent custody at any time prior to the child's reaching eighteen years of age and must dispose of the case according to the child's best interests.[50]

The department may also divest itself of permanent custody of a minor child by discharging him to the exclusive management, control, and custody of a parent or guardian.[51] Prior to discharge, the child must be granted a release from institutional care according to law, and the department must be satisfied that the discharge is consistent with the welfare of the individual and the protection of the public.[52] At least fifteen days before the scheduled discharge date, the department must notify the committing court, in writing, that it intends to discharge the child. Upon discharge it must immediately certify such fact to the committing court, again in writing.[53]

The juvenile court's jurisdiction over the child continues with respect to many decisions regarding both the child's release and postrelease status. In order to release a child prior to the prescribed minimum period of institutionalization, the committing court must grant an early release; not until this is done may the department (1) release the child from the prescribed institutional care; (2) release the child on parole; or (3) assign the child to a family home, group care facility, or other place for treatment and rehabilitation. An early release may be granted upon the court's own motion or upon the request of the department, the child, or the child's parent.[54] A request for early release may be made at any time by the department or upon the court's own motion. The committing

[48]RC 2151.355(A)(4) to (6) use the term "legal custody" rather than "permanent custody" when referring to the status of the department relative to a child committed to it. "Legal custody," as defined in RC 2151.011(B)(10), creates a different status than "permanent custody," defined in RC 2151.011(B)(12). However, RC 5139.05(B), which governs the Department of Youth Services, provides that an order committing a child to the department shall state that the commitment is permanent. RC Ch 5139 also includes definitions of the terms "legal custody" (RC 5139.01(A)(3)) and "permanent commitment" (RC 5139.01(A)(2)), which differ from the meaning of those terms as used in RC Ch 2151. These definitions clearly establish the custodial responsibilities of the department with respect to a child committed to it.
[49]RC 2151.38(A). This statute does not provide parents with the right to file a motion to terminate permanent custody. See State v Clevenger, 19 App(2d) 306, 251 NE(2d) 159 (Clinton 1969). However, RC 5139.05(B) indicates that the permanent custody of the department may be terminated upon motion of the court or petition of the "parent, guardian of the person, or next friend of a child, or upon petition of the department."
[50]RC 2151.38(A).
[51]RC 2151.38(E), RC 5139.05(B), RC 5139.06(C)(4). These statutes make it clear that the act of discharging a child terminates the department's legal custody. Thus, it is uncertain what purpose is served by that part of RC 5139.06(D) which provides, "Upon the discharge from its custody and control, the department may petition the court for an order terminating its custody and control."
[52]See RC 2151.38(B), (C), RC 5139.06(C)(4).
[53]RC 5139.06(C)(4).
[54]RC 2151.38(B)(1), RC 5139.05(B), RC 5139.06(B). Under certain circumstances, the department may transfer a developmentally disabled child to another state institution prior to the minimum period of institutionalization without court approval (RC 5139.06(C)(2)). It may also transfer a child to a less restrictive setting than originally prescribed, with prior consent of the committing court (RC 5139.35). See also RC

court must then either approve the early release by journal entry or must schedule a hearing within thirty days to determine whether the child is to be released.[55] A request by a child or parent for early release may not be made prior to the expiration of thirty days from the day institutional care began.[56] Upon the filing of a timely request by the child or parent, the court may either approve or reject the request without a hearing or may schedule a hearing within thirty days. If the initial request is rejected, the child or parent may make one or more subsequent requests after the expiration of thirty days from the date of the prior rejection. Upon the filing of a subsequent request, the court must either approve the early release or schedule a hearing within thirty days to determine whether to release the child.[57]

If a court schedules a hearing pursuant to a request for an early release or upon its own motion, it must order the department to deliver the child to the court on the hearing date and to present a treatment plan for the child's postinstitutional care.[58] The court then determines whether to grant the early release.

If a child has been institutionalized for the prescribed minimum period of time, the department may release him from institutional care without court approval.[59] Once the child is released, he may be placed on parole[60] or assigned to a family home, group care facility, or other place for treatment or rehabilitation.[61] The department may prescribe such supervision and conditions of parole as it believes conducive to law-abiding conduct, and it may order replacement or renewed parole as often as conditions indicate this to be desirable.[62] Whether the child is released on parole or assigned to a home or treatment facility, the department must give written notification to the committing court of the terms of the release or assignment at least fifteen days prior to the release or assignment.[63]

The department is required to communicate with the appropriate juvenile court or courts regarding a child who has been released from institutional care, regardless of whether the child was granted an early release. Prior to the release of a child, the department must prepare a written treatment and rehabilitation plan for the child, including the conditions of his release.[64] This plan, prepared

---

5139.05(C) regarding the department's authority to utilize a juvenile diagnostic center for observation or treatment.

[55] RC 2151.38(B)(2)(a). This apparently means that the court must conduct the hearing within thirty days and not merely set a hearing date within thirty days.

[56] RC 2151.38(B)(2)(b).

[57] RC 2151.38(B)(2).

[58] RC 2151.38(B)(2)(c).

[59] RC 2151.38(C), RC 5139.06(C)(1).

[60] *Id.* These two statutes apply only when a child has been released after being institutionalized for the prescribed minimum period. However, RC 5139.01(A)(9), which defines the term "release," provides, "A child released pursuant to division (B) of section 2151.38 [i.e., early release] or pursuant to division (C) of section 5139.06 of the Revised Code shall be on parole until discharged ... or until such custody is terminated as otherwise provided by law."

[61] RC 2151.38(C), RC 5139.06(C)(5).

[62] RC 5139.06(C)(1).

[63] *Id.*, RC 5139.06(C)(5).

[64] RC 2151.38(B)(2)(c), (C), RC 5139.06(B), (E). It is not clear whether and how this plan differs from the terms and conditions required when a child is released on parole or

after reviewing the child's rehabilitative progress history and medical and educational records, must be discussed with the child and his parents, guardian, or legal custodian.[65] The plan must be signed by these persons and any authority or person that is to supervise the child upon his release.[66] Prior to the child's release, a copy of the plan must be filed with both the committing court and the juvenile court of the county in which the child is to be placed.[67] The court of the county in which the child is placed may adopt the conditions as a court order and may add any other consistent conditions it considers appropriate.[68]

At least once every thirty days, the department must file a written report with the committing court describing the progress of each child who has been released.[69] The report must describe the treatment and rehabilitative progress of the child and his family, if applicable, and must include any recommendations for alteration of the program, custody, living arrangements, or treatment which the department wishes to implement.[70]

If a child has been assigned, granted early release, or released on parole, and the court of the county where the child has been placed has reason to believe that the child has not followed any of the postrelease conditions, that court may schedule a hearing to determine this issue.[71] If the court determines that the child has seriously violated the conditions of the plan,[72] it may order the child returned to the department for institutionalization or may make any other disposition authorized by law that it considers proper.[73] Any child returned to a department institution must remain there for a minimum of three months.[74] In addition, a child who is returned after having been granted an early release must be institutionalized consistent with the original commitment order. The time during which the child was institutionalized prior to the early release is considered as time served in fulfilling the prescribed minimum period. Thus, if more

---

assigned to a home or treatment facility pursuant to RC 5139.06(C)(1) and (5). However, RC 2151.38(C) provides that the release, discharge, release on parole, or assignment of a child after the minimum period of institutionalization shall be in accordance with RC 5139.06(C).

[65]RC 2151.38(D)(1), (2).

[66]RC 2151.38(D)(3).

[67]RC 2151.38(B)(2)(c), (C), (D)(4), RC 5139.06(B), (E).

[68]RC 2151.38(B)(2)(c), (C), RC 5139.06(B), (E).

[69]RC 2151.38(E). The thirty-day period may be increased or decreased by the court.

[70]RC 2151.38(E).

[71]RC 2151.38(B)(2)(c), (C). If the child was granted an early release, the court must conduct this hearing (RC 2151.38(B)(2)(c)). If the child was released on parole or assigned, the court may, in its discretion, conduct the hearing (RC 2151.38(C)).

[72]The statutes do not define a "serious violation" or specify the standard of proof required in order to make this determination. Although the hearing is not a true "adjudicatory" hearing as defined in Juv R 29, arguably the preponderance of the evidence test established in Juv R 29(E)(4) would apply.

[73]RC 2151.38(B)(2)(c), (C). Presumably, "any other disposition" would include any disposition permitted for a delinquent child under RC 2151.355.

[74]RC 2151.38(B)(2)(c), (C). Because the department's custody automatically terminates when the child attains twenty-one years of age, a child who reaches that age prior to the expiration of the three-month minimum is apparently subject to release. See RC 5139.05(A), (B).

than three months remain of the original commitment order, the child will be held beyond three months.[75]

(F) Commitment to child care agency, custody review proceedings

(1) Semiannual administrative review

Both federal[76] and state[77] laws require periodic reviews of cases of children who are in the custody of public children services agencies and private child-placing agencies.

An agency that is required to prepare a case plan[78] for a child must complete a semiannual administrative review of the case plan no later than six months after the earlier of the date on which the complaint was filed or the date on which the child was first placed in shelter care, and no later than every six months thereafter.[79] If the court issues an order pursuant to the filing of a motion for permanent custody[80] or pursuant to a motion to extend or modify temporary custody,[81] the agency's administrative review must be conducted no later than six months after the court order, and every six months thereafter.[82]

The requirement that agencies must conduct semiannual review may sometimes be satisfied by court review hearings. For instance, the agency's administrative review may be replaced by a hearing held pursuant to the agency's motion to extend or modify a temporary custody order,[83] or it can be replaced by a court hearing to review the child's placement or custody arrangement.[84] If a court hearing is used instead of the agency's semiannual review, the court must determine all of the following:

(1) The continued necessity for and the appropriateness of the child's placement;

(2) The extent of compliance with the child's case plan;

(3) The extent of progress that has been made toward alleviating or mitigating the causes necessitating the child's placement in foster care;

(4) A projected date by which the child may be returned to his home or placed for adoption or legal guardianship; and

(5) The future status of the child.[85]

Administrative reviews which are conducted by the agency rather than the court are to be conducted by a review panel of at least three persons, including the child's caseworker and another person not responsible for the child's case management or service delivery.[86] The review must include a meeting by the

---

[75]RC 2151.38(B).
[76]42 USC 675.
[77]RC 2151.416, RC 2151.417.
[78]See RC 2151.412.
[79]RC 2151.416(A).
[80]RC 2151.414.
[81]RC 2151.415.
[82]RC 2151.416(A).
[83]See RC 2151.415.
[84]See RC 2151.416(A), RC 2151.417.
[85]RC 2151.415(H), RC 2151.417(I).
[86]RC 2151.416(B).

panel with the child's parents, guardian, custodian, guardian ad litem, and foster care provider, unless any of these persons cannot be located or declines to participate.[87] The review must result in a written summary which includes all of the following:

(1) A conclusion regarding the appropriateness of the child's foster care placement;

(2) The extent of the compliance with the case plan of all parties;

(3) The extent of progress that has been made toward alleviating the circumstances that required the agency to assume temporary custody of the child;

(4) An estimated date by which the child may be returned to his home or placed for adoption or legal custody;

(5) An updated case plan that includes any changes that the agency is proposing in the case plan;

(6) The agency's recommendation as to which agency or person should be given custodial rights over the child for the six-month period after the administrative review; and

(7) The names of all persons who participated in the administrative review.[88]

If it is determined at the administrative review that changes in the case plan are needed, the agency and the court must follow the same procedures that apply to any other changes in case plans.[89] Regardless of whether changes in the case plan are needed, the agency must submit its written summary of the administrative review to the court.[90] If the court determines that the custody or care arrangement is not in the child's best interest, it may terminate the agency's custody and place the child in the custody of another public or private organization, society, association, agency, or individual certified pursuant to RC 5103.02 and RC 5103.03.[91]

(2) Juvenile court dispositional review

In addition to the agency's semiannual administrative review, provision is made for the juvenile court to conduct its own custody review proceedings.

Any dispositional order made in abuse, neglect, or dependency proceedings[92] may be reviewed by the court at any time[93] and must be reviewed one year after the earlier of the date on which the complaint was filed or the date on which the child was first placed into shelter care.[94] Such orders must be reviewed by the

---

[87]RC 2151.416(C).
[88]RC 2151.416(D).
[89]See RC 2151.416(E), RC 2151.412(E)(2), (3), RC 2151.417(D).
[90]RC 2151.416(G).
[91]*Id.*
[92]See RC 2151.353, RC 2151.414, RC 2151.415.
[93]RC 2151.417(A).
[94]RC 2151.417(C). The dispositional hearing held pursuant to RC 2151.415 shall take the place of the first review hearing.

court annually thereafter until the child is adopted or returned to his parents, or until the court terminates the child's placement or custody arrangement.[95]

The court may appoint a referee or a citizens review board to conduct the review hearings, subject to the review and approval of the court.[96]

The court must give notice of the review hearings to every interested party and must give them an opportunity to testify and present other evidence at the hearing.[97] The court may even require a party to testify or present other evidence when necessary to a proper determination of the issues.[98] The scope of the court's review includes the following:

(1) The child's placement or custody arrangement;

(2) The child's case plan;

(3) The agency's actions in implementing the case plan;

(4) The action taken by the child's custodian;

(5) The need for a change in the child's custodian or caseworker; and

(6) The need for any specific action to be taken with respect to the child.[99]

After the review hearing, the court may require any party to take any reasonable action that the court determines is necessary and in the best interest of the child, or it may require that a party discontinue any action that is not in the child's best interest.[100] The court must also determine whether the conclusions of the agency's administrative review are supported by a preponderance of the evidence and must approve or modify the case plan based on that evidence.[101] If the child is in temporary custody, the court must determine the child's custody status.[102] If the child is in permanent custody, the court must determine what actions need to be taken to facilitate the child's adoption, including any necessary transfer of permanent custody.[103] Finally, the court must journalize the terms of the child's updated case plan[104] and must send a copy of its determination to all the parties.[105]

CROSS REFERENCES

Text Ch 9, 13.06(A), 13.07(B)(3)

Schroeder-Katz, Ohio Criminal Law, Crim R 32.3, Author's Text, Crim R 34, Author's Text, Crim R 45, Author's Text
Merrick-Rippner, Ohio Probate Law (4th ed), Text Ch 219, 223
Giannelli, Ohio Evidence Manual, Author's Comment 101.07(b), 101.08

---

[95]RC 2151.417(C). The court must schedule the first annual review hearing when it holds the original dispositional hearing, and all subsequent review hearings must be scheduled at the time of the prior review hearing.
[96]RC 2151.417(G).
[97]RC 2151.417(A), (E).
[98]RC 2151.417(E).
[99]RC 2151.417(A), (E).
[100]RC 2151.417(A).
[101]RC 2151.417(F)(1).
[102]RC 2151.417(F)(2).
[103]RC 2151.417(F)(3).
[104]RC 2151.417(F)(4).
[105]RC 2151.417(H).

15.02   Appeals

(A) Types of cases, standing

RC 2501.02 provides that the courts of appeals have jurisdiction over judgments or final orders of courts of record inferior to the court of appeals, "including the finding, order, or judgment of a juvenile court that a child is delinquent, neglected, abused, or dependent, for prejudicial error committed by such lower court."[106] Although juvenile traffic offender proceedings are not specifically included within the statute, the Ohio Supreme Court has held in *In re Hartman*[107] that the statute gives the court of appeals jurisdiction over such proceedings.[108] The court ruled that the classification of juvenile court judgments specifically enumerated following the term "including" in RC 2501.02(A) is not an exhaustive listing, but merely contains examples of appealable juvenile court judgments.

In *Hartman*, the Supreme Court interpreted the term "including" as a word of expansion rather than one of limitation. However, in a prior decision, *In re Becker*,[109] the court stated that absent a finding that a child is delinquent, neglected, or dependent, no appeal is available from the juvenile court.[110] In *Becker*, the court specifically held that a juvenile court order transferring a child to the common pleas court for criminal prosecution is not a final appealable order since no finding of delinquency is made in such a case.[111]

If one follows the rationale of *Hartman*, it appears that a final order adjudicating a child unruly is appealable even though the category of unruly cases is not specifically included in RC 2501.02. The rule[112] that authorizes the stay pending appeal of final orders in unruly cases implicitly recognizes the right of appeal in such cases.[113]

---

[106]RC 2153.17, which applies exclusively to the Cuyahoga County Juvenile Court, provides that the sections of the Revised Code regulating the manner and grounds of appeal from any judgment, order, or decree rendered by the common pleas court in the exercise of juvenile jurisdiction shall apply to the juvenile court.

[107]In re Hartman, 2 OS(3d) 154, 2 OBR 699, 443 NE(2d) 516 (1983).

[108]The meaning of "final orders" is discussed in Text 15.02(B), Final orders.

[109]In re Becker, 39 OS(2d) 84, 314 NE(2d) 158 (1974).

[110]*Becker* was decided prior to the 1975 amendment to RC 2501.02(A), which added abuse cases to the listing.

[111]Accord In re Morales, No. 33919 (8th Dist Ct App, Cuyahoga, 4-24-75). See also Text 9.05, Appeals.

[112]App R 7.

[113]However, there is some support for the argument that unruly cases are not subject to appeal. According to the dissenting opinions in *Hartman*, the *Becker* decision established the rule that the list of appealable orders contained in RC 2501.02 is complete and exclusive. Moreover, one of the dissenting justices argued that there were no constitutional problems inherent in limiting appellate jurisdiction to those juvenile court cases specifically listed in the statute. O Const Art IV, § 3(B)(2) provides that the "courts of appeals shall have jurisdiction *as may be provided by law* to review and affirm, modify, or reverse judgments or final orders of the courts of record inferior to the court of appeals" (emphasis in dissenting opinion of Justice Krupansky, 2 OS(3d) at 158). Although the juvenile court is a court of record pursuant to RC 2151.07, inferior to the court of appeals, the dissent proposed that "as provided by law," only the juvenile proceedings specifically enumerated in RC 2501.02(A) are appealable to the court of appeals. Justice Krupansky further argued that "the majority's analysis conveniently ignores the fact that only *one* category [i.e., juvenile traffic offender] of a mere five

It appears that any party,[114] with the exception of the prosecuting attorney in delinquency cases,[115] may appeal the final order of a juvenile court. Thus, an appeal may be filed by a mother or father who has been denied custody, even if someone else is the child's legal guardian.[116] However, a child's stepfather, who is not a party unless so designated by the court, does not have standing to appeal a permanent custody order.[117]

(B) Final orders

The jurisdiction of the court of appeals over final orders of lower courts includes the finding, order, or judgment of a juvenile court that a child is delinquent, neglected, abused, or dependent.[118] In interpreting this rule, the courts generally have held that a finding of delinquency must be accompanied by an order of disposition to be subject to appeal.[119] Juvenile Rule 34, which governs the procedural aspects of the dispositional hearing, must be followed scrupulously before an appeal may be pursued;[120] absent a disposition, the child has not been prejudiced.[121]

How final the disposition must be in order to permit appeal is an issue often raised. Clearly, an order which finds children neglected and commits them to the permanent custody of a welfare board is a final appealable order.[122]

However, it is not necessary that the dispositional order be final in all respects in order to permit appeal. The Ohio Supreme Court has rejected the argument that a finding of delinquency unaccompanied by a "final dispositional order" is not a final appealable order.[123] The imposition of a penalty pursuant to RC 2151.355 is a dispositional order and, as such, is a final appealable order.[124] In addition, even though a temporary custody order made after an adjudication

---

possible categories is missing from the 'partial' list in RC 2151.02(A)" (emphasis in original). However, a sixth category, that of the unruly child, is also excluded from the list.

[114]The term "party" is defined in Juv R 2(16).

[115]See Text 15.02(E), By the state.

[116]In re Rule, 1 App(2d) 57, 203 NE(2d) 501 (Crawford 1963); In re Neff, No. 1-78-9 (3d Dist Ct App, Allen, 6-14-78). But see In re Soboslay, Nos. 51872, 51873 (8th Dist Ct App, Cuyahoga, 11-13-86), in which the court stated in a footnote that it seriously doubted that the child's mother had standing to raise issues on the appeal of her son's delinquency adjudication, but decided to hear the case since the state had not challenged her standing.

[117]In re Neff, No. 1-78-9 (3d Dist Ct App, Allen, 6-14-78).

[118]RC 2501.02. See Text 15.02(A), Types of cases, standing.

[119]E.g., In re Sekulich, 65 OS(2d) 13, 417 NE(2d) 1014 (1981); In re Short, No. 1568 (4th Dist Ct App, Lawrence, 10-30-81).

[120]State v Wylie, No. 45952 (8th Dist Ct App, Cuyahoga, 8-4-83).

[121]*Id.*

[122]In re Masters, 165 OS 503, 137 NE(2d) 752 (1956).

[123]In re Sekulich, 65 OS(2d) 13, 417 NE(2d) 1014 (1981).

[124]*Id. Sekulich* involved an adjudication of delinquency and an order of disposition requiring the child to pay a fine and court costs, followed by an order that the matter be certified to another juvenile court. Because the court held that the juvenile court was not authorized to certify the matter to another court, a final dispositional order was made.

of neglect is subject to further review,[125] it is a final appealable order, as is a later modification or continuation of that order.[126]

Where a domestic relations court, as part of a final determination of a divorce action, finds it not in the best interest of the child to award custody to either parent and certifies the issue of custody to juvenile court pursuant to RC 3109.04, the certification order is appealable as part of the divorce judgment and constitutes a final appealable order.[127]

On the other hand, where the court order neither fully determines the action nor presents a judgment, it is not a final appealable order as defined by RC 2505.02. Thus, a juvenile court order which overrules the child's objections to the referee's report but defers the issue of restitution for a later time, without specifying the amount of restitution or the method of payment, is a continuing order and thus not a final appealable order.[128] Likewise, a finding of delinquency accompanied only by a commitment to the temporary custody of the Department of Youth Services for the purpose of diagnostic study and report is not a final order subject to appeal, as it is merely a procedural incident.[129] For similar reasons, a juvenile court order transferring a child to the common pleas court for criminal prosecution[130] and a predispositional temporary custody order made pursuant to Juvenile Rule 13 or Juvenile Rule 29(F)(2)(b)[131] are not final appealable orders. Similarly, a juvenile court order overruling a plea in bar in a delinquency proceeding is not a final appealable order and cannot be the vehicle which brings the issue of double jeopardy to the appellate court.[132]

In interpreting Civil Rule 53, the Ohio Supreme Court has held in *Normandy Place Associates v Beyer*[133] that the filing of an objection to a referee's report is not a prerequisite for appellate review of a finding or recommendation made by a referee and adopted by a trial court. This decision was based on the fact that Civil Rule 53(E)(2) makes objections permissible, not mandatory. Because Juvenile Rule 40(D)(2), which governs the filing of objections to referees' reports in juvenile court cases, contains language identical to that found in its civil rule counterpart, the same conclusion would be appropriate in juvenile court cases.

[125]See RC 2151.412, RC 2151.417.

[126]In re Motill, No. 43407 (8th Dist Ct App, Cuyahoga, 10-29-81); In re Rule, 1 App(2d) 57, 203 NE(2d) 501 (Crawford 1963); In re Siniard, No. C-78-063 (6th Dist Ct App, Lucas, 2-9-79); In re Patterson, 16 App(3d) 214, 16 OBR 229, 475 NE(2d) 160 (Madison 1984); In re Myers, No. 85-CA-10 (5th Dist Ct App, Delaware, 3-18-86).

[127]Robinson v Robinson, 19 App(3d) 323, 19 OBR 496 (Franklin 1984).

[128]In re Holmes, 70 App(2d) 277, 434 NE(2d) 747 (Hamilton 1980).

[129]In re Bolden, 37 App(2d) 7, 306 NE(2d) 166 (Allen 1973); In re Whittington, 17 App(2d) 164, 245 NE(2d) 364 (Fairfield 1969). A temporary commitment to the Department of Youth Services is no longer permitted by RC 2151.355.

[130]In re Becker, 39 OS(2d) 84, 314 NE(2d) 158 (1974); In re Morales, No. 33919 (8th Dist Ct App, Cuyahoga, 4-24-75). See also Text 9.05, Appeals.

[131]Morrison v Morrison, 45 App(2d) 299, 344 NE(2d) 144 (Summit 1973). This case involved an application to determine custody filed under RC 2151.23(A)(2).

[132]In re Hampton, 24 App(2d) 69, 263 NE(2d) 910 (Cuyahoga 1970).

[133]Normandy Place Associates v Beyer, 2 OS(3d) 102, 2 OBR 653, 443 NE(2d) 161 (1982). Accord In re Dissolution of Marriage of Sisinger, 5 App(3d) 28, 5 OBR 31, 448 NE(2d) 842 (Franklin 1982); Zacek v Zacek, 11 App(3d) 91, 11 OBR 143, 463 NE(2d) 391 (Franklin 1983).

If a referee fails to file with the trial court a report containing his findings and recommendations, the trial court's judgment is invalid as a matter of law for failure to comply with Civil Rule 53 and, consequently, is not a final order upon which an appeal may be predicated.[134] Moreover, if a report is filed which does not include a statement of the facts on which the referee's recommendation is based, the trial court cannot adopt the recommendation as a court order, since the report lacks the information necessary for an independent analysis of questions of law.[135]

(C) Time of filing notice

To initiate an appeal, a notice of appeal must be filed in the juvenile court within thirty days of the date of entry of the judgment or order subject to appeal.[136] The running of the time for filing a notice of appeal is suspended where a timely motion is filed in the juvenile court for judgment under Civil Rule 50(B) or for a new trial under Civil Rule 59.[137] However, neither a motion for rehearing nor a motion for reconsideration stays the time within which an appeal may be taken.[138]

(D) Stay of proceedings, appeal bond

Unless a juvenile court order is stayed pending the determination of an appeal, it remains in full force and effect. In order to secure a stay of the execution of a court order, the party seeking the stay must apply to the juvenile court which made the order.[139] If application to the juvenile court is not practicable, or if the juvenile court has by journal entry denied an application, a motion to stay may be made to the court of appeals or a judge thereof.[140] No order, judgment, or decree of a juvenile court that concerns a dependent, neglected, unruly, abused, or delinquent child may be stayed upon appeal unless suitable provision is made for the maintenance, care, and custody of such child pending the appeal.[141] Furthermore, appeals concerning such children shall have precedence over all other cases in the court to which the appeal is taken.[142]

In delinquency cases in which the state appeals the granting of a motion to suppress evidence, it is specifically provided that a child in detention or shelter care may be released pending the appeal.[143]

---

[134]Graham v Graham, No. 36318 (8th Dist Ct App, Cuyahoga, 7-7-77). Although based on Civ R 53, the rationale would also apply to children's cases under Juv R 40.

[135]Zacek v Zacek, 11 App(3d) 91, 11 OBR 143, 463 NE(2d) 391 (Franklin 1983); Nolte v Nolte, 60 App(2d) 227, 396 NE(2d) 807 (Cuyahoga 1978).

[136]App R 4(A).

[137]Id. The juvenile rules do not apply to procedures upon appeal. See Juv R 1(C)(1).

[138]In re Motill, No. 43407 (8th Dist Ct App, Cuyahoga, 10-29-81).

[139]App R 7(A).

[140]Id.

[141]App R 7(C). Although the rule does not include abuse or juvenile traffic offender proceedings, it appears that these cases would be subject to their provisions since a final order in such cases is appealable. See Text 15.02(A), Types of cases, standing.

[142]App R 7(C). See also RC 3109.04(E) and RC 3109.06, which provide that appeals taken from custody decisions must be given calendar priority and handled expeditiously by the court of appeals.

[143]Juv R 22(F).

Although bond is not required as a condition of granting a stay, the court of appeals may condition a stay upon the filing of a bond or other appropriate security in the trial court.[144] The procedure for determining the amount and approval of a supersedeas bond pending appeal is the same as that for applying for a stay. The original application is made in the juvenile court, but a motion for such relief may be filed in the appellate court if it shows that application to the juvenile court is not practicable or has been denied.[145] Since there is no constitutional provision guaranteeing the right to an appeal bond, a juvenile court does not err in refusing to grant bail pending appeal to a delinquent child who has been committed to an institution.[146]

The IJA-ABA Standards recommend that once an appeal is filed, the child should be released, with or without conditions, unless the court orders otherwise. The Standards suggest that only children needing secure incarceration should be detained pending appeal and then only if certain conditions exist.[147]

(E) By the state

As a general rule, the state may not appeal the final order of a juvenile court dismissing a delinquency complaint for failure to prove the allegations of the complaint beyond a reasonable doubt. An appeal by the state under such circumstances is barred by the constitutional protection against double jeopardy, since a court proceeding which may result in incarceration places a person, adult or juvenile, in jeopardy.[148]

However, certain decisions in delinquency cases may be appealed by the state. As with other appeals in juvenile court cases,[149] an appeal by the state following the granting of a motion to suppress takes precedence over all other appeals.[150] For example, the state may appeal the grant of a motion to dismiss a complaint and, by leave of the court to which the appeal is taken, any other decision of the juvenile court in a delinquency case except the final verdict.[151] The state may also appeal the juvenile court's granting of a motion to suppress evidence if, in addition to filing a notice of appeal, the prosecuting attorney certifies that (1) the appeal is not taken for the purpose of delay, and (2) the granting of the motion has rendered the state's case so weak that any reasonable possibility of proving the complaint's allegations has been destroyed.[152] In such cases, the notice of appeal and the certification by the prosecutor must be filed with the clerk of the juvenile court within seven days after the date of the entry of the order granting the motion to suppress.[153] Where the state has timely filed a notice of appeal, but has failed to make a proper certification as required by

---

[144]App R 7(B).

[145]App R 7(A).

[146]State v Fullmer, 76 App 335, 62 NE(2d) 268 (Montgomery 1945).

[147]*IJA-ABA Standards Relating to Appeals and Collateral Review* 41 (1980).

[148]In re Gilbert, 45 App(2d) 308, 345 NE(2d) 79 (Summit 1974). See Text 11.15, Double jeopardy.

[149]App R 7(C).

[150]Juv R 22(F).

[151]RC 2945.67(A).

[152]Juv R 22(F). See also RC 2945.67(A).

[153]Juv R 22(F); App R 4(B).

Juvenile Rule 22(F), a court of appeals may allow amendment of the timely filed notice of appeal and certification.[154]

In a criminal case, *State v Felty*,[155] it was held that where a trial court sustains a portion of the defendant's motion to suppress and the state fails to appeal that ruling pursuant to Criminal Rule 12(J) (the equivalent of Juvenile Rule 22(F)) and Appellate Rule 4(B), the state is precluded from contesting that portion of the suppression ruling in the defendant's appeal of his conviction based upon evidence which was not suppressed.

(F) Right to transcript and counsel

In *In re Gault*[156] the United States Supreme Court chose not to rule on the question of whether a child has a right to a transcript on appeal. However, in *Gault* the Court commented that the failure to prepare a transcript imposes a burden upon the reviewing process.

Ohio law provides that in all juvenile court hearings a complete record of all testimony and other oral proceedings must be made upon the request of a party or upon the court's own motion.[157] When a hearing is conducted on a motion for permanent custody pursuant to RC 2151.414, or on a complaint requesting a permanent custody order under RC 2151.353(A)(4), a record is mandatory.[158] No public use may be made of any juvenile court record or transcript except in the course of an appeal or as authorized by the court.[159]

When a transcript of proceedings is requested pursuant to Appellate Rule 9, it is the responsibility of the juvenile court to prepare it.[160] In actions instituted by the state to permanently terminate parental rights, the United States and Ohio Constitutions' guarantees of due process and equal protection require the juvenile court to provide indigent parents with a transcript at public expense for appeals as of right.[161] However, a party's right to a free transcript on appeal turns on that party's status as an indigent, and a motion for a free transcript may be denied where the juvenile court finds that the party has adequate financial means to obtain the transcript.[162] Moreover, since the right to a transcript applies only in a state-instituted permanent custody case, an indigent, noncustodial parent is not entitled to a transcript where temporary custody is given to the other parent.[163]

An indigent parent in a state-instituted action to permanently terminate parental rights is also entitled to appointed counsel on appeal, although the

---

[154]In re Hester, 1 App(3d) 24, 1 OBR 85, 437 NE(2d) 1218 (Franklin 1981).

[155]State v Felty, 2 App(3d) 62, 2 OBR 69, 440 NE(2d) 803 (Hamilton 1981).

[156]In re Gault, 387 US 1, 87 SCt 1428, 18 LEd(2d) 527 (1967).

[157]RC 2151.35(A); Juv R 37(A). State v Eppinger, No. 30798 (8th Dist Ct App, Cuyahoga, 12-9-71).

[158]RC 2151.35(A).

[159]Juv R 37(B).

[160]State ex rel Heller v Miller, 61 OS(2d) 6, 399 NE(2d) 66 (1980). See also In re Lippitt, No. 38421 (8th Dist Ct App, Cuyahoga, 3-9-78).

[161]State ex rel Heller v Miller, 61 OS(2d) 6, 399 NE(2d) 66 (1980).

[162]State ex rel Henry v Grossmann, 5 OS(3d) 235, 5 OBR 496, 450 NE(2d) 1156 (1983).

[163]In re Alexander, No. H-82-23 (6th Dist Ct App, Huron, 12-28-82).

responsibility for affording this right rests with the court of appeals rather than with the juvenile court.[164]

In any delinquency proceeding in which a prosecuting attorney appeals a juvenile court decision granting a motion to dismiss a complaint or a motion to suppress evidence,[165] the juvenile court must appoint counsel in accordance with RC Chapter 120 to represent any indigent person who is not represented by counsel and who has not waived the right to counsel.[166]

(G) Effect of appellate court order on further juvenile court proceedings

If the court of appeals finds that the juvenile court did not commit prejudicial error, it must affirm the ruling of the juvenile court.[167] Following an unsuccessful appeal from the sustaining of a motion to suppress, the state is not barred from continuing its prosecution as long as its Juvenile Rule 22(F) certification, that the suppressed evidence was of such a nature that the prosecution could not be successful without it, was made in good faith.[168] If the certification was not made in good faith, the time consumed in the appeal process, from the grant of the motion, must be charged to the state as undue delay in determining whether the child's constitutional right to a speedy trial has been violated.[169]

If the court of appeals determines that the juvenile court committed prejudicial error and the appellant is entitled to final judgment, the court must reverse the juvenile court order and either enter the appropriate judgment or remand the matter to the juvenile court with instructions to enter an appropriate order.[170] If prejudicial error is found, the court of appeals may also modify the judgment or final order of the juvenile court if appropriate.[171] In In re Ewing,[172] in which a juvenile court adjudged a child delinquent for aggravated burglary and grand theft, a court of appeals modified the judgment by finding the child delinquent for criminal trespass only and remanded the case for a new dispositional hearing. This modification was based on the failure of the evidence to establish a nexus between the child and the alleged stolen property. Similarly, a juvenile court order adjudging a child delinquent for theft and disorderly conduct was modified by a court of appeals to a judgment of delinquency based solely on the theft offense, because the disorderly conduct charge was not proven.[173]

---

[164]State ex rel Heller v Miller, 61 OS(2d) 6, 399 NE(2d) 66 (1980). This holding was not affected by the later decision of the United States Supreme Court in Lassiter v Department of Social Services, 452 US 18, 101 SCt 2153, 68 LEd(2d) 640 (1981), which held that the Due Process Clause of the Fourteenth Amendment does not require appointment of counsel in every parental status termination proceeding. This decision, which was based on narrow factual grounds, dealt with the right to appointed counsel for the juvenile court proceedings and not for purposes of appeal.

[165]See Text 15.02(E), By the state.

[166]RC 2945.67(B).

[167]App R 12(B).

[168]In re Hester, 3 App(3d) 458, 3 OBR 539, 446 NE(2d) 202 (Franklin 1982).

[169]Id.

[170]App R 12(B).

[171]Id.

[172]In re Ewing, No. 46317 (8th Dist Ct App, Cuyahoga, 9-1-83).

[173]In re Brown, No. 34450 (8th Dist Ct App, Cuyahoga, 1-8-76).

If the court of appeals finds (1) that the juvenile court order is against the manifest weight of the evidence, (2) that there is no other prejudicial error, and (3) that the appellee is not entitled to judgment, it must reverse the juvenile court order and either render the appropriate order or remand the case to the juvenile court for further proceedings.[174] Where the testimony presented to a juvenile court in a neglect proceeding indicated that the child was weak and sick but showed no sign of physical neglect, the court of appeals in *In re MacPherson*[175] reversed the neglect adjudication and entered judgment for the appellant-parents. On the other hand, in *In re Grubbs*,[176] where a juvenile court found a child not dependent, the court of appeals reversed the judgment, found the child dependent, and remanded the matter to the juvenile court for further proceedings based on the fact that the evidence established dependency.

When a court of appeals remands the matter of disposition to the juvenile court, there is no specified number of days within which the hearing is to be held. Thus, the juvenile court's delay in conducting the hearing is not a denial of the parents' due process rights, particularly where the parents have failed to object to the time lapse.[177]

In *In re Solarz*,[178] in which a court of appeals reversed for insufficient evidence a juvenile court's dependency adjudication, the court of appeals refused to enter final judgment for the parents. Because the parents had separated during the pendency of the appeal, the cause was remanded to the juvenile court for a determination of the child's custody pursuant to RC 2151.23(A)(2) (to determine the custody of a child not a ward of another court of this state) and (E) (to determine the case of any child certified to the court by any court of competent jurisdiction). The court of appeals further ordered that if the juvenile court found that neither parent was capable of assuming legal custody of the child, new dependency proceedings should be instituted. It has been held that an appellate court's reversal of a juvenile court's permanent custody order leaves a prior temporary custody order in effect.[179]

CROSS REFERENCES

Text 1.02, 9.05, 9.06, 11.15, 15.01(B)

Schroeder-Katz, Ohio Criminal Law, Crim R 46, Author's Text
Merrick-Rippner, Ohio Probate Law (4th ed), Text Ch 223

---

[174]App R 12(C).
[175]In re MacPherson, No. 34106 (8th Dist Ct App, Cuyahoga, 4-3-75).
[176]In re Grubbs, No. 43786 (8th Dist Ct App, Cuyahoga, 4-8-82).
[177]In re Wayne, Nos. 81AP-631, 81AP-632 (10th Dist Ct App, Franklin, 12-10-81).
[178]In re Solarz, Nos. 42275, 42359, 42360 (8th Dist Ct App, Cuyahoga, 11-6-80).
[179]In re Parker, No. 15-79-16 (3d Dist Ct App, Van Wert, 1-26-81); In re Neff, No. 1-78-9 (3d Dist Ct App, Allen, 6-14-78).

15.03 Habeas corpus

Because habeas corpus is an extraordinary remedy,[180] it may not be used either as a substitute for appeal or where an adequate remedy at law exists.[181] Accordingly, when a child has been committed to an institution by the juvenile court in proceedings regular in all particulars, a writ of habeas corpus may not issue from another court on the ground that the child is unlawfully restrained.[182] Similarly, a parent alleging that he failed to receive notice of a hearing concerning the prehearing shelter care of his child must request a rehearing in the juvenile court pursuant to Juvenile Rule 7(G) before seeking habeas corpus relief.[183] Despite the fact that Juvenile Rule 7(G) relates to predispositional detention and shelter care orders, it has been cited as an adequate remedy at law, justifying the denial of a writ of habeas corpus where children were found dependent and committed to the temporary custody of a county human services department.[184] It has also been held that habeas corpus is not an appropriate remedy to challenge a defective dependency complaint where a motion to dismiss pursuant to Juvenile Rule 22(D)(2) could have been filed.[185]

However, where an imprisoned father was not served with a summons for temporary and permanent custody hearings in a dependency case, the order of permanent custody and a subsequent order of adoption were determined to be void in a habeas corpus proceeding.[186] Without proper service of process on the parents, a final dispositional order is void, since the court has no jurisdiction to make such order.[187] It has also been held that habeas is the proper remedy to enforce the due process right of indigent parents to appointed counsel.[188]

The Ohio Supreme Court has ruled that where a juvenile court journal entry stated that "all writs heretofore issued herein have been duly served according to law and that all persons interested are now before the Court," such recital

---

[180]This section covers the use of habeas corpus as an alternative to appeal of juvenile court decisions. It does not include habeas corpus as an original action in juvenile court pursuant to RC 2151.23(A)(3).

[181]Luchene v Wagner, 12 OS(3d) 37, 12 OBR 32, 465 NE(2d) 395 (1984); In re Piazza, 7 OS(2d) 102, 218 NE(2d) 459 (1966). See also State ex rel Spitler v Seiber, 16 OS(2d) 117, 243 NE(2d) 65 (1968); In re Butt, 20 Misc(2d) 15, 20 OBR 399, 486 NE(2d) 255 (1985).

[182]Children's Home of Marion County v Fetter, 90 OS 110, 106 NE 761 (1914).

[183]Linger v Weiss, 57 OS(2d) 97, 386 NE(2d) 1354 (1979), cert denied 444 US 862, 100 SCt 128, 62 LEd(2d) 83 (1979).

[184]Pettry v McGinty, 60 OS(2d) 92, 397 NE(2d) 1190 (1979).

[185]In re Hunt, 46 OS(2d) 378, 348 NE(2d) 727 (1976).

[186]Reynolds v Ross County Children's Services Agency, No. 704 (4th Dist Ct App, Ross, 10-12-79). After service was made on the father and a further hearing was conducted, the court of appeals determined that the father was not a suitable custodian of his children and denied the writ. This judgment was affirmed by the Ohio Supreme Court in Reynolds v Ross County Children's Services Agency, 5 OS(3d) 27, 5 OBR 87, 448 NE(2d) 816 (1983).

[187]In re Frinzl, 152 OS 164, 87 NE(2d) 583 (1949); In re Corey, 145 OS 413, 61 NE(2d) 892 (1945); Lewis v Reed, 117 OS 152, 157 NE 897 (1927); Rarey v Schmidt, 115 OS 518, 154 NE 914 (1926).

[188]Sink v Auglaize County Welfare Dept, No. 2-80-15 (3d Dist Ct App, Auglaize, 4-15-80).

should be taken as true when attacked by a writ of habeas corpus.[189] However, in another habeas corpus proceeding, a father who was imprisoned at the time of a permanent custody hearing regarding his children was permitted to demonstrate that he had not been served with a summons, even though a fill-in-blank form journal entry indicated that all interested parties had been served.[190]

The United States Supreme Court has held that the federal habeas corpus statute[191] does not confer jurisdiction on federal courts to consider collateral challenges to a state court judgment which involuntarily terminates parental rights.[192]

CROSS REFERENCES

Text 7.05, 7.06, 15.01(E)

Merrick-Rippner, Ohio Probate Law (4th ed), Text Ch 223

15.04   Juvenile court records

(A) Confidentiality, use in other proceedings

Both legal and social history information is included in juvenile court records. Legal records, including an appearance docket, a journal, and a cash-book, must be maintained for all official cases.[193] The parents of any child affected, if living, or the nearest of kin, if the parents are deceased, may inspect these records, either in person or by counsel.[194]

Social history records contain the personal and family history of a child or any other party to a juvenile proceeding and may include the prior record of the person with the juvenile court or any other court.[195] Counsel may inspect the social history a reasonable time before any hearing at which it is utilized, although the court may deny inspection for good cause, limit its scope, or order that the contents of the history not be disclosed to specified persons.[196]

As with juvenile court proceedings involving children,[197] the concept of confidentiality applies to juvenile court records involving children. As a general rule, no public use may be made of any juvenile court record except in the course of

---

[189]Linger v Weiss, 57 OS(2d) 97, 386 NE(2d) 1354 (1979), cert denied 444 US 862, 100 SCt 128, 62 LEd(2d) 83 (1979). This ruling was included in a footnote to the decision and was based on the fact that the parent had a right to attack the decision by a direct proceeding under Juv R 7(G). Accord In re Bibb, 70 App(2d) 117, 435 NE(2d) 96 (Hamilton 1980).

[190]Reynolds v Ross County Children's Services Agency, No. 704 (4th Dist Ct App, Ross, 10-12-79).

[191]28 USC 2254.

[192]Lehman v Lycoming County Children's Services Agency, 458 US 502, 102 SCt 3231, 73 LEd(2d) 928 (1982).

[193]RC 2151.18. The statute requires that a separate docket be kept for traffic offenses.

[194]RC 2151.18. It is not clear whether this provision prevents the inspection of these records by anyone other than the parent or next of kin.

[195]Juv R 2(21).

[196]Juv R 32(C).

[197]RC 2151.35; Juv R 27.

an appeal or as authorized by court order.[198] The reports and records of the probation department are also considered confidential and may not be made public.[199]

The confidentiality issue often arises when there is an attempt to introduce juvenile court records into evidence in another proceeding. A juvenile court judgment does not impose any of the civil disabilities ordinarily imposed by conviction of a crime, nor does it operate to disqualify the child in any future civil service examination, appointment, or application. Neither the disposition of the child nor evidence given in the juvenile court is admissible against the child in any proceeding in another court, except for purposes of sentencing and the granting of probation.[200] Thus, a delinquency judgment is not admissible as evidence against a child in a civil action in another court, because the child has neither been charged with a crime nor convicted of a felony.[201] However, the improper admission of such records is not prejudicial error where there is other testimony in the record sufficient to sustain the findings of fact.[202]

The Attorney General is permitted to obtain all juvenile court records relative to a delinquent child in order to comply with RC 2743.51 et seq., the Victims' Reparation Act.[203]

The prohibition against the use of juvenile court records in other cases is not absolute when the subsequent case is a criminal proceeding. Although a state witness's prior juvenile record may not be used to impeach his general credibility,[204] an adjudication of delinquency is admissible under certain circumstances. More particularly, a defendant's right to confront witnesses and to present probative evidence for his defense includes the right to cross-examine a witness about his juvenile record in order to show bias. The specific bias in *Davis v Alaska*[205] was the witness's vulnerable status as a probationer and his possible concern that he might be a suspect in the crime under investigation. In *State v Cox*[206] the juvenile record of a state witness was admissible to demonstrate the

---

[198]Juv R 37(B). See In re Etchell, No. 52880 (8th Dist Ct App, Cuyahoga, 4-30-87), holding that it is not error for a juvenile court to deny a request for a transcript made prior to the filing of the notice of appeal.

[199]RC 2151.14. This provision applies only to the records of the juvenile court probation department and not to those of a state institution to which the child has been committed. State v Sherow, 101 App 169, 138 NE(2d) 444 (Gallia 1956). The records of the Department of Youth Services are confidential, accessible only to department employees, except upon consent of the department or order of the court. See RC 5139.05(D).

[200]RC 2151.358(H); Evid R 609(D).

[201]Beatty v Riegel, 115 App 448, 185 NE(2d) 555 (Montgomery 1961). See also Evid R 609(A).

[202]Allstate Insurance Co v Cook, 324 F(2d) 752 (6th Cir 1963).

[203]In re Flemming, No. 83-5591-09 (Ct of Claims 1983).

[204]State v White, 6 App(3d) 1, 6 OBR 23, 451 NE(2d) 533 (Cuyahoga 1982); State v Mann, No. 1074 (11th Dist Ct App, Ashtabula, 5-28-82); State v Williams, 16 App(3d) 484, 16 OBR 567, 477 NE(2d) 221 (Hamilton 1984), affirmed on other grounds by 21 OS(3d) 33, 21 OBR 320, 487 NE(2d) 560 (1986); State v Marks, No. 1252 (4th Dist Ct App, Athens, 2-17-87).

[205]Davis v Alaska, 415 US 308, 94 SCt 1105, 39 LEd(2d) 347 (1974).

[206]State v Cox, 42 OS(2d) 200, 327 NE(2d) 639 (1975).

deteriorating relationship between the witness and her mother, for whose murder the defendant was being tried.[207]

A federal court has held that where a juvenile confederate of a defendant is called as a prosecution witness, and testimony has already established that the juvenile is in the custody of the Department of Youth Services for his part in the burglary with which the defendant is charged, the jury has sufficient information to appraise the witness's motives and possible bias, and the defendant has no right under the Sixth Amendment to inquire into earlier findings of the juvenile delinquency.[208]

In two cases decided prior to the effective date of the Ohio Rules of Evidence,[209] the juvenile record of a criminal defendant was admitted against his claim of good character.[210] Evidence Rule 609(D), governing the use of evidence of convictions for impeachment, provides that evidence of juvenile adjudications is not admissible except as provided by statute. Thus, it appears that such rebuttal evidence is no longer admissible if it is used merely for impeachment. Moreover, if the defendant does not put his character in issue, but merely testifies in his own behalf, it is prejudicial error to permit cross-examination of him as to the disposition of a juvenile adjudication.[211]

A court of appeals has held that a mere reference to a criminal defendant's juvenile record is not prejudicial if, pursuant to Criminal Rule 52(A), it does not affect substantial rights.[212]

Another exception to the general prohibition against the introduction of a juvenile record in other proceedings arises when the evidence in the record is being used in favor of and not against the minor. Thus, in a civil suit to determine the liability of a defendant insurance company for a judgment rendered against the insured child for injuries in an automobile accident, testimony received in the juvenile court traffic proceeding was admissible.[213]

Because the statutory prohibition against using juvenile records applies only to "any other case or proceeding in any other court,"[214] confessions used in a juvenile court hearing, after which the child was transferred to the general division for criminal prosecution, may be introduced in the criminal court proceedings, since those proceedings are part of the same case.[215]

Although not covered by RC 2151.358(H), it may be permissible in a juvenile court adjudicatory hearing to cross-examine the alleged delinquent child concerning his prior juvenile adjudications for the purpose of impeachment. In two cases decided prior to the adoption of the Ohio Rules of Evidence, the

---

[207]See also State v McGuire, No. 11-192 (11th Dist Ct App, Lake, 12-18-87).

[208]Mann v Gray, 622 FSupp 1225 (ND Ohio 1985), appeal dismissed by 815 F(2d) 78 (1987).

[209]July 1, 1980.

[210]State v Marinski, 139 OS 559, 41 NE(2d) 387 (1942); State v Hale, 21 App(2d) 207, 256 NE(2d) 239 (Franklin 1969).

[211]Malone v State, 130 OS 443 (1936); Workman v Cardwell, 338 FSupp 893 (ND Ohio 1972), cert denied 412 US 932, 93 SCt 2748, 2762, 37 LEd(2d) 161 (1973).

[212]State v Brewster, 1 OO(3d) 372 (App, Franklin 1976).

[213]Bingham v Hartman, 88 Abs 126, 181 NE(2d) 721 (App, Columbiana 1961).

[214]RC 2151.358(H).

[215]State v Lowder, 79 App 237, 72 NE(2d) 785 (Stark 1946).

Cuyahoga County Court of Appeals held that a prior adjudication is admissible for that purpose since the applicability of the statute is limited to all courts exclusive of juvenile courts.[216] However, since juvenile adjudications are not admissible for general impeachment purposes,[217] it appears that a child may not be impeached through the use of a prior juvenile record unless such use is to rebut his claim of good character.[218]

Evidence that a child had been previously adjudicated delinquent for petit theft is admissible for the purposes of disposition to show prior convictions so that the degree of the current theft offense may be enhanced to grand theft.[219]

(B) Expungement and sealing

One of the primary purposes of RC Chapter 2151 is to remove "the consequences of criminal behavior and the taint of criminality from children committing delinquent acts."[220] To this end, Ohio law has provided a means for expunging or sealing the juvenile court and arrest records of children who are adjudged delinquent or unruly, as well as the records of those who are found not delinquent or unruly or who have such complaints dismissed.[221] As a result, once a record is expunged or sealed, the proceedings in the case are treated as if they never occurred. The expungement/sealing process is not available to juvenile traffic offenders[222] nor, apparently, to children whose delinquency or unruly complaint is withdrawn prior to adjudication.[223] Moreover, since the juvenile court's expungement authority arises only after a child comes within its jurisdiction, the statute does not provide for the expungement of arrest records concerning a child who is arrested but has no complaint filed against him.[224]

---

[216]In re Wyrock, Nos. 41827, 41828, 41904 (8th Dist Ct App, Cuyahoga, 10-23-80); State v Eppinger, No. 30798 (8th Dist Ct App, Cuyahoga, 12-9-71).

[217]Evid R 609(D).

[218]See State v Marinski, 139 OS 559, 41 NE(2d) 387 (1942); State v Hale, 21 App(2d) 207, 256 NE(2d) 239 (Franklin 1969).

[219]In re Hayes, 29 App(3d) 162, 29 OBR 191, 504 NE(2d) 491 (Franklin 1986). In dicta, the court indicated that evidence of the child's prior record is not otherwise admissible in juvenile court hearings under RC 2151.358(H).

[220]RC 2151.01(B).

[221]RC 2151.358(C), (F). In considering the expungement process for adults, governed by RC 2953.31, an appellate court held that a trial court does not have discretion to grant judicial (i.e., extrastatutory) expungement relief to adults convicted of an offense. State v Weber, 19 App(3d) 214, 19 OBR 359, 484 NE(2d) 207 (Hamilton 1984).

[222]RC 2151.358(C). See Gebell v Dollison, 57 App(2d) 198, 386 NE(2d) 845 (Clermont 1978), in which it was held that the statute does not prohibit the use of records pertaining to traffic violations, kept pursuant to RC 4507.40, in a driver's license revocation hearing conducted after the accused has attained majority.

[223]According to an opinion of the Ohio Legislative Service Commission (February 24, 1981), the term "dismissed" as used in RC 2151.358(F) has a very limited meaning. The opinion states, in part:

> If a juvenile is arrested, charged with being a delinquent or unruly child, and the court drops the case, or otherwise does not bring the case to a conclusion, without formally dismissing the charges against the juvenile . . . the juvenile cannot have his arrest record expunged under division (F) of section 2151.358.

Such a case could not be expunged under section (C) either, since there has been no adjudication.

[224]An opinion of the Ohio Legislative Service Commission (February 24, 1981) stated that "if a juvenile is arrested and then released without being formally charged in a case,

Once the court issues an order pursuant to RC 2151.358, the juvenile court records are either expunged or sealed. Expungement is available only if the juvenile court proceedings do not result in an adjudication of delinquency or unruliness.[225] Where the child has been adjudicated delinquent or unruly, his records may be sealed but may not be destroyed.[226] Sealed records are removed from the main file of similar records and are secured in a separate file that contains only sealed records and is accessible only to the juvenile court.[227]

The juvenile court's authority to seal a record arises two years after the termination of any court order or two years after the unconditional discharge of a person from the Department of Youth Services or other institution or facility.[228] Once the person has been discharged, the department, institution, or facility must notify the court, and the court must note the date of discharge on a separate record of such discharges.[229] After the prescribed two-year period, the court must order the record of an adjudicated unruly child sealed.[230] If the person was adjudicated a delinquent child, the court must either order the record sealed or send the person notice of his right to have the record sealed. If notice is sent, it must be sent by certified mail to the person's last known address within ninety days after the expiration of the two-year period. The notice must state that the person may apply to the court for an order to seal his record, explain what sealing a record means, and explain the possible consequences of not having the record sealed.[231]

In those cases in which a child timely files an application for an order to seal his record, the court must hold a hearing within sixty days after the application is received. Notice of the hearing must be given to the prosecuting attorney and to any other public office or agency known to have a record of the prior adjudication. If the court finds that the rehabilitation of the person has been attained to a satisfactory degree, it may order the record sealed.[232]

The two-year period does not apply to those cases in which the child has been adjudicated not delinquent or unruly or has had the charges against him dismissed.[233] In such cases the child may at any time apply to the court for expungement of his record. The court must notify the prosecuting attorney of

---

the juvenile cannot have his arrest record expunged under division (F) of section 2151.358."

[225]RC 2151.358(F).

[226]RC 2151.358(C) to (E).

[227]RC 2151.358(A).

[228]RC 2151.358(C).

[229]RC 2151.358(B).

[230]RC 2151.358(C)(1). Because of this mandatory provision, the purpose of RC 2151.358(D) is unclear. Section (D) indicates that after the two-year period an adjudicated unruly child may apply to the court for an order to seal his record and the court must conduct a hearing on the application within sixty days.

[231]RC 2151.358(C)(2).

[232]RC 2151.358(D). In making this finding, the court may rely on the type of information gathered by a probation officer and included in a social history pursuant to Juv R 32.

[233]RC 2151.358(F). This section states that "[a]ny person who has been *arrested* and charged . . . and who is adjudicated *not guilty* of the charges" may apply for expungement (emphasis added). Many delinquent and unruly children are never arrested, and the term "not guilty" is not used in children's cases.

any hearing on the application. In delinquency cases, the court may initiate the expungement proceedings on its own motion. The court must initiate such proceedings in unruly cases if an application for expungement is not filed. If the court determines that the charges were dismissed or the person was adjudicated "not guilty," the court must order the records expunged.[234]

Both expungement and sealing have several beneficial effects for the child. Once the record is expunged or sealed, the proceedings in the case are deemed never to have occurred.[235] With regard to sealed records, all index references to the case and to the person must be deleted, and the person and the court may properly reply to inquiries that no record exists. Sealed records may be inspected with court permission, but only upon application by the person who is the subject of the sealed records and only by the persons that are named in the application.[236] With regard to expunged records, in addition to deleting all index references, the court must also destroy or delete all records of the case, including any pictures and fingerprints taken of the person at arrest. After the expungement order has been issued, the court must, and the person may properly, reply that no record of the case exists.[237]

The expungement/sealing process affects the record-keeping of other governmental bodies in addition to the juvenile court. When a juvenile court record is expunged, the court must order the appropriate persons and governmental agencies to destroy, erase, or delete all index references to the case and all references to the arrest that are maintained by the state or any political subdivision. However, an arrest record may be retained if it is maintained only for purposes of compiling statistical data and does not contain any reference to the person. In addition, if the applicant for an expungement order does not waive in writing his right to bring a civil action based on the arrest to which the expungement order relates, the court must order that a copy of all records of the case, except fingerprints held by the court or a law enforcement agency, be delivered to it. These records are to be sealed with other sealed records and are to be destroyed (1) after the statute of limitations expires for any civil action based on the arrest; (2) after any pending litigation based on the arrest is terminated; or (3) after the applicant files a written waiver of his right to bring the civil action.[238]

The court must send notice of the order to expunge or seal to any public office or agency that it has reason to believe may have a record of the expunged or sealed record.[239] Whereas the disposition of an expunged record depends on whether the waiver of civil action is signed, a sealed record must be destroyed

---

[234]RC 2151.358(F).

[235]RC 2151.358(E), (F).

[236]RC 2151.358(E). Despite this provision, section (H) of the statute provides that "the judgment rendered and the disposition of the child may be considered by any court ... as to the matter of sentence or to the granting of probation." This provision was part of the juvenile law prior to the enactment of the original expungement statute in 1969. When the expungement statute was enacted and then amended, this section was inexplicably included as part of it. Presumably, a record that has been sealed may not be used by any court for any purpose. See RC 2151.358(I).

[237]RC 2151.358(F).

[238]Id.

[239]RC 2151.358(G).

by all persons and governmental bodies except the juvenile court.[240] RC 2151.358(G) provides that an order to seal or expunge applies to all public offices and agencies, regardless of whether they receive notice of the expungement/sealing hearing or a copy of the order to expunge or seal. Despite this language, the statute further indicates that the person whose record has been expunged or sealed may make a written request of the office or agency to have the record destroyed. Upon receipt of the request and a copy of the order, the office or agency must destroy its record of the adjudication or arrest, with the exception of certain statistical data.

In any application for employment, license, or other right or privilege, any appearance as a witness, or any other inquiry, a person may not be questioned with respect to any arrest for which the records were expunged.[241] If such an inquiry is made, the person may respond as if the expunged arrest had not occurred, and the person may not be subjected to any adverse action because of the arrest or the response.[242]

RC 2151.358(J) also establishes the offense of divulging confidential information, a misdemeanor of the fourth degree, for certain governmental officers who release information concerning expunged or sealed records.[243]

CROSS REFERENCES

Text 7.08, 11.11, 11.12, 11.14, 13.04, 13.05

Schroeder-Katz, Ohio Criminal Law, Crim R 55, Author's Text
Merrick-Rippner, Ohio Probate Law (4th ed), Text Ch 223
Giannelli, Ohio Evidence Manual, Author's Comment 609.08, 609.09

15.05   Interstate agreements

(A) Interstate Compact on Juveniles

Ohio law authorizes the governor to enter into compacts with other states with respect to (1) the return of runaways to their home state; (2) the return of juvenile absconders and escapees to the state from which they have absconded or escaped; (3) the out-of-state placement and supervision of delinquent juveniles;[244] and (4) additional cooperative measures for the care and protection of juveniles and the public.[245]

Upon the receipt of a requisition demanding the return of a runaway juvenile, the court or executive authority to whom the requisition is addressed must issue an order to any peace officer or other appropriate person directing that the juvenile be taken into custody and detained. Before the juvenile may be

---

[240]RC 2151.358(A).

[241]RC 2151.358(I). It is not clear why this prohibition does not also apply to sealed records.

[242]RC 2151.358(I). There have been instances in which children whose records were expunged and who enlisted in the armed services were subject to court martial proceedings for not revealing the expunged record. The armed services' argument was that Ohio law did not bind them.

[243]Pursuant to RC 2151.23(A)(5), the juvenile court has exclusive original jurisdiction over such criminal prosecutions.

[244]RC 2151.39, RC 2151.56, RC 5103.20.

[245]RC 2151.56.

returned, he must be taken before a judge of a court in the state in which he is found. If the judge finds that the requisition is in order, the juvenile must be delivered to the officer appointed by the demanding court to receive him.[246]

A juvenile who has run away from another state may be taken into custody without a requisition and brought before the appropriate court. After a hearing, that court must determine whether sufficient cause exists to hold the juvenile, for his own protection and welfare, for up to ninety days until such other state issues a proper requisition. Any criminal or delinquency proceedings pending or anticipated in the state in which the child is found take precedence over the requisition.[247]

Provision is also made for the return of delinquent juveniles who have absconded from probation or parole supervision or who have escaped from institutional custody. The procedures involved in such cases are the same as those for runaways.[248]

Any runaway or delinquent juvenile who has absconded or escaped may consent to his immediate return. The consent must be in writing and signed by the juvenile and his counsel or guardian ad litem, if any. Before the consent may be executed or subscribed, the court must advise the juvenile of his rights under the compact.[249]

Under certain circumstances, a delinquent juvenile placed on probation or parole may be permitted to reside in another state. If the sending state thereafter determines it to be necessary, the juvenile may thereafter be returned to the sending state.[250]

The states that take part in the interstate compact subscribe to the policy that, to the extent possible, no juvenile shall be placed or detained in any prison, jail, or lockup, and shall not be detained or transported in association with criminal, vicious, or dissolute persons.[251]

For the purposes of RC 2151.56, a person over the age of twenty-one may qualify as a "delinquent juvenile," provided that (1) the person has been adjudged delinquent by the sending state, and (2) at the time the provisions of RC 2151.56 are invoked, the person is subject to the jurisdiction of the court in the sending state that made the adjudication or is subject to the jurisdiction or supervision of an agency or institution pursuant to an order of such court.[252]

The payment of any transportation costs involved in the return of runaways, absconders, or escapees is the responsibility of the state to which they are returned.[253] The cost of transporting probationers or parolees to or from the

---

[246]RC 2151.56, Article IV. The term "juvenile" means any person who is a minor under the law of the state of residence of the parent, guardian, person, or agency entitled to the legal custody of the minor.
[247]RC 2151.56, Article V.
[248]*Id.*
[249]RC 2151.56, Article VI.
[250]RC 2151.56, Article VII.
[251]RC 2151.56, Article IX.
[252]OAG 88-50.
[253]RC 2151.56, Articles IV, V.

receiving state is the sending state's responsibility.[254] Any participating state or subdivision thereof may assert any right against any person, agency, or other entity in regard to costs for which that state or subdivision is responsible.[255]

(B) Extradition

The remedies and procedures provided by the interstate compact are in addition to and not in place of other rights, remedies, and procedures.[256] Extradition appears to be another remedy available for the return of alleged or adjudicated delinquents who have escaped or absconded to another state.[257] The attorney general has ruled that when an alleged delinquent flees to another state prior to a final determination of his case, he may be returned to Ohio pursuant to the Uniform Extradition Act.[258] Upon the child's return, he is to be taken before the juvenile court. If the child is taken before any other court, that court must transfer the case to the juvenile court and discontinue all further proceedings with respect to the child.[259]

On the other hand, the Uniform Extradition Act does not apply if the juvenile court has exercised jurisdiction to the extent of ordering a final disposition committing the child to a state institution.[260] Thus, if the child escapes from that institution and flees to another state, the Interstate Compact on Juveniles would be the appropriate remedy to secure his return.[261]

It has been held that RC Chapter 2151 does not confer authority or jurisdiction on a juvenile court to apprehend a child and return him to another state without a hearing as to whether the return is in his best interests.[262]

The expense of transporting children by police or other officers acting upon a juvenile court order is to be paid from the county treasury.[263] In addition, the expense of returning fugitives who have violated RC Chapter 2151 is to be paid from the county general expense fund.[264] This applies to children as well as adults.[265]

CROSS REFERENCES

Text Ch 3

Merrick-Rippner, Ohio Probate Law (4th ed), Text Ch 223
Giannelli, Ohio Evidence Manual, Author's Comment 101.07(a)

---

[254]RC 2151.56, Article VII.

[255]RC 2151.56, Article VIII.

[256]RC 2151.56, Article II.

[257]See RC 2963.20. Extradition might be used in cases where the state to which the child has fled is not a party to the Interstate Compact on Juveniles but is a party to the Uniform Extradition Act. See Extradition of juveniles, 73 ALR3d 700 (1976) (discussion of laws of other states).

[258]RC 2963.01 et seq. See also 1945 OAG 509. This opinion was issued prior to Ohio's adoption of the Interstate Compact on Juveniles on June 18, 1957.

[259]1945 OAG 509.

[260]1946 OAG 770.

[261]RC 2151.56, Article V.

[262]In re Messner, 19 App(2d) 33, 249 NE(2d) 532 (Huron 1969).

[263]RC 2151.54.

[264]RC 2151.45.

[265]1945 OAG 509.

OHIO REVISED CODE
(Selected Provisions)

Chapter
2151   Juvenile Court

Chapter 2151

JUVENILE COURT

Publisher's Note: References to OJur, AmJur, and ALR were compiled from the *Ohio Code Research Guide* (Lawyer's Co-operative Publishing Company).

Publisher's Note: Until 1968, when the Modern Courts Amendment to the Ohio Constitution was adopted, Ohio court procedure was governed entirely by statute and caselaw. The Modern Courts Amendment required the Supreme Court of Ohio, subject to the approval of the General Assembly, to "prescribe rules governing practice and procedure in all courts of the state." Rules of practice and procedure are the Civil, Criminal, Appellate, and Juvenile Rules, Rules of the Court of Claims, and the Ohio Rules of Evidence. Pursuant to Ohio Constitution Article IV, Section 5(B), such rules "shall not abridge, enlarge, or modify any substantive right," and "all laws in conflict with such rules shall be of no further force or effect." Provisions of Chapter 2151 should be read with this in mind.

CROSS REFERENCES

Juvenile court jurisdiction over juvenile capital facilities, 307.021
Curfew for persons under eighteen, 307.71
Humane societies, protection of children, 1717.14
Cuyahoga county juvenile court, jurisdiction and powers, 2153.16
Judges of the division of domestic relations, certain counties; juvenile court powers, 2301.03
Courts of record, premature judgment deemed clerical error, 2701.18
Deception to obtain matter harmful to juveniles, 2907.33
Trial, magistrate courts, applicability to juveniles, 2938.02
When consent not required for adoption, 3107.07
Release of identifying information, consent of biological parents or siblings, procedures, withdrawal of release, 3107.40
Minor employees, conditions on employment, 4109.08
Guardianship of mentally retarded minors, 5123.93
Department of youth services, powers and duties, 5139.04
Youth commission, powers with respect to children, 5139.05
Disposition of child committed to department of youth services, 5139.06
Transfer of child to foster care facility, 5139.39
Judicial power vested in courts O Const Art IV §1
Common pleas courts; probate and other divisions; jurisdiction, O Const Art IV §4
Rules of criminal procedure; scope, applicability, construction, exceptions, Crim R 1
Rules of juvenile procedure, Juv R 1 to 48

LEGAL ENCYCLOPEDIAS AND ALR

Inclusion or exclusion of the day of birth in computing one's age. 5 ALR2d 1143
Marriage as affecting jurisdiction of juvenile court over delinquent or dependent. 14 ALR2d 336
Homicide by juvenile as within jurisdiction of a juvenile court. 48 ALR2d 663

CONSTRUCTION; DEFINITIONS

2151.01   Construction; purpose

The sections in Chapter 2151. of the Revised Code, with the exception of those sections providing for the criminal prosecution of adults, shall be liberally interpreted and construed so as to effectuate the following purposes:

(A) To provide for the care, protection, and mental and physical development of children subject to Chapter 2151. of the Revised Code;

(B) To protect the public interest in removing the consequences of criminal behavior and the taint of criminality from children committing delinquent acts and to substitute therefor a program of supervision, care, and rehabilitation;

(C) To achieve the foregoing purposes, whenever possible, in a family environment, separating the child from its parents only when necessary for his welfare or in the interests of public safety;

(D) To provide judicial procedures through which Chapter 2151. of the Revised Code is executed and enforced, and in which the parties are assured of a fair hearing, and their constitutional and other legal rights are recognized and enforced.

HISTORY: 1969 H 320, eff. 11-19-69

Note: Former 2151.01 repealed by 1969 H 320, eff. 11-19-69; 1953 H 1; GC 1639-1; see now 2151.011 for provisions analogous to former 2151.01.

PRACTICE AND STUDY AIDS

Kurtz & Giannelli, Ohio Juvenile Law, Text 3.06(D), 3.07(B), 7.02, 13.01, 13.06(A), 15.04(B)

CROSS REFERENCES

Judges of the court of domestic relations, juvenile court responsibility, 2301.03
Applicability and construction, Juv R 1
Waiver of rights, Juv R 3
Intake, Juv R 9

LEGAL ENCYCLOPEDIAS AND ALR

OJur 3d: 22, Courts and Judges § 72, 74, 345; 26, Criminal Law § 668; 46, Family Law § 220, 347, 357, 359, 365, 374, 379, 380, 394, 416, 418 to 421, 537, 558

2151.011   Definitions

(A) As used in the Revised Code:

(1) "Juvenile court" means the division of the court of common pleas or a juvenile court separately and independently created having jurisdiction under this chapter.

(2) "Juvenile judge" means a judge of a court having jurisdiction under this chapter.

(B) As used in this chapter:

(1) "Child" means a person who is under the age of eighteen years, except that any person who violates a federal or state law or municipal ordinance prior to attaining eighteen years of age shall be deemed a "child" irrespective of his age at the time the complaint is filed or hearing had on the complaint and except that a person

whose case is transferred for criminal prosecution pursuant to section 2151.26 of the Revised Code and is subsequently convicted in that case shall after the transfer be deemed not to be a child in any case in which he is alleged to have committed an act that if committed by an adult would constitute murder or aggravated murder, an aggravated felony of the first or second degree, or a felony of the first or second degree.

(2) "Adult" means an individual eighteen years of age or older.

(3) "Detention" means the temporary care of children in restricted facilities pending court adjudication or disposition.

(4) "Shelter" means the temporary care of children in physically unrestricted facilities pending court adjudication or disposition.

(5) "Foster home" means a family home in which any child is received apart from his parents for care, supervision, or training.

(6) "Certified foster home" means a foster home operated by persons holding a permit in force, issued under sections 5103.03 to 5103.05 of the Revised Code.

(7) "Approved foster care" means facilities approved by the department of youth services under section 5139.37 of the Revised Code.

(8) "Organization" means any institution, public, semipublic, or private, and any private association, society, or agency located or operating in the state, incorporated or unincorporated, having among its functions the furnishing of protective services or care for children, or the placement of children in foster homes or elsewhere.

(9) "Private child placing agency" means any association, as defined in section 5103.02 of the Revised Code, that is certified pursuant to sections 5103.03 to 5103.05 of the Revised Code to accept temporary, permanent, or legal custody of children and place the children for either foster care or adoption.

(10) "Legal custody" means a legal status which vests in the custodian the right to have physical care and control of the child and to determine where and with whom he shall live, and the right and duty to protect, train, and discipline him and to provide him with food, shelter, education, and medical care, all subject to any residual parental rights, privileges, and responsibilities. An individual granted legal custody shall exercise the rights and responsibilities personally unless otherwise authorized by any section of the Revised Code or by the court.

(11) "Residual parental rights, privileges, and responsibilities" means those rights, privileges, and responsibilities remaining with the natural parent after the transfer of legal custody of the child, including but not necessarily limited to the privilege of reasonable visitation, consent to

adoption, the privilege to determine the child's religious affiliation, and the responsibility for support.

(12) "Permanent custody" means a legal status which vests in a public children services agency or a private child placing agency, all parental rights, duties, and obligations, including the right to consent to adoption, and divests the natural parents or adoptive parents of any and all parental rights, privileges, and obligations, including all residual rights and obligations.

(13) "Temporary custody" means legal custody of a child who is removed from his home, which custody may be terminated at any time at the discretion of the court or, if the legal custody is granted in an agreement for temporary custody, by the person who executed the agreement.

(14) "Commit" means to vest custody as ordered by the court.

(15) "Probation" means a legal status created by court order following an adjudication that a child is delinquent, a juvenile traffic offender, or unruly, whereby the child is permitted to remain in the parent's, guardian's, or custodian's home subject to supervision, or under the supervision of any agency designated by the court and returned to the court for violation of probation at any time during the period of probation.

(16) "Protective supervision" means an order of disposition pursuant to which the court permits an abused, neglected, dependent, unruly, or delinquent child or a juvenile traffic offender to remain in the custody of his parents, guardian, or custodian and stay in his home, subject to any conditions and limitations upon the child, his parents, guardian, or custodian, or any other person that the court prescribes, including supervision as directed by the court for the protection of the child.

(17) "Adequate parental care" means the provision by a child's parent or parents, guardian, or custodian of adequate food, clothing, and shelter to ensure the child's health and physical safety and the provision by a child's parent or parents of specialized services warranted by the child's physical or mental needs.

(18) "Agreement for temporary custody" means a voluntary agreement that is authorized by section 5103.15 of the Revised Code and that transfers the temporary custody of a child to a public children services agency or a private child placing agency.

(19) "Guardian" means a person, association, or corporation that is granted authority by a probate court pursuant to Chapter 2111. of the Revised Code to exercise parental rights over a child to the extent provided in the court's order and subject to the residual parental rights of the child's parents.

(20) "Mental illness" and "mentally ill person subject to hospitalization by court order" have the same meanings as in section 5122.01 of the Revised Code.

(21) "Mentally retarded person" and "mentally retarded person subject to institutionalization by court order" have the same meanings as in section 5123.01 of the Revised Code.

(22) "Permanent surrender" means the act of the parents or, if a child has only one parent, of the parent of a child, by a voluntary agreement authorized by section 5103.15 of the Revised Code, to transfer the permanent custody of the child to a public children services agency or a private child placing agency.

(23) "Placement for foster care" means the arrangement by a public children services agency or a private child placing agency for the out-of-home care of a child of whom the agency has temporary custody or permanent custody.

(24) "Placement for adoption" means the arrangement by a public children services agency or a private child placing agency with a person for the care and adoption by that person of a child of whom the agency has permanent custody.

(25) "Long-term foster care" means an order of a juvenile court pursuant to which both of the following apply:

(a) Legal custody of a child is given to a public children services agency or a private child placing agency without the termination of parental rights;

(b) The agency is permitted to make an appropriate placement of the child and to enter into a written long-term foster care agreement with a foster care provider or with any other person or agency with whom the child is placed.

(26) "Public children services agency" means a children services board or a county department of human services that has assumed the administration of the children services function prescribed by Chapter 5153. of the Revised Code.

(27) "Custodian" means a person who has legal custody of a child or a public children services agency or private child placing agency that has permanent, temporary, or legal custody of a child.

(28) "Counseling" includes general counseling and therapeutic counseling.

(29) "General counseling" means those services performed by a county children services board, county department of human services exercising the children services function, or shelter for victims of domestic violence to assist a child, his parents, and his siblings in alleviating identified problems that may cause or have caused the child to be an abused, neglected, or dependent child.

(30) "Therapeutic counseling" means psychiatric or psychological services performed by a licensed psychiatrist or psychologist or a licensed or certified social worker to correct or alleviate any mental or emotional handicap or disorder of a person.

(31) "Shelter for victims of domestic violence" has the same meaning as in section 3113.33 of the Revised Code.

(32) "Psychiatrist" has the same meaning as in section 5122.01 of the Revised Code.

(33) "Psychologist" has the same meaning as in section 4732.01 of the Revised Code.

(34) "Social worker" means any person who is licensed or certified under Chapter 4757. of the Revised Code to engage in social work.

(35) "Social work" has the same meaning as in section 4757.01 of the Revised Code.

HISTORY: 1988 H 403, eff. 1-1-89

Note: Former 2151.011 repealed by 1988 H 403, eff. 1-1-89; 1988 S 89, H 399; 1986 H 428; 1983 S 210; 1981 H 440; 1980 H 695; 1969 H 320.

Note: 2151.011 contains provisions analogous to former 2151.01 repealed by 1969 H 320, eff. 11-19-69.

Note: 1988 H 403, § 4, eff. 12-15-88, reads: This act is hereby declared to be an emergency measure necessary for the immediate preservation of the public peace, health, and safety. The reason for this necessity is that its enactment into law prior to January 1, 1989, is necessary to make new sections 2151.011 and 2151.412 of the Revised Code effective on that date and thereby prevent confusion in the preparation of case plans for abused, neglected, and dependent children in temporary custody and ensure the provision of necessary services to those children and their families. Therefore, this act shall go into immediate effect.

PRACTICE AND STUDY AIDS

Baldwin's Ohio Legislative Service, 1988 Laws of Ohio, S 89—LSC Analysis, p 5-571

Baldwin's Ohio Domestic Relations Law, Text 29.01

Schroeder-Katz, Ohio Criminal Law, Crim R 1, Author's Text (5)

Kurtz & Giannelli, Ohio Juvenile Law, Text 3.01, 3.06(C), 3.10(A), 7.03(A), 13.06(A), 13.07(B), 15.01(B)(E)

CROSS REFERENCES

Department of public welfare, social services, eligibility of child for subsidized adoption, OAC 5101:2-44-02

Juvenile court jurisdiction over juvenile capital facilities, 307.021

Infant hearing-impairment screening, custodian defined, 3701.503

Placing of child in institution, public children services agency and private children services agency defined, 5103.15

Procedure under Criminal Rules, exceptions, Crim R 1

Additional definitions applicable to juvenile courts, Juv R 2

LEGAL ENCYCLOPEDIAS AND ALR

OJur 3d: 22, Courts and Judges § 72, 345; 26, Criminal Law § 668; 46, Family Law § 359, 365 to 367, 374, 409, 423, 532, 558

Am Jur 2d: 47, Juvenile Courts and Delinquent and Dependent Children § 26, 27

Inclusion or exclusion of the day of birth in computing one's age. 5 ALR2d 1143

Age of child at time of alleged offense or delinquency, or at time of legal proceedings, as criterion of jurisdiction of juvenile court. 89 ALR2d 506

2151.02 "Delinquent child" defined

As used in sections 2151.01 to 2151.54, inclusive, of the Revised Code, "delinquent child" includes any child:

(A) Who violates any law of this state, the United States, or any ordinance or regulation of a political subdivision of the state, which would be a crime if committed by an adult, except as provided in section 2151.021 of the Revised Code;

(B) Who violates any lawful order of the court made under this chapter.

HISTORY: 1969 H 320, eff. 11-19-69
127 v 547; 1953 H 1; GC 1639-2

PRACTICE AND STUDY AIDS

Baldwin's Ohio School Law, Text 24.11

Kurtz & Giannelli, Ohio Juvenile Law, Text 3.02 to 3.04, 7.01, 7.03(D), 7.06(D), 13.07, 13.08, 15.01(C), 15.02(A)

CROSS REFERENCES

Contributing to unruliness or delinquency, 2919.24

Truant pupil, juvenile court proceedings, 3321.22

Construction and operation standards for facilities for rehabilitation of delinquent juveniles, 5139.27, 5139.28

Waiver of rights, Juv R 3

Right to counsel, guardian ad litem, Juv R 4

LEGAL ENCYCLOPEDIAS AND ALR

OJur 3d: 22, Courts and Judges § 345; 26, Criminal Law § 668; 46, Family Law § 416, 418, 558, 560, 568

Am Jur 2d: 47, Juvenile Courts § 23, 25

2151.021 "Juvenile traffic offender" defined

A child who violates any traffic law, traffic ordinance, or traffic regulation of this state, the United States, or any political subdivision of this state, other than a resolution, ordinance, or regulation of a political subdivision of this state the violation of which is required to be handled by a parking violations bureau or a joint parking violations bureau pursuant to Chapter 4521. of the Revised Code, shall be designated as a "juvenile traffic offender."

HISTORY: 1982 H 707, eff. 1-1-83
1969 H 320; 127 v 547

PRACTICE AND STUDY AIDS

Kurtz & Giannelli, Ohio Juvenile Law, Text 3.03, 7.03(D)

CROSS REFERENCES

Waiver of rights, Juv R 3

Right to counsel, guardian ad litem, Juv R 4

LEGAL ENCYCLOPEDIAS AND ALR

OJur 3d: 46, Family Law § 417

Inclusion or exclusion of the day of birth in computing one's age. 5 ALR2d 1143

Marriage as affecting jurisdiction of juvenile court over delinquent or dependent. 14 ALR2d 336

2151.022 "Unruly child" defined

As used in sections 2151.01 to 2151.54, inclusive, of the Revised Code, "unruly child" includes any child:

(A) Who does not subject himself to the reasonable control of his parents, teachers, guardian, or custodian, by reason of being wayward or habitually disobedient;

(B) Who is an habitual truant from home or school;

(C) Who so deports himself as to injure or endanger the health or morals of himself or others;

(D) Who attempts to enter the marriage relation in any state without the consent of his parents, custodian, legal guardian, or other legal authority;

(E) Who is found in a disreputable place, visits or patronizes a place prohibited by law, or associates with vagrant, vicious, criminal, notorious, or immoral persons;

(F) Who engages in an occupation prohibited by law, or is in a situation dangerous to life or limb or injurious to the health or morals of himself or others;

(G) Who has violated a law applicable only to a child.

HISTORY: 1969 H 320, eff. 11-19-69

PRACTICE AND STUDY AIDS

Baldwin's Ohio School Law, Text 20.04, 24.11, 25.02; Forms 20.41

Kurtz & Giannelli, Ohio Juvenile Law, Text 3.02, 3.04, 3.06(D), 7.01

CROSS REFERENCES

Contributing to unruliness or delinquency, 2919.24

Standards of operation and construction for facilities for rehabilitation of delinquent juveniles, 5139.27, 5139.28

Waiver of rights, Juv R 3

Right to counsel, guardian ad litem, Juv R 4

LEGAL ENCYCLOPEDIAS AND ALR

OJur 3d: 22, Courts and Judges § 345; 26, Criminal Law § 668; 46, Family Law § 359, 418, 558

Marriage as affecting jurisdiction of juvenile court over delinquent or dependent. 14 ALR2d 336

Truancy as indicative of delinquency or incorrigibility, justifying commitment of infant or juvenile. 5 ALR4th 1211

2151.03 "Neglected child" defined

As used in sections 2151.01 to 2151.54, inclusive, of the Revised Code, "neglected child" includes any child:

(A) Who is abandoned by his parents, guardian, or custodian;

(B) Who lacks proper parental care because of the faults or habits of his parents, guardian, or custodian;

(C) Whose parents, guardian, or custodian neglects or refuses to provide him with proper or necessary subsistence, education, medical or surgical care, or other care necessary for his health, morals, or well being;

(D) Whose parents, guardian, or custodian neglects or refuses to provide the special care made necessary by his mental condition;

(E) Whose parents, legal guardian, or custodian have placed or attempted to place such child in violation of sections 5103.16 and 5103.17 of the Revised Code.

A child who, in lieu of medical or surgical care or treatment for a wound, injury, disability, or physical or mental condition, is under spiritual treatment through prayer in accordance with the tenets and practices of a well-recognized religion, is not a neglected child for this reason alone.

HISTORY: 1969 H 320, eff. 11-19-69

1953 H 1; GC 1639-3

Note: 1988 S 89, § 3, eff. 1-1-89, reads:

(A) There is hereby created the Abused, Neglected, and Dependent Children Oversight Committee consisting of ten members. Two members shall be members of the House of Representatives appointed by the Speaker, not more than one of whom shall be a member of the same political party, two members shall be members of the Senate appointed by the President of the Senate, not more than one of whom shall be a member of the same political party, one member shall be a juvenile judge appointed by the Ohio Juvenile Judges Association, one member shall be the chief administrative officer of a county children services board or a county department of human services exercising the children services function appointed by the Director of the Department of Human Services, one member shall be a member of a board of county commissioners to be appointed by the Governor, one member shall be appointed by the Governor, and two members shall be appointed by the Committee as provided in division (B) of this section. Except as otherwise provided in division (B) of this section, all of the appointments shall be made before February 1, 1989. Any vacancy occurring on the Committee shall be filled in the same manner as provided for the original appointment.

(B) The Committee shall meet within two weeks after the initial members are appointed at a time and place designated by the Governor. At its first meeting, the Committee shall elect a chairman and vice-chairman from among the legislative members of the Committee and shall adopt rules for its procedures. The Committee shall, by a majority vote of its appointed members, appoint two members to the Committee at the first meeting, one of whom shall be a representative of a public child welfare agency and one of whom shall be a member of a private child placing agency. Thereafter, the Committee shall hold at least four meetings a year in different regions of the state, to be scheduled by the chairman.

(C) The Committee members shall receive no compensation for serving on the Committee but shall receive reimbursement for actual and necessary expenses incurred while discharging the duties of their office.

(D) The Abused, Neglected, and Dependent Children Oversight Committee shall monitor the system for handling children who are alleged or adjudicated to be abused, neglected, or dependent children, evaluate the implementation of the changes in the law as enacted by this act, and the impact of those changes upon the system for handling children who are alleged or adjudicated to be abused, neglected, or dependent children. No later than July 1, 1990, the Committee shall submit a report to the General Assembly evaluating the implementation of the changes to the law made by this act. No later than January 1, 1991, the Committee shall submit a report to the General Assembly evaluating the impact of the changes to the law made by this act. The report shall contain recommendations to the General Assembly for the improvement of the system for handling children who are alleged or adjudicated to be abused, neglected, or dependent children. The Committee shall disband upon the submission of its final report.

(E) Each officer, board, commission, bureau, or department of the state or any of its political subdivisions shall make available to the Committee any information that the Committee reasonably requests and cooperate with the Committee in carrying out its duties.

PRACTICE AND STUDY AIDS

Baldwin's Ohio School Law, Text 24.05(D)

Kurtz & Giannelli, Ohio Juvenile Law, Text 3.05, 3.06, 3.08, 3.10(A), 7.03(L), 13.06(A)

CROSS REFERENCES

Nonsupport of dependents, 2919.21

Duty of husband to support family, wife to assist, duration of duty to support, 3103.03

Waiver of rights, Juv R 3
Right to counsel, guardian ad litem, Juv R 4
Taking into custody, Juv R 6

LEGAL ENCYCLOPEDIAS AND ALR

OJur 2d: 48, Schools § 152
OJur 3d: 22, Courts and Judges § 345; 26, Criminal Law § 668; 46, Family Law § 359, 418, 419, 425, 515, 558, 584
Am Jur 2d: 47, Juvenile Courts and Delinquent and Dependent Children § 24, 25
Inclusion or exclusion of the day of birth in computing one's age. 5 ALR2d 1143
Marriage as affecting jurisdiction of juvenile court over delinquent or dependent. 14 ALR2d 336
Parent's involuntary confinement, or failure to care for child as result thereof, as evincing neglect, unfitness, or the like in dependency or divestiture proceeding. 79 ALR3d 417'

2151.031　"Abused child" defined

As used in this chapter, an "abused child" includes any child who:

(A) Is the victim of "sexual activity" as defined under Chapter 2907. of the Revised Code, where such activity would constitute an offense under that chapter, except that the court need not find that any person has been convicted of the offense in order to find that the child is an abused child;

(B) Is endangered as defined in section 2919.22 of the Revised Code, except that the court need not find that any person has been convicted under that section in order to find that the child is an abused child;

(C) Exhibits evidence of any physical or mental injury or death, inflicted other than by accidental means, or an injury or death which is at variance with the history given of it. Except as provided in division (D) of this section, a child exhibiting evidence of corporal punishment or other physical disciplinary measure by a parent, guardian, custodian, person having custody or control, or person in loco parentis of a child is not an abused child under this division if the measure is not prohibited under section 2919.22 of the Revised Code.

(D) Because of the acts or omissions of his parents, guardian, or custodian, suffers physical or mental injury that harms or threatens the child's health or welfare.

HISTORY:　1988 S 89, eff. 1-1-89
1975 H 85

Note:　See note under 2151.03 from 1988 S 89, § 3.

PRACTICE AND STUDY AIDS

Baldwin's Ohio Legislative Service, 1988 Laws of Ohio, S 89—LSC Analysis, p 5-571

Baldwin's Ohio School Law, Text 24.05(D)
Kurtz & Giannelli, Ohio Juvenile Law, Text 3.05, 3.06(F), 3.08, 13.06(A)

CROSS REFERENCES

Requirement to report child abuse, 2151.421
Sexual activity, defined, 2907.01
Endangering children (child abuse), 2919.22
Failure to report a felony, including child abuse, 2921.22
Prevention of child abuse and child neglect, 3109.13 to 3109.18
Domestic violence, defined, 3113.31

LEGAL ENCYCLOPEDIAS AND ALR

OJur 3d: 22, Courts and Judges § 345; 26, Criminal Law § 668; 46, Family Law § 359, 420, 558
Sexual child abuser's civil liability to child's parent. 54 ALR4th 93

2151.04　"Dependent child" defined

As used in this chapter, "dependent child" includes any child:

(A) Who is homeless or destitute or without proper care or support, through no fault of his parents, guardian, or custodian;

(B) Who lacks proper care or support by reason of the mental or physical condition of his parents, guardian, or custodian;

(C) Whose condition or environment is such as to warrant the state, in the interests of the child, in assuming his guardianship;

(D) To whom both of the following apply:

(1) He is residing in a household in which a parent, guardian, custodian, or other member of the household has abused or neglected a sibling of the child;

(2) Because of the circumstances surrounding the abuse or neglect of the sibling and the other conditions in the household of the child, the child is in danger of being abused or neglected by that parent, guardian, custodian, or member of the household.

HISTORY:　1988 S 89, eff. 1-1-89
1969 H 320; 129 v 1778; 1953 H 1; GC 1639-4

Note:　See note under 2151.03 from 1988 S 89, § 3.

PRACTICE AND STUDY AIDS

Baldwin's Ohio Legislative Service, 1988 Laws of Ohio, S 89—LSC Analysis, p 5-571
Kurtz & Giannelli, Ohio Juvenile Law, Text 3.05 to 3.08, 7.03(C)(L)

CROSS REFERENCES

Nonsupport of dependents, 2919.21
School attendance, juvenile court proceedings, 3321.22
Taking into custody, Juv R 6

LEGAL ENCYCLOPEDIAS AND ALR

OJur 3d: 22, Courts and Judges § 345; 26, Criminal Law § 668; 46, Family Law § 359, 421, 523, 558

Am Jur 2d: 47, Juvenile Courts and Delinquent and Dependent Children § 24, 25

Jurisdiction to award custody of child having legal domicile in another state. 4 ALR2d 7

2151.05   Child without proper parental care

Under sections 2151.01 to 2151.54 of the Revised Code, a child whose home is filthy and unsanitary; whose parents, stepparents, guardian, or custodian permit him to become dependent, neglected, abused, or delinquent; whose parents, stepparents, guardian, or custodian, when able, refuse or neglect to provide him with necessary care, support, medical attention, and educational facilities; or whose parents, stepparents, guardian, or custodian fail to subject such child to necessary discipline is without proper parental care or guardianship.

HISTORY: 1975 H 85, eff. 11-28-75
     1953 H 1; GC 1639-5

PRACTICE AND STUDY AIDS

Kurtz & Giannelli, Ohio Juvenile Law, Text 3.06(C)

CROSS REFERENCES

Taking into custody, Juv R 6

LEGAL ENCYCLOPEDIAS AND ALR

OJur 3d: 22, Courts and Judges § 345; 26, Criminal Law § 668; 46, Family Law § 359, 422, 558

2151.06   Residence or legal settlement

Under sections 2151.01 to 2151.54, inclusive, of the Revised Code, a child has the same residence or legal settlement as his parents, legal guardian of his person, or his custodian who stands in the relation of loco parentis.

HISTORY: 1953 H 1, eff. 10-1-53
     GC 1639-6

PRACTICE AND STUDY AIDS

Kurtz & Giannelli, Ohio Juvenile Law, Text 7.04(A)

LEGAL ENCYCLOPEDIAS AND ALR

OJur 3d: 46, Family Law § 451

ADMINISTRATION, OFFICIALS, AND JURISDICTION

2151.07   Creation and powers of juvenile court; assignment of judge

The juvenile court is a court of record and within the division of domestic relations or probate of the court of common pleas, except that the juvenile courts of Cuyahoga county and Hamilton county shall be separate divisions of the court of common pleas. The juvenile court has and shall exercise the powers and jurisdiction conferred in sections 2151.01 to 2151.99 of the Revised Code.

Whenever the juvenile judge of the juvenile court is absent from the county, or is unable to attend court, or the volume of cases pending in court necessitates it, upon the request of said judge, the presiding judge of the court of common pleas shall assign a judge of the court of common pleas of the county to act in his place or in conjunction with him. If no such judge is available for said purpose, the chief justice of the supreme court shall assign a judge of the court of common pleas, a juvenile judge, or a probate judge from some other county to act in the place of such judge or in conjunction with him, who shall receive such compensation and expenses for his services as is provided by law for judges assigned to hold court in courts of common pleas.

HISTORY: 1972 H 574, eff. 6-29-72
     1969 H 320; 127 v 847; 1953 H 1; GC 1639-7

Note: Guidelines for Assignment of Judges were announced by the Chief Justice of the Ohio Supreme Court on 5-24-88, but not adopted as rules pursuant to O Const Art IV §5. For the full text, see 37 OS(3d) xxxix, 61 OBar A-2 (6-13-88).

PRACTICE AND STUDY AIDS

Baldwin's Ohio Civil Practice, Text 1.03(E)
Kurtz & Giannelli, Ohio Juvenile Law, Text 15.02(A)

CROSS REFERENCES

Compensation and expenses of judges holding court outside county of residence, 141.07
Cuyahoga county juvenile court administrative judge shall be clerk of court, may appoint deputies and clerks, bonds, 2153.08

LEGAL ENCYCLOPEDIAS AND ALR

OJur 3d: 22, Courts and Judges § 72, 75, 97, 100, 345; 26, Criminal Law § 668; 46, Family Law § 359, 374, 394, 558

Am Jur 2d: 47, Juvenile Courts and Delinquent and Dependent Children § 2 to 6

2151.08   Juvenile court in Hamilton county

In Hamilton county the powers and jurisdiction of the juvenile court as conferred by Chapter 2151. of the Revised Code shall be exercised by that judge of the court of common pleas whose term begins on January 1, 1957, and his successors and that judge of the court of common pleas whose term begins on February 14, 1967, and his successors as provided by section 2301.03 of the Revised Code. This conferral of powers and jurisdiction on such judges shall be deemed a creation of a separately and independently created and established juvenile court in Hamilton county, Ohio. Such judges shall serve in each and every position where the statutes permit or require a juvenile judge to serve.

HISTORY: 131 v H 165, eff. 11-16-65
       127 v 84

Note: Former 2151.08 repealed by 126 v 778, eff. 10-11-55; 1953 H 1; GC 1639-8.

2151.09   Separate building and site may be purchased or leased

Upon the advice and recommendation of the juvenile judge, the board of county commissioners may provide by purchase, lease, or otherwise a separate building and site to be known as "the juvenile court" at a convenient location within the county which shall be appropriately constructed, arranged, furnished, and maintained for the convenient and efficient transaction of the business of the court and all parts thereof and its employees, including adequate facilities to be used as laboratories, dispensaries, or clinics for the use of scientific specialists connected with the court.

HISTORY: 1953 H 1, eff. 10-1-53
       GC 1639-15

LEGAL ENCYCLOPEDIAS AND ALR

OJur 3d: 46, Family Law § 375

2151.10   Appropriation for expenses of the court and maintenance of children; hearing; action in court of appeals; limitation of contempt power

The juvenile judge shall annually submit a written request for an appropriation to the board of county commissioners that shall set forth estimated administrative expenses of the juvenile court that the judge considers reasonably necessary for the operation of the court, including reasonably necessary expenses of the judge and such officers and employees as he may designate in attending conferences at which juvenile or welfare problems are discussed, and such sum each year as will provide for the maintenance and operation of the detention home, the care, maintenance, education, and support of neglected, abused, dependent, and delinquent children, other than children entitled to aid under sections 5107.01 to 5107.16 of the Revised Code, and for necessary orthopedic, surgical, and medical treatment, and special care as may be ordered by the court for any neglected, abused, dependent, or delinquent children. The board shall conduct a public hearing with respect to the written request submitted by the judge and shall appropriate such sum of money each year as it determines, after conducting the public hearing and considering the written request of the judge, is reasonably necessary to meet all the administrative expenses of the court. All disbursements from such appropriations shall be upon specifically itemized vouchers, certified to by the judge.

If the judge considers the appropriation made by the board pursuant to this section insufficient to meet all the administrative expenses of the court, he shall commence an action under Chapter 2731. of the Revised Code in the court of appeals for the judicial district for a determination of the duty of the board of county commissioners to appropriate the amount of money in dispute. The court of appeals shall give priority to the action filed by the juvenile judge over all cases pending on its docket. The burden shall be on the juvenile judge to prove that the appropriation requested is reasonably necessary to meet all administrative expenses of the court. If, prior to the filing of an action under Chapter 2731. of the Revised Code or during the pendency of the action, the judge exercises his contempt power in order to obtain the sum of money in dispute, he shall not order the imprisonment of any member of the board of county commissioners notwithstanding sections 2705.02 to 2705.06 of the Revised Code.

HISTORY: 1979 S 63, eff. 7-26-79
       1975 H 85; 1953 H 1; GC 1639-57

CROSS REFERENCES

Board of county commissioners, appropriation for court of common pleas; juvenile court excepted, 307.01

Judicial and court fund, tax levy, 5707.02

LEGAL ENCYCLOPEDIAS AND ALR

OJur 3d: 46, Family Law § 381

2151.11 Court participation in delinquency prevention activities

A juvenile court may participate with other public or private agencies of the county served by the court in programs which have as their objective the prevention and control of juvenile delinquency. The juvenile judge may assign employees of the court, as part of their regular duties, to work with organizations concerned with combatting conditions known to contribute to delinquency, providing adult sponsors for children who have been found delinquent, and developing wholesome youth programs.

The juvenile judge may accept and administer on behalf of the court gifts, grants, bequests, and devises made to the court for the purpose of preventing delinquency.

HISTORY: 131 v H 449, eff. 11-11-65

Note: Former 2151.11 repealed by 129 v 1072, eff. 2-8-61; 1953 H 1; GC 1639-7a.

PRACTICE AND STUDY AIDS

Kurtz & Giannelli, Ohio Juvenile Law, Text 7.02

CROSS REFERENCES

Intake, Juv R 9

LEGAL ENCYCLOPEDIAS AND ALR

OJur 3d: 46, Family Law § 376

2151.12 Clerk; bond; judge as clerk

Whenever the courts of common pleas, division of domestic relations, exercise the powers and jurisdictions conferred in sections 2151.01 to 2151.54 of the Revised Code, or whenever the juvenile judge, or a majority of the juvenile judges of a multi-judge juvenile division, of a court of common pleas, juvenile division and the clerk of the court of common pleas agree in an agreement that is signed by the judge and the clerk and entered formally in the journal of the court, the clerks of courts of common pleas shall keep the records of such courts. In all other cases, the juvenile judge shall be the clerk of his own court.

In counties in which the juvenile judge is clerk of his own court, before entering upon the duties of his office as such clerk, he shall execute and file with the county treasurer a bond in a sum to be determined by the board of county commissioners, with sufficient surety to be approved by the board, conditioned for the faithful performance of his duties as clerk. The bond shall be given for the benefit of the county, the state, or any person who may suffer loss by

reason of a default in any of the conditions of the bond.

HISTORY: 1977 S 336, eff. 3-3-78
      1953 H 1; GC 1639-17

CROSS REFERENCES

Registry of custody documents, duty of clerk of courts, 3109.33

LEGAL ENCYCLOPEDIAS AND ALR

OJur 3d: 46, Family Law § 379

2151.13 Employees; compensation; bond

The juvenile judge may appoint such bailiffs, probation officers, and other employees as are necessary and may designate their titles and fix their duties, compensation, and expense allowances. The juvenile court may by entry on its journal authorize any deputy clerk to administer oaths when necessary in the discharge of his duties. Such employees shall serve during the pleasure of the judge.

The compensation and expenses of all employees and the salary and expenses of the judge shall be paid in semimonthly installments by the county treasurer from the money appropriated for the operation of the court, upon the warrant of the county auditor, certified to by the judge.

The judge may require any employee to give bond in the sum of not less than one thousand dollars, conditioned for the honest and faithful performance of his duties. The sureties on such bonds shall be approved in the manner provided by section 2151.12 of the Revised Code. The judge shall not be personally liable for the default, misfeasance, or nonfeasance of any employee from whom a bond has been required.

HISTORY: 1953 H 1, eff. 10-1-53
      GC 1639-18

CROSS REFERENCES

Peace officer training, 109.73 et seq.
Judges of the court of domestic relations, juvenile court responsibility, 2301.03
Bureau of delinquency prevention, powers and duties, 5139.17

LEGAL ENCYCLOPEDIAS AND ALR

OJur 3d: 22, Courts and Judges § 109, 192, 204; 46, Family Law § 379

2151.14 Duties and powers of probation department; records; command assistance; notice

to victim of accused sex offender's communicable disease

(A) The chief probation officer, under the direction of the juvenile judge, shall have charge of the work of the probation department. The department shall make such investigations as the juvenile court directs, keep a written record of such investigations, and submit the record to the judge or deal with them as he directs. The department shall furnish to any person placed on probation a statement of the conditions of probation and shall instruct him regarding them. The department shall keep informed concerning the conduct and condition of each person under its supervision and shall report thereon to the judge as he directs. Each probation officer shall use all suitable methods to aid persons on probation and to bring about improvement in their conduct and condition. The department shall keep full records of its work, keep accurate and complete accounts of money collected from persons under its supervision, give receipts therefor, and make reports thereon as the judge directs.

(B) Except as provided in division (C) of this section, the reports and records of the department shall be considered confidential information and shall not be made public. A probation officer may serve the process of the court within or without the county, and may make arrests without warrant upon reasonable information or upon view of the violation of sections 2151.01 to 2151.54 of the Revised Code, detain the person arrested pending the issuance of a warrant, and perform such other duties, incident to his office, as the judge directs. All sheriffs, deputy sheriffs, constables, marshals, chiefs of police, and other police officers shall render assistance to probation officers in the performance of their duties when requested to do so by any probation officer.

(C) When a complaint has been filed alleging that a child is delinquent by reason of having committed an act that would constitute a violation of section 2907.02, 2907.03, 2907.04, 2907.05, 2907.06, or 2907.12 of the Revised Code if committed by an adult and the arresting authority, a court, or a probation officer discovers that the child or a person whom the child caused to engage in sexual activity, as defined in section 2907.01 of the Revised Code, has a communicable disease, the arresting authority, court, or probation officer immediately shall notify the victim of the delinquent act of the nature of the disease.

HISTORY: 1986 H 468, eff. 9-17-86
  1953 H 1; GC 1639-19

2151.15   Powers and duties vested in county department of probation

When a county department of probation has been established in the county and the juvenile judge does not establish a probation department within the juvenile court as provided in section 2151.14 of the Revised Code, all powers and duties of the probation department provided for in sections 2151.01 to 2151.54, inclusive, of the Revised Code, shall vest in and be imposed upon such county department of probation.

In counties in which a county department of probation has been or is hereafter established the judge may transfer to such department all or any part of the powers and duties of his own probation department; provided that all juvenile cases shall be handled within a county department of probation exclusively by an officer or division separate and distinct from the officers or division handling adult cases.

HISTORY: 1953 H 1, eff. 10-1-53
  GC 1639-20

2151.151   Juvenile court may contract for services to children on probation

(A) The juvenile judge may contract with any agency, association, or organization, which may be of a public or private, or profit or nonprofit nature, or with any individual for the provision of supervisory or other services to children placed on probation who are under the custody and supervision of the juvenile court.

(B) The juvenile judges of two or more adjoining or neighboring counties may join together for purposes of contracting with any agency, association, or organization, which may be of a public or private, or profit or nonprofit nature, or with any individual for the provision of supervisory or other services to children placed on probation who are under the custody and supervision of the juvenile court of any of the counties that joins [sic] together.

HISTORY:　1981 H 440, eff. 11-23-81

LEGAL ENCYCLOPEDIAS AND ALR

OJur 3d: 46, Family Law § 376

2151.16　Referees; powers and duties

The juvenile judge may appoint and fix the compensation of referees who shall have the usual power of masters in chancery cases, provided, in all such cases submitted to them by the juvenile court, they shall hear the testimony of witnesses and certify to the judge their findings upon the case submitted to them, together with their recommendation as to the judgment or order to be made in the case in question. The court, after notice to the parties in the case of the presentation of such findings and recommendation, may make the order recommended by the referee, or any other order in the judgment of the court required by the findings of the referee, or may hear additional testimony, or may set aside said findings and hear the case anew. In appointing a referee for the trial of females, a female referee shall be appointed where possible.

HISTORY:　1953 H 1, eff. 10-1-53
　　GC 1639-21

PRACTICE AND STUDY AIDS

Kurtz & Giannelli, Ohio Juvenile Law, Text 11.16

CROSS REFERENCES

Judges of the court of domestic relations, juvenile court responsibility, 2301.03
Advertising for children for adoption or foster homes forbidden, 5103.17
Referees, Juv R 40

LEGAL ENCYCLOPEDIAS AND ALR

OJur 3d: 46, Family Law § 496, 498, 502, 564

2151.17　Rules governing practice and procedure

Except as otherwise provided by rules promulgated by the supreme court, the juvenile court may prescribe rules regulating the docketing and hearing of causes, motions, and demurrers, and such other matters as are necessary for the orderly conduct of its business and the prevention of delay, and for the government of its officers and employees, including their conduct, duties, hours, expenses, leaves of absence, and vacations.

HISTORY:　1969 H 320, eff. 11-19-69
　　1953 H 1; GC 1639-11

CROSS REFERENCES

Judges of the court of domestic relations, juvenile court responsibility, 2301.03
Rules of civil procedure; scope, applicability, construction, exceptions, Civ R 1
Procedure not otherwise specified, Juv R 45

LEGAL ENCYCLOPEDIAS AND ALR

OJur 3d: 46, Family Law § 377, 379

2151.18　Records; monthly date report; annual report; copies for distribution; cases in which victim aged or disabled

(A) The juvenile court shall maintain records of all official cases brought before it, including an appearance docket, a journal, and a cashbook. The court shall maintain a separate docket for traffic offenses. All traffic cases shall be recorded on the separate docket instead of on the general appearance docket. The parents of any child affected, if they are living, or the nearest of kin of the child, if the parents are deceased, may inspect these records, either in person or by counsel during the hours in which the court is open.

(B) The clerk of the court shall maintain a statistical record that includes all of the following:

(1) The number of complaints that are filed with the court that allege that a child is delinquent, in relation to which the court determines, under division (D) of section 2151.27 of the Revised Code, that the victim of the alleged delinquent act was sixty-five years of age or older or permanently and totally disabled at the time of the alleged commission of the act;

(2) The number of complaints described in division (B)(1) of this section that result in the child being adjudicated delinquent;

(3) The number of complaints described in division (B)(2) of this section in which the act upon which the adjudication of delinquency is based caused property damage or would be a

theft offense, as defined in division (K) of section 2913.01 of the Revised Code, if committed by an adult;

(4) The number of complaints described in division (B)(3) of this section that result in the child being required, as an order of disposition made under division (A)(8) of section 2151.355 of the Revised Code, to make restitution for all or part of the property damage caused by his delinquent act or for all or part of the value of the property that was the subject of the delinquent act that would be a theft offense if committed by an adult;

(5) The number of complaints described in division (B)(2) of this section in which the act upon which the adjudication of delinquency is based would have been an offense of violence if committed by an adult;

(6) The number of complaints described in division (B)(5) of this section that result in the child being committed, as an order of disposition made under division (A)(3), (4), (5), or (6) of section 2151.355 of the Revised Code, to any facility for delinquent children operated by the county, a district, or a private agency or organization or to the department of youth services;

(7) The number of complaints described in division (B)(1) of this section that result in the case being transferred for criminal prosecution to an appropriate court having jurisdiction of the offense, under division (A) of section 2151.26 of the Revised Code or that involve an act of a child that is required to be prosecuted in an appropriate court having jurisdiction of the offense, under division (G) of that section.

The clerk of the court shall compile an annual summary covering the preceding calendar year showing all of the information for that year contained in the record maintained under this division. The record and the annual summary shall be public records open for inspection. Neither the record nor the annual summary shall include the identity of any party to a case.

(C) The juvenile court shall submit monthly to the department of youth services, on forms provided by the department, any data regarding all official cases of the court that the department reasonably requests. The department shall publish this data on a statewide basis in statistical form at least annually. The department shall not publish the identity of any party to a case.

(D) Not later than June of each year, the court shall prepare an annual report covering the preceding calendar year showing the number and kinds of cases that have come before it, the disposition of the cases, and any other data pertaining to the work of the court that the juvenile judge directs or that the department of youth services requests. Copies of such report shall be filed with the department and with the board of county commissioners. With the approval of the board, copies may be printed for distribution to persons and agencies interested in the court or community program for dependent, neglected, abused, or delinquent children and juvenile traffic offenders. The number of copies ordered printed and the estimated cost of each printed copy shall appear on each copy of the report printed for distribution.

HISTORY: 1984 S 5, eff. 9-26-84
        1981 H 440; 1979 H 394; 1975 H 85; 127 v 547; 1953 H 1; GC 1639-13

PRACTICE AND STUDY AIDS

Kurtz & Giannelli, Ohio Juvenile Law, Text 7.01, 15.04(A)

CROSS REFERENCES

Judges of the court of domestic relations, juvenile court responsibility, 2301.03
Youth services department, powers and duties, 5139.04

LEGAL ENCYCLOPEDIAS AND ALR

OJur 3d: 1, Actions § 103; 46, Family Law § 378

2151.19 Summons; expense

The summons, warrants, citations, subpoenas, and other writs of the juvenile court may issue to a probation officer of any such court or to the sheriff of any county or any marshal, constable, or police officer, and the provisions of law relating to the subpoenaing of witnesses in other cases shall apply in so far as they are applicable.

When a summons, warrant, citation, subpoena, or other writ is issued to any such officer, other than a probation officer, the expense in serving the same shall be paid by the county, township, or municipal corporation in the manner prescribed for the payment of sheriffs, deputies, assistants, and other employees.

HISTORY: 1953 H 1, eff. 10-1-53
        GC 1639-52, 1639-53

PRACTICE AND STUDY AIDS

Kurtz & Giannelli, Ohio Juvenile Law, Text 7.05

CROSS REFERENCES

Right to compulsory process to obtain witnesses, O Const Art I §10
Process, issuance, form, Juv R 15

LEGAL ENCYCLOPEDIAS AND ALR

OJur 3d: 22, Courts and Judges § 345; 26, Criminal Law § 668; 46, Family Law § 359, 474, 483, 545, 558

2151.20 Seal of court; dimensions

Juvenile courts within the probate court shall have a seal which shall consist of the coat of arms of the state within a circle one and one-fourth inches in diameter and shall be surrounded by the words "juvenile court _____ county."

The seal of other courts exercising the powers and jurisdiction conferred in sections 2151.01 to 2151.54, inclusive, of the Revised Code, shall be attached to all writs and processes.

HISTORY: 132 v H 164, eff. 12-15-67
     1953 H 1; GC 1639-9

LEGAL ENCYCLOPEDIAS AND ALR

OJur 3d: 46, Family Law § 376

2151.21 Jurisdiction in contempt

The juvenile court has the same jurisdiction in contempt as courts of common pleas.

HISTORY: 1953 H 1, eff. 10-1-53
     GC 1639-10

PRACTICE AND STUDY AIDS

Kurtz & Giannelli, Ohio Juvenile Law, Text 7.05(B), 13.10, 15.01(D)

CROSS REFERENCES

Contempt of court, Ch 2705

LEGAL ENCYCLOPEDIAS AND ALR

OJur 3d: 22, Courts and Judges § 345; 26, Criminal Law § 668; 46, Family Law § 359, 403, 558
Am Jur 2d: 47, Juvenile Courts and Delinquent and Dependent Children § 5
Court's power to punish for contempt a child within the age group subject to jurisdiction of juvenile court. 77 ALR2d 1004
Interference with enforcement of judgment in criminal or juvenile delinquent case as contempt. 8 ALR3d 657

2151.211 Employee's attendance at delinquency case under subpoena; employer may not penalize

No employer shall discharge or terminate from employment, threaten to discharge or terminate from employment, or otherwise punish or penalize any employee because of time lost from regular employment as a result of the employee's attendance at any proceeding in a delinquency case pursuant to a subpoena. This section generally does not require and shall not be construed to require an employer to pay an employee for time lost as a result of attendance at any proceeding in a delinquency case. However, if an employee is subpoenaed to appear at

a proceeding in a delinquency case and the proceeding pertains to an offense against the employer or an offense involving the employee during the course of his employment, the employer shall not decrease or withhold the employee's pay for any time lost as a result of compliance with the subpoena. Any employer who knowingly violates this section is in contempt of court.

HISTORY: 1984 S 172, eff. 9-26-84

CROSS REFERENCES

Victim's rights pamphlet, publication and distribution, 109.42

LEGAL ENCYCLOPEDIAS AND ALR

OJur 3d: 22, Courts and Judges § 345; 26, Criminal Law § 668; 46, Family Law § 359, 474, 558

2151.22 Terms of court; sessions

The term of any juvenile or domestic relations court, whether a division of the court of common pleas or an independent court, is one calendar year. All actions and other business pending at the expiration of any term of court is automatically continued without further order. The judge may adjourn court or continue any case whenever, in his opinion, such continuance is warranted.

Sessions of the court may be held at such places throughout the county as the judge shall from time to time determine.

HISTORY: 1976 H 390, eff. 8-6-76
     1953 H 1; GC 1639-12

PRACTICE AND STUDY AIDS

Kurtz & Giannelli, Ohio Juvenile Law, Text 15.01(A)

LEGAL ENCYCLOPEDIAS AND ALR

OJur 3d: 46, Family Law § 375

2151.23 Jurisdiction of juvenile court; orders for child support

(A) The juvenile court has exclusive original jurisdiction under the Revised Code:

(1) Concerning any child who on or about the date specified in the complaint is alleged to be a juvenile traffic offender, or a delinquent, unruly, abused, neglected, or dependent child;

(2) To determine the custody of any child not a ward of another court of this state;

(3) To hear and determine any application for a writ of habeas corpus involving the custody of a child;

(4) To exercise the powers and jurisdiction given the probate division of the court of common pleas in Chapters 5122. and 5123. of the Revised Code, if the court has probable cause to believe that a child otherwise within the jurisdiction of the court is a mentally ill person subject to hospitalization by court order, as defined in section 5122.01 of the Revised Code, or a mentally retarded person subject to institutionalization by court order, as defined in section 5123.01 of the Revised Code;

(5) To hear and determine all criminal cases charging adults with the violation of any section of Chapter 2151. of the Revised Code;

(6) Under the interstate compact on juveniles in section 2151.56 of the Revised Code;

(7) Concerning any child who is to be taken into custody pursuant to section 2151.31 of the Revised Code, upon being notified of the intent to take the child into custody and the reasons for taking the child into custody;

(8) To hear and determine requests for the extension of temporary custody agreements, and requests for court approval of permanent custody agreements, that are filed pursuant to section 5103.15 of the Revised Code;

(9) To hear and determine applications for consent to marry pursuant to section 3101.04 of the Revised Code.

(B) The juvenile court has original jurisdiction under the Revised Code:

(1) To hear and determine all cases of misdemeanors charging adults with any act or omission with respect to any child, which act or omission is a violation of any state law or any municipal ordinance;

(2) To determine the paternity of any child alleged to have been born out of wedlock pursuant to sections 3111.01 to 3111.19 of the Revised Code;

(3) Under the uniform reciprocal enforcement of support act in Chapter 3115. of the Revised Code;

(4) To hear and determine an application for an order for the support of any child, if the child is not a ward of another court of this state.

(C) The juvenile court, except as to juvenile courts which are a separate division of the court of common pleas, or a separate and independent juvenile court, has jurisdiction to hear, determine, and make a record of any action for divorce or alimony involving the custody or care of children filed in the court of common pleas and certified by the court of common pleas with all the papers filed therein to the court for trial, provided that no such certification shall be made to any court unless the consent of the juvenile judge is first obtained. After such certification is made and consent obtained, the court shall proceed as if such action were originally begun in that court except as to awards for alimony or support due and unpaid at the time of certification, over which the court has no jurisdiction.

(D) The juvenile court has jurisdiction to hear and determine all matters as to custody and support of children duly certified by the court of common pleas to the juvenile court after a divorce decree has been granted, including jurisdiction to modify the judgment and decree of the common pleas court as the same relate to the custody and support of children.

(E) The juvenile court has jurisdiction to hear and determine the case of any child certified to the court by any court of competent jurisdiction if such child comes within the jurisdiction of the court as defined by this section.

(F)(1) The juvenile court shall exercise its jurisdiction in child custody matters in accordance with sections 3109.04, 3109.21 to 3109.36, and 5103.20 to 5103.28 of the Revised Code.

(2) The juvenile court shall exercise its jurisdiction in child support matters in accordance with section 3109.05 of the Revised Code.

(G) Each order for child support made or modified by a juvenile court on or after December 1, 1986, shall be accompanied by one or more orders described in division (D) or (H) of section 3113.21 of the Revised Code, whichever is appropriate under the requirements of that section, a statement requiring all parties to the order to notify the court in writing of their current mailing address, their current residence address, and of any changes in either address, and a notice that the requirement to notify the court of all changes in either address continues until further notice from the court. If any person required to pay child support under an order made by a juvenile court on or after April 15, 1985, or modified on or after December 1, 1986, is found in contempt of court for failure to make support payments under the order, the court that makes the finding shall, in addition to any other penalty or remedy imposed, assess all court costs arising out of the contempt proceeding against the person and require the person to pay any reasonable attorney's fees of any adverse party, as determined by the court, that arose in relation to the act of contempt.

HISTORY: 1988 S 89, eff. 1-1-89
    1986 H 428, H 509, H 476; 1984 H 614; 1983 H 93; 1982 H 515; 1981 H 1; 1977 S 135; 1976 H 244; 1975 H 85; 1970 H 931; 1969 H 320

   Note: Former 2151.23 repealed by 1969 H 320, eff. 11-19-69; 130 v S 187; 127 v 547; 1953 H 1; GC 1639-16.

PRACTICE AND STUDY AIDS

Baldwin's Ohio Legislative Service, 1988 Laws of Ohio, S 89—LSC Analysis, p 5-571

Baldwin's Ohio Domestic Relations Law, Text Ch 5, Ch 29

Baldwin's Ohio Civil Practice, Text 1.03(E)

Eagle, Ohio Mental Health Law, Text 7.06(B)

Kurtz & Giannelli, Ohio Juvenile Law, Text Ch 3, 7.03(H)(J)(L), 7.06(D), 9.01, 13.06(A), 13.10, 15.04(B)

CROSS REFERENCES

Minor female's complaint for abortion, juvenile court to hear, 2151.85

Support order, defined, 2301.34

Court orders for support, report to human services director, 2301.351

Support order, procedures upon obligor's default, 2301.37

Nonsupport of dependents, 2919.21

Marriage, method of consent, 3101.02

Custody of minor children, 3109.03, 3109.04

Uniform child custody jurisdiction law, 3109.21 to 3109.37

Paternity proceedings, jurisdiction of courts, 3111.06

Payment of child support through withholding of earnings, 3113.21

Payment of support through withholding of earnings, workers' benefits, or bank account; procedures, 3113.21 to 3113.214

Placing of children, 5103.16

Scope of rules, Juv R 1

Rules of procedure do not affect jurisdiction, Juv R 44

LEGAL ENCYCLOPEDIAS AND ALR

OJur 3d: 22, Courts and Judges § 345; 26, Criminal Law § 668; 46, Family Law § 323, 359, 395 to 403, 405, 406, 413, 514, 532, 558; 47, Family Law § 634, 636, 638, 649; 48, Family Law § 1020, 1054, 1055; 53, Habeas Corpus and Post Conviction Remedies § 37

Am Jur 2d: 47, Juvenile Courts and Delinquent and Dependent Children § 16 to 21

Homicide by juvenile as within jurisdiction of a juvenile court. 48 ALR2d 663

Long-arm statutes: obtaining jurisdiction over non-resident parent in filiation or support proceeding. 76 ALR3d 708

Authority of court to order juvenile delinquent incarcerated in adult penal institution. 95 ALR3d 568

2151.24   Separate room for hearings

The board of county commissioners shall provide a special room not used for the trial of criminal or adult cases, when available, for the hearing of the cases of dependent, neglected, abused, and delinquent children.

HISTORY: 1975 H 85, eff. 11-28-75
1953 H 1; GC 1639-14

LEGAL ENCYCLOPEDIAS AND ALR

OJur 3d: 46, Family Law § 375

PRACTICE AND PROCEDURE

2151.25   Transfer to juvenile court

When a child is arrested under any charge, complaint, affidavit, or indictment, whether for a felony or a misdemeanor, proceedings regarding such child shall be initially in the juvenile court in accordance with this chapter. If the child is taken before a judge of a county court, mayor, judge of the municipal court, or judge of the court of common pleas other than a juvenile court, such judge of a county court, mayor, judge of the municipal court, or judge of the court of common pleas shall transfer the case to the juvenile court, whereupon proceedings shall be in accordance with this chapter. Upon such transfer all further proceedings under the charge, complaint, information, or indictment shall be discontinued in the court of said judge of a county court, mayor, municipal judge, or judge of the court of common pleas other than a juvenile court, and the case relating to such child shall thenceforth be within the exclusive jurisdiction of the juvenile court.

HISTORY: 1975 H 205, eff. 1-1-76
1969 H 320; 129 v 582; 1953 H 1; GC 1639-29

PRACTICE AND STUDY AIDS

Gotherman & Babbit, Ohio Municipal Law, Text 55.19

Kurtz & Giannelli, Ohio Juvenile Law, Text 3.10(B), Ch 9

CROSS REFERENCES

Minor under sixteen not to be confined with adult prisoner, 341.11, 2151.34

Right to counsel, 2151.352

Certification to juvenile court, 3109.06

LEGAL ENCYCLOPEDIAS AND ALR

OJur 3d: 22, Courts and Judges § 345; 26, Criminal Law § 668; 46, Family Law § 359, 402, 408, 558

Am Jur 2d: 47, Juvenile Courts and Delinquent and Dependent Children § 16, 20

Homicide by juvenile as within jurisdiction of a juvenile court. 48 ALR2d 663

2151.26   Relinquishment of jurisdiction for purpose of criminal prosecution

(A)(1) Except as provided in division (A)(2) of this section, after a complaint has been filed alleging that a child is delinquent by reason of having committed an act that would constitute a felony if committed by an adult, the court at a hearing may transfer the case for criminal prosecution to the appropriate court having jurisdiction of the offense, after making the following determinations:

(a) The child was fifteen or more years of age at the time of the conduct charged;

(b) There is probable cause to believe that the child committed the act alleged;

(c) After an investigation, including a mental and physical examination of the child made by a public or private agency, or a person qualified to make the examination, that there are reasonable grounds to believe that:

(i) He is not amenable to care or rehabilitation or further care or rehabilitation in any facility designed for the care, supervision, and rehabilitation of delinquent children;

(ii) The safety of the community may require that he be placed under legal restraint, including, if necessary, for the period extending beyond his majority.

(2) After a complaint has been filed alleging that a child is delinquent by reason of having committed an act that would constitute aggravated murder or murder if committed by an adult, the court at a hearing shall transfer the case for criminal prosecution to the appropriate court having jurisdiction of the offense, if the court determines at the hearing that both of the following apply:

(a) There is probable cause to believe that the child committed the alleged act;

(b) The child previously has been adjudicated a delinquent child for the commission of an act that would constitute aggravated murder or murder if committed by an adult.

(B) The court, when determining whether to transfer a case pursuant to division (A)(1) of this section, shall determine if the victim of the delinquent act was sixty-five years of age or older or permanently and totally disabled at the time of the commission of the act and whether the act alleged, if actually committed, would be an offense of violence, as defined in section 2901.01 of the Revised Code, if committed by an adult. Regardless of whether or not the child knew the age of the victim, if the court determines that the victim was sixty-five years of age or older or permanently and totally disabled, that fact shall be considered by the court in favor of transfer, but shall not control the decision of the court. Additionally, if the court determines that the act alleged, if actually committed, would be an offense of violence, as defined in section 2901.01 of the Revised Code, if committed by an adult, that fact shall be considered by the court in favor of transfer, but shall not control the decision of the court.

(C) The child may waive the examination required by division (A)(1)(c) of this section, if the court finds the waiver competently and intelligently made. Refusal to submit to a mental and physical examination by the child constitutes waiver of the examination.

(D) Notice in writing of the time, place, and purpose of any hearing held pursuant to division (A) of this section shall be given to the child's parents, guardian, or other custodian and his counsel at least three days prior to the hearing.

(E) No child, either before or after reaching eighteen years of age, shall be prosecuted as an adult for an offense committed prior to becoming eighteen, unless the child has been transferred as provided in this section. Any prosecution that is had in a criminal court on the mistaken belief that the child was over eighteen years of age at the time of the commission of the offense shall be deemed a nullity, and the child shall not be considered to have been in jeopardy on the offense.

(F) Upon such transfer, the juvenile court shall state the reasons for the transfer and order the child to enter into a recognizance with good and sufficient surety for his appearance before the appropriate court for any disposition that the court is authorized to make for a like act committed by an adult. The transfer abates the jurisdiction of the juvenile court with respect to the delinquent acts alleged in the complaint.

(G) Any child whose case is transferred for criminal prosecution pursuant to this section and who is subsequently convicted in that case shall thereafter be prosecuted as an adult in the appropriate court for any future act that he is alleged to have committed that if committed by an adult would constitute the offense of murder or aggravated murder, or would constitute an aggravated felony of the first or second degree or a felony of the first or second degree.

HISTORY: 1986 H 499, eff. 3-11-87
            1983 S 210; 1981 H 440; 1978 S 119; 1971 S 325; 1969 H 320

Note: Former 2151.26 repealed by 1969 H 320, eff. 11-19-69; 132 v H 343; 1953 H 1; GC 1639-32.

PRACTICE AND STUDY AIDS

Whiteside, Ohio Appellate Practice, Text 5.13
Kurtz & Giannelli, Ohio Juvenile Law, Text 1.04, 3.01, 3.10, Ch 9, 13.07(C), 13.10, 15.01(B)

CROSS REFERENCES

Relinquishment of jurisdiction, procedure, Juv R 30
Social history, physical and mental examinations, custody investigation, Juv R 32

LEGAL ENCYCLOPEDIAS AND ALR

OJur 3d: 22, Courts and Judges § 345; 25, Criminal Law § 379; 26, Criminal Law § 668; 46, Family Law § 359, 409 to 412, 558, 584; 72, Notice and Notices § 1 to 5, 8, 27 to 30

Am Jur 2d: 47, Juvenile Courts and Delinquent and Dependent Children § 19

Right of other person on trial for crime to invoke privilege as to communications by a juvenile delinquent to juvenile court. 2 ALR2d 652

Homicide by juvenile as within jurisdiction of a juvenile court. 48 ALR2d 663

2151.27 Complaint

(A) Any person having knowledge of a child who appears to be a juvenile traffic offender or to be a delinquent, unruly, abused, neglected, or dependent child, may file a sworn complaint with respect to that child in the juvenile court of the county in which the child has a residence or legal settlement, or in which the traffic offense, delinquency, unruliness, abuse, neglect, or dependency allegedly occurred. If an alleged abused, neglected, or dependent child is taken into custody pursuant to division (D) of section 2151.31 of the Revised Code, or is taken into custody pursuant to division (A) of section 2151.31 of the Revised Code without the filing of a complaint and placed into shelter care pursuant to division (C) of section 2151.31 of the Revised Code, a sworn complaint shall be filed with respect to the child before the end of the next business day after the day on which the child was taken into custody. The sworn complaint may be upon information and belief, and in addition to the allegation that the child is a delinquent, unruly, abused, neglected, or dependent child or a juvenile traffic offender, the complaint shall allege the particular facts upon which the allegation that the child is a delinquent, unruly, abused, neglected, or dependent child or a juvenile traffic offender is based.

(B) If a child, before arriving at the age of eighteen years, allegedly commits an act for which he may be adjudged a delinquent child, unruly child, or a juvenile traffic offender and if the specific complaint alleging the act is not filed or a hearing on that specific complaint is not held until after the child arrives at the age of eighteen years, the court has jurisdiction to hear and dispose of the complaint, as if the complaint were filed and the hearing held before the child arrived at the age of eighteen years.

(C) If the complainant in a case in which a child is alleged to be an abused, neglected, or dependent child desires permanent custody of the child or children, temporary custody of the child or children, whether as the preferred or an alternative disposition, or the placement of the child in long-term foster care, the complaint shall contain a prayer specifically requesting permanent custody, temporary custody, or the placement of the child in long-term foster care.

(D) For purposes of the record to be maintained by the clerk under division (B) of section 2151.18 of the Revised Code, when a complaint is filed that alleges that a child is a delinquent child, the court shall determine if the victim of the alleged delinquent act was sixty-five years of age or older or permanently and totally disabled at the time of the alleged commission of the act.

(E) Any person with standing under applicable law may file a complaint for the determination of any other matter over which the juvenile court is given jurisdiction by section 2151.23 of the Revised Code. The complaint shall be filed in the county in which the child who is the subject of the complaint is found or was last known to be found.

HISTORY: 1988 S 89, eff. 1-1-89
            1984 S 5; 1975 H 85; 1969 H 320

Note: Former 2151.27 repealed by 1969 H 320, eff. 11-19-69; 127 v 547; 1953 H 1; GC 1639-23.

PRACTICE AND STUDY AIDS

Baldwin's Ohio Legislative Service, 1988 Laws of Ohio, S 89—LSC Analysis, p 5-571

Kurtz & Giannelli, Ohio Juvenile Law, Text 3.10(A), 7.01, 7.03, 7.04

CROSS REFERENCES

Placing of child in institution, agency filing complaint and case plan, 5103.15
Complaint, Juv R 10

LEGAL ENCYCLOPEDIAS AND ALR

OJur 3d: 22, Courts and Judges § 345; 26, Criminal Law § 668; 46, Family Law § 359, 397, 404, 415, 452, 456, 458, 460, 462, 535, 558

Age of child at time of alleged offense or delinquency, or at time of legal proceedings, as criterion of jurisdiction of juvenile court. 89 ALR2d 506

2151.271 Transfer to juvenile court of another county

If the child resides in a county of the state and the proceeding is commenced in a juvenile court of another county, that court, on its own motion or a motion of a party, may transfer the proceeding to the county of the child's residence upon the filing of the complaint or after the adjudicatory, or dispositional hearing, for such further proceeding as required. The court of the child's residence shall then proceed as if the original complaint had been filed in that court. Transfer may also be made if the residence of the child changes. The proceeding shall be so transferred if other proceedings involving the child are pending in the juvenile court of the county of his residence.

Whenever a case is transferred to the county of the child's residence and it appears to the court of that county that the interests of justice and the convenience of the parties requires that the adjudicatory hearing be had in the county wherein the complaint was filed, the court may return the proceeding to the county wherein the complaint was filed for the purpose of such adjudicatory hearing. The court may thereafter proceed as to the transfer to the county of the child's legal residence as provided in this section.

Certified copies of all legal and social records pertaining to the case shall accompany the transfer.

HISTORY: 1969 H 320, eff. 11-19-69

PRACTICE AND STUDY AIDS

Kurtz & Giannelli, Ohio Juvenile Law, Text 3.01, 7.04(B)

CROSS REFERENCES

Complaint, Juv R 10
Transfer to another county, Juv R 11

LEGAL ENCYCLOPEDIAS AND ALR

OJur 3d: 46, Family Law § 453

2151.28   Summons

(A) After the complaint has been filed, the court shall fix a time for an adjudicatory hearing. The court shall conduct the adjudicatory hearing within one of the following periods of time:

(1) If the complaint alleged that the child is a delinquent or unruly child or a juvenile traffic offender, the adjudicatory hearing shall be held and may be continued in accordance with the Juvenile Rules.

(2) If the complaint alleged that the child is an abused, neglected, or dependent child, the adjudicatory hearing shall be held no later than thirty days after the complaint is filed, except that, for good cause shown, the court may continue the adjudicatory hearing for either of the following periods of time:

(a) For ten days beyond the thirty-day deadline to allow any party to obtain counsel;

(b) For a reasonable period of time beyond the thirty-day deadline to obtain service on all parties or any necessary evaluation, except that the adjudicatory hearing shall not be held later than sixty days after the date on which the complaint was filed.

(B) At an adjudicatory hearing held pursuant to division (A)(2) of this section, the court, in addition to determining whether the child is an abused, neglected, or dependent child, shall determine whether the child should remain or be placed in shelter care until the dispositional hearing. When the court makes the shelter care determination, all of the following apply:

(1) The court shall determine whether there are any relatives of the child who are willing to be temporary custodians of the child. If any relative is willing to be a temporary custodian, the child otherwise would remain or be placed in shelter care, and the appointment is appropriate, the court shall appoint the relative as temporary custodian of the child, unless the court appoints another relative as custodian. If it determines that the appointment of a relative as custodian would not be appropriate, it shall issue a written opinion setting forth the reasons for its determination and give a copy of the opinion to all parties and the guardian ad litem of the child.

The court's consideration of a relative for appointment as a temporary custodian does not make that relative a party to the proceedings.

(2) The court shall make the determination and issue the written finding of facts required by section 2151.419 of the Revised Code.

(3) The court shall schedule the date for the dispositional hearing to be held pursuant to section 2151.35 of the Revised Code. The parents of the child have a right to be represented by counsel; however, in no case shall the dispositional hearing be held later than ninety days after the date on which the complaint was filed.

(C) The court shall direct the issuance of a summons directed to the child except as provided by this section, the parents, guardian, custodian, or other person with whom the child may be and any other persons that appear to the court to be proper or necessary parties to the proceedings, requiring them to appear before the court at the time fixed to answer the allegations of the complaint. The summons shall contain the name and telephone number of the court employee designated by the court pursuant to section 2151.314 of the Revised Code to arrange for the prompt appointment of counsel for indigent persons. A child alleged to be an abused, neglected, or dependent child shall not be summoned unless the court so directs. A summons issued for a child who is under fourteen years of age and who is alleged to be a delinquent child, unruly child, or a juvenile traffic offender shall be served on the parent, guardian, or custodian of the child in his behalf.

If the person who has physical custody of the child, or with whom the child resides, is other than the parent or guardian, then the parents and guardian also shall be summoned. A copy of the complaint shall accompany the summons.

(D) If the complaint contains a prayer for permanent custody, temporary custody, whether as the preferred or an alternative disposition, or long-term foster care in a case involving an alleged abused, neglected, or dependent child, the summons served on the parents shall contain as is appropriate an explanation that the granting of permanent custody permanently divests the parents of their parental rights and privileges, an explanation that an adjudication that the child is an abused, neglected, or dependent child may result in an order of temporary custody that will cause the removal of the child from their legal custody until the court terminates the order of temporary custody or permanently divests the parents of their parental rights, or an explanation that the issuance of an order for long-term foster care will cause the removal of the child from the legal custody of the parents if any of the conditions listed in divisions (A)(5)(a) TO (c) of section 2151.353 of the Revised Code are found to exist.

(E) The court may endorse upon the summons an order directing the parents, guardian, or other person with whom the child may be to appear personally at the hearing and directing the person having the physical custody or control of the child to bring the child to the hearing.

(F) The summons shall contain a statement advising that any party is entitled to counsel in the proceedings and that the court will appoint counsel or designate a county public defender or joint county public defender to provide legal representation if the party is indigent.

(G) If it appears from an affidavit filed or from sworn testimony before the court that the conduct, condition, or surroundings of the child are endangering his health or welfare or those of others, that he may abscond or be removed from the jurisdiction of the court, or that he will not be brought to the court, notwithstanding the service of the summons, the court may endorse upon the summons an order that a law enforcement officer serve the summons and take the child into immediate custody and bring him forthwith to the court.

(H) A party, other than the child, may waive service of summons by written stipulation.

(I) Before any temporary commitment is made permanent, the court shall fix a time for hearing in accordance with section 2151.414 of the Revised Code and shall cause notice by summons to be served upon the parent or guardian of the child and the guardian ad litem of the child, or published, as provided in section 2151.29 of the Revised Code. The summons shall contain an explanation that the granting of permanent custody permanently divests the parents of their parental rights and privileges.

(J) Any person whose presence is considered necessary and who is not summoned may be subpoenaed to appear and testify at the hearing. Any one summoned or subpoenaed to appear who fails to do so may be punished, as in other cases in the court of common pleas, for con-

tempt of court. Persons subpoenaed shall be paid the same witness fees as are allowed in the court of common pleas.

(K) The failure of the court to hold an adjudicatory hearing within any time period set forth in division (A)(2) of this section does not affect the ability of the court to issue any order under this chapter and does not provide any basis for attacking the jurisdiction of the court or the validity of any order of the court.

HISTORY: 1988 S 89, eff. 1-1-89
           1975 H 164, H 85; 1969 H 320

Note: Former 2151.28 repealed by 1969 H 320, eff. 11-19-69; 1953 H 1; GC 1639-24.

PRACTICE AND STUDY AIDS

Baldwin's Ohio Legislative Service, 1988 Laws of Ohio, S 89—LSC Analysis, p 5-571

Giannelli, Ohio Evidence Manual, Author's Comment § 804.07

Kurtz & Giannelli, Ohio Juvenile Law, Text 5.02, 7.05, 7.06(C), 7.07(C), 11.02, 11.03, 13.02, 15.01(D)

CROSS REFERENCES

Right to counsel, O Const Art I §10
Definitions, Juv R 2
Taking into custody, Juv R 6
Process, issuance, form, Juv R 15
Process, service, Juv R 16
Subpoena, Juv R 17
Adjudicatory hearing, Juv R 29

LEGAL ENCYCLOPEDIAS AND ALR

OJur 3d: 22, Courts and Judges § 345; 26, Criminal Law § 668; 46, Family Law § 359, 403, 404, 425, 465 to 470, 475, 509, 515, 545, 558

Am Jur 2d: 47, Juvenile Courts and Delinquent and Dependent Children § 43

Right to and appointment of counsel in juvenile court proceedings. 60 ALR2d 691

Necessity of service of process upon infant itself in juvenile delinquency and dependency proceedings. 90 ALR2d 293

Right of juvenile court defendant to be represented during court proceedings by parent. 11 ALR4th 719

Validity and efficacy of minor's waiver of right to counsel—modern cases. 25 ALR4th 1072

Court appointment of attorney to represent without compensation indigent in civil action. 52 ALR4th 1063

2151.281   Guardian ad litem

(A) The court shall appoint a guardian ad litem to protect the interest of a child in any proceeding concerning an alleged or adjudicated delinquent child or unruly child when:

(1) The child has no parent, guardian, or legal custodian;

(2) The court finds that there is a conflict of interest between the child and his parent, guardian, or legal custodian.

(B)(1) The court shall appoint a guardian ad litem to protect the interest of a child in any proceeding concerning an alleged abused or neglected child, and in any proceeding held pursuant to section 2151.414 of the Revised Code. The guardian ad litem so appointed shall not be the attorney responsible for presenting the evidence alleging that the child is an abused or neglected child and shall not be an employee of any party in the proceeding.

(2) The guardian ad litem appointed for an alleged or adjudicated abused child or neglected child may bring a civil action against any person, who is required by division (A)(1) of section 2151.421 of the Revised Code to file a report of known or suspected child abuse or child neglect, if that person knows or suspects that the child for whom the guardian ad litem is appointed is the subject of child abuse or neglect and does not file the required report and if the child suffers additional injury or harm after the failure to file the report.

(C) In any proceeding concerning an alleged or adjudicated delinquent, unruly, abused, neglected, or dependent child in which the parent appears to be mentally incompetent or is under eighteen years of age, the court shall appoint a guardian ad litem to protect the interest of that parent.

(D) The court shall require the guardian ad litem to faithfully discharge his duties and, upon his failure to faithfully discharge his duties, shall discharge him and appoint another guardian ad litem. The court may fix the compensation for the service of the guardian ad litem, which compensation shall be paid from the treasury of the county.

(E) A parent who is eighteen years of age or older and not mentally incompetent shall be deemed sui juris for the purpose of any proceeding relative to his child who is alleged or adjudicated to be an abused, neglected, or dependent child.

(F) In any case in which a parent of a child alleged or adjudicated to be an abused, neglected, or dependent child is under eighteen years of age, the parents of that parent shall be summoned to appear at any hearing respecting the child, who is alleged or adjudicated to be an abused, neglected, or dependent child.

(G) In any case involving an alleged or adjudicated abused or neglected child or an agreement for the voluntary surrender of temporary or permanent custody of a child that is made in accordance with section 5103.15 of the Revised Code, the court shall appoint the guardian ad litem in each case as soon as possible after the complaint is filed, the request for an extension of the temporary custody agreement is filed with the court, or the request for court approval of

the permanent custody agreement is filed. In any case involving an alleged dependent child in which the parent of the child appears to be mentally incompetent or is under eighteen years of age, there is a conflict of interest between the child and his parents, guardian, or custodian, or the court believes that the parent of the child is not capable of representing the best interest of the child, the court shall appoint a guardian ad litem for the child. The guardian ad litem or his replacement shall continue to serve until any of the following occur:

(1) The complaint is dismissed or the request for an extension of a temporary custody agreement or for court approval of the permanent custody agreement is withdrawn or denied;

(2) All dispositional orders relative to the child have terminated;

(3) The legal custody of the child is granted to a relative of the child, or to another person;

(4) A final decree of adoption is issued with respect to the child;

(5) The child reaches the age of eighteen if the child is not mentally or physically handicapped or the child reaches the age of twenty-one if the child is mentally or physically handicapped;

(6) The guardian ad litem resigns or is removed by the court and a replacement is appointed by the court.

(H) If the guardian ad litem for an alleged or adjudicated abused, neglected, or dependent child is an attorney admitted to the practice of law in this state, he also may serve as counsel to his ward. If a person is serving as guardian ad litem and counsel for a child and either that person or the court finds that a conflict may exist between the person's roles as guardian ad litem and as counsel, the court shall relieve the person of his duties as guardian ad litem and appoint someone else as guardian ad litem for the child. If the court appoints a person who is not an attorney admitted to the practice of law in this state to be a guardian ad litem, the court also may appoint an attorney admitted to the practice of law in this state to serve as counsel for the guardian ad litem.

(I) The guardian ad litem for an alleged or adjudicated abused, neglected, or dependent child shall perform whatever functions are necessary to protect the best interest of the child, including, but not limited to, investigation, mediation, guardian, monitoring court proceedings, and monitoring the services provided the child by the public children services agency or private child placing agency that has temporary or permanent custody of the child, and shall file any motions and other court papers that are in the best interest of the child.

The guardian ad litem shall be given notice of all hearings, administrative reviews, and other proceedings in the same manner as notice is given to parties to the action.

(J)(1) When the court appoints a guardian ad litem pursuant to this section, it shall appoint a qualified volunteer whenever one is available and the appointment is appropriate.

(2) Upon request, the department of human services shall provide for the training of volunteer guardians ad litem.

HISTORY: 1988 S 89, eff. 1-1-89
1986 H 529; 1984 S 321; 1980 H 695; 1975 H 85; 1969 H 320

PRACTICE AND STUDY AIDS

Baldwin's Ohio Legislative Service, 1988 Laws of Ohio, S 89—LSC Analysis, p 5-571
Kurtz & Giannelli, Ohio Juvenile Law, Text 1.04, 11.03

CROSS REFERENCES

Persons required to report injury or neglect, 2151.421
Competency of child as witness, submission of questions to determine, 2317.01
Waiver of rights, Juv R 3
Right to counsel, guardian ad litem, Juv R 4

LEGAL ENCYCLOPEDIAS AND ALR

OJur 3d: 22, Courts and Judges § 345; 26, Criminal Law § 668; 46, Family Law § 359, 446, 447, 465, 549, 558
Am Jur 2d: 47, Juvenile Courts and Delinquent and Dependent Children § 29, 30
Allowance of fees for guardian ad litem appointed for infant defendant, as costs. 30 ALR2d 1148

2151.29   Service of summons

Service of summons, notices, and subpoenas, prescribed by section 2151.28 of the Revised Code, shall be made by delivering a copy to the person summoned, notified, or subpoenaed, or by leaving a copy at his usual place of residence. If the juvenile judge is satisfied that such service is impracticable, he may order service by registered or certified mail. If the person to be served is without the state but he can be found or his address is known, or his whereabouts or address can with reasonable diligence be ascertained, service of the summons may be made by delivering a copy to him personally or mailing a copy to him by registered or certified mail.

Whenever it appears by affidavit that after reasonable effort the person to be served with summons cannot be found or his post-office address ascertained, whether he is within or without a state, the clerk shall publish such summons once in a newspaper of general circulation throughout the county. The summons shall state the substance and the time and place of the hear-

ing, which shall be held at least one week later than the date of the publication. A copy of the summons and the complaint shall be sent by registered or certified mail to the last known address of the person summoned unless it is shown by affidavit that a reasonable effort has been made, without success, to obtain such address.

A copy of the advertisement, summons, and complaint, accompanied by the certificate of the clerk that such publication has been made and that such summons and complaint have been mailed as required by this section, is sufficient evidence of publication and mailing. When a period of one week from the time of publication has elapsed, the juvenile court shall have full jurisdiction to deal with such child as provided by sections 2151.01 to 2151.99, inclusive, of the Revised Code.

HISTORY: 1969 H 320, eff. 11-19-69

Note: Former 2151.29 repealed by 1969 H 320, eff. 11-19-69; 1953 H 1; GC 1639-25.

PRACTICE AND STUDY AIDS

Baldwin's Ohio Civil Practice, Text 3.24; Forms Ch 3
Giannelli, Ohio Evidence Manual, Author's Comment § 804.07
Kurtz & Giannelli, Ohio Juvenile Law, Text 7.05(C), 13.06(B)

CROSS REFERENCES

Process, service, Juv R 16
Subpoena, Juv R 17

LEGAL ENCYCLOPEDIAS AND ALR

OJur 3d: 22, Courts and Judges § 345; 26, Criminal Law § 668; 46, Family Law § 359, 468, 469, 558
Am Jur 2d: 47, Juvenile Courts and Delinquent and Dependent Children § 43
Necessity of service of process upon infant itself in juvenile delinquency and dependency proceedings. 90 ALR2d 293

2151.30   Issuance of warrant

In any case when it is made to appear to the juvenile judge that the service of a citation under section 2151.29 of the Revised Code will be ineffectual or the welfare of the child requires that he be brought forthwith into the custody of the juvenile court, a warrant may be issued against the parent, custodian, or guardian, or against the child himself.

HISTORY: 1953 H 1, eff. 10-1-53
GC 1639-26

CROSS REFERENCES

Process, issuance, form, Juv R 15

Process, service, Juv R 16

LEGAL ENCYCLOPEDIAS AND ALR

OJur 3d: 22, Courts and Judges § 345; 26, Criminal Law § 668; 46, Family Law § 359, 471, 558

2151.31 Apprehension, custody, and detention

(A) A child may be taken into custody in any of the following ways:

(1) Pursuant to an order of the court under this chapter;

(2) Pursuant to the laws of arrest;

(3) By a law enforcement officer or duly authorized officer of the court when any of the following conditions are present:

(a) There are reasonable grounds to believe that the child is suffering from illness or injury and is not receiving proper care, as described in section 2151.03 of the Revised Code, and his removal is necessary to prevent immediate or threatened physical or emotional harm;

(b) There are reasonable grounds to believe that the child is in immediate danger from his surroundings and that his removal is necessary to prevent immediate or threatened physical or emotional harm;

(c) There are reasonable grounds to believe that a parent, guardian, custodian, or other household member of the child's household has abused or neglected another child in the household and to believe that the child is in danger of immediate or threatened physical or emotional harm from that person.

(4) By an enforcement official, as defined in section 4109.01 of the Revised Code, under the circumstances set forth in section 4109.08 of the Revised Code;

(5) By a law enforcement officer or duly authorized officer of the court when there are reasonable grounds to believe that the child has run away from his parents, guardian, or other custodian.

(B) The taking of a child into custody is not and shall not be deemed an arrest except for the purpose of determining its validity under the constitution of this state or of the United States.

(C) A child taken into custody shall not be detained or placed in shelter care prior to the hearing on the complaint, unless his detention or shelter care is required to protect the child from immediate or threatened physical or emotional harm, because the child may abscond or be removed from the jurisdiction of the court, because the child has no parents, guardian, or custodian or other person able to provide supervision and care for him and return him to the court when required, or because an order for placement of the child in detention or shelter care has been made by the court pursuant to this chapter.

(D) Upon receipt of notice from a person that the person intends to take an alleged abused, neglected, or dependent child into custody pursuant to division (A)(3) of this section, a juvenile judge or a designated referee may grant by telephone an ex parte emergency order authorizing the taking of the child into custody if there is probable cause to believe that any of the conditions set forth in divisions (A)(3)(a) to (c) of this section are present. The judge or referee shall journalize any ex parte emergency order issued pursuant to this division. If an order is issued pursuant to this division and the child is taken into custody pursuant to the order, a sworn complaint shall be filed with respect to the child before the end of the next business day after the day on which the child is taken into custody and a hearing shall be held pursuant to division (E) of this section and the Juvenile Rules. A juvenile judge or referee shall not grant an emergency order by telephone pursuant to this division until after he determines that reasonable efforts have been made to notify the parents, guardian, or custodian of the child that the child may be placed into shelter care and of the reasons for placing the child into shelter care, except that, if the requirement for notification would jeopardize the physical or emotional safety of the child or result in the child being removed from the court's jurisdiction, the judge or referee may issue the order for taking the child into custody and placing the child into shelter care prior to giving notice to the parents, guardian, or custodian of the child.

(E) If a judge or referee pursuant to division (D) of this section issues an ex parte emergency order for taking a child into custody, the court shall hold a hearing to determine whether there is probable cause for the emergency order. The hearing shall be held before the end of the next business day after the day on which the emergency order is issued, except that it shall not be held later than seventy-two hours after the emergency order is issued.

If the court determines at the hearing that there is not probable cause for the issuance of the emergency order issued pursuant to division (D) of this section, it shall order the child released to the custody of his parents, guardian, or custodian. If the court determines at the hearing that there is probable cause for the issuance of the emergency order issued pursuant to division (D) of this section, the court shall do all of the following:

(1) Ensure that a complaint is filed or has been filed;

(2) Hold a hearing pursuant to section 2151.314 of the Revised Code to determine if the child should remain in shelter care;

(3) At the hearing held pursuant to section 2151.314 of the Revised Code, make the determination and issue the written finding of facts required by section 2151.419 of the Revised Code.

(F) If the court determines at the hearing held pursuant to division (E) of this section that there is probable cause to believe that the child is an abused child, as defined in division (A) of section 2151.031 of the Revised Code, the court may do any of the following:

(1) Upon the motion of any party, the guardian ad litem, the prosecuting attorney, or an employee of the children services board or the county department of human services exercising the children services function, or its own motion, issue reasonable protective orders with respect to the interviewing or deposition of the child;

(2) Order that the child's testimony be videotaped for preservation of the testimony for possible use in any other proceedings in the case;

(3) Set any additional conditions with respect to the child or the case involving the child that are in the best interest of the child.

(G) This section is not intended, and shall not be construed, to prevent any person from taking a child into custody, if taking the child into custody is necessary in an emergency to prevent the physical injury, emotional harm, or neglect of the child.

HISTORY: 1988 S 89, eff. 1-1-89
1978 H 883; 1969 H 320

Note: Former 2151.31 repealed by 1969 H 320, eff. 11-19-69; 1953 H 1; GC 1639-27.

PRACTICE AND STUDY AIDS

Baldwin's Ohio Legislative Service, 1988 Laws of Ohio, S 89—LSC Analysis, p 5-571

Kurtz & Giannelli, Ohio Juvenile Law, Text 5.02, 7.03(B), 7.06, 7.07(B), 13.04

CROSS REFERENCES

Taking into custody, Juv R 6
Detention and shelter care, Juv R 7

LEGAL ENCYCLOPEDIAS AND ALR

OJur 3d: 22, Courts and Judges § 345; 25, Criminal Law § 339; 26, Criminal Law § 668; 46, Family Law § 359, 425, 426, 428, 430, 558

Am Jur 2d: 47, Juvenile Courts and Delinquent and Dependent Children § 35

2151.311   Procedure upon apprehension

(A) A person taking a child into custody shall, with all reasonable speed, either:

(1) Release the child to his parents, guardian, or other custodian upon their written promise to bring the child before the court when requested by the court, unless his detention or shelter care appears to be warranted or required as provided in section 2151.31 of the Revised Code;

(2) Bring the child to the court or deliver him to a place of detention or shelter care designated by the court and promptly give notice thereof, together with a statement of the reason for taking the child into custody, to a parent, guardian, or other custodian and to the court. Any temporary detention or inquiry of the child necessary to comply with division (A)(1) of this section shall conform to the procedures and conditions prescribed by this chapter and rules of court.

(B) If a parent, guardian, or other custodian fails, when requested, to bring the child before the court as provided by this section, the court may issue its warrant directing that the child be taken into custody and brought before the court.

HISTORY: 1972 S 445, eff. 6-29-72
1970 H 931; 1969 H 320

PRACTICE AND STUDY AIDS

Kurtz & Giannelli, Ohio Juvenile Law, Text 7.06

CROSS REFERENCES

Detention and shelter care, release to parents, procedure, Juv R 7

LEGAL ENCYCLOPEDIAS AND ALR

OJur 3d: 22, Courts and Judges § 345; 26, Criminal Law § 668; 46, Family Law § 359, 426, 430, 558; 72, Notice and Notices § 1 to 5, 27 to 30

Am Jur 2d: 47, Juvenile Courts and Delinquent and Dependent Children § 35

2151.312   Place of detention

(A) A child alleged to be delinquent, unruly, or a juvenile traffic offender may be detained only in the following places:

(1) A certified foster home or a home approved by the court;

(2) A facility operated by a certified child welfare agency;

(3) A detention home or center for delinquent children which is under the direction or supervision of the court or other public authority or of a private agency and approved by the court;

(4) Any other suitable place designated by the court.

A child may be detained in jail or another facility for detention of adults only if the facility described in division (A)(3) of this section is not available and the detention is in a room separate and removed from those for adults. The court may order that a child over the age of fifteen years be detained in a jail in a room separate and removed from adults if public safety and protection reasonably require such detention.

The official in charge of a jail or other facility for the detention of adult offenders or persons charged with crime shall inform the court immediately when a child, who is or appears to be under the age of eighteen years, is received at the facility, and shall deliver him to the court upon request, or transfer him to a detention facility designated by the court.

If a case is transferred to another court for criminal prosecution, the child may be transferred to the appropriate officer or detention facility in accordance with the law governing the detention of persons charged with crime.

(B) Notwithstanding division (A) of this section, no child shall be placed in or committed to any adult jail or other facility for the detention of adults unless a facility described in division (A)(3) of this section is not available and then only if such child is over fifteen years of age, the public safety and protection requires that the detention be in such a place, and the detention is in a room totally separate by both sight and sound from all adult detainees.

(C) A child alleged to be neglected, abused, or dependent shall not be detained in a jail or other facility intended or used for the detention of adults charged with criminal offenses or of children alleged to be delinquent unless upon order of the court.

HISTORY: 1981 H 440, eff. 11-23-81
            1975 H 85; 1969 H 320

PRACTICE AND STUDY AIDS

Kurtz & Giannelli, Ohio Juvenile Law, Text 1.04, 7.06, 9.04(B)

CROSS REFERENCES

Detention and shelter care, Juv R 7

LEGAL ENCYCLOPEDIAS AND ALR

OJur 3d: 22, Courts and Judges § 345; 26, Criminal Law § 668; 46, Family Law § 359, 435 to 438, 558

2151.313 Fingerprinting or photographing child in an investigation; conditions; procedures; offense

(A)(1) Except as provided in division (A)(2) of this section, no child shall be fingerprinted or photographed in the investigation of any violation of law without the consent of the juvenile judge.

(2) Fingerprints and photographs of a child may be taken by law enforcement officers when the child is arrested or otherwise taken into custody for the commission of an act that would be a felony if committed by an adult, without the consent of the juvenile judge, when there is probable cause to believe that the child may have been involved in the commission of the act. A law enforcement officer who takes fingerprints or photographs of a child under this division immediately shall inform the juvenile court that the fingerprints or photographs were taken, and shall provide the court with the identity of the child, the number of fingerprints and photographs taken, and the name and address of each person who has custody and control of the fingerprints or photographs or copies of the fingerprints or photographs.

(B)(1) Subject to division (B)(2) of this section, fingerprints and photographs of a child obtained or taken under division (A)(1) or (2) of this section, and any records of the arrest or custody that was the basis for the taking of the fingerprints or photographs, initially may be retained only until the expiration of thirty days after the date taken, except that the court may limit the initial retention of fingerprints and photographs obtained under division (A)(1) of this section to a shorter period of time. During the initial period of retention, the fingerprints and photographs, copies of the fingerprints and photographs, and records of the arrest or custody shall be used or released only in accordance with division (C) of this section. At the expiration of the initial period for which fingerprints and photographs, copies of fingerprints and photographs, and records of the arrest or custody of a child may be retained under this division, if no complaint is pending against the child in relation to the act for which any such fingerprints and photographs originally were obtained or taken and if the child has neither been adjudicated delinquent in relation to that act nor been convicted of or pleaded guilty to a criminal offense based on that act subsequent to a transfer of the child's case for criminal prosecution pursuant to section 2151.26 of the Revised Code, the fingerprints and photographs, all copies of the fingerprints and photographs, and all records of the arrest or custody that was the basis of the taking of the fingerprints and photographs shall be removed from the file and delivered to the juvenile court. If, at the end of the initial period, such a complaint is pending against the child or the child either has been adjudicated delinquent in relation to the act or has been convicted of or pleaded guilty to a criminal offense based on the act subsequent to transfer of the child's case, the fingerprints and photographs, copies of the fingerprints and photographs, and the records of the arrest or custody that was the basis of the taking of the fingerprints and photographs may further be retained, subject to division (B)(2) of this section, until the expiration of two years after the date on which the fingerprints or photographs were taken or until the child attains eighteen years of age, whichever is earlier.

During this additional period of retention, the fingerprints and photographs, copies of the fingerprints and photographs, and records of the arrest or custody shall be used or released only in accordance with division (C) of this section. At the expiration of the additional period, if no complaint is pending against the child in relation to the act for which any such fingerprints originally were obtained or taken or in relation to any other act for which the fingerprints were used in an investigation authorized by division (C) of this section and that would be a felony if committed by an adult, the fingerprints, all copies of the fingerprints, and all records of the arrest or custody that was the basis of the taking of the fingerprints shall be removed from the file and delivered to the juvenile court, and if no complaint is pending against the child concerning the act for which any such photographs originally were obtained or taken or concerning a similar act that would be a felony if committed by an adult, the photographs and all copies of the photographs, and, if no fingerprints were taken at the time the photographs were taken, all records of the arrest or custody that was the basis of the taking of the photographs shall be removed from the file and delivered to the juvenile court. In either case, if, at the expiration of the applicable additional period, such a complaint is pending against the child, the photographs and copies of the photographs, or the fingerprints and copies of the fingerprints, whichever is applicable, and the records of the arrest or custody may be retained, subject to division (B)(2) of this section, until final disposition of the complaint, and upon final disposition of the complaint, they shall be removed from the file and delivered to the juvenile court.

(2) If a sealing or expungement order issued under section 2151.358 of the Revised Code requires the sealing or destruction of any fingerprints or photographs of a child obtained or taken under division (A)(1) or (2) of this section or of the records of an arrest or custody that was the basis of the taking of any such fingerprints or photographs prior to the expiration of any period for which they otherwise could be retained under division (B)(1) of this section, the fingerprints, photographs, and arrest or custody records that are subject to the order and all copies of the fingerprints, photographs, and arrest

or custody records shall be sealed or destroyed in accordance with the order.

(3) All fingerprints, photographs, records of an arrest or custody, and copies delivered to a juvenile court in accordance with division (B)(1) of this section shall be destroyed by the court.

(C) Until they are delivered to the juvenile court or sealed or destroyed pursuant to a sealing or expungement order, the originals and copies of fingerprints and photographs of a child that are obtained or taken pursuant to division (A)(1) or (2) of this section, and the records of the arrest or custody that was the basis of the taking of the fingerprints or photographs shall be used or released only as follows:

(1) During the initial thirty-day period of retention, originals and copies of fingerprints and photographs, and records of the arrest or custody shall be used, prior to the filing of a complaint against the child in relation to the act for which the fingerprints and photographs were originally obtained or taken, only for the investigation of that act, and shall be released, prior to the filing of such a complaint, only to a court that would have jurisdiction of the child's case under this chapter. Subsequent to the filing of such a complaint, originals and copies of fingerprints and photographs, and records of the arrest or custody shall be used or released during the initial thirty-day period of retention only as provided in division (C)(2)(a), (b), or (c) of this section.

(2) Originals and copies of fingerprints and photographs, and records of the arrest or custody that are retained beyond the initial thirty-day period of retention subsequent to the filing of a complaint, an adjudication of delinquency, or a conviction of or guilty plea to a criminal offense shall be used or released only as follows:

(a) Originals and copies of photographs, and, if no fingerprints were taken at the time the photographs were taken, records of the arrest or custody that was the basis of the taking of any such photographs shall be used only for the investigation of the act for which they originally were obtained or taken or for the investigation of any similar act that would be a felony if committed by an adult;

(b) Originals and copies of fingerprints, and records of the arrest or custody that was the basis of the taking of any such fingerprints shall be used only for the investigation of the act for which they originally were obtained or taken or for the investigation of any other act that would be a felony if commited [sic] by an adult;

(c) Originals and copies of fingerprints, photographs, and records of the arrest or custody that was the basis of the taking of the fingerprints or photographs shall be released only to:

(i) Law enforcement officers of this state or a political subdivision of this state, upon notification to the juvenile court of the name and address of the law enforcement officer or agency to whom or to which they will be released;

(ii) A court that has jurisdiction of the child's case under Chapter 2151. of the Revised Code or subsequent to a transfer of the child's case for criminal prosecution pursuant to section 2151.26 of the Revised Code.

(D) No person shall knowingly do any of the following:

(1) Fingerprint or photograph a child in the investigation of any violation of law other than as provided in division (A)(1) or (2) of this section;

(2) Retain fingerprints or photographs of a child obtained or taken under division (A)(1) or (2) of this section, copies of any such fingerprints or photographs, or records of the arrest or custody that was the basis of the taking of any such fingerprints or photographs other than in accordance with division (B) of this section;

(3) Use or release fingerprints or photographs of a child obtained or taken under division (A)(1) or (2) of this section, copies of any such fingerprints or photographs, or records of the arrest or custody that was the basis of the taking of any such fingerprints or photographs other than in accordance with division (B) or (C) of this section.

HISTORY: 1984 H 258, eff. 9-26-84
    1977 H 315; 1973 S 1; 1969 H 320

Penalty: 2151.99

PRACTICE AND STUDY AIDS

Kurtz & Giannelli, Ohio Juvenile Law, Text 5.05(D)

CROSS REFERENCES

Duties of the superintendent of the bureau of criminal investigation, 109.57

LEGAL ENCYCLOPEDIAS AND ALR

OJur 3d: 22, Courts and Judges § 345; 25, Criminal Law § 89, 90; 26, Criminal Law § 668; 46, Family Law § 359, 428, 429, 521, 558
Expungement of juvenile court records. 71 ALR3d 753

2151.314   Detention hearing

(A) When a child is brought before the court or delivered to a place of detention or shelter care designated by the court, the intake or other authorized officer of the court shall immediately make an investigation and shall release the child unless it appears that his detention or shelter care is warranted or required under section 2151.31 of the Revised Code.

If he is not so released, a complaint under section 2151.27 of the Revised Code shall be filed and an informal detention or shelter care hearing held promptly, not later than seventy-two hours after he is placed in detention or shelter care, to determine whether detention or shelter care is required. Reasonable oral or written notice of the time, place, and purpose of the detention or shelter care hearing shall be given to the child and, if they can be found, to his parents, guardian, or custodian. Prior to the hearing, the court shall inform the parties of their right to counsel and to appointed counsel or to the services of the county public defender or joint county public defender, if they are indigent, of the child's right to remain silent with respect to any allegation of delinquency, and of the name and telephone number of a court employee who can be contacted during the normal business hours of the court to arrange for the prompt appointment of counsel for any party who is indigent. Unless it appears from the hearing that the child's detention or shelter care is required under the provisions of section 2151.31 of the Revised Code, the court shall order his release as provided by section 2151.311 of the Revised Code. If a parent, guardian, or custodian has not been so notified and did not appear or waive appearance at the hearing, upon the filing of his affidavit stating these facts, the court shall rehear the matter without unnecessary delay.

(B) When the court conducts a hearing pursuant to division (A) of this section, all of the following apply:

(1) The court shall determine whether an alleged abused, neglected, or dependent child should remain or be placed in shelter care;

(2) The court shall determine whether there are any relatives of the child who are willing to be temporary custodians of the child. If any relative is willing to be a temporary custodian, the child would otherwise be placed or retained in shelter care, and the appointment is appropriate, the court shall appoint the relative as temporary custodian of the child, unless the court appoints another relative as temporary custodian. If it determines that the appointment of a relative as custodian would not be appropriate, it shall issue a written opinion setting forth the reasons for its determination and give a copy of the opinion to all parties and to the guardian ad litem of the child.

The court's consideration of a relative for appointment as a temporary custodian does not make that relative a party to the proceedings.

(3) The court shall make the determination and issue the written finding of facts required by section 2151.419 of the Revised Code.

(C) If a child is in shelter care following the filing of a complaint pursuant to section 2151.27 of the Revised Code or following a hearing held pursuant to division (A) of this section, any party and the guardian ad litem of the child may file a motion with the court requesting that the child be released from shelter care. The motion shall state the reasons why the child should be released from shelter care and, if a hearing has been held pursuant to division (A) of this section, any changes in the situation of the child or the parents, guardian, or custodian of the child that have occurred since that hearing and that justify the release of the child from shelter care. Upon the filing of the motion, the court shall hold a hearing in the same manner as under division (A) of this section.

(D) Each juvenile court shall designate one court employee to assist persons who are indigent in obtaining appointed counsel. The court shall include in each notice given pursuant to division (A) or (C) of this section and in each summons served upon a party pursuant to this chapter, the name and telephone number at which the designated employee can be contacted during the normal business hours of the court to arrange for prompt appointment of counsel for indigent persons.

HISTORY: 1988 S 89, eff. 1-1-89
  1975 H 164; 1969 H 320

PRACTICE AND STUDY AIDS

Baldwin's Ohio Legislative Service, 1988 Laws of Ohio, S 89—LSC Analysis, p 5-571
Kurtz & Giannelli, Ohio Juvenile Law, Text 1.04, 7.05(A)(B), 7.06(C)(D), 13.04

CROSS REFERENCES

Detention and shelter care, release to parents, hearing, Juv R 7
Temporary disposition, Juv R 13

LEGAL ENCYCLOPEDIAS AND ALR

OJur 3d: 22, Courts and Judges § 345; 26, Criminal Law § 668; 46, Family Law § 359, 430, 432, 433, 558; 72, Notice and Notices § 1 to 5, 8, 27 to 32
Am Jur 2d: 47, Juvenile Courts and Delinquent and Dependent Children § 44
Applicability of rules of evidence in juvenile delinquency proceeding. 43 ALR2d 1128
Right to and appointment of counsel in juvenile court proceedings. 60 ALR2d 691
Right to jury trial in juvenile court delinquency proceedings. 100 ALR2d 1241
Right of bail in proceedings in juvenile courts. 53 ALR3d 848

2151.32 Selection of custodian

In placing a child under any guardianship or custody other than that of its parent, the juvenile court shall, when practicable, select a person or an institution or agency governed by persons of like religious faith as that of the parents of such child, or in case of a difference in the religious faith of the parents, then of the religious faith of the child, or if the religious faith of the child is not ascertained, then of either of the parents.

HISTORY: 1953 H 1, eff. 10-1-53
  GC 1639-33

PRACTICE AND STUDY AIDS

Kurtz & Giannelli, Ohio Juvenile Law, Text 13.01

LEGAL ENCYCLOPEDIAS AND ALR

OJur 3d: 22, Courts and Judges § 345; 26, Criminal Law § 668; 46, Family Law § 359, 528, 558
Consideration and weight of religious affiliations in appointment or removal of guardian for minor child. 22 ALR2d 696

2151.33 Temporary care; emergency medical treatment; reimbursement

(A) Pending hearing of a complaint filed under section 2151.27 of the Revised Code or a motion filed or made under division (B) of this section and the service of citations, the juvenile court may make any temporary disposition of any child that it considers necessary to protect the best interest of the child and that can be made pursuant to division (B) of this section. Upon the certificate of one or more reputable practicing physicians, the court may summarily provide for emergency medical and surgical treatment that appears to be immediately necessary to preserve the health and well-being of any child concerning whom a complaint or an application for care has been filed, pending the service of a citation upon the child's parents, guardian, or custodian. The court may order the parents, guardian, or custodian, if the court finds the parents, guardian, or custodian able to do so, to reimburse the court for the expense involved in providing the emergency medical or surgical treatment. Any person who disobeys the order for reimbursement may be adjudged in contempt of court and punished accordingly.

If the emergency medical or surgical treatment is furnished to a child who is found at the hearing to be a nonresident of the county in which the court is located and if the expense of the medical or surgical treatment cannot be recovered from the parents, legal guardian, or custodian of the child, the board of county commissioners of the county in which the child has a legal settlement shall reimburse the court for the reasonable cost of the emergency medical or surgical treatment out of its general fund.

(B) After a complaint, petition, writ, or other document initiating a case dealing with an alleged or adjudicated abused, neglected, or dependent child is filed and upon the filing or making of a motion pursuant to division (C) of this section, the court, prior to the final disposition of the case, may issue any of the following temporary orders to protect the best interest of the child:

(1) An order granting temporary custody of the child to a particular party;

(2) An order for the taking of the child into custody pursuant to section 2151.31 of the Revised Code pending the outcome of the adjudicatory and dispositional hearings;

(3) An order granting, limiting, or eliminating visitation rights with respect to the child;

(4) An order for the payment of child support for the child and the continued maintenance of any medical, surgical, or hospital policies of insurance for the child that existed at the time of the filing of the complaint, petition, writ, or other document;

(5) An order requiring a party to vacate a residence that will be lawfully occupied by the child;

(6) An order requiring a party to attend an appropriate counseling program that is reasonably available to that party;

(7) Any other order that restrains or otherwise controls the conduct of any party which conduct would not be in the best interest of the child.

(C)(1) A court may issue an order pursuant to division (B) of this section only if a party files a written motion or makes an oral motion requesting the issuance of the order and stating the reasons for it. Any notice sent by the court as a result of the filing or making of a motion pursuant to this division shall contain a notice that any party to a juvenile proceeding has the right to be represented by counsel and to have counsel appointed for him if he is an indigent person.

(2) If a child is taken into custody pursuant to section 2151.31 of the Revised Code and placed in shelter care, the public children services agency or private child placing agency with which the child is placed in shelter care shall file or make a motion as described in division (C)(1) of this section before the end of the next business day immediately after the date on which the child was taken into custody and, at a minimum, shall request an order for temporary custody under division (B)(1)(a) of this section.

(3) Any court that issues an order pursuant to division (B)(2) of this section shall make the determination and issue the written finding of facts required by section 2151.419 of the Revised Code.

(D) If a motion filed or made pursuant to division (C) of this section requests the issuance of an ex parte order, the court may grant an ex parte order if it appears to the court that the best interest and the welfare of the child require that the court issue the order immediately. The person requesting the granting of an ex parte order, to the extent possible, shall give notice of the request to the parents, guardian, or custodian of the child who is the subject of the request. If the court issues the requested ex parte order, the court shall hold a hearing to review the order within seventy-two hours after it is issued or before the end of the next business day after the day on which it is issued, whichever occurs first. The court shall give written notice of the hearing to all parties to the action and shall appoint a guardian ad litem for the child prior to the hearing.

The written notice shall be given by all means that are reasonably likely to result in the party receiving actual notice and shall include all of the following:

(1) The date, time, and location of the hearing;

(2) The issues to be addressed at the hearing;

(3) A statement that every party to the hearing has a right to counsel and to court appointed counsel, if the party is indigent;

(4) The name, telephone number, and address of the person requesting the order;

(5) A copy of the order, except when it is not possible to obtain it because of the exigent circumstances in the case.

If the court does not grant an ex parte order pursuant to a motion filed or made pursuant to division (C) of this section, the court shall hold a shelter care hearing on the motion within ten days after the motion is filed. The court shall give notice of the hearing to all affected parties in the same manner as set forth in the Juvenile Rules.

(E) The court, pending the outcome of the adjudicatory and dispositional hearings, shall not issue an order granting temporary custody of a child to a public children services agency or private child placing agency pursuant to this section, unless the court determines and specifically states in the order that the continued residence of the child in his current home will be contrary to his best interest and welfare and makes the determination and issues the written finding of facts required by section 2151.419 of the Revised Code.

(F) Each public children services agency and private child placing agency that receives temporary custody of a child pursuant to this section shall maintain in the child's case record written documentation that it has placed the child, to the extent that it is consistent with the best interest, welfare, and special needs of the child, in the most family-like setting available and in close proximity to the home of the parents, custodian, or guardian of the child.

(G) For good cause shown, any court order that is issued pursuant to this section may be reviewed by the court at any time upon motion of any party to the action or upon the motion of the court.

HISTORY: 1988 S 89, eff. 1-1-89
        1953 H 1; GC 1639-28

PRACTICE AND STUDY AIDS

Baldwin's Ohio Legislative Service, 1988 Laws of Ohio, S 89—LSC Analysis, p 5-571
Kurtz & Giannelli, Ohio Juvenile Law, Text 3.06(D), 7.06(E), 7.07, 13.04, 13.10

CROSS REFERENCES

Temporary disposition, emergency medical and surgical treatment, Juv R 13
Social history, physical and mental examinations, custody investigation, Juv R 32

LEGAL ENCYCLOPEDIAS AND ALR

OJur 3d: 22, Courts and Judges § 345; 26, Criminal Law § 668; 46, Family Law § 304, 359, 448 to 550, 558; 47, Family Law § 638
Power of court or other public agency to order medical treatment over parental religious objections for child whose life is not immediately endangered. 52 ALR3d 1118
Power of court or other public agency to order medical treatment for child over parental objections not based on religious grounds. 97 ALR3d 421

DETENTION HOMES

2151.34 Treatment of children in custody; detention home

No child under eighteen years of age shall be placed in or committed to any prison, jail, or lockup or brought into any police station, vehicle, or other place where the child can come in contact or communication with any adult who has been convicted of a criminal offense or under arrest and charged with a criminal offense. A child may be confined in a place of juvenile detention for a period not to exceed ninety days, during which time a social history may be prepared to include court record, family history, personal history, school and attendance records, and any other pertinent studies and material that will be of assistance to the juvenile court in its disposition of the charges against that juvenile offender.

Upon the advice and recommendation of the judge, the board of county commissioners shall provide, by purchase, lease, construction, or otherwise, a place to be known as a detention home, which shall be within a convenient distance of the juvenile court and shall not be used for the confinement of adult persons charged with criminal offenses and in which delinquent, unruly, dependent, neglected, abused children, or juvenile traffic offenders may be detained until final disposition. Upon the joint advice and recommendation of the juvenile judges of two or more adjoining or neighboring counties, the boards of county commissioners of the counties shall form themselves into a joint board, and proceed to organize a district for the establishment and support of a detention home for the use of the juvenile courts of those counties, in which delinquent, unruly, dependent, neglected, and abused children, or juvenile traffic offenders may be detained until final disposition, by using a site or buildings already established in one of the counties, or by providing for the purchase of a site and the erection of the necessary buildings thereon.

The county or district detention home shall be maintained as provided in sections 2151.01 to 2151.54 of the Revised Code. In any county in which there is no detention home, or which is not served by a district detention home, the board of county commissioners shall provide funds for the boarding of such children temporarily in private homes. Children who are alleged to be or have been adjudged delinquent, unruly, dependent, neglected, or abused children or juvenile traffic offenders, after a complaint is filed, may be detained in the detention home or certified foster homes until final disposition of their case. The court may arrange for the boarding of such children in certified foster homes or in uncertified foster homes for a period not exceeding sixty days, subject to the supervision of the court, or may arrange with any public children services agency, or private child placing agency to receive for temporary care children within the jurisdiction of the court. A district detention home approved for such purpose by the department of youth services under section 5139.281 of the Revised Code may receive children committed to its temporary custody under section 2151.355 of the Revised Code and provide the care, treatment, and training required.

If a detention home is established as an agency of the court, or a district detention home is established by the courts of several counties as provided in this section, it shall be furnished and carried on, as far as possible, as a family home in charge of a superintendent or matron in a non-punitive neutral atmosphere. The judge, or the directing board of a district detention home, may appoint a superintendent, a matron, and other necessary employees for such home and fix their salaries. During the school year, when possible, a comparable educational program with competent and trained staff shall be provided for those children of school age. A sufficient number of trained recreational personnel shall be included among the staff to assure wholesome and profitable leisure-time activities. Medical and mental health services shall be made available to insure the courts all possible treatment facilities shall be given to those children placed under their care. In the case of a county detention home, such salaries shall be paid in the same manner as is provided by section 2151.13 of the Revised Code for other employees of the court, and the necessary expenses incurred in maintaining such detention home shall be paid by the county. In the case of a district detention home, such salaries and the necessary expenses incurred in maintaining such detention home shall be paid as provided in sections 2151.341 to 2151.3415 of the Revised Code.

If the court arranges for the board of children temporarily detained in such foster homes, or arranges for such board through any private child placing agency, a reasonable sum to be fixed by the court for the board of such children shall be paid by the county. In order to have such foster homes available for service, an agreed monthly subsidy may be paid and a fixed rate per day for care of children actually residing in the foster home.

HISTORY: 1988 S 89, eff. 1-1-89
    1986 H 428; 1981 H 440; 1976 H 1196; 1975 H 85; 1970 H 931; 1969 H 320, S 49; 128 v 1211; 1953 H 1; GC 1639-22

PRACTICE AND STUDY AIDS

Baldwin's Ohio Legislative Service, 1988 Laws of Ohio, S 89—LSC Analysis, p 5-571
    Baldwin's Ohio School Law, Text 23.04(B)
    Kurtz & Giannelli, Ohio Juvenile Law, Text 7.06, 13.07(B)

CROSS REFERENCES

Youth commission, juvenile detention, OAC Ch 5139-7

Uniform bond law, fiscal officer of detention home district designated, 133.01
    Board of county commissioners may submit bond issue to voters for support of detention home, 133.151
    Withdrawal of county from district, continuity of district tax levy, 2151.78
    Actions against political subdivisions, negligence or omission in performing governmental or proprietary functions, Ch 2744
    Division of social administration, examination of institutions, 5103.03

Conditions of financial assistance for construction or acquisition of detention home, 5139.271
    Adoption of rules for payment of assistance, 5139.29
    Tax levy law, detention home districts, 5705.01
    Resolution relative to tax levy in excess of ten-mill limitation, 5705.19
    Detention and shelter care, Juv R 7

LEGAL ENCYCLOPEDIAS AND ALR

OJur 3d: 15, Civil Servants and Other Public Officers and Employees § 253; 22, Courts and Judges § 345; 26, Criminal Law § 668; 46, Family Law § 335, 359, 379, 382, 383, 385, 391 to 393, 435, 436, 530, 532, 558; 73, Penal Institutions § 1; 76, Public Funds § 51, 56
    Am Jur 2d: 60, Penal and Correctional Institutions § 41 et seq.

2151.341 Financing operation of home; department of youth services assistance; tax assessment

A board of county commissioners that provides a detention home and the board of trustees of a district detention home may make application to the department of youth services under section 5139.281 of the Revised Code for financial assistance in defraying the cost of operating and maintaining the home. Such application shall be made on forms prescribed and furnished by the department. The joint boards of county commissioners of district detention homes shall make annual assessments of taxes sufficient to support and defray all necessary expenses of such home not paid from funds made available under section 5139.281 of the Revised Code.

HISTORY: 1981 H 440, eff. 11-23-81
    1977 S 221; 1976 H 1196; 128 v 1211

CROSS REFERENCES

Inspection of facilities by youth commission, 5139.31

LEGAL ENCYCLOPEDIAS AND ALR

OJur 3d: 22, Courts and Judges § 345; 26, Criminal Law § 668; 46, Family Law § 335, 359, 382, 385, 558

2151.342 District detention home may receive donations and bequests

When any person donates or bequeaths his real or personal estate or any part thereof, to the use and benefit of a district detention home, the board of trustees of the home may accept and use such donation or bequest as they deem for the best interests of the institution, and consistent with the conditions of such bequest.

HISTORY: 128 v 1211, eff. 11-2-59

2151.343 District detention home trustees

Immediately upon the organization of the joint board of county commissioners as provided by section 2151.34 of the Revised Code, or so soon thereafter as practicable, such joint board of county commissioners shall appoint a board of not less than five trustees, which shall hold office and perform its duties until the first annual meeting after the choice of an established site and buildings, or after the selection and purchase of a building site, at which time such joint board of county commissioners shall appoint a board of not less than five trustees, one of whom shall hold office for a term of one year, one for the term of two years, one for the term of three years, half of the remaining number for the term of four years, and the remainder for the term of five years. Annually thereafter, the joint board of county commissioners shall appoint one or more trustees, each of whom shall hold office for the term of five years, to succeed the trustee or trustees whose term of office shall expire. A trustee may be appointed to succeed himself upon such board of trustees, and all appointments to such board of trustees shall be made from persons who are recommended and approved by the juvenile court judge or judges of the county of which such person is resident. The annual meeting of the board of trustees shall be held on the first Tuesday in May in each year.

HISTORY: 128 v 1211, eff. 11-2-59

2151.344 Meetings

A majority of the board of trustees appointed under section 2151.343 of the Revised Code constitutes a quorum. Board meetings shall be held at least quarterly. The juvenile court judge of each of the counties of the district organized pursuant to section 2151.34 of the Revised Code shall attend such meetings, or shall designate a member of his staff to do so. The members of the board shall receive no compensation for their services, except their actual traveling expenses, which, when properly certified, shall be allowed and paid by the treasurer.

HISTORY: 128 v 1211, eff. 11-2-59

2151.345 Superintendent of district detention home; duties

The board of trustees of a district detention home shall appoint the superintendent thereof. Before entering upon his duties such superintendent shall give bond to the board, in such sum as it fixes, with sufficient surety, conditioned upon the full and faithful accounting of the funds and properties coming into his hands.

The superintendent shall appoint all employees, who, except for the superintendent, shall be in the classified civil service.

The superintendent under the supervision and subject to the rules and regulations of the board, shall control, manage, operate, and have general charge of the home, and shall have the custody of its property, files, and records.

The children to be admitted for care in such home, the period during which they shall be cared for in such home, and the removal and transfer of children from such home shall be determined by the juvenile courts of the respective counties.

HISTORY: 128 v 1211, eff. 11-2-59

2151.346 Management of home

District detention homes shall be established, operated, maintained, and managed in the same manner so far as applicable as county detention homes.

HISTORY: 128 v 1211, eff. 11-2-59

2151.347 Selection of site

When the board of trustees appointed under section 2151.343 of the Revised Code does not choose an established institution in one of the counties of the district, it may select a suitable site for the erection of a district detention home. Such site must be easily accessible, and when, in the judgment of the board, it is equally conducive to health, economy in purchasing or in building, and to the general interest of the home and inmates, such site shall be as near as practicable to the geographical center of the district. When only two counties form such district the site shall be as near as practicable to the dividing line between such counties.

HISTORY: 128 v 1211, eff. 11-2-59

2151.348   Each county shall be represented on board of trustees

Each county in the district, organized under section 2151.34 of the Revised Code, shall be entitled to one trustee, and in districts composed of but two counties, each county shall be entitled to not less than two trustees. In districts composed of more than four counties, the number of trustees shall be sufficiently increased so that there shall always be an uneven number of trustees constituting such board. The county in which a district detention home is located shall have not less than two trustees, who, in the interim period between the regular meetings of the board of trustees, shall act as an executive committee in the discharge of all business pertaining to the home.

HISTORY: 128 v 1211, eff. 11-2-59

2151.349   Removal of trustees

The joint board of county commissioners organized under section 2151.34 of the Revised Code may remove any trustee appointed under section 2151.343 of the Revised Code, but no such removal shall be made on account of the religious or political opinion of such trustee. The trustee appointed to fill any vacancy shall hold his office for the unexpired term of his predecessor.

HISTORY: 128 v 1211, eff. 11-2-59

2151.3410   Interim powers of board of trustees

In the interim, between the selection and purchase of a site, and the erection and occupancy of the district detention home, the joint board of county commissioners provided by section 2151.34 of the Revised Code may delegate to the board of trustees appointed under section 2151.343 of the Revised Code, such powers and duties as, in its judgment, will be of general interest or aid to the institution. Such joint board of county commissioners may appropriate a trustees' fund, to be expended by the board of trustees in payment of such contracts, purchases, or other expenses necessary to the wants or requirements of the home, which are not otherwise provided for. The board of trustees shall make a complete settlement with the joint board of county commissioners once each six months, or quarterly if required, and shall make a full report of the condition of the home and inmates, to the board of county commissioners and to the juvenile court of each of the counties.

HISTORY: 129 v 582, eff. 1-10-61
128 v 1211

2151.3411   Joint board of county commissioners; powers and duties

The choice of an established site and buildings, or the purchase of a site, stock, implements, and general farm equipment, should there be a farm, the erection of buildings, and the completion and furnishing of the district detention home for occupancy, shall be in the hands of the joint board of county commissioners organized under section 2151.34 of the Revised Code. Such joint board of county commissioners may delegate all or a portion of these duties to the board of trustees provided for under section 2151.343 of the Revised Code, under such restrictions and regulations as the joint board of county commissioners imposes.

HISTORY: 128 v 1211, eff. 11-2-59

2151.3412 Appraisal of detention home's site and buildings; funding of expenses

When an established site and buildings are used for a district detention home the joint board of county commissioners organized under section 2151.34 of the Revised Code shall cause the value of such site and buildings to be properly appraised. This appraisal value, or in case of the purchase of a site, the purchase price and the cost of all betterments and additions thereto, shall be paid by the counties comprising the district, in proportion to the taxable property of each county, as shown by its tax duplicate. The current expenses of maintaining the home not paid from funds made available under section 5139.281 of the Revised Code, and the cost of ordinary repairs thereto shall be paid by each such county in accordance with one of the following methods as approved by the joint board of county commissioners:

(A) In proportion to the number of children from such county who are maintained in the home during the year;

(B) By a levy submitted by the joint board of county commissioners under division (A) of section 5705.19 of the Revised Code and approved by the electors of the district;

(C) In proportion to the taxable property of each county, as shown by its tax duplicate;

(D) In any combination of the methods for payment described in division (A), (B), or (C) of this section.

HISTORY: 1988 H 365, eff. 6-14-88
1976 H 1196; 1972 H 258; 128 v 1211

2151.3413 Withdrawal by county from detention home district; continuity of district tax levy

The board of county commissioners of any county within a detention home district may, upon the recommendation of the juvenile court of such county, withdraw from such district and dispose of its interest in such home by selling or leasing its right, title, and interest in the site, buildings, furniture, and equipment to any counties in the district, at such price and upon such terms as are agreed upon among the boards of county commissioners of the counties concerned. Section 307.10 of the Revised Code does not apply to this section. The net proceeds of any such sale or lease shall be paid into the treasury of the withdrawing county.

Any county withdrawing from such district or from a combined district organized under sections 2151.34 and 2151.65 of the Revised Code shall continue to have levied against its tax duplicate any tax levied by the district during the period in which the county was a member of the district for current operating expenses, permanent improvements, or the retirement of bonded indebtedness. Such levy shall continue to be a levy against such duplicate of the county until such time that it expires or is renewed.

Members of the board of trustees of a district detention home who are residents of a county withdrawing from such district are deemed to have resigned their positions upon the completion of the withdrawal procedure provided by this section. Vacancies then created shall be filled according to sections 2151.343 and 2151.349 of the Revised Code.

HISTORY: 1972 H 258, eff. 1-27-72
128 v 1211

2151.3414 Designation of fiscal officer of detention home district; adjustment of accounts

The county auditor of the county having the greatest population, or, with the unanimous concurrence of the county auditors of the counties composing a district, the auditor of the county wherein the detention home is located, shall be the fiscal officer of a detention home district or a combined district organized under sections 2151.34 and 2151.65 of the Revised Code. The county auditors of the several counties composing a detention home district shall meet at the district detention home not less than once in six months, to review accounts and to transact such other duties in connection with the institution as pertain to the business of their office.

HISTORY: 1974 H 1033, eff. 10-2-74
1972 H 258; 128 v 1211

2151.3415   Board of county commissioners; expenses

Members of the board of county commissioners who meet by appointment to consider the organization of a district detention home, shall, upon presentation of properly certified accounts, be paid their necessary expenses upon a warrant drawn by the county auditor of their county.

HISTORY: 128 v 1211, eff. 11-2-59

LEGAL ENCYCLOPEDIAS AND ALR

OJur 3d: 22, Courts and Judges § 345; 26, Criminal Law § 668; 46, Family Law § 335, 359, 382, 385, 558

2151.3416   Application for financial assistance for detention home

The board of county commissioners of each county which participates in the establishment of a district detention home may apply to the department of youth services for financial assistance to defray the county's share of the cost of acquisition or construction of such home, as provided in section 5139.271 of the Revised Code. Application shall be made in accordance with rules adopted by the department. No county shall be reimbursed for expenses incurred in the acquisition or construction of a district detention home which serves a district having a population of less than one hundred thousand.

HISTORY: 1981 H 440, eff. 11-23-81
            1970 H 1135

CROSS REFERENCES

Inspection of facilities by youth services department, 5139.31

LEGAL ENCYCLOPEDIAS AND ALR

OJur 3d: 22, Courts and Judges § 345; 26, Criminal Law § 668; 46, Family Law § 335, 359, 382, 385, 558

HEARING AND DISPOSITION

2151.35   Hearing procedure; findings; record

(A) The juvenile court may conduct its hearings in an informal manner and may adjourn its hearings from time to time. In the hearing of any case, the general public may be excluded and only those persons admitted who have a direct interest in the case.

All cases involving children shall be heard separately and apart from the trial of cases against adults. The court may excuse the attendance of the child at the hearing in cases involving abused, neglected, or dependent children.

The court shall hear and determine all cases of children without a jury.

If the court at the adjudicatory hearing finds from clear and convincing evidence that the child is an abused, neglected, or dependent child, the court shall proceed, in accordance with division (B) of this section, to hold a dispositional hearing and hear the evidence as to the proper disposition to be made under section 2151.353 of the Revised Code. If the court at the adjudicatory hearing finds beyond a reasonable doubt that the child is a delinquent or unruly child or a juvenile traffic offender, the court shall proceed immediately, or at a postponed hearing, to hear the evidence as to the proper disposition to be made under sections 2151.352 to 2151.355 of the Revised Code. If the court does not find the child to be an abused, neglected, dependent, delinquent, or unruly child or a juvenile traffic offender, it shall order that the complaint be dismissed and that the child be discharged from any detention or restriction theretofore ordered.

A record of all testimony and other oral proceedings in juvenile court shall be made in all proceedings that are held pursuant to section 2151.414 of the Revised Code or in which an order of disposition may be made pursuant to division (A)(4) of section 2151.353 of the Revised Code, and shall be made upon request in any other proceedings. The record shall be made as provided in section 2301.20 of the Revised Code.

(B)(1) If the court at an adjudicatory hearing determines that a child is an abused, neglected, or dependent child, the court shall not issue a dispositional order until after the court holds a separate dispositional hearing. The dispositional hearing for an adjudicated abused, neglected, or dependent child shall be held at least one day but not more than thirty days after the adjudicatory hearing is held, except that the dispositional hearing may be held immediately after the adjudicatory hearing if all parties were served prior to the adjudicatory hearing with all documents required for the dispositional hearing and all parties consent to the dispositional hearing being held immediately after the adjudicatory hearing. The court, upon the request of any party or the guardian ad litem of the child, may continue a dispositional hearing for a reasonable time not to exceed the time limits set forth in this division to enable a party to obtain or consult counsel. The dispositional hearing shall not be held more than ninety days after the date on which the complaint in the case was filed.

If the dispositional hearing is not held within the period of time required by this division, the court, on its own motion or the motion of any party or the guardian ad litem of the child, shall dismiss the complaint without prejudice.

(2) The dispositional hearing shall be conducted in accordance with all of the following:

(a) The judge or referee who presided at the adjudicatory hearing shall preside, if possible, at the dispositional hearing;

(b) The court may admit any evidence that is material and relevant, including, but not limited to, hearsay, opinion, and documentary evidence;

(c) Medical examiners and each investigator who prepared a social history shall not be cross-examined, except upon consent of the parties, for good cause shown, or as the court in its discretion may direct. Any party may offer evidence supplementing, explaining, or disputing any information contained in the social history or other reports that may be used by the court in determining disposition.

(3) After the conclusion of the dispositional hearing, the court shall enter an appropriate judgment within seven days and shall schedule the date for the hearing to be held pursuant to section 2151.415 of the Revised Code. The court may make any order of disposition that is set forth in section 2151.353 of the Revised Code. A copy of the judgment shall be given to each party and to the child's guardian ad litem. If the judgment is conditional, the order shall state the conditions of the judgment. If the child is not returned to his own home, the court shall determine which school district shall bear the cost of his education and may fix an amount of support to be paid by the responsible parent or to be paid from public funds.

(4) As part of its dispositional order, the court may issue any order described in division (B) of section 2151.33 of the Revised Code.

(C) The court shall give all parties to the action and the child's guardian ad litem notice of the adjudicatory and dispositional hearings in accordance with the Juvenile Rules.

(D) If the court issues an order pursuant to division (A)(4) of section 2151.353 of the Revised Code committing a child to the permanent custody of a public children services agency or a private child placing agency, the parents of the child whose parental rights were terminated cease to be parties to the action upon the issuance of the order. This division is not intended to eliminate or restrict any right of the parents to appeal the permanent custody order issued pursuant to division (A)(4) of section 2151.353 of the Revised Code.

(E) Each juvenile court shall schedule its hearings in accordance with the time requirements of this chapter.

(F) In cases regarding abused, neglected, or dependent children, the court may admit any statement of a child that the court determines to be excluded by the hearsay rule if the proponent of the statement informs the adverse party of his intention to offer the statement and of the particulars of the statement, including the name of the declarant, sufficiently in advance of the hearing to provide the party with a fair opportunity to prepare to challenge, respond to, or defend against the statement, and the court determines all of the following:

(1) The statement has circumstantial guarantees of trustworthiness;

(2) The statement is offered as evidence of a material fact;

(3) The statement is more probative on the point for which it is offered than any other evidence that the proponent can procure through reasonable efforts;

(4) The general purposes of the evidence rules and the interests of justice will best be served by the admission of the statement into evidence.

(G) If a child is alleged to be an abused child, the court may order that the testimony of the child be taken by deposition. On motion of the prosecuting attorney, guardian ad litem, or any party, or in its own discretion, the court may order that the deposition be videotaped. Any deposition taken under this division shall be taken with a judge or referee present.

If a deposition taken under this division is intended to be offered as evidence at the hearing, it shall be filed with the court. Part or all of the deposition is admissible in evidence if counsel for all parties had an opportunity and similar motive at the time of the taking of the deposition to develop the testimony by direct, cross, or redirect examination and the judge determines that there is reasonable cause to believe that if the child were to testify in person at the hearing, the child would experience emotional trauma as a result of his participation at the hearing.

HISTORY: 1988 S 89, eff. 1-1-89
          1980 H 695; 1975 H 85; 1969 H 320

Note: Former 2151.35 repealed by 1969 H 320, eff. 11-19-69; 1969 S 49; 132 v S 278; 130 v H 299, H 879; 127 v 547; 125 v 324; 1953 H 1; GC 1639-30; see now 2151.352 for provisions analogous to former 2151.35.

PRACTICE AND STUDY AIDS

Baldwin's Ohio Legislative Service, 1988 Laws of Ohio, S 89—LSC Analysis, p 5-571

Kurtz & Giannelli, Ohio Juvenile Law, Text 7.05(A), 7.07(C), Ch 11, 13.02, 13.03, 15.01(C), 15.02(F), 15.04(A)

CROSS REFERENCES

Juvenile court proceedings for truancy, 3321.22

Disposition of child committed to youth services department, 5139.06

Trial by jury, O Const Art I, § 5

Waiver of rights, Juv R 3
Hearings, Juv R 27
Adjudicatory hearing, Juv R 29
Recordings of proceedings, Juv R 37

LEGAL ENCYCLOPEDIAS AND ALR

OJur 3d: 7, Automobiles and Other Vehicles § 85; 22, Courts and Judges § 345; 26, Criminal Law § 668; 44, Evidence and Witnesses § 926; 46, Family Law § 359, 382, 423, 443, 503 to 506, 515, 522, 523, 530, 558

Am Jur 2d: 47, Juvenile Courts and Delinquent and Dependent Children § 48 to 62

Applicability of rules of evidence in juvenile delinquency proceeding. 43 ALR2d 1128

Propriety of exclusion of press or other media representatives from civil trial. 79 ALR3d 401

Right of juvenile court defendant to be represented during court proceedings by parent. 11 ALR4th 719

2151.351   Limit on holding in secure setting

No child who is not alleged to be, or adjudicated, delinquent by reason of violating any law, ordinance, or regulation, a violation of which would be a crime if committed by an adult shall be held for longer than five days in a secure setting, as defined in rules adopted by the department of youth services.

HISTORY: 1981 H 440, eff. 11-23-81

Note: Former 2151.351 repealed by 1975 H 164, eff. 1-13-76; 1975 H 85; 1969 H 320; 132 v S 383.

PRACTICE AND STUDY AIDS

Kurtz & Giannelli, Ohio Juvenile Law, Text 3.02, 7.06(D)

LEGAL ENCYCLOPEDIAS AND ALR

OJur 3d: 46, Family Law § 435

2151.352   Right to counsel

A child, his parents, custodian, or other person in loco parentis of such child is entitled to representation by legal counsel at all stages of the proceedings and if, as an indigent person, he is unable to employ counsel, to have counsel provided for him pursuant to Chapter 120. of the Revised Code. If a party appears without counsel, the court shall ascertain whether he knows of his right to counsel and of his right to be provided with counsel if he is an indigent person. The court may continue the case to enable a party to obtain counsel or to be represented by the county public defender or the joint county public defender and shall provide counsel upon request pursuant to Chapter 120. of the Revised Code. Counsel must be provided for a child not represented by his parent, guardian, or custodian. If the interests of two or more such parties conflict, separate counsel shall be provided for each of them.

Section 2935.14 of the Revised Code applies to any child taken into custody. The parents, custodian, or guardian of such child, and any attorney at law representing them or the child, shall be entitled to visit such child at any reasonable time, be present at any hearing involving the child, and be given reasonable notice of such hearing.

Any report or part thereof concerning such child, which is used in the hearing and is pertinent thereto, shall for good cause shown be made available to any attorney at law representing such child and to any attorney at law representing the parents, custodian, or guardian of such child, upon written request prior to any hearing involving such child.

HISTORY: 1975 H 164, eff. 1-13-76
           1969 H 320

Note: 2151.352 contains provisions analogous to former 2151.35 repealed by 1969 H 320, eff. 11-19-69.

PRACTICE AND STUDY AIDS

Kurtz & Giannelli, Ohio Juvenile Law, Text 7.08, 9.03(B), 11.03, 11.08

CROSS REFERENCES

Right to counsel, O Const Art I §10
Waiver of rights, Juv R 3
Right to counsel, guardian ad litem, procedure, Juv R 4
Adjudicatory hearing, court to state right to counsel, Juv R 29
Social history, physical and mental examinations, custody investigation, availability of reports to counsel, Juv R 32

LEGAL ENCYCLOPEDIAS AND ALR

OJur 3d: 22, Courts and Judges § 345; 26, Criminal Law § 668; 46, Family Law § 359, 365, 382, 431, 443 to 445, 494, 504, 558

Am Jur 2d: 47, Juvenile Courts and Delinquent and Dependent Children § 38, 39

Right to and appointment of counsel in juvenile court proceedings. 60 ALR2d 691

Right of indigent parent to appointed counsel in proceeding for involuntary termination of parental rights. 80 ALR3d 1141

Right of juvenile court defendant to be represented during court proceedings by parent. 11 ALR4th 719

Validity and efficacy of minor's waiver of right to counsel—modern cases. 25 ALR4th 1072

2151.353 Disposition of abused, neglected, or dependent child

(A) If a child is adjudicated an abused, neglected, or dependent child, the court may make any of the following orders of disposition:

(1) Place the child in protective supervision;

(2) Commit the child to the temporary custody of a public children services agency, a private child placing agency, either parent, a relative residing within or outside the state, or a probation officer for placement in a certified foster home or approved foster care;

(3) Award legal custody of the child to either parent or to any other person who, prior to the dispositional hearing, files a motion requesting legal custody of the child;

(4) Commit the child to the permanent custody of a public children services agency or private child placing agency, if the court determines in accordance with division (E) of section 2151.414 of the Revised Code that the child cannot be placed with one of his parents within a reasonable time or should not be placed with either parent and determines in accordance with division (D) of section 2151.414 of the Revised Code that the permanent commitment is in the best interest of the child. If the court grants permanent custody under this division, the court, upon the request of any party, shall file a written opinion setting forth its findings of fact and conclusions of law in relation to the proceeding;

(5) Place the child in long-term foster care with a public children services agency or private child placing agency, if a public children services agency or private child placing agency requests the court to place the child in long-term foster care and if the court finds, by clear and convincing evidence, that long-term foster care is in the best interest of the child and that one of the following exists:

(a) The child, because of physical, mental, or psychological problems or needs, is unable to function in a family-like setting and must remain in residential or institutional care;

(b) The parents of the child have significant physical, mental, or psychological problems and are unable to care for the child because of those problems, adoption is not in the best interest of the child, as determined in accordance with division (D) of section 2151.414 of the Revised Code, and the child retains a significant and positive relationship with a parent or relative;

(c) The child is sixteen years of age or older, has been counseled on the permanent placement options available to him, is unwilling to accept or unable to adapt to a permanent placement, and is in an agency program preparing him for independent living.

(B) No order for permanent custody or temporary custody of a child or the placement of a child in long-term foster care shall be made pursuant to this section, unless the complaint alleging the abuse, neglect, or dependency contains a prayer requesting permanent custody, temporary custody, or the placement of the child in long-term foster care as desired, the summons served on the parents of the child contains as is appropriate a full explanation that the granting of an order for permanent custody permanently divests them of their parental rights, a full explanation that an adjudication that the child is an abused, neglected, or dependent child may result in an order of temporary custody that will cause the removal of the child from their legal custody until the court terminates the order of temporary custody or permanently divests the parents of their parental rights, or a full explanation that the granting of an order for long-term foster care will result in the removal of the child from their legal custody if any of the conditions listed in divisions (A)(5)(a) to (c) of this section are found to exist, and the summons served on the parents contains a full explanation of their right to be represented by counsel and to have counsel appointed pursuant to Chapter 120. of the Revised Code if they are indigent.

If after making disposition as authorized by division (A)(2) of this section, a motion is filed that requests permanent custody of the child, the court may grant permanent custody of the child to the movant in accordance with section 2151.414 of the Revised Code.

(C) If the court issues an order for protective supervision pursuant to division (A)(1) of this section, the court may place any reasonable restrictions upon the child, the child's parents, guardian, or custodian, or any other person, including, but not limited to, any of the following:

(1) Order a party, within forty-eight hours after the issuance of the order, to vacate the child's home indefinitely or for a specified period of time;

(2) Order a party, a parent of the child, or a physical custodian of the child to prevent any particular person from having contact with the child;

(3) Issue an order restraining or otherwise controlling the conduct of any person which conduct would not be in the best interest of the child.

(D) As part of its dispositional order, the court shall journalize a case plan for the child. The journalized case plan shall not be changed except as provided in section 2151.412 of the Revised Code.

(E)(1) The court shall retain jurisdiction over any child for whom the court issues an order of disposition pursuant to division (A) of this section or pursuant to section 2151.414 or 2151.415 of the Revised Code until the child attains the age of eighteen if the child is not mentally or physically handicapped, the child attains the age of twenty-one if the child is mentally or physically handicapped, or the child is adopted and a final decree of adoption is issued, except that the court may retain jurisdiction over the child and continue any order of disposition under division (A) of this section or under section 2151.414 or 2151.415 of the Revised Code for a specified period of time to enable the child to graduate from high school or vocational school. The court shall make an entry continuing its jurisdiction under this division in the journal.

(2) Any public children services agency, any private child placing agency, the department of human services, or any party, other than any parent whose parental rights with respect to the child have been terminated pursuant to an order issued under division (A)(4) of this section, by filing a motion with the court, may at any time request the court to modify or terminate any order of disposition issued pursuant to division (A) of this section or section 2151.414 or 2151.415 of the Revised Code. The court shall hold a hearing upon the motion as if the hearing were the original dispositional hearing and shall give all parties to the action and the guardian ad litem notice of the hearing pursuant to the Juvenile Rules.

(F) Any temporary custody order issued pursuant to division (A) of this section shall terminate one year after the earlier of the date on which the complaint in the case was filed or the child was first placed into shelter care, except that, upon the filing of a motion pursuant to section 2151.415 of the Revised Code, the temporary custody order shall continue and not terminate until the court issues a dispositional order under that section.

(G) Any order for protective supervision issued pursuant to division (A)(1) of this section shall terminate one year after the earlier of the date on which the complaint in the case was filed or the child was first placed into shelter care, unless the public children services agency or private child placing agency that prepared the child's case plan files a motion with the court requesting the extension for a period of up to six months of the original dispositional order or the extension of a previously granted extension for an additional period of up to six months. Upon the filing of the motion and the court's giving notice of the date, time, and location of the hearing to all parties and the guardian ad litem, the court shall hold a hearing on the motion. If the court determines at the hearing that the extension of the orginal dispositional order or of any previously granted extension is in the best interest of the child, the court shall issue an order extending the original dispositional order or previously granted extension for an additional period of up to six months.

At any time after the court issues an order extending an original order for protective supervision issued under division (A)(1) of this sec-

tion or a previously granted extension, the agency that filed the motion requesting the extension may request the court to terminate the dispositional order, and the court, upon receipt of the moticn, shall terminate the dispositional order.

(H) The court shall not issue a dispositional order pursuant to division (A) of this section that removes a child from his home unless the court makes the determination required by section 2151.419 of the Revised Code and includes in the dispositional order the finding of facts required by that section.

HISTORY: 1988 S 89, eff. 1-1-89
              1986 H 428; 1981 H 440; 1980 H 695; 1975 H 85; 1969 H 320

PRACTICE AND STUDY AIDS

Baldwin's Ohio Legislative Service, 1988 Laws of Ohio, S 89—LSC Analysis, p 5-571
Baldwin's Ohio School Law, Text 20.04
Kurtz & Giannelli, Ohio Juvenile Law, Text Ch 3, 7.05(B), 11.03, 11.14, 13.03 to 13.06, 13.10, 15.01(B)(F), 15.02(F)

CROSS REFERENCES

Preschool programs, employee not to have had child removed from home, 3301.54
Lists of prospective adoptive children and parents, 5103.152
Day-care facilities, certain persons not to be employed by, 5104.09
Adjudicatory hearing, Juv R 29
Dispositional hearing, procedure, Juv R 34

LEGAL ENCYCLOPEDIAS AND ALR

OJur 3d: 22, Courts and Judges § 345; 26, Criminal Law § 668; 46, Family Law § 359, 382, 397, 421, 466, 506, 514, 530, 536, 558
Am Jur 2d: 42, Infants § 56, 57; 47, Juvenile Courts and Delinquent and Dependent Children § 29 to 33
Physical abuse of child by parent as ground for termination of parent's right to child. 53 ALR3d 605
Sexual abuse of child by parent as ground for termination of parent's right to child. 58 ALR3d 1074
Liability of parent for support of child institutionalized by juvenile court. 59 ALR3d 636
Parent's involuntary confinement, or failure to care for child as result thereof, as evincing neglect, unfitness, or the like in dependency or divestiture proceeding. 79 ALR3d 417
Right of indigent parent to appointed counsel in proceeding for involuntary termination of parental rights. 80 ALR3d 1141
Validity of state statute providing for termination of parental rights. 22 ALR4th 774
Validity and application of statute allowing endangered child to be temporarily removed from parental custody. 38 ALR4th 756
Failure of state or local government entity to protect child abuse victim as violation of federal constitutional right. 79 ALR Fed 514

2151.354 Disposition of unruly child; operator's license suspension or revocation

(A) If the child is adjudged unruly the court may:

(1) Make any of the dispositions authorized under section 2151.353 of the Revised Code;

(2) Place the child on probation under such conditions as the court prescribes;

(3) Suspend or revoke the operator's or chauffeur's license issued to such child; suspend or revoke the registration of all motor vehicles registered in the name of such child.

If after making such disposition the court finds, upon further hearing, that the child is not amenable to treatment or rehabilitation under such disposition, the court may make a disposition otherwise authorized under section 2151.355 of the Revised Code.

(B) If a child is adjudged unruly for having committed any act that if committed by an adult would be a drug abuse offense as defined in section 2925.01 of the Revised Code, or a violation of division (B) of section 2917.11, or section 4511.19 of the Revised Code, the court shall suspend or revoke the temporary instruction permit or probationary operator's license issued to the child until the child attains the age of eighteen years or attends, at the discretion of the court, and satisfactorily completes a drivers' intervention program certified pursuant to section 3720.06 of the Revised Code. During the time the child is attending the program, the court shall retain any temporary instruction permit or probationary license issued to the child and shall return the permit or license when the child satisfactorily completes the program.

HISTORY: 1989 H 329, eff. 6-30-89
  1988 H 643; 1969 H 320

Note: 1989 H 329 suspended the operation of the amendment of this section by 1988 H 643, as printed above, from 3-17-89 to 6-30-89. See *Baldwin's Ohio Revised Code Annotated* for version in effect until 6-30-89.

PRACTICE AND STUDY AIDS

Baldwin's Ohio School Law, Text 20.04; Forms 20.41
Kurtz & Giannelli, Ohio Juvenile Law, Text 3.04, 3.09(A), 7.03(I), 13.08

CROSS REFERENCES

Deception to obtain matter harmful to juveniles, 2907.33
Registrar of motor vehicles, revocation of probationary driver's license, 4507.162
Adjudicatory hearing, Juv R 29
Dispositional hearing, procedure, Juv R 34

LEGAL ENCYCLOPEDIAS AND ALR

OJur 3d: 22, Courts and Judges § 345; 26, Criminal Law § 668; 46, Family Law § 359, 382, 397, 421, 506, 514, 530, 531, 536, 558

Am Jur 2d: 42, Infants § 56, 57; 47, Juvenile Courts and Delinquent and Dependent Children § 29 to 33
Physical abuse of child by parent as ground for termination of parent's right to child. 53 ALR3d 605
Sexual abuse of child by parent as ground for termination of parent's right to child. 58 ALR3d 1074
Liability of parent for support of child institutionalized by juvenile court. 59 ALR3d 636
Parent's involuntary confinement, or failure to care for child as result thereof, as evincing neglect, unfitness, or the like in dependency or divestiture proceeding. 79 ALR3d 417
Right of indigent parent to appointed counsel in proceeding for involuntary termination of parental rights. 80 ALR3d 1141
Validity of state statute providing for termination of parental rights. 22 ALR4th 774
Validity and application of statute allowing endangered child to be temporarily removed from parental custody. 38 ALR4th 756
Failure of state or local government entity to protect child abuse victim as violation of federal constitutional right. 79 ALR Fed 514

2151.355 Orders of disposition for delinquent child; records; notice to victims

(A) If a child is found by the court to be a delinquent child, the court may make any of the following orders of disposition:

(1) Any order that is authorized by section 2151.353 of the Revised Code;

(2) Place the child on probation under any conditions that the court prescribes. If the child is adjudicated a delinquent child because he violated section 2909.05, 2909.06, or 2909.07 of the Revised Code and if restitution is appropriate under the circumstances of the case, the court shall require the child to make restitution for the property damage caused by his violation as a condition of the child's probation. If the child is adjudicated a delinquent child because he violated any other section of the Revised Code, the court may require the child as a condition of his probation to make restitution for the property damage caused by his violation and for the value of the property that was the subject of the violation he committed, if it would be a theft offense, as defined in division (K) of section 2913.01 of the Revised Code, if committed by an adult. The restitution may be in the form of a cash reimbursement paid in a lump sum or in installments, the performance of repair work to restore any damaged property to its original condition, the performance of a reasonable amount of labor for the victim approximately equal to the value of the property damage caused by his violation or to the value of the property that is the subject of the violation if it would be a theft offense if committed by an adult, the performance of community service or community work, any other form of restitution devised by the

court, or any combination of the previously described forms of restitution.

(3) Commit the child to the temporary custody of any school, camp, institution, or other facility for delinquent children operated for the care of delinquent children by the county, by a district organized under section 2151.34 or 2151.65 of the Revised Code, or by a private agency or organization, within or without the state, that is authorized and qualified to provide the care, treatment, or placement required;

(4) If the child was adjudicated delinquent by reason of having committed an act that would be an aggravated felony of the third degree or a felony of the third or fourth degree if committed by an adult, commit the child to the legal custody of the department of youth services for institutionalization for an indefinite term consisting of a minimum period of six months and a maximum period not to exceed the child's attainment of the age of twenty-one years;

(5) If the child was adjudicated delinquent by reason of having committed an act that would be an aggravated felony of the first or second degree or a felony of the first or second degree if committed by an adult, commit the child to the legal custody of the department of youth services for institutionalization in a secure facility for an indefinite term consisting of a minimum period of one year and a maximum period not to exceed the child's attainment of the age of twenty-one years;

(6) If the child was adjudicated delinquent by reason of having committed an act that would be the offense of murder or aggravated murder if committed by an adult, commit the child to the legal custody of the department of youth services for institutionalization in a secure facility until the child's attainment of the age of twenty-one years;

(7) Impose a fine not to exceed fifty dollars and costs;

(8) Require the child to make restitution for all or part of the property damage caused by his delinquent act and for all or part of the value of the property that was the subject of any delinquent act that he committed and that would be a theft offense, as defined in division (K) of section 2913.01 of the Revised Code, if committed by an adult. If the court determines that the victim of the child's delinquent act was sixty-five years of age or older or permanently and totally disabled at the time of the commission of the act, the court shall, regardless of whether or not the child knew the age of the victim, consider this fact in favor of imposing restitution, but that fact shall not control the decision of the court. The restitution may be in the form of a cash reimbursement paid in a lump sum or in installments, the performance of repair work to restore any damaged property to its original con-

dition, the performance of a reasonable amount of labor for the victim, the performance of community service or community work, any other form of restitution devised by the court, or any combination of the previously described forms of restitution.

(9) Suspend or revoke the operator's license or temporary instruction permit issued to the child, or suspend or revoke the registration of all motor vehicles registered in the name of the child;

(10) Make any further disposition that the court finds proper.

(B) If a child is adjudicated delinquent for having committed any act that if committed by an adult would be a drug abuse offense as defined in section 2925.01 of the Revised Code, or a violation of division (B) of section 2917.11, or section 4511.19 of the Revised Code, the court shall suspend or revoke the temporary instruction permit or probationary operator's license issued to the child until the child attains the age of eighteen years or attends, at the discretion of the court, and satisfactorily completes a drivers' intervention program certified pursuant to section 3720.06 of the Revised Code. During the time the child is attending the program, the court shall retain any temporary instruction permit or probationary license issued to the child and shall return the permit or license when the child satisfactorily completes the program.

(C) At the dispositional hearing and prior to making any disposition pursuant to division (A) of this section, the court shall determine whether the victim of the delinquent act committed by the child was sixty-five years of age or older or permanently and totally disabled at the time the delinquent act was committed and whether the delinquent act would have been an offense of violence if committed by an adult. If the victim was sixty-five years of age or older or permanently and totally disabled at the time the act was committed, regardless of whether or not the child knew the age of the victim, and if the act would have been an offense of violence if committed by an adult, the court shall consider these facts in favor of imposing commitment under division (A)(3), (4), (5), or (6) of this section, but these facts shall not control the court's decision.

(D)(1) When a juvenile court commits a delinquent child to the custody of the department of youth services pursuant to this section, the court shall not designate the specific institution in which the child is to be placed by the department, but instead shall specify that the child is to be institutionalized or that the institutionalization is to be in a secure facility if that is required by division (A) of this section.

(2) When a juvenile court commits a delinquent child to the custody of the department of

youth services, the court shall provide the department with the child's social history, medical records, section or sections of the Revised Code violated and the degree of the violation, and any other records of the child that the department reasonably requests. The court at that time also shall give notice to the school attended by the child of the child's commitment by sending to that school a copy of the court's journal entry ordering the commitment. As soon as possible after receipt of the notice described in this section, the school shall provide the department of youth services with the child's school transcript. However, the department shall not refuse to accept a child committed to it, nor shall a child committed to it be held in a county or district detention home because of the court's failure to provide the records it is required to provide under this division or because of a school's failure to provide the records it is required to provide under this division. The department of youth services shall provide the court and the school with an updated copy of the child's school transcript and shall provide the court with a summary of the institutional record of the child when it releases the child from institutional care. The department also shall provide the court with a copy of any portion of the child's institutional record that the court specifically requests within five working days of the request.

(E) At any hearing at which a child is adjudicated delinquent, or as soon as possible after the hearing, the court shall notify all victims of the delinquent act, who may be entitled to a recovery under any of the following sections, of the right of the victims to recover, pursuant to section 3109.09 of the Revised Code, compensatory damages from the child's parents; of the right of the victims to recover, pursuant to section 3109.10 of the Revised Code, compensatory damages from the child's parents for willful and malicious assaults committed by the child; and of the right of the victims to recover an award of reparations pursuant to sections 2743.51 to 2743.72 of the Revised Code.

HISTORY: 1989 H 329, eff. 6-30-89
     1988 H 643; 1983 S 210; 1982 H 209; 1981 H 440; 1978 H 565, S 119; 1977 H 1; 1976 H 1196; 1974 H 1067; 1973 S 324; 1972 H 494; 1970 H 931; 1969 H 320

Note: 1989 H 329 suspended the operation of the amendment of this section by 1988 H 643, as printed above, from 3-17-89 to 6-30-89. See *Baldwin's Ohio Revised Code Annotated* for version in effect until 6-30-89.

PRACTICE AND STUDY AIDS

Gotherman & Babbit, Ohio Municipal Law, Text 41.07

Kurtz & Giannelli, Ohio Juvenile Law, Text 1.04, 3.02, 3.09(A), 7.03(I), 13.07, 13.08(B), 13.10, 15.01(B)(E)
Painter & Looker, Ohio Driving Under the Influence Law, Text 19.04(D)

CROSS REFERENCES

Youth commission, revocation of aftercare, OAC 5139-5-13

Victims' rights pamphlet, publication and distribution, 109.42
Political subdivision's immunity from liability, injury or death of delinquent child performing community service work, 2744.03
Department of youth services as legal custodian, commitment, 5139.01, 5139.05, 5139.06
Department of youth services, early releases in emergency overcrowding, 5139.20
Return of child to committing court, 5139.32
Placement of child in less restrictive setting, court approval required, 5139.35
Hearings, Juv R 27
Adjudicatory hearing, procedure, Juv R 29
Dispositional hearing, procedure, Juv R 34

LEGAL ENCYCLOPEDIAS AND ALR

OJur 3d: 22, Courts and Judges § 345; 26, Criminal Law § 411, 668; 46, Family Law § 359, 382, 527, 532, 537, 558; 73, Penal Institutions § 65
Am Jur 2d: 47, Juvenile Courts and Delinquent and Dependent Children § 29 to 33
Authority of court to order juvenile delinquent incarcerated in adult penal institution. 95 ALR3d 568

2151.356   Disposition of juvenile traffic offender

(A) Unless division (C) of this section applies, if a child is found to be a juvenile traffic offender, the court may make any of the following orders of disposition:

(1) Impose a fine not to exceed fifty dollars and costs;

(2) Suspend the child's probationary operator's license or the registration of all motor vehicles registered in the name of such child for such period as the court prescribes;

(3) Revoke the child's probationary operator's license or the registration of all motor vehicles registered in the name of such child;

(4) Place the child on probation;

(5) Require the child to make restitution for all damages caused by his traffic violation or any part thereof.

If after making such disposition the court finds upon further hearing that the child has failed to comply with the orders of the court and his operation of a motor vehicle constitutes him a danger to himself and to others, the court may make any disposition authorized by section 2151.355 of the Revised Code.

(B) If a child is found to be a juvenile traffic offender for having committed any act that if committed by an adult would be a drug abuse offense as defined in section 2925.01 of the Revised Code, or a violation of division (B) of section 2917.11, or section 4511.19 of the Revised Code, the court shall suspend or revoke the temporary instruction permit or probationary operator's license issued to the child until the child attains the age of eighteen years or attends, at the discretion of the court, and satisfactorily completes a drivers' intervention program certified pursuant to section 3720.06 of the Revised Code. During the time the child is attending the program, the court shall retain any temporary instruction permit or probationary license issued to the child and shall return the permit or license when the child satisfactorily completes the program.

(C) If a child is found to be a juvenile traffic offender for having committed an act that if committed by an adult would be a violation of division (B)(1) or (2) of section 4513.263 of the Revised Code, the court shall impose the appropriate fine set forth in section 4513.99 of the Revised Code. If a child is found to be a juvenile traffic offender for having committed an act that if committed by an adult would be a violation of division (B)(3) of section 4513.263 of the Revised Code, and the child is sixteen years of age or older, the court shall impose the fine set forth in division (H) of section 4513.99 of the Revised Code. If a child is found to be a juvenile traffic offender for having committed an act that if committed by an adult would be a violation of division (B)(3) of section 4513.263 of the Revised Code, and the child is under sixteen years of age, the court shall not impose a fine but may place the child on probation. Any fine imposed under this division is subject to waiver in accordance with division (F) of section 4513.263 of the Revised Code.

(D) A juvenile traffic offender is subject to sections 4509.01 to 4509.78 of the Revised Code.

HISTORY: 1989 H 329, eff. 6-30-89
     1988 H 643; 1986 H 428, S 54; 1977 H 222, H 1; 1970 H 931; 1969 H 320

Note: 1989 H 329 suspended the operation of the amendment of this section by 1988 H 643, as printed above, from 3-17-89 to 6-30-89. See *Baldwin's Ohio Revised Code Annotated* for version in effect until 6-30-89.

PRACTICE AND STUDY AIDS

Kurtz & Giannelli, Ohio Juvenile Law, Text 13.09(A) to (D), (G)

Painter & Looker, Ohio Driving Under the Influence Law, Text 19.04(C)(D)

CROSS REFERENCES

Adjudicatory hearing, procedure, Juv R 29
Dispositional hearing, procedure, Juv R 34

LEGAL ENCYCLOPEDIAS AND ALR

OJur 3d: 7, Automobiles and Other Vehicles § 85, 120; 22, Courts and Judges § 345; 26, Criminal Law § 668; 28, Criminal Law § 1680; 46, Family Law § 359, 382, 533, 558

Am Jur 2d: 47, Juvenile Courts and Delinquent and Dependent Children § 29

2151.357   Cost of education

In the manner prescribed by division (C)(2) of section 3313.64 of the Revised Code, the court shall, at the time of making any order that removes a child from his own home or that vests legal or permanent custody of the child in a person or government agency other than his parent, determine the school district that is to bear the cost of educating the child. Such determination shall be made a part of the order that provides for the child's placement or commitment.

Whenever a child is placed in a detention home established under section 2151.34 of the Revised Code or a juvenile facility established under section 2151.65 of the Revised Code, his school district as determined by the court shall pay the cost of educating the child based on the per capita cost of the educational facility within such detention home or juvenile facility. Whenever a child is placed by the court in a private institution, school, residential treatment center, or other private facility, the state shall pay to the court a subsidy to help defray the expense of educating the child in an amount equal to the product of the daily per capita educational cost of such facility and the number of days the child resides at the facility, provided that such subsidy shall not exceed five hundred dollars per year. The subsidy shall be paid quarterly to the court.

HISTORY: 1981 S 140, eff. 7-1-81
     1970 S 518; 1969 H 320

PRACTICE AND STUDY AIDS

Baldwin's Ohio School Law, Text 23.02(B), 23.03(C), 23.04(B)

Kurtz & Giannelli, Ohio Juvenile Law, Text 7.06(E), 13.01

CROSS REFERENCES

Boards of education, residency for attendance purposes, acceptance of certain tuition requirements, enforcement, 3313.64

Education of handicapped children, definitions, 3323.01

Dispositional hearing, Juv R 34

LEGAL ENCYCLOPEDIAS AND ALR

OJur 3d: 46, Family Law § 552

2151.358   Under what conditions records are to be sealed or expunged; procedures; effects; offense of divulging confidential information

(A) As used in this section, "seal a record" means to remove a record from the main file of similar records and to secure it in a separate file that contains only sealed records and that is accessible only to the juvenile court. A record that is sealed shall be destroyed by all persons and governmental bodies except the juvenile court.

(B) The department of youth services and any other institution or facility that unconditionally discharges a person who has been adjudicated a delinquent or unruly child shall immediately give notice of the discharge to the court that committed the person. The court shall note the date of discharge on a separate record of such discharges.

(C) Two years after the termination of any order made by the court or two years after the unconditional discharge of a person from the department of youth services or other institution or facility to which the person may have been committed, the court that issued the order or committed the person shall:

(1) If the person was adjudicated an unruly child, order the record of the person sealed;

(2) If the person was adjudicated a delinquent child, either order the record of the person sealed or send the person notice of his right to have his record sealed.

The court shall send the notice within ninety days after the expiration of the two-year period by certified mail to the person at his last known address. The notice shall state that the person may apply to the court for an order to seal his record, explain what sealing a record means, and explain the possible consequences of not having his record sealed.

(D) At any time after the two-year period has elapsed, any person who has been adjudicated an unruly or delinquent child may apply to the court for an order to seal his record. The court shall hold a hearing on each application within sixty days after the application is received. Notice of the hearing on the application shall be given to the prosecuting attorney and to any other public office or agency known to have a record of the prior adjudication. If the court finds that the rehabilitation of the person who was adjudicated a delinquent child has been attained to a satisfactory degree, the court may order the record of the person sealed.

(E) If the court orders the adjudication record of a person sealed pursuant to division (C) or (D) of this section, the court shall order that the proceedings in the case in which the person was adjudicated a delinquent or unruly child be deemed never to have occurred. All index references to the case and the person shall be deleted and the person and the court may properly reply that no record exists with respect to the person upon any inquiry in the matter. Inspection of records that have been ordered sealed may be permitted by the court only upon application by the person who is the subject of the sealed records and only by the persons that are named in his application.

(F) Any person who has been arrested and charged with being a delinquent child, and who is adjudicated not guilty of the charges against him in the case or who has the charges against him in the case dismissed, may apply to the court for an expungement of his record in the case. The application may be filed at any time after the person is adjudicated not guilty or the charges against the person are dismissed. The court shall give notice to the prosecuting attorney of any hearing on the application. The court may initiate the expungement proceedings on its own motion.

Any person who has been arrested and charged with being an unruly child, and who is adjudicated not guilty of the charges against him in the case or who has the charges against him in the case dismissed, may apply to the court for an expungement of his record. The court shall initiate the expungement proceedings on its own motion if an application for expungement is not filed.

If the court upon receipt of an application for expungement or upon its own motion determines that the charges against any person in any case were dismissed or that any person was adjudicated not guilty in any case, the court shall order that the records of the case be expunged and that the proceedings in the case be deemed never to have occurred. If the applicant for the expungement order, with the written consent of his parents or guardian if he is a minor and with the written approval of the court, waives in writing his right to bring any civil action based on the arrest for which the expungement order is applied, the court shall order the appropriate persons and governmental agencies to delete all index references to the case; destroy or delete all court records of the case; destroy all copies of any pictures and fingerprints taken of the person pursuant to the expunged arrest; and destroy, erase, or delete any reference to the arrest that is maintained by the state or any political subdivision of the state, except a record of the arrest that is maintained for compiling statistical data and that does not contain any reference to the person.

If the applicant for an expungement order does not waive in writing his right to bring any civil action based on the arrest for which the expungement order is applied, the court shall, in addition to ordering the deletion, destruction, or erasure of all index references and court records of the case and of all references to the arrest that are maintained by the state or any political subdivision of the state, order that a copy of all records of the case except fingerprints held by the court or a law enforcement agency be delivered to the court. The court shall seal all of the records delivered to the court in a separate file in which only sealed records are maintained. The sealed records shall be kept by the court until the statute of limitations expires for any civil action based on the arrest, any pending litigation based on the arrest is terminated, or the applicant files a written waiver of his right to bring a civil action based on the arrest. After the expiration of the statute of limitations, the termination of the pending litigation, or the filing of the waiver, the court shall destroy the sealed records.

After the expungement order has been issued, the court shall, and the person may properly, reply that no record of the case with respect to the person exists.

(G) The court shall send notice of the order to expunge or seal to any public office or agency that the court has reason to believe may have a record of the expunged or sealed record. An order to seal or expunge under this section applies to every public office or agency that has a record of the prior adjudication or arrest, regardless of whether it receives notice of the hearing on the expungement or sealing of the record or a copy of the order to expunge or seal the record. Upon the written request of a person whose record has been expunged or sealed and the presentation of a copy of the order to expunge or seal, a public office or agency shall destroy its record of the prior adjudication or arrest, except a record of the adjudication or arrest that is maintained for compiling statistical data and that does not contain any reference to the person who is the subject of the order to expunge or seal.

(H) The judgment rendered by the court under this chapter shall not impose any of the civil disabilities ordinarily imposed by conviction of a crime in that the child is not a criminal by reason of the adjudication, nor shall any child be charged or convicted of a crime in any court except as provided by this chapter. The disposition of a child under the judgment rendered or any evidence given in court is not admissible as evidence against the child in any other case or proceeding in any other court, except that the judgment rendered and the disposition of the child may be considered by any court only as to the matter of sentence or to the granting of probation. The disposition or evidence shall not operate to disqualify a child in any future civil service examination, appointment, or application.

(I) In any application for employment, license, or other right or privilege, any appearance as a witness, or any other inquiry, a person may not be questioned with respect to any arrest for which the records were expunged. If an inquiry is made in violation of this division, the person may respond as if the expunged arrest did not occur, and the person shall not be subject to any adverse action because of the arrest or the response.

(J) An officer or employer of the state or any of its political subdivisions who knowingly releases, disseminates, or makes available for any purpose involving employment, bonding, licensing, or education to any person or to any department, agency, or other instrumentality of the state, or of any of its political subdivisions, any information or other data concerning any arrest, complaint, trial, hearing, adjudication, or correctional supervision, the records of which have been expunged or sealed pursuant to this section, is guilty of divulging confidential information, a misdemeanor of the fourth degree.

HISTORY: 1984 H 37, eff. 6-22-84
          1981 H 440; 1977 H 315; 1969 H 320

PRACTICE AND STUDY AIDS

Gotherman & Babbit, Ohio Municipal Law, Text 47.47

Giannelli, Ohio Evidence Manual, Author's Comment § 501.04, 609.08, 609.09

Kurtz & Giannelli, Ohio Juvenile Law, Text 11.11(F), 13.09(G), 15.04

CROSS REFERENCES

Expungement in adult cases, 2953.31 to 2953.55
Advising child of right to expungement, Juv R 34

LEGAL ENCYCLOPEDIAS AND ALR

OJur 3d: 22, Courts and Judges § 345; 26, Criminal Law § 668; 27, Criminal Law § 1160, 1174, 1216; 28, Criminal Law § 1572; 39, Employment Relations § 34; 46, Family Law § 359, 382, 508, 526, 541, 542, 558; 72, Notice and Notices § 1 to 5, 27 to 30

Am Jur 2d: 47, Juvenile Courts and Delinquent and Dependent Children § 59

Use of judgment in prior juvenile court proceeding to impeach credibility of witness. 63 ALR3d 1112

2151.359   Control of conduct of parent, guardian, or custodian

In any proceeding wherein a child has been adjudged delinquent, unruly, abused, neglected, or dependent, on the application of a party, or the court's own motion, the court may make an order restraining or otherwise controlling the conduct of any parent, guardian, or other custodian in the relationship of such individual to the child if the court finds that such an order is necessary to:

(A) Control any conduct or relationship that will be detrimental or harmful to the child;

(B) Where such conduct or relationship will tend to defeat the execution of the order of disposition made or to be made.

Due notice of the application or motion and the grounds therefor, and an opportunity to be heard shall be given to the person against whom such order is directed.

HISTORY: 1975 H 85, eff. 11-28-75
1969 H 320

PRACTICE AND STUDY AIDS

Kurtz & Giannelli, Ohio Juvenile Law, Text 13.10

CROSS REFERENCES

Temporary disposition, Juv R 13
Dispositional hearing, Juv R 34

LEGAL ENCYCLOPEDIAS AND ALR

OJur 3d: 46, Family Law § 534

2151.3511 Deposition of child sex offense victim; presence of charged child; additional depositions; videotaped deposition; admissibility of deposition; televised or recorded testimony

(A)(1) In any proceeding in juvenile court involving a complaint in which a child is charged with a violation of section 2907.02, 2907.03, 2907.04, 2907.05, 2907.06, 2907.12, 2907.21, 2907.31, 2907.32, 2907.321, 2907.322, or 2907.323, or division (B)(5) of section 2919.22 of the Revised Code and in which an alleged victim was a child who was under eleven years of age when the complaint was filed, the juvenile judge, upon motion of an attorney for the prosecution, shall order that the testimony of the child victim be taken by deposition. The prosecution also may request that the deposition be videotaped in accordance with division (A)(2) of this section. The judge shall notify the child victim whose deposition is to be taken, the prosecution, and the attorney for the child who is charged of the date, time, and place for taking the deposition, which notice shall identify the child victim who is to be examined, and whether a request that the deposition be videotaped has been made. The child who is charged shall have the right to attend the deposition and the right to be represented by counsel. Depositions shall be taken in the manner provided in civil cases, except that the judge in the proceeding shall preside at the taking of the deposition and shall rule at that time on any objections of the prosecution or the attorney for the child charged. The prosecution and the attorney for the child charged shall have the right, as at an adjudication hearing, to full examination and cross-examination of the child victim whose deposition is to be taken. If a deposition taken under this division is intended to be offered as evidence in the proceeding it shall be filed in the juvenile court in which the action is pending, and is admissible in the manner described in division (B) of this section. If a deposition of a child victim taken under this division is admitted as evidence at the proceeding under division (B) of this section, the child victim shall not be required to testify in person at the proceeding. However, at any time before the conclusion of the proceeding, the attorney for the child charged may file a motion with the judge requesting that another deposition of the child victim be taken because new evidence material to the defense of the child charged has been discovered that the attorney for the child charged could not with reasonable diligence have discovered prior to the taking of the admitted deposition. Any such motion shall be accompanied by supporting affidavits. Upon the filing of such a motion and affidavits, the court may order that additional testimony of the child victim relative to the new evidence be taken by another deposition. If the court orders the taking of another deposition under this provision, the deposition shall be taken in accordance with this division; if the admitted deposition was a videotaped deposition taken in accordance with division (A)(2) of this section, the new deposition also shall be videotaped in accordance with that division and in other cases, the new deposition may be videotaped in accordance with that division.

(2) If the prosecution requests that a deposition to be taken under division (A)(1) of this section be videotaped, the juvenile judge shall order that the deposition be videotaped in accordance with this division. If a juvenile judge issues such an order, the judge shall exclude from the room in which the deposition is to be taken every person except the child victim giving the testimony, the judge, one or more interpreters if needed, the attorneys for the prosecution and the child who is charged with the violation, any person needed to operate the equipment to be used, one person chosen by the child victim giving the deposition, and any person whose presence the judge determines would contribute to the welfare and well-being of the child victim giving the deposition. The person chosen by the child victim shall not himself be a witness in the proceeding, and both before and during the deposition shall not discuss the testimony of the child victim with any other witness in the proceeding. To the extent feasible, any person operating the recording equipment shall be restricted to a room adjacent to the room in which the deposition is being taken, or to a location in the room in which the deposition is being taken that is behind a screen or mirror so that any such person can see and hear, but cannot be seen or heard by, the child victim giving the deposition during his deposition. The child who is charged with the violation shall be permitted

to observe and hear the testimony of the child victim giving the deposition on a monitor and shall be provided with an electronic means of immediate communication with his attorney during the testimony, but shall be restricted to a location that is such that he cannot be seen or heard by the child victim giving the deposition, except on a monitor provided for that purpose. The child victim giving the deposition shall be provided with a monitor on which he can observe, during his testimony, the child who is charged with the violation. The judge, at his discretion, may preside at the deposition by electronic means from outside the room in which the deposition is to be taken; if the judge presides in such a manner, the judge shall be provided with monitors on which he can see each person in the room in which the deposition is to be taken and with an electronic means of communication with each such person, and each person in the room shall be provided with a monitor on which he can see the judge and an electronic means of communication with the judge. A deposition that is videotaped under this division shall be taken and filed in the manner described in division (A)(1) of this section and is admissible in the manner described in this division and division (B) of this section, and if such a videotaped deposition is admitted as evidence at the proceeding, the child victim shall not be required to testify in person at the proceeding. No deposition videotaped under this division shall be admitted as evidence at any proceeding unless division (B) of this section is satisfied relative to the deposition and all of the following apply relative to the recording:

(a) The recording is both aural and visual and is recorded on film or videotape, or by other electronic means;

(b) The recording is authenticated under the Rules of Evidence and the Rules of Criminal Procedure as a fair and accurate representation of what occurred, and the recording is not altered other than at the direction and under the supervision of the judge in the proceeding;

(c) Each voice on the recording that is material to the testimony on the recording or the making of the recording, as determined by the judge, is identified;

(d) Both the prosecution and the child who is charged with the violation are afforded an opportunity to view the recording before it is shown in the proceeding.

(B)(1) At any proceeding in relation to which a deposition was taken under division (A) of this section, the deposition or a part of it is admissible in evidence upon motion of the prosecution if the testimony in the deposition or the part to be admitted is not excluded by the hearsay rule and if the deposition or the part to be admitted otherwise is admissible under the Rules of Evidence. For purposes of this division, testimony is not excluded by the hearsay rule if the testimony is not hearsay under Evidence Rule 801; if the testimony is within an exception to the hearsay rule set forth in Evidence Rule 803; if the child victim who gave the testimony is unavailable as a witness, as defined in Evidence Rule 804, and the testimony is admissible under that rule; or if both of the following apply:

(a) The child who is charged with the violation had an opportunity and similar motive at the time of the taking of the deposition to develop the testimony by direct, cross, or redirect examination;

(b) The judge determines that there is reasonable cause to believe that if the child victim who gave the testimony in the deposition were to testify in person at the proceeding, the child victim would experience serious emotional trauma as a result of his participation at the proceeding.

(2) Objections to receiving in evidence a deposition or a part of it under division (B) of this section shall be made as provided in civil actions.

(3) The provisions of divisions (A) and (B) of this section are in addition to any other provisions of the Revised Code, the Rules of Juvenile Procedure, the Rules of Criminal Procedure, or the Rules of Evidence that pertain to the taking or admission of depositions in a juvenile court proceeding, and do not limit the admissibility under any such other provisions of any deposition taken under division (A) of this section or otherwise taken.

(C) In any proceeding in juvenile court involving a complaint in which a child is charged with a violation listed in division (A)(1) of this section and in which an alleged victim was a child who was under eleven years of age when the complaint was filed, the prosecution may file a motion with the juvenile judge requesting the judge to order the testimony of the child victim to be taken in a room other than the room in which the proceeding is being conducted and be televised, by closed circuit equipment, into the room in which the proceeding is being conducted to be viewed by the child who is charged with the violation and any other persons who are not permitted in the room in which the testimony is to be taken but who would have been present during the testimony of the child victim had it been given in the room in which the proceeding is being conducted. Except for good cause shown, the prosecution shall file such a motion at least seven days before the date of the proceeding. The juvenile judge may issue such an order, upon motion of the prosecution, if the judge determines that the child victim is unavailable to testify in the room in which the proceeding is being conducted in the physical presence of the child charged with the violation, due to one or more of the reasons set forth in division (E) of this section. If a juvenile judge issues such an order, the judge shall exclude from the room in which the testimony is to be taken every person except a person described in division (A)(2) of this section. The judge, at his discretion, may preside during the giving of the testimony by electronic means from outside the room in which it is being given, subject to the limitations set forth in division (A)(2) of this section. To the extent feasible, any person operating the televising equipment shall be hidden from the sight and hearing of the child victim giving the testimony, in a manner similar to that described in division (A)(2) of this section. The child who is charged with the violation shall be permitted to observe and hear the testimony of the child victim giving the testimony on a monitor and shall be provided with an electronic means of immediate communication with his attorney during the testimony, but shall be restricted to a location that is such that he cannot be seen or heard by the child victim giving the testimony, except on a monitor provided for that purpose. The child victim giving the testimony shall be provided with a monitor on which he can observe, during his testimony, the child who is charged with the violation.

(D) In any proceeding in juvenile court involving a complaint in which a child is charged with a violation listed in division (A)(1) of this section and in which an alleged victim was a child who was under eleven years of age when the complaint was filed, the prosecution may file a motion with the juvenile judge requesting the judge to order the testimony of the child victim to be taken outside of the room in which the proceeding is being conducted and be recorded for showing in the room in which the proceeding is being conducted before the judge, the child who is charged with the violation, and any other persons who would have been present during the testimony of the child victim had it been given in the room in which the proceeding is being conducted. Except for good cause shown, the prosecution shall file such a motion at least seven days before the date of the proceeding. The juvenile judge may issue such an order, upon motion of the prosecution, if the judge determines that the child victim is unavailable to testify in the room in which the proceeding is being conducted in the physical presence of the child charged with the violation, due to one or more of the reasons set forth in division (E) of this section. If a juvenile judge issues such an order, the judge shall exclude from the room in which the testimony is to be taken every person except a person described in

division (A)(2) of this section. To the extent feasible, any person operating the recording equipment shall be hidden from the sight and hearing of the child victim giving the testimony, in a manner similar to that described in division (A)(2) of this section. The child who is charged with the violation shall be permitted to observe and hear the testimony of the child victim giving the testimony on a monitor and shall be provided with an electronic means of immediate communication with his attorney during the testimony, but shall be restricted to a location that is such that he cannot be seen or heard by the child victim giving the testimony, except on a monitor provided for that purpose. The child victim giving the testimony shall be provided with a monitor on which he can observe, during his testimony, the child who is charged with the violation. No order for the taking of testimony by recording shall be issued under this division unless the provisions set forth in divisions (A)(2)(a), (b), (c), and (d) of this section apply to the recording of the testimony.

(E) For purposes of divisions (C) and (D) of this section, a juvenile judge may order the testimony of a child victim to be taken outside of the room in which a proceeding is being conducted if the judge determines that the child victim is unavailable to testify in the room in the physical presence of the child charged with the violation due to one or more of the following circumstances:

(1) The persistent refusal of the child victim to testify despite judicial requests to do so;

(2) The inability of the child victim to communicate about the alleged violation because of extreme fear, failure of memory, or another similar reason;

(3) The substantial likelihood that the child victim will suffer serious emotional trauma from so testifying.

(F)(1) If a juvenile judge issues an order pursuant to division (C) or (D) of this section that requires the testimony of a child victim in a juvenile court proceeding to be taken outside of the room in which the proceeding is being conducted, the order shall specifically identify the child victim to whose testimony it applies, the order applies only during the testimony of the specified child victim, and the child victim giving the testimony shall not be required to testify at the proceeding other than in accordance with the order. The authority of a judge to close the taking of a deposition under division (A)(2) of this section or a proceeding under division (C) or (D) of this section is in addition to the authority of a judge to close a hearing pursuant to section 2151.35 of the Revised Code.

(2) A juvenile judge who makes any determination regarding the admissibility of a deposi-

tion under divisions (A) and (B) of this section, the videotaping of a deposition under division (A)(2) of this section, or the taking of testimony outside of the room in which a proceeding is being conducted under division (C) or (D) of this section, shall enter his determination and findings on the record in the proceeding.

HISTORY:　1986 H 108, eff. 10-14-86

PRACTICE AND STUDY AIDS

Kurtz & Giannelli, Ohio Juvenile Law, Text 11.12

CROSS REFERENCES

Bureau of criminal identification and investigation, recording and televising equipment for child sex offense victims, 109.54

LEGAL ENCYCLOPEDIAS AND ALR

Am Jur 2d: 21A, Criminal Law § 960; 47, Juvenile Courts and Delinquent and Dependent Children § 49, 52

2151.36　Support of child

When a child has been committed as provided by this chapter, the juvenile court may make an examination regarding the income of the parents, guardian, or person charged with the child's support, and may then order that the parent, guardian, or person pay for the care, maintenance, and education of the child and for expenses involved in providing orthopedic, medical or surgical treatment for, or special care of, the child. The court may enter judgment for the money due and enforce the judgment by execution as in the court of common pleas.

Any expenses incurred for the care, support, maintenance, education, medical or surgical treatment, special care of a child, who has a legal settlement in another county, shall be at the expense of the county of legal settlement, if the consent of the juvenile judge of the county of legal settlement is first obtained. When the consent is obtained, the board of county commissioners of the county in which the child has a legal settlement shall reimburse the committing court for the expense out of its general fund. If the department of human services considers it to be in the best interest of any delinquent, dependent, unruly, abused, or neglected child who has a legal settlement in a foreign state or country, that the child be returned to the state or country of legal settlement, the child may be committed to the department for the return.

Any expense ordered by the court for the care, maintenance, and education of dependent, neglected, abused, unruly, or delinquent children, or for orthopedic, medical or surgical treatment, or special care of such children under this chapter, except the part of the expense as may be paid by the state or federal government, shall be paid from the county treasury upon specifically itemized vouchers, certified to by the judge. The court shall not be responsible for any expense resulting from the commitment of children to any home, public children services agency, private child placing agency, or other institution, association, or agency, unless such expense has been authorized by the court at the time of commitment.

HISTORY:　1988 S 89, eff. 1-1-89
　　　　　　1986 H 428; 1975 H 85; 1969 S 49, H 320; 1953 H 1; GC 1639-34

PRACTICE AND STUDY AIDS

Baldwin's Ohio Legislative Service, 1988 Laws of Ohio, S 89—LSC Analysis, p 5-571
Baldwin's Ohio Domestic Relations Law, Text 37.01
Baldwin's Ohio School Law, Forms 20.41
Kurtz & Giannelli, Ohio Juvenile Law, Text 13.10

CROSS REFERENCES

Duty of husband to support family, wife to assist, 3103.03
Payment of support through withholding of earnings, workers' benefits, or bank account; procedures, 3113.21 to 3113.214
Division of social administration, disposition of money paid, 5103.11

LEGAL ENCYCLOPEDIAS AND ALR

OJur 3d: 22, Courts and Judges § 345; 26, Criminal Law § 668; 46, Family Law § 359, 382, 543, 553, to 555, 558; 47, Family Law § 636, 638
Liability of parent for support of child institutionalized by juvenile court. 59 ALR3d 636

2151.37　Institution receiving children required to make report

At any time the juvenile judge may require from an association receiving or desiring to receive children, such reports, information, and statements as he deems necessary. He may at any time require from an association or institution reports, information, or statements concerning any child committed to it by such judge under sections 2151.01 to 2151.54, inclusive, of the Revised Code.

HISTORY:　1953 H 1, eff. 10-1-53
　　　　　　GC 1639-36

LEGAL ENCYCLOPEDIAS AND ALR

OJur 3d: 46, Family Law § 376

2151.38 Custody of child by public agency; limits on authority to release; procedures

(A) When a child is committed to the legal custody of the department of youth services, the jurisdiction of the juvenile court in respect to the child so committed shall cease and terminate at the time of commitment, except as provided in divisions (B) and (C) of this section and except that if the department of youth services makes a motion to the court for the termination of permanent custody, the court upon the motion, after notice and hearing and for good cause shown, may terminate permanent custody at any time prior to the child's attainment of age eighteen. The court shall make disposition of the matter in whatever manner will serve the best interests of the child.

(B)(1) If a child is committed to the department of youth services pursuant to division (A)(4) or (5) of section 2151.355 of the Revised Code, the department shall not release the child from institutional care or institutional care in a secure facility, whichever is applicable, and as a result shall not discharge the child, order his release on parole, or assign him to a family home, group care facility, or other place for treatment or rehabilitation, prior to the expiration of the prescribed minimum periods of institutionalization unless the department, the child, or the child's parent requests an early release from institutional care or institutional care in a secure facility, whichever is applicable, from the court that committed the child and the court approves the early release in a journal entry, or unless the court on its own motion grants an early release. A request for early release by the department, the child, or the child's parent shall be made only in accordance with division (B)(2) of this section.

If a child is committed to the department of youth services pursuant to division (A)(6) of section 2151.355 of the Revised Code, the department shall not release the child from institutional care in a secure facility, and as a result shall not discharge the child, order his release on parole, or assign him to a family home, group care facility, or other place for treatment or rehabilitation, prior to the child's attainment of the age of twenty-one years unless the department, the child, or the child's parent requests an early release from institutional care in a secure facility from the court that committed the child and the court approves the early release in a journal entry, or unless the court on its own motion grants an early release. A request for early release by the department, the child, or the child's parent shall be made only in accordance with division (B)(2) of this section.

(2)(a) If the department of youth services desires to release a child committed to it pursuant to division (A)(4) or (5) of section 2151.355 of the Revised Code from institutional care or institutional care in a secure facility, whichever is applicable, prior to the expiration of the prescribed minimum periods of institutionalization or if it desires to release a child committed to it pursuant to division (A)(6) of that section from institutional care in a secure facility prior to the child's attainment of the age of twenty-one years, it shall request the court that committed the child for an early release from institutional care or institutional care in a secure facility, whichever is applicable.

Upon receipt of a request for a child's early release filed by the department at any time, or upon its own motion at any time, the court that committed the child to the department shall either approve the early release from institutional care or institutional care in a secure facility, whichever is applicable, by journal entry or schedule a time within thirty days for a hearing on whether the child is to be released.

(b) If a child who has been committed to the department pursuant to division (A)(4), (5), or (6) of section 2151.355 of the Revised Code or the parents of such a child seek his release from institutional care or institutional care in a secure facility, whichever is applicable, prior to the expiration of the prescribed minimum period of institutionalization or prior to the child's attainment of the age of twenty-one years, whichever is applicable, the child or the child's parent shall request the court that committed the child to grant such an early release. No such request initially may be made prior to the expiration of thirty days from the day on which the child began his institutional care or institutional care in a secure facility, whichever is applicable. Upon the filing of such an initial request for early release, the court either shall approve the early release, by journal entry, shall schedule a time within thirty days for a hearing on whether the child is to be released, or shall reject the request without conducting a hearing. If an initial request for early release is rejected, the child or the child's parent may make one or more subsequent requests for early release, provided that no such request shall be made prior to the expiration of thirty days from the day on which a hearing was conducted on any previous request filed by the child or the child's parent, or, in relation to a request filed immediately after an initial request, prior to the expiration of thirty days from the day on which the initial request was rejected without hearing or the day on which a hearing was conducted on the initial request. Upon the filing of any request for early release subsequent to an initial request, the court shall either approve the early release, by journal entry, or schedule a time within thirty days for a hearing on whether the child is to be released.

(c) If a court schedules a hearing to determine whether a child committed to the department should be granted an early release, either upon receipt of a request filed by the department under division (B)(2)(a) of this section or filed by the child or the child's parent in accordance with the time periods prescribed in division (B)(2)(b) of this section, or upon its own motion, it shall order the department to deliver the child to the court on the date set for the hearing and present to the court at that time a treatment plan for the child's post-institutional care. The court shall determine at the hearing whether the child should be released from institutionalization or institutionalization in a secure facility, whichever is applicable. If the court approves the early release, the department shall prepare a written treatment and rehabilitation plan for the child pursuant to division (D) of this section, which shall include the terms and conditions of his release. It shall send the committing court and the juvenile court of the county in which the child is placed a copy of the plan and the terms and conditions that it fixed. The court of the county in which the child is placed may adopt the terms and conditions set by the department as an order of the court and may add any additional consistent terms and conditions it considers appropriate. If a child is released under this division and the court of the county in which the child is placed has reason to believe that the child has not deported himself in accordance with any post-release terms and conditions established by the court in its journal entry, the court of the county in which the child is placed shall schedule a time for a hearing on whether the child violated any of the post-release terms and conditions. If the court of the county in which the child is placed determines at the hearing that the child violated any of the post-release terms and conditions established by the court in its journal entry, the court may, if it determines that the violation of the terms and conditions was a serious violation, order the child to be returned to the department for institutionalization or institutionalization in a secure facility, consistent with the original order of commitment of the child, or in any case, may make any other disposition of the child authorized by law that the court considers proper. If the court of the county in which the child is placed orders the child to be returned to a department of youth services institution, the time during which the child was institutionalized or institutionalized in a secure facility, whichever is applicable, prior to his early release shall be considered as time served in fulfilling the prescribed minimum period of institutionalization or institutionalization in a secure facility that is applicable to the child under his original order of commitment. If the court orders the child returned to a department of youth services institution, the child shall remain in institutional care for a minimum period of three months.

(C) If a child is committed to the department of youth services pursuant to division (A)(4) or (5) of section 2151.355 of the Revised Code and the child has been institutionalized or institutionalized in a secure facility, whichever is applicable, for the prescribed minimum periods of time under those divisions, the department, without approval of the court that committed the child, may release the child from institutional care or discharge the child. If the department releases the child from institutional care and then orders his release on parole or assigns him to a family home, group care facility, or other place for treatment or rehabilitation, the department also shall prepare a written treatment and rehabilitation plan for the child pursuant to division (D) of this section, which shall include the terms and conditions of his release or assignment, and shall send the committing court and the juvenile court of the county in which the child is placed a copy of the plan and the terms and conditions that it fixed. The court of the county in which the child is placed may adopt the terms and conditions as an order of the court, and may add any additional consistent terms and conditions it considers appropriate. The release, discharge, release on parole, or assignment shall be in accordance with division (C) of section 5139.06 of the Revised Code. Upon notification of a pending release, discharge, release on parole, or assignment in accordance with that division, the committing court shall enter the notification in its journal. If a child is released on parole or is assigned subject to specified terms and conditions and the court of the county in which the child is placed has reason to believe that the child has not deported himself in accordance with any post-release terms and conditions established by the court in its journal entry, the court of the county in which the child is placed may, in its discretion, schedule a time for a hearing on whether the child violated any of the post-release terms and conditions. If the court of the county in which the child is placed conducts a hearing and determines at the hearing that the child violated any of the post-release terms and conditions established in its journal entry, the court may, if it determines that the violation of the terms and conditions was a serious violation, order the child to be returned to the department of youth services for institutionalization, or in any case, may make any other disposition of the child authorized by law that the court considers proper. If the court of the county in which the child is placed orders the child to be returned to a department of youth services institution, the child shall remain institutionalized for a minimum period of three months.

(D) The department of youth services shall, prior to the release of a child pursuant to division (B) or (C) of this section:

(1) After reviewing the child's rehabilitative progress history and medical and educational records, prepare a written treatment and rehabilitation plan for the child, which shall include terms and conditions of the release;

(2) Completely discuss the terms and conditions of the plan prepared pursuant to division (D)(1) of this section and the possible penalties for violation of the plan with the child and his parents, guardian, or legal custodian;

(3) Have the plan prepared pursuant to division (D)(1) of this section signed by the child, his parents, legal guardian, or custodian, and any authority or person that is to supervise, control, and provide supportive assistance to the child at the time of the child's release pursuant to division (B) or (C) of this section;

(4) File a copy of the treatment plan prepared pursuant to division (D)(1) of this section, prior to the child's release, with the committing court and the juvenile court of the county in which the child is to be placed.

(E) The department of youth services shall file a written progress report with the committing court regarding each child released pursuant to division (B) or (C) of this section, at least once every thirty days unless specifically directed otherwise by the court. The report shall indicate the treatment and rehabilitative progress of the child and his family, if applicable, and shall include any suggestions and recommendations for alteration of the program, custody, living arrangements, or treatment. The department shall retain legal custody of a child so released until it discharges the child or until the custody is terminated as otherwise provided by law.

HISTORY: 1988 S 89, eff. 1-1-89
     1986 H 428; 1983 H 291; 1981 H 440, H 1;
     1980 H 695; 1969 H 320, S 49; 130 v H 299;
     1953 H 1; GC 1639-35

PRACTICE AND STUDY AIDS

Baldwin's Ohio Legislative Service, 1988 Laws of Ohio, S 89—LSC Analysis, p 5-571
Baldwin's Ohio Civil Practice, Text 1.03(E)
Kurtz & Giannelli, Ohio Juvenile Law, Text 13.07(B), 15.01(B)(E), 15.02(B)

CROSS REFERENCES

Department of youth services as legal custodian, release and placement defined, 5139.01

Commitment of child to department of youth services, 5139.05 to 5139.10
Duties of the department of youth services to reduce and control delinquency, 5139.11
Department of youth services, early releases in emergency overcrowding condition, 5139.20

LEGAL ENCYCLOPEDIAS AND ALR

OJur 3d: 22, Courts and Judges § 345; 26, Criminal Law § 668; 46, Family Law § 359, 382, 536, 537, 558; 73, Penal Institutions § 65
Am Jur 2d: 47, Juvenile Courts and Delinquent and Dependent Children § 32, 33

2151.39   Placement of children from other states

No person, association or agency, public or private, of another state, incorporated or otherwise, shall place a child in a family home or with an agency or institution within the boundaries of this state, either for temporary or permanent care or custody or for adoption, unless such person or association has furnished the department of human services with a medical and social history of the child, pertinent information about the family, agency, association, or institution in this state with whom the sending party desires to place the child, and any other information or financial guaranty required by the department to determine whether the proposed placement will meet the needs of the child. The department may require the party desiring the placement to agree to promptly receive and remove from the state a child brought into the state whose placement has not proven satisfactorily responsive to the needs of the child at any time until the child is adopted, reaches majority, becomes self-supporting or is discharged with the concurrence of the department. All placements proposed to be made in this state by a party located in a state which is a party to the interstate compact on the placement of children shall be made according to the provisions of sections 5103.20 to 5103.28 of the Revised Code.

HISTORY: 1986 H 428, eff. 12-23-86
     1975 H 247; 126 v 1165; 1953 H 1; GC
     1639-37

PRACTICE AND STUDY AIDS

Kurtz & Giannelli, Ohio Juvenile Law, Text 15.05(A)

CROSS REFERENCES

Placing of children, 5103.16
Advertising child placement, restriction, 5103.17

LEGAL ENCYCLOPEDIAS AND ALR

OJur 3d: 46, Family Law § 372

2151.40 Cooperation with court

Every county, township, or municipal official or department, including the prosecuting attorney, shall render all assistance and co-operation within his jurisdictional power which may further the objects of sections 2151.01 to 2151.54 of the Revised Code. All institutions or agencies to which the juvenile court sends any child shall give to the court or to any officer appointed by it such information concerning such child as said court or officer requires. The court may seek the co-operation of all societies or organizations having for their object the protection or aid of children.

On the request of the judge, when the child is represented by an attorney, or when a trial is requested the prosecuting attorney shall assist the court in presenting the evidence at any hearing or proceeding concerning an alleged or adjudicated delinquent, unruly, abused, neglected, or dependent child or juvenile traffic offender.

HISTORY: 1975 H 85, eff. 11-28-75
1969 H 320; 1953 H 1; GC 1639-55

CROSS REFERENCES

Adjudicatory hearing, Juv R 29

LEGAL ENCYCLOPEDIAS AND ALR

OJur 3d: 46, Family Law § 424

GENERAL PROVISIONS

2151.41 Abusing or contributing to delinquency of a child—Repealed

HISTORY: 1985 H 349, eff. 3-6-86
1969 H 320; 1953 H 1; GC 1639-45

Note: See now 2919.24 for provisions analogous to former 2151.41.

2151.411 Liability of parent for acts of delinquent child

A parent or guardian having custody of a child is charged with the control of such child and shall have the power to exercise parental control and authority over such child. In any case where a child is found delinquent and placed on probation, if the court finds at the hearing that the parent having custody of such child has failed or neglected to subject him to reasonable parental control and authority, and that such failure or neglect is the proximate cause of the act or acts of the child upon which the finding of delinquency is based, the court may require such parent to enter into a recogni-

zance with sufficient surety, in an amount of not more than five hundred dollars, conditioned upon the faithful discharge of the conditions of probation of such child. If the child thereafter commits a second act and is by reason thereof found delinquent, or violates the conditions of probation, and the court finds at the hearing that the failure or neglect of such parent to subject him to reasonable parental control and authority or to faithfully discharge the conditions of probation of such child on the part of such parent, is the proximate cause of the act or acts of the child upon which such second finding of delinquency is based, or upon which such child is found to have violated the conditions of his probation, the court may declare all or a part of the recognizance forfeited and the amount of such forfeited recognizance shall be applied in payment of any damages which may have been caused by such child, if there be such damages, otherwise, the proceeds therefrom, or part remaining after the payment of damages as aforesaid, shall be paid into the county treasury.

The provisions of this section as it relates to failure or neglect of parents to subject a child to reasonable parental control and authority shall be in addition to and not in substitution for any other sections of this chapter relating to failure or neglect to exercise such parental control or authority. The provisions of this section shall not apply to foster parents.

HISTORY: 127 v 21, eff. 9-13-57

PRACTICE AND STUDY AIDS

Kurtz & Giannelli, Ohio Juvenile Law, Text 13.10

CROSS REFERENCES

Victims' rights pamphlet, publication and distribution, 109.42

Damages recoverable against parent of minor who willfully damages property or commits theft offense, 3109.09

Liability of parents for assaults by their children, 3109.10

LEGAL ENCYCLOPEDIAS AND ALR

OJur 3d: 22, Courts and Judges § 345; 26, Criminal Law § 668; 46, Family Law § 301, 359, 382, 529, 558

Am Jur 2d: 59, Parent and Child § 130 to 138

Criminal responsibility of parent for act of child. 12 ALR4th 673

2151.412 Case plans

(A) Each public children services agency and private child placing agency shall prepare and maintain a case plan for any child to whom the agency is providing services and to whom any of the following applies:

(1) The agency filed a complaint pursuant to section 2151.27 of the Revised Code alleging that the child is an abused, neglected, or dependent child;

(2) The agency has temporary or permanent custody of the child;

(3) The child is living at home subject to an order for protective supervision;

(4) The child is in long-term foster care.

(B)(1) The department of human services shall adopt rules pursuant to Chapter 119. of the Revised Code setting forth the content and format of case plans required by division (A) of this section and establishing procedures for developing, implementing, and changing the case plans. The rules shall at a minimum comply with the requirements of Title IV-E of the "Social Security Act," 94 Stat. 501, 42 U.S.C. 671 (1980), as amended.

(2) The department of human services shall adopt rules pursuant to Chapter 119. of the Revised Code requiring public children services agencies and private child placing agencies to maintain case plans for children and their families who are receiving services in their homes from the agencies and for whom case plans are not required by division (A) of this section. The agencies shall maintain case plans as required by those rules; however, the case plans shall not be subject to any other provision of this section except as specifically required by the rules.

(C) Each public children services agency and private child placing agency that is required by division (A) of this section to maintain a case plan shall file the case plan with the court prior to the child's adjudicatory hearing but no later than thirty days after the earlier of the date on which the complaint in the case was filed or the child was first placed into shelter care. If the agency does not have sufficient information prior to the adjudicatory hearing to complete any part of the case plan, the agency shall specify in the case plan the additional information necessary to complete each part of the case plan and the steps that will be taken to obtain that information. All parts of the case plan shall be completed by the earlier of thirty days after the adjudicatory hearing or the date of the dispositional hearing for the child.

(D) Any agency that is required by division (A) of this section to prepare a case plan shall attempt to obtain an agreement among all parties, including, but not limited to, the parents, guardian, or custodian of the child and the guardian ad litem of the child regarding the content of the case plan. If all parties agree to the content of the case plan and the court approves it, the court shall journalize it as part of its dispositional order. If the agency cannot obtain an agreement upon the contents of the case plan or

the court does not approve it, the parties shall present evidence on the contents of the case plan at the dispositional hearing. The court, based upon the evidence presented at the dispositional hearing and the best interest of the child, shall determine the contents of the case plan and journalize it as part of the dispositional order for the child.

(E)(1) All parties are bound by the terms of the journalized case plan.

(2) No party shall change a substantive part of the case plan, including, but not limited to, the child's placement and the visitation rights of any party, unless the proposed change has been approved by all parties and the guardian ad litem. The proposed change shall be submitted to the court within seven days of approval. If the court approves the proposed change, it shall journalize the case plan with the change within fourteen days after receipt of the proposed change. The agency may implement the proposed change fourteen days after it is submitted to the court for approval, unless the court schedules a hearing under section 2151.417 of the Revised Code to consider the proposed change. If the court does not approve the proposed change to the case plan, it shall schedule a hearing under section 2151.417 of the Revised Code to be held no later than thirty days after the expiration of the fourteen-day time period and give notice of the date, time, and location of the hearing to all parties and the guardian ad litem of the child. The agency shall not implement any proposed change to a case plan pursuant to this division, unless the proposed change has been approved by the court or the court has failed to either approve and journalize the proposed change or schedule a hearing pursuant to section 2151.417 of the Revised Code on the proposed change within fourteen days after the proposed change was submitted to the court.

(3) If an agency has reasonable cause to believe that a child is suffering from illness or injury and is not receiving proper care and that an appropriate change in the child's case plan is necessary to prevent immediate or threatened physical or emotional harm, to believe that a child is in immediate danger from his surroundings and that an immediate change in the child's case plan is necessary to prevent immediate or threatened physical or emotional harm to the child, or to believe that a parent, guardian, custodian, or other member of the child's household has abused or neglected the child and that the child is in danger of immediate or threatened physical or emotional harm from that person unless the agency makes an appropriate change in the child's case plan, it may implement the change without prior agreement or a court hearing and, before the end of the next business day

after the change is made, give all parties, the guardian ad litem of the child, and the court notice of the change. If the agency, within seven days after implementing the change pursuant to this division, can obtain an agreement on the change to the case plan that is signed by all parties and the child's guardian ad litem, it shall immediately file the change with the court. If the court approves the change, it shall journalize the case plan with the change within fourteen days after receipt of the change. If the court does not approve the change to the case plan, it shall schedule a hearing under section 2151.417 of the Revised Code to be held no later than thirty days after the expiration of the fourteen-day time period and give notice of the date, time, and location of the hearing to all parties and the guardian ad litem of the child. If the agency cannot obtain the approval of all parties and the child's guardian ad litem to a change to the case plan, it shall request the court to schedule a hearing under section 2151.417 of the Revised Code to consider the change. The court shall schedule the requested hearing to be held within fourteen days after the request and give notice of the date, time, and location of the hearing to all parties and the guardian ad litem of the child.

(F)(1) All case plans for children in temporary custody shall have the following general goals:

(a) Consistent with the best interest and special needs of the child, to achieve an out-of-home placement in the least restrictive, most family-like setting available and in close proximity to the home from which the child was removed or the home in which the child will be permanently placed;

(b) To do either of the following:

(i) With all due speed eliminate the need for the out-of-home placement so that the child can return home;

(ii) If return to the child's home is not imminent and desirable, develop and implement an alternative permanent living arrangement for the child.

(2) The department of human services shall adopt rules pursuant to Chapter 119. of the Revised Code setting forth the general goals of case plans for children subject to dispositional orders for protective supervision, long-term foster care, or permanent custody.

(G) In the agency's development of a case plan and the court's review of the case plan, the agency and the court shall be guided by the following general priorities:

(1) A child who is residing with or can be placed with his parents within a reasonable time should remain in their legal custody even if an order of protective supervision is required for a reasonable period of time;

(2) If both parents of the child have abandoned the child, have relinquished custody of the child, have become incapable of supporting or caring for the child even with reasonable assistance, or have a detrimental effect on the health, safety, and best interest of the child, the child should be placed in the legal custody of a suitable member of the child's extended family.

(3) If a child described in division (G)(2) of this section has no suitable member of his extended family to accept legal custody, the child should be placed in the legal custody of a suitable nonrelative who shall be made a party to the proceedings after being given legal custody of the child;

(4) If the child has no suitable member of his extended family to accept legal custody of the child and no suitable nonrelative is available to accept legal custody of the child and, if the child temporarily cannot or should not be placed with his parents, guardian, or custodian, the child should be placed in the temporary custody of a public children services agency or a private child placing agency;

(5) If the child cannot be placed with either of his parents within a reasonable period of time or should not be placed with either, if no suitable member of the child's extended family or suitable nonrelative is available to accept legal custody of the child, and if the agency has a reasonable expectation of placing the child for adoption, the child should be committed to the permanent custody of the public children services agency or private child placing agency.

(H) The case plan for a child in temporary custody shall include at a minimum the following requirements if the child is or has been the victim of abuse or neglect or if the child witnessed the commission in the child's household of abuse or neglect against a sibling of the child, a parent of the child, or any other person in the child's household:

(1) A requirement that the child's parents, guardian, or custodian participate in mandatory counseling;

(2) A requirement that the child's parents, guardian, or custodian participate in any supportive services that are required by or provided pursuant to the child's case plan.

HISTORY: 1988 H 403, eff. 1-1-89

Note: Former 2151.412 repealed by 1988 H 403, eff. 1-1-89; 1988 S 89. Prior 2151.412 repealed by 1988 S 89, eff. 1-1-89; 1988 H 399; 1986 H 428; 1980 H 695.

Note: 1988 H 403, § 4, eff. 12-15-88, reads: This act is hereby declared to be an emergency measure necessary for the immediate preservation of the public peace, health, and safety. The reason for this necessity is that its enactment into law prior to January 1, 1989, is necessary to make new sections 2151.011 and

2151.412 of the Revised Code effective on that date and thereby prevent confusion in the preparation of case plans for abused, neglected, and dependent children in temporary custody and ensure the provision of necessary services to those children and their families. Therefore, this act shall go into immediate effect.

Note: 1988 S 89, § 5 and 7, eff. 1-1-89, read:

Section 5. If a child is in the temporary custody of a public children services agency or private child placing agency on the effective date of this act and the child is in the custody of one of his parents, his guardian, or his custodian the agency may file a motion with the court at any time prior to March 1, 1989, requesting the court to terminate the temporary custody order and to issue an order for the protective supervision of the child and give all interested parties notice of the filing of the motion. If an agency files a motion pursuant to this section, the court shall terminate the temporary custody order and issue an order for the protective supervision of the child if no interested party files a written objection to the motion at any time within thirty days after the filing of the motion. If any interested party files a written objection to the motion within the thirty-day period, the court shall hold a hearing on the motion with notice to all interested parties and issue appropriate dispositional orders after the hearing. If the agency does not file a motion pursuant to his section prior to March 1, 1989, the court shall conduct a hearing no later than April 1, 1989, with notice to all interested parties to determine whether to issue an order for the protective supervision of the child or an order requiring the child to be removed from the home of his parent or parents.

If an agency files a motion pursuant to this section, the agency shall file with the motion a case plan that is prepared pursuant to section 2151.412 of the Revised Code, as enacted by this act.

Section 7. If a public children services agency or a private child placing agency has temporary custody of a child on the effective date of this act and the child is not in the custody of one of his parents, his guardian, or his custodian on the effective date of this act, all of the following apply:

(A) The agency shall do all of the following:

(1) Prepare and file with the court a case plan for the child in accordance with section 2151.412 of the Revised Code, as enacted by this act, on or before July 1, 1989, and, after the case plan is prepared and filed with the court, comply with all provisions of section 2151.412 of the Revised Code, as enacted by this act;

(2) Conduct an administrative review of the child's case plan in accordance with section 2151.416 of the Revised Code, as renumbered and amended by this act, on or before the sixth month after the court conducts its first review hearing as required by division (B) of this section and continue to conduct internal agency reviews of the child's case plan no later than every six months in accordance with that section until the child attains the age of eighteen if the child is not mentally or physically handicapped, the child attains the age of twenty-one if the child is mentally or physically handicapped, the child is adopted and a final decree of adoption is issued, or the court otherwise terminates the custody arrangement.

(B) The court with jurisdiction over the child shall conduct its first review hearing under division (C) of section 2151.417 of the Revised Code to review the child's case plan after the case plan is filed pursuant to division (A)(1) of this section on or before July 1, 1989, and shall continue to hold review hearings no later than every twelve months in accordance with division (C) of section 2151.417 of the Revised Code until the child attains the age of eighteen if the child is not mentally or physically handicapped, the child attains the age of twenty-one if the child is mentally or physically handicapped, the child is adopted and a final decree of adoption is issued, or the court otherwise terminates the custody arrangement.

(C) The temporary custody order shall terminate on or before the earlier of January 1, 1990, or eighteen months after the last annual review was held or should have been held with respect to the child under section 5103.151 of the Revised Code, as that section existed immediately prior to the effective date of this act.

Note: See note under 2151.414 from 1988 S 89, § 4.

PRACTICE AND STUDY AIDS

Baldwin's Ohio Legislative Service, 1988 Laws of Ohio, S 89—LSC Analysis, p 5-571

Kurtz & Giannelli, Ohio Juvenile Law, Text 3.09(C), 13.05, 13.06(B), 13.07(B), 15.01(F), 15.02(B)

CROSS REFERENCES

Placing of child in institution, agency filing complaint and case plan, 5103.15

LEGAL ENCYCLOPEDIAS AND ALR

OJur 3d: 46, Family Law § 530, 536; 72, Notice and Notices § 1 to 5, 8, 27 to 30

2151.413　Motion for permanent custody

(A) A public children services agency or private child placing agency that, pursuant to an order of disposition under division (A)(2) of section 2151.353 of the Revised Code or under any version of section 2151.353 of the Revised Code that existed prior to the effective date of this amendment, is granted temporary custody of a child who is not abandoned or orphaned or of an abandoned child whose parents have been located may file a motion in the court that made the disposition of the child requesting permanent custody of the child if a period of at least six months has elapsed since the order of temporary custody was issued or the initial filing of the case plan with the court if the child is an abandoned child whose parents have been located.

(B) A public children services agency or private child placing agency that, pursuant to an order of disposition under division (A)(2) of section 2151.353 of the Revised Code or under any version of section 2151.353 of the Revised Code that existed prior to the effective date of this amendment, is granted temporary custody of a child who is abandoned or orphaned may file a motion in the court that made the disposition of the child requesting permanent custody of the child, if the child is abandoned, whenever it can show the court that the parents cannot be located and, if the child is orphaned, whenever it can show that no relative of the child is able to take legal custody of the child.

(C) Any agency that files a motion for permanent custody under this section shall include in the case plan of the child who is the subject of the motion, a specific plan of the agency's actions to seek an adoptive family for the child and to prepare the child for adoption.

HISTORY: 1988 S 89, eff. 1-1-89
    1980 H 695

PRACTICE AND STUDY AIDS

Baldwin's Ohio Legislative Service, 1988 Laws of Ohio, S 89—LSC Analysis, p 5-571
    Kurtz & Giannelli, Ohio Juvenile Law, Text 7.03(I), 13.06

LEGAL ENCYCLOPEDIAS AND ALR

OJur 3d: 46, Family Law § 536

2151.414   Procedures upon motion

(A) Upon the filing of a motion pursuant to section 2151.413 of the Revised Code for permanent custody of a child by a public children services agency or private child placing agency that has temporary custody of the child, the court shall schedule a hearing and give notice of the filing of the motion and of the hearing, in accordance with section 2151.29 of the Revised Code, to all parties to the action and to the child's guardian ad litem. The notice also shall contain a full explanation that the granting of permanent custody permanently divests the parents of their parental rights, a full explanation of their right to be represented by counsel and to have counsel appointed pursuant to Chapter 120. of the Revised Code if they are indigent, and the name and telephone number of the court employee designated by the court pursuant to section 2151.314 of the Revised Code to arrange for the prompt appointment of counsel for indigent persons. The court shall conduct a hearing in accordance with section 2151.35 of the Revised Code to determine if it is in the best interest of the child to permanently terminate parental rights and grant permanent custody to the agency that filed the motion. The adjudication that the child is an abused, neglected, or dependent child and the grant of temporary custody to the agency that filed the motion shall not be readjudicated at the hearing and shall not be affected by a denial of the motion for permanent custody.

(B) The court may grant permanent custody of a child to a movant if the court determines at the hearing held pursuant to division (A) of this section, by clear and convincing evidence, that it is in the best interest of the child to grant permanent custody of the child to the agency that filed the motion for permanent custody and that any of the following apply:

(1) The child is not abandoned or orphaned and the child cannot be placed with either of his parents within a reasonable time or should not be placed with his parents;

(2) The child is abandoned and the parents cannot be located;

(3) The child is orphaned and there are no relatives of the child who are able to take permanent custody.

(C) In making the determinations required by this section or division (A)(4) of section 2151.353 of the Revised Code, a court shall not consider the effect the granting of permanent custody to the agency would have upon any parent of the child. A written report of the guardian ad litem of the child shall be submitted to the court prior to or at the time of the hearing held pursuant to division (A) of this section or section 2151.35 of the Revised Code but shall not be submitted under oath.

If the court grants permanent custody of a child to a movant under this division, the court, upon the request of any party, shall file a written opinion setting forth its findings of fact and conclusions of law in relation to the proceeding. The court shall not deny an agency's motion for permanent custody solely because the agency failed to implement any particular aspect of the child's case plan.

(D) In determining the best interest of a child at a hearing held pursuant to division (A) of this section or for the purposes of division (A)(4) of section 2151.353 of the Revised Code, the court shall consider all relevant factors, including, but not limited to, the following:

(1) The reasonable probability of the child being adopted, whether an adoptive placement would positively benefit the child, and whether a grant of permanent custody would facilitate an adoption;

(2) The interaction and interrelationship of the child with his parents, siblings, relatives, foster parents and out-of-home providers, and any other person who may significantly affect the child;

(3) The wishes of the child, as expressed directly by the child or through his guardian ad litem, with due regard for the maturity of the child;

(4) The custodial history of the child;

(5) The child's need for a legally secure permanent placement and whether that type of

placement can be achieved without a grant of permanent custody to the agency.

(E) In determining at a hearing held pursuant to division (A) of this section or for the purposes of division (A)(4) of section 2151.353 of the Revised Code whether a child cannot be placed with either of his parents within a reasonable period of time or should not be placed with his parents, the court shall consider all relevant evidence. If the court determines, by clear and convincing evidence, at a hearing held pursuant to division (A) of this section or for the purposes of division (A)(4) of section 2151.353 of the Revised Code that one or more of the following exist as to each of the child's parents, the court shall enter a finding that the child cannot be placed with either of his parents within a reasonable time or should not be placed with his parents:

(1) Following the placement of the child outside his home and notwithstanding reasonable case planning and diligent efforts by the agency to assist the parents to remedy the problems that initially caused the child to be placed outside the home, the parent has failed continuously and repeatedly for a period of six months or more to substantially remedy the conditions causing the child to be placed outside his home. In determining whether the parents have substantially remedied those conditions, the court shall consider parental utilization of medical, psychiatric, psychological, and other social and rehabilitative services and material resources that were made available to the parents for the purpose of changing parental conduct to allow them to resume and maintain parental duties.

(2) The severe and chronic mental illness, severe and chronic emotional illness, severe mental retardation, severe physical disability, or chemical dependency of the parent makes the parent unable to provide an adequate permanent home for the child at the present time and in the forseeable future;

(3) The parent committed any abuse as described in section 2151.031 of the Revised Code against the child, caused the child to suffer any neglect as described in section 2151.03 of the Revised Code, or allowed the child to suffer any neglect as described in section 2151.03 of the Revised Code between the date that the original complaint alleging abuse or neglect was filed and the date of the filing of the motion for permanent custody;

(4) The parent has demonstrated a lack of commitment toward the child by failing to regularly support, visit, or communicate with the child when able to do so, or by other actions showing an unwillingness to provide an adequate permanent home for the child;

(5) The parent is incarcerated for an offense committed against the child or a sibling of the child;

(6) The parent is incarcerated at the time of the filing of the motion for permanent custody or the dispositional hearing of the child and will not be available to care for the child for at least eighteen months after the filing of the motion for permanent custody or the dispositional hearing;

(7) The parent is repeatedly incarcerated and the repeated incarceration prevents the parent from providing care for the child;

(8) The parent for any reason is unwilling to provide food, clothing, shelter, and other basic necessities for the child or to prevent the child from suffering physical, emotional, or sexual abuse or physical, emotional, or mental neglect.

(F) The parents of a child for whom the court has issued an order granting permanent custody pursuant to this section, upon the issuance of the order, cease to be parties to the action. This division is not intended to eliminate or restrict any right of the parents to appeal the granting of permanent custody of their child to a movant pursuant to this section.

HISTORY: 1988 S 89, eff. 1-1-89
1980 H 695

Note: Per In re Vickers Children, 14 App(3d) 201, 14 OBR 228, 470 NE(2d) 438 (Butler 1983), 2151.414 is in conflict with Juvenile Rule 29 and 34.

Note: 1988 S 89, § 4, eff. 1-1-89, reads:
If a child is in the permanent custody of a public children services agency or private child placing agency on the effective date of this act, both of the following apply:
(A) The agency shall do both of the following:
(1) Prepare and file with the court a case plan for the child in accordance with section 2151.412 of the Revised Code, as enacted by this act, on or before July 1, 1989, and, after the case plan is prepared and filed with the court, comply with all provisions of section 2151.412 of the Revised Code, as enacted by this act.
(2) Conduct an administrative review of the child's case plan in accordance with section 2151.416 of the Revised Code, as renumbered and amended by this act, on or before the sixth month after the court conducts its first review hearing as required by division (B) of this section and continue to conduct administrative reviews of the child's case plan no later than every six months in accordance with that section until the child attains the age of eighteen if the child is not mentally or physically handicapped, the child attains the age of twenty-one if the child is mentally or physically handicapped, the child is adopted and a final decree of adoption is issued, or the court otherwise terminates the custody arrangement.
(B) The court with jurisdiction over the child shall conduct its first review hearing in accordance with division (C) of section 2151.417 of the Revised Code to review the child's case plan after the case plan is filed pursuant to division (A)(1) of this section and on

or before July 1, 1989, and shall continue to hold review hearings no later than every twelve months in accordance with division (C) of section 2151.417 of the Revised Code until the child attains the age of eighteen if the child is not mentally or physically handicapped, the child attains the age of twenty-one if the child is mentally or physically handicapped, the child is adopted and a final decree of adoption is issued, or the court otherwise terminates the custody arrangement.

PRACTICE AND STUDY AIDS

Baldwin's Ohio Legislative Service, 1988 Laws of Ohio, S 89—LSC Analysis, p 5-571
Kurtz & Giannelli, Ohio Juvenile Law, Text 7.05(A)(B), 11.14, 13.03, 13.06, 15.01(F), 15.02(F)

CROSS REFERENCES

Adjudicatory hearing, Juv R 29
Dispositional hearing, Juv R 34

LEGAL ENCYCLOPEDIAS AND ALR

OJur 3d: 22, Courts and Judges § 345; 26, Criminal Law § 668; 46, Family Law § 359, 382, 469, 506, 536, 558; 72, Notice and Notices § 1 to 5, 8, 27 to 30
Right of indigent parent to appointed counsel in proceeding for involuntary termination of parental rights. 80 ALR3d 1141

2151.415 Motions for dispositional orders; procedure

(A) Any public children services agency or private child placing agency that has been given temporary custody of a child pursuant to section 2151.353 of the Revised Code, not later than thirty days prior to the earlier of the date for the termination of the custody order pursuant to division (F) of section 2151.353 of the Revised Code or the date set at the dispositional hearing for the hearing to be held pursuant to this section, shall file a motion with the court that issued the order of disposition requesting that any of the following orders of disposition of the child be issued by the court:

(1) An order that the child be returned to his home and the custody of his parents, guardian, or custodian without any restrictions;

(2) An order for protective supervision;

(3) An order that the child be placed in the legal custody of a relative or other interested individual;

(4) An order permanently terminating the parental rights of the child's parents;

(5) An order that the child be placed in long-term foster care;

(6) In accordance with division (D) of this section, an order for the extension of temporary custody.

(B) Upon the filing of a motion pursuant to division (A) of this section, the court shall hold a dispositional hearing on the date set at the dispositional hearing held pursuant to section 2151.35 of the Revised Code, with notice to all parties to the action in accordance with the Juvenile Rules. After the dispositional hearing or at a date after the dispositional hearing that is not later than one year after the earlier of the date on which the complaint in the case was filed or the child was first placed into shelter care, the court, in accordance with the best interest of the child as supported by the evidence presented at the dispositional hearing, shall issue an order of disposition as set forth in division (A) of this section, except that all orders for permanent custody shall be made in accordance with sections 2151.413 and 2151.414 of the Revised Code.

(C)(1) If an agency pursuant to division (A) of this section requests the court to place a child into long-term foster care, the agency shall present evidence to indicate why long-term foster care is appropriate for the child, including, but not limited to, evidence that the agency has tried or considered all other possible dispositions for the child. A court shall not place a child in long-term foster care, unless it finds, by clear and convincing evidence, that long-term foster care is in the best interest of the child and that one of the following exists:

(a) The child, because of physical, mental, or psychological problems or needs, is unable to function in a family-like setting and must remain in residential or institutional care;

(b) The parents of the child have significant physical, mental, or psychological problems and are unable to care for the child because of those problems, adoption is not in the best interest of the child, as determined in accordance with division (D) of section 2151.414 of the Revised Code, and the child retains a significant and positive relationship with a parent or relative;

(c) The child is sixteen years of age or older, has been counseled on the permanent placement options available to him, is unwilling to accept or unable to adapt to a permanent placement, and is in an agency program preparing him for independent living.

(2) If the court issues an order placing a child in long-term foster care, both of the following apply:

(a) The court shall issue a finding of fact setting forth the reasons for its finding;

(b) The agency may make any appropriate placement for the child and shall develop a case plan for the child that is designed to assist the child in finding a permanent home outside of the home of the parents.

(D)(1) If an agency pursuant to division (A) of this section requests the court to grant an extension of temporary custody for a period of up to six months, the agency shall include in the motion an explanation of the progress on the case plan of the child and of its expectations of reunifying the child with its family, or placing the child in a permanent placement, within the extension period. The court shall schedule a hearing on the motion, give notice of its date, time, and location to all parties and the guardian ad litem of the child, and at the hearing consider the evidence presented by the parties and the guardian ad litem. The court may extend the temporary custody order of the child for a period of up to six months, if it determines at the hearing, by clear and convincing evidence, that the extension is in the best interest of the child, there has been significant progress on the case plan of the child, and there is reasonable cause to believe that the child will be reunified with one of his parents or otherwise permanently placed within the period of extension. If the court extends the temporary custody of the child pursuant to this division, upon request it shall issue findings of fact.

(2) Prior to the end of the extension granted pursuant to division (D)(1) of this section, the agency that received the extension shall file a motion with the court requesting the issuance of one of the orders of disposition set forth in divisions (A)(1) to (5) of this section or requesting the court to extend the temporary custody order of the child for an additional period of up to six months. If the agency requests the issuance of an order of disposition under divisions (A)(1) to (5) of this section or does not file any motion prior to the expiration of the extension period, the court shall conduct a hearing in accordance with division (B) of this section and issue an appropriate order of disposition.

If the agency requests an additional extension of up to six months of the temporary custody order of the child, the court shall schedule and conduct a hearing in the manner set forth in division (D)(1) of this section. The court may extend the temporary custody order of the child for an additional period of up to six months if it determines at the hearing, by clear and convincing evidence, that the additional extension is in the best interest of the child, there has been substantial additional progress since the original extension of temporary custody in the case plan of the child, there has been substantial additional progress since the original extension of temporary custody toward reunifying the child with one of his parents or otherwise permanently placing the child, and there is reasonable cause to believe that the child will be reunified with one of his parents or otherwise placed in a permanent setting before the expiration of the additional extension period. If the court extends the temporary custody of the child for an additional period pursuant to this division, upon request it shall issue findings of fact.

(3) Prior to the end of the extension of a temporary custody order granted pursuant to division (D)(2) of this section, the agency that received the extension shall file a motion with the court requesting the issuance of one of the orders of disposition set forth in divisions (A)(1) to (5) of this section. Upon the filing of the motion by the agency or, if the agency does not file the motion prior to the expiration of the extension period, upon its own motion, the court, prior to the expiration of the extension period, shall conduct a hearing in accordance with division (B) of this section and issue an appropriate order of disposition.

(4) No court shall grant an agency more than two extensions of temporary custody pursuant to division (D) of this section.

(E) After the issuance of an order pursuant to division (B) of this section, the court shall retain jurisdiction over the child until the child attains the age of eighteen if the child is not mentally or physically handicapped, the child attains the age of twenty-one if the child is mentally or physically handicapped, or the child is adopted and a final decree of adoption is issued, unless the court's jurisdiction over the child is extended pursuant to division (E) of section 2151.353 of the Revised Code.

(F) The court, on its own motion or the motion of the agency or person with legal custody of the child, the child's guardian ad litem, or any other party to the action, may conduct a hearing with notice to all parties to determine whether any order issued pursuant to this section should be modified or terminated or whether any other dispositional order set forth in divisions (A)(1) to (5) of this section should be issued. After the hearing and consideration of all the evidence presented, the court, in accordance with the best interest of the child, may modify or terminate any order issued pursuant to this section or issue any dispositional order set forth in divisions (A)(1) to (5) of this section.

(G) If the court places a child in long-term foster care with a public children services agency or a private child placing agency pursuant to this section, the agency with which the child is placed in long-term foster care shall not remove the child from the residential placement in which the child is originally placed pursuant to the case plan for the child or in which the child is placed with court approval pursuant to this division, unless the court and the guardian ad litem are given notice of the intended removal and the court issues an order approving the removal or unless the removal is necessary to protect the child from physical or emotional harm and the agency gives the court notice of the removal and of the reasons why the removal is necessary to protect the child from physical or emotional harm immediately after the removal of the child from his prior setting.

(H) If the hearing held under this section takes the place of an administrative review that otherwise would have been held under section 2151.416 of the Revised Code, the court at the hearing held under this section shall do all of the following in addition to any other requirements of this section:

(1) Determine the continued necessity for and the appropriateness of the child's placement;

(2) Determine the extent of compliance with the child's case plan;

(3) Determine the extent of progress that has been made toward alleviating or mitigating the causes necessitating the child's placement in foster care;

(4) Project a likely date by which the child may be returned to his home or placed for adoption or legal guardianship;

(5) Determine the future status of the child.

HISTORY: 1988 S 89, eff. 1-1-89

PRACTICE AND STUDY AIDS

Baldwin's Ohio Legislative Service, 1988 Laws of Ohio, S 89—LSC Analysis, p 5-571

Kurtz & Giannelli, Ohio Juvenile Law, Text 1.04, 13.06(A), 15.01(B)(F)

2151.416 Administrative review of case plans

(A) Each agency that is required by section 2151.412 of the Revised Code to prepare a case plan for a child shall complete a semiannual administrative review of the case plan no later than six months after the earlier of the date on which the complaint in the case was filed or the child was first placed in shelter care. After the first administrative review, the agency shall complete semiannual administrative reviews no later than every six months. If the court issues an order pursuant to section 2151.414 or 2151.415 of the Revised Code, the agency shall complete an administrative review no later than six months after the court's order and continue to complete administrative reviews no later than every six months after the first review, except that the court hearing held pursuant to section 2151.417 of the Revised Code may take the place of any administrative review that would otherwise be held at the time of the court hearing.

(B) Each administrative review required by division (A) of this section shall be conducted by a review panel of at least three persons, including, but not limited to, both of the following:

(1) A caseworker with day-to-day responsibility for, or familiarity with, the management of the child's case plan;

(2) A person who is not responsible for the management of the child's case plan or for the delivery of services to the child or the parents, guardian, or custodian of the child.

(C) Each semiannual administrative review shall include, but not be limited to, a joint meeting by the review panel with the parents, guardian, or custodian of the child, the guardian ad litem of the child, and the child's foster care provider and shall include an opportunity for those persons to submit any written materials to be included in the case record of the child. If a parent, guardian, custodian, guardian ad litem, or foster care provider of the child cannot be located after reasonable efforts to do so or declines to participate in the administrative review after being contacted, the agency does not have to include them in the joint meeting.

(D) The agency shall prepare a written summary of the semiannual administrative review that shall include, but not be limited to, all of the following:

(1) A conclusion regarding the appropriateness of the child's foster care placement;

(2) The extent of the compliance with the case plan of all parties;

(3) The extent of progress that has been made toward alleviating the circumstances that required the agency to assume temporary custody of the child;

(4) An estimated date by which the child may be returned to his home or placed for adoption or legal custody;

(5) An updated case plan that includes any changes that the agency is proposing in the case plan;

(6) The recommendation of the agency as to which agency or person should be given custodial rights over the child for the six-month period after the administrative review;

(7) The names of all persons who participated in the administrative review.

(E)(1) If the agency, the parents, guardian, or custodian of the child, and the guardian ad litem and the attorney of the child agree to the need for changes in the case plan of the child and the terms of the changes, the revised case plan shall be signed by all parties and the guardian ad litem of the child and filed with the court together with the written summary of the administrative review no later than seven days after the completion of the administrative review. If the court does not object to the revised case plan, it shall journalize the case plan, within fourteen days after it is filed with the court. The agency may implement the proposed changes fourteen days after they are submitted to the court for approval, unless the court schedules a hearing under section 2151.417 of the Revised Code to consider the proposed changes. If the court does not approve of the revised case plan, it shall schedule a review hearing to be held pursuant to section 2151.417 of the Revised Code no later than thirty days after the filing of the case plan and written summary and give notice of the date, time, and location of the hearing to all parties and the guardian ad litem of the child.

(2) If the agency, the parents, guardian, or custodian of the child, and the guardian ad litem and the attorney of the child do not agree to the need for changes to the case plan and to all of the proposed changes, the agency shall file its written summary of the administrative review with the court no later than seven days after the completion of the administrative review and request the court to conduct a review hearing pursuant to section 2151.417 of the Revised Code. The court shall schedule the hearing to be held no later than thirty days after the written summary was filed with the court and shall give notice of the date, time, and location of the hearing to all parties and the guardian ad litem of the child.

(F) The department of human services may adopt rules pursuant to Chapter 119. of the Revised Code for procedures and standard forms for conducting administrative reviews pursuant to this section.

(G) The juvenile court that receives the written summary of the administrative review, upon determining, either from the written summary, case plan, or otherwise, that the custody or care arrangement is not in the best interest of the child, may terminate the custody of an agency and place the child in the custody of another public or private organization, society, association, agency, or individual certified pursuant to sections 5103.02 and 5103.03 of the Revised Code.

(H) The department of human services shall report annually to the public and to the general assembly on the results of the review of case plans of each agency and on the results of the summaries submitted to the department under section 3107.10 of the Revised Code. The annual report shall include any information that is required by the department, including, but not limited to, all of the following:

(1) A statistical analysis of the administrative reviews conducted pursuant to this section and section 2151.417 of the Revised Code;

(2) The number of children in temporary or permanent custody for whom an administrative review was conducted, the number of children whose custody status changed during the period, the number of children whose residential placement changed during the period, and the number of residential placement changes for each child during the period;

(3) An analysis of the utilization of public social services by agencies and parents or guardians, and the utilization of the adoption listing service of the department pursuant to section 5103.152 of the Revised Code;

(4) A compilation and analysis of data submitted to the department under section 3107.10 of the Revised Code.

HISTORY: 1988 S 89, eff. 1-1-89

Note: 2151.416 is former 5103.151 amended and recodified by 1988 S 89, eff. 1-1-89; 1986 H 428; 1980 H 695; 1978 H 832; 1976 H 156.

Note: See note under 2151.414 from 1988 S 89, § 4.

Note: See note under 2151.412 from 1988 S 89, § 5.

PRACTICE AND STUDY AIDS

Baldwin's Ohio Legislative Service, 1988 Laws of Ohio, S 89—LSC Analysis, p 5-571

Kurtz & Giannelli, Ohio Juvenile Law, Text 1.04, 15.01(F)

CROSS REFERENCES

Definitions used for public welfare personal information systems, OAC 5101-9-30

Use and disclosure of personal information concerning recipients, providers, OAC 5101-9-35, 5101-9-36

Participation in interconnected or combined systems, OAC 5101-9-41

Requirement of annual review for each child in care or custody, OAC 5101:2-42-45

LEGAL ENCYCLOPEDIAS AND ALR

OJur 3d: 46, Family Law § 339, 449

Am Jur 2d: 47, Juvenile Courts and Delinquent and Dependent Children § 33

2151.417 Review by court issuing dispositional orders

(A) Any court that issues a dispositional order pursuant to section 2151.353, 2151.414, or 2151.415 of the Revised Code may review at any time the child's placement or custody arrangement, the case plan prepared for the child pursuant to section 2151.412 of the Revised Code, the actions of the public children services agency or private child placing agency in implementing that case plan, and any other aspects of the child's placement or custody arrangement. In conducting the review, the court shall determine the appropriateness of any agency actions, the appropriateness of continuing the child's placement or custody arrangement, and whether any changes should be made with respect to the child's placement or custody arrangement or with respect to the actions of the agency under the child's placement or custody arrangement. Based upon the evidence presented at a hearing held after notice to all parties and the guardian ad litem of the child, the court may require the agency, the parents, guardian, or custodian of the child, and the physical custodians of the child to take any reasonable action that the court determines is necessary and in the best interest of the child or to discontinue any action that it determines is not in the best interest of the child.

(B) If a court issues a dispositional order pursuant to section 2151.353, 2151.414, or 2151.415 of the Revised Code, the court has continuing jurisdiction over the child as set forth in division (E)(1) of section 2151.353 of the Revised Code. The court may amend a dispositional order in accordance with division (E)(2) of section 2151.353 of the Revised Code at any time upon its own motion or upon the motion of any interested party.

(C) Any court that issues a dispositional order pursuant to section 2151.353, 2151.414, or 2151.415 of the Revised Code shall hold a review hearing one year after the earlier of the date on which the complaint in the case was filed or the child was first placed into shelter care to review the case plan prepared pursuant to section 2151.412 of the Revised Code and to review the child's placement or custody arrangement. The court shall schedule the review hearing at the time that it holds the dispositional hearing pursuant to section 2151.35 of the Revised Code.

The court shall hold a similar review hearing no later than every twelve months after the initial review hearing until the child is adopted, returned to his parents, or the court otherwise terminates the child's placement or custody arrangement, except that the dispositional hearing held pursuant to section 2151.415 of the Revised Code shall take the place of the first review hearing to be held under this section. The court shall schedule each subsequent review hearing at the conclusion of the review hearing immediately preceding the review hearing to be scheduled.

(D) If, within fourteen days after a written summary of an administrative review is filed with the court pursuant to section 2151.416 of the Revised Code, the court does not approve the revised case plan filed pursuant to division (E)(1) of section 2151.416 of the Revised Code or the agency requests a review hearing pursuant to division (E)(2) of section 2151.416 of the Revised Code, the court shall hold a review hearing in the same manner that it holds review hearings pursuant to division (C) of this section,

except that if a review hearing is required by this division and if a hearing is to be held pursuant to division (C) of this section or section 2151.415 of the Revised Code, the hearing held pursuant to division (C) of this section or section 2151.415 of the Revised Code shall take the place of the review hearing required by this division.

(E) The court shall give notice of the review hearings held pursuant to this section to every interested party, including, but not limited to, the appropriate agency employees who are responsible for the child's care and planning, the child's parents, any person who had guardianship or legal custody of the child prior to the custody order, the child's guardian ad litem, and the child. The court shall summon every interested party to appear at the review hearing and give them an opportunity to testify and to present other evidence with respect to the child's custody arrangement, including, but not limited to, the case plan for the child, the actions taken by the child's custodian, the need for a change in the child's custodian or caseworker, or the need for any specific action to be taken with respect to the child. The court shall require any interested party to testify or present other evidence when necessary to a proper determination of the issues presented at the review hearing.

(F) After the review hearing, the court shall take the following actions based upon the evidence presented:

(1) Determine whether the conclusions of the administrative review are supported by a preponderance of the evidence and approve or modify the case plan based upon that evidence;

(2) If the child is in temporary custody, do all of the following:

(a) Determine whether the child can and should be returned home with or without an order for protective supervision;

(b) If the child can and should be returned home with or without an order for protective supervision, terminate the order for temporary custody;

(c) If the child cannot or should not be returned home with an order for protective supervision, determine whether the agency currently with custody of the child should retain custody or whether another public children services agency, private child placing agency, or an individual should be given custody of the child.

(3) If the child is in permanent custody, determine what actions are required by the custodial agency and of any other organizations or persons in order to facilitate an adoption of the child and make any appropriate orders with respect to the custody arrangement or conditions of the child, including, but not limited to, a transfer of permanent custody to another public

children services agency or private child placing agency;

(4) Journalize the terms of the updated case plan for the child.

(G) The court may appoint a referee or a citizens review board to conduct the review hearings that the court is required by this section to conduct, subject to the review and approval by the court of any determinations made by the referee or citizens review board. If the court appoints a citizens review board to conduct the review hearings, the board shall consist of one member representing the general public and four members who are trained or experienced in the care or placement of children and have training or experience in the fields of medicine, psychology, social work, education, or any related field. Of the initial appointments to the board, two shall be for a term of one year, two shall be for a term of two years, and one shall be for a term of three years, with all the terms ending one year after the date on which the appointment was made. Thereafter, all terms of the board members shall be for three years and shall end on the same day of the same month of the year as did the term that they succeed. Any member appointed to fill a vacancy occurring prior to the expiration of the term for which his predecessor was appointed shall hold office for the remainder of the term.

(H) A copy of the court's determination following any review hearing held pursuant to this section shall be sent to the custodial agency, the guardian ad litem of the child who is the subject of the review hearing, and, if that child is not the subject of a permanent commitment hearing, the parents of the child.

(I) If the hearing held under this section takes the place of an administrative review that otherwise would have been held under section 2151.416 of the Revised Code, the court at the hearing held under this section shall do all of the following in addition to any other requirements of this section:

(1) Determine the continued necessity for and the appropriateness of the child's placement;

(2) Determine the extent of compliance with the child's case plan;

(3) Determine the extent of progress that has been made toward alleviating or mitigating the causes necessitating the child's placement in foster care;

(4) Project a likely date by which the child may be returned to his home or placed for adoption or legal guardianship;

(5) Determine the future status of the child.

HISTORY: 1988 S 89, eff. 1-1-89

Note: See note under 2151.414 from 1988 S 89, § 4.

Note: See note under 2151.412 from 1988 S 89, § 5.

PRACTICE AND STUDY AIDS

Baldwin's Ohio Legislative Service, 1988 Laws of Ohio, S 89—LSC Analysis, p 5-571
Kurtz & Giannelli, Ohio Juvenile Law, Text 1.04, 13.05(D), 15.01(B)(F)

CROSS REFERENCES

Placing of child in institution, review hearing, 5103.15

2151.418 Foster homes considered residential property use

Any foster home shall be considered to be a residential use of property for purposes of municipal, county, and township zoning and shall be a permitted use in all zoning districts in which residential uses are permitted. No municipal, county, or township zoning regulation shall require a conditional permit or any other special exception certification for any foster home.

HISTORY: 1988 S 89, eff. 1-1-89

PRACTICE AND STUDY AIDS

Baldwin's Ohio Legislative Service, 1988 Laws of Ohio, S 89—LSC Analysis, p 5-571
Kurtz & Giannelli, Ohio Juvenile Law, Text 13.06(A)

2151.419 Hearings on efforts of agencies to prevent removal of children from homes

(A) At any hearing held pursuant to section 2151.28, division (E) of section 2151.31, or section 2151.314, 2151.33, or 2151.353 of the Revised Code at which the court removes a child from his home or continues the removal of a child from his home, the court shall determine whether the public children services agency or private child placing agency that filed the complaint in the case, removed the child from his home, has custody of the child, or will be given custody of the child has made reasonable efforts to prevent the removal of the child from his home, to eliminate the continued removal of the child from his home, or to make it possible for the child to return home. The agency shall have the burden of proving that it has made those reasonable efforts. If the agency removed the child from his home during an emergency in which the child could not safely remain at home and the agency did not have prior contact with the child, the court is not prohibited, solely because the agency did not make the reasonable efforts during the emergency to prevent the removal of the child, from determining that the agency made those reasonable efforts.

(B) The court shall issue written finding of facts setting forth its determination under division (A) of this section. In its written finding of facts, the court shall briefly describe the relevant services provided by the agency to the family of the child and why those services did not prevent the removal of the child from his home or enable the child to return home.

HISTORY: 1988 S 89, eff. 1-1-89

PRACTICE AND STUDY AIDS

Baldwin's Ohio Legislative Service, 1988 Laws of Ohio, S 89—LSC Analysis, p 5-571
Kurtz & Giannelli, Ohio Juvenile Law, Text 1.04, 13.04

2151.42   Prohibition against neglecting or mistreating child—Repealed

HISTORY: 1972 H 511, eff. 1-1-74
       130 v H 83; 1953 H 1; GC 1639-46

Note: See now 2919.21 and 2919.22 for provisions analogous to former 2151.42.

2151.421   Persons required to report injury or neglect; procedures on receipt of report

(A)(1) No attorney, physician, including a hospital intern or resident, dentist, podiatrist, practitioner of a limited branch of medicine or surgery as defined in section 4731.15 of the Revised Code, registered nurse, licensed practical nurse, visiting nurse, other health care professional, licensed psychologist, licensed school psychologist, speech pathologist or audiologist, coroner, administrator or employee of a child day-care center, administrator or employee of a certified child care agency or other public or private children services agency, school teacher, school employee, school authority, social worker, or person rendering spiritual treatment through prayer in accordance with the tenets of a well-recognized religion, who is acting in his official or professional capacity and knows or suspects that a child under eighteen years of age or a physically or mentally handicapped child under twenty-one years of age has suffered any wound, injury, disability, or condition of a nature that reasonably indicates abuse or neglect of the child, shall recklessly fail immediately to report or cause reports to be made of that knowledge or suspicion to the children services board, the county department of human services exercising the children services function, or a municipal or county peace officer in the county in which the child resides or in which the abuse or neglect is occurring or has occurred.

(2) An attorney is not required to make a report pursuant to division (A)(1) of this section concerning any communication made to him by one of his clients in the attorney-client relationship, if, in accordance with division (A) of section 2317.02 of the Revised Code, the attorney could not testify with respect to that communication in a civil or criminal proceeding, except that the client is deemed to have waived any testimonial privilege under division (A) of section 2317.02 of the Revised Code with respect to that communication and the attorney shall make a report pursuant to division (A)(1) of this section with respect to that communication, if all of the following apply:

(a) The client, at the time of the communication, is either a child under eighteen years of age or a physically or mentally handicapped person under twenty-one years of age;

(b) The attorney knows or suspects, as a result of the communication or any observations made during that communication, that the client has suffered any wound, injury, disability, or condition of a nature that reasonably indicates abuse or neglect of the client;

(c) The attorney-client relationship does not arise out of the client's attempt to have an abortion without the notification of her parents, guardian, or custodian in accordance with section 2151.85 of the Revised Code.

(3) A physician is not required to make a report pursuant to division (A)(1) of this section concerning any communication made to him by one of his patients in the physician-patient relationship, if, in accordance with division (B) of section 2317.02 of the Revised Code, the physician could not testify with respect to that communication in a civil or criminal proceeding, except that the patient is deemed to have waived any testimonial privilege under division (B) of section 2317.02 of the Revised Code with respect to that communication and the physician shall make a report pursuant to division (A)(1) of this section with respect to that communication, if all of the following apply:

(a) The patient, at the time of the communication, is either a child under eighteen years of age or a physically or mentally handicapped child under twenty-one years of age;

(b) The physician knows or suspects, as a result of the communication or any observations made during that communication, that the patient has suffered any wound, injury, disability, or condition of a nature that reasonably indicates abuse or neglect of the patient;

(c) The physician-patient relationship does not arise out of the patient's attempt to have an abortion without the notification of her parents, guardian, or custodian in accordance with section 2151.85 of the Revised Code.

(B) Anyone, who has reason to believe that a child under eighteen years of age or a physically or mentally handicapped child under twenty-one years of age has suffered any wound, injury, disability, or other condition of a nature that reasonably indicates abuse or neglect of the child, may report or cause reports to be made of that knowledge or suspicion to the children services board, the county department of human services exercising the children services function, or to a municipal or county peace officer.

(C) Any report made pursuant to division (A) or (B) of this section shall be made forthwith by telephone or in person forthwith, and shall be followed by a written report, if requested by the receiving agency or officer. The written report shall contain:

(1) The names and addresses of the child and his parents or the person or persons having custody of the child, if known;

(2) The child's age and the nature and extent of the child's injuries, abuse, or neglect, including any evidence of previous injuries, abuse, or neglect;

(3) Any other information that might be helpful in establishing the cause of the injury, abuse, or neglect.

Any person, who is required by division (A) of this section to report known or suspected child abuse or child neglect, may take or cause to be taken color photographs of areas of trauma visible on a child and, if medically indicated, cause to be performed radiological examinations of the child.

(D) Upon the receipt of a report concerning the possible abuse or neglect of a child, the municipal or county peace officer who receives the report shall refer the report to the appropriate county department of human services or children services board.

(E) No child about whom a report is made pursuant to this section shall be removed from his parents, his stepparents, his guardian, or any other persons having custody of the child by a municipal or county peace officer without consultation with the children services board or the county department of human services exercising the children services function, unless, in the judgment of the reporting physician and the officer, immediate removal is considered essential to protect the child from further abuse or neglect.

(F) The county department of human services or children services board shall investigate, within twenty-four hours, each report of known or suspected child abuse or child neglect that is referred to it under this section to determine the circumstances surrounding the injuries, abuse,

or neglect, the cause of the injuries, abuse, or neglect, and the person or persons responsible. The investigation shall be made in cooperation with the law enforcement agency. The county department of human services or children services board shall report each case to a central registry which the state department of human services shall maintain in order to determine whether prior reports have been made in other counties concerning the child or other principals in the case. The department or board shall submit a report of its investigation, in writing to the law enforcement agency.

The county department of human services or children services board shall make any recommendations to the county prosecutor or city director of law that it considers necessary to protect any children that are brought to its attention.

(G) Anyone or any hospital, institution, school, health department, or agency participating in the making of reports under this section, or anyone participating in a judicial proceeding resulting from the reports, shall be immune from any civil or criminal liability that otherwise might be incurred or imposed as a result of such actions. Notwithstanding section 4731.22 of the Revised Code, the physician-patient privilege shall not be a ground for excluding evidence regarding a child's injuries, abuse, or neglect, or the cause of the injuries, abuse, or neglect in any judicial proceeding resulting from a report submitted pursuant to this section.

(H) Nothing in this section shall be construed to define as an abused or neglected child any child who is under spiritual treatment through prayer in accordance with the tenets and practice of a well-recognized religion in lieu of medical treatment.

(I)(1) Any report made under this section is confidential.

(2) No person shall permit or encourage the unauthorized dissemination of the contents of any report made under this section.

(J) Any report that is required by this section shall result in protective services and emergency supportive services being made available by the county department of human services or children services board on behalf of the children about whom the report is made, in an effort to prevent further neglect or abuse, to enhance their welfare, and, whenever possible, to preserve the family unit intact. The department of human services shall exercise rule-making authority under Chapter 119. of the Revised Code to aid in the implementation of this section.

(K) There shall be placed on file with the juvenile court in each county and the department of human services an initial plan of cooperation jointly prepared and subscribed to by a committee consisting of the county peace officer, all chief municipal peace officers within the county, the prosecuting attorney of the county and the director of law of each city, and the children services board or county department of human services exercising the children services function as convened by the county director of human services. The plan shall set forth the normal operating procedure to be employed by all concerned officials in the execution of their respective responsibilities under this section and division (B) of section 2919.21, division (B)(1) of section 2919.22, division (B) of section 2919.23, and section 2919.24 of the Revised Code. The plan shall include a system for cross-referral of reported cases of abuse and neglect as necessary, and also shall include the name and title of the official directly responsible for making reports to the central registry.

HISTORY: 1986 H 529, eff. 3-11-87
     1986 H 528; 1985 H 349; 1984 S 321; 1977 H 219; 1975 H 85; 1969 H 338, S 49; 131 v H 218; 130 v H 765

Penalty: 2151.99(A)

PRACTICE AND STUDY AIDS

Baldwin's Ohio Domestic Relations Law, Text 11.08, 73.02
Baldwin's Ohio School Law, Text 5.08(A), 24.05, 24.06
Giannelli, Ohio Evidence Manual, Author's Comment § 501.04, 501.08
Kurtz & Giannelli, Ohio Juvenile Law, Text 7.03(A), 7.08(A), 11.11(A)

CROSS REFERENCES

Alleged child abuse and neglect, OAC 5101:2-34
Child abuse and neglect, interstate and intrastate referral procedures, protective service alerts, locating the child, OAC 5101:2-35-62 et seq.
Disabled infants, alleged withholding of nutrition or medical treatment as neglect, reporting procedures, OAC 5101:2-35-77
Children's protective services, OAC Ch 5101:2-36
Supportive services, OAC Ch 5101:2-39
Child abuse and neglect reporting law for approved child day care centers, OAC 5101:2-41-17

Evidence, privileged communications and acts, duty to report child abuse, 2317.02
Failure to report a felony or certain suspicious circumstances, 2921.22
Prevention of child abuse and child neglect, 3109.13 to 3109.18
Petition alleging domestic violence against minor children, 3113.31
Child abuse prevention, in-service training for school employees, 3319.073
Outpatient mental health services for minors, obligations of mental health professionals, 5122.04

LEGAL ENCYCLOPEDIAS AND ALR

OJur 3d: 22, Courts and Judges § 345; 26, Criminal Law § 668; 46, Family Law § 359, 382, 558, 563; 47, Family Law § 886
Civil liability of physician for failure to diagnose or report battered child syndrome. 97 ALR3d 338
Validity, construction, and application of statute limiting physician-patient privilege in judicial proceedings relating to child abuse or neglect. 44 ALR4th 649

ADULT CASES

2151.422   Mentally ill, mentally deficient, or psychopathic offenders—Repealed

HISTORY: 1978 H 565, eff. 11-1-78
     132 v S 316

2151.43   Charges against adults; defendant bound over to grand jury

In cases against an adult under sections 2151.01 to 2151.54 of the Revised Code, any person may file an affidavit with the clerk of the juvenile court setting forth briefly, in plain and ordinary language, the charges against the accused who shall be tried thereon. When the child is a recipient of aid pursuant to Chapter 5107. or 5113. of the Revised Code, the county department of human services shall file charges against any person who fails to provide support to a child in violation of section 2919.21 of the Revised Code, unless the department files charges under section 3113.06 of the Revised Code, or unless charges of nonsupport are filed by a relative or guardian of the child, or unless action to enforce support is brought under Chapter 3115. of the Revised Code.

In such prosecution an indictment by the grand jury or information by the prosecuting attorney shall not be required. The clerk shall issue a warrant for the arrest of the accused, who, when arrested, shall be taken before the juvenile judge and tried according to such sections.

The affidavit may be amended at any time before or during the trial.

The judge may bind such adult over to the grand jury, where the act complained of constitutes a felony.

HISTORY: 1986 H 428, eff. 12-23-86
     1972 H 511; 1969 H 361; 132 v H 390; 127 v 847; 1953 H 1; GC 1639-39

CROSS REFERENCES

Failure to pay maintenance cost, 3113.06

LEGAL ENCYCLOPEDIAS AND ALR

OJur 3d: 46, Family Law § 567, 568, 570; 78, Public Welfare § 120

Civil liability of physician for failure to diagnose or report battered child syndrome. 97 ALR3d 338

Validity, construction, and application of statute limiting physician-patient privilege in judicial proceedings relating to child abuse or neglect. 44 ALR4th 649

2151.44   Complaint after hearing

If it appears at the hearing of a child that any person has abused or has aided, induced, caused, encouraged, or contributed to the dependency, neglect, or delinquency of a child or acted in a way tending to cause delinquency in such child, or that a person charged with the care, support, education, or maintenance of any child has failed to support or sufficiently contribute toward the support, education, and maintenance of such child, the juvenile judge may order a complaint filed against such person and proceed to hear and dispose of the case as provided in sections 2151.01 to 2151.54, inclusive, of the Revised Code.

On the request of the judge, the prosecuting attorney shall prosecute all adults charged with violating such sections.

HISTORY: 1953 H 1, eff. 10-1-53
     GC 1639-40, 1639-42

LEGAL ENCYCLOPEDIAS AND ALR

OJur 3d: 46, Family Law § 566

Civil liability of physician for failure to diagnose or report battered child syndrome. 97 ALR3d 338

Validity, construction, and application of statute limiting physician-patient privilege in judicial proceedings relating to child abuse or neglect. 44 ALR4th 649

2151.45   Expense of extradition

When a person charged with the violation of sections 2151.01 to 2151.54, inclusive, of the Revised Code, has fled to another state or territory, and the governor has issued a requisition for such person, the board of county commissioners shall pay from the general expense fund of the county to the agent designated in such requisition all necessary expenses incurred in pursuing and returning such prisoner.

HISTORY: 1953 H 1, eff. 10-1-53
     GC 1639-41

PRACTICE AND STUDY AIDS

Kurtz & Giannelli, Ohio Juvenile Law, Text 15.05(B)

LEGAL ENCYCLOPEDIAS AND ALR

OJur 3d: 46, Family Law § 547, 581

Civil liability of physician for failure to diagnose or report battered child syndrome. 97 ALR3d 338

Validity, construction, and application of statute limiting physician-patient privilege in judicial proceedings relating to child abuse or neglect. 44 ALR4th 649

2151.46   Bail

Sections 2937.21 to 2937.45, inclusive, of the Revised Code, relating to bail in criminal cases in the court of common pleas, shall apply to adults committed or held under sections 2151.01 to 2151.54, inclusive, of the Revised Code.

HISTORY: 1953 H 1, eff. 10-1-53
     GC 1639-43

CROSS REFERENCES

Bail, Crim R 46

LEGAL ENCYCLOPEDIAS AND ALR

OJur 3d: 46, Family Law § 572

Civil liability of physician for failure to diagnose or report battered child syndrome. 97 ALR3d 338

Validity, construction, and application of statute limiting physician-patient privilege in judicial proceedings relating to child abuse or neglect. 44 ALR4th 649

2151.47   Jury trial; procedure

Any adult arrested under section 2151.01 to 2151.54, inclusive, of the Revised Code, may demand a trial by jury, or the juvenile judge upon his own motion may call a jury. A demand for a jury trial must be made in writing in not less than three days before the date set for trial, or within three days after counsel has been retained, whichever is later. Sections 2945.17 and 2945.22 to 2945.36, inclusive, of the Revised Code, relating to the drawing and impaneling of jurors in criminal cases in the court of common pleas, other than in capital cases, shall apply to such jury trial. The compensation of jurors and costs of the clerk and sheriff shall be taxed and paid as in criminal cases in the court of common pleas.

HISTORY: 1969 H 1, eff. 3-18-69
     132 v S 55; 1953 H 1; GC 1639-44

CROSS REFERENCES

Jury trial, Crim R 23

LEGAL ENCYCLOPEDIAS AND ALR

OJur 3d: 22, Courts and Judges § 345; 26, Criminal Law § 668; 46, Family Law § 359, 382, 558, 573, 581

Am Jur 2d: 47, Jury § 7 et seq.

Right of accused, in state criminal trial, to insist, over prosecutor's or court's objection, on trial by court without jury. 37 ALR4th 304

2151.48 Commitment to women's reformatory in lieu of jail or workhouse

When any female over the age of eighteen years is found guilty of a misdemeanor under sections 2151.01 to 2151.54, inclusive, of the Revised Code, the juvenile judge may order such female confined to the women's reformatory at Marysville for the same term for which said female could be committed to a workhouse or jail.

HISTORY: 1953 H 1, eff. 10-1-53
GC 1639-48

CROSS REFERENCES

Sentencing procedure, Crim R 32
Presentence investigation, Crim R 32.2

LEGAL ENCYCLOPEDIAS AND ALR

OJur 3d: 46, Family Law § 578
Jurisdiction to award custody of child having legal domicil in another state. 4 ALR2d 7

2151.49 Suspension of sentence

In every case of conviction under sections 2151.01 to 2151.54 of the Revised Code, where imprisonment is imposed as part of the punishment, the juvenile judge may suspend sentence, before or during commitment, upon such condition as he imposes. In the case of conviction for non-support of a child who is receiving aid under Chapter 5107. or 5113. of the Revised Code, if the juvenile judge suspends sentence on condition that the person make payments for support, the payment shall be made to the county department of human services rather than to the child or custodian of the child.

HISTORY: 1986 H 428, eff. 12-23-86
132 v H 390; 1953 H 1; GC 1639-49

CROSS REFERENCES

Support order, defined, 2301.34
Support payments to bureau of support, 2301.36
Modification of sentence, 2929.51
Payment of support through withholding of earnings, workers' benefits, or bank account; procedures, 3113.21 to 3113.214
Support of dependents, withholding personal earnings to pay support, bond, 3115.23
Sentencing procedure, Crim R 32
Presentence investigation, Crim R 32.2

LEGAL ENCYCLOPEDIAS AND ALR

OJur 3d: 22, Courts and Judges § 345; 26, Criminal Law § 668; 46, Family Law § 359, 382, 558, 579, 580; 47, Family Law § 636, 638
Am Jur 2d: 21, Criminal Law § 557 to 566
Inherent power of court to suspend for indefinite period execution of sentence in whole or in part. 73 ALR3d 474

2151.50 Forfeiture of bond

When, as a condition of suspension of sentence under section 2151.49 of the Revised Code, bond is required and given, upon the failure of a person giving such bond to comply with the conditions thereof, such bond may be forfeited, the suspension terminated by the juvenile judge, the original sentence executed as though it had not been suspended, and the term of any sentence imposed in such case shall commence from the date of imprisonment of such person after such forfeiture and termination of suspension. Any part of such sentence which may have been served shall be deducted from any such period of imprisonment. When such bond is forfeited the judge may issue execution thereon without further proceedings.

HISTORY: 1953 H 1, eff. 10-1-53
GC 1639-50

LEGAL ENCYCLOPEDIAS AND ALR

OJur 3d: 46, Family Law § 580

2151.51 Provision for dependent children of person sentenced to workhouse or jail

When an adult is sentenced to imprisonment for any violation of section 2919.21 or 2919.22 of the Revised Code, the county from which such person is sentenced, on the order of the juvenile judge, shall pay from the general revenue fund fifty cents for each day such prisoner is confined to the juvenile court of such county, for the maintenance of the dependent children of such prisoner. Such expenditure shall be made under the direction of the judge, who shall designate an employee for such purpose. The board of county commissioners of such county shall make an appropriation for such cases, and allowances therefrom shall be paid from the county treasury upon the warrant of the county auditor.

HISTORY: 1975 H 1, eff. 6-13-75
1953 H 1; GC 1639-47

2151.52 Appeals on questions of law

The sections of the Revised Code and rules relating to appeals on questions of law from the court of common pleas shall apply to prosecutions of adults under this chapter, and from such prosecutions an appeal on a question of law may be taken to the court of appeals of the county under laws or rules governing appeals in other criminal cases to such court of appeals.

HISTORY: 1986 H 412, eff. 3-17-87
129 v 290; 1953 H 1; GC 1639-51

Applicability of rules of appellate procedure, scope, App R 1

LEGAL ENCYCLOPEDIAS AND ALR

OJur 3d: 46, Family Law § 589

2151.53 Physical and mental examinations; records of examination; expenses

Any person coming within sections 2151.01 to 2151.54, inclusive, of the Revised Code, may be subjected to a physical and mental examination by competent physicians, psychologists, and psychiatrists to be appointed by the juvenile court. Whenever any child is committed to any institution by virtue of such sections, a record of such examinations shall be sent with the commitment to such institution. The compensation of such physicians, psychologists, and psychiatrists and the expenses of such examinations shall be paid by the county treasurer upon specifically itemized vouchers, certified by the juvenile judge.

HISTORY: 1953 H 1, eff. 10-1-53
GC 1639-54

CROSS REFERENCES

Social history, physical or mental examination, custody investigation, procedure, Juv R 32

LEGAL ENCYCLOPEDIAS AND ALR

OJur 3d: 46, Family Law § 492, 551, 564

2151.54 Fees and costs

The juvenile court shall tax and collect the same fees and costs as are allowed the clerk of the court of common pleas for similar services. No fees or costs shall be taxed in cases of delinquent, unruly, dependent, abused, or neglected children except as required by section 2743.70 of the Revised Code or when specifically ordered by the court. The expense of transportation of children to places to which they have been committed, and the transportation of children to and from another state by police or other officers, acting upon order of the court, shall be paid from the county treasury upon specifically itemized vouchers certified to by the judge.

HISTORY: 1980 H 238, eff. 8-8-80
1975 H 85; 1970 H 931; 1953 H 1; GC 1639-56

PRACTICE AND STUDY AIDS

Kurtz & Giannelli, Ohio Juvenile Law, Text 15.05(B)

CROSS REFERENCES

Common pleas court, fees and costs, Ch 2335

LEGAL ENCYCLOPEDIAS AND ALR

OJur 3d: 46, Family Law § 544, 547, 581

2151.55 Purpose and construction— Repealed

HISTORY: 130 v H 299, eff. 10-7-63
1953 H 1; GC 1639-59

INTERSTATE COMPACT ON JUVENILES

2151.56 Interstate compact on juveniles

The governor is hereby authorized to execute a compact on behalf of this state with any other state or states legally joining therein in the form substantially as follows:

THE INTERSTATE COMPACT ON JUVENILES

The contracting states solemnly agree:

Article I — Findings and Purposes

That juveniles who are not under proper supervision and control, or who have absconded, escaped or run away, are likely to endanger their own health, morals and welfare, and the health, morals and welfare of others. The cooperation of the states party to this compact is therefore necessary to provide for the welfare and protection of juveniles and of the public with respect to (1) cooperative supervision of delinquent juveniles on probation or parole; (2) the return, from one state to another, of delinquent juveniles who have escaped or absconded; (3) the return, from one state to another, of nondelinquent juveniles who have run away from home; and (4) additional measures for the protection of juveniles and of the public, which any two or more of the party states may find desirable to undertake cooperatively. In carrying out the provisions of this compact the party states shall be guided by the noncriminal, reformative and protective policies which guide their laws concerning delinquent, neglected or dependent juveniles generally. It shall be the policy of the states party to this compact to cooperate and observe their respective responsibilities for the prompt return and acceptance of juveniles and delinquent juveniles who become subject to the provisions of this compact. The provisions of this compact shall be reasonably and liberally construed to accomplish the foregoing purposes.

Article II — Existing Rights and Remedies

That all remedies and procedures provided by this compact shall be in addition to and not in substitution for other rights, remedies and procedures, and shall not be in derogation of parental rights and responsibilities.

Article III — Definitions

That, for the purposes of this compact, "delinquent juvenile" means any juvenile who has been adjudged delinquent and who, at the time the provisions of this compact are invoked, is still subject to the jurisdiction of the court that has made such adjudication or to the jurisdiction or supervision of an agency or institution pursuant to an order of such court; "probation or parole" means any kind of conditional release of juveniles authorized under the laws of the states party hereto; "court" means any court having jurisdiction over delinquent, neglected or dependent children; "state" means any state, territory or possessions of the United States, the District of Columbia, and the Commonwealth of Puerto Rico; and "residence" or any variant thereof means a place at which a home or regular place of abode is maintained.

Article IV — Return of Runaways

(a) That the parent, guardian, person or agency entitled to legal custody of a juvenile who has not been adjudged delinquent but who has run away without the consent of such parent, guardian, person or agency may petition the appropriate court in the demanding state for the issuance of a requisition for his return. The petition shall state the name and age of the juvenile, the name of the petitioner and the basis of entitlement to the juvenile's custody, the circumstances of his running away, his location if known at the time application is made, and such other facts as may tend to show that the juvenile who has run away is endangering his own welfare or the welfare of others and is not an emancipated minor. The petition shall be verified by affidavit, shall be executed in duplicate, and shall be accompanied by two certified copies of the document or documents on which the petitioner's entitlement to the juvenile's custody is based, such as birth records, letters of guardianship, or custody decrees. Such further affidavits and other documents as may be deemed proper may be submitted with such petition. The judge of the court to which this application is made may hold a hearing thereon to determine whether for the purposes of this compact the petitioner is entitled to the legal custody of the juvenile, whether or not it appears that the juvenile has in fact run away without consent, whether or not he is an emancipated minor, and whether or not it is in the best interest of the juvenile to compel his return to the state. If the judge determines, either with or without a hearing, that the juvenile should be returned, he shall present to the appropriate court or to the executive authority of the state where the juvenile is alleged to be located a written requisition for the return of such juvenile. Such requisition shall set forth the name and age of the juvenile, the determination of the court that the juvenile has run away without the consent of a parent, guardian, person or agency entitled to his legal custody, and that it is in the best interest and for the protection of such juvenile that he be returned. In the event that a proceeding for the adjudication of the juvenile as a delinquent, neglected or dependent juvenile is pending in the court at the time when such juvenile runs away, the court may issue a requisition for the return of such juvenile upon its own motion, regardless of the consent of the parent, guardian, person or agency entitled to legal custody, reciting therein the nature and circumstances of the pending proceeding. The requisition shall in every case be executed in duplicate and shall be signed by the judge. One copy of the requisition shall be filed with the compact administrator of the demanding state, there to remain on file subject to the provisions of law governing records of such court. Upon the receipt of a requisition demanding the return of a juvenile who has run away, the court or the executive authority to whom the requisition is addressed shall issue an order to any peace officer or other appropriate person directing him to take into custody and detain such juvenile. Such detention order must substantially recite the facts necessary to the validity of its issuance hereunder. No juvenile detained upon such order shall be delivered over to the officer whom the court demanding him shall have appointed to receive him, unless he shall first be taken forthwith before a judge of a court in the state, who shall inform him of the demand made for his return, and who may appoint counsel or guardian ad litem for him. If the judge of such court shall find that the requisition is in order, he shall deliver such juvenile over to the officer whom the court demanding him shall have appointed to receive him. The judge, however, may fix a reasonable time to be allowed for the purpose of testing the legality of the proceeding.

Upon reasonable information that a person is a juvenile who has run away from another state party to this compact without the consent of a parent, guardian, person or agency entitled to his legal custody, such juvenile may be taken into custody without a requisition and brought forthwith before a judge of the appropriate court who may appoint counsel or guardian ad litem for such juvenile and who shall determine after a hearing whether sufficient cause exists to hold the person, subject to the order of the court, for his own protection and welfare, for such a time not exceeding ninety days as will enable his return to another state party to this compact pursuant to a requisition for his return from a court of that state. If, at the time when a state seeks the return of a juvenile who has run away, there is pending in the state wherein he is found any criminal charge, or any proceeding to have him adjudicated a delinquent juvenile for an act committed in such state, or if he is suspected of having committed within such state a criminal offense or an act of juvenile delinquency, he shall not be returned without the consent of such state until discharged from prosecution or other form of proceeding, imprisonment, detention or supervision for such offense or juvenile delinquency. The duly accredited officers of any state party to this compact, upon the establishment of their authority and the identity of the juvenile being returned, shall be permitted to transport such juvenile through any and all states party to this compact, without interference. Upon his return to the state from which he ran away, the juvenile shall be subject to such further proceedings as may be appropriate under the laws of that state.

(b) That the state to which a juvenile is returned under this Article shall be responsible for payment of the transportation costs of such return.

(c) That "juvenile" as used in this Article means any person who is a minor under the law of the state of residence of the parent, guardian, person or agency entitled to the legal custody of such minor.

Article V — Return of Escapees and Absconders

(a) That the appropriate person or authority from whose probation or parole supervision a delinquent juvenile has absconded or from whose institutional custody he has escaped shall present to the appropriate court or to the executive authority of the state where the delinquent juvenile is alleged to be located a written requisition for the return of such delinquent juvenile. Such requisition shall state the name and age of the delinquent juvenile, the particulars of his adjudication as a delinquent juvenile, the circumstances of the breach of the terms of his probation or parole or of his escape from an institution or agency vested with his legal custody or supervision, and the location of such delinquent juvenile, if known, at the time the requisition is made. The requisition shall be ver-

ified by affidavit, shall be executed in duplicate, and shall be accompanied by two certified copies of the judgment, formal adjudication, or order of commitment which subjects such delinquent juvenile to probation or parole or to the legal custody of the institution or agency concerned. Such further affidavits and other documents as may be deemed proper may be submitted with such requisition. One copy of the requisition shall be filed with the compact administrator of the demanding state, there to remain on file subject to the provisions of law governing records of the appropriate court. Upon the receipt of a requisition demanding the return of a delinquent juvenile who has absconded or escaped, the court or the executive authority to whom the requisition is addressed shall issue an order to any peace officer or other appropriate person directing him to take into custody and detain such delinquent juvenile. Such detention order must substantially recite the facts necessary to the validity of its issuance hereunder. No delinquent juvenile detained upon such order shall be delivered over to the officer whom the appropriate person or authority demanding him shall have appointed to receive him, unless he shall first be taken forthwith before a judge of an appropriate court in the state, who shall inform him of the demand made for his return and who may appoint counsel or guardian ad litem for him. If the judge of such court shall find that the requisition is in order, he shall deliver such delinquent juvenile over to the officer whom the appropriate person or authority demanding him shall have appointed to receive him. The judge, however, may fix a reasonable time to be allowed for the purpose of testing the legality of the proceeding.

Upon reasonable information that a person is a delinquent juvenile who has absconded while on probation or parole, or escaped from an institution or agency vested with his legal custody or supervision in any state party to this compact, such person may be taken into custody in any other state party to this compact without a requisition. But in such event, he must be taken forthwith before a judge of the appropriate court, who may appoint counsel or guardian ad litem for such person and who shall determine, after a hearing, whether sufficient cause exists to hold the person subject to the order of the court for such a time, not exceeding ninety days, as will enable his detention under a detention order issued on a requisition pursuant to this Article. If, at the time when a state seeks the return of a delinquent juvenile who has either absconded while on probation or parole or escaped from an institution or agency vested with his legal custody or supervision, there is pending in the state wherein he is detained any criminal charge or any proceeding to have him adjudicated a delinquent juvenile for an act committed in such state, or if he is suspected of having committed within such state a criminal offense or an act of juvenile delinquency, he shall not be returned without the consent of such state until discharged from prosecution or other form of proceeding, imprisonment, detention or supervision for such offense or juvenile delinquency. The duly accredited officers of any state party to this compact, upon the establishment of their authority and the identity of the delinquent juvenile being returned, shall be permitted to transport such delinquent juvenile through any and all states party to this compact, without interference. Upon his return to the state from which he escaped or absconded, the delinquent juvenile shall be subject to such further proceedings as may be appropriate under the laws of that state.

(b) That the state to which a delinquent juvenile is returned under this Article shall be responsible for the payment of the transportation costs of such return.

Article VI — Voluntary Return Procedure

That any delinquent juvenile who has absconded while on probation or parole, or escaped from an institution or agency vested with his legal custody or supervision in any state party to this compact, and any juvenile who has run away from any state party to this compact, who is taken into custody without a requisition in another state party to this compact under the provisions of Article IV (a) or of Article V (a), may consent to his immediate return to the state from which he absconded, escaped or ran away. Such consent shall be given by the juvenile or delinquent juvenile and his counsel or guardian ad litem if any, by executing or subscribing a writing, in the presence of a judge of the appropriate court, which states that the juvenile or delinquent juvenile and his counsel or guardian ad litem, if any, consent to his return to the demanding state. Before such consent shall be executed or subscribed, however, the judge, in the presence of counsel or guardian ad litem, if any, shall inform the juvenile or delinquent juvenile of his rights under this compact. When the consent has been duly executed, it shall be forwarded to and filed with the compact administrator of the state in which the court is located and the judge shall direct the officer having the juvenile or delinquent juvenile in custody to deliver him to the duly accredited officer or officers of the state demanding his return, and shall cause to be delivered to such officer or officers a copy of the consent. The court may, however, upon the request of the state to which the juvenile or delinquent juvenile is being

returned, order him to return unaccompanied to such state and shall provide him with a copy of such court order; in such event a copy of the consent shall be forwarded to the compact administrator of the state to which said juvenile or delinquent juvenile is ordered to return.

Article VII — Cooperative Supervision of Probationers and Parolees

(a) That the duly constituted judicial and administrative authorities of a state party to this compact (herein called "sending state") may permit any delinquent juvenile within such state, placed on probation or parole, to reside in any other state party to this compact (herein called "receiving state") while on probation or parole, and the receiving state shall accept such delinquent juvenile, if the parent, guardian or person entitled to the legal custody of such delinquent juvenile is residing or undertakes to reside within the receiving state. Before granting such permission, opportunity shall be given to the receiving state to make such investigations as it deems necessary. The authorities of the sending state shall send to the authorities of the receiving state copies of pertinent court orders, social case studies and all other available information which may be of value to and assist the receiving state in supervising a probationer or parolee under this compact. A receiving state, in its discretion, may agree to accept supervision of a probationer or parolee in cases where the parent, guardian or person entitled to the legal custody of the delinquent juvenile is not a resident of the receiving state, and if so accepted the sending state may transfer supervision accordingly.

(b) That each receiving state will assume the duties of visitation and of supervision over any such delinquent juvenile and in the exercise of those duties will be governed by the same standards of visitation and supervision that prevail for its own delinquent juveniles released on probation or parole.

(c) That, after consultation between the appropriate authorities of the sending state and of the receiving state as to the desirability and necessity of returning such a delinquent juvenile, the duly accredited officers of a sending state may enter a receiving state and there apprehend and retake any such delinquent juvenile on probation or parole. For that purpose, no formalities will be required, other than establishing the authority of the officer and the identity of the delinquent juvenile to be retaken and returned. The decision of the sending state to retake a delinquent juvenile on probation or parole shall be conclusive upon and not reviewable within the receiving state, but if, at the time the sending state seeks to retake a delinquent juvenile on probation or parole, there is pending against him within the receiving state any criminal charge or any proceeding to have him adjudicated a delinquent juvenile for any act committed in such state, or if he is suspected of having committed within such state a criminal offense or an act of juvenile delinquency, he shall not be returned without the consent of the receiving state until discharged from prosecution or other form of proceeding, imprisonment, detention or supervision for such offense or juvenile delinquency. The duly accredited officers of the sending state shall be permitted to transport delinquent juveniles being so returned through any and all states party to this compact, without interference.

(d) That the sending state shall be responsible under this Article for paying the costs of transporting any delinquent juvenile to the receiving state or of returning any delinquent juvenile to the sending state.

Article VIII — Responsibility for Costs

(a) That the provisions of Articles IV(b), V(b) and VII(d) of this compact shall not be construed to alter or affect any internal relationship among the departments, agencies and officers of and in the government of a party state, or between a party state and its subdivisions, as to the payment of costs, or responsibilities therefor.

(b) That nothing in this compact shall be construed to prevent any party state or subdivision thereof from asserting any right against any person, agency or other entity in regard to costs for which such party state or subdivision thereof may be responsible pursuant to Articles IV(b), V(b) or VII(d) of this compact.

Article IX — Detention Practices

That, to every extent possible, it shall be the policy of states party to this compact that no juvenile or delinquent juvenile shall be placed or detained in any prison, jail or lockup nor be detained or transported in association with criminal, vicious or dissolute persons.

Article X — Supplementary Agreements

That the duly constituted administrative authorities of a state party to this compact may enter into supplementary agreements with any other state or states party hereto for the cooperative care, treatment and rehabilitation of delinquent juveniles whenever they shall find that such agreements will improve the facilities or programs available for such care, treatment and rehabilitation. Such care, treatment and rehabilitation may be provided in an institution located within any state entering into such supplementary agreement. Such supplementary agreements shall (1) provide the rates to be paid for the care, treatment and custody of such delinquent

juveniles, taking into consideration the character of facilities, services and subsistence furnished; (2) provide that the delinquent juvenile shall be given a court hearing prior to his being sent to another state for care, treatment and custody; (3) provide that the state receiving such a delinquent juvenile in one of its institutions shall act solely as agent for the state sending such delinquent juvenile; (4) provide that the sending state shall at all times retain jurisdiction over delinquent juveniles sent to an institution in another state; (5) provide for reasonable inspection of such institutions by the sending state; (6) provide that the consent of the parent, guardian, person or agency entitled to the legal custody of said delinquent juvenile shall be secured prior to his being sent to another state; and (7) make provision for such other matters and details as shall be necessary to protect the rights and equities of such delinquent juveniles and of the cooperating states.

Article XI — Acceptance of Federal and Other Aid

That any state party to this compact may accept any and all donations, gifts and grants of money, equipment and services from the federal or any local government, or any agency thereof and from any person, firm or corporation, for any of the purposes and functions of this compact, and may receive and utilize the same subject to the terms, conditions and regulations governing such donations, gifts and grants.

Article XII — Compact Administrators

That the governor of each state party to this compact shall designate an officer who, acting jointly with like officers of other party states, shall promulgate rules and regulations to carry out more effectively the terms and provisions of this compact.

Article XIII — Execution of Compact

That this compact shall become operative immediately upon its execution by any state as between it and any other state or states so executing. When executed it shall have the full force and effect of law within such state, the form of execution to be in accordance with the laws of the executing state.

Article XIV — Renunciation

That this compact shall continue in force and remain binding upon each executing state until renounced by it. Renunciation of this compact shall be by the same authority which executed it, by sending six months' notice in writing of its intention to withdraw from the compact to the other states party hereto. The duties and obligations of a renouncing state under Article VII hereof shall continue as to parolees and probationers residing therein at the time of withdrawal until retaken or finally discharged. Supplementary agreements entered into under Article X hereof shall be subject to renunciation as provided by such supplementary agreements, and shall not be subject to the six months' renunciation notice of the present Article.

Article XV — Severability

That the provisions of this compact shall be severable and if any phrase, clause, sentence or provision of this compact is declared to be contrary to the constitution of any participating state or of the United States or the applicability thereof to any government, agency, person or circumstance is held invalid, the validity of the remainder of this compact and the applicability thereof to any government, agency, person or circumstance shall not be affected thereby. If this compact shall be held contrary to the constitution of any state participating therein, the compact shall remain in full force and effect as to the remaining states and in full force and effect as to the state affected as to all severable matters.

HISTORY: 1988 H 790, eff. 3-16-89
     127 v 530

PRACTICE AND STUDY AIDS

Kurtz & Giannelli, Ohio Juvenile Law, Text 15.05

CROSS REFERENCES

Jurisdiction of juvenile court under interstate compact, 2151.23
Procedure not otherwise specified, Juv R 45

LEGAL ENCYCLOPEDIAS AND ALR

OJur 3d: 22, Courts and Judges § 345; 26, Criminal Law § 668; 46, Family Law § 359, 371, 372, 382, 425
Extradition of juveniles. 73 ALR3d 700

2151.57   Compact administrator; powers and duties

Pursuant to section 2151.56 of the Revised Code, the governor is hereby authorized and empowered, with the advice and consent of the senate, to designate an officer who shall be the compact administrator and who, acting jointly with like officers of other party states, shall promulgate rules and regulations to carry out more effectively the terms of the compact. Such compact administrator shall serve subject to the pleasure of the governor. The compact administrator is hereby authorized, empowered and directed to cooperate with all departments, agencies and officers of and in the government of this state and its subdivisions in facilitating the proper administration of the compact or of any supplementary agreement or agreements entered into by this state thereunder.

HISTORY: 127 v 530, eff. 9-17-57

LEGAL ENCYCLOPEDIAS AND ALR

OJur 3d: 22, Courts and Judges § 345; 26, Criminal Law § 668; 46, Family Law § 359, 371, 372, 382, 425
Extradition of juveniles. 73 ALR3d 700

2151.58   Supplementary agreements

The compact administrator is hereby authorized and empowered to enter into supplementary agreements with appropriate officials of other states pursuant to the compact. In the event that such supplementary agreement shall require or contemplate the use of any institution or facility of this state or require or contemplate the provision of any service by this state, said supplementary agreement shall have no force or effect until approved by the head of the department or agency under whose jurisdiction the institution or facility is operated or whose department or agency will be charged with the rendering of such service.

HISTORY: 127 v 530, eff. 9-17-57

LEGAL ENCYCLOPEDIAS AND ALR

OJur 3d: 22, Courts and Judges § 345; 26, Criminal Law § 668; 46, Family Law § 359, 371, 372, 382, 425
Extradition of juveniles. 73 ALR3d 700

2151.59   Discharge of financial obligations

The compact administrator, subject to the approval of the director of budget and management, may make or arrange for any payments necessary to discharge any financial obligations imposed upon this state by the compact or by any supplementary agreement entered into thereunder.

HISTORY: 1985 H 201, eff. 7-1-85
     127 v 530

LEGAL ENCYCLOPEDIAS AND ALR

OJur 3d: 22, Courts and Judges § 345; 26, Criminal Law § 668; 46, Family Law § 359, 371, 372, 382, 425
Extradition of juveniles. 73 ALR3d 700

2151.60   Enforcement by agencies of state and subdivisions

The courts, departments, agencies and officers of this state and its subdivisions shall enforce this compact and shall do all things appropriate to the effectuation of its purposes and intent which may be within their respective jurisdictions.

HISTORY: 127 v 530, eff. 9-17-57

LEGAL ENCYCLOPEDIAS AND ALR

OJur 3d: 22, Courts and Judges § 345; 26, Criminal Law § 668; 46, Family Law § 359, 371 to 373, 382, 425

2151.61   Additional article

In addition to any procedure provided in Articles IV and VI of the compact for the return of any runaway juvenile, the particular states, the juvenile or his parents, the courts, or other legal custodian involved may agree upon and adopt any other plan or procedure legally authorized under the laws of this state and the other respective party states for the return of any such runaway juvenile.

Article XVI—Additional Article

That this Article shall provide additional remedies, and shall be binding only as among and between those party states which specifically execute the same.

For the purposes of this Article, "child," as used herein, means any minor within the jurisdictional age limits of any court in the home state.

When any child is brought before a court of a state of which such child is not a resident, and such state is willing to permit such child's return to the home state of such child, such home state, upon being so advised by the state in which such proceeding is pending, shall immediately institute proceedings to determine the residence and jurisdictional facts as to such child in such home state, and upon finding that such child is in fact a resident of said state and subject to the jurisdiction of the court thereof, shall within five days authorize the return of such child to the home state, and to the parent or custodial agency legally authorized to accept such custody in such home state, and at the expense of such home state, to be paid from such funds as such home state may procure, designate, or provide, prompt action being of the essence.

HISTORY: 127 v 530, eff. 9-17-57

CROSS REFERENCES

Judges of the division of domestic relations, 2301.03

LEGAL ENCYCLOPEDIAS AND ALR

OJur 3d: 22, Courts and Judges § 345; 26, Criminal Law § 668; 46, Family Law § 359, 371, 372, 382, 425

FACILITIES FOR TRAINING, TREATMENT, AND REHABILITATION OF JUVENILES

2151.65   Facilities for treatment of juveniles; joint boards; admission

Upon the advice and recommendation of the juvenile judge, the board of county commissioners may provide by purchase, lease, construction, or otherwise a school, forestry camp, or other facility or facilities where delinquent, as defined in section 2151.02 of the Revised Code, dependent, abused, unruly, as defined in section 2151.022 of the Revised Code, or neglected children or juvenile traffic offenders may be held for training, treatment, and rehabilitation. Upon the joint advice and recommendation of the juvenile judges of two or more adjoining or neighboring counties, the boards of county commissioners of such counties may form themselves into a joint board and proceed to organize a district for the establishment and support of a school, forestry camp, or other facility or facilities for the use of the juvenile courts of such counties, where delinquent, dependent, abused, unruly, or neglected children, or juvenile traffic offenders may be held for treatment, training, and rehabilitation, by using a site or buildings already established in one such county, or by providing for the purchase of a site and the erection of the necessary buildings thereon. Such county or district school, forestry camp, or other facility or facilities shall be maintained as provided in sections 2151.01 to 2151.80 of the Revised Code. Children who are adjudged to be delinquent, dependent, neglected, abused, unruly, or juvenile traffic offenders may be committed to and held in any such school, forestry camp, or other facility or facilities for training, treatment, and rehabilitation.

The juvenile court shall determine:

(A) The children to be admitted to any school, forestry camp, or other facility maintained under this section;

(B) The period such children shall be trained, treated, and rehabilitated at such facility;

(C) The removal and transfer of children from such facility.

HISTORY: 1980 S 168, eff. 10-2-80
    1975 H 85; 130 v H 879

PRACTICE AND STUDY AIDS

Baldwin's Ohio School Law, Text 23.04(B)

CROSS REFERENCES

Board of county commissioners may submit bond issue to voters for support of school, detention home, forestry camp or other facilities, 133.151

Acquisition, construction, or renovation of facilities, 307.021

Withdrawal by county from detention home district, continuity of district tax levy, 2151.3413

Designation of fiscal officer of detention home district, adjustment of accounts, 2151.3414

Disposition of delinquent child, 2151.355

Withdrawal of county from district, continuity of district tax levy, 2151.78

Standards of construction prerequisite to financial assistance of facilities for rehabilitation of delinquent juveniles, 5139.27

Operation standards necessary for financial assistance in defraying cost of operation and maintenance of facilities, 5139.28

Adoption of rules for payment of assistance, 5139.29

Transfer of child committed to facility, 5139.30

Tax levy law, detention home district is "subdivision," 5705.01

Resolution relative to tax levy in excess of ten-mill limitation, 5705.19

LEGAL ENCYCLOPEDIAS AND ALR

OJur 3d: 15, Civil Servants and Other Public Officers and Employees § 253; 46, Family Law § 552; 73, Penal Institutions § 42; 76, Public Funds § 51, 56

2151.651　Application for financial assistance for acquisition or construction of facilities

The board of county commissioners of a county which, either separately or as part of a district, is planning to establish a school, forestry camp, or other facility under section 2151.65 of the Revised Code, to be used exclusively for the rehabilitation of children between the ages of twelve to eighteen years, other than psychotic or mentally retarded children, who are designated delinquent[1] as defined in section 2151.02 of the Revised Code, or unruly, as defined in section 2151.022 of the Revised Code, by order of a juvenile court, may make application to the department of youth services, created under division (B) of section 5139.01 of the Revised Code, for financial assistance in defraying the county's share of the cost of acquisition or construction of such school, camp, or other facility, as provided in section 5139.27 of the Revised Code. Such application shall be made on forms prescribed and furnished by the department.

HISTORY:　1981 H 440, eff. 11-23-81
　1980 S 168; 131 v H 943

[1]Prior and current versions differ although no amendment to this punctuation was indicated in 1981 H 440; "delinquent" appeared as "delinquent," in 1980 S 168.

CROSS REFERENCES

Standards of construction prerequisite to financial assistance of facilities for rehabilitation of delinquent juveniles, 5139.27

Inspection of youth rehabilitation facilities, 5139.31

LEGAL ENCYCLOPEDIAS AND ALR

OJur 3d: 73, Penal Institutions § 45

2151.652　Application for financial assistance to maintain facilities

The board of county commissioners of a county or the board of trustees of a district maintaining a school, forestry camp, or other facility established under section 2151.65 of the Revised Code, used exclusively for the rehabilitation of children between the ages of twelve to eighteen years, other than psychotic or mentally retarded children, who are designated delinquent, as defined in section 2151.02 of the Revised Code, or unruly, as defined in section 2151.022 of the Revised Code, by order of a juvenile court, may make application to the department of youth services, created under division (B) of section 5139.01 of the Revised Code, for financial assistance in defraying the cost of operating and maintaining such school, forestry camp, or other facility, as provided in section 5139.28 of the Revised Code.

Such application shall be made on forms prescribed and furnished by the department.

HISTORY:　1981 H 440, eff. 11-23-81
　1980 S 168; 131 v H 943

CROSS REFERENCES

Operation standards necessary for financial assistance in defraying cost of operation and maintenance of facilities, 5139.28

Inspection of youth rehabilitation facilities, 5139.31

LEGAL ENCYCLOPEDIAS AND ALR

OJur 3d: 73, Penal Institutions § 45

2151.653　Program of education; teachers

The board of county commissioners of a county or the board of trustees of a district maintaining a school, forestry camp, or other facility established under section 2151.65 of the Revised Code, shall provide a program of education for the youths admitted to such school, forestry camp, or other facility. Either of such boards and the board of education of any school district may enter into an agreement whereby such board of education provides teachers for such school, forestry camp, or other facility, or permits youths admitted to such school, forestry camp, or other facility to attend a school or schools within such school district, or both. Either of such boards may enter into an agreement with the appropriate authority of any university, college, or vocational institution to assist in providing a program of education for the youths admitted to such school, forestry camp, or other facility.

HISTORY: 131 v H 943, eff. 8-10-65

2151.654   Agreements for admission of children from counties not maintaining facilities

The board of county commissioners of a county or the board of trustees of a district maintaining a school, forestry camp, or other facility established under section 2151.65 of the Revised Code, may enter into an agreement with the board of county commissioners of a county which does not maintain such a school, forestry camp, or other facility, to admit to such school, forestry camp, or other facility a child from the county not maintaining such a school, forestry camp, or other facility.

HISTORY: 131 v H 943, eff. 8-10-65

2151.66   Annual tax assessments

The joint boards of county commissioners of district schools, forestry camps, or other facility or facilities created under section 2151.65 of the Revised Code, shall make annual assessments of taxes sufficient to support and defray all necessary expenses of such school, forestry camp, or other facility or facilities.

HISTORY: 130 v H 879, eff. 10-14-63

LEGAL ENCYCLOPEDIAS AND ALR

OJur 3d: 73, Penal Institutions § 45

2151.67   Receipt and use of gifts, grants, devises, bequests and public moneys

The board of county commissioners of a county or the board of trustees of a district maintaining a school, forestry camp, or other facility established or to be established under section 2151.65 of the Revised Code may receive gifts, grants, devises, and bequests, either absolutely or in trust, and may receive any public moneys made available to it. Each of such boards shall use such gifts, grants, devises, bequests, and public moneys in whatever manner it determines is most likely to carry out the purposes for which such school, forestry camp, or other facility was or is to be established.

HISTORY: 132 v H 1, eff. 2-21-67
     131 v H 943

Note: Former 2151.67 repealed by 131 v H 943, eff. 8-10-65; 130 v H 879.

LEGAL ENCYCLOPEDIAS AND ALR

OJur 3d: 73, Penal Institutions § 45

2151.68   Board of trustees

Immediately upon the organization of the joint board of county commissioners as provided by section 2151.65 of the Revised Code, or so soon thereafter as practicable, such joint board of county commissioners shall appoint a board of not less than five trustees, which shall hold office and perform its duties until the first annual meeting after the choice of an established site and buildings, or after the selection and purchase of a building site, at which time such joint board of county commissioners shall appoint a board of not less than five trustees, one of whom shall hold office for a term of one year, one for the term of two years, one for the term of three years, half of the remaining number for the term of four years, and the remainder for the term of five years. Annually thereafter, the joint board of county commissioners shall appoint one or more trustees, each of whom shall hold office for the term of five years, to succeed any trustee whose term of office expires. A trustee may be appointed to succeed himself upon such board of trustees, and all appointments to such board of trustees shall be made from persons who are recommended and approved by the juvenile court judge or judges of the county of which such person is a resident. The annual meeting of the board of trustees shall be held on the first Tuesday in May in each year.

HISTORY: 130 v H 879, eff. 10-14-63

LEGAL ENCYCLOPEDIAS AND ALR

OJur 3d: 73, Penal Institutions § 43

2151.69   Board meetings; compensation

A majority of the trustees appointed under section 2151.68 of the Revised Code constitutes a quorum. Board meetings shall be held at least quarterly. The presiding juvenile court judge of each of the counties of the district organized pursuant to section 2151.65 of the Revised Code shall attend such meetings, or shall designate a member of his staff to do so. The members of the board shall receive no compensation for their services, except their actual traveling expenses, which, when properly certified, shall be allowed and paid by the treasurer.

HISTORY: 130 v H 879, eff. 10-14-63

2151.70 Appointment of superintendent; bond; compensation; duties

The judge, in a county maintaining a school, forestry camp, or other facility or facilities created under section 2151.65 of the Revised Code, shall appoint the superintendent of any such facility. In the case of a district facility created under such section, the board of trustees shall appoint the superintendent. A superintendent, before entering upon his duties, shall give bond with sufficient surety to the judge or to the board, as the case may be, in such amount as may be fixed by the judge or the board, such bond being conditioned upon the full and faithful accounting of the funds and properties coming into his hands.

Compensation of the superintendent and other necessary employees of a school, forestry camp, or other facility or facilities shall be fixed by the judge in the case of a county facility, or by the board of trustees in the case of a district facility. Such compensation and other expenses of maintaining the facility shall be paid in the manner prescribed in section 2151.13 of the Revised Code in the case of a county facility, or in accordance with rules and regulations provided for in section 2151.77 of the Revised Code in the case of a district facility.

The superintendent of a facility shall appoint all employees of such facility. All such employees, except the superintendent, shall be in the classified civil service.

The superintendent of a school, forestry camp, or other facility shall have entire executive charge of such facility, under supervision of the judge, in the case of a county facility, or under supervision of the board of trustees, in the case of a district facility. The superintendent shall control, manage, and operate the facility, and shall have custody of its property, files, and records.

HISTORY: 130 v H 879, eff. 10-14-63

2151.71   Operation of facilities

District schools, forestry camps, or other facilities created under section 2151.65 of the Revised Code shall be established, operated, maintained, and managed in the same manner, so far as applicable, as county schools, forestry camps, or other facilities.

HISTORY: 130 v H 879, eff. 10-14-63

2151.72   Selection of site for district facility

When the board of trustees appointed under section 2151.68 of the Revised Code does not choose an established institution in one of the counties of the district, it may select a suitable site for the erection of a district school, forestry camp, or other facility or facilities created under section 2151.65 of the Revised Code.

HISTORY: 130 v H 879, eff. 10-14-63

2151.73   Apportionment of trustees; executive committee

Each county in the district, organized under section 2151.65 of the Revised Code, shall be entitled to one trustee, and in districts composed of but two counties, each county shall be entitled to not less than two trustees. In districts composed of more than four counties, the number of trustees shall be sufficiently increased so that there shall always be an uneven number of trustees constituting such board. The county in which a district school, forestry camp, or other facility created under section 2151.65 of the Revised Code is located shall have not less than two trustees, who, in the interim period between the regular meetings of the board of trustees, shall act as an executive committee in the discharge of all business pertaining to the school, forestry camp, or other facility.

HISTORY: 130 v H 879, eff. 10-14-63

2151.74   Removal of trustee

The joint board of county commissioners organized under section 2151.65 of the Revised Code may remove any trustee appointed under section 2151.68 of the Revised Code, but no such removal shall be made on account of the religious or political convictions of such trustee. The trustee appointed to fill any vacancy shall hold his office for the unexpired term of his predecessor.

HISTORY: 130 v H 879, eff. 10-14-63

2151.75 Interim duties of trustees; trustees fund; reports

In the interim, between the selection and purchase of a site, and the erection and occupancy of a district school, forestry camp, or other facility or facilities created under section 2151.65 of the Revised Code, the joint board of county commissioners provided by section 2151.65 of the Revised Code may delegate to a board of trustees appointed under section 2151.68 of the Revised Code, such powers and duties as, in its judgment, will be of general interest or aid to the institution. Such joint board of county commissioners may appropriate a trustees' fund, to be expended by the board of trustees in payment of such contracts, purchases, or other expenses necessary to the wants or requirements of the school, forestry camp, or other facility or facilities which are not otherwise provided for. The board of trustees shall make a complete settlement with the joint board of county commissioners once each six months, or quarterly if required, and shall make a full report of the condition of the school, forestry camp, or other facility or facilities and inmates, to the board of county commissioners, and to the juvenile court of each of the counties.

HISTORY: 130 v H 879, eff. 10-14-63

2151.76 Authority for choice, construction, and furnishing of district facility

The choice of an established site and buildings, or the purchase of a site, stock, implements, and general farm equipment, should there be a farm, the erection of buildings, and the completion and furnishing of the district school, forestry camp, or other facility or facilities for occupancy, shall be in the hands of the joint board of county commissioners organized under section 2151.65 of the Revised Code. Such joint board of county commissioners may delegate all or a portion of these duties to the board of trustees provided for under section 2151.68 of the Revised Code, under such restrictions and regulations as the joint board of county commissioners imposes.

HISTORY: 130 v H 879, eff. 10-14-63

2151.77 Capital and current expenses of district

When an established site and buildings are used for a district school, forestry camp, or other facility or facilities created under section 2151.65 of the Revised Code the joint board of county commissioners organized under section 2151.65 of the Revised Code shall cause the value of such site and buildings to be properly appraised. This appraisal value, or in case of the purchase of a site, the purchase price and the cost of all betterments and additions thereto, shall be paid by the counties comprising the district, in proportion to the taxable property of each county, as shown by its tax duplicate. The current expenses of maintaining the school, forestry camp, or other facility or facilities and the cost of ordinary repairs thereto shall be paid by each such county in accordance with one of the following methods as approved by the joint board of county commissioners:

(A) In proportion to the number of children from such county who are maintained in the school, forestry camp, or other facility or facilities during the year;

(B) By a levy submitted by the joint board of county commissioners under division (A) of section 5705.19 of the Revised Code and approved by the electors of the district;

(C) In proportion to the taxable property of each county, as shown by its tax duplicate;

(D) In any combination of the methods for payment described in division (A), (B), or (C) of this section.

The board of trustees shall, with the approval of the joint board of county commissioners, adopt rules for the management of funds used for the current expenses of maintaining the school, forestry camp, or other facility or facilities.

HISTORY: 1988 H 365, eff. 6-14-88
    1972 H 258; 130 v H 879

2151.78 Withdrawal of county from district; continuity of district tax levy

The board of county commissioners of any county within a school, forestry camp, or other facility or facilities district may, upon the recommendation of the juvenile court of such county, withdraw from such district and dispose of its interest in such school, forestry camp, or other facility or facilities selling or leasing its right, title, and interest in the site, buildings, furniture, and equipment to any counties in the district, at such price and upon such terms as are agreed upon among the boards of county commissioners of the counties concerned. Section 307.10 of the Revised Code does not apply to this section. The net proceeds of any such sale or lease shall be paid into the treasury of the withdrawing county.

Any county withdrawing from such district or from a combined district organized under sections 2151.34 and 2151.65 of the Revised Code shall continue to have levied against its tax duplicate any tax levied by the district during the period in which the county was a member of the district for current operating expenses, permanent improvements, or the retirement of bonded indebtedness. Such levy shall continue to be a levy against such duplicate of the county until such time that it expires or is renewed.

Members of the board of trustees of a district school, forestry camp, or other facility or facilities who are residents of a county withdrawing from such district are deemed to have resigned their positions upon the completion of the withdrawal procedure provided by this section. Vacancies then created shall be filled according to sections 2151.68 and 2151.74 of the Revised Code.

HISTORY: 1972 H 258, eff. 1-27-72
130 v H 879

LEGAL ENCYCLOPEDIAS AND ALR

OJur 3d: 73, Penal Institutions § 42

2151.79 Designation of fiscal officer of district; duties of county auditors

The county auditor of the county having the greatest population, or, with the unanimous concurrence of the county auditors of the counties composing a facilities district, the auditor of the county wherein the facility is located, shall be the fiscal officer of a district organized under section 2151.65 of the Revised Code or a combined district organized under sections 2151.34 and 2151.65 of the Revised Code. The county auditors of the several counties composing a school, forestry camp, or other facility or facili-

ties district, shall meet at the district school, forestry camp, or other facility or facilities not less than once in each six months, to review accounts and to transact such other duties in connection with the institution as pertain to the business of their office.

HISTORY: 1974 H 1033, eff. 10-2-74
1972 H 258; 130 v H 879

LEGAL ENCYCLOPEDIAS AND ALR

OJur 3d: 73, Penal Institutions § 45

2151.80 Expenses of members of boards of county commissioners

Each member of the board of county commissioners who meets by appointment to consider the organization of a district school, forestry camp, or other facility or facilities shall, upon presentation of properly certified accounts, be paid his necessary expenses upon a warrant drawn by the county auditor of his county.

HISTORY: 130 v H 879, eff. 10-14-63

MISCELLANEOUS PROVISIONS

2151.85 Minor female's complaint for abortion; hearing; appeal

(A) A woman who is pregnant, unmarried, under eighteen years of age, and unemancipated and who wishes to have an abortion without the notification of her parents, guardian, or custodian may file a complaint in the juvenile court of the county in which she has a residence or legal settlement, in the juvenile court of any county that borders to any extent the county in which she has a residence or legal settlement, or in the juvenile court of the county in which the hospital, clinic, or other facility in which the abortion would be performed or induced is located, requesting the issuance of an order authorizing her to consent to the performance or inducement of an abortion without the notification of her parents, guardian, or custodian.

The complaint shall be made under oath and shall include all of the following:

(1) A statement that the complainant is pregnant;

(2) A statement that the complainant is unmarried, under eighteen years of age, and unemancipated;

(3) A statement that the complainant wishes to have an abortion without the notification of her parents, guardian, or custodian;

(4) An allegation of either or both of the following:

(a) That the complainant is sufficiently mature and well enough informed to intelligently decide whether to have an abortion without the notification of her parents, guardian, or custodian;

(b) That one or both of her parents, her guardian, or her custodian was engaged in a pattern of physical, sexual, or emotional abuse against her, or that the notification of her parents, guardian, or custodian otherwise is not in her best interest.

(5) A statement as to whether the complainant has retained an attorney and, if she has retained an attorney, the name, address, and telephone number of her attorney.

(B)(1) The court shall fix a time for a hearing on any complaint filed pursuant to division (A) of this section and shall keep a record of all testimony and other oral proceedings in the action. The court shall hear and determine the action and shall not refer any portion of it to a referee. The hearing shall be held at the earliest possible time, but not later than the fifth business day after the day that the complaint is filed. The court shall enter judgment on the complaint immediately after the hearing is concluded. If the hearing required by this division is not held by the fifth business day after the complaint is filed, the failure to hold the hearing shall be considered to be a constructive order of the court authorizing the complainant to consent to the performance or inducement of an abortion without the notification of her parent, guardian, or custodian, and the complainant and any other person may rely on the constructive order to the same extent as if the court actually had issued an order under this section authorizing the complainant to consent to the performance or inducement of an abortion without such notification.

(2) The court shall appoint a guardian ad litem to protect the interests of the complainant at the hearing that is held pursuant to this section. If the complainant has not retained an attorney, the court shall appoint an attorney to represent her. If the guardian ad litem is an attorney admitted to the practice of law in this state, the court also may appoint him to serve as the complainant's attorney.

(C)(1) If the complainant makes only the allegation set forth in division (A)(4)(a) of this section and if the court finds, by clear and convincing evidence, that the complainant is sufficiently mature and well enough informed to decide intelligently whether to have an abortion, the court shall issue an order authorizing the complainant to consent to the performance or inducement of an abortion without the notification of her parents, guardian, or custodian. If the

court does not make the finding specified in this division, it shall dismiss the complaint.

(2) If the complainant makes only the allegation set forth in division (A)(4)(b) of this section and if the court finds, by clear and convincing evidence, that there is evidence of a pattern of physical, sexual, or emotional abuse of the complainant by one or both of her parents, her guardian, or her custodian, or that the notification of the parents, guardian, or custodian of the complainant otherwise is not in the best interest of the complainant, the court shall issue an order authorizing the complainant to consent to the performance or inducement of an abortion without the notification of her parents, guardian, or custodian. If the court does not make the finding specified in this division, it shall dismiss the complaint.

(3) If the complainant makes both of the allegations set forth in divisions (A)(4)(a) and (b) of this section, the court shall proceed as follows:

(a) The court first shall determine whether it can make the finding specified in division (C)(1) of this section and, if so, shall issue an order pursuant to that division. If the court issues such an order, it shall not proceed pursuant to division (C)(3)(b) of this section. If the court does not make the finding specified in division (C)(1) of this section, it shall proceed pursuant to division (C)(3)(b) of this section.

(b) If the court pursuant to division (C)(3)(a) of this section does not make the finding specified in division (C)(1) of this section, it shall proceed to determine whether it can make the finding specified in division (C)(2) of this section and, if so, shall issue an order pursuant to that division. If the court does not make the finding specified in division (C)(2) of this section, it shall dismiss the complaint.

(D) The court shall not notify the parents, guardian, or custodian of the complainant that she is pregnant or that she wants to have an abortion.

(E) If the court dismisses the complaint, it immediately shall notify the complainant that she has a right to appeal under section 2505.073 of the Revised Code.

(F) Each hearing under this section shall be conducted in a manner that will preserve the anonymity of the complainant. The complaint and all other papers and records that pertain to an action commenced under this section shall be kept confidential and are not public records under section 149.43 of the Revised Code.

(G) The clerk of the supreme court shall prescribe complaint and notice of appeal forms that shall be used by a complainant filing a complaint under this section and by an appellant filing an appeal under section 2505.073 of the Revised Code. The clerk of each juvenile court shall furnish blank copies of the forms, without charge, to any person who requests them.

(H) No filing fee shall be required of, and no court costs shall be assessed against, a complainant filing a complaint under this section or an appellant filing an appeal under section 2505.073 of the Revised Code.

(I) As used in this section, "unemancipated" means that a woman who is unmarried and under eighteen years of age has not entered the armed services of the United States, has not become employed and self-subsisting, or has not otherwise become independent from the care and control of her parent, guardian, or custodian.

HISTORY: 1985 H 319, eff. 3-24-86

CROSS REFERENCES

Attempt to have abortion without parental notice not creating patient-physician relationship, 2151.421

Appeal from dismissal of minor female's complaint for abortion, 2505.073

LEGAL ENCYCLOPEDIAS AND ALR

Right of minor to have abortion performed without parental consent. 42 ALR3d 1406

2151.99   Penalties

(A) Whoever violates division (D)(2) or (3) of section 2151.313 or division (A)(1) or (I)(2) of section 2151.421 of the Revised Code is guilty of a misdemeanor of the fourth degree.

(B) Whoever violates division (D)(1) of section 2151.313 of the Revised Code is guilty of a minor misdemeanor.

HISTORY: 1986 H 529, eff. 3-11-87
            1985 H 349; 1984 H 258; 1972 H 511; 1969 H 320; 130 v H 765; 1953 H 1

PRACTICE AND STUDY AIDS

Baldwin's Ohio School Law, Text 24.05(A)

CROSS REFERENCES

Alleged child abuse and neglect, persons mandated to report, OAC 5101:2-34-04

Judges of the court of domestic relations, juvenile court responsibility, 2301.03

Penalties for misdemeanor, 2929.21

Imposing sentence for misdemeanor, 2929.22

LEGAL ENCYCLOPEDIAS AND ALR

OJur 3d: 46, Family Law § 577

OHIO RULES OF PROCEDURE

(Selected Provisions)

Rules of Juvenile Procedure

Edited by WILLIAM A. KURTZ, A.B., J.D.
Deputy Court Administrator,
Cuyahoga County Court of Common Pleas,
Juvenile Court Division

Publisher's Note: References to OJur, AmJur, and ALR were compiled from the *Ohio Code Research Guide* (Lawyer's Co-operative Publishing Company).

Publisher's Note: These Rules are published as they appear in the *Ohio Official Reports*.

Publisher's Note: Until 1968, when the Modern Courts Amendment to the Ohio Constitution was adopted, Ohio court procedure was governed entirely by statute and caselaw. The Modern Courts Amendment required the Supreme Court of Ohio, subject to the approval of the General Assembly, to "prescribe rules governing practice and procedure in all courts of the state." Rules of practice and procedure are the Civil, Criminal, Appellate, and Juvenile Rules, Rules of the Court of Claims, and the Ohio Rules of Evidence. Pursuant to Ohio Constitution Article IV, Section 5(B), such rules "shall not abridge, enlarge, or modify any substantive right," and "all laws in conflict with such rules shall be of no further force or effect."

CROSS REFERENCES

Humane societies, protection of children, 1717.14

Cuyahoga county juvenile court, jurisdiction, 2153.16

Judges of the court of domestic relations, juvenile court responsibility, 2301.03

Trial, magistrate courts, applicability of chapter, 2938.02

Youth commission, commitment of children, assignment to juvenile diagnostic center, 5139.05

LAW REVIEW ARTICLES

31 Cin Law Rev 131 (1962). A synopsis of Ohio Juvenile Court Law, Hon. Don J. Young, Jr.

18 WRU Law Rev 1239 (1967). The Juvenile Court—A Court of Law, Walter G. Whitlatch.

18 Clev St L Rev 599 (1969). Role of the Attorney in Juvenile Court, Julian Greenspun.

10 Cleve Mar L Rev 524 (1961). Evidence in Cuyahoga County Juvenile Court, Elaine J. Columbro.

55 Am Bar Assn Jour 1151 (1969). Right of Children: The Legal Vacuum, Lois G. Forer.

54 Am Bar Assn Jour 33 (1968). A Way Out of Juvenile Delinquency, Roman C. Pucinski.

53 Am Bar Assn Jour 811 (1967). In re Gault, Juvenile Courts and Lawyers, Norman Lefstein.

53 Am Bar Assn Jour 456 (1967). An Answer to the Challenge of Kent, Daniels W. McLean.

53 Am Bar Assn Jour 31 (1967). The Juvenile Court: Effective Justice or Benevolent Despotism?, Bertram Polow.

52 Am Bar Assn Jour 923 (1966). The Kent Case and the Juvenile Court: A Challenge to Lawyers, Robert Gardner.

Clev Bar Jour 257 (Sept. 1966). Juvenile Court: Neglected Child of the Judiciary, Hon. Albert A. Woldman.

Clev Bar Jour 179 (June 1966). Juvenile Court: Time for Change, Charles Auerbach.

Clev Bar Jour, August 1956, Vol. 27, No. 10. A legal look at Juvenile Court, Paul W. Alexander.

Vol 33 Cuyahoga County Bar Assn Bull, No. 8. Rules of the Juvenile Court of Cuyahoga County.

Juv R 1

Scope of rules: applicability; construction; exceptions

(A) Applicability.

These rules prescribe the procedure to be followed in all juvenile courts of this state in all proceedings coming within the jurisdiction of such courts, with the exceptions stated in subdivision (C).

(B) Construction.

These rules shall be liberally interpreted and construed so as to effectuate the following purposes:

(1) to effect the just determination of every juvenile court proceeding by ensuring the parties a fair hearing and the recognition and enforcement of their constitutional and other legal rights;

(2) to secure simplicity and uniformity in procedure, fairness in administration, and the elimination of unjustifiable expense and delay;

(3) to provide for the care, protection, and mental and physical development of children subject to the jurisdiction of the juvenile court, and to protect the welfare of the community; and

(4) to protect the public interest by treating children as persons in need of supervision, care and rehabilitation.

(C) Exceptions.

These rules shall not apply to procedure (1) upon appeal to review any judgment, order or ruling, (2) upon the trial of criminal actions, (3) upon the trial of divorce, annulment, and alimony actions, (4) in proceedings to determine the paternity of any child born out of wedlock and (5) in the commitment of the mentally ill and mentally retarded; provided that when any statute provides for procedure by general or specific reference to the statutes governing procedure in juvenile court actions such procedure shall be in accordance with these rules.

Adopted eff. 7-1-72

Editor's Comment

1. Applicability
2. Construction
3. Exceptions

1. Applicability

Juv R 1(A) follows the format of both Civ R 1(A) and Crim R 1(A) and prescribes the procedure to be followed by all juvenile courts of Ohio and those exercising juvenile jurisdiction in all proceedings within their jurisdiction except those exceptions stated in Juv R 1(C). There are only two courts in Ohio exercising exclusively juvenile jurisdiction. These are the Cuyahoga and Hamilton county courts which are now juvenile divisions of their respective common pleas courts. Juvenile jurisdiction in all other counties in Ohio is exercised either by the probate division or the domestic relations division of the court of common pleas.

2. Construction

Juv R 1(B) restates the purposes of the Juvenile Court Act, Ch 2151, and follows the language used in 2151.01. Juv R 1(B)(1) adopts the language of 2151.01(D); Juv R 1(B)(2) is new and follows the general format of Crim R 1(B) and Civ R 1(B) and clearly outlines the thrust of the rules to secure simplicity and uniformity, fairness in administration and the elimination of unjustifiable expense and delay. Juv R 1(B)(3) adopts the language of 2151.01(A) with the added phrase "to protect the welfare of the community". Juv R 1(B)(4) is a rephrasing of 2151.01(B) in that the language "removing the consequences of criminal behavior and the taint of criminality from children committing delinquent acts and to substitute therefor a program" has been deleted so as to make it clear that juvenile proceedings are not criminal actions. The language of 2151.01(C) has been deleted as being superfluous as the best interest of the child still permeates the entire juvenile proceeding with the protection of the community also a major consideration.

3. Exceptions

The Rules of Juvenile Procedure are clearly applicable to all juvenile proceedings except as stated herein to appeals which are governed by the Appellate Rules; criminal actions within the jurisdiction of juvenile courts pursuant to 2151.23(A)(5) and 2151.23(B)(1) which are governed by the Criminal Rules; divorce, annulment and alimony actions which are governed by Ch 3105 and Civ R 75; paternity actions pursuant to 2151.23(B)(2) which are governed by the provisions of Ch 3115 and the Civil Rules; and commitment proceedings regarding the mentally ill or mentally retarded in which the juvenile court has jurisdiction pursuant to 2151.23(A)(4) but which are governed by the provisions of Ch 5122 and 5125.

Juv R 1(C) like Crim R 1(C) and Civ R 1(C) is both a rule of exclusion and a rule of inclusion. The rule states the general exclusions from applicability but also by stating "when any statute provides for procedure by general or specific reference to the statutes governing procedure in juvenile court actions such procedure shall be in accordance with these rules" it becomes a rule of inclusion. The Juvenile Rules apply not only because of this proviso but also because O Const Art IV, § 5(B) states "all laws in conflict with such rules shall be of no further force or effect after such rules have taken effect".

Juv R 1(C) makes it clear that when jurisdiction is transferred to the juvenile court by any other court pursuant to 3107.12, 3109.04 or 3109.06, these Rules of Juvenile Procedure apply.

CROSS REFERENCES

Kurtz & Giannelli, Ohio Juvenile Law, Text 1.04, 7.02, 13.10

Powers and duties of supreme court, administrative director, rules, O Const Art IV §5
Rules of Criminal Procedure, application to juvenile proceedings limited, Crim R 1

OJur 3d: 23, Courts and Judges § 428; 25, Criminal Law § 38; 46, Family Law § 363, 364
Procedural requirements under Federal Constitution in juvenile delinquency proceedings—federal cases. 25 LEd(2d) 950

NOTES ON DECISIONS AND OPINIONS

1. Cases interpreting Juvenile Rule 1
2. Cases interpreting law analogous to Juvenile Rule 1

1. Cases interpreting Juvenile Rule 1

14 App(3d) 201, 14 OBR 228, 470 NE(2d) 438 (Butler 1983), In re Vickers Children. A hearing on a complaint for permanent custody must be bifurcated according to Juv R 29 and 34 into separate adjudicatory and dispositional hearings, notwithstanding the contrary provisions of RC 2151.414, since Juv R 1(A) provides that all proceedings in a juvenile court are governed by the Rules of Juvenile Procedure.

61 App(2d) 44, 398 NE(2d) 800 (1978), In re Gantt. When, in an adjudicatory hearing held pursuant to Juv R 29, the only evidence of guilt utilized by the court is testimony presented at the preliminary hearing, where the accused exercised adequate rights of cross-examination, he is denied no constitutional right.

52 App(2d) 312, 369 NE(2d) 1054 (1976), State v Eddington. A juvenile judge has no authority to commit the trial of a criminal charge against an adult to a referee, and any proceedings so committed are null and void.

45 App(2d) 191, 341 NE(2d) 853 (1975), State ex rel Leis v Black. The juvenile and general divisions of a court of common pleas possess concurrent jurisdiction over a juvenile accused of a crime, and the juvenile division has not been divested of personal jurisdiction over one whose disposition is returned to it after the accused initially waived his right to be judged in that tribunal.

2. Cases interpreting law analogous to Juvenile Rule 1

2151.01 CONSTRUCTION; PURPOSE

29 Misc 71, 278 NE(2d) 701 (CP Columbiana 1971), In re Morris. The matter of unlawful search and seizure under US Const Am 4 applies to juveniles.

OAG 70-143. A judge of a juvenile court may not commit a child who has been found to be a delinquent child, or a juvenile traffic offender, to the county jail upon the failure, refusal, or inability of such child to pay a fine and court costs.

OAG 70-015. If the county adult detention facility is designed with a space which is enclosed on all sides, that is distinct, set apart and disconnected so that no child over the age of fifteen placed in that space will come in contact or communication with any adult convicted of or arrested for a crime, and the public interest and safety require the detention of such child when a delinquent detention facility is not available, the use of such adult facility is authorized.

2151.05 CHILD WITHOUT PROPER PARENTAL CARE

28 NP(NS) 433 (1930), In re Decker. The juvenile statutes are designed primarily for the protection of dependent and reformation of delinquent children and must be given a liberal construction.

2151.23 JURISDICTION OF JUVENILE COURT

12 CC(NS) 374, 21 CD 492 (1909), Travis v State; affirmed by 82 OS 439, 92 NE 1125 (1910). Act 96 v 314, creating juvenile courts and establishing procedure therein, is not void for lack of definiteness in stating the offenses therein proscribed.

Juv R 2
Definitions

As used in these rules:

(1) "Adjudicatory hearing" means a hearing to determine whether a child is a juvenile traffic offender, delinquent, unruly, neglected, or dependent or is otherwise within the jurisdiction of the court or whether temporary legal custody should be converted to permanent custody.

(2) "Child" means a person who is under the age of eighteen years. A child who violates a federal or state law or municipal ordinance prior to attaining eighteen years of age shall be deemed a child irrespective of his age at the time the complaint is filed or hearing had thereon.

(3) "Complaint" means the legal document which sets forth the allegations which form the basis for juvenile court jurisdiction.

(4) "Court proceeding" means all action taken by a court from the earlier of (a) the time a complaint is filed and (b) the time a person first appears before an officer of a juvenile court until the court relinquishes jurisdiction over such child.

(5) "Custodian" means a person who has been granted custody of a child by a court.

(6) "Detention" means the temporary care of children in restricted facilities pending court adjudication or disposition, or execution of a court order.

(7) "Detention hearing" means a hearing to determine whether a child shall be held in detention or shelter care prior to or pending execution of a final dispositional order.

(8) "Dispositional hearing" means a hearing to determine what action shall be taken concerning a child who is within the jurisdiction of the court.

(9) "Guardian" means a court appointed guardian of the person of a child.

(10) "Guardian ad litem" means a person appointed to protect the interests of a party in a juvenile court proceeding.

(11) "Hearing" means any portion of a juvenile court proceeding before the court, whether summary in nature or by examination of witnesses.

(12) "Indigent person" means a person who, at the time his need is determined, is unable by reason of lack of property or income to provide for full payment of legal counsel and all other necessary expenses of representation.

(13) "Juvenile court" means a division of the court of common pleas, or a juvenile court separately and independently created, having jurisdiction under R.C. Chapter 2151.

(14) "Juvenile judge" means a judge of a court having jurisdiction under R.C. Chapter 2151.

(15) "Mental examination" means an examination by a psychiatrist or psychologist.

(16) "Party" means a child who is the subject of a juvenile court proceeding, his spouse, if any, his parent, or if the parent of a child be himself a child, the parent of such parent and, in appropriate cases, his custodian, guardian or guardian ad litem, the state and any other person specifically designated by the court.

(17) "Person" includes an individual, association, corporation, or partnership and the state or any of its political subdivisions, departments, or agencies.

(18) "Physical examination" means an examination by a physician.

(19) "Rule of court" means a rule promulgated by the supreme court or a rule concerning local practice adopted by another court which is not inconsistent with the rules promulgated by the supreme court and which rule is filed with the supreme court.

(20) "Shelter care" means the temporary care of children in physically unrestricted facilities pending court adjudication or disposition, or execution of a court order.

(21) "Social history" means the personal and family history of a child or any other party to a juvenile proceeding and may include the prior record of the person with the juvenile court or any other court.

(22) "Ward of court" means a child over whom the court assumes continuing jurisdiction.

Adopted eff. 7-1-72

Editor's Comment

1. Adjudicatory hearing
2. Child
3. Complaint
4. Court proceeding
5. Custodian
6. Detention

7. Detention hearing
8. Dispositional hearing
9. Guardian
10. Guardian ad litem
11. Hearing
12. Indigent person
13. Juvenile court
14. Juvenile judge
15. Mental examination
16. Party
17. Person
18. Physical examination
19. Rule of court
20. Shelter care
21. Social history
22. Ward of court

Juv R 2 is the definitions rule. The inclusion of a definitions rule follows the pattern of Ch 2151 (2151.011), the Minnesota Rules and the National Council on Crime and Delinquency Model Rules. This departure from the pattern of the Ohio Civil Rules and Criminal Rules was adopted by the committee because a number of crucial terms occur throughout the Juvenile Rules. Once a definition rule was included for such terms, it made sense to include all definitions in the rule.

The definitions are organized alphabetically because of their number and the impossibility of finding any fully satisfactory conceptual order. In this regard, they follow the Minnesota Rules, but not the Model Rules or 2151.011.

1. Adjudicatory hearing

This definition determines the scope of Juv R 29 (Adjudicatory hearing), so as to make it clear that the procedural safeguards connected with that type of hearing are applicable in the cases so defined. The definition includes any hearing to establish that a person is within the jurisdiction of the juvenile court, mentioning specifically the five most usual types of cases: delinquency, unruliness, neglect, dependency, and juvenile traffic offender. The phrase "otherwise within the jurisdiction" is added to catch the other categories of cases over which the juvenile court has jurisdiction under 2151.23. The most significant part of the definition is the inclusion within Juv R 29 of hearings to determine whether a temporary legal custody commitment should be changed to permanent custody. This is a hearing which has the effect of completely terminating parental rights, and its importance requires that the full procedural protection of an adjudicatory hearing be provided even though the child is already within the jurisdiction of the court once there has been a temporary legal custody commitment.

The definition is adapted to the Ohio setting from Minnesota Rule 1-2(a).

2. Child

The term "child" is used throughout the rules and so is defined here.

The definition is taken from 2151.011(B)(1). The only change is that the definition is stated in two sentences rather than one in order to more accurately reflect the logical relationship of its two parts. No change in substance is intended.

3. Complaint

This definition provides that the document by which juvenile court proceedings are commenced is to be called a complaint.

The form of the definition is taken from Minnesota Rule 1-2(q) and NCCD Model Rule 1(7), although the term "complaint" is used in place of the term "petition" which is used in those rules, so as to conform to the terminology of the Civil Rules.

4. Court proceeding

The term "court proceeding" is used many places in the rules (see Juv R 3, 4, 37). The intent of the definition is to indicate that the term has a broad scope. A significant example of the effect of the definition is to be seen in conjunction with Juv R 4(A) on the time when the right to counsel arises.

5. Custodian

This term is used in many cases and is defined so as to clearly indicate the difference between one who has physical custody and one who has been granted legal custody by a court.

6. Detention

This definition, together with that of "shelter care" (Juv R 2(20)), defines the scope of Juv R 7 (Detention and shelter). In many respects, detention is treated differently from shelter care within that rule. Thus, the definitions of the two terms and the differences between them are important. The essence of detention is the presence of physically restrictive facilities for children found to be delinquent or unruly while the essence of shelter care is the absence of restrictive facilities and is designed for children found to be dependent or neglected.

The definition is taken from 2151.011(B)(3). The only change is the addition of the language "or execution of a court order", which is required to make it clear that a child may be detained, for example, after a dispositional order that he be committed to the Ohio Youth Commission until the Ohio Youth Commission can take custody of him.

7. Detention hearing

Detention hearing is required by Juv R 7(F).

8. Dispositional hearing

This definition determines the scope of the hearing provided for in Juv R 34.

9. Guardian

This definition provides a special, limited meaning for the term "guardian" within the Juvenile Rules. The guardian is included as a party under Juv R 2(16), and the present definition limits this to the guardian of the person rather than the guardian of the property, where two guardians exist under the law of guardianship. It further limits the guardian who is automatically a party under Juv R 2(16) to guardians appointed by a court, as contrasted with natural guardians under the law of guardianship.

10. Guardian ad litem

The appointment and functions of the guardian ad litem are dealt with in Juv R 4. The definition here indicates clearly that the "guardian ad litem" is conceptually different from the "guardian" as defined in Juv R 2(9).

This definition is consistent with the use of the term in 2151.281.

11. Hearing

This definition provides a general meaning for the term "hearing" as used in the rules. It should make it clear that the adjudicatory and dispositional hearings are not the only types of hearings in juvenile court. Some rules refer to all hearings (*see*, particularly, Juv R 27).

The definition is taken from the Minnesota Rules.

12. Indigent person

The definition is an exact restatement of the definition found in 2151.352. The definition provides that the court should look not only to the expense of employing counsel to determine indigency, but should also consider the other expenses of juvenile court proceedings, such as those involved in securing expert evaluations and testimony.

The juvenile court has a strong interest in having parties in juvenile court represented by counsel, and a more realistic flexible standard was thus required in the juvenile court. While one might assume that some adults can reasonably protect their own interests without counsel, that assumption clearly cannot be indulged with respect to a child.

13. Juvenile court

This definition must be seen in conjunction with the definition of "juvenile judge," from which it is distinguished. The latter term has been used whenever a particular rule applies only to a judge of the juvenile court, while the broader terms "juvenile court" and "court" are used when a rule applies to the court in general, judges and referees.

The definition is taken from 2151.011(A)(1).

14. Juvenile judge

The function of this definition is described in connection with the preceding definition.

The definition is taken from 2151.011(A)(2).

15. Mental examination

The definition is particularly important and relates to Juv R 30 dealing with transfer of jurisdiction for the purposes of criminal prosecution.

16. Party

The term "party" is used throughout the Juvenile Rules and so is a centrally important definition.

This definition creates two categories of parties. Persons in the first group are always parties in a juvenile proceeding covered by these rules. This includes the child who is the subject of the proceed-ing, his spouse, if any, and his parents. The second category consists of persons who may be parties in appropriate cases; they are a custodian, guardian or guardian ad litem for the child, the state, and any other person the court may designate.

The effect of the rule should be to erase any doubt that both parent and child are parties to all types of juvenile court proceedings covered by these rules. This is significant in that the various aspects of procedural due process are accorded to parties to juvenile court proceedings, but depend on the definition of this crucial term.

By indicating that where the state is involved in a juvenile court proceeding it too becomes a party, the rules make it clear that such mechanisms as juvenile court discovery are available against the state.

The flexibility provided in the last phrase in the rule is crucial in juvenile court, where the welfare of a child may be directly affected by the conduct of some person outside the legal family. The most obvious category of person the court might wish to make a party is a stepparent or person living with a parent of the child and contributing to his neglect. In some cases, the court might also wish to make a children's services board or other agency a party in order to facilitate the use of dispositional alternatives available only through such agency.

The definition is taken directly from 2151.011(B)(12). The only change is the deletion of the words "natural or adoptive" before the word "parent" in the final clause. The words were deleted because they would be surplusage.

17. Person

This definition indicates clearly that the term "person" as used in these rules is not limited to physical persons.

The definition is taken from the Minnesota Rules.

18. Physical examination

This definition determines the scope of part of Juv R 32 and is especially important in neglect and child abuse proceedings.

19. Rule of court

Local rules of court may be used to supplement these rules in such areas as that of intake procedure, which is only dealt with here in the most general terms (Juv R 9).

The definition is taken from Civ R 83.

20. Shelter care

The function of this definition is discussed in connection with Juv R 2(6) dealing with detention.

The definition is taken from 2151.011(B)(4). The term "shelter care" has been used here instead of the term "shelter" used in the Revised Code, as being more expressive of the concept involved. The only material change from the Code definition is the addition of the language "or execution of a court order", which is required to make it clear that a child may be placed in shelter care after a disposition order of the court until the order can be carried out. For example, in a custody dispute, the court might order that a child be turned over to a parent in another state; the child would need to be held in shelter care until the arrival of the parent to take custody of him.

21. Social history

This definition provides a broad scope for a term that is used extensively in Juv R 32. The social history provides the juvenile court with the basis for making a disposition in the best interest of a child found to be within the court's jurisdiction.

22. Ward of court

This term is used in Juv R 42(G) and is used but not defined in Ch 2151.

Some terms defined in 2151.011 have not been defined in this rule as their meaning has been established in other statutes and case decisions. Terms which are used but not defined in this rule shall be given a meaning consistent with the purposes outlined in Juv R 1(B).

CROSS REFERENCES

Schroeder-Katz, Ohio Criminal Law, Crim R 1, Author's Text

Kurtz & Giannelli, Ohio Juvenile Law, Text 1.04, 7.03, 7.05(A), 7.06(A)(C)(D), 9.03(B)(C)(E), 11.03, 11.11(C), 13.09(E), 13.10, 15.02(A), 15.04(A)

OJur 3d: 22, Courts and Judges § 72; 23, Courts and Judges § 428; 26, Criminal Law § 637; 46, Family Law § 365 to 368, 374, 423, 465

NOTES ON DECISIONS AND OPINIONS

1. Cases interpreting Juvenile Rule 2
2. Cases interpreting law analogous to Juvenile Rule 2

1. Cases interpreting Juvenile Rule 2

45 App(2d) 299, 344 NE(2d) 144 (1973), Morrison v Morrison. A temporary order of a juvenile court changing custody under Juv R 13 or 29 is not a dispositional order under Juv R 34, and hence is not a final appealable order.

37 App(2d) 7, 306 NE(2d) 166 (1973), In re Bolden. Error cannot be predicated on the juvenile court's holding a dispositional hearing immediately following an adjudicatory hearing and its failure to continue the dispositional hearing for a reasonable time to enable the party to obtain or consult counsel, as prescribed by Juv R 34(A), unless it affirmatively appears in the record that the affected nonindigent party has requested such continuance.

No. 87-CA-12 (5th Dist Ct App, Delaware, 10-22-87), In re Dague. The father of a juvenile adjudged delinquent is a party as defined in Juv R 2(16) and is subject to orders of the court.

No. 1388 (4th Dist Ct App, Scioto, 3-28-83), In re Knipp. In an adjudicatory hearing to convert temporary custody of a minor to permanent custody pursuant to Juv R 2(1), the trial court erred in admitting into evidence reports of a child welfare agency where no foundation was laid to admit such report as a business records exception or public records exception to hearsay.

2. Cases interpreting law analogous to Juvenile Rule 2

2151.011 DEFINITIONS

OAG 70-015. If the county detention facility is designed with a space which is enclosed on all sides, that is distinct, set apart and disconnected so that no child over the age of fifteen placed in that space will come in contact or communication with any adult convicted of or arrested for a crime, and the public interest and safety require the detention of such child when a delinquent detention facility is not available, the use of such adult facility is authorized.

1957 OAG 880. The office of probate and juvenile judge is incompatible with the office of county court judge.

1956 OAG 7008. The term "legal settlement," as used in Ch 2151, with respect to parents, guardians, or persons standing in the relationship of loco parentis of children within the jurisdiction of the juvenile court, has reference to that term as defined in 5113.05.

1937 OAG 871. After the effective date of GC 1639-1 (RC 2151.01) et seq., in all counties of Ohio not having a juvenile court or division of domestic relations, all juvenile jurisdiction is reposed in a juvenile court within the probate court of such county.

2151.07 CREATION AND POWERS OF JUVENILE COURT

1945 OAG 247. When a girl commits an act of delinquency before arriving at the age of eighteen, and the complaint is not filed or hearing held until after said child arrives at the age of eighteen years, the juvenile court has jurisdiction to hear and dispose of such complaint, except that GC 2101 (RC 5141.31) prohibits the commitment of such child to the Girls' Industrial School if, at the time of such hearing, she has arrived at the age of eighteen years.

2151.25 TRANSFER TO JUVENILE COURT

1939 OAG 726. Under authority of this act, juvenile court has exclusive jurisdiction of all persons under eighteen charged with arson or other burnings as contained in GC 12433 (RC 2907.02) and GC 12436 (RC 2907.07).

Juv R 3

Waiver of rights

A child's right to be represented by counsel at a hearing to determine whether the juvenile court shall relinquish its jurisdiction for purposes of criminal prosecution may not be waived. No other right of a child may be waived without the permission of the court.

Adopted eff. 7-1-72

Editor's Comment

Juv R 3 deals with basic rights in juvenile court and the waiver of those rights. The provision that the child's right to counsel may not be waived at a hearing under Juv R 30 dealing with relinquishment of jurisdiction for purposes of criminal prosecution is mandated by the ruling in *Kent v United States,* 383 US 541, 86 SCt 1045, 16 LEd(2d) 84 (1966), holding that at such a critical stage of the proceedings due process of law and fundamental fairness require that the child be represented by counsel. All other rights can be waived if the waiver is knowingly and intelligently made and is voluntary. This is always a fact determination and whether waiver is proper depends on the particular facts in each instance. The rule provides that the judge may deny a waiver if it is against the best interest of the child or if there is any question whether the waiver is knowingly and intelligently made and is voluntary.

CROSS REFERENCES

Kurtz & Giannelli, Ohio Juvenile Law, Text 5.04(B), 7.05(D), 9.03(B), 11.03

Relinquishment of jurisdiction for purposes of criminal prosecution, Juv R 30

OJur 3d: 23, Courts and Judges § 428; 46, Family Law § 441

Am Jur 2d: 47, Juvenile Courts and Delinquent and Dependent Children § 39

Validity and efficacy of minor's waiver of right to counsel—modern cases. 25 ALR4th 1072

Procedural requirements under Federal Constitution in juvenile delinquency proceedings—federal cases. 25 LEd(2d) 950

NOTES ON DECISIONS AND OPINIONS

1. Cases interpreting Juvenile Rule 3
2. Cases interpreting law analogous to Juvenile Rule 3

1. Cases interpreting Juvenile Rule 3

No. 3430 (9th Dist Ct App, Lorain, 5-11-83), In re Hawkins. Where a fourteen-year-old minor, without counsel, made a statement to police implicating herself in setting a fire which killed her father, and the court psychologist testified that such minor was of average intelligence, the minor's statement is properly admitted into evidence where the minor had waived her Miranda rights and during the course of such statement the minor answered intelligently, coherently, and gave no indication of undue influence.

2. Cases interpreting law analogous to Juvenile Rule 3

2151.35 HEARING PROCEDURE; FINDINGS; RECORD

18 App(2d) 276, 248 NE(2d) 620 (1969), In re Baker; modified by 20 OS(2d) 142, 254 NE(2d) 363 (1969). Where a juvenile has received the following essentials of due process and fair treatment, (1) written notice of the specific charge or factual allegations, given to the juvenile and his parents or guardian sufficiently in advance of the hearing to permit preparation; (2) notification to the juvenile and his parents of the juvenile's right to be represented by counsel retained by them, or, if they are unable to afford counsel, that counsel will be appointed to represent the juvenile; (3) application of the constitutional privileges against self-incrimination; and (4), absent a valid confession, a determination of delinquency and an order of commitment based only on sworn testimony subjected to the opportunity for cross-examination in accordance with constitutional requirements, such juvenile has not been deprived of due process under either the Constitution of the United States or the Constitution of the State of Ohio.

Juv R 4

Right to counsel; guardian ad litem

(A) Right to counsel; when arises.

Every party shall have the right to be represented by counsel and every child, parent, custodian, or other person in loco parentis the right to appointed counsel if indigent. These rights shall arise when a person becomes a party to a juvenile court proceeding. When the complaint alleges that a child is an abused child, the court must appoint an attorney to represent the interests of the child.

(B) Guardian ad litem; when appointed.

The court shall appoint a guardian ad litem to protect the interests of a child or incompetent adult in a juvenile court proceeding when:

(1) The child has no parent, guardian, or legal custodian;

(2) The interests of the child and the interests of the parent may conflict;

(3) The parent is under eighteen years of age or appears to be mentally incompetent;

(4) Appointment is otherwise necessary to meet the requirements of a fair hearing.

(C) Guardian ad litem as counsel.

When the guardian ad litem is an attorney admitted to practice in this state, he may also serve as counsel to his ward.

(D) Appearance of attorneys.

An attorney shall enter his appearance by filing a written notice with the court or by appearing personally at a court hearing and informing the court that he represents a party.

(E) Withdrawal of counsel or guardian ad litem.

An attorney or guardian ad litem may withdraw only with the consent of the court upon good cause shown.

(F) Costs.

The court may fix compensation for the services of appointed counsel and guardians ad litem, tax the same as a part of the costs and assess them against the child, his parents, custodian, or other person in loco parentis of such child.

Adopted eff. 7-1-72; amended eff. 7-1-76

Editor's Comment

1. Right to counsel; guardian ad litem
2. Right to counsel; when arises
3. Guardian ad litem; when appointed
4. Guardian ad litem as counsel
5. Appearance of attorneys
6. Withdrawal of counsel or guardian ad litem
7. Costs

1. Right to counsel; guardian ad litem

Juv R 4 governs the right to counsel and guardian ad litem and tries to coordinate the two more clearly than is done in Ch 2151.

2. Right to counsel; when arises

Juv R 4(A) first states the right of all parties to counsel and to appointed counsel if indigent. The terms "party" and "indigent person" are broadly defined in Juv R 2(16) and 2(12) respectively.

The rule then provides that these rights arise as soon as a person becomes a party to a juvenile court proceeding as defined in Juv R 2(4). These rights arise also whenever a child is taken into custody pursuant to Juv R 6. The rule restates 2151.351 (Repealed) and 2151.352.

Juv R 4(A) further provides that in child abuse cases (2151.031) the court must appoint an attorney to represent the interests of the child. When considering this provision in conjunction with the statutory requirement (2151.281) that a guardian ad litem be appointed to protect the interests of an alleged abused or neglected child, it appears that the proper procedure would be to appoint an attorney to act as both legal counsel and guardian ad litem for an alleged abused child. If the court finds that a conflict may exist between the attorney's dual role of legal counsel and guardian ad litem, the court should relieve the attorney of one of the roles and appoint someone else to assume those responsibilities.

3. Guardian ad litem; when appointed

Juv R 4(B) continues Ohio practice, as represented by 2151.281, by handling the problem of conflict between interests of parents and their children through the appointment of a guardian ad litem rather than simply by appointment of a second counsel. The guardian ad litem can then act as

counsel under Juv R 4(C) if he is an attorney or may ask the court to appoint a separate attorney for the child.

On the other hand, Juv R 4(B) expands the cases in which a guardian ad litem is to be appointed. The cases mentioned in Juv R 4(B)(1) and 4(B)(3) are already covered in 2151.281. Juv R 4(B)(4), however, is new and Juv R 4(B)(2) is significantly broader than the first paragraph of 2151.281(B), which provides that a guardian ad litem shall be appointed where the court finds there *is* a conflict of interest. Juv R 4(B)(2) substitutes "may" for "is" on the theory that a possibility of conflict should be sufficient to appoint someone to insure that the child is adequately represented. The court should consider the appointment of a guardian ad litem whenever a child so requests, on the theory that when the child perceives a conflict of interest he is entitled to individual representation.

Absent from the rules is the statutory provision (2151.281) that a guardian ad litem must be appointed to protect the interests of any child who is the subject of a motion for permanent custody filed pursuant to 2151.414.

4. Guardian ad litem as counsel

Juv R 4(C) provides that a guardian ad litem may serve as counsel to his ward where he is an attorney admitted to practice in this state. The rule also implies that whether or not he is an attorney, he could request the court to appoint independent counsel for his client if his client is indigent, as defined in Juv R 2(12).

5. Appearance of attorneys

Juv R 4(D) provides the means by which an attorney is to enter his appearance in a case. The rule is taken from the Minnesota Rules and the National Council on Crime and Delinquency Model Rules.

6. Withdrawal of counsel or guardian ad litem

Juv R 4(E) gives the court discretion to disallow a request for withdrawal by an attorney or guardian ad litem unless there is good cause shown. The rule is consistent with 2151.281.

7. Costs

Juv R 4(F) supplements the costs provision of 2151.351 (Repealed) in that it includes compensation for guardians ad litem and provides for assessment against other parties where appropriate.

CROSS REFERENCES

Kurtz & Giannelli, Ohio Juvenile Law, Text 1.04, 5.04(C), 7.01, 9.03(B), 11.03, 13.10

Paternity proceedings, representation of child's interests, 3111.07

OJur 3d: 23, Courts and Judges § 428; 46, Family Law § 443 to 447, 548, 549
Am Jur 2d: 47, Juvenile Courts and Delinquent and Dependent Children § 22, 38, 58
Right to and appointment of counsel in juvenile court proceeding. 60 ALR2d 691

Right of indigent parent to appointed counsel in proceeding for involuntary termination of parental rights. 80 ALR3d 1141

LAW REVIEW ARTICLES

8 Nor Ky L Rev 513 (1981). Lassiter v Department of Social Services: The Due Process Right to Appointed Counsel Left Hanging in the Mathews v Eldrodge Balance, Jane E. Jackson.

NOTES ON DECISIONS AND OPINIONS

1. Cases interpreting Juvenile Rule 4
2. Cases interpreting law analogous to Juvenile Rule 4

1. Cases interpreting Juvenile Rule 4

66 OS(2d) 123, 420 NE(2d) 116 (1981), State ex rel Butler v Demis. 120.33(B) does not impose a clear legal duty upon a judge to appoint as counsel of record the attorney personally selected by an indigent party.

33 App(3d) 318, 515 NE(2d) 987 (Franklin 1986), Nationwide Mutual Insurance Co v Wymer. In an action brought against a parent and his child for damages caused by a fire in a rental unit, where the court finds the child alone liable for such damages in that the child was responsible for starting the fire, the fees and expenses of a court-appointed guardian ad litem are properly charged to the indigent minor child and not to his parent, as part of the court costs.

54 App(2d) 137, 376 NE(2d) 603 (1977), In re Christopher. Where an infant child has been in the custody of prospective adoptive parents as a result of a permanent order of custody in a dependency action and that permanent order is subsequently vacated and the parent moves to terminate temporary custody, it appears that the interests of the child and parent may conflict and a guardian ad litem must be appointed for the child pursuant to Juv R 4(B) prior to the hearing on the mother's motion to terminate custody.

54 App(2d) 137, 376 NE(2d) 603 (1977), In re Christopher. The guardian ad litem appointed for a child in a dependency action where the interest of the child and the parent may conflict must have no ties or loyalties to anyone with an adversary interest in the outcome such as a natural parent or the prospective adoptive parents.

47 App(2d) 203, 353 NE(2d) 887 (1975), In re Height. Where a court, having acquired jurisdiction over a child by virtue of a divorce action between the child's parents, certifies the matter of the child's custody to a juvenile court, the consent of the juvenile court having been first obtained, the juvenile court has exclusive jurisdiction over the child's custody by virtue of 3109.06 and 2151.23(D) and a finding of unfitness of the parents or that there is no suitable relative to have custody is not a necessary prerequisite to such certification, and while such certification shall be deemed to be the complaint in the juvenile court, it does not constitute a complaint in the juvenile court that such child is dependent or neglected and those dispositions provided for under 2151.353, 2151.354, and 2151.355 are not applicable to the disposition of such a child,

disposition thereof being subject to and controlled by 3109.04.

37 App(2d) 7, 306 NE(2d) 166 (1973), In re Bolden. The guarantee of the right to be represented by counsel set forth in Juv R 4(A) does not, as to a nonindigent party, require that trial be continued indefinitely until counsel can be obtained, but merely requires, if it does not appear that counsel could not be obtained through the exercise of reasonable diligence and a willingness to enter into reasonable contractual arrangements for counsel's services, that a reasonable opportunity be given to the party before trial to employ such counsel.

2. Cases interpreting law analogous to Juvenile Rule 4

2111.23 GUARDIAN AD LITEM

33 App(3d) 318, 515 NE(2d) 987 (Franklin 1986), Nationwide Mutual Insurance Co v Wymer. No statutory authority exists authorizing the payment of guardian ad litem fees from county funds in a civil action involving negligent or intentional acts of an indigent minor in causing fire damage to a rental unit.

2151.35 HEARING PROCEDURE; FINDINGS; RECORD

19 OS(2d) 70, 249 NE(2d) 808 (1969), In re Agler. In order to sustain commitment of a juvenile offender to a state institution in a delinquency proceeding, where such commitment will deprive the child of his liberty, the alleged delinquent must have been afforded representation by counsel, appointed at state expense in case of indigency.

18 App(2d) 276, 248 NE(2d) 620 (1969), In re Baker; modified by 20 OS(2d) 142, 254 NE(2d) 363 (1969). Where a juvenile has received the following essentials of due process and fair treatment, (1) written notice of the specific charge or factual allegations, given to the juvenile and his parents or guardian sufficiently in advance of the hearing to permit preparation; (2) notification to the juvenile and his parents of the juvenile's right to be represented by counsel retained by them, or, if they are unable to afford counsel, that counsel will be appointed to represent the juvenile; (3) application of the constitutional privileges against self-incrimination; and (4), absent a valid confession, a determination of delinquency and an order of commitment based only on sworn testimony subjected to the opportunity for cross-examination in accordance with constitutional requirements, such juvenile has not been deprived of due process under either the Constitution of the United States or the Constitution of the State of Ohio.

2151.351 ASSIGNMENT OF COUNSEL

OAG 69-110. When the court deems it necessary to appoint counsel for a juvenile, pursuant to 2151.351, such counsel's services shall be paid for by the county as is stated therein.

2151.352 RIGHT TO COUNSEL

12 OS(3d) 40, 12 OBR 35, 465 NE(2d) 397 (1984), Beard v Williams County Dept of Social Services. There is no constitutional right to

appointment of counsel for indigent parents in a hearing on a complaint by a county social services department for temporary custody of allegedly neglected children.

OAG 84-023. Pursuant to RC 2151.352, a child, his parents, custodian, or other persons in loco parentis, if indigent, is entitled to be represented in all juvenile proceedings by a public defender in accordance with the comprehensive system set forth in RC Ch 120, regardless of whether the outcome of the proceeding could result in a loss of liberty.

Juv R 5
[Reserved]

Juv R 6
Taking into custody

A child may be taken into custody: (1) pursuant to an order of the court, (2) pursuant to the law of arrest, (3) by a law enforcement officer or duly authorized officer of the court when there are reasonable grounds to believe that the child is suffering from illness or injury and is not receiving proper care, or is in immediate danger from his surroundings, and that his removal is necessary, (4) by a law enforcement officer or duly authorized officer of the court when there are reasonable grounds to believe that the child has run away from his parents, guardian, or other custodian, and (5) where, during the pendency of court proceedings, it appears to the court that the conduct, condition or surroundings of the child are endangering the health, welfare, person or property of himself or others, or that he may abscond or be removed from the jurisdiction of the court or will not be brought to the court.

Adopted eff. 7-1-72

Editor's Comment

Juv R 6 is a virtual reproduction of the procedural provisions of 2151.31 and 2151.28(D).

2151.28(D) provides that "If it appears from the affidavit filed or from sworn testimony before the court, that the conduct, condition or surroundings of the child are endangering his health or welfare or those of others, or that he may abscond or be removed from the jurisdiction of the court or will not be brought to the court, notwithstanding the service of the summons, the court may endorse upon the summons an order that a law enforcement officer shall serve the summons and shall take the child into immediate custody and bring him forthwith to the court."

CROSS REFERENCES

Kurtz & Giannelli, Ohio Juvenile Law, Text 5.02, 7.06(C)

OJur 3d: 23, Courts and Judges § 428; 46, Family Law § 323, 425, 426, 430 to 437, 439, 493, 535, 540

Am Jur 2d: 47, Juvenile Courts and Delinquent and Dependent Children § 35, 44 to 48

Validity and application of statute allowing endangered child to be temporarily removed from parental custody. 38 ALR4th 756

LAW REVIEW ARTICLES

9 Akron L Rev 257 (1975). The Plight of the Interstate Child in American Courts, Leona Mary Hudak.

NOTES ON DECISIONS AND OPINIONS

1. Cases interpreting Juvenile Rule 6
2. Cases interpreting law analogous to Juvenile Rule 6

1. Cases interpreting Juvenile Rule 6

OAG 87-105. Under Ohio law, unless matters of public safety are involved, a child alleged to be abused, neglected, or dependent may be removed from his home by court order only upon a judicial determination that continuation in the home would be contrary to the child's best interest.

2. Cases interpreting law analogous to Juvenile Rule 6

2151.25 TRANSFER TO JUVENILE COURT

43 App 44, 182 NE 519 (1932), Durst v Griffith. The statute relating to the arrest of minors has application only to arrests in criminal cases.

2151.31 APPREHENSION, CUSTODY, AND DETENTION

9 OS(2d) 1, 222 NE(2d) 620 (1966), State v Carder. The purpose of 2151.31 is not to determine the admissibility into evidence of a child's fingerprints, but rather to conform to the theory that juvenile proceedings are not criminal in nature.

127 OS 333, 188 NE 550 (1933), Ex parte Province. When a mother voluntarily appears at and participates in a hearing in which the dependency of the child is considered, she waives all prior notice of proceedings upon such complaint of dependency to which she was entitled under the statute.

19 App(2d) 292, 251 NE(2d) 153 (1969), Garland v Dustman. Under 2151.14 and 2151.31 it is the manifest duty of enforcement officers to cooperate with and assist the juvenile authorities in the performance of their duties when such officers are specifically requested to do so by the juvenile authorities; and such officers may avoid liability in an action for false imprisonment by showing that they were justified in the detention or restraint of the juvenile made under the specific direction and order of the juvenile authorities.

3 App(2d) 381, 210 NE(2d) 714 (1965), State v Carder; affirmed by 9 OS(2d) 1, 222 NE(2d) 620 (1966). A voluntary confession to the perpetration of murder obtained from a sixteen and three-fourths year old high school junior, which confession was made before indictment and while the accused was detained for investigation, is admissible in evidence (1) where the accused had been allowed to consult with an attorney prior to being questioned; (2) where the accused first was advised that he did not have to talk; (3) where the accused, when told that his parents and another attorney were there and waiting to see him, stated that he did not want to see them; and (4) where there is no showing that the confession was obtained by inquisitorial processes.

120 App 199, 201 NE(2d) 793 (1963), State v Stewart; affirmed by 176 OS 156, 198 NE(2d) 439 (1964). A voluntary confession to the perpetration of murder, obtained from a seventeen-year-old high school senior, which confession was made before indictment on said charge and while the accused was under arrest for a misdemeanor, is admissible in evidence (1) where the accused was first advised that "he would not be compelled to give a statement . . . if he wanted to give a statement it would be by his own free will and that statement would be used for or against him in court;" (2) where the accused was further advised that "he could secure the services of an attorney;" and (3) where there is no showing that the confession was obtained by inquisitorial processes, without the procedural safeguards of due process, and by such compulsion that the confession is irreconcilable with the possession of mental freedom. (120 App 199 superseded by statute as stated in State v Humphries, 51 OS(2d) 95, 364 NE(2d) 1354 (1977).)

114 App 319, 182 NE(2d) 631 (1961), In re Jones. 2151.28 and 2151.31 do not require a hearing as a condition precedent to the taking of a child into custody, pursuant to order of a juvenile court, during pendency of an action in such court.

79 App 237, 72 NE(2d) 785 (1946), State v Lowder. Three minors, suspected of murder, were apprehended; prior to their being taken before any court and before any charges were filed against them, signed confessions were obtained from each of them; they were then taken before juvenile court which conducted investigation, and nature of crime being apparent, cases were referred to common pleas court where accused were indicted, tried and convicted; in each instance confession obtained was used against one making it, in both juvenile court and court of common pleas; held: confessions were admissible in evidence, even though accused were not taken immediately before juvenile court as directed by this section; fact that confessions were used in juvenile court did not render them inadmissible in court of common pleas under GC 1639-30 (RC 2151.35) because there was but one case or proceeding.

92 Abs 475, 194 NE(2d) 797 (Juv Cuyahoga 1963), In re Long, Jr. The statutory law of arrest does not apply to special statutory proceedings in the juvenile court which are civil in nature and have for their purpose the securing for each child under the jurisdiction of the juvenile court such care, guidance and control as will best serve the child's welfare.

66 Abs 403, 115 NE(2d) 849 (App Montgomery 1952), State ex rel Peaks v Allaman. A minor detained on delinquency charges is not charged with an offense and hence is not entitled to release on bail.

61 Abs 311, 104 NE(2d) 182 (App Franklin 1950), Harris v Alvis. A minor charged with a felony who fails to object to the jurisdiction of the common pleas court by a plea in abatement because of his age waives his right to object.

Juv R 7
Detention and shelter care

(A) Detention: standards.

A child taken into custody shall not be placed in detention or shelter care prior to final disposition unless his detention or care is required to protect the person and property of others or those of the child, or the child may abscond or be removed from the jurisdiction of the court, or he has no parent, guardian, or custodian or other person able to provide supervision and care for him and return him to the court when required.

(B) Priorities in placement prior to hearing.

A person taking a child into custody shall, with all reasonable speed, either:

(1) Release the child to his parent, guardian, or other custodian; or

(2) Where his detention or shelter care appears to be required under the standards of subdivision (A) bring the child to the court or deliver him to a place of detention or shelter care designated by the court.

(C) Initial procedure upon detention.

Any person who delivers a child to a shelter or detention facility shall give the admissions officer at the facility a signed report stating why the child was taken into custody and why he was not released to his parent, guardian or custodian, and shall assist the admissions officer, if necessary, in notifying the parent pursuant to subdivision (E)(3).

(D) Admission.

The admissions officer in a shelter or detention facility, upon receipt of a child, shall review the report submitted pursuant to subdivision (C), make such further investigation as is feasible and either:

(1) Release the child to the care of his parents, guardian or custodian; or

(2) Where detention or shelter care is required under the standards of subdivision (A), admit the child to the facility or place him in some appropriate facility.

(E) Procedure after admission.

When a child has been admitted to detention or shelter care the admissions officer shall:

(1) Prepare a report stating the time the child was brought to the facility and the reasons he was admitted;

(2) Advise the child of (a) his right to telephone his parents and counsel immediately and at reasonable times thereafter and (b) the time, place and purpose of the detention hearing; and

(3) Use reasonable diligence to contact the child's parent, guardian or custodian and advise him of:

(a) The place of and reasons for detention;

(b) The time the child may be visited;

(c) The time, place and purpose of the detention hearing; and

(d) The right to counsel and appointed counsel in the case of indigency.

(F) Detention hearing.

(1) Hearing: time; notice. When a child has been admitted to detention or shelter care, a detention hearing shall be held promptly, not later than seventy-two hours after the child is placed in detention or shelter care or the next court day, whichever is earlier, to determine whether detention or shelter care is required. Reasonable oral or written notice of the time, place, and purpose of the detention hearing shall be given to the child and, if he can be found, to his parent, guardian, or other custodian.

(2) Hearing: advisement of rights. Prior to the hearing, the court shall inform the parties as to: (a) the right to counsel and to appointed counsel if indigent and (b) the child's right to remain silent with respect to any allegation of a juvenile traffic offense, delinquency, or unruliness.

(3) Hearing procedure. The court may consider any evidence, including the reports filed by the person who brought the child to the facility and the admissions officer, without regard to formal rules of evidence. Unless it appears from the hearing that the child's detention or shelter care is required under subdivision (A), the court shall order his release to his parent, guardian or custodian.

(G) Rehearing.

Any decision relating to detention or shelter care may be reviewed at any time upon motion of any party. If a parent, guardian, or custodian did not receive notice of the initial hearing and did not appear or waived appearance at the hearing, the court shall rehear the matter promptly.

(H) Separation from adults.

No child shall be placed in or committed to any prison, jail, lockup or any other place where he can come in contact or communication with any adult convicted of crime, under arrest or charged with crime.

A child may be detained in jail or other facility for detention of adults only if the child is alleged to be delinquent, there is no detention center for delinquent children under the supervision of the court or other agency approved by the court, and the detention is in a room separate and removed from those for adults. The court may order that a child over the age of fifteen years who is alleged to be delinquent be detained in a jail in a room separate and removed from adults if public safety or protection of the child or others reasonably requires such detention.

A child alleged to be neglected or dependent shall not be detained in a jail or other facility intended or used for the detention of adults charged with criminal offenses or of children alleged to be delinquent unless upon order of the court.

(I) Medical examination.

The supervisor of a shelter or detention facility may provide for a physical examination of a child placed therein.

(J) Telephone and visitation rights.

A child may telephone his parents and attorney immediately after being admitted to a shelter or detention facility and at reasonable times thereafter.

The child may be visited at reasonable visiting hours by his parents and adult members of his family, his pastor and his teachers. He may be visited by his attorney at any time.

Adopted eff. 7-1-72

Editor's Comment

1. Detention and shelter care
2. Detention: standards
3. Priorities in placement prior to hearing
4. Initial procedure upon detention
5. Admission
6. Procedure after admission
7. Detention hearing
8. Rehearing
9. Separation from adults
10. Medical examination
11. Telephone and visitation rights

1. Detention and shelter care

Juv R 7 governs detention and shelter care, which are defined in Juv R 2. Detention involves physically restricted facilities and shelter care involves physically unrestricted facilities. Generally, the rule is a restatement of present law and is drawn from 2151.31 through 2151.314.

The rule sets forth the standard to be employed in deciding whether detention or shelter care is required in subdivision (A). Subdivisions (B) through (C) provide the procedure through which the standards are to be implemented. Subdivision (G) provides for a rehearing at any time upon motion of any party and mandates a rehearing if a parent, guardian, or custodian failed to receive notice of the detention hearing and does not waive appearance. Subdivision (H) deals with the type of facilities required for detention. Subdivision (I) authorizes medical examinations for detained children. Subdivision (J) deals with a child's visitation and telephone rights while in detention.

The rule proceeds on the assumption, as does Ch 2151, that the state is empowered to provide interim shelter care or detention, prior to a hearing on the merits of the complaint, for a child who is not receiving adequate care in his home or who is accused of illegal behavior, without the right to bail normally available to adult defenders. The rule requires no finding of probable cause that an offense has been committed as a prerequisite to detention.

2. Detention: standards

Juv R 7(A) provides the standards that are to be employed in determining whether or not a child is to be held in detention or shelter care prior to final disposition. This standard is then employed by reference throughout Juv R 7 (See Juv R 7(B)(2), 7(D)(2) and 7(F)(3)).

Detention or shelter care in a pending case are permitted in three situations: (a) where required in order to protect the person or property of the child or others; (b) where required to prevent the child's leaving or being removed from the jurisdiction; and (c) where the child has no parent, guardian or custodian.

The standards are taken from 2151.31 (final paragraph) and represent a continuation of present law. Two changes have been made from 2151.31.

First, the rule provides that the standards are to apply until the time when final disposition takes place, whereas 2151.31 provides that they apply "prior to the hearing on the complaint." Since these rules deal with the whole of juvenile court proceedings, it is necessary to deal with detention from the beginning to the end of those proceedings.

Secondly, the language of the provision in 2151.31, which reads "or because an order for his detention or shelter care has been made by the court pursuant to this chapter" was deleted. This language created circuity in the rule and could be confusing. The standards provided are the only standards according to which a child may be detained, and the open-ended final clause could be understood to authorize an order for detention according to some other criteria.

3. Priorities in placement prior to hearing

Juv R 7(B) provides that an initial decision is to be made by the person taking the child into custody and that he is to release the child to his parent, guardian, or custodian unless detention or shelter care is justified and required under the standards provided in subdivision (A). Juv R 7(B) is taken from 2151.311(A) and (A)(1). The only change made is a restriction on the release provision. Section 2151.311(A)(1) says that the child may be released to the named persons "upon their written promise to bring the child before the court when requested by the court". The committee felt that this was an undesirable restriction, since the person taking a child into custody might find it unnecessary to require such a commitment in writing. Such a commitment would still be required if it was felt to be necessary to insure that the child would appear in court when requested.

4. Initial procedure upon detention

Juv R 7(C) requires the person delivering a child to a shelter or detention facility to give the admissions officer of the facility a written report of the reasons the child was taken into custody and the reasons he was not released to his parent, guardian, or custodian. It further requires such person to assist the admissions officer in informing parents of the child's detention under subdivision (E).

Juv R 7(C) is a modification of 2151.311(A)(2) in its requirements of a written report and in its procedure for notification. 2151.311(A)(2) places upon the person delivering the child to the facility the responsibility for notifying the parent. Juv R 7(C), with 7(E), places that responsibility on the admissions officer of the facility and only requires that the person delivering the child to the facility assist the admissions officer in a notification, which is broader than the notification under 2151.311(A)(2).

5. Admission

Juv R 7(D) is a restatement of 2151.314, paragraph one, and requires the admissions officer of a detention or shelter facility to make a determination of the appropriateness of detention or shelter care under the standards provided in subdivision (A). The only change from the Revised Code is the specification of the admissions officer as the person to make this determination, while the Revised Code refers to "the intake or other authorized officer of the court."

6. Procedure after admission

Juv R 7(E) provides that the admissions officer is to prepare a report on the reasons for admission when a child is admitted to the facility and to advise the child and his parents, if possible, of certain basic information. Under subdivision (C) the person delivering the child to the facility is to assist the admissions officer in advising the parent.

The requirement of a written report is not stated in the Revised Code, although it is standard practice in most courts of the state.

Juv R 7(E)(2) and (3) expand upon 2151.314, paragraph two, which only requires that the child and parent be advised of the time, place and purpose of the detention hearing. In addition, the rule requires that they be notified of their right to counsel at the hearing and of their telephone and visitation rights, which are further specified in subdivision (J).

7. Detention hearing

Juv R 7(F) provides the procedure by which the detention hearing is to be held. It is taken from 2151.314, paragraph two, with two changes. 2151.314 simply provides that the hearing shall be informal. Juv R 7(F)(3) makes it clear that the reports prepared by the person delivering the child and the admissions officer may be considered at the detention hearing.

The most important change that the rule makes over present law is that 2151.314 provides that the hearing shall be held not later than seventy-two hours after the child is placed in detention, while the rule provides that the hearing shall be held "promptly, not later than seventy-two hours after the child is placed in detention or the next court day, whichever is earlier".

8. Rehearing

Juv R 7(G) provides for rehearings on detention and shelter care decisions. It allows the court to rehear such matters upon motion of a party and requires a prompt rehearing where a parent, guardian, or custodian did not receive notice, appear or waive appearance at the hearing. The latter provision is taken from 2151.314, paragraph two, and the discretionary rehearing is a codification of current practice in most large courts.

9. Separation from adults

Juv R 7(H) places limitations on the type of facility within which a child may be detained. It requires separation from adults and places limitations on the possibility of detention in a jail or other facility for the detention of adults. It is taken from 2151.312.

10. Medical examination

Juv R 7(I) authorizes the supervisor of a shelter or detention facility to provide for a physical examination of a child placed therein. The term physical examination is defined in Juv R 2 and requires that the examination be by a physician.

Juv R 7(I) outlines the authority of the supervisor of a detention or shelter facility to control health conditions within the facility. This is particularly important because of the incidence of drug problems, venereal disease and other infectious diseases of those persons who come into such facilities. While the supervisor is permitted to provide for an examination on his own authority, medical treatment is only authorized by court order under Juv R 13.

11. Telephone and visitation rights

Juv R 7(J) defines the telephone and visitation rights of a child held in detention or shelter care. The policy behind the rule is the need to have the incarceration of a child involve as little separation from his family as possible.

CROSS REFERENCES

Giannelli, Ohio Evidence Manual, Author's Comment § 101.07, 101.10

Kurtz & Giannelli, Ohio Juvenile Law, Text 7.06, 7.08(B), 15.03

OJur 3d: 23, Courts and Judges § 428; 46, Family Law § 323, 425, 426, 430 to 437, 439, 493, 535, 540; 72, Notice and Notices § 1 to 5

Am Jur 2d: 47, Juvenile Courts and Delinquent and Dependent Children § 35, 44 to 54

Validity and application of statute allowing endangered child to be temporarily removed from parental custody. 38 ALR4th 756

Procedural requirements under Federal Constitution in juvenile delinquency proceedings—federal cases. 25 LEd(2d) 950

NOTES ON DECISIONS AND OPINIONS

1. Cases interpreting Juvenile Rule 7
2. Cases interpreting law analogous to Juvenile Rule 7

1. Cases interpreting Juvenile Rule 7

24 OS(3d) 22, 24 OBR 18, 492 NE(2d) 805 (1986), In re Moloney. Where an allegedly neglected, dependent, or abused child is committed to the temporary, emergency custody of a children services board after a shelter care hearing under Juv R 7, the court need not order a reunification plan where it has not finally adjudged and disposed of the matter under RC 2151.353.

60 OS(2d) 92, 397 NE(2d) 1190 (1979), Pettry v McGinty. Habeas corpus will not lie at the request of the father of children found to be dependent and placed in the temporary care and custody of the county welfare department.

57 OS(2d) 97, 386 NE(2d) 1354 (1979), Linger v Weiss. A parent, alleging that he failed to receive notice of a hearing concerning the shelter care of his child, must move the juvenile court for a rehearing,

pursuant to Juv R 7(G), before seeking a writ of habeas corpus.

No. 3430 (9th Dist Ct App, Lorain, 5-11-83), In re Hawkins. Where police apprehended a fourteen-year-old minor for questioning following a fire, police may properly question such minor at the police station before delivering her to a place of detention or bringing her to court.

No. 3430 (9th Dist Ct App, Lorain, 5-11-83), In re Hawkins. Where a fourteen-year-old minor, without counsel, made a statement to police implicating herself in setting a fire which killed her father, and the court psychologist testified that such minor was of average intelligence, the minor's statement is properly admitted into evidence where the minor had waived her Miranda rights and during the course of such statement the minor answered intelligently, coherently, and gave no indication of undue influence.

OAG 87-105. Under Ohio law, unless matters of public safety are involved, a child alleged to be abused, neglected, or dependent may be removed from his home by court order only upon a judicial determination that continuation in the home would be contrary to the child's best interest.

2. Cases interpreting law analogous to Juvenile Rule 7

US CONST AM 14

467 US 253, 104 SCt 2403, 81 LEd(2d) 207 (1984), Schall v Martin. The due process clause of US Const Am 14 is not violated where a state statute provides for: (1) the pretrial detention of a juvenile delinquent where there is a finding, following notice and a hearing, and a statement of reasons and facts, that there is a "serious risk" that the child might commit a crime before return date; and (2) a more formal hearing within a maximum of seventeen days where detention is ordered. (Ed. note: New York law construed in light of federal constitution.)

2151.23 JURISDICTION OF JUVENILE COURT

OAG 70-143. A judge of a juvenile court may not commit a child who has been found to be a delinquent child, or a juvenile traffic offender, to the county jail upon the failure, refusal, or inability of such child to pay a fine and court costs.

2151.27 COMPLAINT

66 Abs 403, 115 NE(2d) 849 (App Montogery 1952), State ex rel Peaks v Allaman. A minor detained on delinquency charges is not charged with an offense and hence is not entitled to release on bail.

2151.312 PLACE OF DETENTION

OAG 70-015. If the county adult detention facility is designed with a space which is enclosed on all sides, that is distinct, set apart and disconnected so that no child over the age of fifteen placed in that space will come in contact or communication with any adult convicted of or arrested for a crime, and the public interest and safety require the detention of such child when a delinquent detention facility is

not available, the use of such adult facility is authorized.

2151.314 DETENTION HEARING

25 App(2d) 78, 266 NE(2d) 589 (1970), State ex rel Harris v Common Pleas Court. The commitment of a fifteen year old to a state institution pursuant to 2151.26 for the purpose of examination is not an act for which a writ of prohibition will issue.

2151.34 TREATMENT OF CHILDREN IN CUSTODY; DETENTION HOME

1962 OAG 2814. A juvenile detention home is a place not used for the confinement of adult persons, and such a home should be separate and apart from buildings in which adult persons are confined; accordingly, such a juvenile detention home may not properly be established in a county jail, even though one complete floor of the jail would be used for such purpose, and the intention would be to keep the one floor separate and apart from the rest of the jail.

2151.35 HEARING PROCEDURE; FINDINGS; RECORD

1963 OAG 553. The placement or detention of delinquent, dependent, neglected children, or juvenile traffic offenders, is upon final disposition of the juvenile court and does not include placement in a detention home provided under 2151.34.

Juv R 8
[Reserved]

Juv R 9
Intake

(A) Court action to be avoided.

In all appropriate cases formal court action should be avoided and other community resources utilized to ameliorate situations brought to the attention of the court.

(B) Screening; referral.

Information that a child is within the court's jurisdiction may be informally screened prior to the filing of a complaint to determine whether the filing of a complaint is in the best interest of the child and the public.

Adopted eff. 7-1-72

Editor's Comment

Juv R 9 is a very general rule requiring juvenile courts to make every effort to avoid the use of formal court proceedings in cases involving children and to utilize alternative community resources to ameliorate situations brought to the attention of the court. The philosophy behind this rule is that formal court action should be a last resort in juvenile problems.

Pre-judicial screening of juvenile court cases was a primary recommendation of the Task Force Report on Juvenile Delinquency and Youth Crime to the President's Commission on Law Enforcement and the Administration of Justice (1967) and the National Council of Crime and Delinquency, Model Rules.

Most juvenile courts in the state have evolved and continue to experiment with procedures for the implementation of this principle of diversion.

CROSS REFERENCES

Kurtz & Giannelli, Ohio Juvenile Law, Text 7.01, 7.02

Scope of rules, applicability, construction, exceptions, Juv R 1

OJur 3d: 23, Courts and Judges § 428; 46, Family Law § 423, 452, 456, 458 to 462

Am Jur 2d: 47, Juvenile Courts and Delinquent and Dependent Children § 40

NOTES ON DECISIONS AND OPINIONS

38 OS(3d) 149, 527 NE(2d) 286 (1988), In re M.D. The prosecution of a twelve-year-old girl as a delinquent based on a charge of complicity to commit rape violates RC Ch 2151, Juv R 9(A), local court intake policy, public policy, and due process of law where such prosecution arises from an incident of three children "playing doctor," with the adjudicated delinquent directing a five-year-old boy to drop his pants and place his penis in a five-year-old girl's mouth in order to take her temperature, because no offense was actually committed and the failure to raise the issue of the constitutionality of applying the rape statute to children under the age of thirteen does not preclude consideration of the constitutional challenge on appeal.

Juv R 10
Complaint

(A) Filing.

Any person having knowledge of a child who appears to be a juvenile traffic offender, delinquent, unruly, neglected, dependent, or abused may file a complaint with respect to such child in the juvenile court of the county in which the child has a residence or legal settlement, or in which the traffic offense, delinquency, unruliness, neglect, dependency, or abuse occurred.

Any person may file a complaint to have determined the custody of a child not a ward of another court of this state, and any person entitled to the custody of a child and unlawfully deprived of such custody

may file a complaint requesting a writ of habeas corpus. Complaints concerning custody shall be filed in the county where the child is found or was last known to be.

When a case concerning a child is transferred or certified from another court, the certification from the transferring court shall be deemed to be the complaint. The juvenile court may order the certification supplemented upon its own motion or that of a party.

(B) Complaint: general form.

The complaint, which may be upon information and belief, shall:

(1) State in ordinary and concise language the essential facts which bring the proceeding within the jurisdiction of the court and in juvenile traffic offense and delinquency proceedings shall contain the numerical designation of the statute or ordinance alleged to have been violated;

(2) Contain the name and address of the parent, guardian, or custodian of the child or, if such name or address is unknown, shall so state; and

(3) Be made under oath.

(C) Complaint: Juvenile traffic offense.

A Uniform Traffic ticket shall be used as a complaint in juvenile traffic offense proceedings.

(D) Complaint: permanent custody.

A complaint seeking permanent custody of a child shall so state.

(E) Complaint: habeas corpus.

Where a complaint for a writ of habeas corpus involving the custody of a child is based on the existence of a lawful court order, a certified copy of such order shall be attached to the complaint.

Adopted eff. 7-1-72; amended eff. 7-1-75, 7-1-76

Editor's Comment

Juv R 10 spells out the procedure to be followed in initiating a proceeding in the juvenile court and uses the same appellation for the formal filing as Crim R 3, i.e., complaint for uniformity.

The first paragraph of subdivision (A) is based on the first sentence of 2151.27, which defines venue in a juvenile proceeding. The second and third paragraphs have no specific statutory basis, but are included to provide specific procedure for habeas corpus and custody cases, and cases transferred from another court to a juvenile court pursuant to 3109.04, 3109.06 (Domestic Relations) and

3107.12 (Probate). (*See* 2151.23(A)(2) and (3) and 2151.25.)

Venue in the custody and habeas corpus situation differs from the more typical delinquency, unruly, neglect, dependency or juvenile traffic offender case because the matter does not involve conduct by a child. Rather, the concern is to find a proper place for a child who may be found without a legal custodian. Hence, the reference in this rule to venue being "where the child is found or was last known to be." When considering a child custody case in which a child from an Ohio county is removed to another state, the venue provisions of Juv R 10 should be read in conjunction with the Uniform Child Custody Jurisdiction Act (3109.21 et seq.) which, under certain circumstances, permits an Ohio court to assume jurisdiction even though the child is absent from this state.

To avoid unnecessary delays and repetitious pleadings, the rule provides that the certification of the transferring court shall be the complaint in juvenile court, upon transfer of the case from a court without juvenile jurisdiction to the juvenile court.

The provision of subdivision (B) that the complaint may be on information and belief originates in the second sentence of 2151.27. The use of "ordinary and concise language" appears in Crim R 7(B), as does the requirement that the complaint include a reference to the statute or ordinance alleged to have been violated in delinquency cases. (*See* Crim R 3.)

The language of subdivision (B)(2) requiring the name and address of the parent, if known, requires what is presently being practiced in many, if not all, counties. The requirement of subdivision (B)(3) that the complaint be made under oath comes from 2151.27.

Subdivision (D), requiring that a complaint seeking permanent custody must so state, follows the last paragraph of 2151.27.

The language of subdivision (E) requiring the attachment of a certified copy of an order which is the basis of a complaint for habeas corpus is similar to Civ R 10(D) and follows the holding in the case of *In re McTaggart*, 2 App(2d) 214, 207 NE(2d) 562 (1965).

CROSS REFERENCES

Kurtz & Giannelli, Ohio Juvenile Law, Text 7.01, 7.03, 7.04(A), 15.03

Complaint, Crim R 3
Warrant or summons, Crim R 7
Adjudicatory hearing, Juv R 29

OJur 3d: 23, Courts and Judges § 428; 46, Family Law § 423, 452, 456, 458 to 462
Am Jur 2d: 47, Juvenile Courts and Delinquent and Dependent Children § 40 to 42

NOTES ON DECISIONS AND OPINIONS

1. Cases interpreting Juvenile Rule 10
2. Cases interpreting law analogous to Juvenile Rule 10

1. Cases interpreting Juvenile Rule 10

46 OS(2d) 378, 348 NE(2d) 727 (1976), In re Hunt. A complaint under Juv R 10 and 2151.27 alleging that a child is dependent must state the essential facts which bring the proceeding within the jurisdiction of the court.

31 App(3d) 1, 31 OBR 14, 508 NE(2d) 190 (Hamilton 1987), In re Howard. A delinquency complaint which alleges that a juvenile "knowingly" aided another to commit robbery is sufficient to state a charge of complicity under Juv R 10(B).

21 App(3d) 36, 21 OBR 38, 486 NE(2d) 152 (Huron 1984), In re Wilson. A properly served summons containing the "full explanation" required by RC 2151.353(B) must be accompanied by a copy of the complaint, amended or not, if the complaint seeks, temporarily or permanently, to divest a parent of his parental rights.

14 App(3d) 353, 14 OBR 420, 471 NE(2d) 516 (Defiance 1984), In re Snider. When a case concerning a child is transferred or certified from another court, such certification does not constitute a complaint in the juvenile court that such a child is neglected, dependent, or abused, and those dispositions provided for under RC 2151.353 pertaining to neglected, dependent, or abused children, including an award of permanent custody to a county welfare department which has assumed the administration of child welfare, are not applicable to such a child, disposition thereof being subject to and controlled by RC 3109.04.

13 App(3d) 37, 13 OBR 40, 468 NE(2d) 111 (Preble 1983), In re Sims. Juv R 10(B) is not meant to force a complainant to state every fact surrounding every incident described in the complaint, and therefore, in proving its case in a neglect and dependency proceeding, the state need not limit its proof to the habits and faults of the custodial parent that are actually listed in the complaint.

No. 6-81-12 (3d Dist Ct App, Hardin, 7-14-82), In re Baker. In an action to remove a child from her mother's custody, the mere allegation that such child is dependent, where the complaint fails to state the essential facts upon which the allegation of dependency is based and which allegations bring the proceeding within the jurisdiction of the court, such complaint is insufficient to confer jurisdiction upon the trial court.

No. L-81-187 (6th Dist Ct App, Lucas, 1-15-82), Harris v Hopper. Any person has standing to bring an action for child custody under 2151.23; such a person need not be a parent, need not have established paternity and need not have legitimized the child.

52 Misc 4, 367 NE(2d) 931 (CP Cuyahoga 1977), In re Wright. There is a distinction between a "putative" father and a father who has been adjudicated as such by his own admission, in that a father adjudicated as such by his own admission has legal standing to seek custody of his illegitimate child against the world, including the mother.

2. Cases interpreting law analogous to Juvenile Rule 10
_____

2151.03 NEGLECTED CHILD DEFINED

7 App(2d) 79, 218 NE(2d) 757 (1964), Union County Child Welfare Bd v Parker. An allegation in a motion filed in juvenile court seeking to have that court "determine and award the future care and custody" of a child, that "neither parent is a suitable person to have the care and custody of said child," does not constitute a charge that such child is "neglected" or "dependent" and is not sufficiently definite to constitute the "complaint" necessitated by 2151.27.

2151.04 DEPENDENT CHILD DEFINED

112 App 361, 176 NE(2d) 252 (1960), In re Minton. In a proceeding in the juvenile court, instituted by the filing of a complaint under 2151.27, a finding by the court that a child is "neglected," in that it "lacked proper parental care because of the faults and habits of his parents" and "dependent " in that its "condition and environment . . . is such as to warrant the court . . . in assuming his guardianship" must be based on evidence with respect to whether the child was receiving proper parental care in a proper environment in its home at the time of the hearing.

2151.23 JURISDICTION OF JUVENILE COURT

175 OS 513, 196 NE(2d) 588 (1964), Byington v Byington. Habeas corpus will not lie where a child has been adjudicated a neglected and dependent child and committed by a juvenile court.

19 App(2d) 33, 249 NE(2d) 532 (1969), In re Messner. Habeas corpus in a court of competent jurisdiction as prescribed in Ch 2725 is the proper proceeding to raise the question of rightful custody of minor children, where it is alleged that the restraint is illegal, or where a parent or other person claims that he or she has been unlawfully deprived of custody of a minor child; and, as part of such proceedings, the best interests and welfare of the child is a primary question and determining factor, and all other matters must yield accordingly, including the comity existing between states.

2 App(2d) 214, 207 NE(2d) 562 (1965), In re McTaggart; modified by 4 App(2d) 359, 212 NE(2d) 663 (1965). Where, in an action in habeas corpus instituted by the natural mother to gain custody of her minor child, the respondents, who have the child in their custody, are unable to show a valid judgment or order of the court that has jurisdiction to issue such order, it is error for the trial court to determine on the principle "what is for the best interests of the child" that the custody of such child should remain in the respondents and to deny custody to the natural mother.

67 App 66, 35 NE(2d) 887 (1941), In re Evans. Writ of habeas corpus will not be granted to release from the state reformatory a minor who stated his age to be 19 years, when in fact he was but 17 years of age, and thereafter was indicted, pleaded guilty and was convicted in the common pleas court on a criminal charge.

28 Misc 200, 270 NE(2d) 678 (CP Preble 1970), Baker v Rose. Where a juvenile court assumes jurisdiction in a habeas corpus proceeding relating to the rights of a parent to custody of his children, it may exercise such further powers as are necessary to the complete resolution of the entire issue, including retention of continuing jurisdiction to make further orders, although the petition for writ of habeas corpus is denied.

95 Abs 101, 199 NE(2d) 765 (Juv Cuyahoga 1964), Matter of Robert O. Where a child is placed for adoption and the mother's consent is subsequently withdrawn, a certification of the case to the juvenile court upon dismissal of the petition does not of itself give the juvenile court jurisdiction to determine the child's custody.

88 Abs 1, 176 NE(2d) 187 (CP Fayette 1961), In re Ruth. Where a juvenile court has acquired jurisdiction over the question of custody of a child, the court of common pleas may not thereafter inquire into such custody in a habeas corpus proceeding.

72 Abs 323, 135 NE(2d) 285 (CP Licking 1956), In re Justice. Court not bound to deliver a child to a parent upon the claim of mere legal right but should in the exercise of sound discretion and after careful consideration of the facts award custody to one other than the parent.

2151.27 COMPLAINT

19 App(2d) 33, 249 NE(2d) 532 (1969), In re Messner. An Ohio juvenile court, in a dependency proceeding pursuant to 2151.27 et seq., has no jurisdiction to interfere with a mother's legal custody of her children, in the absence of proof and a finding of unfitness of such parent, merely for the purpose of releasing such children to the officers of the court of a foreign state, and the court need not give full faith and credit to a Michigan decree where that decree was obtained by the husband in an ex parte custody determination, subsequent to a divorce decree, in which the Michigan court had no personal jurisdiction over the nonresident wife.

16 App(2d) 164, 243 NE(2d) 111 (1968), In re Laricchiuta. Proceedings declaring a child neglected by the juvenile court of another county do not prevent a child from thereafter becoming a school resident in a county to which he moves with his family.

16 App(2d) 164, 243 NE(2d) 111 (1968), In re Laricchiuta. The school board of the district in which a child has a school residence at the time of his placement in another district must pay his tuition, whether such placement was by order of court or by the child welfare board in whose care the parent had voluntarily left him, and subsequent proceedings by the juvenile court declaring such child neglected will not end the obligation of the district of his school residence to continue paying his tuition.

9 App(2d) 299, 224 NE(2d) 358 (1967), James v Child Welfare Board. An application for a writ of habeas corpus will be denied where a complaint is duly filed in the county of legal residence, pursuant to 2151.27, charging a child with being a dependent or neglected child, notwithstanding the court of common pleas of another county in this state, as a result of a divorce action there heard, gave custody

of the child to the mother who subsequently moved with the child to the county where the affidavit of dependency and neglect was filed.

7 App(2d) 79, 218 NE(2d) 757 (1964), Union County Child Welfare Bd v Parker. Proceedings, wherein the juvenile court determines in response to such motion that such child is a neglected and dependent child and orders such child placed in the temporary custody of the county welfare board, are void ab initio for want of a complaint filed as prescribed by 2151.27, and such proceedings cannot be the foundation for a determination of dependency or neglect necessary to support an order awarding custody of such child.

114 App 248, 181 NE(2d) 503 (1960), In re Small. Where a neglected child proceeding is instituted in the juvenile court by a parent of such child, and a divorce action is later instituted by such parent, the juvenile court has exclusive original jurisdiction to determine whether the child is neglected, the power to determine his custody and the authority to place the child with a relative.

114 App 248, 181 NE(2d) 503 (1960), In re Small. In an appeal on questions of law from a judgment in a neglected-child proceeding, the court of appeals may not substitute its judgment for that of the trial court as to what order of custody would be for the best interest of the child.

114 App 248, 181 NE(2d) 503 (1960), In re Small. 3109.04 is not applicable to a neglected-child proceeding under 2151.27.

112 App 361, 176 NE(2d) 252 (1960), In re Minton. A proceeding, instituted in the juvenile court under 2151.27 may not be used by the complainant either to force an adoption or as a substitute for an adoption proceeding.

97 App 114, 123 NE(2d) 757 (1954), In re Belk. The juvenile court of the county in which acts constituting neglect or dependency of a minor child occur has jurisdiction over complaints concerning such child whether or not the parent or minor child was a nonresident of such county.

93 App 251, 114 NE(2d) 65 (1952), In re Lorok. The juvenile court is given original jurisdiction in a proper proceeding to determine the right of custody of any child where such child is not a ward of another court, and it is not necessary in the exercise of such jurisdiction that the juvenile court first determine that such child is a dependent, neglected or delinquent child.

87 App 101, 90 NE(2d) 394 (1950), State ex rel Clark v Allaman; affirmed by 154 OS 296, 95 NE(2d) 753 (1950). Juvenile court has no jurisdiction to adjudicate a child as a dependent child until after filing of a complaint charging such dependency and notice given to the parent or parents.

86 App 377, 86 NE(2d) 501 (1949), State ex rel Sparto v Williams; affirmed by 153 OS 64, 90 NE(2d) 598 (1950), Sparto v Juvenile Court of Drake County. Where an affidavit is filed in support of a motion for a new trial, alleging that the child was a neglected child within the meaning of this section, on which charges a hearing was had, the juvenile court has jurisdiction in such matter and may grant a motion for new trial.

67 App 117, 36 NE(2d) 47 (1941), In re Anteau. In complaint under this section, that a child of separated parents is dependent, a judgment of common pleas court that the child is dependent awarding its custody to its father "until further order of the court," is a final order from which appeal to the court of appeals may be taken.

23 App 348, 155 NE 499 (1926), State ex rel Brown v Hoffman. Under GC 1639 (GC 1639-7; RC 2151.07), GC 1647 (GC 1639-23; RC 2151.27), and GC 1681 (GC 1639-32; RC 2151.26), transfer by court of common pleas of felony case against minor to court of domestic relations merely gives latter court information and authority to act thereon.

12 Misc 251, 231 NE(2d) 253 (Juv Cuyahoga 1967), In re Gail L. The juvenile court has the authority to hear and determine the case of a "neglected child" notwithstanding the fact that the child is at the time within the continuing jurisdiction of the common pleas court by virtue of a divorce decree.

95 Abs 101, 199 NE(2d) 765 (Juv Cuyahoga 1964), Matter of Robert O. Placement of an illegitimate child for adoption and subsequent withdrawal of consent thereto by the mother does not of itself warrant a finding that the child is neglected.

92 Abs 357, 194 NE(2d) 912 (App Scioto 1962), State ex rel Burchett v Juvenile Court. In order for a juvenile court to have jurisdiction to declare a child to be dependent, it must be shown that either the residence of the child is in the county or that the acts constituting neglect or dependency occurred in the county.

89 Abs 243, 185 NE(2d) 329 (App Columbiana 1959), Hartshorne v Hartshorne. A certification by a common pleas court of its record to the juvenile court constitutes a filing of a complaint within the meaning of 2151.27.

87 Abs 222, 179 NE(2d) 198 (Juv Marion 1961), In re Davis. Where a juvenile court in the jurisdiction in which an offender resides waives jurisdiction so that the offender will be tried by a common pleas court, such defendant is entitled to a trial in the county where the offense occurred.

82 Abs 599, 167 NE(2d) 148 (Juv Columbiana 1959), In re Goshorn. Where an affidavit was filed charging that children were neglected and dependent and the mother unfit, and such children were taken into custody by the county welfare department at a time when the mother and children were residents of the county, the juvenile court had jurisdiction of such proceedings even though citation was not served on the mother until after her removal to another county.

66 Abs 403, 115 NE(2d) 849 (App Montgomery 1952), State ex rel Peaks v Allaman. A minor detained on delinquency charges is not charged with an offense and hence is not entitled to release on bail.

3109.04 CUSTODY

115 App 186, 184 NE(2d) 228 (1961), In re Howland. An award of custody of a child in a divorce action is conclusive only as to the parties to such action, and the remedy of habeas corpus is

available to obtain such child where a party other than the parties to the divorce action is involved; and it is not necessary to apply to the court which originally awarded custody of such child.

73 Abs 91, 134 NE(2d) 474 (CP Muskingum 1956), Trout v Trout. On the evidence in a habeas corpus action the court will permit two boys to remain with their father rather than being given to their mother or separated.

Juv R 11
Transfer to another county

(A) Residence in another county; transfer optional.

If the child resides in a county of this state and the proceeding is commenced in a court of another county, that court, on its own motion or a motion of a party, may transfer the proceeding to the county of the child's residence upon the filing of the complaint or after the adjudicatory or dispositional hearing for such further proceeding as required. The court of the child's residence shall then proceed as if the original complaint had been filed in that court. Transfer may also be made if the residence of the child changes.

(B) Proceedings in another county; transfer required.

The proceedings shall be so transferred if other proceedings involving the child are pending in the juvenile court of the county of his residence.

(C) Adjudicatory hearing in county where complaint filed.

Where either the transferring or receiving court finds that the interests of justice and the convenience of the parties so require, the adjudicatory hearing shall be held in the county wherein the complaint was filed. Thereafter the proceeding may be transferred to the county of the child's residence for disposition.

(D) Transfer of records.

Certified copies of all legal and social records pertaining to the proceeding shall accompany the transfer.

Adopted eff. 7-1-72

Editor's Comment

1. Residence in another county; transfer optional
2. Proceedings in another county; transfer required

1. Residence in another county; transfer optional

Subdivision (A) is taken from the first two sentences of 2151.271.

2. Proceedings in another county; transfer required

Subdivision (B) is the same as the fourth sentence of the first paragraph of 2151.271.

The rule clarifies the authority of the court having venue to transfer jurisdiction to the juvenile court of residence of the child at any stage of the proceedings. It also mandates transfer if proceedings are pending in the juvenile court of the child's residence.

CROSS REFERENCES

Kurtz & Giannelli, Ohio Juvenile Law, Text 7.03(J), 7.04(B)

OJur 3d: 23, Courts and Judges § 428; 46, Family Law § 453, 454

NOTES ON DECISIONS AND OPINIONS

1. Cases interpreting Juvenile Rule 11
2. Cases interpreting law analogous to Juvenile Rule 11

1. Cases interpreting Juvenile Rule 11

12 App(3d) 138, 12 OBR 460, 468 NE(2d) 73 (Preble 1983), Squires v Squires. Venue in a custody proceeding in the juvenile division of common pleas court is governed by Juv R 11, which provides for an optional transfer of venue where the child resides in one county and the custody proceeding is brought in another county.

No. 81-CA-22 (4th Dist Ct App, Pickaway, 7-28-82), State v Payne. Where a case is pending against a juvenile in a foreign county, such case must be transferred to the juvenile's home county, if, at any time prior to dispositional order, proceedings against the juvenile are pending in his home county. Furthermore, such mandatory transfer may not be avoided by the foreign county through the use of a bindover proceeding.

2. Cases interpreting law analogous to Juvenile Rule 11

2151.23 JURISDICTION OF JUVENILE COURT
97 App 114, 123 NE(2d) 757 (1954), In re Belk. The juvenile court of the county in which acts constituting neglect or dependency of a minor child occur has jurisdiction over complaints concerning such child whether or not the parent or minor child was a nonresident of such county.

1935 OAG 4172; 1929 OAG 755. A juvenile court has jurisdiction to declare any child dependent which is found within the county under facts and circumstances constituting dependency. The legal residence of the child or its parents, or those standing in loco parentis does not determine the jurisdiction of the court. The county in which such court assumes jurisdiction and declares such child to be dependent will be responsible for the support of such child.

2151.27 COMPLAINT

92 Abs 357, 194 NE(2d) 912 (App Scioto 1962), State ex rel Burchett v Juvenile Court. In order for a juvenile court to have jurisdiction to declare a child to be dependent, it must be shown that either the residence of the child is in the county or that the acts constituting neglect or dependency occurred in the county.

Juv R 12
[Reserved]

Juv R 13
Temporary disposition; temporary orders; emergency medical and surgical treatment

(A) Temporary disposition.

Pending hearing on a complaint, the court may make such temporary orders concerning the custody or care of a child who is the subject of the complaint as the child's interest and welfare may require.

(B) Temporary orders.

Pending hearing on a complaint, the court may issue such temporary orders with respect to the relations and conduct of other persons toward a child who is the subject of the complaint as the child's interest and welfare may require.

(C) Emergency medical and surgical treatment.

Upon the certification of one or more reputable practicing physicians, the court may order such emergency medical and surgical treatment as appears to be immediately necessary for any child concerning whom a complaint has been filed.

(D) Ex parte proceedings.

Where it appears to the court that the interest and welfare of the child require that action be taken immediately, the court may proceed summarily and without notice under subdivision (A), (B) or (C).

(E) Hearing; notice.

Wherever possible, the court shall provide an opportunity for hearing before proceeding under subdivision (A), (B) or (C) and shall give notice of the time and place of the hearing to the parties and any other person who may be affected by the proposed action. Where the court has proceeded without notice under subdivision (D), it shall give notice of the action it has taken to the parties and any other affected person and provide them an opportunity for a hearing concerning the continuing effects of such action.

(F) Payment.

The court may order the parent, guardian or custodian, if able, to pay for any emergency medical or surgical treatment provided pursuant to subdivision (C). Such order of payment may be enforced by judgment, upon which execution may issue, and a failure to pay as ordered may be punished as for a contempt of court.

Adopted eff. 7-1-72

Editor's Comment

1. Temporary disposition; temporary orders; emergency medical and surgical treatment
2. Ex parte proceedings
3. Hearing; notice
4. Payment

1. Temporary disposition; temporary orders; emergency medical and surgical treatment

Juv R 13 provides for temporary orders with respect to a child who is the subject of a juvenile court complaint. These temporary orders can deal with custody or care of the child (subdivision (A)), and the relations and conduct of other persons toward a child (subdivision (B)), and emergency medical and surgical treatment (subdivision (C)).

2. Ex parte proceedings

Subdivision (D) provides for summary procedure without notice in issuing such temporary orders, where required in the interest of the child.

3. Hearing; notice

Subdivision (E) provides that notice and hearing shall be given prior to the temporary order where possible and after the issuance of the order in all cases.

4. Payment

Subdivision (F) provides a mechanism for getting reimbursement for medical and surgical treatment provided pursuant to subdivision (C).

This rule is taken from 2151.33 and represents present law. Subdivisions (A) and (B) provide additional detail to 2151.33, which simply provides that the court can make "such temporary disposition of any child as it deems best". Subdivisions (D) and (E) provide greater detail to the notion of summary procedure and notice contained in 2151.33.

CROSS REFERENCES

Kurtz & Giannelli, Ohio Juvenile Law, Text 3.06(D), 7.06(E), 7.07, 7.08(B), 15.02(B)

OJur 3d: 4, Appellate Review § 105; 23, Courts and Judges § 428; 46, Family Law § 448 to 450, 550, 584

Am Jur 2d: 47, Juvenile Court and Delinquent and Dependent Children § 29 to 33, 35, 36

Validity and application of statute allowing endangered child to be temporarily removed from parental custody. 38 ALR4th 756

LAW REVIEW ARTICLES

10 Capital U Law Rev 309 (1981). Consent to Medical Treatment for Minors Under Care of Children Services Board, Stephen D. Freedman, Esq.

NOTES ON DECISIONS AND OPINIONS

1. Cases interpreting Juvenile Rule 13
2. Cases interpreting law analogous to Juvenile Rule 13

1. Cases interpreting Juvenile Rule 13

44 OS(2d) 28, 336 NE(2d) 426 (1975), Williams v Williams. Where a court of another state has awarded custody of a minor child pursuant to a valid in personam order, and there is no evidence of a subsequent change in circumstances affecting the best interests of the child, the courts of this state will give full faith and credit to that order.

21 App(3d) 115, 21 OBR 123, 487 NE(2d) 341 (Trumbull 1984), Parker v Trumbull County Children Services Bd. Due process is not denied to the parent of a severely abused child by a court holding a temporary custody hearing ex parte under Juv R 13 without appointing a guardian ad litem under RC 2151.281.

45 App(2d) 299, 344 NE(2d) 144 (1973), Morrison v Morrison. A temporary order of a juvenile court changing custody under Juv R 13 or 29 is not a dispositional order under Juv R 34, and hence is not a final appealable order.

Nos. 48417 and 48480 (8th Dist Ct App, Cuyahoga, 1-24-85), In re Koballa. A comprehensive reunification plan need be prepared only when a child is committed to the temporary custody of the department of public welfare under RC 2151.353(A)(2) or RC 2151.353(A)(3); this is the plain meaning of RC 2151.412(C), which does not, it follows, require preparation of a plan when a temporary custody order is based on Juv R 13(A) and Juv R 13(D).

OAG 87-105. Under Ohio law, unless matters of public safety are involved, a child alleged to be abused, neglected, or dependent may be removed from his home by court order only upon a judicial determination that continuation in the home would be contrary to the child's best interest.

2. Cases interpreting law analogous to Juvenile Rule 13

2151.33 TEMPORARY CARE; EMERGENCY MEDICAL TREATMENT; REIMBURSEMENT

90 Abs 21, 185 NE(2d) 128 (CP Lucas 1962), In re Clark. Juvenile court properly authorized hospital to administer blood transfusions to child over religious objections of parents.

1951 OAG 898. When a complaint or application for care concerning a child has been filed with the juvenile court, such court may, pending service of a citation on the child's parents, guardian or custodian, order the provision of emergency medical or surgical treatment.

2151.35 HEARING PROCEDURE; FINDINGS; RECORD

1951 OAG 898. Where a child has been permanently committed to a child welfare board by order of the juvenile court, such board may properly consent to medical and surgical treatment of such child; where a child has been temporarily so committed, the child remains a ward of juvenile court, and such court may properly consent to medical and surgical treatment of such child.

Juv R 14
[Reserved]

Juv R 15
Process: issuance, form

(A) Summons: issuance.

After the complaint has been filed, the clerk shall promptly issue summons to the parties and to any person with whom the child may be, requiring the parties or person to appear before the court at the time fixed for hearing. A copy of the complaint shall accompany the summons.

(B) Summons: form.

The summons shall contain:

(1) The name of the party or person with whom the child may be or, if unknown, any name or description by which the party or person can be identified with reasonable certainty.

(2) A summary statement of the complaint and in juvenile traffic offense and delinquency proceedings the numerical designation of the applicable statute or ordinance.

(3) A statement that any party is entitled to be represented by an attorney and that upon request the court will appoint an attorney for an indigent party entitled to appointed counsel under Rule 4(A).

(4) An order to the party or person to appear at a stated time and place with a warning that the party or person may lose valuable rights or be subject to court sanction if he fails to appear at the time and place stated in the summons.

(5) If a complaint requests permanent custody a statement that the parent, guardian or other custodian may be permanently divested of all parental rights.

(C) Summons: endorsement.

The court may endorse upon the summons an order directed to the party, or person with whom the child may be, to appear personally and bring the child to the hearing.

(D) Warrant: issuance.

If it appears that summons will be ineffectual or the welfare of the child requires that he be brought forthwith to the court, a warrant may be issued against the child. A copy of the complaint shall accompany the warrant.

(E) Warrant: form.

The warrant shall contain the name of the child or, if that is unknown, any name or description by which he can be identified with reasonable certainty. It shall contain a summary statement of the complaint and in juvenile traffic offense and delinquency proceedings the numerical designation of the applicable statute or ordinance. A copy of the complaint shall be attached to the warrant. The warrant shall command that the child be taken into custody and be brought before the court issuing such warrant without unnecessary delay.

Adopted eff. 7-1-72

Editor's Comment

  1. Summons: issuance
  2. Summons: form
  3. Summons: endorsement
  4. Warrant: issuance
  5. Warrant: form

1. Summons: issuance

"Summons: issuance" is a restatement of the second sentence of the first paragraph of 2151.28(A) and the last sentence of paragraph two of 2151.28(A), and requires the clerk to promptly issue process upon the filing of the complaint.

2. Summons: form

Juv R 15(B)(1) and 15(B)(2) "Summons: form," adopts the language of Crim R 4(C) and the provisions of 2935.18.

Juv R 15(B)(3) is simply restating RC 2151.28(C).

Juv R 15(B)(4) follows Crim R 4(C)(2) but expands the warning beyond the arrest feature and adds to Ohio law the language of Federal Rule 4.

Juv R 15(B)(5) merely restates the language of the third paragraph of 2151.28(A).

3. Summons: endorsement

Juv R 15(C) restates the provision of 2151.28(B).

4. Warrant: issuance

Juv R 15(D) is a restatement of 2151.30 and adds the requirement that a copy of the complaint shall accompany the warrant.

5. Warrant: form

Juv R 15(E) is taken from Crim R 4(C)(1), substituting the word "custody" instead of "arrest" and "child" in lieu of "defendant." Juv R 6 states the other reasons in addition to the law of arrest for which a child can be deprived of his liberty and taken into custody. Juvenile proceedings are not criminal proceedings, and a child is never referred to as a defendant.

CROSS REFERENCES

Kurtz & Giannelli, Ohio Juvenile Law, Text 7.05, 11.03, 15.01(D)

Warrant or summons, Crim R 4

OJur 3d: 23, Courts and Judges § 428; 46, Family Law § 465 to 467, 471 to 473

Am Jur 2d: 47, Juvenile Courts and Delinquent and Dependent Children § 43

Necessity of service of process upon infant itself in juvenile delinquency and dependency proceedings. 90 ALR2d 293

Failure to give adequate notice to juvenile's parents as ground for reversal of determination of juvenile delinquency under Federal Juvenile Delinquency Act (18 USCS secs. 5031-5042). 30 ALR Fed 745

NOTES ON DECISIONS AND OPINIONS

1. Cases interpreting Juvenile Rule 15
2. Cases interpreting law analogous to Juvenile Rule 15

1. Cases interpreting Juvenile Rule 15

44 OS(2d) 28, 336 NE(2d) 426 (1975), Williams v Williams. Where a court of another state has awarded custody of a minor child pursuant to a valid in personam order, and there is no evidence of a subsequent change in circumstances affecting the best interests of the child, the courts of this state will give full faith and credit to that order.

21 App(3d) 36, 21 OBR 38, 486 NE(2d) 152 (Huron 1984), In re Wilson. A properly served summons containing the "full explanation" required by RC 2151.353(B) must be accompanied by a copy of the complaint, amended or not, if the complaint seeks, temporarily or permanently, to divest a parent of his parental rights.

2. Cases interpreting law analogous to Juvenile Rule 15

2151.19 SUMMONS; EXPENSE

OAG 70-130. The sheriff is required to serve summons, notices, and subpoenas which are directed to him by the juvenile court, and whether the juvenile court requests the summons, notices or subpoenas to be served personally or to be delivered by registered or certified mail, the sheriff's office is legally required to serve them in accordance with such directions of the juvenile court; and if the person to be served is out of the state and his address is known, service of summons may be made by the sheriff by delivering a copy to him personally or mailing a copy to him by registered or certified mail.

2151.28 SUMMONS

145 OS 413, 61 NE(2d) 892 (1945), In re Corey. Under this section, the parents of a minor child or children are entitled to notice, actual or constructive, in a proceeding instituted in the juvenile court upon a complaint of dependency of such children; without such notice jurisdiction of the court does not attach and a judgment of commitment in proceeding is void.

126 OS 526, 186 NE 362 (1933), State ex rel Heth v Moloney. Under this section, a juvenile court may either issue a citation, requiring a minor charged with being dependent, neglected or delinquent and its parents or guardian or other person to appear, or the judge may in the first instance issue a warrant for the arrest of such minor.

126 OS 526, 186 NE 362 (1933), State ex rel Heth v Moloney. In case of arrest of a minor, upon a warrant issued by a juvenile court, arising out of a complaint charging such minor with delinquency, the juvenile court has jurisdiction of the proceedings even though a citation has not been issued to the parents, guardian or other person having custody and control of such child.

115 OS 518, 154 NE 914 (1926), Rarey v Schmidt. The words "other person having custody of such child," as used in former GC 1648 (GC 1639-10; RC 2151.21), meant a person having custody created by operation of law or awarded to such person by judicial order, judgment, or decree.

1 App(2d) 57, 203 NE(2d) 501 (1963), In re Rule. A father is a party to proceedings in a juvenile court in which his children are found to be neglected and in which temporary custody is given to the mother; and he is also a party to a subsequent proceeding in the same court modifying such temporary custody order and is entitled to appear in an appeal from such order and to move to dismiss such appeal.

1 App(2d) 57, 203 NE(2d) 501 (1963), In re Rule. An order modifying a previously-entered temporary custody order, which was made in disposition of a finding that a child is neglected, constitutes a final appealable order.

114 App 319, 182 NE(2d) 631 (1961), In re Jones. 2151.28 and 2151.31 do not require a hearing as a condition precedent to the taking of a child into custody, pursuant to order of a juvenile court, during pendency of an action in such court.

87 App 101, 90 NE(2d) 394 (1950), State ex rel Clark v Allaman; affirmed by 154 OS 296, 95 NE(2d) 753 (1950). Juvenile court has no jurisdiction to adjudicate a child as dependent until after filing of a complaint charging such dependency and notice given to the parent or parents.

27 App 306, 160 NE 733 (1927), In re Cunningham. Where warrant was issued requiring infant daughter to be produced in court, and subpoena was issued for mother, and mother appeared at hearing, the mother, under former GC 1648 (GC 1639-24; RC 2151.28), received due notice in dependency proceeding against daughter.

22 App 528, 154 NE 55 (1926), In the Matter of Veselich. In complaint under former GC 1647 (GC 1639-23; RC 2151.27), GC 1648 (GC 1639-24; RC 2151.28), alleging dependency of child, paramount duty of juvenile court is conservation of child's interests.

89 Abs 473, 184 NE(2d) 707 (Prob Montgomery 1961), Mobley v Allaman. Where the mother of an illegitimate child was served with notice of a hearing on the motion of a county child welfare board for permanent custody of the child, and then married the father, who acknowledged paternity, and said father and mother appeared together at the hearing, the father could not thereafter complain that he had no notice of said hearing.

77 Abs 487, 150 NE(2d) 67 (Juv Wayne 1958) State v Hershberger; reversed by 83 Abs 63, 168 NE(2d) 12 (App Wayne 1958). Where parents passively resisted an order of the juvenile court, both could be held for contempt, not just the husband.

77 Abs 487, 150 NE(2d) 671 (Juv Wayne 1958), State v Hershberger; reversed by 83 Abs 63, 168 NE(2d) 12 (App Wayne 1958). Where a juvenile court found that a child was neglected, and committed such child to the temporary custody of the local child welfare board, the parents of such child could be punished for contempt for passively resisting such order. (Ed. Note: This was an Amish school attendance case.)

72 Abs 519, 135 NE(2d) 638 (App Franklin 1954), In re McCoy. Where the father of a child is named as a defendant in a divorce proceeding and is properly served, the court has jurisdiction to find the child to be a dependent child and to place it in a foster home.

33 Abs 8 (CP Delaware 1940), In re Flickinger. Regular legal notice by service of process on the parent is an indispensable prerequisite to jurisdiction of juvenile court to make commitment of a minor child in delinquency cases.

OAG 70-130. The sheriff is required to serve summons, notices, and subpoenas which are directed to him by the juvenile court, and whether the juvenile court requests the summons, notices or subpoenas to be served personally or to be delivered by registered or certified mail, the sheriff's office is legally required to serve them in accordance with such directions of the juvenile court; and if the person to be served is out of the state and his address is known, service of summons may be made by the sheriff by delivering a copy to him personally or mailing a copy to him by registered or certified mail.

1925 OAG 2451. A new citation to the parents or guardian is not necessary at the time a juvenile judge wishes to change a temporary order to a permanent one.

2151.35 HEARING PROCEDURE; FINDINGS; RECORD

1 App(2d) 57, 203 NE(2d) 501 (1963), In re Rule. A father is a party to proceedings in a juvenile court in which his children are found to be neglected and in which temporary custody is given to the mother; and he is also a party to a subsequent proceeding in the same court modifying such temporary custody order and is entitled to appear in an appeal from such order and to move to dismiss such appeal.

2151.36 SUPPORT OF CHILD

1929 OAG 281. A juvenile court does not have jurisdiction to make commitments of children under former GC 1653 (Repealed) unless service, either actual or constructive, is first had on the father of such child or on the person having the custody of such child.

Juv R 16
Process: service

(A) Summons: service, return.

Summons shall be served as provided in Civil Rules 4(A), (C) and (D), 4.1, 4.2, 4.3, 4.5 and 4.6. The summons shall direct the party served to appear at a stated time and place; where service is by certified mail such time shall not be less than twenty-one days after the date of mailing.

When the residence of a party is unknown, and cannot with reasonable diligence be ascertained, service shall be made by publication. Before service by publication can be made, an affidavit of a party or his counsel must be filed with the court. The affidavit shall aver that service of summons cannot be made because the residence of the defendant is unknown to the affiant and cannot with reasonable diligence be ascertained.

Upon the filing of the affidavit the clerk shall cause service of notice to be made by publication in a newspaper of general circulation in the county in which the complaint is filed. If no newspaper is published in that county, then publication shall be in a newspaper published in an adjoining county. The publication shall contain the name and address of the court, the case number, the name of the first party on each side, and the name and last known address, if any, of the person or persons whose residence is unknown. The publication shall also contain a summary statement of the object of the complaint and shall notify the person to

be served that he is required to appear at the time and place stated; such time shall not be less than fourteen days after the date of publication. The publication shall be published once and service shall be complete on the date of publication.

After the publication, the publisher or his agent shall file with the court an affidavit showing the fact of publication together with a copy of the notice of publication. The affidavit and copy of the notice shall constitute proof of service.

(B) Warrant: execution; return.

(1) By whom. The warrant shall be executed by any officer authorized by law.

(2) Territorial limits. The warrant may be executed at any place within this state.

(3) Manner. The warrant shall be executed by taking the party against whom it is issued into custody. The officer need not have the warrant in his possession at the time he executes it, but in such case he shall inform the party of the complaint made and the fact that the warrant has been issued. A copy of the warrant shall be given to the person named therein as soon as possible.

(4) Return. The officer executing a warrant shall make return thereof to the issuing court. Unexecuted warrants shall upon request of the issuing court be returned to that court.

A warrant returned unexecuted and not cancelled or a copy thereof may, while the complaint is pending, be delivered by the court to an authorized officer for execution.

An officer executing a warrant shall take the person named therein without unnecessary delay before the court which issued the warrant.

Adopted eff. 7-1-72

Editor's Comment

1. Summons: service, return
2. Warrant: execution; return

1. Summons: service, return

Juv R 16(A) incorporates the provisions of Civ R 4 by reference specifically to this rule and adds the requirement that the summons shall direct the party served to appear at a stated time and place. The main reason for adoption of this rule was the rationale that uniformity in the manner in which service of process was accomplished was desirable and in this respect juvenile procedure does not require any differentiation.

The manner of perfecting service by publication adopts the language of 2151.29 but alters the time for hearing requirement from one week to fourteen days.

The adoption of the rule also changes the provision of 2151.28 requiring that summons issued for a child under fourteen years of age be served on his parent, guardian or custodian in his behalf. Civ R 4.2(2) requires that service of process upon a person under sixteen years of age be effected by serving either his guardian or anyone of the following persons with whom he lives or resides: the father, mother, or the individual having the care of such person; or by serving such person if he neither has a guardian nor lives or resides with a parent or a person having his care.

Civ R 4 through 4.6 cover, modify and expand the service of process principles generally set forth in Ch 2703. These are now the same principles applicable to a juvenile court proceeding which commences with the filing of the complaint pursuant to Juv R 10(A).

Refer to staff notes under Civ R 4 for further discussion of effect and clarification of the methods of service of process provided for by Juv R 16(A).

2. Warrant: execution; return

Juv R 16(B) dealing with the execution and return of warrants is identical with the provisions of Crim R 4(D).

Juv R 16(B)(2) adopts the provision of 2935.02 which permits a warrant to be executed at any place in the state.

Juv R 16(B)(3) providing that an officer need not have the warrant in his possession at the time he executes it is consistent with the provisions of 2151.14 and is similar to Crim R 4(D)(3).

CROSS REFERENCES

Baldwin's Ohio Civil Practice, Text 3.24 to 3.29
Schroeder-Katz, Ohio Criminal Law, Text 31.11(B)
Kurtz & Giannelli, Ohio Juvenile Law, Text 1.04, 7.05

Process: summons, Civ R 4 et seq.
Warrant or summons, Crim R 4

OJur 3d: 23, Courts and Judges § 428; 46, Family Law § 465 to 467, 471 to 473
Am Jur 2d: 47, Juvenile Courts and Delinquent and Dependent Children § 43
Necessity of service of process upon infant itself in juvenile delinquency and dependency proceedings. 90 ALR2d 293
Failure to give adequate notice to juvenile's parents as ground for reversal of determination of juvenile delinquency under Federal Juvenile Delinquency Act (18 USCS secs. 5031-5042). 30 ALR Fed 745
Procedural requirements under Federal Constitution in juvenile delinquency proceedings—federal cases. 25 LEd(2d) 950

NOTES ON DECISIONS AND OPINIONS

1. Cases interpreting Juvenile Rule 16
2. Cases interpreting law analogous to Juvenile Rule 16

1. Cases interpreting Juvenile Rule 16

44 OS(2d) 28, 336 NE(2d) 426 (1975), Williams v Williams. Where a court of another state has awarded custody of a minor child pursuant to a valid in personam order, and there is no evidence of a subsequent change in circumstances affecting the best interests of the child, the courts of this state will give full faith and credit to that order.

33 App(3d) 224, 515 NE(2d) 635 (Cuyahoga 1986), In re Miller. Service by publication pursuant to Juv R 16(A) is defective when the notice fails to include the last known address of the party to be served and where only minimal efforts are made discover the whereabouts of the party to be served.

33 App(3d) 224, 515 NE(2d) 635 (Cuyahoga 1986), In re Miller. Where a challenge to a party's claim that reasonable diligence was exercised to locate a party served by publication under Juv R 16(A) is raised, the party claiming use of reasonable diligence must support such a claim.

21 App(3d) 36, 21 OBR 38, 486 NE(2d) 152 (Huron 1984), In re Wilson. Service of summons by publication is defective if the published notice fails to include a last known address, when such an address is known, and fails to include a summary statement of the object of the complaint.

No. C-830874 (1st Dist Ct App, Hamilton, 8-15-84), In re Marshall. Service of a complaint alleging that children are dependent and neglected and notice of hearing by regular mail the day before the hearing and receipt of same the day after the hearing deprives the defending parent of sufficient notice and due process under the law; the report of the referee and judgment of the juvenile court are rendered a nullity, despite the fact that such service complies with the letter of the procedural rules.

2. Cases interpreting law analogous to Juvenile Rule 16

2151.29 SERVICE OF SUMMONS

152 OS 164, 87 NE(2d) 583 (1949), In re Frinzl. Where only notice given mother of hearing to change child's temporary commitment to a permanent one was served on mother within an hour before such hearing, and she had no opportunity to either prepare for such hearing or to engage counsel to represent her, such notice is insufficient in law, and an order for permanent custody made at such hearing is void for want of jurisdiction of court in making it, even though mother was present at hearing; attack made upon it by an application for a writ of habeas corpus is proper even though judgment appears to be regular and valid upon its face.

152 OS 164, 87 NE(2d) 583 (1949), In re Frinzl. Juvenile court is without jurisdiction to make permanent a temporary commitment of child unless notice of time and place of hearing is served on parent or guardian either by delivering a copy to the person to be notified, by leaving a copy at his

usual place of residence, by service by registered mail, or by publication, as provided by this section; such notice must be served sufficiently in advance of hearing to allow reasonable time to obtain counsel and prepare for participation in such hearing.

117 OS 152, 157 NE 897 (1927), Lewis v Reed. The matters required to be shown under former GC 1648 (GC 1639-24; RC 2151.28) as a prerequisite to notice by publication of proceedings as to dependency of minor children were jurisdictional. In such case an attack upon a judgment for fraud in its procurement is direct, and is permitted, notwithstanding that the judgment questioned may appear on its face regular and valid.

117 OS 152, 157 NE 897 (1927), Lewis v Reed. Under GC 1648 (GC 1639-24; RC 2151.28), the mother of an illegitimate child is entitled to notice, actual or constructive, of proceedings upon a complaint of dependency instituted in the juvenile court in reference to such child; and until notice of such proceedings has been given to the mother, the jurisdiction of the juvenile court does not attach and a judgment of permanent commitment rendered in such dependency proceeding is void.

115 OS 518, 154 NE 914 (1926), Rarey v Schmidt. Where a minor child has neither legal guardian nor custodian, other than a parent, and the residence of the parent is known, service, actual or constructive, must be had upon such parent before a juvenile court has jurisdiction to declare such child a dependent child.

115 OS 518, 154 NE 914 (1926), Rarey v Schmidt. An order of a juvenile court declaring a minor child to be a dependent child and awarding its custody to a stranger, obtained without service upon the parent, the guardian, or a person having the custody of such child by operation of law or awarded by a judicial order, judgment, or decree, confers upon such stranger no power to consent to the adoption of such child by any one.

33 Abs 8 (CP Delaware 1940), In re Flickinger. Knowledge by a mother that her girl was being held and that a complaint might or even probably would be made against her was not sufficient to meet the requirements of this section.

OAG 70-130. The sheriff is required to serve summons, notices, and subpoenas which are directed to him by the juvenile court, and whether the juvenile court requests the summons, notices or subpoenas to be served personally or to be delivered by registered or certified mail, the sheriff's office is legally required to serve them in accordance with such directions of the juvenile court; and if the person to be served is out of the state and his address is known, service of summons may be made by the sheriff by delivering a copy to him personally or mailing a copy to him by registered or certified mail.

Juv R 17
Subpoena
(A) For attendance of witnesses; form; issuance.

Every subpoena issued by the clerk shall be under the seal of the court, shall state the name of the court and the title of the action, and shall command each person to whom it is directed to attend and give testimony at a time and place therein specified. The clerk shall issue a subpoena, or a subpoena for the production of documentary evidence, signed and sealed but otherwise in blank, to a party requesting it, who shall fill it in and file a copy thereof with the clerk before service.

(B) Parties unable to pay.

The court shall order at any time that a subpoena be issued for service on a named witness upon an ex parte application of a party upon a satisfactory showing that the presence of the witness is necessary and that the party is financially unable to pay the witness fees required by subdivision (D). If the court orders the subpoena to be issued the costs incurred by the process and the fees of the witness so subpoenaed shall be paid in the same manner in which similar costs and fees are paid in case of a witness subpoenaed in behalf of the state in a criminal prosecution.

(C) For production of documentary evidence.

A subpoena may also command the person to whom it is directed to produce the books, papers, documents or other objects designated therein; but the court upon motion made promptly and in any event at or before the time specified in the subpoena for compliance therewith may quash or modify the subpoena if compliance would be unreasonable or oppressive. The court may direct that the books, papers, documents or other objects designated in the subpoena be produced before the court at a time prior to the hearing or prior to the time they are offered in evidence and may upon their production permit them or portions thereof to be inspected by the parties or their attorneys.

(D) Service.

A subpoena may be served by a sheriff, bailiff, coroner, clerk of court, constable, probation officer or a deputy of any, by an attorney-at-law or his agent or by any person designated by order of the court who is not a party and is not less than eighteen years of age. Service of a subpoena upon a person named therein shall be made by delivering a copy thereof to such person or by reading it to him in person or by leaving it at his usual place of residence, and by tendering to him upon demand the fees for one day's attendance and the mileage allowed by law. The person serving the subpoena shall file a return thereof with the clerk. If the witness being subpoenaed resides outside the county in which the court is located, the fees for one day's attendance and mileage shall be tendered without demand. The return may be forwarded through the postal service, or otherwise.

(E) Subpoena for taking depositions; place of examination.

When the attendance of a witness before an official authorized to take depositions is required, the subpoena shall be issued by such person and shall command the person to whom it is directed to attend and give testimony at a time and place specified therein. The subpoena may command the person to whom it is directed to produce designated books, papers, documents or tangible objects which constitute or contain evidence relating to any of the matters within the scope of the examination permitted by Rule 25.

A person whose deposition is to be taken may be required to attend an examination in the county wherein he resides or is employed or transacts his business in person, or at such other convenient place as is fixed by an order of court.

(F) Subpoena for a hearing.

At the request of any party subpoenas for attendance at a hearing shall be issued by the clerk of the court in which the hearing is held. A subpoena requiring the attendance of a witness at a hearing may be served at any place within this state.

(G) Contempt.

Failure by any person without adequate excuse to obey a subpoena served upon him may be deemed a contempt of the court or officer issuing the subpoena.

Adopted eff. 7-1-72

Editor's Comment

1. For attendance of witnesses; form; issuance
2. Parties unable to pay
3. For production of documentary evidence
4. Service
5. Subpoena for taking depositions; place of examination; subpoena for a hearing

1. For attendance of witnesses; form; issuance

Juv R 17 follows closely the provisions of Civ R 45 and Crim R 17. Juv R 17(A) adopts the identical language of both Civ R 45(A) and Crim R 17(A).

2. Parties unable to pay

Juv R 17(B) adopts the language of Crim R 17(B) as to parties unable to pay fees. There is no such provision in Civ R 45.

3. For production of documentary evidence

Juv R 17(C) adopts the language of Crim R 17(C).

4. Service

Juv R 17(D) is similar to Crim R 17(D) and Civ R 45(D) and adds "probation officer" to those who may serve a subpoena as provided in 2151.14.

5. Subpoena for taking depositions; place of examination; subpoena for a hearing

Juv R 17(E) and 17(F) are identical with both Civ R 45 and Crim R 17 as is Juv R 17(G) regarding power of the juvenile court to treat as contempt the failure of any person to obey a subpoena without adequate excuse and follows the requirement of 2151.21.

The rule covers subpoenas for hearing, for production of materials and for depositions. The Ohio procedure closely follows Federal Rule 45 and is similar to 2317.11 through 2317.20. It provides for a uniform and flexible method for the issuance of subpoenas, changes and expands portions of the statutory law and supersedes 2317.11 through 2317.20.

Prior to the adoption of the rule there was no specific procedure for the issuance of subpoenas in the juvenile court except a reference in paragraph (G) of 2151.28.

(See Staff Notes under Civ R 45, *Baldwin's Ohio Revised Code Annotated*.)

CROSS REFERENCES

Giannelli, Ohio Evidence Manual, Author's Comment § 804.07, 1004.04

Kurtz & Giannelli, Ohio Juvenile Law, Text 15.01(D)

Subpoena, Civ R 45
Subpoena, Crim R 17

OJur 3d: 23, Courts and Judges § 428; 46, Family Law § 403, 474 to 478, 499, 545

Am Jur 2d: 47, Juvenile Courts and Delinquent and Dependent Children § 44, 49

LAW REVIEW ARTICLES

19 Am Crim L Rev 193 (1981). Subpoena, Dona A. Nutini and Patricia J. Pannell.

NOTES ON DECISIONS AND OPINIONS

2151.19 SUMMONS; EXPENSE

OAG 70-130. The sheriff is required to serve summons, notices, and subpoenas which are directed to him by the juvenile court, and whether the juvenile court requests the summons, notices or subpoenas to be served personally or to be delivered by registered or certified mail, the sheriff's office is legally required to serve them in accordance with such directions of the juvenile court; and if the person to be served is out of the state and his address is known, service of summons may be made by the sheriff by delivering a copy to him personally or mailing a copy to him by registered or certified mail.

Juv R 18

Time

(A) Time: computation.

In computing any period of time prescribed or allowed by these rules, by the local rules of any court, by order of court, or by any applicable statute, the date of the act or event from which the designated period of time begins to run shall not be included. The last day of the period so computed shall be included, unless it is a Saturday, a Sunday, or a legal holiday, in which event the period runs until the end of the next day which is not a Saturday, a Sunday or a legal holiday. When the period of time prescribed or allowed is less than seven days, intermediate Saturdays, Sundays, and legal holidays shall be excluded in computation.

(B) Time: enlargement.

When an act is required or allowed to be performed at or within a specified time, the court for cause shown may at any time in its discretion (1) with or without motion or notice, order the period enlarged if application therefor is made before expiration of the period originally prescribed or of that period as extended by a previous order, or (2) upon motion permit the act to be done after expiration of the specified period if the failure to act on time was the result of excusable neglect or would result in injustice to a party, but the court may not extend the time for taking any action under

Rule 7(F)(1), Rule 22(F), Rule 29(A) and Rule 29(F)(2)(b), except to the extent and under the conditions stated in them.

(C) Time: unaffected by expiration of term.

The period of time provided for the doing of any act or the taking of any proceeding is not affected or limited by the expiration of a term of court. The expiration of a term of court in no way affects the power of a court to do any act in a juvenile proceeding.

(D) Time: for motions; affidavits.

A written motion, other than one which may be heard ex parte, and notice of the hearing thereof, shall be served not later than seven days before the time specified for the hearing unless a different period is fixed by rule or order of the court. For cause shown such an order may be made on ex parte application. When a motion is supported by affidavit, the affidavit shall be served with the motion, and opposing affidavits may be served not less than one day before the hearing unless the court permits them to be served at a later time.

(E) Time: additional time after service by mail.

Whenever a party has the right or is required to do an act within a prescribed period after the service of a notice or other paper upon him and the notice or other paper is served upon him by mail, three days shall be added to the prescribed period. This subdivision does not apply to service of summons.

Adopted eff. 7-1-72

Editor's Comment

Juv R 18 is identical with Civ R 6 and Crim R 45. Juv R 18 differs only in that Juv R 18(B) provides that the court may not extend the time for taking any action under Juv R 7(F)(1) pertaining to a detention hearing; Juv R 22(F) pertaining to the time for filing pleadings; Juv R 29(A) pertaining to the adjudicatory hearing; and Juv R 29(F)(2)(b) pertaining to the dispositional hearing; except to the extent and under the conditions stated in them.

The rule is very similar in principle to Federal Rule 6 but does provide that computations of periods of time are unaffected by the expiration of a term of court. In the federal court system, terms of court have been abolished.

Computation of a period of time set forth in the rule varies slightly from 1.14 in that if the final day of the period falls on Saturday, that day shall be excluded in the computation of time. The term "legal holidays" refers to those legal holidays set forth in 1.14.

Under the rule the court has discretionary control over any time extensions provided request is made to the court before the expiration of the period originally prescribed or of that period as extended by a previous order. After the prescribed period of time the court may only extend the time required to perform an act if the party's failure was the result of excusable neglect or would result in an injustice to the party. The court may not extend the time in the instances enumerated in Juv R 18(B).

The rule follows generally the requirements of 2309.42.

CROSS REFERENCES

Kurtz & Giannelli, Ohio Juvenile Law, Text 7.06(D), 15.01(A)

Time, Civ R 6
Time, Crim R 45

OJur 3d: 23, Courts and Judges § 428; 46, Family Law § 369, 370, 481, 485

Juv R 19
Motions

An application to the court for an order shall be by motion. A motion other than one made during trial or hearing shall be in writing unless the court permits it to be made orally. It shall state with particularity the grounds upon which it is made and shall set forth the relief or order sought. It shall be supported by a memorandum containing citations of authority and may be supported by an affidavit.

To expedite its business, the court may make provision by rule or order for the submission and determination of motions without oral hearing upon brief written statements of reasons in support and opposition.

Adopted eff. 7-1-72

Editor's Comment

Juv R 19 adopts the language generally of Civ R 7(B) and differs only in providing that a motion shall be supported by a memorandum containing citations of authority rather than by a brief as in the civil rule. The court may by adoption of a local rule provide for the submission and determination of motions without oral hearing upon brief written statements of reasons in support and opposition and is based upon Federal Rule 78. This provision is consistent with Juv R 1(B)(2) pertaining to the elimination of unjustifiable expense and delay.

The rule requires that an application to the court shall be by motion which unless made during the hearing shall be in writing and shall state the grounds with particularity.

The rule covers motion practice in juvenile court.

CROSS REFERENCES

Kurtz & Giannelli, Ohio Juvenile Law, Text 7.06(C)

Pleadings and motions, Civ R 7

OJur 3d: 23, Courts and Judges § 428; 46, Family Law § 479, 482
Am Jur 2d: 56, Motions, Rules, and Orders § 1 et seq.

Juv R 20
Service and filing of papers

(A) Service: when required.

Written notices, requests for discovery, designation of record on appeal and written motions, other than those which are heard ex parte, and similar papers shall be served upon each of the parties.

(B) Service: how made.

Whenever under these rules or by an order of the court service is required or permitted to be made upon a party represented by an attorney, the service shall be made upon the attorney unless service upon the party himself is ordered by the court. Service upon the attorney or upon the party shall be made in the manner provided in Civil Rule 5(B).

(C) Filing.

All papers required to be served upon a party shall be filed simultaneously with or immediately after service. Papers filed with the court shall not be considered until proof of service is endorsed thereon or separately filed. The proof of service shall state the date and the manner of service and shall be signed and filed in the manner provided in Civil Rule 5(D).

Adopted eff. 7-1-72

Editor's Comment

Juv R 20 is substantially like Crim R 49 and closely follows Civ R 5. Juv R 20(A) is more limited in the types of pleadings that may be filed in a juvenile proceeding and requires that necessary pleadings shall be served on each party. It follows the civil rule in providing for service upon an attorney of record unless service upon the party is ordered by the court. When service is upon the attorney it shall be made as provided in Civ R 5.

The rule differs from the civil rule in that it requires that all pleadings shall be filed simultaneously with or immediately after service rather than within three days after service.

Juv R 20 governs the filing with the court of pleadings and papers subsequent to the filing of the original complaint.

CROSS REFERENCES

Kurtz & Giannelli, Ohio Juvenile Law, Text 7.08(A)

Service and filing of pleadings and other papers subsequent to the original complaint, Civ R 5
Service and filing of papers, Crim R 49

OJur 3d: 23, Courts and Judges § 428; 46, Family Law § 484, 486
Necessity of service of process upon infant itself in juvenile delinquency and dependency proceedings. 90 ALR2d 293

Juv R 21

Preliminary conferences

At any time after the filing of a complaint, the court upon motion of any party or upon its own motion may order one or more conferences to consider such matters as will promote a fair and expeditious proceeding.

Adopted eff. 7-1-72

Editor's Comment

This is a modification of Crim R 17.1, intended to encourage the expanded use of the preliminary conference technique in a manner appropriate to the purposes of the Juvenile Court Act. The requirement of the criminal rule that a memorandum be prepared and filed was deemed unwieldy and unnecessary in the juvenile setting.

CROSS REFERENCES

Indictment and information, Crim R 7

OJur 3d: 46, Family Law § 487

Juv R 22

Pleadings and motions; defenses and objections

(A) Pleadings and motions.

Pleadings in juvenile proceedings shall be the complaint and the answer, if any, filed by a party. A party may move to dismiss the complaint or for other appropriate relief.

(B) Amendment of pleadings.

Any pleading may be amended at any time prior to the adjudicatory hearing. After the commencement of the adjudicatory hearing, a pleading may be amended upon agreement of the parties, or if the interests of justice require, upon order of court. Such order shall where requested grant a party reasonable time in which to respond to an amendment.

(C) Answer.

No answer shall be necessary. A party may file an answer to the complaint, which, if filed, shall contain specific and concise admissions or denials of each material allegation of the complaint.

(D) Prehearing motions.

Any defense, objection or request which is capable of determination without hearing on the allegations of the complaint may be raised before the adjudicatory hearing by motion. The following must be heard before the adjudicatory hearing, though not necessarily on a separate date:

(1) Defenses or objections based on defects in the institution of the proceeding;

(2) Defenses or objections based on defects in the complaint (other than failure to show jurisdiction in the court or to charge an offense which objections shall be noticed by the court at any time during the pendency of the proceeding);

(3) Motions to suppress evidence on the ground that it was illegally obtained;

(4) Motions for discovery.

(E) Motion time.

All prehearing motions shall be filed by the earlier of (1) seven days prior to hearing, or (2) ten days after the appearance of counsel. The court in the interest of justice may extend the time for making prehearing motions.

The court for good cause shown may permit a motion to suppress evidence under subsection (D)(3) to be made at the time such evidence is offered.

(F) State's right to appeal upon granting a motion to suppress.

In delinquency proceedings the state may take an appeal as of right from the granting of a motion to suppress evidence if, in addition to filing a notice of appeal, the prosecuting attorney certifies that (1) the appeal is not taken for the purpose of delay and (2) the granting of the motion has rendered proof available to the state so weak in its entirety that any reasonable possibility of proving the complaint's allegations has been destroyed.

Such appeal shall not be allowed unless the notice of appeal and the certification by the prosecuting attorney are filed with the clerk of the juvenile court within seven days after the date of the entry of the judgment or order granting the motion. Any appeal which may be taken under this rule shall be diligently prosecuted.

A child in detention or shelter care may be released pending this appeal when the state files the notice of appeal and certification.

This appeal shall take precedence over all other appeals.

Adopted eff. 7-1-72; amended eff. 7-1-77

Editor's Comment

1. Pleadings and motions
2. Amendment of pleadings
3. Answer
4. Prehearing motions
5. Motion time
6. State's right to appeal upon granting a motion to suppress

1. Pleadings and motions

Subdivision (A) is similar to Crim R 12(A), modified to conform with juvenile court practice.

2. Amendment of pleadings

Subdivision (B) is an amalgamation of Crim R 7(D) and Civ R 15(B), and is intended to provide the parties with broad latitude in amending pleadings, while complying with the due process requirements of adequate notice. The prohibition contained in Crim R 7(D) against changing the name or identity of the crime charged is not included in the juvenile rule. The defense of variance is probably not appropriate in delinquency cases, and the opportunity for a party to obtain time in which to respond to the amendment avoids due process complications.

3. Answer

Subdivision (C) conforms to present practice, in that no answer is required. If an answer is filed, the requirement of concise admissions or denials contained in Civ R 8(B) attaches.

4. Prehearing motions

Subdivision (D) is basically Crim R 12(B), slightly modified grammatically and follows the holding in *State v Davis*, 1 OS(2d) 28, 203 NE(2d) 357 (1964).

5. Motion time

Subdivision (E) adopts the structure of Crim R 12(C), but with time periods shortened to conform with the need for expeditious action in juvenile proceedings. Though it may appear to set extremely short periods, time extensions are available.

6. State's right to appeal upon granting a motion to suppress

Subdivision (F) is basically Crim R 12(J) providing the right of appeal to the state. Also, the mandatory release of a criminal defendant required by Crim R 12(J) pending appeal has not been adopted. A child in detention or shelter care may be kept there pending the appellate decision.

The rule provides that appeal on the granting of a motion to suppress shall take precedence over all other appeals in order to avoid delay in prosecution of the matter.

CROSS REFERENCES

Whiteside, Ohio Appellate Practice, Forms 9.26, 9.30
Kurtz & Giannelli, Ohio Juvenile Law, Text 3.10(C), 5.01, 7.03(K)(L), 7.08(A), 11.15, 15.02(D)(E)(G), 15.03

Pleadings and motions, Civ R 7
General rules of pleading, Civ R 8
Amended and supplemental pleadings, Civ R 15
Indictment and information, Crim R 7
Pleadings and motions before trial: defenses and objections, Crim R 12

OJur 3d: 23, Courts and Judges § 428; 26, Criminal Law § 846; 46, Family Law § 455, 463, 464, 480, 482, 588
Am Jur 2d: 47, Juvenile Courts and Delinquent and Dependent Children § 40 to 43

LAW REVIEW ARTICLES

32 Case WRU Law Rev 443 (1982). The Fourth Amendment Exclusionary Rule: The Desirability of a Good Faith Exception, Donald L. Willits.

14 Jour of Family Law 535 (1976). Access to "Confidential" Welfare Records in the Course of Child Protection Proceedings, Stephen Levine.

NOTES ON DECISIONS AND OPINIONS

46 OS(2d) 378, 348 NE(2d) 727 (1976), In re Hunt. A complaint under Juv R 10 and 2151.27 alleging that a child is dependent must state the essential facts which bring the proceeding within the jurisdiction of the court.

3 App(3d) 458, 3 OBR 539, 446 NE(2d) 202 (Franklin 1982), In re Hester. The state is not barred from prosecution following an unsuccessful appeal from the sustaining of a motion to suppress so long as the state's certification upon appeal pursuant to Juv R 22(F) or Crim R 12(J), that the evidence suppressed was of such nature that the prosecution could not be successful without it, was made in good faith; if such certification were not made in good faith, the time consumed in determining the appeal from the motion to suppress

must be charged to the state as undue delay in prosecution of the accused with respect to a determination of whether there has been a violation of the
accused's right to a speedy trial.

1 App(3d) 24, 1 OBR 85, 437 NE(2d) 1218
(1981), In re Hester. Where the state has timely
filed a notice of appeal from the granting of a
motion to suppress, but has failed to make a proper
certification as required by Juv R 22(F), a court of
appeals may, pursuant to App R 3(E), allow the
amendment of the timely filed notice of appeal and
certification so that there may be full compliance
with Juv R 22(F).

59 App(2d) 129, 392 NE(2d) 1262 (1977), In re
Fudge. In a juvenile proceeding an objection, raised
after trial and submission, based on a failure of the
testimony to establish the age of the accused juvenile, relates to jurisdiction over the person and not
to jurisdiction in the court, and is waived under Juv
R 22(D)(2).

45 App(2d) 308, 345 NE(2d) 79 (1974), In re
Gilbert. An appeal by the state from a finding of
not guilty, on a charge of "delinquency by reason of
murder," by the juvenile division of the court of
common pleas is barred by the constitutional protection against former jeopardy.

No. C-830874 (1st Dist Ct App, Hamilton,
8-15-84), In re Marshall. Service of a complaint
alleging that children are dependent and neglected
and notice of hearing by regular mail the day before
the hearing and receipt of same the day after the
hearing deprives the defending parent of sufficient
notice and due process under the law; the report of
the referee and judgment of the juvenile court are
rendered a nullity, despite the fact that such service
complies with the letter of the procedural rules.

No. 7998 (2d Dist Ct App, Montgomery,
10-25-83), In re Johnson. Where a juvenile is asked
to take a polygraph examination as a potential witness to a murder but is not charged, arrested, photographed, fingerprinted or considered a suspect,
such juvenile is not in custody and Miranda has no
application.

Juv R 23

Continuance

Continuances shall be granted only
when imperative to secure fair treatment
for the parties.

Adopted eff. 7-1-72

Editor's Comment

This rule is unique, and states the policy that
juvenile cases are to be heard and determined as
expeditiously as possible. Juvenile courts are of
equal rank with common pleas courts, and a conflicting engagement of counsel in a municipal court
or other lower court is not an adequate basis for a
continuance in juvenile court.

CROSS REFERENCES

Kurtz & Giannelli, Ohio Juvenile Law, Text
11.02, 13.02, 13.03

OJur 3d: 23, Courts and Judges § 428; 46, Family Law § 503

NOTES ON DECISIONS AND OPINIONS

54 App(2d) 195, 376 NE(2d) 970 (1977), In re
Therklidsen. The ten-day period of limitations in
Juv R 29(A) is procedural only and such rule confers no substantive right upon an accused to have
his case dismissed if he is not tried within the designated time.

37 App(2d) 7, 306 NE(2d) 166 (1973), In re
Bolden. The guarantee of the right to be represented by counsel set forth in Juv R 4(A) does not,
as to a nonindigent party, require that trial be continued indefinitely until counsel can be obtained,
but merely requires, if it does not appear that counsel could not be obtained through the exercise of
reasonable diligence and a willingness to enter into
reasonable contractual arrangements for counsel's
services, that a reasonable opportunity be given to
the party before trial to employ such counsel.

Juv R 24

Discovery

(A) Request for discovery.

Upon written request, each party of
whom discovery is requested shall forthwith produce for inspection, copying or
photographing the following information,
documents and material in his custody,
control or possession:

(1) The names and last known addresses
of each witness to the occurrence which
forms the basis of the charge or defense;

(2) Copies of any written statements
made by any party or witness;

(3) Transcriptions, recordings and summaries of any oral statements of any party
or witness, except the work product of
counsel;

(4) Any scientific or other reports which
a party intends to introduce at the hearing,
or which pertain to physical evidence
which a party intends to introduce;

(5) Photographs and any physical evidence which a party intends to introduce at
the hearing.

(B) Order granting discovery: limitations; sanctions.

If a request for discovery is refused,
application may be made to the court for a
written order granting the discovery.

Motions for discovery shall certify that a request for discovery has been made and refused. An order granting discovery may make such discovery reciprocal for all parties to the proceeding, including the party requesting discovery. Notwithstanding the provisions of subdivision (A), the court may deny, in whole or part, or otherwise limit or set conditions on the discovery authorized by such subdivision, upon its own motion, or upon a showing by a party upon whom a request for discovery is made that granting discovery may jeopardize the safety of a party, witness, or confidential informant, result in the production of perjured testimony or evidence, endanger the existence of physical evidence, violate a privileged communication, or impede the criminal prosecution of a minor as an adult or of an adult charged with an offense arising from the same transaction or occurrence.

(C) Failure to comply.

If at any time during the course of the proceedings it is brought to the attention of the court that a person has failed to comply with an order issued pursuant to this rule, the court may grant a continuance, prohibit the person from introducing in evidence the material not disclosed, or enter such other order as it deems just under the circumstances.

Adopted eff. 7-1-72

Editor's Comment

1. Request for discovery
2. Order granting discovery: limitations; sanctions
3. Failure to comply

1. Request for discovery

Juv R 24(A) establishes a procedure similar to that under Crim R 16(A), by which the discovery authorized by the rule is to proceed upon request of one party upon another, without prior court order.

Juv R 24(A)(1) is similar to Crim R 16(B)(1)(e), requiring the production of occurrence witnesses' names and addresses. The protection against witness harassment contained in Crim R 16(B)(1)(e) is provided in subdivision (B) of the Juvenile Rule.

Juv R 24(A)(2) and (3), requiring the production of transcriptions, recordings and summaries of witnesses' oral statements, authorizes broader discovery than would be available under Crim R 16(B)(1)(c). The juvenile rule would make such items as police arrest reports (*i.e.,* non-privileged investigation reports) available to counsel. The scope of its coverage is similar to that contained in Civ R 34.

Juv R 24(A)(4) authorizes production of scientific reports, and is similar to the discovery allowed by Crim R 16(B)(1)(d).

Juv R 24(A)(5), authorizing discovery of photographs and physical evidence intended for use at a hearing, is similar to Crim R 16(B)(1)(c).

2. Order granting discovery: limitations; sanctions

Juv R 24(B) regulates the procedure by which discovery can be obtained by court order, in the event that the person upon whom discovery is made refuses to comply with a request for discovery. It contains the restrictions of Crim R 16(B)(1)(e), which protects against witness harassment, and it provides additional protections against abuse of the discovery process. It is an effort to anticipate the main objections to broad discovery, and provide a procedure by which the discovery authorized in subdivision (A) can be effectuated fairly and expeditiously.

3. Failure to comply

Juv R 24(C) provides for remedies where an order for discovery has not been complied with.

The rule gives the court the power to deny in whole or in part or otherwise limit or set conditions regarding discovery either on its own motion or upon the motion of a party showing that the discovery requested may jeopardize the safety of a party, witness, or a confidential informant; result in production of perjured testimony or evidence; endanger the existence of physical evidence; violate a privileged communication; or impede the criminal prosecution of a minor or adult charged with an offense arising from the same transaction or occurrence.

The rule adopts the liberal discovery philosophy of the federal rules and is very similar to that expressed in *Ex Parte Oliver,* 173 OS 125, 180 NE(2d) 599 (1962). In this case the Supreme Court noted "any discovery proceeding ... has inherent in it the possibility of revealing information or data helpful to one side or another even though such information or data would be inadmissible in a subsequent trial. Any disadvantage to one party from another's gaining such information is offset, however, by the possible advantage therefrom of arriving at the truth of the situation, which is, and must remain, the ultimate goal. ..." (*See* Civ R 26.)

Policies considered as supportive of the broad discovery of this rule include the following: the "open file" approach conforms to general, but informal practice in our juvenile courts; discovery along the lines suggested by the rule reduce the adversary quality of the hearings; the hearing process will be expedited; and regulation of discovery by rules will avoid litigation on the issue.

CROSS REFERENCES

Kurtz & Giannelli, Ohio Juvenile Law, Text 7.01, 7.08

General provisions governing discovery, Civ R 26

Production of documents and things for inspection, copying, testing and entry upon land for inspection and other purposes, Civ R 34

Discovery and inspection, Crim R 16

OJur 3d: 23, Courts and Judges § 428; 46, Family Law § 477, 488 to 491

Am Jur 2d: 23, Depositions and Discovery § 400 to 467

NOTES ON DECISIONS AND OPINIONS

34 OS(2d) 55, 295 NE(2d) 659 (1973), State ex rel Daggett v Gessaman. Under the discovery provisions of the Civil Rules, the court has a discretionary power, not a ministerial duty; an interlocutory order, overruling a motion to compel answers to interrogatories involving opinions, contentions, and legal conclusions, is not a final appealable order.

Juv R 25

Depositions

The court upon good cause shown may grant authority to take the deposition of a party or other person upon such terms and conditions and in such manner as the court may fix.

Adopted eff. 7-1-72

Editor's Comment

The rule provides that a request to take a deposition in a juvenile proceeding is within the sound discretion of the court and shall be granted only upon a showing of good cause. If the deposition is ordered, the court shall determine the procedure for notice, attendance, time and place. This rule has no statutory basis, though it is based generally on 2945.50 and Crim R 15.

CROSS REFERENCES

Giannelli, Ohio Evidence Manual, Author's Comment § 804.07, 804.08

Kurtz & Giannelli, Ohio Juvenile Law, Text 7.08(A), 15.01(D)

Perpetuation of testimony, depositions before action or pending appeal, Civ R 27

Deposition, Crim R 15

OJur 3d: 23, Courts and Judges § 428; 46, Family Law § 477, 488 to 491

Am Jur 2d: 23, Depositions and Discovery § 400 to 467

Juv R 26
[Reserved]

Juv R 27
Hearings: general

The juvenile court may conduct its hearings in an informal manner and may adjourn such hearings from time to time. In the hearing of any case the general public may be excluded and only such persons admitted as have a direct interest in the case.

All cases involving children shall be heard separate and apart from the trial of cases against adults. The court may excuse the attendance of the child at the hearing in neglect, dependency, or abuse cases. The court shall hear and determine all cases of children without a jury.

Adopted eff. 7-1-72; amended eff. 7-1-76

Editor's Comment

The rule is identical to the first two paragraphs of 2151.35 and provides for informal hearings and continuances of hearings. Continuances should only be granted for good cause shown. (*See* Juv R 23.) Privacy of the hearings is essential and in the best interest of the child, but the rule gives the court discretion in permitting persons admission to the hearing. Most courts have by agreement with the news media permitted reporters to attend hearings provided the confidential nature of the hearing is preserved and no names are released without permission of the court.

It is important to separate children's hearings from adult trials to avoid the taint of criminality and to serve the best interest of the child while still affording protection to the community.

The provision permitting the court to excuse the attendance of the child at neglect, dependency, and abuse hearings is advisable as many of the children involved are of tender age and unable to participate in the hearing. Where the child may be older, the question of disruption of the parental relationship is important and must be considered by the court.

The denial of the right to a jury in juvenile proceedings has been held to be constitutionally permissible by the U.S. Supreme Court. See *McKeiver, et al v Pennsylvania*, 403 US 528, 91 SCt 1976, 29 LEd(2d) 647 (1971). In this case, the U.S. Supreme Court held "the applicable due process standard in juvenile proceedings is fundamental fairness as developed in *In re Gault*, 387 US 1, 87 SCt 1428, 18 LEd(2d) 527 (1967), and *In re Winship*, 397 US 358, 90 SCt 1068, 25 LEd(2d) 368 (1970), which emphasized factfinding procedures, but in our legal system, the jury is not a necessary component of accurate fact finding." The court further stated:

"Equating the adjudicative phase of the juvenile proceeding with a criminal trial ignores the aspect of fairness, concern, sympathy and paternal attention inherent in the juvenile court system."

CROSS REFERENCES

Kurtz & Giannelli, Ohio Juvenile Law, Text 7.05(A), Ch 11, 13.01 to 13.03, 15.04(A)

OJur 3d: 23, Courts and Judges § 428; 46, Family Law § 503 to 505
Am Jur 2d: 47, Juvenile Courts and Delinquent and Dependent Children § 44 to 48
Propriety of exclusion of press or other media representatives from civil trial. 79 ALR3d 401

LAW REVIEW ARTICLES

6 U Tol L Rev 1 (1974). The Effect of the Double Jeopardy Clause on Juvenile Proceedings, James G. Carr.

NOTES ON DECISIONS AND OPINIONS

1. Cases interpreting Juvenile Rule 27
2. Cases interpreting law analogous to Juvenile Rule 27

1. Cases interpreting Juvenile Rule 27

40 OS(3d) 8 (1988), State ex rel Fyffe v Pierce. It is within the discretion of a juvenile court judge to determine whether or not to close from the general public a hearing on the transfer of jurisdiction from the juvenile division to the court of common pleas, and thus a writ of prohibition to prevent the judge from conducting an open hearing will not lie.

2. Cases interpreting law analogous to Juvenile Rule 27

2151.23 JURISDICTION OF JUVENILE COURT
19 OS(2d) 70, 249 NE(2d) 808 (1969), In re Agler. Delinquency proceedings in juvenile court do not require indictment or trial by jury under US Const Am 5, 6, and 14, or under O Const Art I, § 5 and 10.

Juv R 28
[Reserved]

Juv R 29
Adjudicatory hearing

(A) Scheduling the hearing.

The date for the adjudicatory hearing shall be set when the complaint is filed, or as soon thereafter as is practicable. If the child who is the subject of the complaint is in detention or shelter care, the hearing shall be held not later than ten days after the filing of the complaint; upon a showing of good cause the adjudicatory hearing may be continued and detention or shelter care extended.

(B) Advisement and findings at the commencement of the hearing.

At the beginning of the hearing, the court shall:

(1) Ascertain whether notice requirements have been complied with, and if not, whether the affected parties waive compliance;

(2) Inform the parties of the substance of the complaint, the purpose of the hearing and possible consequences thereof, including the possibility that the cause may be transferred to the appropriate adult court under Rule 30 where the complaint alleges that a child fifteen years of age or over is delinquent by conduct which would constitute a felony if committed by an adult;

(3) Inform unrepresented parties of their right to counsel, and determine if such parties are waiving their right to counsel;

(4) Appoint counsel for any unrepresented party entitled thereto under Rule 4(A) who does not waive his right to counsel; and

(5) Inform any unrepresented party who waives counsel of his rights: to obtain counsel at any stage of the proceedings, to remain silent, to offer evidence, to cross-examine witnesses, and, upon request, to have a record of all proceedings made, at public expense if indigent.

(C) Entry of admission or denial.

The court shall request each party against whom allegations are made in the complaint to admit or deny the allegations. A failure or refusal to admit the allegations shall be deemed a denial.

(D) Initial procedure upon entry of an admission.

The court may refuse to accept an admission and shall not accept an admission without addressing the party personally and determining that:

(1) He is making the admission voluntarily with understanding of the nature of the allegations and the consequences of the admission; and

(2) He understands that by entering his admission he is waiving his rights to challenge the witnesses and evidence against

him, to remain silent and to introduce evidence at the adjudicatory hearing.

The court may hear testimony, review documents, or make further inquiry, as it deems appropriate, or it may proceed directly to the action required by subdivision (F).

(E) Initial procedure upon entry of a denial.

If a party denies the allegations, the court shall:

(1) Direct the prosecuting attorney or another attorney-at-law to assist the court by presenting evidence in support of the allegations of a complaint;

(2) Order the separation of witnesses, upon request of any party;

(3) Take all testimony under oath or affirmation in either question-answer or narrative form; and

(4) Determine the issues by proof beyond a reasonable doubt in juvenile traffic offense, delinquency, and unruly proceedings, by clear and convincing evidence in dependency, neglect, and child abuse proceedings, and by a preponderance of the evidence in all other cases.

(F) Procedure upon determination of the issues.

Upon the determination of the issues, the court shall:

(1) If the allegations of the complaint were not proved, dismiss the complaint;

(2) If the allegations of the complaint are admitted or proved:

(a) enter an adjudication and proceed forthwith to disposition; or

(b) enter an adjudication and continue the matter for disposition for not more than six months and may make appropriate temporary orders; or

(c) postpone judgment or adjudication for not more than six months; or

(d) dismiss the complaint if such action is in the best interests of the child and the community;

(3) Upon request make written findings of fact and conclusions of law pursuant to Civil Rule 52.

Adopted eff. 7-1-72; amended eff. 7-1-76

Editor's Comment

1. Scheduling the hearing
2. Advisement and findings at the commencement of the hearing

3. Entry of admission or denial
4. Initial procedure upon entry of an admission
5. Initial procedure upon entry of denial
6. Procedure upon determination of the issues

1. Scheduling the hearing

Juv R 29(A) contains the substance of the first sentence of 2151.28, with the additional requirements that the adjudicatory hearing shall be heard within ten days if the child is in detention, and that the hearing date shall be set in all cases as soon as practicable after the complaint is filed. There is an apparent conflict between Juv R 29(A) and Juv R 16(A) in cases in which a child is in detention and a party needs to be served by certified mail (because the party resides outside the county) or by publication (because the party's whereabouts are unknown). As indicated, Juv R 29(A) requires the adjudicatory hearing to be held within ten days if the child is detained. However, pursuant to Juv R 16(A), where service is by certified mail the hearing date shall not be less than twenty-one days after the date of mailing; and where service is by publication the hearing date shall not be less than fourteen days after the date of publication. (The fourteen day requirement where publication is required supersedes 2151.29, which requires only a one week period between publication and the hearing date.) Many courts resolve this conflict between the rules by providing a hearing for the child within ten days, at which time a determination may be made as to whether further detention is required pending the completion of service of process.

2. Advisement and findings at the commencement of the hearing

Juv R 29(B) repeats the format of other hearing provisions, by stating the specific advisements and findings required at the commencement of the hearing. This format follows the pattern of Crim R 10 and Minnesota Rule 5-1.

3. Entry of admission or denial

Juv R 29(C), which authorizes the court to call upon the parties to admit or deny the allegations of the complaint, is based on general practice. (See Crim R 10 and 11.) The major distinction between the juvenile rules and the criminal rules is that Juv R 29(C) permits the entry of either an admission or denial, whereas Crim R 11(A) permits the defendant to enter any one of four separate pleas: guilty, not guilty by reason of insanity, not guilty, or with the court's consent, no contest.

4. Initial procedure upon entry of an admission

Juv R 29(D), regulating the procedure upon entry of an admission, is based on Crim R 11. It differs from the criminal rule, however, in that it requires in all cases that the court determine that the party understands that his admission acts to waive the enumerated rights. Crim R 11 distinguishes among felony cases, serious misdemeanor cases, and petty misdemeanor cases. Only in felony cases is the court required to determine that the guilty plea results in a waiver of those rights.

5. Initial procedure upon entry of denial

The structure of Juv R 29(E), regulating initial procedure upon entry of a denial, is based on Minnesota Juvenile Rule 5-2. Juv R 29(E)(1) requires participation of the prosecuting attorney or other attorney-at-law in contested cases. 2151.40 requires the prosecuting attorney to render "all assistance and cooperation within his jurisdictional power" to the juvenile court and to "assist the court in presenting the evidence at any hearing or proceeding concerning an alleged or adjudicated delinquent, unruly, abused, neglected, or dependent child or juvenile traffic offender." Appearance of the prosecutor in contested cases has been made mandatory by this rule.

Juv R 29(E)(2) and (3) conform to present practice. Subdivision (E)(4), regulating the standard of proof complies with *In re Winship*, 397 US 358, 90 SCt 1068 , 25 LEd(2d) 368 (1970), which requires proof beyond a reasonable doubt in delinquency cases. The rule has expanded the requirements of *Winship* by providing for proof beyond a reasonable doubt in juvenile traffic offense and unruly proceedings as well. In dependency, neglect, and abuse proceedings, the standard of proof is clear and convincing evidence. The same provisions are contained in 2151.35.

6. Procedure upon determination of the issues

Juv R 29(F), regulating procedure upon determination of the issues, provides a variety of alternatives, in conformity with present and preferred practice.

Subdivision (F)(3) provides that written findings of fact and conclusions of law shall be prepared in accordance with Civ R 52 upon the request of a party. Civ R 52 provides that the court may in its discretion require the party to submit proposed findings of fact and conclusions of law which when made by the court shall form part of the record. This requirement may be satisfied by the filing of an opinion or memorandum of decision prior to entry of judgment. Since there is no jury in juvenile proceedings, findings of fact and conclusions of law are not mandatory, but are within the sound discretion of the court.

The rule expands on the holding of the U.S. Supreme Court *In re Gault,* 387 US 1, 87 SCt 1428, 18 LEd(2d) 527 (1967), in being more liberal and in meeting all requirements of fundamental fairness and due process of law. In *In re Gault* although the issues of right to a record and right to appeal were raised, the court did not decide these questions. Right to a record in juvenile proceedings in Ohio is governed by both statute (2151.35) and rule (Juv R 37(A)) as is the right to appeal (*See* 2505.17, Juv R 34(E), App R 7(C).)

The requirement of subdivision (E)(4) that the court determine all issues beyond a reasonable doubt in delinquency proceedings is mandated by the U.S. Supreme Court. *See In re Winship*, 397 US 358, 90 SCt 1068, 25 LEd(2d) 368 (1970).

CROSS REFERENCES

Schroeder-Katz, Ohio Criminal Law, Text 31.11(B)

Giannelli, Ohio Evidence Manual, Author's Comment § 615.01, 615.03

Kurtz & Giannelli, Ohio Juvenile Law, Text 1.04, 7.05(A)(C), 7.06(D), 7.07(C), Ch 11, 13.02, 13.03, 15.02(B)

Arraignment, Crim R 10
Pleas, rights upon plea, Crim R 11

OJur 3d: 4, Appellate Review § 105; 23, Courts and Judges § 428; 46, Family Law § 509 to 513, 522, 523, 584
Am Jur 2d: 47, Juvenile Courts and Delinquent and Dependent Children § 44 to 57
Applicability of rules of evidence in juvenile court proceeding. 43 ALR2d 1128
Procedural requirements under Federal Constitution in juvenile delinquency proceedings—federal cases. 25 LEd(2d) 950

LAW REVIEW ARTICLES

24 Clev St L Rev 602 (1975). Juvenile Delinquent and Unruly Proceedings in Ohio: Unconstitutional Adjudications, Patricia Simia Kleri.

24 Clev St L Rev 356 (1975). Juvenile Delinquency Proceedings in Ohio: Due Process and the Hearsay Dilemma, Sara E. Strattan. (See Ohio Rules of Evidence, Art VIII, Hearsay.)

NOTES ON DECISIONS AND OPINIONS

1. Cases interpreting Juvenile Rule 29
2. Cases interpreting law analogous to Juvenile Rule 29

1. Cases interpreting Juvenile Rule 29

17 OS(3d) 229, 17 OBR 469, 479 NE(2d) 257 (1985), In re Baby Girl Baxter. In proceedings where parental rights are subject to termination, it is reversible error not to provide separate adjudicatory and dispositional hearings as required by RC 2151.35, Juv R 29(F)(2)(a), and Juv R 34.

5 OS(3d) 27, 5 OBR 87, 448 NE(2d) 816 (1983), Reynolds v Ross County Childrens' Services Agency. A juvenile court's determination of parental unsuitability for custody of minor children must be supported by a preponderence of the evidence.

57 OS(2d) 97, 386 NE(2d) 1354 (1979), Linger v Weiss. The juvenile court has exclusive original jurisdiction, pursuant to 2151.23(A), concerning any child who is alleged in a proper complaint to be neglected, and the court does not lose jurisdiction by failing to adhere to the time limits set forth in Juv R 29(A) and 34(A).

36 App(3d) 241, 523 NE(2d) 540 (Lucas 1987), Elmer v Lucas County Children Services Bd. Although a finding of dependency may be made only upon the presentation of clear and convincing evidence, if the parties agree to waive such a hearing and stipulate to certain facts, then Juv R 29(D) must be fully complied with and the facts set forth in the record must sufficiently support a finding of dependency.

36 App(3d) 241, 523 NE(2d) 540 (Lucas 1987), Elmer v Lucas County Children Services Bd. A bifurcated hearing on a permanent custody complaint is required due to the evidentiary and waiver

requirements of Juv R 29 and due to the different standards of proof applicable to the adjudicatory and dispositional stages, and where the record does not reflect separate stages, a remand for further proceedings on the matter is proper.

14 App(3d) 201, 14 OBR 228, 470 NE(2d) 438 (Butler 1983), In re Vickers Children. A hearing on a complaint for permanent custody must be bifurcated according to Juv R 29 and 34 into separate adjudicatory and dispositional hearings, notwithstanding the contrary provisions of RC 2151.414, since Juv R 1(A) provides that all proceedings in a juvenile court are governed by the Rules of Juvenile Procedure.

13 App(3d) 37, 13 OBR 40, 468 NE(2d) 111 (Preble 1983), In re Sims. Where a complaint alleges that a child is neglected or dependent within the meaning of RC 2151.03(B) and 2151.04(A), (B), and (C), the child's mother is not prohibited by Juv R 29(D)(2) from taking part in the adjudicatory hearing by the fact that she entered a plea of "admitted" to the allegations in the complaint.

13 App(3d) 37, 13 OBR 40, 468 NE(2d) 111 (Preble 1983), In re Sims. Although Juv R 29 provides for juvenile proceedings to be conducted in an informal manner, hearsay evidence that is otherwise inadmissible will not be admitted at the adjudicatory stage of a neglect and dependency proceeding since the importance of parental interests requires an accurate finding of the facts underlying a complaint which alleges neglect or dependency and requires substantial compliance with the Ohio Rules of Evidence.

4 App(3d) 196, 4 OBR 300, 447 NE(2d) 129 (Franklin 1982), In re Green. Juv R 29(C) provides that a failure or refusal to admit the allegations of the complaint shall be deemed a denial.

4 App(3d) 196, 4 OBR 300, 447 NE(2d) 129 (Franklin 1982), In re Green. Where a juvenile entered a no contest plea to a delinquency complaint apparently on the basis that she would be able to appeal the juvenile court's ruling on the pretrial motion to suppress, as would be true in an adult criminal case, the court erroneously disposed of the case on such a plea.

4 App(3d) 196, 4 OBR 300, 447 NE(2d) 129 (Franklin 1982), In re Green. The no contest plea in a juvenile proceeding is not the unequivocal admission of the allegations of the complaint contemplated by Juv R 29(D), and it must be construed as a denial and the prosecuting attorney must prove the issues of delinquency beyond a reasonable doubt.

4 App(3d) 196, 4 OBR 300, 447 NE(2d) 129 (Franklin 1982), In re Green. There is no statement in Crim R 11 that a no contest plea results in a waiver of a defendant's right to challenge evidence against him as is specifically provided for by Juv R 29(D)(2) in relation to an admission of allegations of the complaint.

61 App(2d) 44, 398 NE(2d) 800 (1978), In re Gantt. There are no constitutional violations in an adjudicatory hearing held pursuant to Juv R 29 when the court uses evidence of guilt that was presented at the preliminary hearing where the accused was afforded cross-examination of witnesses.

54 App(2d) 195, 376 NE(2d) 970 (1977), In re Therklidsen. The ten day period of limitations in Juv R 29(A) is procedural only and such rule confers no substantive right upon an accused to have his case dismissed if he is not tried within the designated time.

45 App(2d) 299, 344 NE(2d) 144 (1973), Morrison v Morrison. A temporary order of a juvenile court changing custody under Juv R 13 or 29 is not a dispositional order under Juv R 34, and hence is not a final appealable order.

37 App(2d) 7, 306 NE(2d) 166 (1973), In re Bolden. The guarantee of the right to be represented by counsel set forth in Juv R 4(A) does not, as to a nonindigent party, require that trial be continued indefinitely until counsel can be obtained, but merely requires, if it does not appear that counsel could not be obtained through the exercise of reasonable diligence and a willingness to enter into reasonable contractual arrangements for counsel's services, that a reasonable opportunity be given to the party before trial to employ such counsel.

No. 3301 (11th Dist Ct App, Trumbull, 3-9-84), In re Becker. The finding of a juvenile court in an adjudicatory hearing is a final appealable order.

2. Cases interpreting law analogous to Juvenile Rule 29

US CONST AM 4

469 US 325, 105 SCt 733, 83 LEd(2d) 720 (1985), New Jersey v T.L.O. The exclusion on Fourth Amendment grounds of the contents of a fourteen-year-old schoolgirl's purse from delinquency proceedings is erroneous where a teacher discovered the pupil smoking in violation of school rules inasmuch as: (1) the teacher's report supported a suspicion on the part of the principal that the pupil had violated school rules; (2) the principal's suspicion gave him reason to suspect that the pupil had cigarettes in her purse, her denials notwithstanding, and a search of the purse for cigarettes was, therefore, proper; (3) the discovery in plain view of rolling papers on removal of the cigarette pack gave the principal reason to suspect the presence of marijuana; and (4) reasonable suspicion of the presence of marijuana justified a thorough search which turned up marijuana, letters implicating the pupil in dope dealing, and other evidence of drug-related activities.

2151.35 HEARING PROCEDURE; FINDINGS; RECORD

18 App(2d) 276, 248 NE(2d) 620 (1969), In re Baker; modified by 20 OS(2d) 142, 254 NE(2d) 363 (1969). Where a juvenile has received the following essentials of due process and fair treatment, (1) written notice of the specific charge or factual allegations given to the juvenile and his parents or guardian sufficiently in advance of the hearing to permit preparation; (2) notification to the juvenile and his parents of the juvenile's right to be represented by counsel retained by them, or, if they are unable to afford counsel, that counsel will be

appointed to represent the juvenile; (3) application of the constitutional privileges against self-incrimination; and (4), absent a valid confession, a determination of delinquency and an order of commitment based only on sworn testimony subjected to the opportunity for cross-examination in accordance with constitutional requirements, such juvenile has not been deprived of due process under either the Constitution of the United States or the Constitution of the State of Ohio.

18 App(2d) 276, 248 NE(2d) 620 (1969), In re Baker; modified by 20 OS(2d) 142, 254 NE(2d) 363 (1969). Proof of possession, use, or control by a juvenile of a hallucinogen is sufficient evidence upon which a juvenile court can find such juvenile a delinquent under Ch 2151.

Juv R 30
Relinquishment of jurisdiction for purposes of criminal prosecution

(A) Preliminary hearing.

In any proceeding where the court may transfer a child fifteen or more years of age for prosecution as an adult, the court shall hold a preliminary hearing to determine if there is probable cause to believe that the child committed the act alleged and that such act would be a felony if committed by an adult. Such hearing may be upon motion of the court, the prosecuting attorney or the child.

(B) Investigation.

If the court finds probable cause, it shall continue the proceedings for full investigation. Such investigation shall include a mental and physical examination of the child by the Ohio Youth Commission, a public or private agency, or by a person qualified to make such examination. When the investigation is completed, a hearing shall be held to determine whether to transfer jurisdiction. Written notice of the time, place and nature of the hearing shall be given to the parties at least three days prior to the hearing.

(C) Prerequisites to transfer.

The proceedings may be transferred if the court finds there are reasonable grounds to believe:

(1) The child is not amenable to care or rehabilitation in any facility designed for the care, supervision and rehabilitation of delinquent children; and

(2) The safety of the community may require that the child be placed under legal restraint for a period extending beyond the child's majority.

(D) Retention of jurisdiction.

If the court retains jurisdiction, it shall set the proceedings for hearing on the merits.

(E) Determination of amenability to rehabilitation.

In determining whether the child is amenable to the treatment or rehabilitative processes available to the juvenile court, the court shall consider:

(1) The child's age and his mental and physical health;

(2) The child's prior juvenile record;

(3) Efforts previously made to treat or rehabilitate the child;

(4) The child's family environment; and

(5) School record.

(F) Waiver of mental and physical examination.

The child may waive the mental and physical examination required under subdivision (B). Refusal to submit to a mental and physical examination or any part thereof by the child shall constitute waiver thereof.

(G) Order of transfer.

The order of transfer shall state the reasons therefor.

(H) Release of transferred child.

The juvenile court shall set terms and conditions for the release of the transferred child in accordance with Criminal Rule 46.

Adopted eff. 7-1-72; amended eff. 7-1-76

Editor's Comment

It is provided by statute (2151.26) that jurisdiction of cases of children fifteen years of age or over who are alleged to have committed a felony may be transferred to the appropriate court for criminal prosecution. Juv R 30 contains the procedural provisions governing the transfer.

Prior to making the transfer order, subdivision (A) requires the court to conduct a preliminary hearing to determine if there is probable cause to believe that the child committed the act alleged and that such act would be a felony if committed by an adult. This is in conformity with the U.S. Supreme Court decision in *Breed v Jones*, 421 US 519, 95 SCt 1779, 44 LEd(2d) 346 (1975) which held that the criminal prosecution of a juvenile in the adult court pursuant to an order of transfer made subsequent to an adjudicatory hearing in the juvenile court constitutes double jeopardy. Prior to *Breed* and the 1976 amendment to Juv R 30, the rule permitted the juvenile court to make the order of transfer at any time prior to the entry of an order of final disposition, even after adjudicatory hearing. *Breed* has been held to have retroactive application to pre-*Breed* cases in which an adjudicatory hearing was held prior to the order of transfer (*Sims v Engle*, 619 F(2d) 598 (6th Cir 1980), cert. denied, 101 SCt 1403, 67 LEd(2d) 372 (1981)).

If probable cause is found at the preliminary hearing, subdivision (B) requires the court to continue the proceedings for further hearing and for a full investigation, including mental and physical examinations of the child. Pursuant to subdivision (F), the child may waive the mental and physical examinations. A child's refusal to submit to the examinations constitutes a waiver. Written notice must be provided to the parties at least three days prior to the next hearing, at which time a decision will be made whether to transfer jurisdiction.

In order to transfer jurisdiction, subdivision (C) requires the court to find reasonable grounds to believe that the child is not amenable to care or rehabilitation in any facility designed for the care, supervision, and rehabilitation of delinquent children and that the safety of the community may require the minor's confinement beyond his majority. This requirement is also mandated by 2151.26(A)(3).

Subdivision (E) lists the specific factors to be considered in determining whether the child is to be deemed amenable to rehabilitation, as required by 2151.26(A)(3). This is in conformity with the U.S. Supreme Court mandate. *See Kent v U.S.*, 383 US 451, 86 SCt 1045, 16 LEd(2d) 84 (1966). In this case, the court held that the question of transfer of jurisdiction was a critical stage of the proceedings, and that fundamental fairness and due process required representation by counsel (*See* Juv R 3) and opportunity to inspect all records considered by the court (*See* Juv R 32), and an examination by a psychiatrist or psychologist of his own choosing. The court also set down guidelines for the court to consider as a basis for transfer.

If the court decides to transfer jurisdiction, subdivision (G) requires the court to recite the basis for transfer. If the court decides to retain jurisdiction, subdivision (D) requires the court to conduct a full hearing on the merits.

CROSS REFERENCES

Kurtz & Giannelli, Ohio Juvenile Law, Text 7.08(B), Ch 9, 13.07(C), 13.10

OJur 3d: 23, Courts and Judges § 428; 26, Criminal Law § 668; 46, Family Law § 409 to 412

Am Jur 2d: 47, Juvenile Courts and Delinquent and Dependent Children § 19, 20

LAW REVIEW ARTICLES

6 U Tol L Rev 1 (1974). The Effect of the Double Jeopardy Clause on Juvenile Proceedings, James G. Carr.

NOTES ON DECISIONS AND OPINIONS

20 OS(3d) 34, 20 OBR 282, 485 NE(2d) 711 (1985), State v Douglas. Where the record before a juvenile court contains sufficient credible evidence pertaining to each factor listed in Juv R 30(E), the court's determination to transfer the case for trial of the juvenile as an adult will be upheld, absent an abuse of discretion, even without any written statement of the court on those factors.

69 OS(2d) 120, 431 NE(2d) 326 (1982), State v Adams. Once a juvenile is bound over in any county in Ohio pursuant to 2151.26 and Juv R 30, that juvenile is bound over for all felonies committed in other counties of this state, as well as for future felonies he may commit.

69 OS(2d) 120, 431 NE(2d) 326 (1982), State v Adams. When a minor is transferred from the juvenile court to the court of common pleas on a charge which would constitute a felony if committed by an adult, the grand jury is empowered to return any indictment under the facts submitted to it and is not confined to returning indictments only on charges originally filed in the juvenile court.

39 OS(2d) 84, 314 NE(2d) 158 (1974), In re Becker. An order by a juvenile court pursuant to 2151.26 transferring a child to the court of common pleas for criminal prosecution is not a final appealable order.

29 App(3d) 194, 29 OBR 237, 504 NE(2d) 1121 (Cuyahoga 1985), State v Smith. A minor does not have the right to be tried as an adult and there is no provision for bind-over upon motion of a minor.

5 App(3d) 168, 5 OBR 351, 450 NE(2d) 700 (Wood 1982), State v Oviedo. When a juvenile court determines whether a juvenile is amenable to rehabilitation, all five factors of Juv R 30(E) must be considered, but the court is not required to resolve all five factors against the juvenile in order to justify his transfer for prosecution as an adult.

5 App(3d) 168, 5 OBR 351, 450 NE(2d) 700 (Wood 1982), State v Oviedo. Pursuant to Juv R 30(G), an order of transfer is sufficient if it demonstrates that the statutory requirement of "full investigation" has been met and that the issue has received the full attention of the juvenile court.

61 App(2d) 44, 398 NE(2d) 800 (1978), In re Gantt. When, in an adjudicatory hearing held pursuant to Juv R 29, the only evidence of guilt utilized by the court is testimony presented at the preliminary hearing, where the accused exercised adequate rights of cross-examination, he is denied no constitutional right.

55 App(2d) 285, 380 NE(2d) 1350 (1977), State v Sims. Informal proceedings conducted in a juvenile court in 1962 for the purpose of determining whether or not to bind over a juvenile defendant to be tried as an adult do not constitute an "adjudicatory hearing" as described in Breed v Jones, 421 US 519, 95 SCt 1779, 44 LEd(2d) 346 (1975). (Ed. note: But see Sims v Engle, 619 F(2d) 598 (6th Cir 1980).)

44 App(2d) 387, 339 NE(2d) 668 (1975), State v Young. An accused in a court of common pleas who has been bound over from a juvenile court is entitled to have his "jail time," service while under the jurisdiction of the latter, deducted from his sentence.

No. 52757 (8th Dist Ct App, Cuyahoga, 10-8-87), State v Brown. Statutes are presumed

Ohio Rules of Procedure

constitutional and the burden is on a defendant to demonstrate the contrary; therefore, where a defendant alleges, without analysis, that RC 2151.26 and Juv R 30(E) are unconstitutionally void for vagueness, because they fail to provide a workable standard to insure equal treatment among juvenile defendants, that burden is not met.

No. 12967 (9th Dist Ct App, Summit, 9-23-87), State v Dickens. The decision to relinquish juvenile court jurisdiction rests with the juvenile court; expert testimony as to the amenability of a defendant to rehabilitation in juvenile facilities is not binding on the court.

No. F-82-17 (6th Dist Ct App, Fulton, 6-10-83), State v Newton. Juvenile court's failure to state with reasonable specificity the factual basis underlying its order to transfer a juvenile to common pleas court for prosecution as an adult renders the common pleas court without jurisdiction.

No. 81-CA-22 (4th Dist Ct App, Pickaway, 7-28-82), State v Payne. Where a case is pending against a juvenile in a foreign county, such case must be transferred to the juvenile's home county, if, at any time prior to dispositional order, proceedings against the juvenile are pending in his home county. Furthermore, such mandatory transfer may not be avoided by the foreign county through the use of a bindover proceeding.

No. 81-C-60 (7th Dist Ct App, Columbiana, 6-22-82), State v Barnum. A judge is only required to find reasonable grounds to believe the accused would be amenable to rehabilitation, not that the accused cannot be rehabilitated.

1 OBR 377 (CP, Cuyahoga 1982), In the Matter of Terry H. It would be apex juris and unreasonable to hold that every judge who presides over a preliminary hearing in a criminal or juvenile matter must thereafter disqualify himself because his impartiality might "reasonably" be questioned.

644 F(2d) 573 (6th Cir 1981), Johnson v Perini. Where the order of a juvenile court contained a finding only that there was probable cause to believe that the juvenile had committed an act which would be a felony if committed by an adult, the hearing in juvenile court was not an adjudicatory hearing and the subsequent trial of defendant as an adult in the court of common pleas did not subject him to double jeopardy.

640 F(2d) 839 (6th Cir 1981), Keener v Taylor. A juvenile court proceeding to determine whether petitioner should be treated as a juvenile or transferred to the court of common pleas to be tried as an adult on a murder charge was not an adjudicatory proceeding to which double jeopardy attached and hence did not preclude a subsequent trial of petitioner as an adult, notwithstanding that the state presented evidence of probable cause in proceeding to believe that petitioner had committed the alleged offense, where probable cause evidence was heard solely for juvenile court to decide which judicial treatment of petitioner would serve his interests and those of the community, not for juvenile court to decide petitioner's guilt.

619 F(2d) 598 (6th Cir 1980), Sims v Engle. Where Ohio statute required full investigation of facts underlying charge of delinquency and finding of delinquency prior to bindover of juvenile for trial as an adult, once juvenile court, possessing jurisdiction and power to enter final orders levying a wide range of possible sanctions, began a hearing, not limited in scope by statute to preliminary or probable cause hearing, jeopardy attached, with the result that subsequent criminal prosecution for the same acts contravened his constitutional protection against double jeopardy.

Juv R 31
[Reserved]

Juv R 32
Social history; physical examination; mental examination; custody investigation

(A) Social history and physical or mental examination: availability before adjudication.

The court may order and utilize a social history or physical or mental examination at any time after the filing of a complaint:

(1) upon the request of the party concerning whom the history or examination is to be made;

(2) where transfer of a child for adult prosecution is an issue in the proceeding;

(3) where a material allegation of a neglect, dependency, or abused child complaint relates to matters that such a history or examination may clarify;

(4) where a party's legal responsibility for his acts or his competence to participate in the proceedings is an issue;

(5) where a physical or mental examination is required to determine the need for emergency medical care under Rule 13; or

(6) where authorized under Rule 7(I).

(B) Limitations on preparation and use.

Until there has been an admission or adjudication that the child who is the subject of the proceedings is a juvenile traffic offender, delinquent, unruly, neglected, dependent, or abused, no social history, physical examination or mental examination shall be ordered except as authorized under subdivision (A) and any social history, physical examination or mental examination ordered pursuant to subdivision (A) shall be utilized only for the limited purposes therein specified. The person preparing a social history or making a physical or mental examination shall not testify about the history or examination or information received in its preparation in any juvenile traffic offender, delinquency, or unruly child adjudicatory hearing, except as may be required in a hearing to determine whether a child should be transferred to an adult court for criminal prosecution.

(C) Availability of social history or investigation report.

A reasonable time before the dispositional hearing, or any other hearing at which a social history or physical or mental examination is to be utilized, counsel shall be permitted to inspect any social history or report of a mental or physical examination. The court may, for good cause shown, deny such inspection or limit its scope to specified portions of the history or report. The court may order that the contents of the history or report, in whole or part, not be disclosed to specified persons. If inspection or disclosure is denied or limited, the court shall state its reasons for such denial or limitation to counsel.

(D) Investigation: custody; habeas corpus.

On the filing of a complaint for custody or for a writ of habeas corpus to determine the custody of a child, or on the filing of a motion for change of custody, the court may cause an investigation to be made as to the character, health, family relations, past conduct, present living conditions, earning ability and financial worth of the parties to the action. The report of such investigation shall be confidential, but shall be made available to the parties or their counsel upon written request not less than three days before hearing. The court may tax as costs all or any part of the expenses of each investigation.

Adopted eff. 7-1-72; amended eff. 7-1-73, 7-1-76

Editor's Comment

1. Social history and physical or mental examination availability before adjudication
2. Limitations on preparation and use
3. Availability of social history or investigation report
4. Investigation: custody; habeas corpus

1. Social history and physical or mental examination availability before adjudication

Juv R 32(A) sets forth a list of situations in which the court may order a social history or physical or mental examination prior to an adjudication on the allegations of the complaint. These are all situations in which the history or examination is important to the proper resolution of issues that may arise prior to the adjudication.

2. Limitations on preparation and use

Juv R 32(B) specifies that the cases listed in subdivision (A) are the only cases in which a history or examination may be ordered prior to an adjudication and that even in those cases the history or report may be used prior to adjudication only for the purpose specified in subdivision (A).

3. Availability of social history or investigation report

Juv R 32(C) provides a general principle that the social history and reports on a physical or mental examination are to be available to counsel prior to their use. It also provides for limitations on that availability for good cause shown. The rule is drawn from 2151.352.

4. Investigation: custody; habeas corpus

Juv R 32(D) provides for an investigation very similar to those provided for in subdivisions (A) through (C), but does so in language taken from Civ R 75(D), so that there will be no conflict in procedure in custody disputes depending on the court in which they are placed. A few minor modifications in the language of Civ R 75(D) have been made. These changes are:

(1) the addition of "health" and "present living conditions" to the items that may be included in the report;

(2) the statement that the report shall be confidential;

(3) the shortening of the time when a written request to see the report must be submitted from seven days to three days.

Jurisdiction in custody cases may be transferred from the domestic relations court to the juvenile court pursuant to 3109.04 where both parents are declared unfit or unsuited without the consent of the juvenile court and pursuant to 3109.06 on motion of either party or the court with the consent of the juvenile court. Uniformity of procedure is desirable.

The juvenile court has exclusive original jurisdiction to determine the custody of a child not a ward of another court of this state pursuant to 2151.23(A)(2) and to hear and determine any application for a writ of habeas corpus involving the custody of a child pursuant to 2151.23(A)(3).

CROSS REFERENCES

Kurtz & Giannelli, Ohio Juvenile Law, Text 7.08(B), 9.03, 11.04, 11.09, 11.11(B), 15.04

Divorce, annulment and alimony actions, Civ R 75

Detention, and shelter care, Juv R 7

Temporary disposition, temporary orders, emergency medical and surgical treatment, Juv R 13

Relinquishment of jurisdiction for purposes of criminal prosecution, Juv R 30

OJur 3d: 23, Courts and Judges § 428; 46, Family Law § 493 to 495, 546

LAW REVIEW ARTICLES

24 Clev St L Rev 356 (1975). Juvenile Delinquency Proceedings in Ohio: Due Process and the Hearsay Dilemma, Sara E. Strattan.

NOTES ON DECISIONS AND OPINIONS

24 App(3d) 180, 24 OBR 270, 493 NE(2d) 1011 (Trumbull 1985), Davis v Trumbull County Children Services Bd. In a hearing to determine whether a child is dependent, hearsay evidence contained in a social history report may not be used as evidence of the truth of the complaint, although, pursuant to Juv R 32(A)(3), the report may be used to clarify allegations of the complaint.

18 App(3d) 43, 18 OBR 155, 480 NE(2d) 492 (Montgomery 1984), In re Green. Where a court orders a psychological evaluation on the request of an indigent party, pursuant to Juv R 32(A)(1), the court may admit the evaluation into evidence over the objection of the party.

Juv R 33
[Reserved]

Juv R 34
Dispositional hearing

(A) Scheduling the hearing.
The dispositional hearing may be held immediately following the adjudicatory hearing or at a later time fixed by the court. Where the dispositional hearing is to be held immediately following the adjudicatory hearing, the court, upon the request of a party shall continue the hearing for a reasonable time to enable the party to obtain or consult counsel.

(B) Hearing procedure.
The hearing shall be conducted in the following manner:

(1) The judge who presided at the adjudicatory hearing shall, if possible, preside;

(2) The court may admit any evidence that is material and relevant, including hearsay, opinion and documentary evidence; and

(3) Medical examiners and each investigator who prepared a social history shall not be cross-examined, except upon consent of all parties, for good cause shown, or as the court in its discretion may direct. Any party may offer evidence supplementing, explaining, or disputing any information contained in the social history or other reports which may be used by the court in determining disposition.

(C) Judgment.
After the conclusion of the hearing, the court shall enter an appropriate judgment within seven days. A copy of the judgment shall be given to any party requesting such copy. In all cases where a child is placed on probation, the child shall receive a written statement of the conditions of probation. If the judgment is conditional, the order shall state the conditions. If the child is not returned to his own home, the court shall determine which school district shall bear the cost of his education and may fix an amount of support to be paid by the responsible parent, or to be paid from public funds.

(D) Restraining orders.
In any proceeding where a child is made a ward of the court, the court may grant a restraining order controlling the conduct of any party if the court finds that such order is necessary to control any conduct or relationship which may be detrimental or harmful to the child and tend to defeat the execution of a dispositional order.

(E) Advisement of rights after hearing.
At the conclusion of the hearing, the court shall advise the child of his right to record expungement and, where any part of the proceeding was contested, advise the parties of their right to appeal.

Adopted eff. 7-1-72

Editor's Comment

1. Dispositional hearing
2. Judgment
3. Restraining orders
4. Advisement of rights after hearing

1. Dispositional hearing

This rule follows the same structure as the rules regulating the detention and adjudicatory hearing, and establishes procedure which is generally followed. Until the adoption of this rule there was no uniform procedure to be followed by all courts. The rule is in conformity with Juv R 1(B)(2) to secure uniformity in procedure.

2. Judgment

Juv R 34(C) as to the requirement that a child placed on probation receive a written statement of the conditions of probation is drawn from 2151.14.

3. Restraining orders

Juv R 34(D) restraining orders follows the provision of 2151.359 which it supersedes.

4. Advisement of rights after hearing

Juv R 34(E) requires that a child adjudged delinquent or unruly shall be advised of the right to have his record expunged in accordance with 2151.358. Application to expunge a record shall not be made any sooner than two years after the termination of any order made by the court, or two years after his unconditional discharge from the Ohio Youth Commission or other institution or facility to which he may have been committed. (*See* 2151.358.)

CROSS REFERENCES

Giannelli, Ohio Evidence Manual, Author's Comment § 101.10, 802.06

Kurtz & Giannelli, Ohio Juvenile Law, Text 7.07(C), 11.01, Ch 13, 15.01(C), 15.02(B)

OJur 3d: 4, Appellate Review § 105; 23, Courts and Judges § 428; 46, Family Law § 524 to 526, 534, 584

Am Jur 2d: 47, Juvenile Courts and Delinquent and Dependent Children § 44 to 62

LAW REVIEW ARTICLES

24 Clev St L Rev 356 (1975). Juvenile Delinquency Proceedings in Ohio: Due Process and the Hearsay Dilemma, Sara E. Strattan.

14 Jour of Family Law 535 (1976). Access to "Confidential" Welfare Records in the Course of Child Protection Proceedings, Stephen Levine.

NOTES ON DECISIONS AND OPINIONS

1. Cases interpreting Juvenile Rule 34
2. Cases interpreting law analogous to Juvenile Rule 34

1. Cases interpreting Juvenile Rule 34

17 OS(3d) 229, 17 OBR 469, 479 NE(2d) 257 (1985), In re Baby Girl Baxter. In proceedings where parental rights are subject to termination, it is reversible error not to provide separate adjudicatory and dispositional hearings as required by RC 2151.35, Juv R 29(F)(2)(a), and Juv R 34.

57 OS(2d) 97, 386 NE(2d) 1354 (1979), Linger v Weiss. The juvenile court has exclusive original jurisdiction, pursuant to 2151.23(A), concerning any child who is alleged in a proper complaint to be neglected, and the court does not lose jurisdiction by failing to adhere to the time limits set forth in Juv R 29(A) and 34(A).

30 App(3d) 228, 30 OBR 386, 507 NE(2d) 384 (Fayette 1986), Christman v Washington Court House School Dist. When a child is placed in the permanent custody of the youth services department, the court shall determine the school district responsible for the costs of educating the child as provided by RC 2151.357; Juv R 34(C) is not inconsistent with RC 2151.357, and gives the court no discretion to determine such school district in any other manner.

16 App(3d) 214, 16 OBR 229, 475 NE(2d) 160 (Madison 1984), In re Patterson. A further dispositional order which continues an original order of temporary custody constitutes a final appealable order within the meaning of RC 2505.02.

14 App(3d) 201, 14 OBR 228, 470 NE(2d) 438 (Butler 1983), In re Vickers Children. A hearing on a complaint for permanent custody must be bifurcated according to Juv R 29 and 34 into separate adjudicatory and dispositional hearings, notwithstanding the contrary provisions of RC 2151.414, since Juv R 1(A) provides that all proceedings in a juvenile court are governed by the Rules of Juvenile Procedure.

45 App(2d) 299, 344 NE(2d) 144 (1973), Morrison v Morrison. A temporary order of a juvenile court changing custody under Juv R 13 or 29 is not a dispositional order under Juv R 34, and hence is not a final appealable order.

45 App(2d) 187, 341 NE(2d) 638 (1975), In re Haas. Where no part of a proceeding conducted pursuant to Juv R 34(E) is contested, a juvenile court is not required to advise an accused of his right to appeal.

37 App(2d) 7, 306 NE(2d) 166 (1973), In re Bolden. Error cannot be predicated on the juvenile court's holding a dispositional hearing immediately following an adjudicatory hearing and its failure to continue the dispositional hearing for a reasonable time to enable the party to obtain or consult counsel, as prescribed by Juv R 34(A), unless it affirmatively appears in the record that the affected nonindigent party has requested such continuance.

37 App(2d) 7, 306 NE(2d) 166 (1973), In re Bolden. The guarantee of the right to be represented by counsel set forth in Juv R 4(A) does not, as to a nonindigent party, require that trial be continued indefinitely until counsel can be obtained, but merely requires, if it does not appear that counsel could not be obtained through the exercise of reasonable diligence and a willingness to enter into reasonable contractual arrangements for counsel's services, that a reasonable opportunity be given to the party before trial to employ such counsel.

OAG 88-023. A court that commits a child to the custody of the youth services department is required to determine which school district shall bear the cost of educating the child.

2. Cases interpreting law analogous to Juvenile Rule 34

2151.02 DELINQUENT CHILD DEFINED

17 App(2d) 183, 245 NE(2d) 358 (1969), State v Fisher. Division (E) of 2151.35 (RC 2151.355(E)) which authorizes the juvenile court to commit a male child over sixteen years of age, who has committed an act which if committed by an adult would

be a felony, to the Ohio state reformatory (the same institution to which adults convicted of a felony are committed), without providing to such juvenile equal rights of due process of law, is an unconstitutional denial of rights secured by United States Constitution, Amendment XIV.

2151.10 APPROPRIATION FOR EXPENSES OF THE COURT AND MAINTENANCE OF CHILDREN

87 App 36, 89 NE(2d) 605 (1949), City of Cleveland v Gorman. Authorization of the juvenile court at time of commitment is a condition precedent to the accrual of liability against the county for expenses resulting from commitment of children to any institution.

1962 OAG 3489. A juvenile court may, upon finding that a child is neglected, dependent, or delinquent, commit the child to any person or institution meeting the requirements of 5103.02 and 5103.03, even though a county child welfare board exists and could provide care and support for the child; and the board of county commissioners has a duty to appropriate each year such sum as will provide the court with necessary funds for the care, maintenance, education, and support of neglected, dependent, and delinquent children.

2151.35 HEARING PROCEDURE; FINDINGS; RECORD

19 App(2d) 33, 249 NE(2d) 532 (1969), In re Messner. An Ohio juvenile court, in a dependency proceeding pursuant to 2151.27 et seq., has no jurisdiction to interfere with a mother's legal custody of her children, in the absence of proof and a finding of unfitness of such parent, merely for the purpose of releasing such children to the officers of the court of a foreign state, and the court need not give full faith and credit to a Michigan decree where that decree was obtained by the husband in an ex parte custody determination, subsequent to a divorce decree, in which the Michigan court had no personal jurisdiction over the nonresident wife.

1962 OAG 3461. Where a juvenile court commits a child to the boys' industrial school, the jurisdiction of the court over the child ceases; and the fact that the court may have attempted to put a condition upon the release of the child, such as making restitution for damages, does not affect the exclusive power of the school and the department of mental hygiene and correction to release the child for satisfactory behavior and progress in training; and the department may so release the child regardless of whether or not such condition has been fulfilled.

1962 OAG 2938. Where a juvenile court commits a child to a specialized school in another state, the court must itself pay expenses occasioned by the commitment and authorized by the court at the time of commitment, which expenses are paid out of funds appropriated to the court by the board of county commissioners under 2151.10; and the court may order the parents, guardian, or person charged with the child's support to reimburse the court for such payments.

1962 OAG 2871. A person who is committed to the Ohio state reformatory as a juvenile delinquent is not serving a "sentence" within the meaning of the aggregate sentence provision of 2965.35.

1961 OAG 2704. A male juvenile delinquent over sixteen years of age who has been committed to the Ohio state reformatory until he arrives at the age of twenty-one years, unless sooner released for satisfactory behavior and progress in training, may be released by the superintendent upon the granting of a parole by the pardon and parole commission, and may be granted a certificate of final release by the commission if he has faithfully performed all of the conditions and obligations of his parole and has obeyed all the rules and regulations adopted by the commission; but such final release may not be issued before one year after the release from the reformatory unless the said prisoner has attained the age of twenty-one years.

1950 OAG 2529. The juvenile court, under this section, may commit children directly to a district children's home.

1941 OAG 3353. Juvenile court is empowered to commit a child to a foster home and to make such terms respecting such commitment as may be proper and suitable under the circumstances.

Juv R 35
Proceedings after judgment

(A) Continuing jurisdiction; invoked by motion.

The continuing jurisdiction of the court shall be invoked by motion filed in the original proceeding, notice of which shall be served in the manner provided for the service of process.

(B) Revocation of probation.

The court shall not revoke probation except after a hearing at which the child shall be present and apprised of the grounds on which such action is proposed. The parties shall have the right to counsel and the right to appointed counsel where entitled thereto under Rule 4(A). Probation shall not be revoked except upon a finding that the child has violated a condition of probation of which he had, pursuant to Rule 34(C), been notified.

(C) Detention.

During the pendency of proceedings under this rule, a child may be placed in detention in accordance with the provisions of Rule 7.

Adopted eff. 7-1-72

Editor's Comment

1. Continuing jurisdiction; invoked by motion
2. Revocation of probation
3. Detention

1. Continuing jurisdiction; invoked by motion

The rule states that the continuing jurisdiction of the court shall be invoked by motion filed in the original proceeding with notice of the filing being served as provided in Juv R 16. The rule is generally applicable to cases involving custody and allows the continuing jurisdiction of the court to be invoked without reference to a time limitation.

Subdivision (A) is based on Civ R 75(J), and adopts a procedure similar to that in domestic relations cases.

2. Revocation of probation

Subdivision (B) is based on Crim R 32.3, regulating probation revocation procedures. Case law clearly establishes the right of a person to proper notice, a hearing, representation by counsel and an opportunity to be heard on the issue of probation revocation.

3. Detention

Subdivision (C) restates the requirement that placement of a child in detention or shelter care during the pendency of proceedings under this rule is governed by Juv R 7.

CROSS REFERENCES

Kurtz & Giannelli, Ohio Juvenile Law, Text 13.08(B), 15.01(A)(C)

Divorce, annulment and alimony actions, Civ R 75

Sentence, Crim R 32

OJur 3d: 23, Courts and Judges § 428; 46, Family Law § 536, 539, 540; 72, Notice and Notices § 1 to 5, 31 to 36
Am Jur 2d: 47, Juvenile Courts and Delinquent Children § 60 to 62
Probation revocation: insanity as defense. 56 ALR4th 1178

Juv R 36

[Reserved]

Juv R 37

Recording of proceedings

(A) Recording of hearings.

In all juvenile court hearings, upon request of a party, or upon the court's own motion, a complete record of all testimony, or other oral proceedings shall be taken in shorthand, stenotype or by any other adequate mechanical or electronic recording device.

(B) Restrictions on use of recording or transcript.

No public use shall be made by any person, including a party, of any juvenile court record, including the recording or a transcript thereof of any juvenile court hearing, except in the course of an appeal or as authorized by order of the court.

Adopted eff. 7-1-72

Editor's Comment

Juv R 37(A) follows the provision of 2151.35 and the Ohio Supreme Court Rules of Superintendence, No. 10, and provides that a complete transcript of juvenile court proceedings shall be taken when requested by a party, or upon the court's own motion.

Juv R 37(B) further provides that no public use shall be made of a transcript except upon appeal or upon authorization of the court.

The preparation of a transcript shall be at public expense if the party is indigent in accordance with Juv R 29(B)(5).

CROSS REFERENCES

Kurtz & Giannelli, Ohio Juvenile Law, Text 9.03(J), 11.14, 15.02(F), 15.04(A)

OJur 3d: 23, Courts and Judges § 428; 46, Family Law § 501, 506, 507
Am Jur 2d: 47, Juvenile Courts and Delinquent and Dependent Children § 56

NOTES ON DECISIONS AND OPINIONS

1. Cases interpreting Juvenile Rule 37
2. Cases interpreting law analogous to Juvenile Rule 37

1. Cases interpreting Juvenile Rule 37

OAG 84-077. Under RC 1347.08, a juvenile court must permit a juvenile or a duly authorized attorney who represents the juvenile to inspect court records pertaining to the juvenile unless the records are exempted under RC 1347.04(A)(1)(e) or 1347.08(C) or (E)(2). Under Juv R 37(B), the records may not, however, be put to any public use except in the course of an appeal or as authorized by order of the court.

2. Cases interpreting law analogous to Juvenile Rule 37

2151.07 CREATION AND POWERS OF JUVENILE COURT
OAG 68-123. The juvenile court is now a part of a division of the court of common pleas and subject to the requirement that it provide a court reporter for its proceedings if so requested.

2151.16 REFEREES; POWERS AND DUTIES
22 App(2d) 125, 259 NE(2d) 128 (1969), In re Gutman. A juvenile court is not required to provide, at state expense, a bill of exceptions in a cus-

tody proceeding, especially absent a demand for the taking of testimony by a court reporter.

2151.26 RELINQUISHMENT OF JURISDICTION FOR PURPOSE OF CRIMINAL PROSECUTION

23 App(2d) 215, 262 NE(2d) 427 (1970), State v Ross. An indigent juvenile offender is entitled to a record in a hearing conducted for the purpose of determining whether the juvenile court may waive jurisdiction and bind the offender over to the court of common pleas for criminal prosecution.

Juv R 38
[Reserved]

Juv R 39
[Reserved]

Juv R 40
Referees: appointment; powers; duties

(A) Appointment.

The juvenile judge may appoint one or more referees. The appointment of a referee may empower him to act in a single proceeding or in a specified class of proceedings or portions thereof. The juvenile judge shall not appoint as referee any person who has contemporaneous responsibility for working with, or supervising the behavior of, children who are subject to dispositional orders of the appointing court or any other juvenile court.

(B) Powers.

An order of reference to a referee may specify or limit his powers and may direct him to report only upon particular issues or to do or perform particular acts or to receive and report evidence only and may fix the time and place for beginning and closing the hearings and for the filing of his report. Subject to the specifications and limitations stated in the order, the referee has and shall exercise the power of the court to regulate all proceedings in every hearing before him and to do all acts and take all measures necessary or proper for the efficient performance of his duties under the order. He may summon and compel the attendance of witnesses and may require the production before him of

evidence upon all matters embraced in the reference, including the production of all books, papers, vouchers, documents and writings applicable thereto. He may rule upon the admissibility of evidence unless otherwise directed by the order of reference and has the authority to put witnesses on oath and may himself examine them and may call parties to the action and examine them upon oath. The referee shall make a report of the proceeding, including evidence offered and excluded, in the same manner and subject to the same limitations as provided in Rule 37 for hearings by the court.

(C) Proceedings.

(1) Meetings. When a special reference is made in a specific case, the clerk shall forthwith furnish the referee with a copy of the order of reference. Upon receipt thereof unless the order of reference otherwise provides, the referee shall forthwith set a time and place for the first meeting of the parties or their attorneys, or for the hearing of the case, to be held promptly after the date of the order of reference and shall notify the parties or their attorneys or both. When a general reference has been made for a specified class of proceedings or portions thereof, the clerk or the referee shall forthwith upon receiving the case set a time and place for hearing of the case, to be held promptly after receiving the case, and shall notify the parties or their attorneys or both.

Any party, on notice to the other parties and to the referee, may apply to the court for an order requiring the referee to expedite the matter and to make his report. If a party fails to appear at the time and place appointed, the referee may proceed ex parte, or, in his discretion, may take appropriate steps to have the absent party brought before him forthwith or at a future day, or may adjourn the proceedings to a future day, giving notice to the absent party of the adjournment.

(2) Witnesses. The parties may procure the attendance of witnesses before the referee by the issuance and service of subpoenas as provided in Juv R 17. If without adequate excuse a witness fails to appear or to give evidence, he may be punished as for a contempt and be subject to the conse-

quences, penalties, and remedies provided in Rule 17.

(D) Report.

(1) Contents and filing. The referee shall prepare a report upon the matters submitted by the order of reference or otherwise. The referee shall file the report with the judge and forthwith provide copies to the parties. The report shall set forth the findings of the referee upon the case submitted together with a recommendation as to the judgment or order to be made in the case in question, but the referee shall file with the report a transcript of the proceedings and of the evidence only if the court so directs.

(2) Objections to report. A party may, within fourteen days of the filing of the report, serve and file written objections to the referee's report. Such objections shall be considered a motion. Objections shall be specific and state with particularity the grounds therefor. Upon consideration of the objections the court may: adopt, reject or modify the report; hear additional evidence; return the report to the referee with instructions; or hear the matter itself.

(3) Stipulation as to findings. The effect of a referee's report is the same whether or not the parties have consented to the reference. When the parties stipulate in writing that a referee's findings of fact shall be final, only questions of law arising upon the report shall thereafter be considered.

(4) Draft report. Before filing the report a referee may submit a draft thereof to counsel for all parties for the purpose of receiving their suggestions. The referee shall sign any findings or decision and file it together with any exceptions.

(5) When effective. The report of a referee shall be effective and binding only when approved and entered as a matter of record by the court. The referee's findings of fact must be sufficient for the court to make an independent analysis of the issues and to apply appropriate rules of law in reaching a judgment order. The court may adopt the referee's recommendations about appropriate conclusions of law and the appropriate resolution of any issues. However, the court shall determine whether there is any error of law or other defect on the face of the referee's report even if no party objects to such an error or defect. The court shall enter its own judgment on the issues submitted for action and report by the referee.

(6) Factual findings. A party may not assign as error the court's adoption of a referee's finding of fact unless an objection to that finding is contained in that party's written objections to the referee's report. The court may adopt any finding of fact in the referee's report without further consideration unless the party who objects to that finding supports that objection with a copy of all relevant portions of the transcript from the referee's hearing or an affidavit about evidence submitted to the referee if no transcript is available. In deciding whether to adopt a referee's finding of fact, the court may disregard any evidence which was not submitted to the referee unless the complaining party demonstrates that with reasonable diligence he or she could not have discovered and produced that evidence for the referee's consideration.

(7) Permanent and interim orders. The court may enter judgment on the basis of findings of fact contained in the referee's report without waiting for timely objections by the parties, but the filing of timely written objections to the referee's report shall operate as an automatic stay of execution of that judgment until the court disposes of those objections and thereby vacates, modifies or adheres to the judgment previously entered. The court may make an interim order on the basis of findings of facts contained in the referee's report without waiting for or ruling on timely objections by the parties where immediate relief is justified and such an interim order shall not be subject to the automatic stay caused by the filing of timely objections to the report, but no interim order shall extend more than twenty-eight (28) days, unless within that time, for good cause shown, the court extends it for one like period.

Adopted eff. 7-1-72; amended eff. 7-1-75, 7-1-85

Editor's Comment

1. Referees: appointment; powers; duties
2. Appointment
3. Powers
4. Proceedings
5. Report

1. Referees: appointment; powers; duties

Juv R 40 governs the appointment, powers and duties of juvenile court referees. It is modeled very closely on Civ R 53, with modifications only to reflect the different use of referees in juvenile court. The rule is in accordance with present law and practice in Ohio.

2. Appointment

Juv R 40(A) follows the pattern of Civ R 53(A), but contains several significant differences.

While it is highly desirable for referees to be attorneys at law, in some small counties this is impossible and referees who are not attorneys at law can serve a very useful function under the supervision of the juvenile judge.

Juv R 40(A) permits the court to appoint a referee for "a specified class of proceedings or portions thereof", a possibility that does not exist in Civ R 53. This is in fact the most common use of referees in juvenile court.

The last sentence in the subdivision was taken from Minnesota Rule 1-6. It requires that the functions of referees and probation officers or other court workers cannot be mingled in one person.

Civ R 53(B) on compensation has been omitted in Juv R 40, because the referee acts in a public capacity and it would be inappropriate to tax the cost of his service to the parties.

A provision of 2151.16 that states a preference for female referees in cases involving female children has been eliminated in this rule.

3. Powers

Juv R 40(B) is taken directly from Civ R 53(C), except that the provision on making a record of the proceedings is changed to fit the special role of juvenile court referees and the requirements of Juv R 37.

4. Proceedings

Juv R 40(C) is patterned on Civ R 53(D), with changes to accord with juvenile court practice.

First, the referee is empowered to set a time for "the hearing of the case" in addition to the power in Civ R 53 to "set a time and place for the first meeting of the parties or their attorneys."

Second, the time for such hearing or meeting is to be "promptly" rather than "within a reasonable time."

Third, the final sentence in Juv R 40(C)(1), first paragraph, was added to deal with the situation where the order of reference deals with a class of cases.

Fourth, in the second paragraph of Juv R 40(C)(1), the referee is given the power to order the party brought before him where he has failed to appear for the initial hearing.

Fifth, Civ R 53(D)(3) on statement of accounts is omitted from Juv R 40 as inapplicable in this context.

5. Report

Juv R 40(D) is modeled after Civ R 53(E), with some differences.

In subdivision (D)(1), the report is to be filed with the judge instead of the clerk and copies are to be "provided" rather than "mailed" to the parties. Subdivision (D)(1) also provides that the referee's report shall contain the referee's findings in the case and his recommendation. This provision is taken from 2151.16.

Subdivisions (D)(2), (D)(3), (D)(4), and (D)(5) are substantially similar to Civ R 53(E)(2), (E)(3), (E)(4), and (E)(5).

CROSS REFERENCES

Giannelli, Ohio Evidence Manual, Author's Comment § 101.03

Kurtz & Giannelli, Ohio Juvenile Law, Text 1.04, 7.07(B), 11.16, 15.02(B)

Referees, Civ R 53

OJur 3d: 23, Courts and Judges § 428; 46, Family Law § 496 to 502

NOTES ON DECISIONS AND OPINIONS

1. Cases interpreting Juvenile Rule 40
2. Cases interpreting law analogous to Juvenile Rule 40

1. Cases interpreting Juvenile Rule 40

36 OS(2d) 139, 304 NE(2d) 596 (1973), In re Stall. An evidentiary hearing before the juvenile court judge after a hearing before a juvenile court referee is not mandatory.

30 App(3d) 87, 30 OBR 185, 506 NE(2d) 925 (Franklin 1986), In re Bradford. Juv R 40(D) does not contemplate that a trial court rubber-stamp all reports by referees; thus, a court may, upon consideration of objections properly made, reject a referee's report.

19 App(3d) 130, 19 OBR 219, 483 NE(2d) 173 (Cuyahoga 1984), In re Weimer. The requirement of Juv R 40(D)(1) that the report of the referee set forth his findings in the case is satisfied where a supplemental report provides necessary material lacking in the original.

19 App(3d) 130, 19 OBR 219, 483 NE(2d) 173 (Cuyahoga 1984), In re Weimer. Juv R 40(D)(1), which requires copies of juvenile court referee reports to be furnished to the parties, comprehends a supplemental report filed at the request of the court to correct deficiencies in the original; approval of a supplemental report is prejudicial error where a copy of the supplement was not provided to the defending party.

52 App(2d) 312, 369 NE(2d) 1054 (1976), State v Eddington. A juvenile judge has no authority to commit the trial of a criminal charge against an adult to a referee and any proceedings so committed are null and void.

438 US 204, 98 SCt 2699, 57 LEd(2d) 705 (1978), Swisher v Brady. A juvenile is placed in jeopardy at a hearing before a master whose duty is to determine whether he has committed acts that

violate a criminal law, and where the potential consequences are stigma and the deprivation of liberty. (Ed. note: Maryland law construed in light of federal Constitution.) (Followed by United States v DiFrancesco, 101 SCt 426, 66 LEd(2d) 328 (1980).)

2. Cases interpreting law analogous to Juvenile Rule 40

2151.16 REFEREES; POWERS AND DUTIES

22 App(2d) 125, 259 NE(2d) 128 (1969), In re Gutman. The action of a juvenile court in postponing a hearing on a matter submitted to a referee who failed to file findings and recommendations, and in rectifying such deficiency by taking additional testimony and, thereafter, rendering a decision constitutes a substantial compliance with 2151.16.

22 App(2d) 125, 259 NE(2d) 128 (1969), In re Gutman. A juvenile court is not required to provide, at state expense, a bill of exceptions in a custody proceeding, especially absent a demand for the taking of testimony by a court reporter.

1 App(2d) 430, 205 NE(2d) 106 (1965), Dolgin v Dolgin. While the juvenile court has authority to appoint a referee with power of masters in chancery to hear a case and report his findings and recommendations to the judge, there is no such authority with reference to an investigating counselor, and the action and report of such counselor is ex parte and does not constitute the hearing of "additional testimony" by the judge under such statute.

87 App 220, 94 NE(2d) 474 (1949), De Ville v De Ville. A referee of the juvenile court appointed pursuant to this section has functions and duties similar to those of a master commissioner appointed pursuant to GC 11487 to 11492 (RC 2315.38 to 2315.43; Civ R 53).

44 Abs 86, 62 NE(2d) 510 (App Franklin 1945), In re Hobson. Notice required by this section to be given to parties must be in writing.

324 F(2d) 752 (1963), Allstate Insurance v Cook. A judgment of the juvenile court in the form of journalized recommendations of the referee is not rendered invalid because it was not immediately signed by the judge.

SUPREME COURT RULES FOR THE GOVERNMENT OF THE JUDICIARY

Bd of Commrs on Grievances & Discipline Op 87-041 (9-25-87). At present, referees are not required to comply with Gov Jud R IV, which mandates continuing legal education for judges. Both part-time and full-time referees are encouraged to participate in continuing legal education in order to increase their knowledge and understanding of their position as referees and their knowledge of the area of law over which they preside as referee.

Bd of Commrs on Grievances & Discipline Op 87-032 (6-22-87). A part-time referee is considered a part-time judge for purposes of the Code of Judicial Conduct and may serve as a member or officer of a local board of education, provided such activity does not reflect adversely upon his impartiality or interfere with the performance of his judicial duties. A part-time referee should not serve as a member or officer of a local board of education if it is likely that said board will be engaged in proceedings that would ordinarily come before him or will be regularly engaged in adversary proceedings in any court. Additionally, a part-time referee should disqualify himself in any case in which his decision could affect any organization which he serves as either an officer or member of its board and he should avoid even the appearance of impropriety in all his activities.

Bd of Commrs on Grievances & Discipline Op 87-014 (6-22-87). Referees are considered judges for purposes of complying with the Code of Judicial Conduct. In this regard, part-time referees may not practice before the court division on which they serve or before the judge or judges to whom they owe their appointment; however, part-time referees serving the domestic relations division of common pleas court may practice law before other judges in the general, probate, and juvenile divisions of that court so long as they avoid the appearance of impropriety. (See also Bd of Commrs on Grievances & Discipline Op 87-036 (9-25-87).)

Juv R 41
[Reserved]

Juv R 42
Consent to marry

(A) Application where parental consent not required.

When a minor desires to contract matrimony and has no parent, guardian, or custodian whose consent to the marriage is required by law, the minor shall file an application under oath in the county where the female resides requesting that the judge of the juvenile court give consent and approbation in the probate court for such marriage.

(B) Contents of application.

The application required by subdivision (A) shall contain:

(1) The name and address of the person for whom consent is sought;

(2) The age of said person;

(3) The reason why consent of a parent is not required; and

(4) The name and address, if known, of the parent, where the minor alleges that his parent's consent is unnecessary because the parent has neglected or abandoned him for one year or longer immediately preceding the application.

(C) Application where female pregnant or delivered of child born out of wedlock.

Where a female is pregnant or delivered of a child born out of wedlock and the parents of such child seek to marry even though one or both of them is under the minimum age prescribed by law for persons who may contract marriage, such persons shall file an application under oath in the county where the female resides requesting that the judge of the juvenile court give consent in the probate court to such marriage.

(D) Contents of application.

The application required by subdivision (C) shall contain:

(1) The name and address of the person or persons for whom consent is sought;

(2) The age of such person;

(3) An indication of whether the female is pregnant or has already been delivered;

(4) An indication of whether or not any applicant under eighteen years of age is already a ward of the court; and

(5) Any other facts which may assist the court in determining whether to consent to such marriage.

If pregnancy is asserted, a certificate from a physician verifying pregnancy shall be attached to the application. If an illegitimate child has been delivered, the birth certificate of such child shall be attached.

The consent to the granting of the application by each parent whose consent to the marriage is required by law shall be indorsed on the application.

(E) Investigation.

Upon receipt of an application under subdivision (C), the court shall set a date and time for hearing thereon at its earliest convenience and shall direct that an inquiry be made as to the circumstances surrounding the applicants.

(F) Notice.

If neglect or abandonment is alleged in an application under subdivision (A) and the address of the parent is known, the court shall cause notice of the date and time of hearing to be served upon such parent.

(G) Judgment.

If the court finds that the allegations stated in the application are true, and that the granting of the application is in the best interest of the applicants, the court shall grant the consent and shall make the applicant referred to in subdivision (C) a ward of the court.

(H) Certified copy.

A certified copy of the judgment entry shall be transmitted to the probate court.

Adopted eff. 7-1-72; amended eff. 7-1-80

Editor's Comment

1. Consent to marry
2. Application where parental consent not required
3. Contents of application
4. Application where minor female pregnant or delivered of a child born out of wedlock
5. Contents of application
6. Investigation
7. Notice
8. Judgment
9. Certified copy

1. Consent to marry

Juv R 42 was adopted pursuant to Juv R 1 (B)(2) to provide for simplicity and uniformity in procedure. Prior to the adoption of the rule no procedure was mandated. 3101.04 now superseded by the rule provides that the juvenile judge may give his consent and approbation in the probate court for the marriage of (A) a minor who has no parent, guardian, or custodian whose consent is required upon application of both parties in the county in which the marriage license is applied for. Pursuant to 3101.01 male persons of the age of eighteen and female persons of the age of sixteen, not nearer than second cousins, and not having a husband or wife living may be joined in marriage. The statute requires that a minor, that is one not having attained his twenty-first birthday, must first obtain the consent of his parents, surviving parent, guardian, etc. An exception to the age requirements of 3101.01 is provided by 3101.04(B) which states that "when the condition of a minor female is such as imperatively to impel the marriage estate by reason of approaching maternity, or when an illegitimate child has been born, the matter shall be inquired into by the juvenile court. If as a result of the inquiry one or both parties are made wards of the court, said court may, with the consent of said wards, their parents, if any are living, or of any guardian or custodian give consent in the probate court."

2. Application where parental consent not required

Juv R 42(A) provides that an application under oath be filed in the juvenile court of the county where the female resides for consent to marry when parental consent is not required.

3. Contents of application

Juv R 42(B) sets forth what information shall be furnished the court in the application for consent to marry.

4. Application where minor female pregnant or delivered of a child born out of wedlock

Juv R 42(C) provides for the filing of an application for consent to marry when the female is under sixteen years of age and is pregnant or has been delivered of a child born out of wedlock.

5. Contents of application

Juv R 42(D) outlines what the application for consent to marry, where a female is under sixteen, is pregnant or has been delivered of an illegitimate child, shall contain.

6. Investigation

Juv R 42(E) requires that the court conduct an inquiry as to the circumstances and to set a date and time for the hearing.

7. Notice

Juv R 42(F) provides for notice to a parent whose address is known regarding the hearing when the application under subdivision (A) alleges that consent is not required because neglect for a period of one year or abandonment has occurred.

8. Judgment

Juv R 42(G) makes it clear that the court has discretionary authority to grant or deny the application. The best interests of the applicants is the determinative issue.

9. Certified copy

Juv R 42(H) requires that a certified copy of the judgment entry be furnished the probate court which may issue the marriage license upon the applicants' complying with the other provisions. (*See* Ch 3101 regarding marriage.)

CROSS REFERENCES

Persons who may marry, 3101.01

OJur 3d: 23, Courts and Judges § 428; 45, Family Law § 17; 46, Family Law § 395

NOTES ON DECISIONS AND OPINIONS

3101.04 CONSENT OF JUVENILE JUDGE

76 App 338, 64 NE(2d) 428 (1945), Carlton v Carlton. The marriage of a male person seventeen years of age is void except under the conditions provided for in section.

Juv R 43
[Reserved]

Juv R 44
Jurisdiction unaffected

These rules shall not be construed to extend or limit the jurisdiction of the juvenile court.

Adopted eff. 7-1-72

Editor's Comment

Juv R 44 makes it clear that the Rules of Juvenile Procedure do not affect the jurisdiction of the juvenile court. Jurisdiction is established by the Constitution of Ohio and 2151.23.

CROSS REFERENCES

Scope of rules, exceptions, Juv R 1

OJur 3d: 46, Family Law § 364

NOTES ON DECISIONS AND OPINIONS

438 US 204, 98 SCt 2699, 57 LEd(2d) 705 (1978), Swisher v Brady. A procedure which allows a juvenile court master to file written findings of fact with the juvenile court judge who may then make supplemental findings in response to the state's exceptions, the juvenile's exceptions or sua sponte, either on the record or a record supplemented by evidence to which the parties do not object, does not violate the double jeopardy clause. (Ed. note: Maryland law construed in light of federal constitution.) (Followed by United States v DiFrancesco, 101 SCt 426, 66 LEd(2d) 328 (1980).)

Juv R 45
Procedure not otherwise specified

If no procedure is specifically prescribed by these rules, the court shall proceed in any lawful manner not inconsistent therewith.

Adopted eff. 7-1-72

Editor's Comment

Juvenile court has jurisdiction over many different types of proceedings pursuant to 2151.23 for which no specific procedure has been provided in these rules, either because they are related to matters in the probate or domestic relations divisions of the common pleas court or the issue is seldom raised in the juvenile court.

Examples of this are transfer of jurisdiction from the probate division pursuant to 3107.12; transfer of jurisdiction from domestic relations division under 3109.04 and 3109.06; and the jurisdiction of the juvenile court to exercise the powers and jurisdiction of the probate division granted in Ch 5122 and 5125 of the Ohio Revised Code, if a child is otherwise within the jurisdiction of the juvenile court. An example of seldom used procedure is proceedings under the Interstate Compact under 2151.56. Juv R 45 is designed to apply to these kinds of procedures.

CROSS REFERENCES

OJur 3d: 46, Family Law § 364

Juv R 46

Forms

The forms contained in the Appendix of Forms which the supreme court from time to time may approve are illustrative and not mandatory.

Adopted eff. 7-1-72

Editor's Comment

Juv R 46 provides that forms approved by the Supreme Court are not mandatory. The rule permits local courts to devise forms to meet local conditions.

CROSS REFERENCES

Merrick-Rippner, Ohio Probate Law (4th Ed.), Forms Ch 217, Ch 221, Ch 223

Juv R 47

Effective date

(A) Effective date of rules.

These rules shall take effect on the first day of July, 1972. They govern all proceedings in actions brought after they take effect and also all further proceedings in actions then pending, except to the extent that their application in a particular action pending when the rules take effect would not be feasible or would work injustice, in which event the former procedure applies.

(B) Effective date of amendments.

The amendments submitted by the Supreme Court to the general assembly on January 12, 1973, shall take effect on the first day of July, 1973. They govern all proceedings in actions brought after they take effect and also all further proceedings in actions then pending, except to the extent that their application in a particular action pending when the amendments take effect

would not be feasible or would work injustice, in which event the former procedure applies.

(C) Effective date of amendments.

The amendments submitted by the Supreme Court to the General Assembly on January 10, 1975, and on April 29, 1975, shall take effect on July 1, 1975. They govern all proceedings in actions brought after they take effect and also all further proceedings in actions then pending, except to the extent that their application in a particular action pending when the amendments take effect would not be feasible or would work injustice, in which event the former procedure applies.

(D) Effective date of amendments.

The amendments submitted by the Supreme Court to the General Assembly on January 9, 1976 shall take effect on July 1, 1976. They govern all proceedings in actions brought after they take effect and also all further proceedings in actions then pending, except to the extent that their application in a particular action pending when the amendments take effect would not be feasible or would work injustice, in which event the former procedure applies.

(E) Effective date of amendments.

The amendments submitted by the Supreme Court to the General Assembly on January 14, 1980, shall take effect on July 1, 1980. They govern all proceedings in actions brought after they take effect and also all further proceedings in actions then pending, except to the extent that their application in a particular action pending when the amendments take effect would not be feasible or would work injustice, in which event the former procedure applies.

(F) Effective date of amendments.

The amendments submitted by the Supreme Court to the General Assembly on December 24, 1984 and January 8, 1985 shall take effect on July 1, 1985. They govern all proceedings in actions brought after they take effect and also all further proceedings in actions then pending, except to the extent that their application in a particular action pending when the amendments take effect would not be feasible or would work injustice, in which event the former procedure applies.

Adopted eff. 7-1-72; amended eff. 7-1-73, 7-1-75, 7-1-76, 7-1-80, 7-1-85

Editor's Comment

Juv R 47 is based upon O Const Art IV, § 5(B), which provides that rules approved by the Supreme Court and not disapproved by the legislature shall take effect on the first day of July in the year in which the rules were submitted to the legislature.

CROSS REFERENCES

OJur 3d: 46, Family Law § 363

Juv R 48
Title

These rules shall be known as the Ohio Rules of Juvenile Procedure and may be cited as "Juvenile Rules" or "Juv. R. —."

Adopted eff. 7-1-72

Ohio Rules of Evidence

Publisher's Note: These Rules are published as they appear in the *Ohio Official Reports.*

Publisher's Note: Until 1968, when the Modern Courts Amendment to the Ohio Constitution was adopted, Ohio court procedure was governed entirely by statute and caselaw. The Modern Courts Amendment required the Supreme Court of Ohio, subject to the approval of the General Assembly, to "prescribe rules governing practice and procedure in all courts of the state." Rules of practice and procedure are the Civil, Criminal, Appellate, and Juvenile Rules, Rules of the Court of Claims, and the Ohio Rules of Evidence. Pursuant to Ohio Constitution Article IV, Section 5(B), such rules "shall not abridge, enlarge, or modify any substantive right," and "all laws in conflict with such rules shall be of no further force or effect."

Article I
GENERAL PROVISIONS

Evid R 101

Scope of rules: applicability; privileges; exceptions

(A) Applicability.

These rules govern proceedings in the courts of this state and before court-appointed referees of this state subject to the exceptions stated in subdivision (C) of this rule.

(B) Privileges.

The rule with respect to privileges applies at all stages of all actions, cases, and proceedings conducted under these rules.

(C) Exceptions.

These rules (other than with respect to privileges) do not apply in the following situations:

(1) Admissibility determinations. Determinations prerequisite to rulings on the admissibility of evidence when the issue is to be determined by the court under Rule 104.

(2) Grand jury. Proceedings before grand juries.

(3) Miscellaneous criminal proceedings. Proceedings for extradition or rendition of fugitives; sentencing; granting or revoking probation; issuance of warrants for arrest, criminal summonses and search warrants; and proceedings with respect to release on bail or otherwise.

(4) Contempt. Contempt proceedings in which the court may act summarily.

(5) Arbitration. Proceedings for those mandatory arbitrations of civil cases authorized by the rules of superintendence and governed by local rules of court.

(6) Other rules. Proceedings in which other rules prescribed by the supreme court govern matters relating to evidence.

(7) Special non-adversary statutory proceedings. Special statutory proceedings of a non-adversary nature in which these rules would by their nature be clearly inapplicable.

(8) Small claims division. Proceedings in the small claims division of a county or municipal court.

Adopted eff. 7-1-80

Evid R 102

Purpose and construction

The purpose of these rules is to provide procedures for the adjudication of causes to the end that the truth may be ascertained and proceedings justly determined. These rules shall be construed to state the common law of Ohio unless the rule clearly indicates that a change is intended and shall not supersede substantive statutory provisions.

Adopted eff. 7-1-80

Evid R 103

Rulings on evidence

(A) Effect of erroneous ruling.

Error may not be predicated upon a ruling which admits or excludes evidence unless a substantial right of the party is affected, and

(1) Objection. In case the ruling is one admitting evidence, a timely objection or motion to strike appears of record stating the specific ground of objection, if the specific ground was not apparent from the context; or

(2) Offer of proof. In case the ruling is one excluding evidence, the substance of the evidence was made known to the court by offer or was apparent from the context within which questions were asked. Offer of proof is not necessary if evidence is excluded during cross-examination.

(B) Record of offer and ruling.

At the time of making the ruling, the court may add any other or further statement which shows the character of the evidence, the form in which it was offered, the objection made, and the ruling thereon. It may direct the making of an offer in question and answer form.

(C) Hearing of jury.

In jury cases, proceedings shall be conducted, to the extent practicable, so as to prevent inadmissible evidence from being suggested to the jury by any means, such as making statements or offers of proof or asking questions in the hearing of the jury.

(D) Plain error.

Nothing in this rule precludes taking notice of plain errors affecting substantial rights although they were not brought to the attention of the court.

Adopted eff. 7-1-80

Evid R 104

Preliminary questions

(A) Questions of admissibility generally.

Preliminary questions concerning the qualification of a person to be a witness, the existence of a privilege, or the admissibility of evidence shall be determined by the court, subject to the provisions of subdivision (B). In making its determination it is not bound by the rules of evidence except those with respect to privileges.

(B) Relevancy conditioned on fact.

When the relevancy of evidence depends upon the fulfillment of a condition of fact, the court shall admit it upon, or subject to, the introduction of evidence sufficient to support a finding of the fulfillment of the condition.

(C) Hearing of jury.

Hearings on the admissibility of confessions shall in all cases be conducted out of the hearing of the jury. Hearings on other preliminary matters shall also be conducted out of the hearing of the jury when the interests of justice require.

(D) Testimony by accused.

The accused does not, by testifying upon a preliminary matter, subject himself to cross-examination as to other issues in the case.

(E) Weight and credibility.

This rule does not limit the right of a party to introduce before the jury evidence relevant to weight or credibility.

Adopted eff. 7-1-80

Evid R 105

Limited admissibility

When evidence which is admissible as to one party or for one purpose but not admissible as to another party of[1] for another purpose is admitted, the court, upon request of a party, shall restrict the evidence to its proper scope and instruct the jury accordingly.

Adopted eff. 7-1-80

[1]So in original; should this read "or"?

Evid R 106

Remainder of or related writings or recorded statements

When a writing or recorded statement or part thereof is introduced by a party, an adverse party may require him at that time to introduce any other part or any other writing or recorded statement which is otherwise admissible and which ought in fairness to be considered contemporaneously with it.

Adopted eff. 7-1-80

Article II
JUDICIAL NOTICE

Evid R 201

Judicial notice of adjudicative facts

(A) Scope of rule.

This rule governs only judicial notice of adjudicative facts; i.e., the facts of the case.

(B) Kinds of facts.

A judicially noticed fact must be one not subject to reasonable dispute in that it is either (1) generally known within the territorial jurisdiction of the trial court or (2) capable of accurate and ready determination by resort to sources whose accuracy cannot reasonable[1] be questioned.

(C) When discretionary.

A court may take judicial notice, whether requested or not.

(D) When mandatory.

A court shall take judicial notice if requested by a party and supplied with the necessary information.

(E) Opportunity to be heard.

A party is entitled upon timely request to an opportunity to be heard as to the propriety of taking judicial notice and the tenor of the matter noticed. In the absence of prior notification, the request may be made after judicial notice has been taken.

(F) Time of taking notice.

Judicial notice may be taken at any stage of the proceeding.

(G) Instructing jury.

In a civil action or proceeding, the court shall instruct the jury to accept as conclusive any fact judicially noticed. In a criminal case, the court shall instruct the jury that it may, but is not required to, accept as conclusive any fact judicially noticed.

Adopted eff. 7-1-80

[1]So in original; should this read "reasonably"?

Article III
PRESUMPTIONS

Evid R 301

Presumptions in general in civil actions and proceedings

In all civil actions and proceedings not otherwise provided for by statute enacted by the General Assembly or by these rules, a presumption imposes on the party against whom it is directed the burden of going forward with evidence to rebut or meet the presumption, but does not shift to such party the burden of proof in the sense of the risk of non-persuasion, which remains throughout the trial upon the party on whom it was originally cast.

Adopted eff. 7-1-80

Evid R 302
[Reserved]

Article IV
RELEVANCY AND ITS LIMITS

Evid R 401	Definition of "relevant evidence"
Evid R 402	Relevant evidence generally admissible; irrelevant evidence inadmissible
Evid R 403	Exclusion of relevant evidence on grounds of prejudice, confusion, or waste of time
Evid R 404	Character evidence not admissible to prove conduct; exceptions; other crimes
Evid R 405	Methods of proving character
Evid R 406	Habit; routine practice
Evid R 407	Subsequent remedial measures
Evid R 408	Compromise and offers to compromise
Evid R 409	Payment of medical and similar expenses
Evid R 410	Inadmissibility of pleas, offers of pleas, and related statements
Evid R 411	Liability insurance

Evid R 401

Definition of "relevant evidence"

"Relevant evidence" means evidence having any tendency to make the existence of any fact that is of consequence to the determination of the action more probable or less probable than it would be without the evidence.

Adopted eff. 7-1-80

Evid R 402

Relevant evidence generally admissible; irrelevant evidence inadmissible

All relevant evidence is admissible, except as otherwise provided by the Constitution of the United States, by the Constitution of the State of Ohio, by statute enacted by the General Assembly not in conflict with a rule of the Supreme Court of Ohio, by these rules, or by other rules prescribed by the Supreme Court of Ohio. Evidence which is not relevant is not admissible.

Adopted eff. 7-1-80

Evid R 403

Exclusion of relevant evidence on grounds of prejudice, confusion, or waste of time

(A) Exclusion mandatory.

Although relevant, evidence is not admissible if its probative value is substantially outweighed by the danger of unfair prejudice, of confusion of the issues, or of misleading the jury.

(B) Exclusion discretionary.

Although relevant, evidence may be excluded if its probative value is substantially outweighed by considerations of undue delay, or needless presentation of cumulative evidence.

Adopted eff. 7-1-80

Evid R 404

Character evidence not admissible to prove conduct; exceptions; other crimes

(A) Character evidence generally.

Evidence of a person's character or a trait of his character is not admissible for the purpose of proving that he acted in conformity therewith on a particular occasion, subject to the following exceptions:

(1) Character of accused. Evidence of a pertinent trait of his character offered by an accused, or by the prosecution to rebut the same is admissible; however, in prosecutions for rape, gross sexual imposition, and prostitution, the exceptions provided by statute enacted by the General Assembly are applicable.

(2) Character of victim. Evidence of a pertinent trait of character of the victim of the crime offered by an accused, or by the prosecution to rebut the same, or evidence of a character trait of peacefulness of the victim offered by the prosecution in a homicide case to rebut evidence that the victim was the first aggressor is admissible; however, in prosecutions for rape, gross sexual imposition, and prostitution, the exceptions provided by statute enacted by the General Assembly are applicable.

(3) Character of witness. Evidence of the character of a witness on the issue of credi-bility is admissible as provided in Rules 607, 608, and 609.

(B) Other crimes, wrongs or acts.

Evidence of other crimes, wrongs, or acts is not admissible to prove the character of a person in order to show that he acted in conformity therewith. It may, however, be admissible for other purposes, such as proof of motive, opportunity, intent, preparation, plan, knowledge, identity, or absence of mistake or accident.

Adopted eff. 7-1-80

Evid R 405

Methods of proving character

(A) Reputation or opinion.

In all cases in which evidence of character or a trait of character of a person is admissible, proof may be made by testimony as to reputation or by testimony in the form of an opinion. On cross-examination, inquiry is allowable into relevant specific instances of conduct.

(B) Specific instances of conduct.

In cases in which character or a trait of character of a person is an essential element of a charge, claim, or defense, proof may also be made of specific instances of his conduct.

Adopted eff. 7-1-80

Evid R 406

Habit; routine practice

Evidence of the habit of a person or of the routine practice of an organization, whether corroborated or not and regardless of the presence of eyewitnesses, is relevant to prove that the conduct of the person or organization on a particular occasion was in conformity with the habit or routine practice.

Adopted eff. 7-1-80

Evid R 407

Subsequent remedial measures

When, after an event, measures are taken which, if taken previously, would have made the event less likely to occur, evidence of the subsequent measures is not admissible to prove negligence or culpable conduct in connection with the event. This rule does not require the exclusion of evidence of subsequent measures when offered for another purpose, such as proving ownership, control, or feasibility of precautionary measures, if controverted, or impeachment.

Adopted eff. 7-1-80

Evid R 408

Compromise and offers to compromise

Evidence of (1) furnishing or offering or promising to furnish, or (2) accepting or offering or promising to accept, a valuable consideration in compromising or attempting to compromise a claim which was disputed as to either validity or amount, is not admissible to prove liability for or invalidity of the claim or its amount. Evidence of conduct or statements made in compromise negotiations is likewise not admissible. This rule does not require the exclusion of any evidence otherwise discoverable merely because it is presented in the course of compromise negotiations. This rule also does not require exclusion when the evidence is offered for another purpose, such as proving bias or prejudice of a witness, negativing a contention of undue delay, or proving an effort to obstruct a criminal investigation or prosecution.

Adopted eff. 7-1-80

Evid R 409

Payment of medical and similar expenses

Evidence of furnishing or offering or promising to pay medical, hospital, or similar expenses occasioned by an injury is not admissible to prove liability for the injury.

Adopted eff. 7-1-80

Evid R 410

Inadmissibility of pleas, offers of pleas, and related statements

Except as otherwise provided in this rule, evidence of a plea of guilty, later withdrawn, or a plea of no contest, or the equivalent plea from another jurisdiction, or a plea of guilty in a violations bureau, or of an offer to plead guilty or no contest to the crime charged or any other crime, or of statements made in connection with, and relevant to, any of the foregoing pleas or offers, is not admissible in any civil or criminal proceeding against the person who made the plea or offer. However, evidence of a statement made in connection with, and relevant to, a plea of guilty, later withdrawn, a plea of no contest, or an offer to plead guilty or no contest to the crime charged or any other crime, is admissible in a criminal proceeding for perjury or false statement if the statement was made by the defendant under oath, on the record, and in the presence of counsel.

Adopted eff. 7-1-80

Evid R 411

Liability insurance

Evidence that a person was or was not insured against liability is not admissible upon the issue whether he acted negligently or otherwise wrongfully. This rule does not require the exclusion of evidence of insurance against liability when offered for another purpose, such as proof of agency, ownership or control, if controverted, or bias or prejudice of a witness.

Adopted eff. 7-1-80

Article V
PRIVILEGES

Evid R 501
General rule

The privilege of a witness, person, state or political subdivision thereof shall be governed by statute enacted by the General Assembly or by principles of common law as interpreted by the courts of this state in the light of reason and experience.

Adopted eff. 7-1-80

Article VI
WITNESSES

Evid R 601
General rule of competency

Every person is competent to be a witness except:

(A) Those of unsound mind, and children under ten (10) years of age, who appear incapable of receiving just impressions of the facts and transactions respecting which they are examined, or of relating them truly and;

(B) A spouse testifying against the other spouse charged with crimes except crimes against the testifying spouse or the children of either and;

(C) An officer, while on duty for the exclusive or main purpose of enforcing traffic laws, arresting or assisting in the arrest of a person charged with a traffic violation punishable as a misdemeanor where the officer at the time of the arrest was not using a properly marked motor vehicle as defined by statute or was not wearing a legally distinctive uniform as defined by statute.

(D) A person giving expert testimony on the issue of liability in any claim asserted in any civil action against a physician, podiatrist, or hospital arising out of the diagnosis, care or treatment of any person, unless the person testifying is licensed to practice medicine and surgery, osteopathic medicine and surgery, or podiatric medicine and surgery by the state medical board or by the licensing authority of any state, and unless such person devotes three-fourths of his professional time to the active clinical practice in his field of licensure, or to its instruction in an accredited university.

(E) As otherwise provided in these rules.

Adopted eff. 7-1-80

Evid R 602

Lack of personal knowledge

A witness may not testify to a matter unless evidence is introduced sufficient to support a finding that he has personal knowledge of the matter. Evidence to prove personal knowledge may, but need not, consist of the testimony of the witness himself. This rule is subject to the provisions of Rule 703, relating to opinion testimony by expert witnesses.

Adopted eff. 7-1-80

Evid R 603

Oath or affirmation

Before testifying, every witness shall be required to declare that he will testify truthfully, by oath or affirmation administered in a form calculated to awaken his conscience and impress his mind with his duty to do so.

Adopted eff. 7-1-80

Evid R 604

Interpreters

An interpreter is subject to the provisions of these rules relating to qualification as an expert and the administration of an oath or affirmation that he will make a true translation.

Adopted eff. 7-1-80

Evid R 605

Competency of judge as witness

The judge presiding at the trial may not testify in that trial as a witness. No objection need be made in order to preserve the point.

Adopted eff. 7-1-80

Evid R 606

Competency of juror as witness

(A) At the trial.

A member of the jury may not testify as a witness before that jury in the trial of the case in which he is sitting as a juror. If he is called so to testify, the opposing party shall be afforded an opportunity to object out of the presence of the jury.

(B) Inquiry into validity of verdict or indictment.

Upon an inquiry into the validity of a verdict or indictment, a juror may not testify as to any matter or statement occurring during the course of the jury's deliberations or to the effect of anything upon his or any other juror's mind or emotions as influencing him to assent to or dissent from the verdict or indictment or concerning his mental processes in connection therewith. A juror may testify on the question whether extraneous prejudicial information was improperly brought to the jury's attention or whether any outside influence was improperly brought to bear on any juror, only after some outside evidence of that act or event has been presented. However a juror may testify without the presentation of any outside evidence concerning any threat, any bribe, any attempted threat or bribe, or any improprieties of any officer of the court. His affidavit or evidence of any statement by him concerning a matter about which he would be precluded from testifying will not be received for these purposes.

Adopted eff. 7-1-80

Evid R 607

Who may impeach

The credibility of a witness may be attacked by any party except that the credibility of a witness may be attacked by the party calling the witness by means of a prior inconsistent statement only upon a showing of surprise and affirmative damage. This exception does not apply to statements admitted pursuant to Rules 801(D)(1)(a), 801(D)(2), or 803.

Adopted eff. 7-1-80

Evid R 608

Evidence of character and conduct of witness

(A) Opinion and reputation evidence of character.

The credibility of a witness may be attacked or supported by evidence in the form of opinion or reputation, but subject to these limitations: (1) the evidence may refer only to character for truthfulness or untruthfulness, and (2) evidence of truthful character is admissible only after the character of the witness for truthfulness has been attacked by opinion or reputation evidence or otherwise.

(B) Specific instances of conduct.

Specific instances of the conduct of a witness, for the purpose of attacking or supporting his credibility, other than conviction of crime as provided in Rule 609, may not be proved by extrinsic evidence. They may, however, in the discretion of the court, if clearly probative of truthfulness or untruthfulness, be inquired into on cross-examination of the witness (1) concerning his character for truthfulness or untruthfulness, or (2) concerning the character for truthfulness or untruthfulness of another witness as to which character the witness being cross-examined has testified.

The giving of testimony, whether by an accused or by any other witness, does not operate as a waiver of his privilege against self-incrimination when examined with respect to matters which relate only to credibility.

Adopted eff. 7-1-80

Evid R 609

Impeachment by evidence of conviction of crime

(A) General rule.

For the purpose of attacking the credibility of a witness, evidence that he has been convicted of a crime shall be admitted if elicited from him or established by public record during cross-examination but only if the crime (1) was punishable by death or imprisonment in excess of one year under the law under which he was convicted, or (2) involved dishonesty or false statement, regardless of the punishment whether based upon state or federal statute or ordinance.

(B) Time limit.

Evidence of a conviction under this rule is not admissible if a period of more than ten years has elapsed since the date of the conviction or of the release of the witness from the confinement, or the termination of probation, or shock probation, or parole, or shock parole imposed for that conviction, whichever is the later date, unless the court determines, in the interests of justice, that the probative value of the conviction supported by specific facts and circumstances substantially outweighs its prejudicial effect. However, evidence of a conviction more than ten years old as calculated herein, is not admissible unless the proponent gives to the adverse party sufficient advance written notice of intent to use such evidence to provide the adverse party with a fair opportunity to contest the use of such evidence.

(C) Effect of pardon, annulment, expungement, or certificate of rehabilitation.

Evidence of a conviction is not admissible under this rule if (1) the conviction has been the subject of a pardon, annulment, expungement, certificate of rehabilitation, or other equivalent procedure based on a finding of the rehabilitation of the person convicted, and that person has not been convicted of a subsequent crime which was punishable by death or imprisonment in excess of one year, or (2) the conviction has been the subject of a pardon, annulment, expungement, or other equivalent procedure based on a finding of innocence.

(D) Juvenile adjudications.

Evidence of juvenile adjudications is not admissible except as provided by statute enacted by the General Assembly.

(E) Pendency of appeal.

The pendency of an appeal therefrom does not render evidence of a conviction inadmissible. Evidence of the pendency of an appeal is admissible.

Adopted eff. 7-1-80

Evid R 610

Religious beliefs or opinions

Evidence of the beliefs or opinions of a witness on matters of religion is not admissible for the purpose of showing that by reason of their nature his credibility is impaired or enhanced.

Adopted eff. 7-1-80

Evid R 611

Mode and order of interrogation and presentation

(A) Control by court.

The court shall exercise reasonable control over the mode and order of interrogating witnesses and presenting evidence so as to (1) make the interrogation and presentation effective for the ascertainment of the truth, (2) avoid needless consumption of time, and (3) protect witnesses from harassment or undue embarrassment.

(B) Scope of cross-examination.

Cross-examination shall be permitted on all relevant matters and matters affecting credibility.

(C) Leading questions.

Leading questions should not be used on the direct examination of a witness except as may be necessary to develop his testimony. Ordinarily leading questions should be permitted on cross-examination. When a party calls a hostile witness, an adverse party, or a witness identified with an adverse party, interrogation may be by leading questions.

Adopted eff. 7-1-80

Evid R 612

Writing used to refresh memory

Except as otherwise provided in criminal proceedings by Rule 16(B)(1)(g) and 16(C)(1)(d) of Ohio Rules of Criminal Procedure, if a witness uses a writing to refresh his memory for the purpose of testifying, either: (1) while testifying; or (2) before testifying, if the court in its discretion determines it is necessary in the interests of justice, an adverse party is entitled to have the writing produced at the hearing. He is also entitled to inspect it, to cross-examine the witness thereon, and to introduce in evidence those portions which relate to the testimony of the witness. If it is claimed that the writing contains matters not related to the subject matter of the testimony the court shall examine the writing *in camera*, excise any portions not so related, and order delivery of the remainder to the party entitled thereto. Any portion withheld [*sic*] over objections shall be preserved and made available to the appellate court in the event of an appeal. If a writing is not produced or delivered pursuant to order under this rule, the court shall make any order justice requires, except that in criminal cases when the prosecution elects not to comply, the order shall be one striking the testimony or, if the court in its discretion determines that the interests of justice so require, declaring a mistrial.

Adopted eff. 7-1-80

Evid R 613

Prior statements of witnesses

(A) Examining witness concerning prior statement.

In examining a witness concerning a prior statement made by him, whether written or not, the statement need not be shown nor its contents disclosed to him at that time, but on request the same shall be shown or disclosed to opposing counsel.

(B) Extrinsic evidence of prior inconsistent statement of witness.

Extrinsic evidence of a prior inconsistent statement by a witness is not admissible unless the witness is afforded a prior opportunity to explain or deny the same and the opposite party is afforded an opportunity to interrogate him thereon, or the interests of justice otherwise require. This provision does not apply to admissions of a party-opponent as defined in Rule 801(D)(2).

Adopted eff. 7-1-80

Evid R 614
Calling and interrogation of witnesses by court

(A) Calling by court.

The court may, on its own motion or at the suggestion of a party, call witnesses, and all parties are entitled to cross-examine witnesses thus called.

(B) Interrogation by court.

The court may interrogate witnesses, in an impartial manner, whether called by itself or by a party.

(C) Objections.

Objections to the calling of witnesses by the court or to interrogation by it may be made at the time or at the next available opportunity when the jury is not present.

Adopted eff. 7-1-80

Evid R 615
Exclusion of witnesses

At the request of a party the court shall order witnesses excluded so that they cannot hear the testimony of other witnesses, and it may make the order of its own motion. This rule does not authorize exclusion of (1) a party who is a natural person, or (2) an officer or employee of a party which is not a natural person designated as its representative by its attorney, or (3) a person whose presence is shown by a party to be essential to the presentation of his cause.

Adopted eff. 7-1-80

Article VII
OPINIONS AND EXPERT TESTIMONY

Evid R 701   Opinion testimony by lay witnesses
Evid R 702   Testimony by experts
Evid R 703   Bases of opinion testimony by experts
Evid R 704   Opinion on ultimate issue
Evid R 705   Disclosure of facts or data underlying expert opinion

Evid R 701
Opinion testimony by lay witnesses

If the witness is not testifying as an expert, his testimony in the form of opinions or inferences is limited to those opinions or inferences which are (1) rationally based on the perception of the witness and (2) helpful to a clear understanding of his testimony or the determination of a fact in issue.

Adopted eff. 7-1-80

Evid R 702
Testimony by experts

If scientific, technical, or other specialized knowledge will assist the trier of fact to understand the evidence or to determine a fact in issue, a witness qualified as an expert by knowledge, skill, experience, training, or education, may testify thereto in the form of an opinion or otherwise.

Adopted eff. 7-1-80

Evid R 703

Bases of opinion testimony by experts

The facts or data in the particular case upon which an expert bases an opinion or inference may be those perceived by him or admitted in evidence at the hearing.

Adopted eff. 7-1-80

Evid R 704

Opinion on ultimate issue

Testimony in the form of an opinion or inference otherwise admissible is not objec-tionable solely because it embraces an ulti-mate issue to be decided by the trier of fact.

Adopted eff. 7-1-80

Evid R 705

Disclosure of facts or data underlying expert opinion

The expert may testify in terms of opin-ion or inference and give his reasons there-for after disclosure of the underlying facts or data. The disclosure may be in response to a hypothetical question or otherwise.

Adopted eff. 7-1-80

Article VIII
HEARSAY

Evid R 801

Definitions

The following definitions apply under this article:

(A) Statement.

A "statement" is (1) an oral or written assertion or (2) nonverbal conduct of a per-son, if it is intended by him as an assertion.

(B) Declarant.

A "declarant" is a person who makes a statement.

(C) Hearsay.

"Hearsay" is a statement, other than one made by the declarant while testifying at the trial or hearing, offered in evidence to prove the truth of the matter asserted.

(D) Statements which are not hearsay.

A statement is not hearsay if:

(1) Prior statement by witness. The declarant testifies at the trial or hearing and is subject to cross-examination concerning the statement, and the statement is (a) inconsistent with his testimony, and was given under oath subject to cross-examina-tion by the party against whom the state-ment is offered and subject to the penalty of perjury at a trial, hearing, or other pro-ceeding, or in a deposition, or (b) consis-tent with his testimony and is offered to rebut an express or implied charge against him of recent fabrication or improper influ-ence or motive, or (c) one of identification of a person soon after perceiving him, if the circumstances demonstrate the reliability of the prior identification.

(2) Admission by party-opponent. The statement is offered against a party and is (a) his own statement, in either his individ-ual or a representative capacity, or (b) a statement of which he has manifested his adoption or belief in its truth, or (c) a state-ment by a person authorized by him to make a statement concerning the subject, or (d) a statement by his agent or servant

concerning a matter within the scope of his agency or employment, made during the existence of the relationship, or (e) a statement by a co-conspirator of a party during the course and in furtherance of the conspiracy upon independent proof of the conspiracy.

Adopted eff. 7-1-80

Evid R 802
Hearsay rule

Hearsay is not admissible except as otherwise provided by the Constitution of the United States, by the Constitution of the State of Ohio, by statute enacted by the General Assembly not in conflict with a rule of the Supreme Court of Ohio, by these rules, or by other rules prescribed by the Supreme Court of Ohio.

Adopted eff. 7-1-80

Evid R 803
Hearsay exceptions; availability of declarant immaterial

The following are not excluded by the hearsay rule, even though the declarant is available as a witness:

(1) Present sense impression.

A statement describing or explaining an event or condition made while the declarant was perceiving the event or condition, or immediately thereafter unless circumstances indicate lack of trustworthiness.

(2) Excited utterance.

A statement relating to a startling event or condition made while the declarant was under the stress of excitement caused by the event or condition.

(3) Then existing, mental, emotional, or physical condition.

A statement of the declarant's then existing state of mind, emotion, sensation, or physical condition (such as intent, plan, motive, design, mental feeling, pain, and bodily health), but not including a statement of memory or belief to prove the fact remembered or believed unless it relates to the execution, revocation, identification, or terms of declarant's will.

(4) Statements for purposes of medical diagnosis or treatment.

Statements made for purposes of medical diagnosis or treatment and describing medical history, or past or present symptoms, pain, or sensations, or the inception or general character of the cause or external source thereof insofar as reasonably pertinent to diagnosis or treatment.

(5) Recorded recollection.

A memorandum or record concerning a matter about which a witness once had knowledge but now has insufficient recollection to enable him to testify fully and accurately, shown by the testimony of the witness to have been made or adopted when the matter was fresh in his memory and to reflect that knowledge correctly. If admitted, the memorandum or record may be read into evidence but may not itself be received as an exhibit unless offered by an adverse party.

(6) Records of regularly conducted activity.

A memorandum, report, record, or data compilation, in any form, of acts, events, or conditions, made at or near the time by, or from information transmitted by, a person with knowledge, if kept in the course of a regularly conducted business activity, and if it was the regular practice of that business activity to make the memorandum, report, record, or data compilation, all as shown by the testimony of the custodian or other qualified witness or as provided by Rule 901(B)(10), unless the source of information or the method or circumstances of preparation indicate lack of trustworthiness. The term "business" as used in this paragraph includes business, institution, association, profession, occupation, and calling of every kind, whether or not conducted for profit.

(7) Absence of entry in record kept in accordance with the provisions of paragraph (6).

Evidence that a matter is not included in the memoranda, reports, records, or data compilations, in any form, kept in accordance with the provisions of paragraph (6), to prove the nonoccurrence or nonexistence of the matter, if the matter was of a kind of which a memorandum, report, record, or data compilation was regularly made and preserved, unless the sources of information or other circumstances indicate lack of trustworthiness.

(8) Public records and reports.

Records, reports, statements, or data compilations, in any form, of public offices or agencies, setting forth (a) the activities of the office or agency, or (b) matters observed pursuant to duty imposed by law as to which matters there was a duty to report, excluding, however, in criminal cases matters observed by police officers and other law enforcement personnel, unless offered by defendant, unless the sources of information or other circumstances indicate lack of trustworthiness.

(9) Records of vital statistics.

Records or data compilations, in any form, of births, fetal deaths, deaths, or marriages, if the report thereof was made to a public office pursuant to requirement of law.

(10) Absence of public record or entry.

To prove the absence of a record, report, statement, or data compilation, in any form, or the nonoccurrence or nonexistence of a matter of which a record, report, statement, or data compilation, in any form, was regularly made and preserved by a public office or agency, evidence in the form of a certification in accordance with Rule 901(B)(10) or testimony, that diligent search failed to disclose the record, report, statement, or data compilation, or entry.

(11) Records of religious organizations.

Statements of births, marriages, divorces, deaths, legitimacy, ancestry, relationship by blood or marriage, or other similar facts of personal or family history, contained in a regularly kept record of religious organization[1].

(12) Marriage, baptismal, and similar certificates.

Statements of fact contained in a certificate that the maker performed a marriage or other ceremony or administered a sacrament, made by a clergyman, public official, or other person authorized by the rules or practices of a religious organization or by law to perform the act certified, and purporting to have been issued at the time of the act or within a reasonable time thereafter.

(13) Family records.

Statements of fact concerning personal or family history contained in family Bibles, genealogies, charts, engravings on rings, inscriptions on family portraits, engravings on urns, crypts, or tombstones, or the like.

(14) Records of documents affecting an interest in property.

The record of a document purporting to establish or affect an interest in property, as proof of the content of the original recorded document and its execution and delivery by each person by whom it purports to have been executed, if the record is a record of a public office and an applicable statute authorizes the recording of documents of that kind in that office.

(15) Statements in documents affecting an interest in property.

A statement contained in a document purporting to establish or affect an interest in property if the matter stated was relevant to the purpose of the document, unless dealings with the property since the document was made have been inconsistent with the truth of the statement or the purport of the document.

(16) Statements in ancient documents.

Statements in a document in existence twenty years or more the authenticity of which is established.

(17) Market reports, commercial publications.

Market quotations, tabulations, lists, directories, or other published compilations, generally used and relied upon by the public or by persons in particular occupations.

(18) Reputation concerning personal or family history.

Reputation among members of his family by blood, adoption, or marriage or among his associates, or in the community, concerning a person's birth, adoption, marriage, divorce, death, legitimacy, relationship by blood, adoption or marriage, ancestry, or other similar fact of his personal or family history.

(19) Reputation concerning boundaries or general history.

Reputation in a community, arising before the controversy, as to boundaries of or customs affecting lands in the community, and reputation as to events of general history important to the community or state or nation in which located.

(20) Reputation as to character.

Reputation of a person's character among his associates or in the community.

(21) Judgment of previous conviction.

Evidence of a final judgment, entered after a trial or upon a plea of guilty (but not upon a plea of no contest or the equivalent plea from another jurisdiction), adjudging a person guilty of a crime punishable by death or imprisonment in excess of one year, to prove any fact essential to sustain the judgment, but not including, when offered by the Government in a criminal prosecution for purposes other than impeachment, judgments against persons other than the accused. The pendency of an appeal may be shown but does not affect admissibility.

(22) Judgment as to personal, family, or general history, or boundaries.

Judgments as proof of matters of personal, family or general history, or boundaries, essential to the judgment, if the same would be provable by evidence of reputation.

Adopted eff. 7-1-80

[1] So in 62 OS(2d) xlvi; federal rule reads "a religious organization."

Evid R 804

Hearsay exceptions; declarant unavailable

(A) Definition of unavailability.

"Unavailability as a witness" includes situations in which the declarant:

(1) is exempted by ruling of the court on the ground of privilege from testifying concerning the subject matter of his statement; or

(2) persists in refusing to testify concerning the subject matter of his statement despite an order of the court to do so; or

(3) testifies to a lack of memory of the subject matter of his statement; or

(4) is unable to be present or to testify at the hearing because of death or then existing physical or mental illness or infirmity; or

(5) is absent from the hearing and the proponent of his statement has been unable to procure his attendance (or in the case of a hearsay exception under subdivision (B)(2), (3), or (4), his attendance or testimony) by process or other reasonable means. A declarant is not unavailable as a witness if his exemption, refusal, claim of lack of memory, inability, or absence is due to the procurement or wrongdoing of the proponent of his statement for the purpose of preventing the witness from attending or testifying.

(B) Hearsay exceptions.

The following are not excluded by the hearsay rule if the declarant is unavailable as a witness:

(1) Former testimony. Testimony given as a witness at another hearing of the same or a different proceeding, or in a deposition taken in compliance with law in the course of the same or another proceeding, if the party against whom the testimony is now offered, or, in a civil action or proceeding, a predecessor in interest, had an opportunity and similar motive to develop the testimony by direct, cross, or redirect examination. Testimony given at a preliminary hearing must satisfy the right to confrontation and exhibit indicia of reliability.

(2) Statement under belief of impending death. In a prosecution for homicide or in a civil action or proceeding, a statement made by a declarant while believing that his death was imminent, concerning the cause or circumstances of what he believed to be his impending death.

(3) Statement against interest. A statement which was at the time of its making so far contrary to the declarant's pecuniary or proprietary interest, or so far tended to subject him to civil or criminal liability, or to render invalid a claim by him against another, that a reasonable man in his position would not have made the statement unless he believed it to be true. A statement tending to expose the declarant to criminal liability, whether offered to exculpate or inculpate the accused, is not admissible unless corroborating circumstances clearly

indicate the trustworthiness of the statement.

(4) Statement of personal or family history. (a) A statement concerning the declarant's own birth, adoption, marriage, divorce, legitimacy, relationship by blood, adoption, or marriage, ancestry, or other similar fact of personal or family history, even though declarant had no means of acquiring personal knowledge of the matter stated; or (b) a statement concerning the foregoing matters, and death also, of another person, if the declarant was related to the other by blood, adoption, or marriage or was so intimately associated with the other's family as to be likely to have accurate information concerning the matter declared.

(5) Statement by a deceased, deaf-mute, or incompetent person. The statement was made by a decedent, or a deaf-mute who is now unable to testify, or a mentally incompetent person, where (a) the estate or personal representative of the decedent's estate, or the guardian or trustee of the deaf-mute or incompetent person is a party, and (b) the statement was made before the death or the development of the deaf-mute condition or the incompetency, and (c) the statement is offered to rebut testimony by an adverse party on a matter which was within the knowledge of the decedent, deaf-mute, or incompetent person.

Adopted eff. 7-1-80; amended eff. 7-1-81

Evid R 805

Hearsay within hearsay

Hearsay included within hearsay is not excluded under the hearsay rule if each part of the combined statements conforms with an exception to the hearsay rule provided in these rules.

Adopted eff. 7-1-80

Evid R 806

Attacking and supporting credibility of declarant

When a hearsay statement, or a statement defined in Rule 801(D)(2), (c), (d), or (e), has been admitted in evidence, the credibility of the declarant may be attacked, and if attacked may be supported, by any evidence which would be admissible for those purposes if declarant had testified as a witness. Evidence of a statement or conduct by the declarant at any time, inconsistent with his hearsay statement, is not subject to any requirement that he may have been afforded an opportunity to deny or explain. If the party against whom a hearsay statement has been admitted calls the declarant as a witness, the party is entitled to examine him on the statement as if under cross-examination.

Adopted eff. 7-1-80

Article IX
AUTHENTICATION AND IDENTIFICATION

Evid R 901

Requirement of authentication or identification

(A) General provision.

The requirement of authentication or identification as a condition precedent to admissibility is satisfied by evidence suffi-

cient to support a finding that the matter in question is what its proponent claims.

(B) Illustrations.

By way of illustration only, and not by way of limitation, the following are examples of authentication or identification conforming with the requirements of this rule:

(1) Testimony of witness with knowledge. Testimony that a matter is what it is claimed to be.

(2) Nonexpert opinion on handwriting. Nonexpert opinion as to the genuineness of handwriting, based upon familiarity not acquired for purposes of the litigation.

(3) Comparison by trier or expert witness. Comparison by the trier of fact or by expert witness with specimens which have been authenticated.

(4) Distinctive characteristics and the like. Appearance, contents, substance, internal patterns, or other distinctive characteristics, taken in conjunction with circumstances.

(5) Voice identification. Identification of a voice, whether heard firsthand or through mechanical or electronic transmission or recording, by opinion based upon hearing the voice at any time under circumstances connecting it with the alleged speaker.

(6) Telephone conversations. Telephone conversations, by evidence that a call was made to the number assigned at the time by the telephone company to a particular person or business, if (a) in the case of a person, circumstances, including self-identification, show the person answering to be the one called, or (b) in the case of a business, the call was made to a place of business and the conversation related to business reasonably transacted over the telephone.

(7) Public records or reports. Evidence that a writing authorized by law to be recorded or filed and in fact recorded or filed in a public office, or a purported public record, report, statement, or data compilation, in any form, is from the public office where items of this nature are kept.

(8) Ancient documents or data compilation. Evidence that a document or data compilation, in any form, (a) is in such condition as to create no suspicion concerning its authenticity, (b) was in a place where it, if authentic, would likely be, and (c) has been in existence twenty years or more at the time it is offered.

(9) Process or system. Evidence describing a process or system used to produce a result and showing that the process or system produces an accurate result.

(10) Methods provided by statute or rule. Any method of authentication or identification provided by statute enacted by the General Assembly not in conflict with a rule of the Supreme Court of Ohio or by other rules prescribed by the Supreme Court.

Adopted eff. 7-1-80

Evid R 902
Self-authentication

Extrinsic evidence of authenticity as a condition precedent to admissibility is not required with respect to the following:

(1) Domestic public documents under seal.

A document bearing a seal purporting to be that of the United States, or of any State, district, Commonwealth, territory, or insular possession thereof, or the Panama Canal Zone, or the Trust Territory of the Pacific Islands, or of a political subdivision, department, officer, or agency thereof, and a signature purporting to be an attestation or execution.

(2) Domestic public documents not under seal.

A document purporting to bear the signature in his official capacity of an officer or employee of any entity included in paragraph (1) hereof, having no seal, if a public officer having a seal and having official duties in the district or political subdivision of the officer or employee certifies under seal that the signer has the official capacity and that the signature is genuine.

(3) Foreign public documents.

A document purporting to be executed or attested in his official capacity by a person authorized by the laws of a foreign country to make the execution or attestation, and accompanied by a final certification as to the genuineness of the signature and official position (a) of the executing or attesting person, or (b) of any foreign official whose certificate of genuineness of signature and official position relates to the execution or attestation or is in a chain of certificates of genuineness of signature and official position relating to the execution or attestation. A final certification may be made by a secretary of embassy or legation, consul general, consul, vice consul, or consular agent of the United States, or a diplomatic or consular official of the foreign country assigned or accredited to the United States. If reasonable opportunity has been given to all parties to investigate the authenticity and accuracy of official documents, the court may, for good cause shown, order that they be treated as presumptively authentic without final certification or permit them to be evidenced by an attested summary with or without final certification.

(4) Certified copies of public records.

A copy of an official record or report or entry therein, or of a document authorized by law to be recorded or filed and actually recorded or filed in a public office, including data compilations in any form, certified as correct by the custodian or other person authorized to make the certification, by certificate complying with paragraph (1), (2), or (3) of this rule or complying with any law of a jurisdiction, state or federal, or rule prescribed by the Supreme Court of Ohio.

(5) Official publications.

Books, pamphlets, or other publications purporting to be issued by public authority.

(6) Newspapers and periodicals.

Printed materials purporting to be newspapers or periodicals, including notices and advertisements contained therein.

(7) Trade inscriptions and the like.

Inscriptions, signs, tags, or labels purporting to have been affixed in the course of business and indicating ownership, control, or origin.

(8) Acknowledged documents.

Documents accompanied by a certificate of acknowledgment executed in the manner provided by law by a notary public or other officer authorized by law to take acknowledgments.

(9) Commercial paper and related documents.

Commercial paper, signatures thereon, and documents relating thereto to the extent provided by general commercial law.

(10) Presumptions created by law.

Any signature, document, or other matter declared by any law of a jurisdiction, state or federal, to be presumptively or prima facie genuine or authentic.

Adopted eff. 7-1-80

Evid R 903

Subscribing witness' testimony unnecessary

The testimony of a subscribing witness is not necessary to authenticate a writing unless required by the laws of the jurisdiction whose laws govern the validity of the writing.

Adopted eff. 7-1-80

Article X
CONTENTS OF WRITINGS, RECORDINGS AND PHOTOGRAPHS

Evid R 1001
Definitions

For purposes of this article the following definitions are applicable:

(1) Writings and recordings.

"Writings" and "recordings" consist of letters, words, or numbers, or their equivalent, set down by handwriting, typewriting, printing, photostating, photographing, magnetic impulse, mechanical or electronic recording, or other forms of date[1] compilation.

(2) Photographs.

"Photographs" include still photographs, X-ray films, video tapes, and motion pictures.

(3) Original.

An "original" of a writing or recording is the writing or recording itself or any counterpart intended to have the same effect by a person executing or issuing it. An "original" of a photograph includes the negative or any print therefrom. If data are stored in a computer or similar device, any printout or other output readable by sight, shown to reflect the data accurately, is an "original".

(4) Duplicate.

A "duplicate" is a counterpart produced by the same impression as the original, or from the same matrix, or by means of photography, including enlargements and miniatures, or by mechanical or electronic re-recording, or by chemical reproduction, or by other equivalent techniques which accurately reproduce the original.

Adopted eff. 7-1-80

[1]So in original; should this read "data"?

Evid R 1002
Requirement of original

To prove the content of a writing, recording, or photograph, the original writing, recording, or photograph is required, except as otherwise provided in these rules or by statute enacted by the General Assembly not in conflict with a rule of the Supreme Court of Ohio.

Adopted eff. 7-1-80

Evid R 1003
Admissibility of duplicates

A duplicate is admissible to the same extent as an original unless (1) a genuine question is raised as to the authenticity of the original or (2) in the circumstances it would be unfair to admit the duplicate in lieu of the original.

Adopted eff. 7-1-80

Evid R 1004
Admissibility of other evidence of contents

The original is not required, and other evidence of the contents of a writing, recording, or photograph is admissible if:

(1) Originals lost or destroyed.

All originals are lost or have been destroyed, unless the proponent lost or destroyed them in bad faith; or

(2) Original not obtainable.

No original can be obtained by any available judicial process or procedure; or

(3) Original in possession of opponent.

At a time when an original was under the control of the party against whom offered, he was put on notice, by the pleadings or otherwise, that the contents would be subject of proof at the hearing, and he does not produce the original at the hearing; or

(4) Collateral matters.

The writing, recording, or photograph is not closely related to a controlling issue.

Adopted eff. 7-1-80

Evid R 1005
Public records

The contents of an official record, or of a document authorized to be recorded or filed and actually recorded or filed, including data compilations in any form if otherwise admissible, may be proved by copy, certified as correct in accordance with Rule 902, Civ. R. 44, Crim. R. 27 or testified to be correct by a witness who has compared it with the original. If a copy which complies with the foregoing cannot be obtained by the exercise of reasonable diligence, then other evidence of the contents may be given.

Adopted eff. 7-1-80

Evid R 1006
Summaries

The contents of voluminous writings, recordings, or photographs which cannot conveniently be examined in court may be presented in the form of a chart, summary, or calculation. The originals, or duplicates, shall be made available for examination or copying, or both, by other parties at a reasonable time and place. The court may order that they be produced in court.

Adopted eff. 7-1-80

Evid R 1007
Testimony or written admission of party

Contents of writings, recordings, or photographs may be proved by the testimony or deposition of the party against whom offered or by his written admission, without accounting for the nonproduction of the original.

Adopted eff. 7-1-80

Evid R 1008
Functions of court and jury

When the admissibility of other evidence of contents of writings, recordings, or photographs under these rules depends upon the fulfillment of a condition of fact, the question whether the condition has been fulfilled is ordinarily for the court to determine in accordance with the provisions of Rule 104. However, when an issue is raised (a) whether the asserted writing ever existed, or (b) whether another writing, recording, or photograph produced at the trial is the original, or (c) whether other evidence of contents correctly reflects the contents, the issue is for the trier of fact to determine as in the case of other issues of fact.

Adopted eff. 7-1-80

Article XI
MISCELLANEOUS RULES

Evid R 1101
[Reserved]

Evid R 1102
Effective date

(A) Effective date of rules.

These rules shall take effect on the first day of July, 1980. They govern all proceedings in actions brought after they take effect and also all further proceedings in actions then pending, except to the extent that in the opinion of the court their application in a particular action pending when the rules take effect would not be feasible or would work injustice, in which event former evidentiary principles apply.

(B) Effective date of amendments.

The amendments submitted by the Supreme Court to the General Assembly on January 14, 1981, and on April 29, 1981, shall take effect on July 1, 1981. They govern all proceedings in actions brought after they take effect and also all further proceedings in actions then pending, except to the extent that their application in a particular action pending when the amendments take effect would not be feasible or would work injustice, in which event the former procedure applies.

Adopted eff. 7-1-80; amended eff. 7-1-81

Evid R 1103
Title

These rules shall be known as the Ohio Rules of Evidence and may be cited as "Evidence Rules" or "Evid. R. ___."

Adopted eff. 7-1-80

APPENDICES

A. Table of Cases
B. Table of Laws and Rules Construed
C. Glossary
D. Bibliography

Appendix A
Table of Cases

This table is arranged alphabetically letter-by-letter; i.e., each group of words comprising a casename is considered as a continuous series of letters. For example, *Harrison; State v* would precede *Harris; United States v.*

For citation and subsequent case history, consult the Text Section(s) listed.

Casename	Text Section(s)
A	
Adams; State v	9.01, 9.04(B)
Adoption of McDermitt, In re	7.03(L)
Adoption of Schoeppner, In re	3.06(C)
Agler, In re	1.04, 3.02, 11.03, 11.07, 11.10, 11.11, 11.13
Agosto, In re	11.11(A)
Ake v Oklahoma	11.11(E)
Alabama; Boykin v	11.06
Alabama; Taylor v	5.04
Alaska; Davis v	1.02(I), 11.12, 15.04(A)
Albin; State ex rel Turner v	7.05(B), 15.01(D)
Alderman v United States	5.01
Alexander, In re	15.02(F)
Allaman; Mobley v	7.05(D)
Allaman; State ex rel Clark v	7.03(J), (L)
Allaman; State ex rel Peaks v	1.04, 7.06(E)
Allen; Illinois v	11.12
Allstate Insurance Co v Cook	15.04(A)
Alvis; Harris v	3.10(B)
Alvis; Mellot v	3.10(B)
Anderson v Charles	5.04(B)
Anderson; Jenkins v	5.04(B)
Anderson; Raleigh Fitkin-Paul Morgan Memorial Hospital v	3.06(D)
Andresen v Maryland	5.03(B)
Angle v Holmes County Welfare Dept Children's Services Div	3.09(E)
Anonymous, In re	9.03(E)
Anteau, In re	7.03(C)
Anthony P., In re	11.02
Anthony S., In re	7.01
Appeal in Pima County, Juvenile Action, In re	11.15

Casename	Text Section(s)
Appeal No. 245, In re	5.04
Appeal No. 544, In re	11.06
Appeal of a Juvenile, In re	11.03
Application of A. and M., In re	11.11(A)
Argersinger v Hamlin	9.03(B)
Arizona; Edwards v	5.04(B), (C), 5.05(B)
Arizona v Hicks	5.03(C)
Arizona v Mauro	5.04(B)
Arizona; Mincey v	5.04(A), (B)
Arizona; Miranda v	1.02(E), 5.04
Arizona v Roberson	5.04(B)
Arkansas; Cole v	9.03(C)
Arkansas; Holloway v	11.03
Arnold; State v	9.02(D)
Artler, In re	3.06(A), (D)
Ashtabula County Children Services Board; Howser v	7.03(A)
Ash; United States v	5.05(B)
Atkinson v Grumman Ohio Corp	13.03
Atwell, In re	3.10(C), 11.04
Auger; Speck v	9.02
Auglaize County Welfare Dept; Sink v	15.03
Auterson, In re	3.10(C)
Azure; United States v	11.11(E)
B	
Baby Girl Baxter, In re	11.01, 11.03, 11.11
Baby Girl S., In re	3.05, 3.07(D), 13.06(A)
Baker, In re (1982)	7.03(C), (L)
Baker, In re (1969)	3.02, 5.01, 11.11
Bambrick; State ex rel Wilson v	11.03
Banks, In re	7.03(I), 7.05(B), 11.06, 13.06(A)
Barbine; Moran v	5.04(B)
Barker v Wingo	11.02
Barrett; Connecticut v	5.04(B)
Barzak, In re	11.03, 11.11(A), (B)

Casename	Text Section(s)	Casename	Text Section(s)
Baumgartner, In re	13.06(A)	Breed v Jones	1.02(E), 9.02,
Baxter, In re	13.02		9.06, 11.01,
Bayer; Clark v	13.06(A)		11.15
Beatty v Riegel	15.04(A)	Brenda H., In re	3.06(C)
Becker, In re	9.05, 15.02(A),	Brenson v Havener	9.06
	(B)	Brent, In re	5.03(D)
Beckwith v United States	5.04(B)	Brewer; Morrissey v	9.03(C), 11.12
Beheler; California v	5.04(B)	Brewer v Williams	5.04(C), 5.05(B)
Bell, In re	7.03(I), 7.05(A)	Brewster; State v	15.04(A)
Bell; State v	5.04(A), (B)	Bridges, In re	7.03(F)
Belton; New York v	5.03(C)	Bridges v Lucas County	
Bennett, In re	3.05	Children Services Bd	7.03(L)
Benn, In re	11.07	Brinegar v United States	5.03(B)
Benton v Maryland	11.15	Brookhart v Janis	11.12
Berkemer v McCarty	5.04(B)	Brown v Illinois	5.01, 5.04
Bernstein, In re	3.03, 7.03(F),	Brown, In re (1986)	11.11(E)
	7.08(A)	Brown, In re (1979)	7.03(C),
Bertine; Colorado v	5.03(C)		7.05(C), (D),
Beyer; Normandy Place			13.02
Associates v	15.02(B)	Brown, In re (1976)	15.02(G)
Bibb, In re	3.07(A), (C),	Brown, In re (1971)	9.03(H)
	11.10, 13.02,	Brown; Mill v	1.01(B)
	15.03	Brown v Ohio	11.15
Bickerstaff; State v	9.04(B), 11.02	Brown; State v	9.02
Biedenharn; State v	7.03(A)	Brown; Texas v	5.03(C)
Biggers; Neil v	5.05(C)	Brown v Wainwright	9.01
Bingham v Hartman	15.04(A)	Bryan, In re	9.06
Birch v Birch	7.03(J)	Bryan v Superior Court	9.03(F)
Bishop v Ezzone	7.03(A)	Bryant, In re	3.07(D),
Bishop, In re	3.05, 3.07(A),		7.03(L), 7.05(B),
	(D), 11.10		13.02
Black; Holt v	9.06	Buchholtz; State v	5.04(B)
Black, In re (1981)	13.02	Bullard, In re	9.01, 9.02
Black, In re (1980)	11.11(D)	Bumper v North Carolina	5.03(D)
Black; State v	11.11(G)	Bundy, In re	7.03(L)
Black; State ex rel Leis v	3.10(B)	Bundy; Ironton v	7.03(K)
Blankenship, In re	7.03(I)	Burchett, State ex rel v	
Bleier v Crouse	1.04, 7.05(A)	Juvenile Court for	
Board of—See name of		Scioto County	7.04(A)
particular board.		Burdeau v McDowell	5.03(A)
Bolan; State v	5.04(B)	Bureau of—See name of	
Bolden, In re	11.03, 13.02,	particular bureau.	
	13.07(B), (C),	Burgess, In re (1984)	3.02, 7.03(C),
	15.02(B)		(K)
Bortree; State v	5.03(D)	Burgess, In re (1980)	3.04
Bourjaily v United States	11.12	Burgun; State v	7.03(C), (D)
Bowen, In re	7.04(A)	Burkhart, In re	3.05, 3.07(B)
Bowers; United States v	11.11(E)	Burrell, In re	3.06(C), 3.07(B)
Bowman, In re	3.07(B), 13.02,	Bustamonte; Schneckloth	
	13.06(A)	v	5.03(D)
Boyer, In re	3.02, 3.07(A),	Butler; North Carolina v	5.04(B)
	15.01(C)	Butler; State v	3.02
Boykin v Alabama	11.06	Butler, State ex rel v	
Bradford, In re	11.16	Demis	11.03
Bradshaw; Oregon v	5.04(B)	Butt, In re	15.03
Brady; Swisher v	1.02(E), 11.01,	Byrd, In re	7.03(J),
	11.15		13.06(A)
Brathwaite; Manson v	5.05(C)		

Casename	Text Section(s)	Casename	Text Section(s)
Cox; James v	9.03(B), (C)	Deiz; State ex rel Oregonian Publishing Co v	11.08
Cox; State v	11.11(F), 15.04(A)	DeLong; State v	11.11(A)
Cox v Turley	7.06(A)	Demis; State ex rel Butler v	11.03
Coy v Iowa	11.12		
Cradle v Peyton	9.01	Dennis M., In re	5.04(B)
Crandell v State	9.03(C)	Denno; Stovall v	5.05(C)
Creek, In re	5.04(B)	Department of—See also name of particular department.	
Crisp, In re	3.07(B)		
Crose, In re	7.03(I), (L), 11.11(B), 13.03	Department of Social Services; Lassiter v	1.02(F), 11.01, 11.03, 15.02(F)
Crouse; Bleier v	1.04, 7.05(A)		
Crouse, Ex parte	1.01(B)	De Pasquale; Gannett Co v	11.08
Crowe, In re	3.02	DeSanti; J.P. v (1981)	7.08(B)
Crowell; State v	3.03	DeSanti; J.P. v (1978)	7.08(B)
Culombe v Connecticut	5.04(A)	D.H.; State v	3.10(A)
Cunningham, In re	3.05, 11.01, 13.01, 13.02, 13.06(A)	Diana A., In re	11.09
		Diane P., In re	5.01
Cunningham; State v	3.10(C)	Dickerson, In re	3.06(B)
Cuyahoga County Welfare Dept; Watts v	3.08	Diebler v State	7.03(K)
		Dillon, In re	3.07(B)
Cuyler v Sullivan	11.03	Dillon Jr., In re	3.08
D		Dingfelt; Commonwealth v	5.03(E)
Dague, In re	13.10	Dionisio; United States v	5.03(A), 5.05(A)
Daily Mail Publishing Co; Smith v	1.02(I), 11.08	Dissolution of Marriage of Sisinger, In re	15.02(B)
Dake, In re	3.07(B)	District Court of Oklahoma; Oklahoma Publishing Co v	1.02(I)
Dalton; R.W.T. v	7.06(C)		
Dandoy, State ex rel v Superior Court of County of Pima	11.04	Dodez; Gishwiler v	13.06(A)
		Doe, In re (NM)	9.03(H)
Daniels, In re	7.03(L)	Doe, In re (Hawaii)	3.04
Daniel T., In re	5.05(B), (C)	Doe, In re (Ohio)	13.01
Darnell, In re	1.04, 11.07	Dolibor, In re	7.03(K)
Darst, In re	3.05, 3.07(A), (B), 13.02	Dollison; Gebell v	13.09(G), 15.04(B)
Daudt v Daudt	13.07(B)	Donald L. v Superior Court of Los Angeles County	9.02, 9.04(A), 11.09
Daudt, In re	13.07(B), 13.10		
Davis v Alaska	1.02(I), 11.12, 15.04(A)		
		Donaldson, In re	5.03(E)
Davis, In re (1984)	13.06(A)	Douglas, In re	3.06(C), 3.07(A), 7.01, 7.07(A)
Davis, In re (1982)	7.03(C)		
Davis, In re (1961)	3.10(A), 7.04(B)		
Davis v State	9.02	Douglas; State v	1.04, 9.01, 9.02(D), 9.03(D), (I)
Davis; State v	5.03, 5.05(D)		
Davis v Trumbull County Children Services Bd	3.07(D)		
Day, In re	13.07(B)	Doyle v Ohio	5.04(B)
Day; Kenton Bd of Ed v	13.01	Draper v United States	5.03(B)
Deborah C., In re	5.04(B)	Draper v Washington	13.03
Decker, In re (App)	11.11(A)	Drope v Missouri	11.04
Decker, In re (Juv)	7.03(C)	Drushal v Drushal	13.06(A)
DeGeronimo, In re	3.02, 3.10(A), 13.07(B), 15.01(B)	Du Bose v Court of Common Pleas	9.06

Casename	Text Section(s)
Garth D., In re	5.04(A)
Gates; Illinois v	5.03(B)
Gault, In re	1.02(B), 5.02,
	7.03(C),
	7.05(A), 7.06(E),
	9.01, 9.03(B),
	(C), (F), 11.01,
	11.03, 11.12 to
	11.14, 15.02(F)
Gebell v Dollison	13.09(G),
	15.04(B)
Geboy v Gray	9.01, 9.03(B),
	(C)
Georgia; Waller v	11.08
Gerstein v Pugh	5.02
Gibbs; State v	9.02, 9.03(C)
Gideon v Wainwright	5.05(B), 9.03(B)
Gilbert v California	5.05(A), (B)
Gilbert, In re (1987)	7.08(A)
Gilbert, In re (1974)	11.15, 15.02(E)
Gillies; Von Moltke v	11.03
Gilman; Williams County	
Dept of Soc Services v	11.03
Gishwiler v Dodez	13.06(A)
Gladys R., In re	3.10(A)
Glenn, In re	11.14
Globe Newspaper Co v	
Superior Court for	
County of Norfolk	11.08
G.M.K. v State	11.06
Goldberg v Kelly	11.12
Goshorn, In re	7.04(A)
Gossick, In re	7.06(D)
Grady; State v	13.07(B)
Graham v Graham	15.02(B)
Grand Jury Proceedings,	
In re	11.11(A)
Gray; Geboy v	9.01, 9.03(B),
	(C)
Gray; Mann v	15.04(A)
Gray; State v	3.06(D)
Green; California v	11.12
Green, In re (1984)	7.08(B), 11.10,
	11.11(E)
Green, In re (1982)	11.05
Greenwood; California v	5.03(A)
Gregory v Flowers	1.04
Gregory W. and Gerald	
S., In re	1.01(C)
Griffin v California	9.03(F), 11.13
Griffin v Illinois	11.14
Griffin; State v	3.07(A)
Grooms; State v	9.02(D),
	9.03(D)
Grossmann; Smith v	11.01
Grossmann; State ex rel	
Henry v	15.02(F)

Casename	Text Section(s)
Grubbs, In re	3.07(B),
	15.02(G)
Grumman Ohio Corp;	
Atkinson v	13.03
Gustafson v Florida	5.03(C)
Guthrie, In re	3.05, 13.02,
	13.03
Gutman, In re	3.07(B), (D),
	13.01

H

Casename	Text Section(s)
Haas, In re	13.03
Hadsell, In re	3.07(C), 7.03(I),
	13.06(A)
Hale, In re	13.07(B)
Hale; State v	11.11(F),
	15.04(A)
Haley v Ohio	1.01(C), 5.04(A)
Hall, In re	13.07(B)
Hamil, In re	13.10
Hamlin; Argersinger v	9.03(B)
Hampton, In re	11.15, 15.02(B)
Handelsman v	
Handelsman	3.01
Hardesty v Hardesty	3.01
Harris v Alvis	3.10(B)
Harris, In re	9.03(E)
Harris v New York	5.04(A), (B)
Harris; State v (App)	9.02(D), 9.03(J)
Harris; State v (OS)	5.04(B)
Harshey, In re	3.06(F)
Hartman; Bingham v	15.04(A)
Hartman, In re	15.02(A)
Hartshorne v Hartshorne	3.01, 7.03(J)
Harvey, In re	5.02
Haslam v Haslam	7.03(J)
Hass; Oregon v	5.04(B)
Havener; Brenson v	9.06
Hawkins, In re (1983)	5.04, 7.06(A),
	11.11(A)
Hawkins, In re (1981)	3.07(B)
Hawkins; State v	9.02(D)
Hayden; Warden,	
Maryland Penitentiary	
v	5.03(C)
Hayes, In re (1986)	3.02, 11.11(F),
	15.04(A)
Hayes, In re (1939)	3.06(C),
	3.07(B), 7.03(C)
Hayes v Municipal Court	
of Oklahoma City	3.04
Haziel v United States	9.03(B)
Heard; Port v	11.11(A)
Hederson, In re	13.06(A)
Height, In re	7.03(J), 11.03
Heightland, In re	3.07(B)
Heising, In re	9.03(I)
Heist, In re	1.04

Casename	Text Section(s)
Larry and Scott H., In re	3.05, 3.07(B), (C)
Lassiter v Department of Social Services	1.02(F), 11.01, 11.03, 15.02(F)
Lathan; State v	5.05(B)
Lavrich; Lesher v	13.05(F)
Leach v State	5.04(B)
Lee, In re	3.07(B), 7.03(L), 13.06(B)
Lee; State v (App(3d))	11.11(D)
Lee; State v (8th Dist App)	3.02, 7.08(A)
Lefkowitz v Turley	9.03(F)
Lehman v Lycoming County Children's Services Agency	15.03
Leis, State ex rel v Black	3.10(B)
Leonard v Licker	1.04
Leonard; State v	9.03(D)
Leon; United States v	5.01
Lesher v Lavrich	13.05(F)
Lewandowski, In re	7.03(F)
Lewis, In re	7.03(I)
Lewis v Reed	7.05(A), 15.03
Lewis; State v	11.11(D)
Lewis v United States	11.12
Licker; Leonard v	1.04
Likens, In re	3.01, 3.07(D), 7.03(K)
Lindsay v Lindsay	1.01(B)
Lindsay; State v	3.02
Linger, In re	3.05, 7.07(C)
Linger v Weiss	1.04, 7.06(C), (D), 7.07(C), 11.02, 13.02, 15.03
L., In re	11.08
Lipker; State v	5.04(B)
Lippitt, In re	3.01, 3.06(D), 15.02(F)
Livingston, In re	3.07(C)
Lockhart, In re	7.03(L)
Long; State v	3.03
Louisiana; Duncan v	11.07
Louisiana; Tague v	5.04(B)
Lowder; State v	15.04(A)
Loyd; State v	5.04(B)
Luallen, In re	3.07(D), 7.05(A)
Lucas County Children Serv Bd; Elmer v	11.01, 11.06
Lucas County Children Services Bd; Bridges v	7.03(L)
Lucas, In re (1985)	11.11(B)
Lucas, In re (1982)	13.06(A)
Luchene v Wagner	15.03
Ludy v Ludy	3.07(B), 7.03(I)

Casename	Text Section(s)
Luke, In re	3.07(D), 13.06(A), (B), 15.01(A)
Lycoming County Children's Services Agency; Lehman v	15.03

M

Mack, In re	9.01, 11.15
MacPherson, In re	3.06(D), 7.04(A), 15.02(G)
Madison; State v	5.05(C)
Maine v Moulton	5.04(C)
Majoros; State v	3.02
Malloy v Hogan	5.05(A), 11.13
Malone v State	15.04(A)
Mann v Gray	15.04(A)
Mann; State v	15.04(A)
Manson v Brathwaite	5.05(C)
Mara; United States v	5.03(A), 5.05(A)
Marinski; State v	11.11(F), 15.04(A)
Mark J., In re	5.05(C)
Marks; State v	15.04(A)
Maroney; Chambers v	5.03(C)
Marshall, In re	3.08
Marsh, In re	5.03(C)
Martin, In re	13.09(G)
Martin v Ohio	11.10
Martin; Schall v	1.02(G), 7.06(C)
Mary B., In re	11.06
Maryland; Andresen v	5.03(B)
Maryland; Benton v	11.15
Maryland v Garrison	5.03(B)
Maryland; Kemplen v	1.02(B), 9.01, 9.03(B), (C), 9.05
Maryland; Smith v	5.03(A)
Massachusetts; Prince v	3.06(D)
Massachusetts v Sheppard	5.01
Massachusetts v Upton	5.03(B)
Massiah v United States	5.04(C)
Massie, In re	7.03(I)
Masters, In re	3.06(B), (C), 15.02(B)
Mathiason; Oregon v	5.04(B)
Matlock; United States v	5.03(D)
Mauro; Arizona v	5.04(B)
Maxwell; Sopko v	7.03(A)
Mayer v Chicago	11.14
McCall, In re	3.07(B), (C)
McCallister; State v	15.01(E)
McCarthy, In re	3.07(B), (D)
McCarthy v United States	11.06
McCarty; Berkemer v	5.04(B)
McCourt, In re	3.10(C)
McDonnell; Wolff v	9.03(C), (H)

Casename	Text Section(s)	Casename	Text Section(s)
McDowell; Burdeau v	5.03(A)	Morales, In re	15.02(A), (B)
McFadden v Kendall	3.01	Moran v Barbine	5.04(B)
McGinty; Pettry v	15.03	Morgan; Henderson v	11.06
McGuire; State v	15.04(A)	Morgan; State v	11.11(D)
McKeiver v Pennsylvania	1.02(B), (D), 11.01, 11.03, 11.07, 11.08	Morgan; St. Thomas Medical Center v	13.10
McKelvin, In re	5.05(B)	Morris, In re	5.03
McMann v Richardson	11.03	Morrison v Morrison	7.07(C), 15.02(B)
M.D., In re	3.10(A), 7.01	Morris; People v	9.03(E)
Medina v Coles	7.03(G)	Morrissey v Brewer	9.03(C), 11.12
Mellot v Alvis	3.10(B)	Morris; State v	5.03(A)
Mendenhall; State v	3.10(C)	Mosley; Michigan v	5.04(B)
Meng, State ex rel v Todaro	3.10(A)	Moss v Weaver	7.06(C)
Menich, In re	11.14	Motill, In re	15.02(B), (C)
Mercer v State	5.03(E)	Moulton; Maine v	5.04(C)
Messner, In re	15.05(B)	Mucci; People ex rel Guggenheim v	9.03(E)
Meyers; Florida v	5.03(C)	Mullaney v Wilbur	11.10
Michael C.; Fare v	1.02(E), 5.04(B)	Mullins; State v	11.11(G)
Michael P., In re	5.04(B)	Municipal Court of Oklahoma City; Hayes v	3.04
Michigan v Jackson	5.04(C)		
Michigan v Mosley	5.04(B)	Murchison, In re	11.09
Mill v Brown	1.01(B)	Murphy; Minnesota v	5.04(B)
Miller, In re (App(3d))	3.01, 7.05(C)	Murray; State ex rel Thompson v	3.01
Miller, In re (OS(3d))	11.03		
Miller, In re (1st Dist App)	7.05(A), 13.06(B)	Murray v United States	5.01
		Myer, In re	11.03
Miller, In re (OS(2d))	3.09(E)	Myers, In re	15.02(B)
Miller, In re (Juv)	3.06(D)		
Miller v Quatsoe	9.03(C)	**N**	
Miller; State v	11.06		
Miller; State ex rel Heller v	3.05, 11.03, 11.14, 13.01, 15.02(F)	Nagle, State ex rel v Olin	3.06(D)
		Nance, In re	7.03(L)
		Nardone v United States	5.01
		Neff, In re	7.03(C), (I), 15.02(A), (G)
Miller; United States v	5.03(A)	Neil v Biggers	5.05(C)
Mincey v Arizona	5.04(A), (B)	New Hampshire; Coolidge v	5.03(B), (C)
Minnesota v Murphy	5.04(B)		
Minor Boy v State	5.02	New Jersey v T.L.O.	1.02(H), 5.03
M., In re (1979)	13.06(A), (B)	Newton, In re	15.01(D)
M., In re (1972)	5.03(C)	Newton; State v	1.04, 7.06(D), 9.03(A), (I), 11.02
Minton, In re	3.05		
Miranda v Arizona	1.02(E), 5.04		
Missouri; Drope v	11.04	New York v Belton	5.03(C)
Mobley v Allaman	7.05(D)	New York; Dunaway v	5.02, 5.04
Moloney; State ex rel Heth v	3.10(A), 15.01(B)	New York; Harris v	5.04(A), (B)
		New York; Patterson v	11.10
Monfreda, In re	15.01(B)	New York v Quarles	5.04(B)
Montgomery County Children Services Board v Kiszka	13.06(A), (B)	Nicholson, In re	3.06(D)
		Nix v Williams	5.01
		Nolte v Nolte	11.16, 15.02(B)
Moody; State v	5.05(C)	Normandy Place Associates v Beyer	15.02(B)
Moore v Illinois	5.05(B)		
Moore, In re	7.03(L), 13.02	North Carolina; Bumper v	5.03(D)
Moore v State	9.06	North Carolina v Butler	5.04(B)

Appendix B
Table of Laws and Rules Construed

ABBREVIATIONS

App R—Rules of Appellate Procedure
Civ R—Rules of Civil Procedure
Crim R—Rules of Criminal Procedure
Evid R—Rules of Evidence
Juv R—Rules of Juvenile Procedure
OAC—Ohio Administrative Code
O Const—Ohio Constitution
RC—Ohio Revised Code
Traf R—Traffic Rules
USC—United States Code
US Const—United States Constitution

O Const	Text Section(s)
Art I, § 5	11.07
Art I, § 9	7.06(E)
Art I, § 10	5.05(A), (B), 11.02, 11.08, 11.12, 11.13, 11.15, 15.02(F)
Art I, § 14	5.03
Art IV, § 3(B)(2)	15.02(A)
Art IV, § 5(B)	1.04, 7.05(C)

RC	Text Section(s)
3.20	7.03(F)
329.01	3.06(D)
341.11	7.06(A)
1347.04(A)(1)(e)	7.08(B)
1347.08	7.08(B)
2111.46	7.03(J)
Ch 2151	1.04
2151.01	3.07(B), 7.02
2151.01(A)	3.06(D), 13.01
2151.01(B)	13.01, 15.04(B)
2151.01(C)	13.01, 13.06(A)
2151.011	3.10(A), 13.07(B)
2151.011(A)(12)	13.10
2151.011(B)(1)	3.01, 3.10(A), 7.03(A), 9.01, 13.07(B), 15.01(B)
2151.011(B)(2)	7.03(A), 13.07(B)
2151.011(B)(5)	13.06(A)
2151.011(B)(6)	13.06(A)
2151.011(B)(9)	13.06(A)
2151.011(B)(10)	13.06(A), 15.01(B), (E)
2151.011(B)(11)	13.06(A)
2151.011(B)(12)	13.06(A), 15.01(B), (E)
2151.011(B)(13)	13.06(A)
2151.011(B)(15)	13.07(B)
2151.011(B)(16)	13.06(A)
2151.011(B)(17)	3.06(C)
2151.011(B)(25)	13.06(A)
2151.011(B)(26)	13.06(A)
2151.02	3.02, 3.03, 7.01, 7.03(D), 13.08(B), 13.09(A)

RC	Text Section(s)
2151.02(A)	7.06(D), 15.02(A)
2151.02(B)	3.02, 3.04, 7.06(D), 13.08(B), 15.01(C)
2151.021	3.03, 7.03(D), 13.07(A), 13.08(A)
2151.022	3.02, 3.04, 7.01
2151.022(B)	3.06(D)
2151.03	3.05, 3.06(A), (D), (F), 3.08, 3.10(A), 7.03(L), 13.06(A)
2151.03(A)	3.06(C), 3.06(F)
2151.03(B)	3.06(C), 3.06(D)
2151.03(C)	3.06(D)
2151.03(D)	3.06(E), 3.08
2151.03(E)	3.06(C), 3.06(F)
2151.031	3.05, 3.08, 13.06(A)
2151.031(D)	3.06(F)
2151.04	3.05, 3.07(A), 3.08, 7.03(L)
2151.04(A)	3.07(B)
2151.04(B)	3.06(C), 3.07(A), (C)
2151.04(C)	3.06(D), (E), 3.07, 7.03(C)
2151.04(D)	3.07(E)
2151.05	3.06(C)
2151.06	7.04(A)
2151.07	15.02(A)
2151.11	7.02
2151.12	7.01
2151.13	7.01, 7.03(F)
2151.14	13.07(B), 15.04(A)
2151.16	11.16
2151.18	7.01, 15.04(A)
2151.21	7.05(B), 13.10, 15.01(D)
2151.22	15.01(A)
2151.23	3.01, 7.06(D)
2151.23(A)(1)	3.01, 3.05, 7.03(L), 9.01
2151.23(A)(2)	3.05, 7.03(J), 13.06(A), 15.02(B), (G)
2151.23(A)(3)	15.03

RC	Text Section(s)	RC	Text Section(s)
2151.23(A)(4)	13.10	2151.312(A)	7.06(A), 9.04(B)
2151.23(A)(5)	15.04(B)	2151.312(B)	1.04, 7.06(A)
2151.23(A)(8)	3.09(A)	2151.312(C)	7.06(A)
2151.23(D)	3.01, 7.03(J)	2151.313	5.05(D)
2151.23(E)	7.03(J), 15.02(G)	2151.314	1.04, 7.03(B), 7.06(D),
2151.23(F)	7.03(H), (J)		13.04
2151.25	3.10(B), 9.01, 9.02(D),	2151.314(A)	7.06(C), 7.06(D)
	9.03(I)	2151.314(B)	7.06(C)
2151.26	1.04, 3.01, 3.02,	2151.314(B)(2)	7.05(A)
	3.10(A), 7.08(B), 9.01,	2151.314(C)	7.06(C)
	9.02(D), 9.03(A),	2151.314(D)	7.05(B)
	13.07(C)	2151.32	13.01
2151.26(A)	9.02(B), (C)	2151.33	3.06(D), 7.07(A), (C),
2151.26(A)(1)	9.02(D)		13.04, 13.06(A)
2151.26(A)(1)(a)	9.02(A)	2151.33(A)	7.06(E), 7.07(A), 13.10
2151.26(A)(2)	9.02(A), (D), 9.03(A)	2151.33(B)	7.07(A)
2151.26(A)(3)	9.03(A), (D)	2151.33(C)	7.07(A)
2151.26(B)	9.02(D), 13.10	2151.33(D)	7.07(B), (C)
2151.26(C)	9.03(A)	2151.33(E)	7.07(C)
2151.26(D)	9.03(C)	2151.33(F)	7.07(C)
2151.26(E)	3.10(B), 9.01, 15.01(B)	2151.34 to	
2151.26(F)	9.03(I), 9.04(B)	2151.3416	7.06(A)
2151.26(G)	9.04(B)	2151.34	7.06(A), (D), (E),
2151.27	3.10(A), 7.01, 7.03(A),		13.07(B)
	(B), (F), (I), (J), (L),	2151.35	3.05, 9.03(K), 11.01,
	7.05(C)		11.07, 11.08, 11.10,
2151.27(A)	7.03(A), (C), (F), (I),		11.12, 11.14, 13.06(A),
	(J), 7.04(A)		15.01(C), 15.04(A)
2151.27(C)	7.03(I)	2151.35(A)	7.05(A), 13.02, 13.03,
2151.271	3.01, 7.04(B)		15.02(F)
2151.28	7.05(C), (D)	2151.35(B)(1)	7.07(C), 13.02
2151.28(A)(1)	7.06(D), 11.02	2151.35(B)(2)	13.03
2151.28(A)(2)	7.07(C), 11.02	2151.35(B)(2)(a)	13.02
2151.28(B)	13.04	2151.35(B)(2)(c)	13.03
2151.28(B)(1)	7.05(A)	2151.35(B)(3)	13.03, 13.06(A)
2151.28(B)(3)	7.07(C), 13.02	2151.35(B)(4)	13.06(A)
2151.28(C)	7.05(A) to (C)	2151.35(C)	7.05(A)
2151.28(D)	5.02, 7.05(B)	2151.35(D)	7.03(E), 7.05(A)
2151.28(E)	7.05(B)	2151.35(F)	11.11(B)
2151.28(F)	7.05(B), 11.03	2151.35(G)	11.11(B)
2151.28(G)	7.06(C)	2151.351	3.02, 7.06(D)
2151.28(H)	7.05(D)	2151.3511	11.11(B), 11.12
2151.28(J)	7.05(B), (C), 15.01(D)	2151.352	7.08(A), (B), 9.03(B),
2151.281	1.04, 11.03		11.03, 11.08
2151.281(H)	11.03	2151.353 to	
2151.29	7.05(C), 13.06(B)	2151.356	13.01
2151.31 to		2151.353	3.05, 3.07(A), 7.03(J),
2151.314	7.06(E)		11.14, 13.07(B),
2151.31	5.02		13.08(B), 15.01(B), (F)
2151.31(A)	7.03(B), 7.06(C)	2151.353(A)	3.09(A), 7.03(E),
2151.31(A)(3)(c)	5.02		13.06(A), 15.01(B)
2151.31(A)(4)	5.02	2151.353(A)(4)	3.06(C), 7.03(E), 13.03,
2151.31(C)	7.06(B), (C)		13.06(A), (B), 13.07(B),
2151.31(D)	7.03(B), 7.07(B), 11.16		15.02(F)
2151.31(E)	7.07(B), 13.04	2151.353(B)	7.03(I), 7.05(B), 11.03,
2151.31(F)	7.07(B)		13.07(B)
2151.311(A)	7.06(A)	2151.353(C)	13.06(A), 13.10
2151.311(A)(1)	7.06(E)	2151.353(D)	13.05(C)

RC	Text Section(s)
2151.353(E)	15.01(B)
2151.353(F)	1.04, 13.06(A)
2151.353(G)	1.04, 13.06(A)
2151.353(H)	13.04
2151.354	3.02, 7.03(J), 13.08(B)
2151.354(A)	3.09(A), 7.03(I), 13.08(B)
2151.354(A)(2)	3.04, 13.08(B)
2151.354(A)(3)	13.08(B)
2151.354(B)	13.08(A)
2151.355	1.04, 3.02, 7.03(J), 13.07(B), (C), 15.01(E), 15.02(B)
2151.355(A)	3.02, 3.09(A), 13.07(B)
2151.355(A)(1)	7.03(I)
2151.355(A)(2) to (6)	13.10
2151.355(A)(4) to (6)	13.08(B), 15.01(B), (E)
2151.355(A)(4)	3.02, 13.07(C)
2151.355(A)(5)	3.02
2151.355(A)(8)	13.07(C), 13.10
2151.355(A)(10)	13.08(B)
2151.355(B)	13.07(A)
2151.355(C)	13.10
2151.355(D)(1)	13.07(B)
2151.355(E)	13.10
2151.356	13.08(B), 13.09(D), (G)
2151.356(A)(1)	13.09(B)
2151.356(A)(2)	13.09(B), (E), (G)
2151.356(A)(3) to (5)	13.09(B)
2151.356(B)	13.09(A)
2151.356(C)	13.09(C)
2151.356(D)	13.09(G)
2151.357	7.06(E), 13.01
2151.358	11.11(F), 13.09(G), 15.04(B)
2151.358(H)	11.11(F), 15.04(A)
2151.359	13.10
2151.36	13.10
2151.38	13.07(B), 15.01(B), (E)
2151.39	15.05(A)
2151.40	7.05(A)
2151.411	13.10
2151.412	1.04, 3.09(C), 13.06(B), 15.01(F), 15.02(B)
2151.412(A)	13.05(A)
2151.412(A)(2)	13.07(B)
2151.412(C)	13.05(B)
2151.412(D)	13.05(C)
2151.412(E)(1)	13.05(C)
2151.412(E)(2)	13.05(D), 15.01(F)
2151.412(E)(3)	13.05(D), 15.01(F)
2151.412(F) to (H)	13.05(E)
2151.413	1.04, 7.03(I), 13.06(A), (B)

RC	Text Section(s)
2151.414	1.04, 11.14, 13.03, 13.06(A), (B), 15.01(F), 15.02(F)
2151.414(A)	7.05(B)
2151.414(F)	7.03(E), 7.05(A)
2151.415	1.04, 13.06(A), 15.01(B), (F)
2151.416	1.04, 15.01(F)
2151.417	1.04, 13.05(D), 15.01(F), 15.02(B)
2151.417(B)	15.01(B)
2151.418	13.06(A)
2151.419	1.04, 7.06(C), 7.07(B), (C)
2151.419(A)	13.04
2151.419(B)	13.04
2151.421	7.03(A), 7.08(A), 11.11(A)
2151.45	15.05(B)
2151.54	13.07(B), 15.05(B)
2151.56	7.04(B), 15.05(A), (B)
2151.65	13.01, 13.07(B)
2151.99	7.03(A)
2151.99(B)	5.05(D)
2153.08	7.01
2153.09	7.01
2153.15	15.01(A)
2153.17	15.02(A)
2301.20	13.03
2307.70	13.07(B)
2317.01	11.11(D)
2317.02	11.11(A)
2501.02	15.02(A), (B)
2505.02	15.02(B)
2505.17	15.02(D)
2705.01 to 2705.10	7.05(B), 15.01(D)
2739.04	11.11(A)
2739.12	11.11(A)
2743.51 et seq.	15.04(A)
2743.51 to 2743.72	13.10
2743.70	13.07(B)
2901.02(A)	3.02
2901.02(D)	9.02(B)
2901.02(E)	9.02(B)
2901.02(G)	3.02
2901.03(A)	9.02(B)
2903.06	3.03, 13.09(E)
2903.07	3.03, 13.09(E)
2907.04	3.02
2907.07(C)	3.02
2907.31	3.02
2907.321	3.02
2907.33(A)	3.02
2907.33(B)	3.04
2909.05 to 2909.07	13.07(B)
2911.01	7.03(C)
2913.02	3.02

OAC	Text Section(s)
5139-19-02	7.02
5139-19-02(C)	7.06(D)

Civ R	Text Section(s)
4(A)	7.05(C)
4(C)	7.05(C)
4(D)	7.05(C), (D)
4.1	7.05(C)
4.2	7.05(C)
4.3 to 4.6	7.05(C)
5(B)	7.08(A)
50(B)	15.02(C)
53	15.02(B)
59	15.02(C)
60	15.01(A)

Crim R	Text Section(s)
3	7.03(D)
4	5.02
7(D)	7.03(K)
12(J)	15.02(E)
16	7.08(A)
29	3.10(C)
31(C)	7.03(K)
46	9.04(B)
52(A)	15.04(A)

App R	Text Section(s)
4(A)	15.02(C)
4(B)	15.02(E)
7	15.02(A)
7(A) to (C)	15.02(D)
7(C)	15.02(E)
9	15.02(F)
9(C)	13.03
12(B)	15.02(G)
12(C)	15.02(G)

Juv R	Text Section(s)
1	1.04
1(B)	7.02
1(B)(3)	3.06(D), 13.10
1(C)(1)	15.02(C)
2(1)	11.01
2(2)	3.01, 3.10(A), 13.09(E)
2(3)	7.03(A)
2(4)	7.01
2(5)	7.03(E)
2(6)	7.06(A), (D)
2(7)	7.06(C)
2(8)	13.02
2(9)	7.03(E)
2(12)	9.03(B), 11.03
2(16)	1.04, 3.10(A), 7.01, 7.03(E), 7.04(B), 7.05(A), 9.03(C),

Juv R	Text Section(s)
	11.11(C), 13.10, 15.02(A)
2(17)	7.03(A)
2(20)	7.06(A), (D)
2(21)	9.03(E), 15.04(A)
3	5.04(B), 7.05(D)
4(A)	7.01, 7.05(B), 9.03(B), 11.03
4(B)	1.04, 11.03
4(C)	11.03
4(F)	13.10
6	5.02, 7.06(C)
7	1.04, 7.06(D), (E), 15.01(A)
7(A)	5.04, 7.06(B), (C)
7(B)	5.02, 7.06(A), (E)
7(C) to (E)	7.06(B)
7(E)(2)(a)	7.06(E)
7(F)	1.04, 7.06(C)
7(F)(1) to (3)	7.06(C), (D)
7(G)	7.06(C), 15.03
7(H)	1.04, 7.06(A)
7(I)	7.06(E), 7.08(B)
7(J)	7.06(E)
9	3.10(A)
9(A)	7.01, 7.02
9(B)	7.02
10	7.01, 7.03(A), (F)
10(A)	7.03(J), 7.04(A)
10(B)	7.03(C), (E), (I)
10(B)(1)	7.03(C), (D), (G), (I), (J)
10(B)(2)	7.03(E)
10(B)(3)	7.03(F)
10(C)	7.03(G)
10(D)	7.03(I)
11	7.03(J), 7.04(B)
13	7.06(E), 7.07(C), 7.08(B), 15.02(B)
13(A)	3.06(D), 7.07(A)
13(C)	7.07(A)
15	1.04
15(A)	7.05(A), (B)
15(B)	7.05(B)
15(B)(3)	11.03
15(B)(4)	15.01(D)
15(C)	7.05(B), 15.01(D)
15(D)	5.02
16	1.04, 13.06(B)
16(A)	7.05(C), (D)
17	7.05(C)
17(G)	15.01(D)
18(B)	7.06(D)
18(C)	15.01(A)
19	7.06(C), 15.01(A)
20(A) to (C)	7.08(A)
22	3.10(C)
22(A)	7.03(K)

Appendix C
Glossary

Adjudicatory hearing—A hearing to determine whether a child is a juvenile traffic offender, delinquent, unruly, neglected, dependent, or abused, or is otherwise within the court's jurisdiction, or whether temporary legal custody should be converted to permanent custody. Juv R 2(1), Juv R 29.

Agreement for temporary custody—A voluntary agreement that is authorized by RC 5103.15 and that transfers the temporary custody of a child to a public children services agency or a private child placing agency. RC 2151.011(B)(18).

Bind-over—See **Transfer**.

Child—A person who is under the age of eighteen years. Any child who violates a law prior to attaining age eighteen is deemed a child irrespective of his age at the time a complaint is filed or a hearing is held on the complaint. A person whose case is transferred for criminal prosecution and who is subsequently convicted in that case is deemed not to be a child in any subsequent case in which he is alleged to have committed the offense of aggravated murder, murder, an aggravated felony of the first or second degree, or a felony of the first or second degree. RC 2151.011(B)(1); Juv R 2(2).

Commit—To vest custody as ordered by the court. RC 2151.011(B)(14).

Complaint—The legal document which sets forth the allegations which form the basis for juvenile court jurisdiction. Juv R 2(3), Juv R 10.

Court proceeding—All action taken by a court from the earlier of (a) the time a complaint is filed or (b) the time a person first appears before an officer of the court until the court relinquishes jurisdiction over the child. Juv R 2(4).

Custodian—A person who has legal custody of a child or a public children services agency or private child placing agency that has permanent, temporary, or legal custody of a child. RC 2151.011(B)(27); Juv R 2(5).

Detention—The temporary care of children in restricted facilities pending court adjudication or disposition, or execution of a court order. RC 2151.011(B)(3); Juv R 2(6), Juv R 7.

Detention hearing—A hearing to determine whether a child shall be held in detention or shelter care prior to or pending execution of a final dispositional order. Juv R 2(7), Juv R 7(F).

Discovery—A process enabling one party to a court proceeding to gain information from another party. Juv R 24.

Dispositional hearing—A hearing to determine what action shall be taken concerning a child who is within the jurisdiction of the court. Juv R 2(8), Juv R 34.

Ex parte proceeding—A court proceeding done for, or on behalf of, one of the parties. Juv R 13.

Expungement—An erasure or destruction of a child's court record. RC 2151.358.

Felony—Any offense specifically classified as a felony, and any offense for which imprisonment of an adult for more than one year may be imposed as a penalty. RC 2901.02(D) and (E); Crim R 2.

Guardian—A person, association, or corporation that is granted authority by a probate court to exercise parental rights over a child to the extent provided in the court's order and subject to the residual parental rights of the child's parents. RC 2151.011(B)(19); Juv R 2(9).

Guardian ad litem—A person appointed to protect the interests of a party in a juvenile court proceeding. RC 2151.281; Juv R 2(10), Juv R 4(B).

Hearing—Any portion of a juvenile court proceeding before the court, whether summary in nature or by examination of witnesses. Juv R 2(11).

Indigent person—A person who, at the time his need is determined, is unable by reason of lack of property or income to provide for full payment of legal counsel and all other necessary expenses of representation. Juv R 2(12), Juv R 4(A).

Juvenile court—A division of the court of common pleas, or a juvenile court separately and independently created, having jurisdiction under RC Chapter 2151; Juv R 2(13).

Juvenile judge—A judge of a court having jurisdiction under RC Chapter 2151; Juv R 2(14).

Legal custody—A legal status created by court order which vests in the custodian the right to have physical care and control of the child and to determine where and with whom he shall live, and the right and duty to protect, train, and discipline him and to provide him with food, shelter, education, and medical care, all subject to any residual parental rights, privileges, and responsibilities. RC 2151.011(B)(10).

Long-term foster care—A juvenile court order pursuant to which legal custody of a child is given to a public children services agency or private child placing agency without the termination of parental rights, and in which the agency is permitted to make an appropriate placement of the child and enter into a written long-term foster care agreement with a foster care provider or with any other person or agency with whom the child is placed. RC 2151.011(B)(25).

Mental examination—An examination by a psychiatrist or psychologist. Juv R 2(15).

Misdemeanor—Any offense specifically classified as a misdemeanor, and any offense for which imprisonment for not more than one year may be imposed as a penalty. RC 2901.02(D) and (F); Crim R 2.

Party—A child who is the subject of a juvenile court proceeding, his spouse, if any, his parent, or if the parent of a child be himself a child, the parent of such parent and, in appropriate cases, his custodian, guardian or guardian ad litem, the state and any other person specifically designated by the court. Juv R 2(16).

Permanent custody—A legal status which vests in a public children services agency or a private child placing agency all parental rights, duties, and obligations, including the right to consent to adoption, and divests the natural or adoptive parents of any and all parental rights, privileges, and obligations, including all residual rights and obligations. RC 2151.011(B)(12).

Permanent surrender—The act of a child's parent(s), by a voluntary agreement authorized by RC 5103.15, to transfer the permanent custody of the child to a public children services agency or a private child placing agency. RC 2151.011(B)(22).

Person—An individual, association, corporation, or partnership and the state or any of its political subdivisions, departments, or agencies. Juv R 2(17).

Physical examination—An examination by a physician. Juv R 2(18).

Private child placing agency—Any association, as defined in RC 5103.02, that is certified pursuant to RC 5103.03 to RC 5103.05 to accept temporary, permanent, or legal custody of children for either foster care or adoption. RC 2151.011(B)(9).

Probation—A legal status created by court order following an adjudication that a child is delinquent, a juvenile traffic offender, or unruly whereby the child is permitted to remain in the parent's, guardian's, or custodian's home subject to supervision, or under the supervision of any agency designated by the court and returned to the court for violation of probation at any time during the period of probation. RC 2151.011(B)(15).

Protective supervision—An order of disposition pursuant to which the court permits a child to remain in the custody of his parents, guardian, or custodian and stay in his home, subject to any conditions and limitations upon the child, his parents, guardian, or custodian, or any other person that the court prescribes, including supervision as directed by the court for the protection of the child. RC 2151.011(B)(16).

Public children services agency—A children services board or a county department of human services that has assumed the administration of the children services function prescribed by RC Chapter 5153. RC 2151.011(B)(26).

Rule of court—A rule promulgated by the Supreme Court or a rule concerning local practice adopted by another court which is not inconsistent with the rules promulgated by the Supreme Court and which rule is filed with the Supreme Court. Juv R 2(19).

Seal a record—Removal of a child's record from the main court file and securing it in a separate file accessible only to the court and certain persons. RC 2151.358(A).

Shelter care—The temporary care of children in physically unrestricted facilities pending court adjudication or disposition, or execution of a court order. RC 2151.011(B)(4); Juv R 2(20), Juv R 7.

Social history—The personal and family history of a child or any other party to a juvenile proceeding which may include the prior record of the person with the juvenile court or any other court. Juv R 2(21), Juv R 32.

Subpoena—A document issued by a court commanding the person to whom it is directed to attend and give testimony at a time and place therein specified. Juv R 17.

Summons—A document issued by a court requiring the party or person to whom it is directed to appear before the court at the time fixed for hearing. Juv R 15.

Temporary custody—Legal custody of a child who is removed from his home, which custody may be terminated at any time at the discretion of the court or, if the legal custody is granted in an agreement for temporary custody, by the person who executed the agreement. RC 2151.011(B)(13).

Transfer—The process by which a juvenile court relinquishes jurisdiction and transfers a juvenile case to the criminal courts for prosecution. RC 2151.26; Juv R 30.

Waiver—See Transfer.

Ward of court—A child over whom the court assumes continuing jurisdiction. Juv R 2(22).

Appendix D
Bibliography

Books

Bailey, F., and H. Rothblatt. *Handling Juvenile Delinquency Cases.* Rochester, NY: Lawyer's Cooperative, 1982.

Davis, S. *Rights of Juveniles: The Juvenile Justice System.* 2d ed. New York: C. Boardman Co, 1980.

Fox, S. *Juvenile Courts in a Nutshell.* 3d ed. St. Paul, Minn: West Publishing Co, 1984.

Fox, S. *Modern Juvenile Justice.* 2d ed. St. Paul, Minn: West Publishing Co, 1981.

Kadish, S.H., ed. *Encyclopedia of Crime and Justice.* Vol. 3. New York: Free Press, 1983.

Katz, L.R. *Ohio Arrest, Search and Seizure.* 2d ed. Cleveland: Banks-Baldwin Law Publishing Co, 1987.

Katz, L.R. *Schroeder-Katz, Ohio Criminal Law and Practice.* 2 vols. Cleveland: Banks-Baldwin Law Publishing Co, 1974-88.

LaFave, W.R. *Search and Seizure: A Treatise on the Fourth Amendment.* St. Paul, Minn: West Publishing Co, 1987.

LaFave, W.R., and J.H. Israel. *Criminal Procedure.* 3 vols. St. Paul, Minn: West Publishing Co, 1984.

Loftus, E. *Eyewitness Testimony.* New York: Cambridge University Press, 1984.

Lou, H.H. *Juvenile Courts in the United States.* Chapel Hill: University of North Carolina Press, 1927.

McCarthy, F., and J. Carr. *Juvenile Law and Its Processes.* Indianapolis: Bobbs-Merrill Co, 1980.

Miller, F., R. Dawson, G. Dix, and R. Parnas. *The Juvenile Justice Process.* 2d ed. Mineola, NY: Foundation Press, 1976.

Paulsen, M., and C. Whitebread. *Juvenile Law and Procedure.* Reno, Nev: National Council of Juvenile Court Judges, 1974.

Piersma, P., J. Ganousis, A. Volenik, H. Swanger, and P. Connell. *Law and Tactics in Juvenile Cases.* 3d ed. Philadelphia: ALI-ABA, 1977.

Sobel, N. *Eye-Witness Identification: Legal and Practical Problems.* 2d ed. New York: C. Boardman Co, 1987.

Wadlington, W., C. Whitebread, and S. Davis. *Children in the Legal System.* Mineola, NY: Foundation Press, 1983.

Articles

Alexander, P. "A Legal Look at Juvenile Court." *Clev Bar J* 27 (August 1956): 171-72, 181-83.

Auerbach, C. "Juvenile Court: Time for a Change." *Clev Bar J* 37 (June 1966): 179-83.

Blank, N. "Reunification Planning for Children in Custody of Ohio's Children Services Boards: What Does the Law Require?" *Akron L Rev* 16 (Spring 1983): 681-704.

Columbro, E. "Evidence in Cuyahoga County Juvenile Court." *Clev Mar L Rev* 10 (September 1961): 524-32.

Erickson, N.S. "Preventing Foster Care Placement: Supportive Services in the Home." *J Fam L* 19 (1980-81): 569-613.

Greenspun, J. "Role of the Attorney in Juvenile Court." *Clev St L Rev* 18 (September 1969): 599-608.

Grisso, T. "Juveniles' Capacity to Waive Miranda Rights." *Calif L Rev* 68 (1980): 1134-66.

Hartman, J.F. " 'Unusual' Punishment: The Domestic Effects of International Norms Restricting the Application of the Death Penalty." *Cin L Rev* 52 (1983): 655-99.

Hazelkorn, D. "In re Barzak: Access to Children Services Board Files." *Akron L Rev* 19 (Fall 1985): 237-49.

Kravitz, M. "Due Process in Ohio for the Delinquent and Unruly Child." *Capital L Rev* 2 (1973): 53-85.

Note. "Juvenile Delinquent and Unruly Proceedings in Ohio: Unconstitutional Adjudications." *Clev St L Rev* 24 (1975): 602-34.

Streib, V.L. "Capital Punishment of Children in Ohio: 'They'd Never Send a Boy of Seventeen to the Chair in Ohio Would They?' " *Akron L Rev* 18 (Summer 1984): 51-102.

Sylvester, B.E. "The Law of Adoption in Ohio." *Capital L Rev* 2 (1973): 23-51.

Whitlatch, W. "The Juvenile Court—A Court of Law." *Case WR L Rev* 18 (May 1967): 1239-50.

Willey, R.J. "The History of Juvenile Law Reform in Ohio Since *Gault.*" *Ohio North L Rev* 12 (1985): 469-590.

Woldman, A.A. "Juvenile Court: 'Neglected Child' of the Judiciary." *Clev Bar J* 37 (September 1966): 257, 270-75.

Young, D.J. "A Synopsis of Ohio Juvenile Court Law." *Cin L Rev* 31 (Spring 1962): 131-50.

Zaremski, M.J. "Blood Transfusions and Elective Surgery: A Custodial Function of an Ohio Juvenile Court." *Clev St L Rev* 23 (Spring 1974): 231-44.

Reports

IJA-ABA Juvenile Justice Standards, A Summary and Analysis (2d ed 1982).

IJA-ABA Standards Relating to Abuse and Neglect (1981).

IJA-ABA Standards Relating to Adjudication (1980).

IJA-ABA Standards Relating to Appeals and Collateral Review (1980).

IJA-ABA Standards Relating to Dispositional Procedures (1980).

IJA-ABA Standards Relating to Dispositions (1980).

IJA-ABA Standards Relating to Interim Status: The Release, Control, and Detention of Accused Juvenile Offenders Between Arrest and Disposition (1980).

IJA-ABA Standards Relating to Juvenile Delinquency and Sanctions (1980).

IJA-ABA Standards Relating to the Juvenile Probation Function: Intake and Predisposition Investigative Services (1980).

IJA-ABA Standards Relating to Noncriminal Misbehavior (1982).

IJA-ABA Standards Relating to Police Handling of Juvenile Problems (1980).

IJA-ABA Standards Relating to Pretrial Court Proceedings (1980).

IJA-ABA Standards Relating to Prosecution (1980).

IJA-ABA Standards Relating to Rights of Minors (1980).

IJA-ABA Standards Relating to Transfer Between Courts (1980).

National Advisory Committee on Criminal Justice Standards and Goals, *Juvenile Justice and Delinquency Prevention* (1976).

President's Commission on Law Enforcement and Administration of Justice, *Task Force Report: Juvenile Delinquency and Youth Crime* (1967).

INDEX

Revised Code sections are cited by number.

EvR   Rules of Evidence
JuvR   Rules of Juvenile Procedure
T   Text

Cross references to another main heading are in CAPITAL LETTERS.

ADMISSIONS, EvR 801(D)
    See also GUILTY PLEAS.
Adjudicatory hearings, T 11.05, T 11.06; JuvR
    29(C), JuvR 29(D)
Admissibility hearings, EvR 104

ADOLESCENTS—See JUVENILES.

ADOPTION
Case plans, seeking and preparing child for
    adoption, 2151.413(C)
Certification of case to juvenile court following
    dismissal of petition
  Complaint for custody, not considered to be,
    T 7.03(J)
Declarants, hearsay exception, EvR 804(B)(4)
Definition, 2151.011(R)(24)
Nonresident children, placement, 2151.39
Unlawful placement, neglect finding due to, T
    3.06(F)
Withdrawal of consent to adoption not consid-
    ered "neglect" of child, T 3.06(B)

ADOPTION ASSISTANCE AND CHILD
    WELFARE ACT OF 1980
State compliance with federal law, T 1.04

ADULT CASES
Appeals, 2151.52
Bail, 2151.46
Bonds for suspended sentences, 2151.50
Charges, 2151.43
Complaints, 2151.44
Defined, 2151.011(B)
Extradition, 2151.45
Hearing charges against, JuvR 27
Imprisonment, support of children, 2151.51
Jurisdiction, 2151.23(A), 2151.23(B)
Jury trials, 2151.47
Sentences, 2151.48 to 2151.51
Suspension of sentence, 2151.49

AFFIDAVITS
Continuing jurisdiction, filing in support of
    motion to invoke, T 15.01(A)
Service of process, JuvR 18(D)
  Publication, by; filing with court, T 7.05(C)

AFFIRMATIONS—See OATHS AND AFFIR-
    MATIONS.

AFFIRMATIVE DEFENSES
Burden of proof, T 11.10

AGE JURISDICTION—See JURISDIC-
    TIONAL AGE.

AGED PERSONS
Victims of crime—See VICTIMS OF CRIME,
    at Age 65 or over.

AGGRAVATED VEHICULAR HOMICIDE
Minor committing, prosecution as delinquent,
    T 3.03

AIDING AND ABETTING
Commitment, aiding escape from, 2151.422 to
    2151.54, 2151.99(A)
Delinquency, 2151.99(A)

ALCOHOLIC BEVERAGES
Possession or purchase by minor as delinquent
    act, T 3.02

ALCOHOLISM
Adequate parental care lacking, factor in deter-
    mination, 2151.914(A)

ALIMONY
Juvenile procedure rules, applicability, JuvR
    1(C)
Modification of award, juvenile court's juris-
    diction, 2151.23(C)

ALIUNDE RULE, EvR 606

"AMENABILITY TO TREATMENT"
    DETERMINATION—See TRANS-
    FER FOR CRIMINAL PROSECU-
    TION.

AMENDMENTS OF PLEADINGS, T
    7.03(K); JuvR 22(B)

ANCIENT DOCUMENTS
Authentication, EvR 901
Hearsay exception, EvR 803(16)

ANNUAL REPORTS OF JUVENILE
    COURTS, 2151.18(D)

ANNULMENT OF MARRIAGE
Juvenile procedure rules, applicability, JuvR
    1(C)

ANSWERS—See COMPLAINTS.

APPEALS, T 15.02
Abortion, complaint for in juvenile court
  Fees and costs, 2151.85(H)
  Forms, 2151.85(G)
  Right to, 2151.85(E)
Adult cases, 2151.52
Affirming juvenile court ruling, T 15.02(G)
Age of majority reached while appeal pending,
    effect on court's jurisdiction, T
    15.01(B)
  Transfer of case for criminal proceedings,
    appeal from, T 9.06
Appropriations for, 2151.10
Bonds, T 15.02(D)
Complaints, refusal to file, T 7.01
Detention hearings, T 7.06(C)

ARRESTS—*continued*
Warrants for, T 5.02
  Evidence rules, applicability, EvR 101

ASSAULT AND BATTERY
Minor committing, parental liability, T 13.10;
  2151.355(E)

ASSESSMENTS, SPECIAL
Detention homes, funding, 2151.341
Juvenile rehabilitation facilities, to support,
  2151.66, 2151.78

ATTORNEY-CLIENT PRIVILEGE
Child abuse, applicability to reports of,
  2151.421(A)
Neglected children, applicability to reports of,
  2151.421(A)

ATTORNEY GENERAL
Federal law violation by juvenile, certification
  of cases for prosecution in federal district court, T 3.02
Juvenile court records of delinquent child,
  obtaining for reparation of victims of
  crimes, T 15.04(A)

ATTORNEYS—See also RIGHT TO COUN-
  SEL.
Abused child, JuvR 4(A)
Adjudicatory hearing, JuvR 29(B)
Appearance, JuvR 4(D)
Child abuse to be reported by, 2151.421(A),
  2151.99(B)
Court-appointed—See INDIGENT PERSONS,
  at Attorney appointed for.
Court employee appointed to assist indigent
  persons in obtaining, 2151.314(D)
Detention hearing, JuvR 7(F)
Guardian ad litem as, T 11.03; 2151.281(H);
  JuvR 4(C)
  Conflict of interest, T 11.03
  Withdrawal of counsel, T 11.03
Indigents, for—See INDIGENT PERSONS.
Ineffective assistance of counsel—See INEF-
  FECTIVE ASSISTANCE OF COUN-
  SEL.
Inspection of records by, T 15.04(A)
Prosecuting—See PROSECUTORS.
Right to—See RIGHT TO COUNSEL.
Runaway consenting to return, guardian's sig-
  nature required, T 15.05(A)
Service of process on, JuvR 20(B)
Termination of parental rights, T 15.02(F);
  2151.353(B)
Waiver of right to, JuvR 3
Withdrawal from case, JuvR 4(E)

AUDITORS, COUNTY
Detention homes, powers and duties,
  2151.3414

AUDITORS, COUNTY—*continued*
Juvenile rehabilitation facilities, powers and
  duties, 2151.79

AUTHENTICATION OF EVIDENCE, EvR
  901 to EvR 903
Acknowledged documents, EvR 902
Ancient documents, EvR 901
Commercial paper, EvR 902
Comparison of authenticated specimens, EvR
  901
Congressional acts, presumptions under, EvR
  902
Expert witness comparing authenticated speci-
  mens, EvR 901
Foreign public documents, EvR 902
Handwriting, nonexpert opinion, EvR 901
Illustrations, EvR 901
Methods provided by statute or rule, EvR 901
Newspapers, EvR 902
Official publications, EvR 902
Periodicals, EvR 902
Public records, EvR 901, EvR 902
Requirement, EvR 901
Seal, domestic public documents under, EvR
  902
Self-authentication, EvR 902
Subscribing witness' testimony, EvR 903
Telephone conversations, EvR 901
Trade inscriptions, EvR 902
Voice identification, EvR 901

AUTOMOBILES—See MOTOR VEHICLES.

BAIL
Adult offenders, juvenile proceedings, 2151.46
Delinquency cases, T 7.06(E)
  Denial, T 15.02(D)
Evidence rules, applicability, EvR 101
Recognizance
  Juvenile on probation, parent required to
    post, T 13.10; 2151.411
  Transfer from juvenile court, 2151.26(F)
Unruly children, T 7.06(E)

BAILIFFS, 2151.13
Service of process by, JuvR 17(D)

BANK RECORDS
Warrantless searches, T 5.03(A)

BAPTISMAL CERTIFICATES
Hearsay exceptions, EvR 803(12)

BATTERED CHILDREN—See CHILD
  ABUSE.

BEST EVIDENCE RULE, EvR 1001

BEST INTERESTS OF CHILD
Dependency determination, T 13.02; 2151.414

COUNTY COURTS
Child brought before, transfer to juvenile court, 2151.25

COURT COSTS, 2151.54
Abortion, complaint for in juvenile court, 2151.85(H)
  Appeals, 2151.85(H)
Counsel, JuvR 4(F)
Counties, reimbursement by, 2151.36
Custody investigation, JuvR 32(D)
Guardian ad litem, JuvR 4(F)
Service of process, 2151.19
Support of dependents of imprisoned adults, 2151.51
Witness, 2151.28(J); JuvR 17(B), JuvR 17(D)

COURTHOUSES, 2151.09

COURTS—See particular court by name.
Contempt—See CONTEMPT.
Costs—See COURT COSTS.
Federal—See FEDERAL COURTS.
Juvenile courts—See JUVENILE COURTS.

COURTS OF APPEALS—See also APPEALS.
Docket priority, actions concerning juvenile court appropriations, 2151.10
Jurisdiction, T 15.02(A)

COURTS OF COMMON PLEAS
Child brought before, transfer to juvenile court, 2151.25
Clerks as juvenile court clerks, 2151.12
Judges, assignment to juvenile courts, 2151.07

CRIME VICTIMS—See VICTIMS OF CRIME.

CRIMINAL DAMAGING
Restitution as probation condition, T 13.07(B)(2)

CRIMINAL MISCHIEF
Restitution as probation condition, T 13.07(B)(2)

CRIMINAL PROSECUTIONS
Confidential information divulged, T 15.04(B)
Evidence rules, applicability, EvR 101
Juveniles—See TRANSFER FOR CRIMINAL PROSECUTION.
Obstruction, evidence of compromise to prove, EvR 408

CROSS-EXAMINATIONS, JuvR 34(B)
Adjudicatory hearings, T 11.12
Confidentiality not to limit right to cross-examine witness, T 11.12
Dispositional hearings, T 13.03; JuvR 34(B)
Expert witnesses, EvR 705
Leading questions, EvR 611(B)

CROSS-EXAMINATIONS—*continued*
Prior juvenile record, concerning, T 15.04(A)
Right to cross-examine overrides confidentiality of juvenile records, T 11.12
Scope, EvR 611

CRYPTS
Inscriptions, hearsay exceptions, EvR 803(13)

CURFEWS
Constitutionality, T 3.04
Exceptions, T 3.04
Unruly child, determination as due to violation, T 3.04

CUSTODIAL INTERROGATION, T 5.04(B)(1)

CUSTODIANS
Definitions, 2151.011(B)(27)

CUSTODY OF CHILDREN, DOMESTIC
Certification of cases to juvenile court, T 3.01; 2151.23(C) to 2151.23(F)
Investigative reports, JuvR 32(D)

**CUSTODY OF CHILDREN, INSTITU-
TIONAL**
Permanent custody—See PERMANENT CUS-
TODY.
Removal of child from placement with parents
  Ex parte proceeding, 2151.31(D)
  Temporary order, 2151.33(B)
Temporary custody—See TEMPORARY CUS-
TODY.

CUSTOMS
Evidence of, EvR 406

CUYAHOGA COUNTY JUVENILE COURT, T 1.04; 2151.07

DAMAGES—See also RESTITUTION.
Parental liability for acts of child, T 13.07(B)(6), T 13.10; 2151.355(E), 2151.411

DATA PROCESSING
Evidence generated by, defined, EvR 1001

DAY CARE CENTERS
Employees reporting child abuse, 2151.421(A), 2151.99(B)

DEAD MAN'S STATUTE, EvR 601

DEAF PERSONS
Hearsay exception, applicability, EvR 804(B)(5)

DEATH
Abused child, determination, T 3.08

DELINQUENCY—*continued*
Persons over age twenty-one, T 15.05(A)
Photographs, T 15.04(B); 2151.313, 2151.99(C)
Plural findings, T 13.07(C)
Prevention programs—See DIVERSION PRO-
    GRAMS.
Prior adjudications
  Confederate delinquent, inquiry into, T
    15.04(A)
  Conviction, as; misdemeanor elevated to fel-
    ony, T 3.02
  Theft adjudication as element, proof beyond
    reasonable doubt, T 3.02
Probation, T 3.02, T 13.07(B)(2), T
    13.07(B)(6); 2151.355(A), 2151.356(A)
  See also PROBATION, generally.
Reasonable doubt standard of proof, T 1.02(C),
    T 11.10
Recognizance
  Parent to enter into, T 13.10; 2151.411
  Transfer of case from juvenile court,
    2151.26(F)
Records and reports
  Annual report by juvenile court, 2151.18(D)
  Expungement of records, 2151.358
    Fingerprints and photographs, 2151.313
  Physical and mental examinations, 2151.53
  Sealing of records, 2151.358
    Fingerprints and photographs, 2151.313
  Social histories—See SOCIAL HISTORIES.
Rehabilitation, 2151.65 to 2151.80
  See also REHABILITATION.
Release from commitment
  Jurisdiction, T 15.01(E)
  School transcript provided to child's prior
    school, T 13.07(B)(4); 2151.355(D)
  Youth services department, from—See
    YOUTH SERVICES DEPARTMENT.
Removal of child from home, reasonable
    efforts to prevent, T 13.04
Repair of damaged property as restitution, T
    13.07(B)(2)
Repeat offender
  Bond posted by parents, forfeiture, T 13.10
  Parent's liability, 2151.411
Restitution by, T 13.07(B)(2); 2151.355(A)
  Complaints resulting in, statistical record,
    2151.18(B)
School transcripts, provision to youth services
    department upon commitment, T
    13.07(B)(4); 2151.355(D)
Sealing of records, T 15.04(B); 2151.358
  Fingerprints and photographs, 2151.313
Sex offenses, minor victims
  Deposition testimony, T 11.11(B)
Shelter care, T 7.06
  See also SHELTER CARE, generally.
Silence, advising parties of rights prior to
    detention hearing, T 7.06(C)
Social histories—See SOCIAL HISTORIES.
Statute violated providing to youth services
    department upon commitment, T
    13.07(B)(4); 2151.38(C)

DELINQUENCY—*continued*
Stay pending appeal, T 15.02(D)
Summons, T 7.05
  See also SUMMONS, generally.
Temporary custody as disposition of case, T
    13.07(B)(3); 2151.355(A)
Theft offenses, restitution as probation condi-
    tion, T 13.07(B)(2); 2151.355(A)
Traffic offenders—See also TRAFFIC
    OFFENDERS, JUVENILE.
  Delinquent act, traffic offense as, T 3.03;
    2151.356(A)
Unfit parents, 2151.05
Unruly child, disposition as delinquent, T
    13.08(B); 2151.354(A)
Venue—See VENUE, generally.
Violation of court order or law as delinquent
    act, T 3.02; 2151.02
Warrant against, JuvR 15(E)
Witness at proceeding, penalization by
    employer prohibited, 2151.211
Youth services department, powers and
    duties—See YOUTH SERVICES
    DEPARTMENT.

DENIALS
Adjudicatory hearings, T 11.05; JuvR 29(C),
    JuvR 29(E)

DENTISTS
Child abuse to be reported, 2151.421(A),
    2151.99(B)

DEPARTMENTS, STATE
Human services—See HUMAN SERVICES
    DEPARTMENT, STATE.
Youth services—See YOUTH SERVICES
    DEPARTMENT.

**DEPENDENT AND NEGLECTED CHIL-
    DREN**, T 3.05 to T 3.07
Abandoned children
  Defined, T 3.06(B)
  Illegal placement of child distinguished from,
    T 3.06(F)
  Neglect, defined as, T 3.06(A); 2151.03(A)
  Permanent custody—See PERMANENT
    CUSTODY, generally.
Abuse or neglect, danger of; detention due to,
    T 5.02
Abuse or neglect of sibling, detention due to, T
    5.02
Address of child, inclusion in pleadings, T
    7.03(H)
Appeals, T 15.02
  See also APPEALS, generally.
Case plans, T 13.05(A)
Child's attendance at dispositional hearing, T
    13.03
"Clear and convincing evidence" standard of
    proof, T 11.10

EVIDENCE—*continued*
Search warrants to obtain—See SEARCH WARRANTS.
Seizure—See SEARCH AND SEIZURE.
Social histories as—See SOCIAL HISTORIES.
Suppression—See SUPPRESSION OF EVIDENCE.
Transcripts—See TRANSCRIPTS.
Transfer of case for criminal proceedings
  Evidence rules, applicability, T 9.03(E)
  Right to present evidence, T 9.03(H)
Witnesses—See WITNESSES AND TESTIMONY.

EX PARTE PROCEEDINGS, JuvR 13(D)
Removal of child, authorizing, 2151.31(D)
Temporary orders, 2151.33(D)

EXCITED UTTERANCES, EvR 803(2)
Abused children, T 11.11(B)

EXCLUSIONARY RULE—See also SUPPRESSION OF EVIDENCE.
Derivative evidence doctrine, T 5.01
"Good faith" exception, T 5.01

EXECUTION OF JUDGMENT
Adult cases tried in juvenile courts, 2151.50
Support of juveniles committed in juvenile proceedings, 2151.36

EXPERT WITNESSES, EvR 702 to EvR 705
Authentication, EvR 901
Basis of testimony, EvR 703
Competency of witness, to prove, T 11.11(D)
Cross-examination, disclosing facts behind opinion, EvR 705
Dependency and neglect cases, T 11.11(E)
Due process right to, T 11.11(E)
Facts, disclosure, EvR 705
Hypothetical questions, T 11.11(E)
Interpreters as, EvR 604
Objections to testimony, EvR 704
Personal observations as basis for opinion, T 11.11(E)
Qualifications for, T 11.11(E)
Ultimate issues, opinion concerning admissible, T 11.11(E)

EXPUNGEMENT OF RECORDS, T 15.04(B); 2151.313(B), 2151.358
Admissibility as evidence, EvR 609
Dismissal of complaint, following, T 15.04(B); 2151.358(F)
Dispositional hearing, advising child of rights, T 13.03; JuvR 34(E)
Effect, T 15.04(B)
Fingerprints, 2151.313
Impeachment of evidence, EvR 609
Index references deleted, T 15.04(B)
"Not guilty" determination, T 15.04(B)
Photographs, 2151.313

EXPUNGEMENT OF RECORDS—*continued*
Traffic offenders, juvenile, T 15.04(B)
Violations, T 15.04(B); 2151.358, 2151.99(C)
Withdrawal of complaint, following, T 15.04(B)

EXTRADITION, T 15.05(B)
Hearings, T 15.05(B)
Juvenile proceedings, adult offenders, 2151.45

FAIR TRIALS—See DUE PROCESS.

FAITH HEALING
Children, of, T 3.06(D); 2151.03, 2151.421(H)

FALSE ARREST
Records to be delivered to court when right to bring action not waived, T 15.04(B)

FEDERAL COURTS
District courts, prosecution of juveniles in, T 3.02
Juvenile Justice and Delinquency Prevention Act of 1974 governing, T 1.01(A)
Supreme court cases, T 1.02

FEES AND COSTS—See also particular subject concerned.
Abortion, complaint for in juvenile court, 2151.85(H)
  Appeals, 2151.85(H)
Court costs—See COURT COSTS.
Delinquency cases, T 13.07(B)(5)
Extradition, T 15.05(B)
  Juvenile proceedings, adult offenders, 2151.45
Failure to pay, imprisonment due to, T 13.07(B)(5)
Transportation costs, return of runaway or escapee to former state, T 15.04(A)

FELONIES
Arrests, authority to make, T 5.02
Minor committing—See DELINQUENCY.
Miranda rights, T 5.04(B)
Prior conviction elevating crime to, delinquency adjudication as "conviction", T 3.02
Transfer to adult court—See TRANSFER FOR CRIMINAL PROSECUTION.

FEMALES
Delinquent, commitment to women's reformatory, 2151.48
Pregnant, consent of juvenile court for marriage, JuvR 42
Trials, female referee appointed for female defendant, 2151.16

FINAL ORDERS
Appeals from, T 15.02(A)
Custody, certification of issue to juvenile court, T 15.02(B)

FINAL ORDERS—*continued*
Delinquency finding as, T 15.02(B)
Disposition of case required, T 15.02(B)
Referees' reports
    Failure to file findings of fact, effect on
        determination of judgment as final
        order, T 15.02(B)
    Objections to, requirement for appeal, T
        15.02(B)
Temporary custody as, T 7.07(C), T 15.02(B)
Transfer of case for criminal prosecution, T
    9.05, T 15.02(A), T 15.02(B)

**FINANCIAL RESPONSIBILITY, MOTOR
    VEHICLE**
Juvenile traffic offenders, T 13.09(G)

FINDINGS OF FACT, 2151.353(A),
    2151.35(A); JuvR 29(F)
Detention hearings, T 7.06(C)
Judicial notice, EvR 201
Removal of child from home, reasonable
    efforts to prevent, T 13.04
Shelter care hearings, T 7.06(C)
Temporary orders, written findings required,
    2151.33(C)
Transfer for criminal prosecution, amenability
    to treatment
    Not required, T 9.02(D), T 9.03(I)

FINES AND FORFEITURES
Delinquency cases, T 13.07(B)(5); 2151.355(A)
Failure to pay, imprisonment due to, T
    13.07(B)(5)
Traffic offenders, T 13.09(B); 2151.356(A)
Transfer of case following imposition of fine, T
    13.07(B)(5), T 13.07(C)

FINGERPRINTS, 2151.313
Arrest of minor, exception, T 5.05(D)
Due process not violated by, T 5.05(A)
Expungement of record, destruction, T
    15.04(B)
Felony exception, T 5.05(D)
Retention, T 5.05(D)
Violations, 2151.99(C)

FIRSTHAND KNOWLEDGE RULE, EvR
    602

FORESTRY CAMPS
Juveniles, for, 2151.65 to 2151.80
    See also REHABILITATION, generally.

FORMS, JuvR 46
Abortion, complaint for in juvenile court,
    2151.85(G)
    Appeals, 2151.85(G)
Complaint, JuvR 10(B)
Subpoena, JuvR 17(A)
Summons, JuvR 15(B)
Warrant against child, JuvR 15(E)

FOSTER CARE
Abused children, T 13.06(A)(5)
    Placement, 2151.353(A)
Case plans, T 13.05(A); 2151.412(A)
Children services agencies
    Placement, factors to consider, 2151.415(C)
    Removal of child from residential placement,
        2151.415(G)
Complaints, T 7.03(I)
Defined, 2151.011(B)
Dependent children, T 13.06(A)(5)
    Placement, 2151.353(A)
Detention, foster home as place of,
    2151.312(A)
Drift, prevention, T 1.04
Funding, T 7.02; 2151.34
Long-term foster care
    Complaint, 2151.27(C)
    Definition, 2151.011(B)(25)
Neglected children, T 13.06(A)(5)
    Placement, 2151.353(A)
Nonresident children, 2151.39
Parties to actions, foster parents as, T 7.05(A)
Permanent custody motion, effect on, T
    13.06(B)(4)
Placement of children in, T 7.06(A);
    2151.415(C)
    Definitions, 2151.011(B)(23)
    Factors to consider, 2151.415(C)
    Temporary, 2151.34
    Youth services department—See Youth ser-
        vices department placing child in, this
        heading.
Removal from detrimental, factor in depen-
    dency determination, T 3.07(C), T
    3.07(D)
Removal of child from residential placement,
    2151.415(G)
Residential use of property, foster homes con-
    sidered for zoning purposes, 2151.418
Right to counsel during proceedings,
    2151.353(B)
Summons to explain effect of, T 7.05(B)
Temporary custody, commitment of child as
    disposition of case, 2151.34
Youth services department placing child in
    Early release, following, T 15.01(E)
    Funding, T 7.02
    Minimum time for commitment served, fol-
        lowing, T 15.01(E)
Zoning, foster homes considered residential use
    of property for purposes of, 2151.418

FRAUD
Modification or vacation of judgment due to, T
    15.01(A)

FREEDOM OF PRESS
Newspaper publishing name of alleged juvenile
    offender, T 1.02(H)

FRUIT OF THE POISONOUS TREE, T 5.01

HEARINGS—*continued*
Bifurcated procedure, T 1.01(C), T 11.01, T 13.02
    See also ADJUDICATORY HEARINGS; DISPOSITIONAL HEARINGS.
Contempt proceedings, T 15.01(D)
Continuing jurisdiction invoked by filing new complaint, T 15.01(A)
Criminal prosecution of juvenile, determination—See TRANSFER FOR CRIMINAL PROSECUTION.
Definitions, JuvR 2
Detention hearings—See DETENTION HEARINGS.
Discovery motion, on, JuvR 22(D)
Dispositional—See DISPOSITIONAL HEARINGS.
Early release from youth services department custody, T 15.01(E); 2151.38(B)
Ex parte orders, T 7.07(B)
    Removal of child, authorizing, 2151.31(E)
Exclusion from, JuvR 27
    General public, T 9.03(K)
Expungement of records, 2151.358(D)
Extradition, T 15.05(B)
Notice—See NOTICE.
Parents' right to attend, 2151.352
Permanent custody—See PERMANENT CUSTODY, generally.
Placement of child prior to—See DETENTION AND DETENTION HOMES.
Probation revocation, T 15.01(C)
Proposed actions, JuvR 13(E)
Public, exclusion of, T 9.03(K)
Recording—See TRANSCRIPTS.
Referees—See REFEREES.
Release of child from youth services department institution, 2151.38(A), 2151.38(B)
    Violation of terms of release, T 15.01(E)
Relinquishing jurisdiction for criminal prosecution, right to counsel, JuvR 3
Removal of child from placement with parents
    Ex parte order, 2151.31
Restitution, hearing on existence of damages and amount of restitution, T 13.07(B)(6)
Restraining orders on parents, T 13.10; 2151.359
Revocation of probation, JuvR 35(B)
Right to counsel—See RIGHT TO COUNSEL.
Runaways, holding in custody while awaiting requisition, T 15.05(A)
Scheduling, 2151.35(E)
Sealing of records—See SEALING OF RECORDS.
Separation of children and adults, 2151.24; JuvR 27
Subpoena for attendance, JuvR 17(F)
Summons to appear, 2151.28; JuvR 15, JuvR 16(A)

HEARINGS—*continued*
Temporary orders, T 7.07(A); 2151.33; JuvR 13(E)
    Ex parte orders, 2151.33(D)
Transcripts—See TRANSCRIPTS.
Transfer of jurisdiction—See TRANSFER FOR CRIMINAL PROSECUTION.
Venue—See VENUE.
Violations by child released from youth services department institution, 2151.38(B), 2151.38(C)
Waiver of rights, JuvR 3
Youth services department, T 15.01(E)

HEARSAY, EvR 801 to EvR 806
Absence of document, proving, EvR 803(7), EvR 803(10)
Abused children, admissibility of statements, 2151.35(F)
Adjudicatory hearings, admissibility, T 11.11(B)
Ancient documents, exception, EvR 803(16)
Baptismal certificates, exception, EvR 803(12)
Birth records, exception, EvR 803(9)
Boundaries, reputation of; exception, EvR 803(19)
Business records, exception, EvR 803(6)
    Hospital and medical records as, T 11.11(B)
Character evidence, EvR 803(20)
Co-conspirators, statements of, T 11.12
Commercial publications, exception, EvR 803(17)
Confrontation rights, considerations, T 11.12
Convictions, final judgments; exception, EvR 803(21)
Crypts, inscriptions; exception, EvR 803(13)
Deaf-mute's statement, exception, EvR 804(B)(5)
Death records, exception, EvR 803(9)
Decedent's statement, exception, EvR 804(B)(5)
Definition, EvR 801
Dependent children, admissibility of statements, 2151.35(F)
Dispositional hearings, admissibility, T 13.03
Dying declarations, EvR 804(B)(2)
Emotional condition, exception, EvR 803(3)
Exceptions, EvR 803, EvR 804
Excited utterance, exception, EvR 803(2)
    Abused children, T 11.11(B)
Family history records or statements, exceptions, EvR 803(13), EvR 804(B)(4)
Genealogies, exception, EvR 803(13)
Judgments, exception, EvR 803(21), EvR 803(22)
Market reports, exception, EvR 803(17)
Marriage certificates, exception, EvR 803(9), EvR 803(12)
Medical statements, exception, EvR 803(4)
    Abused children, T 11.11(B)
Memorandum, exception, EvR 803(5) to EvR 803(7)
Mental condition, exception, EvR 803(3)

JAILS—See also PRISONERS.
Detention of minors in, T 13.07(B)(8);
  2151.312(B), 2151.34; JuvR 7(H)
  Interstate compact states, policy concerning,
    T 15.05(A)
  Separation from adults, T 7.06(A)
Warrantless search of cells, T 5.03(A)

JEOPARDY—See DOUBLE JEOPARDY.

JOURNALS
Juvenile courts to maintain, T 15.04(A)

JUDGES
Adjudicatory hearings, transfer hearing judge as
    judge, T 9.04(A), T 11.09
Assignment, 2151.07
Bond when acting as clerk, 2151.12
Clerk, as, 2151.12
Compensation, 2151.13
Competency as witnesses, EvR 605
Defined, 2151.011(A)
Dispositional hearings, retention of adjudica-
    tory hearing judge, T 13.02; JuvR
    34(B)
Expenses, 2151.13
Hamilton county, 2151.08
Impartiality, T 11.09
Transfer hearing, disqualification upon reten-
    tion of juvenile court jurisdiction, T
    9.04(A), T 11.09
"Wise and merciful father," as, T 1.01(B)
Witness, as; competency, EvR 605

JUDGMENT ENTRIES
Dispositional hearings, T 13.03; JuvR 34(C)
School attended by child, commitment order
    sent to, T 13.07(B)(4)

**JUDGMENT NOTWITHSTANDING VER-
DICT**
Appeals, time for filing notice suspended by
    motion, T 15.02(C)

JUDGMENTS
Civil disabilities not imposed on juvenile by, T
    15.04(A)
Conditional judgments, T 13.03
Convictions, prior; hearsay exception, EvR
    803(21)
Dispositional hearing
  Time requirements, 2151.35(B)
Dispositional hearing, entry following, T 13.03;
    JuvR 34(C)
Entries—See JUDGMENT ENTRIES.
Execution—See EXECUTION OF JUDG-
    MENT.
Hearsay exception, EvR 803(21), EvR 803(22)
Modification grounds, T 15.01(A)
Vacating—See VACATION OF JUDG-
    MENTS.

JUDICIAL NOTICE
Adjudicative facts, EvR 201

JURISDICTION, T 3.01 to T 3.10; 2151.07,
    2151.23; JuvR 44
Abused children, T 3.08; 2151.23(A)
  Age jurisdiction—See JURISDICTIONAL
    AGE.
Adult cases, 2151.23
Age jurisdiction—See JURISDICTIONAL
    AGE.
Appeals, T 15.02(A)
  Age twenty-one reached while appeal pend-
    ing, effect, T 15.01(B)
Certification of cases to juvenile court, T 3.01,
    T 7.03(J); 2151.23(C) to 2151.23(F),
    2151.25
  Jurisdiction continuing and exclusive, T 3.01
"Child" defined, T 3.10(A)
Complaints
  Continuing jurisdiction invoked by filing, T
    15.01(A)
  Filed after child reaches age eighteen, juve-
    nile court jurisdiction, T 3.10(A)
Contempt, T 15.01(D); 2151.21
Continuing, T 3.01, T 15.01; JuvR 35(A)
  Duration, T 15.01(B)(1)
  Termination, T 15.01(B)(1)
Criminal capacity, minimum age, T 3.10(A)
Criminal prosecution, transfer of jurisdiction
    for—See TRANSFER FOR CRIMI-
    NAL PROSECUTION.
Custody action, 2151.23
  Domestic relations courts, T 3.01
  Juvenile court not exercising, T 3.01
  Permanent custody proceeding, T 15.01(B)
  Probate courts, T 3.01
Delinquent children, T 3.01, T 3.02
  Age jurisdiction, T 3.10
Dependent and neglected children, T 3.05 to T
    3.07; 2151.23(A)
  Age jurisdiction, T 3.10
  Exclusive original jurisdiction of juvenile
    court, T 3.01
  Notice of intention to apprehend, 2151.23(A)
  Time of dependency or neglect, establishing,
    T 3.05
Detention homes, child placed in pending con-
    tinuing jurisdiction proceedings, T
    15.01(A)
Domestic relations courts
  Certification of jurisdiction to juvenile court,
    T 3.01, T 7.03(J)
  Custody of children, T 3.01
Double jeopardy
  Transfer of cases to juvenile court, T 3.10(B)
Early release of child from youth services
    department custody, T 15.01(E)
Exclusive and continuing when cases certified
    to juvenile court, T 3.01
Extradition, T 15.05(B)
Federal law violation, procedure for prosecu-
    tion, T 3.02

UNRULY CHILDREN—*continued*
Motion to review original disposition order, T 13.08(B)
Motor vehicle registration, suspension or revocation, T 13.08(B)
"Not guilty" determination, expungement of records, T 15.04(B); 2151.358
Notice, motion to review original disposition order when child not amenable to treatment, T 13.08(B)
Parents, failure to obey, T 3.04; 2151.022(A)
Pattern of misconduct required for finding, T 3.04
Photographs—See PHOTOGRAPHS.
Probation, T 13.08(B); 2151.354(A)
    See also PROBATION, generally.
  Revocation, jurisdiction, T 15.01(C)
  Violations regarded as delinquency, T 3.02
Reasonable doubt standard of proof, T 11.10
Removal of child from home, reasonable efforts to prevent, T 13.04
Restitution ordered as disposition of case, T 13.08(B)
Review of original disposition order, motion for, T 13.08(B)
Right to counsel, applicability, T 11.03
Sealing of records—See SEALING OF RECORDS.
Sexual promiscuity, T 3.04; 2151.022(C)
Shelter care, T 7.06
    See also DETENTION AND DETENTION HOMES, generally.
Stay pending appeal, T 15.02(D)
Summons, T 7.05
    See also SUMMONS, generally.
Teachers, failure to obey, T 3.04; 2151.022(A)
Treatment, child not amenable to; disposition as delinquent, T 13.08(B); 2151.354(A)
Truancy, T 3.04; 2151.022(B)
Youth services department, commitment to not permitted, T 13.08(B)

UTTERANCES, EXCITED, EvR 803(2)

VACATION OF JUDGMENTS
Fraud as grounds, T 15.01(A)
Grounds, T 15.01(A)
Jurisdiction lacking as grounds, T 15.01(A)
Misrepresentation as grounds, T 15.01(A)

VANDALISM
Parental liability, T 13.10

VEHICULAR HOMICIDE
Minor committing, prosecution as delinquent, T 3.03

VENUE
Adjudicatory hearings, T 7.04(B)
  Transfer of cases, T 7.04(B); JuvR 11
Change of, T 7.04(B); 2151.271

VENUE—*continued*
County of behavior's occurrence, T 7.04(A); 2151.27(A)
Criminal prosecution, transfer of case for, T 7.04(B)
    See also TRANSFER FOR CRIMINAL PROSECUTION, generally.
Disposition following adjudicatory hearing, transfer of case for, T 7.04(B)
Fine, imposition; transfer following not permitted, T 7.04(B)
Move by parents or child, effect, T 7.04(A)
  Change of venue following, T 7.04(B)
Proceedings pending in other juvenile court, transfer to court of child's residence, T 7.04(B); JuvR 11(B)
Records to accompany transfer of case, T 7.04(B); JuvR 11(D)
Residence of child, T 7.04(A); JuvR 11
  Change in, transfer of case due to, T 7.04(B)
Transfer—See Change of, this heading; TRANSFER TO ANOTHER COUNTY.

VERDICTS
Impeachment, testimony by jurors, EvR 606

VICTIMS OF CRIME
Age 65 or over
  Effect in cases of juvenile delinquents, T 13.10; 2151.26(B), 2151.27(D), 2151.355(A), 2151.355(C)
  Juvenile court actions transferred to adult court, 2151.26(B)
  Restitution ordered for, T 13.07(B)(6); 2151.355(A)
Character evidence, admissibility, EvR 404
Handicapped persons, effect in juvenile delinquency cases, T 13.10; 2151.26(B), 2151.355(A), 2151.355(C)
Juvenile court records of delinquent child, attorney general obtaining, T 15.04(A)
Notice, entitlement to restitution, T 13.10; 2151.355(E)
Restitution, T 13.07(B)(6), T 13.10; 2151.355(A)
  Unruly child ordered to pay, T 13.08(B)
Unborn children, jurisdiction, T 3.10(A)

VIDEOTAPE RECORDING
Depositions
  Sex offenses, minor victims, T 11:11(B)
Juvenile proceedings, JuvR 37
  Minor sex offense victims, 2151.3511
Minor sex offense victims
  Juvenile proceedings, 2151.3511

VISITATION RIGHTS
Detention or shelter facilities, T 7.06(B), T 7.06(E); JuvR 7(J)
Temporary orders, 2151.33(B)